CURRENT LEGAL PROBLEMS 2009

VOLUME 62

CURRENT LEGAL PUBLICATIONS

CURRENT LEGAL PROBLEMS 2009

VOLUME 62

Edited by
COLM O'CINNEIDE

Deputy Editor
GEORGE LETSAS

Assistant Editor
CHRISTOPHER CAMPBELL-HOLT

On Behalf of the Faculty of Laws
University College London

OXFORD
UNIVERSITY PRESS

OXFORD
UNIVERSITY PRESS

Great Clarendon Street, Oxford OX2 6DP

Oxford University Press is a department of the University of Oxford.
It furthers the University's objective of excellence in research, scholarship,
and education by publishing worldwide in

Oxford New York

Auckland Cape Town Dar es Salaam Hong Kong Karachi
Kuala Lumpur Madrid Melbourne Mexico City Nairobi
New Delhi Shanghai Taipei Toronto

With offices in

Argentina Austria Brazil Chile Czech Republic France Greece
Guatemala Hungary Italy Japan Poland Portugal Singapore
South Korea Switzerland Thailand Turkey Ukraine Vietnam

Oxford is a registered trade mark of Oxford University Press
in the UK and in certain other countries

Published in the United States
by Oxford University Press Inc., New York

First published 2010

British Library Cataloguing in Publication Data
Data available

Library of Congress Cataloging in Publication Data
Library of Congress Control Number: 2009942187

Typeset by MPS Limited, A Macmillan Company
Printed in Great Britain
on acid-free paper by
CPI Antony Rowe,
Chippenham, Wiltshire

ISBN 978–0–19–958373–7

1 3 5 7 9 10 8 6 4 2

Editor's Preface

Since its establishment in 1947, *Current Legal Problems* has showcased cutting-edge academic research in law. Contributors are invited to present their research, first, in a public lecture and then subsequently in extended paper form, on the basis that they are engaged in ground-breaking scholarship that engages with current issues relating to the place of law within contemporary society. As a result, over the years, leading scholars have published an impressive array of papers in the successive volumes of the series, which have provided readers with an annual taste of the changing focus and concerns of top-class legal research. This year is no exception. It is, therefore, a great pleasure to introduce the incisive, rigorous and wide-ranging scholarship contained in the fourteen papers that make up this sixty-second volume of *Current Legal Problems*.

The papers that follow are arranged on the basis of subject matter, so as to provide the reader with an unfolding range of perspectives on the interlinked and intertwined relationship between law and the wider society it both shapes and is shaped by. The volume opens with a series of critical and reflective pieces by Susan Marks, William Lucy, and Sean Coyle that aim to interrogate various aspects of how law and law's place within the existing social order is conventionally conceptualized and understood.

In a compelling example of sustained critical analysis, Marks examines how legal analysis often turns a blind eye to deeply-engrained patterns of power relations and social practices that shape the 'current arrangements' of our society, preferring to assume that the world we are given is the product of luck and chance and circumstance, and thereby falling into the trap of 'false contingency'. She suggests that this tendency often has its roots in a denial or downplaying of determinism and a failure to confront the limits of incremental reform that does not acknowledge the deeper currents that shape our collective history. Marks calls for an intellectual 'anti-anti-Marxism' as a step towards addressing 'false contingency': in so doing, her focus is on the work of those in the international law field, but the analysis offered here is of pressing relevance across the full spectrum of legal engagement.

William Lucy examines how law purports to judge all its addressees as identical abstract beings and apply general and objective standards equally to all, permitting only a limited range of exculpatory claims. Given that this abstraction runs counter to our desire to be judged by our specific personal characteristics in so many other facets of our individual and particular lives, he assesses what might be said in favour of 'law's abstract judgement'. In so doing, Lucy presents a fascinating analysis of the normative arguments in support of the positive case for this abstraction and suggests that '[o]nly when such a case has been considered shall we know if anything of significance will be lost by excising this familiar feature of familiar legal systems'.

Similar, themes of how to reconcile the abstract and rational character of law with the human society it emerges from and forms an integral part of recur in Sean Coyle's contemplative and insightful arguments questioning the existence of any meaningful dichotomy between the 'humanly-created aspect of legal order and its principled, rational character'. For Coyle, it is exactly in 'law's systematic and rational nature that the human face of law is most fully comprehended'. He contends as a result that a central question for jurisprudence must be how plural visions of the good come together and are combined together within national traditions of civility and respect for liberty, exemplified by the 'English national spirit' that provided the fertile soil for the growth of the common law.

Turning to the sphere of constitutional law and its deepening engagement with human rights, Aileen Kavanagh confronts the 'democratic sceptics' that question the legitimacy of judicial review which limit democratically-derived decision-making in the name of human rights. In a hard-hitting analysis, she argues the moral arguments made by 'democratic sceptics' against rights review are flawed, while the empirical arguments on which their case often ultimately rests are outmoded. David Cole examines the similarities and differences between the measures adopted by the US and UK governments in response to the terrorist threat after 9/11. In a compelling piece of comparative analysis which is informed by his ground-breaking scholarship on US counter-terrorism laws, Cole concludes on a hopeful note that 'an irreversible downward spiral in rights protections is not necessarily inevitable', suggesting that lessons can be learnt by democratic governments from the mistakes they make in fighting terrorism.

The next two chapters explore themes relating to the relationship between law and individual expression and self-creation. Sarah

Worthington brings her well-established expertise in the sphere of private law to bear on the question of whether law provides a supportive environment for artistic creativity, concluding after a wide-ranging and thought-provoking analysis that if a goal of private law is to create incentives for 'artists to deliver more and better art, and to have that art exposed to public scrutiny', then it is 'doubtful that the current legal rules succeed'.

Melanie Williams, in a compelling and fascinating paper, sets out to explore the discourses and narratives which link law and the 'sciences of the psyche', with a view to assessing whether these 'professional narratives' and law in particular succeed in engaging and identifying the 'truth' of those individuals who become subject to their focus. Using a combination of case studies, critical analysis and multi-disciplinary research, she concludes that the 'truths' of individuals 'spring from complex internal narratives which may not correlate readily to the doctrines of medicine and law', especially when it comes to questions of mental responsibility and agency. In this paper again we see the themes of law's abstraction and its relation to the human condition re-surface, with Williams critiquing the way in which law and psychiatry place excessive reliance upon conventional accounts of free will and the psyche that have at best a tangential relationship with the complex realities of the operation of individual psyches.

Turning to issues of the place of law within regulatory frameworks, Maria Lee in her inaugural paper examines what she identifies as a 'consistent mismatch between the rhetoric and practice of regulation', whereby broad social, political and ethical considerations are given lip service in regulatory debates but sidelined 'when it comes to the crunch' in favour of reliance upon the narrower horizons of technical expertise on 'safety' and 'risk'. In an impressively wide-ranging and sustained critique of regulatory practice, she argues that this denial of space to wider perspectives in regulation has important normative implications, not least because there is often more at stake than can be grasped through the limited parameters of risk and safety.

Thomas Gibbons also confronts issues of accountability and regulation in his innovative and hard-hitting paper on media distortions, an often-neglected field in the realm of freedom of speech analysis and media law. Unwilling to give the media free rein without closer scrutiny, he suggests that where distortions occur as a result of commercial and institutional pressures in the media industry, there are no grounds for privileging the media on the grounds of freedom of speech.

Gibbons proceeds to consider a number of regulatory options which might minimise media distortion, preferring approaches based on a system of 'enforced ethics'.

Rebecca Probert is also unwilling to accept received wisdom without critical scrutiny. In an impressive piece of scholarship, she concludes that the current state of English family law is 'inconsistent and inadequate' in its application to cohabiting couples. However, she then proceeds to question whether the appropriate solution is to confer on such couples the same rights as if they were married. Probert proceeds to examine how the position of cohabiting couples could be improved within the current legal framework, but also identifies the need for a more wide-ranging review of the legal treatment of marriage and cohabitation. This paper provides an invaluable outline of the pressing current legal issues that such a reform must engage with.

Ioannis Lianos brings a rigorous comparative and multidisciplinary focus to bear on questions of 'economic transplants', specific economic concepts that are incorporated into legal discourse by what he describes as an act of 'translation'. This paper examines the special characteristics of these particular types of 'transplant' and what distinguishes them from other instances where economic analysis is integrated into legal discourse and in particular competition law. Lianos also argues that the 'paradigm' of translation is the most adequate explanatory framework for taking into account the dual legal/economic nature of economic transplants and also can serve as a conceptual base for a wider examination of the interaction of law with other social sciences.

Damian Chalmers focuses on the factors that explain the often 'cumbersome' nature of EU law, which he attributes to the raised level of expectation and the demanding standards that are generated by virtue of pursuit of a European *eudaimonia*, ie the aspirations of EU law to grant individuals the structures, entitlements, responsibilities and protection to make better and more successful lives for themselves. In a compelling and wide-ranging analysis, Chalmers suggests that this ambition has the effect of ensuring that EU law acquires a 'shrill feel' in which it 'judges itself and others according to parameters that cannot be met', while entitlements are granted in highly selective ways to those who have the resources and drive to meet these demanding goals. In addition, he argues that this ambition diverts attention from the pressing need to develop conceptions of justice or institutions for mediating political difference within the framework of EU law. In this paper, Chalmers poses serious questions and makes some far-reaching points about the ambition and goals of EU law, thereby rising to the challenge of confronting pressing and current legal problems head on.

Ken Oliphant focuses upon the different 'planes' of European Tort Law, including academic restatements of common Europe-wide rules and principles of tortuous liability, tort liability under EU law and through national incorporation of the European Convention on Human Rights, and the 'search for a common core of principles in the court practice of different national systems'. He examines the state of academic research in this area, and argues that the interaction between these different planes of European Tort Law and the common law is 'potentially explosive, but nevertheless positive', because 'explosive charges may assist in the demolition of outmoded and dilapidated structures to make way for renewal'. In another wide-ranging piece of sustained analysis, he concludes that the English law of tort should be fundamentally deconstructed and redeveloped employing models derived from the various planes of its European counterpart.

Finally, David Wilkins brings a trans-Atlantic perspective to bear on the shifting, complex and often problematic nature of the relationship between corporate lawyers and their clients. He brings both his academic scholarship and his impressive grasp of the reality of legal practice in both North America and Europe to bear in challenging what he describes as the tendency to conflate 'the standards of advocacy appropriate to the criminal context with those that should govern in civil or regulatory matters.' Wilkins goes further in arguing for the 'fundamental unfairness of the traditional agency model in a world in which lawyers are almost as vulnerable to client manipulation as the other way around', and closes by exploring the new types of corporate attorney/client relationship emerging in current practice. By engaging with these cutting-edge issues, his paper provides a fitting conclusion to a volume characterised by rigorous and challenging legal scholarship of the highest rank.

Colm O'Cinneide
October 2009

Contents

List of Contributors

Damian Chalmers Professor of European Union Law, London School of Economics and Political Science

David Cole Professor of Law, Georgetown Law School

Sean Coyle Professor of Jurisprudence, School of Law, University of Exeter

Thomas Gibbons Halliwells Professor of Law, University of Manchester

Aileen Kavanagh Reader in Law and Fellow of St Edmund Hall, University of Oxford

Maria Lee Professor of Law, University College London

Ioannis Lianos Reader in European and Competition Law, University College London

William Lucy Professor of Law, Law School, University of Manchester

Susan Marks Professor of Public International Law, London School of Economics and Political Science

Ken Oliphant Director of the Institute for European Tort Law in the Austrian Academy of Sciences, Vienna; Professor of Law at the University of Bristol

Rebecca Probert Associate Professor, School of Law, University of Warwick

David B Wilkins Lester Kissel Professor of Law, Harvard Law School

Melanie Williams Professor of Law, School of Law, University of Exeter

Sarah Worthington Professor of Law, London School of Economics and Political Science

List of Abbreviations

ATCSA	[UK] Anti-terrorism, Crime and Security Act 2001
CCS	Carbon Capture Storage
CDPA	[UK] Copyright Designs and Patents Act 1988
CFCs	Chlorofluorocarbons
CLP	*Current Legal Problems*
CoRWM	Committee on Radioactive Waste Management
DCFR	Draft Common Frame of Reference
ECTIL	European Centre of Tort and Insurance Law
ECHR	European Convention of Human Rights
ECtHR	European Court of Human Rights
ECJ	European Court of Justice
EFSA	European Food Safety Authority
FI	Food Information [provision of, to consumers]
FISA	[US] Foreign Intelligence Surveillance Act 1978
GC	General Counsel
GMO	Genetically Modified Organism
HRA	[UK] Human Rights Act 1998
IPPC	Integrated Pollution Prevention and Control
NSA	National Security Agency
PACE	[UK] Police and Criminal Evidence Act 1984
PCC	Press Complaints Commission
PETL	Principles of European Tort Law
PR	Patients' Rights [in cross-border health care]
SCORE	Supplier Cost Reduction Effort
SEC	Securities and Exchange Commission
SOX	[US] Sarbanes-Oxley Act 2002
SPS	Sanitary and Phytosanitary
SSNIP	Small but Significant Non Transitory Increase in Price test
WTO	World Trade Organization

Table of Cases

UNITED KINGDOM

EUROPEAN COURT OF HUMAN RIGHTS

EUROPEAN UNION

WORLD TRADE ORGANISATION

AUSTRALIA

CANADA

UNITED STATES

False Contingency

*Susan Marks**

In his text *The Eighteenth Brumaire of Louis Bonaparte* Karl Marx writes of the 'circumstances and relationships that [as he saw it] made it possible for a grotesque mediocrity to play a hero's part'.[1] The grotesque mediocrity was Louis Bonaparte, later the Emperor Napoleon III, and 18 Brumaire was, of course, the date in the revolutionary calendar when Louis's uncle, the first Emperor Napoleon, seized power in 1799. For Marx the story of Louis Bonaparte's own later *coup d'état* in 1851 showed how tragedy may repeat itself as farce. But it also showed, more generally, how historical processes are at once open and determined. The course of events is not fixed; indeed, it is very often strange and unexpected. On the other hand, to be unexpected is not necessarily to be inexplicable, since the past shapes the possibilities of the present. As Marx famously put it, '[men] make their own history, but they do not make it just as they please in circumstances they choose for themselves; rather they make it in present circumstances, given and inherited'.[2] My argument in this paper can be summarized with reference to that passage. It concerns what I have come to see as a problematic tendency in my own work and in that of others in the international legal field writing in a similar register. This is that we are very alert to the issue Marx highlights in the first part of the statement I just quoted—that men make their own history—but we are rather less focused than we should be on the issue he highlights in the second part—that they do not make it just as they please in circumstances of their own choosing but rather in circumstances they inherit.

* Professor of Public International Law, London School of Economics and Political Science.

[1] K Marx, *The Eighteenth Brumaire of Louis Bonaparte* (3rd edn, Lawrence and Wishart: London, 1954) 6.

[2] K Marx, '*The Eighteenth Brumaire of Louis Bonaparte*' in T Carver (ed), *Marx: Later Political Writings* (Cambridge University Press: Cambridge, 1996) 32. (I use a different edition here from that cited in the previous footnote, as this contains the more familiar English rendering of this passage.)

To be clear at the outset, I believe it is quite right to hammer the point that history is a social product, not given but made. For if it has been made, then it can be remade differently. This is surely a cardinal principle of all progressive thought, and the work of drawing out its multifarious implications is as urgent as it is endless. The worry I want to explore here, however, is that we may be undertaking this work in a way which causes us to neglect the equally important progressive point that possibilities are framed by circumstances. While current arrangements can indeed be changed, change unfolds within a context that includes systematic constraints and pressures. In general terms, what I wish to re-evoke is the idea that things can be, and quite frequently are, contingent without being random, accidental, or arbitrary. From another angle, there is a kind of necessity which must be reckoned into, rather than always contrasted with, our sense of what it is to be an artefact of history. I will use the term 'false contingency' to denote the failure to take that idea adequately into account. In the discussion that follows I will explain more precisely how I intend this phrase, and will try to illustrate something of its significance and ramifications. Along the way I will also offer some speculative comments on why false contingency may need, as I suggest, re-evoking—why this second half of the critical equation seems to have got forgotten or put aside. But first, I need to begin with the backstory.

False Necessity

The inspiration for my term 'false contingency' comes from the established concept of false necessity. As is, I think, well known, this is the subject of an eponymous book by Roberto Unger, first published in 1987.[3] Part of his multi-volume study entitled 'Politics: A Work in Constructive Social Theory', *False Necessity* is in every sense of the word a colossal work, and its analysis is at times rather recondite. When it comes to the exposition of this central concept, however, Unger expresses himself with great clarity and concision. 'The illusions of false necessity arise', he writes, 'because we surrender to the social world, and then begin to mistake present society for possible humanity, giving in to the ideas and attitudes that make the established order seem natural,

[3] R Unger, *False Necessity* (2nd edn, Verso: London, 2004).

necessary, or authoritative.'[4] Yet 'what seems to be given and presupposed is merely what we have temporarily refrained from challenging and remaking'.[5] Far from representing a natural order of things, social reality is best understood as characterized by 'permanent incompleteness, perennial conflict and inescapable choice'.[6] Unger explains that, as an analytical concept, false necessity helps to bring into focus the 'fatalistic myths'[7] which mask the historicity of existing arrangements and prevent us from grasping their contingency, provisionality and hence, most importantly, their mutability. He invites his readers to join him in a 'campaign against false necessity',[8] dedicated to subverting these resignation-inducing myths one by one.

The basic idea of false necessity, then, is that things do not have to be as they are. Actuality is not destiny, and we need to search out and expose the various forms of thought which obscure that fact and lend an aura of solidity and self-evidence to what must instead be revealed as precarious and contingent. Although Unger develops his arguments in his own very distinctive way, he does not, of course, claim this as an original insight; his project is to recover it, and imbue it with new emphasis and new meaning. Certainly the basic idea here long predates the name Unger gives to it. A defining theme of social theory in a 'critical' mode, it has a history in many different disciplines and today carries the banner of many different traditions and concepts, or indeed none. To take the case of writing about international law, the phrase 'false necessity' has to my knowledge rarely, if ever, been used, but the claim it is meant to express serves as the premise or explicit argument of much contemporary scholarship. Thus, scholars highlight the contested character of what appears as beyond dispute—the humanitarianism of humanitarian intervention, for example, and indeed its categorization as intervention. Or they point up the political stakes behind technical-legal description—what happens when having foreign students in your class becomes trade in services, for instance, or when soya bean seeds become intellectual property. Or yet, to mention just one other familiar move, they show how analyses—in areas such as development policy—can work as 'progress narratives' that encourage us to assume that all is for the best in this best of all possible worlds. The idioms, projects and

[4] Ibid, xx. My citations are mostly to Unger's 'Introduction to the New Edition', where his argument is summarized.
[5] Ibid, xxviii.
[6] Ibid, xxix.
[7] Ibid, xxx.
[8] Ibid, xx.

fields of study vary widely, but the ambition of challenging what Unger terms false necessity is very widely shared.

Standing behind the concept of false necessity is obviously an idea of necessity and its postulated alternative, contingency. In philosophy, and especially the philosophy of history, debates about necessity and contingency have mostly revolved around determinism, accident and the 'role of the individual in history'. It will be instructive for my later argument if we review something of these issues. As a starting point for doing so, we can take Isaiah Berlin's influential essay entitled 'Historical Inevitability'.[9] Writing in 1953, Berlin criticizes what he sees as the renewed currency of determinism in approaches to historical enquiry. By determinism he means, as he somewhat archly puts it, the effort 'to bring us to our senses by showing where the true, the impersonal and unalterable machinery of life and thought is to be found'.[10] That is to say, it refers to the notion that history obeys laws, that these laws set us on an irresistible course with inevitable outcomes, and that events are accordingly to be attributed to impersonal forces beyond the control of individual human beings. Berlin observes that this kind of approach is both inaccurate and dangerous. It is inaccurate because there are no such laws: individual will and action, not to mention accident, are in fact, and have always been, at the heart of historical processes. And it is dangerous because, where individual agency is denied, so too is the basis for personal responsibility. In his words:

> . . .if the history of the world is due to the operation of identifiable forces other than, or little affected by, free human wills and free choices, then the proper explanation of what happens must be given in terms of the evolution of such forces. . . [W]hat can a single individual . . . be expected to do?[11]

Berlin is worried about the weakening of our capacity to evaluate conduct, and ascribe praise or blame where it is due.

Is he right to worry about this? A notable riposte to Berlin was delivered by EH Carr in his book *What is History?* first published in 1961.[12] It is always easier, Carr remarks, to blame catastrophes on individual wickedness and credit achievements to individual genius than to study historical processes at the level of deeper causes and wider contexts.[13] He agrees with Berlin that 'the facts of history are indeed facts about individuals', but counters that these facts are not generally

[9] I Berlin, *Four Essays on Liberty* (Oxford University Press: Oxford, 1969) 41.
[10] Ibid, 106. [11] Ibid, 63.
[12] EH Carr, *What is History?* (London: Penguin, 2nd edn, 1990). [13] Ibid, 46.

about 'actions of individuals performed in isolation', and nor are they only about conscious motives and willed outcomes.[14] For Carr, any adequate theory of history has to take into account that people's actions often have results they do not intend or even desire. This is not to maintain that they are the unconscious tools of some all-powerful force, but it is to note that social circumstances matter in historical explanation. In this regard, Carr contends that determinism is a 'red herring'.[15] Clearly, we can no longer imagine that history obeys laws. But historians can, and most do, imagine that causation can be investigated, and for Carr, determinism refers simply to the belief underpinning this that everything that happens has a cause and could not have happened differently without some difference in that antecedent cause. Or rather, most things that happen have multiple causes, so that the key issue is to establish the relative significance of various determining factors. If the most significant factors generally have more to do with institutions and policies than with the actions and wishes of particular individuals, then Carr insists that this is not to negate the reality or relevance of the latter. As he recalls, one who studies the causes of crime does not by that fact alone deny the moral responsibility of individual offenders.[16]

Determinism and Determination

In the contributions of these two scholars we can see already that determinism is a complex concept with more than one meaning and more than one bearing with respect to necessity and contingency. Of course, necessity and contingency are themselves complex concepts. *Necessity* refers, in broad terms, to the phenomenon of constraint. In some usages, this is simply a matter of pointing to the existence of external forces that mould, structure or check. In other usages, the constraint rises to the level of compulsion, so that what is necessary is fixed and unavoidable, and must simply be accommodated, as it cannot be altered. Linked to that, the metaphysical doctrine of necessitarianism asserts that the world is as it must be (whether for reasons to do with God, nature, rationality, convention, or some other circumstance), in contrast to voluntarism which stresses the role in human affairs of free will and choice. For its part, *contingency* has a fascinating etymology, which brings with it a literal sense of 'touching' or 'coming into

[14] Ibid, 52. [15] Ibid, 91 *et seq.* [16] Ibid, 95.

contact'. More figuratively, it denotes uncertain occurrence or fortuitousness. Something is contingent if it may or may not happen. This could be because it is dependent on some prior event, the incidence or timing of which is indefinite—as in the legal concept of a 'contingent remainder'. Or it could simply be because there is no scheme prescribing, proscribing or otherwise influencing its occurrence. But either way, the emphasis is thrown on chance, accident and all that is random, indeterminate and up in the air.

What then of *determinism*? It is clear that for Berlin determinism implies compulsion. It names the belief that dynamics are at work which are driving history inevitably and inexorably towards outcomes that are bound to result, no matter what people may do. This notion of determinism—let us call it 'fatalistic determinism'[17]—has wide currency, both in academic writing and ordinary speech, and is perhaps especially valued as a critical concept, invoked to challenge 'deterministic' approaches when we want to reassert the capacity of human beings to influence the conditions of their own lives. Fatalistic determinism has relevance to the analysis of many different bodies of thought. During the second half of the 20th century, however, it came to be associated for many with one body of thought in particular, seen as its pre-eminent exemplar: Marxism. Berlin appears to be among those who hold this view, for it is above all against 'Marx and Marxists'[18] that he stresses the role of the individual in history. At the same time, it needs hardly to be recalled that Marxism is far from unitary as a tradition, and the problem of determinism has long exercised historical materialists as well. If Marx followed the classical economists in dubbing his theory a 'law', he also wrote (to mention again the passage I quoted at the beginning) that 'men make their own history'.[19] At any rate, few Marxists today would defend the idea that the processes he describes are inevitable, predictable, or fated.[20] For most, Marx's 'economic law of motion of modern society'[21] is to be understood not as a

[17] I take this term from Harry Ritter, who himself draws it from William Dray. See H Ritter, *Dictionary of Concepts in History* (Greenwood Press: Westport, Conn, 1986) 105, and WH Dray, 'Determinism in History', in P Edwards (ed), *The Encyclopedia of Philosophy*, Vol 2 (Collier-Macmillan: New York, 1967) 373–6.

[18] I Berlin, *Four Essays on Liberty* (Oxford University Press: Oxford, 1969) 46.

[19] See Marx, n 2 above, 32.

[20] See R Bhaskar, 'Determinism' in T Bottomore (ed), *A Dictionary of Marxist Thought* (2nd edn, Blackwell: Oxford, 1991) 139, to which the present discussion is heavily indebted.

[21] K Marx, *Capital, Volume 1* (Penguin: London, 1990) 92.

universal principle that can explain the past and foretell the future, but rather as a far more specific and limited set of claims about capitalism.

Fatalistic determinism is a very familiar sense of determinism. To many of us, it is what comes most readily to mind when the word is heard. But it is not the only sense. At the least, Carr reminds us that there also exists a notion of determinism which is concerned with causation. This older sense, for which a common label is 'scientific determinism', has a more neutral connotation than fatalistic determinism. It refers to the belief that events occur in accordance with observable relationships of cause and effect. To some scholars, Carr among them, the main point of scientific determinism is that it justifies the ongoing work of studying causal relations and elaborating explanatory theories. In the context of historical and other social scientific enquiry, it can also moderate a voluntarist preoccupation with the role of the individual and encourage the exploration of diverse causal factors affecting social processes, including institutional and systemic factors. As we have seen, that aspect is important to Carr. How does scientific determinism relate to fatalistic determinism? Well, philosophers remind us that causes may be sufficient without being necessary, and that effects may be conditioned on causes without necessarily being produced by them. Thus, 'because an event was caused to happen, [this does not mean] it was bound to happen before it was caused'.[22] Equally, states of affairs may be explained by reference to the effects they produce in the future, as in the functional mode of explanation. All this said, scientific determinism takes many forms, and in some of them fatalistic determinism is not so very far away, inasmuch as the emphasis is on interlinked causal chains which effectively predetermine outcomes.

Let us now try another tack. What if we shift the focus from determinism (the belief) to determination (the process), or indeed determine (the action)? Perhaps that will give us a clearer view of what is in issue. The verb 'determine' has its roots in the Latin word *terminare*, meaning 'to set bounds' to something. This takes us in various directions. I may *determine* a dispute. But in doing so, I may need to *determine* exactly what happened on that terrible day. To this end, I may *determine*, or *be determined upon*, a somewhat unconventional course of action. And in turn, that course of action may *determine* my professional future—or the lack of it. Determination, then, is the

[22] See Bhaskar, n 20 above, 139.

process of settling disputes, ascertaining facts, resolving upon actions, and conditioning outcomes. In some usages there is the implication of bringing things to a close, or fixing things in such a way that the end becomes a foregone conclusion. But, as Raymond Williams emphasizes in his discussion of the term as a 'keyword', the roots of determination in bound-setting mean that there has always remained another sense in which the accent is instead on limits and pressures.[23] Thus, determining conditions (or 'determinants') that 'set certain limits or exert certain pressures' are contrasted with 'accidental' or 'voluntary' factors.[24] Williams observes that, when determination is understood in this manner, we are able to avoid both the 'fatalism' of believing that 'everything is already decided'—in our terms, fatalistic determinism—and what he describes as a 'vague and indifferent state in which no necessary factors . . . can be admitted to exist'. To his mind, that latter attitude is 'in real terms . . . a kind of madness' which only our confidence in criticizing other views as determinist prevents us from recognizing.[25]

This idea of determination as the setting of limits and the exertion of pressures is also useful in another way. It steers us away from reductive or over-simplified accounts of the processes involved. In debates about determinism within Marxist circles, Louis Althusser is perhaps the theorist most closely associated with the insight that determination is almost always *overdetermination*. Hence, to refer only to one aspect of this, that which is determined is generally also itself determining. In Althusser's work during the 1960s, the context for these observations is explication of the concept of base and superstructure. Against currents of economic or technological determinism, he argued that base and superstructure are to be understood as referring to determinant factors of various sorts and to their effectivity and relationship in particular circumstances. More specifically, the reference is to 'an accumulation of effective determinations', with production—the economic base—determining 'in the last instance', as Engels is said to have insisted.[26] What are we to make of this idea of determination 'in the last instance'? Althusser explains that it means that 'the economy is determinant . . . in the long run, the run of History'. 'But'—and he now adds a crucial qualification—'History "asserts itself" through the multiform world

[23] R Williams, *Keywords* (2nd edn, Fontana: London, 1983) 98. [24] Ibid, 101.
[25] Ibid
[26] L Althusser, *For Marx* (Verso: London, 2005) 113 (emphasis omitted).

of the superstructures, from local tradition to international circumstance'.[27] Thus, he continues:

> the economic dialectic is never active *in the pure state*; in History . . . the superstructures etc. are never seen to step respectfully aside when their work is done or, when the Time comes, . . . to scatter before His Majesty the Economy as he strides along the royal road of the Dialectic.

No, he writes, '[f]rom the first moment to the last, the lonely hour of the "last instance" never comes'.[28] Whilst often overlooked and easily elided, this proviso makes plain that what is in issue is not prediction, but orientation—not a vision of an end-state or teleology, but a claim about the direction and dynamics of change. To speak with a more recent scholar, analysis focuses on the 'tendencies of mechanisms rather than [on] the invariant conjunctions of events', for once again determination is seen to 'set limits, rather than [prescribing] uniquely fixed results'.[29]

Althusser is by no means, of course, the only Marxist theorist to have challenged reductive accounts of the concept of base and superstructure, now viewed in historical perspective as belonging with the effort to rationalize Soviet economic policy. For our purposes, however, the main interest of all this is less how it affects conceptions of historical materialism than what is revealed about necessity and contingency. And what is revealed about necessity and contingency is that neither will do. If Berlin is right to criticize fatalistic determinism, Carr is also right that fatalistic determinism is a red herring which distracts us from the key issue of causation—or, I would prefer, determination. As we have seen, determination can mean different things, but in one notable definition it signals that the course of events is not necessary in the sense of being inevitable, predictable and impervious to 'modification by human intervention'.[30] At the same time, nor is it the case that history is 'altogether contingent, unpatterned, [and] accidental . . . only a succession of . . . events, produced by a combination of chance and will'.[31] Rather, there exist some 'necessary factors', as Williams calls them, in the shape of limits and pressures which orient change without actually predetermining it. The issue then becomes to investigate in particular circumstances what individual and collective action can achieve, what relation is established between structure and agency, how the world works as an organic totality. Vocabularies and preoccupations vary but

27 Ibid, 112. 28 Ibid, 113. 29 Bhaskar, n 20 above, 139.

30 R Miliband, *Class Power and State Power* (Verso: London, 1983) 132.

31 Ibid

the common theme, expressed pithily by Ellen Wood, is that '[w]e are not obliged to accept a Manichaean choice between determinism and contingency'.[32] For Wood, '[t]he real alternative to both is *history*'.[33] Once we have rejected the inevitability of specific outcomes, while also recognizing that the range of outcomes is not indeterminate, what is left—she contends—is the category of 'possibility'. But it is '*historical* possibility, that is, the existence of . . . social and material conditions which make something possible that was impossible before'.[34]

False Contingency

We have come quite a long way from Unger and false necessity, but hopefully the point is now clear: if we need to be on guard against false necessity, we need also to be on guard against what might correspondingly be termed false contingency. For just as things do not have to be as they are, so too history is not simply a matter of chance and will. The concept of false contingency refers to this idea, and to the limits and pressures, tendencies and orientations, over-determination and determination in the last instance, that shape both realities and possibilities. It bears underlining that the analysis of false contingency is not meant to replace the analysis of false necessity; the argument is that they must be pursued in tandem. Or rather, the argument actually goes further than that, insofar as anti-necessitarian critique depends on showing that current arrangements are not simply arbitrary or accidental, but belong with the logics of a system which must also be brought within the analytical frame. It follows that enquiry into false necessity becomes itself necessitarian when false contingency is ignored. (Note, incidentally, that in what I have just said I have referred both to the 'analysis' and simply to the 'concept' of false contingency. This is one of those concepts, like reification and indeed false necessity, which enact a critique, in the sense that to use the word is already to call into

[32] E Wood, *Democracy Against Capitalism* (Cambridge University Press: Cambridge, 1995) 145. In contrast, Alexander Chryssis argues that the choice between determinism and contingency is not Manichaean in this context, but Hegelian, insofar as Marx followed Hegel in opting for a conception of possibility as the 'maturation of conditions for transition of the Idea to next stage of its necessary development'. See A Chryssis, 'The Cunning of Production and the Proletarian Revolution' in M Cowling (ed) *The Communist Manifesto: New Interpretations* (Edinburgh University Press: Edinburgh, 1998) 97, 102.

[33] Ibid, 145.

[34] Ibid, 144 (some emphasis omitted).

question its referent. It is characteristic of such concepts that whether one speaks of their analysis or simply of them, the gist is roughly the same insofar as what is signalled is the existence of a problem, to be specified and explored.)

I recalled earlier that the idea behind false necessity long predates the name Unger invents for it. The same applies to false contingency. This too is no original insight, as some of the writings on which I have drawn already make clear. Indeed, its history would be hard to disentangle from that of false necessity, for which it serves as a complement and corrective. So again the project is one of recovery, not discovery, aiming to imbue an old idea with new emphasis and new meaning. An immediate question that arises is: why is this required? How is it that false necessity today names a widespread preoccupation, while false contingency does not? What has happened to make us forget the problem of false contingency, or perhaps even deliberately blot it out? No doubt many things contribute, but among them may be a tendency to elide determination with determinism. As we have seen, false contingency is concerned with determination. And determination, while obviously related to determinism, is quite distinct from it. In any event, determinism itself has many variants, of which, as we have also seen, belief in historical inevitability is only one. Despite these points, the idea appears to have taken root that to investigate 'necessary factors'—limits, pressures, systemic constraints, and so on—is to commit yourself to determinism in the fatalistic sense. Contingency—and nothing but contingency—or (fatalistic) determinism: as Wood observes, that seems to be the choice. There is also another aspect to this. Recall that for Berlin, among many others, determinism came to be associated—never exclusively, but nonetheless quite strongly—with Marxism. It may even have served at times as a code word for Marxism. This points in an obvious direction. If the investigation of false contingency commits you to determinism, and if determinism associates you with Marxism, then false contingency becomes very much a minority concern.

Something of this line of thought seems to inform Unger's work on false necessity. Unger is certainly aware of the problem of false contingency. His constant talk is of 'frameworks', 'routines' and 'formative contexts' and, in agglutinative mode, of 'context-transforming struggle', 'structure-revising capabilites', 'framework-preserving routines', and 'institutional disentrenchment'. This language could scarcely be more redolent of the existence of limits and pressures. Yet we are never invited or encouraged to scrutinize these, at least not in any sustained fashion. They remain in the background, casting long shadows but rarely coming directly into view. To be sure, the burden of Unger's story is that there are limits to the limits and pressures on the pressures—in his phrase, 'structure-defying resistance' is always possible.[35] But that does not explain why false necessity is allowed to occupy the whole field of analytical enquiry, for surely—and this is the burden of false contingency—you need to know what the structure is that can be resistently defied. A better explanation may have to do with the way Unger sets up his argument. The 'campaign against false necessity'[36] is counterposed to the 'fatalism' of what Unger terms 'deep structure social theory', and the 'most relentless and influential exponent' of deep structure social theory is identified as Marxism.[37] On Unger's account, 'in Marxist social theory, the apparition of fate may describe a temporary—albeit unavoidable—stage in the evolution of humanity'.[38] Unger is, of course, right to highlight and challenge the fatalistic determinism that characterizes notable currents within Marxism, especially those which have done duty as state socialist ideology. But, as we have seen, he is wrong to write as though the study of false contingency were tarred with that same brush.

So much for speculations and abstractions. Let me now try to make things more concrete by giving a couple of examples. I mentioned at the beginning that my subject was a problematic tendency which I have come to recognize in my own work, among other places. So my first example is offered in the spirit of self-criticism. Some time ago I wrote about the claim, current in the early 1990s and to some degree still today, that there exists under post-Cold War international law an emergent right to democratic governance.[39] I took issue with the conception of democracy that seemed to underpin both this claim and the arguments put forward to refute it. More generally, I objected that the meaning of democracy was being treated as given and self-evident, whereas in fact it is deeply contested. Against the false necessity that made it seem as if this one conceptualization belonged to the order of nature, I reasserted the contingency of democratic ideas. But how did that particular idea come to be privileged, and what would it take to

[35] Unger, n 3 above, 319. [36] Ibid, xx. [37] Ibid, xxx.

[38] Ibid. For further discussion of Unger's 'complicated relation to Marx's own ideas', see especially ibid, 38.

[39] S Marks, *The Riddle of All Constitutions* (Oxford University Press: Oxford, 2000).

dethrone it? The 'thin' or formal conception of democracy I criticized was not just a random choice. I examined its implications at some length, but never said anything about the extent to which there was a logic to it. I do not just mean a logic within the argument; I mean a logic stretching beyond it, a 'bigger picture' of which this was a part. I never provided reasons for seeing the problem of democratic ideas in international law as other than isolated, free-floating and very possibly anomalous.

My second example comes from the work of one of the most influential and inspirational people writing on international law today, David Kennedy.[40] In an important text, Kennedy sets out his critique of the international human rights movement. Is it the solution, he asks, or also itself part of the problem? He shows that, in a variety of ways, the international human rights movement is indeed itself part of the problem, and that we can begin to grasp this only if we weigh initiatives pragmatically, by considering their benefits and costs in particular contexts. Against the false necessity that makes it seem as if international human rights initiatives reflect the universal interest, Kennedy reasserts the instability of arrangements that in fact produce winners and losers. But how do people come to be winners and losers, and what would it take to alter that situation? Reading his analysis, we are left to imagine that who is a winner and who a loser is in each case entirely arbitrary, something that is just a matter of how the chips fall on that particular occasion. Early on in the text, Kennedy makes the following comment, aimed at qualifying what may seem as investment in the philosophy of rational choice:

> In weighing initiatives pragmatically, it is often more useful to focus on 'distributional consequences among individuals or groups' than 'costs and benefits'. The costs/benefits vocabulary suggests (incorrectly) that one could know at an abstract level what to count as a cost or a benefit. In fact, of course, the 'costs' and the 'benefits' will look different and be evaluated differently by different people.[41]

But the problem with rational choice is not just that it fails to register that costs and benefits will look different and be evaluated differently by different people. It is also that it fails to register that costs and

[40] D Kennedy, 'The International Human Rights Movement: Part of the Problem?' (2001) *European Human Rights Law Review* 245 (reproduced in slightly modified form in D Kennedy, *The Dark Sides of Virtue* (Princeton University Press: Princeton, NJ, 2004) ch 1.

[41] Ibid, 249.

benefits are linked, both to one another and to a larger set of systemic processes, the upshot of which is that some people always enjoy social benefits while bearing very few social costs, and the reverse applies to others. Kennedy's account has more in common with the rational choice perspective than he suggests, insofar as it does little to make us understand the relationality and systematicity of privilege and deprivation.

False contingency is a little difficult to illustrate because for the most part it is in the nature of an absent presence. But these examples are perhaps enough to illustrate the way in which, at a certain point, discussion stops and the subject gets changed. There is a great deal of talk about how things that are contingent are made to seem as if they were necessary, in virtue of being natural, universal, rational, eternal, etc, but much less discussion of voluntarist mystifications. Terry Eagleton brings out something of the significance of this omission when, writing about literary history, he asks: 'For whom exactly does experience seem like a swirl of vivid odds and ends? It might have seemed this way to Virginia Woolf, but it is unlikely that it did so to the servants who rose not long after dawn to lay her fires and polish her fenders.'[42] To those at the less comfortable end of social relations, Eagleton implies, the patterning of privilege and deprivation will be quite plain, or at any rate of interest and worth investigation. In passing, we may note here the link with ideology critique. I mentioned a moment ago the way false necessity may be produced through practices of naturalization, universalization, and the like. These are not only modes of producing false necessity. They are also typical operations of ideology. (I use that term to refer to discursive manoeuvres that help to legitimate and hence stabilize existing configurations of power). To this extent, false necessity and ideology can be understood as overlapping concepts—overlapping, but not coextensive. For, as Slavoj Žižek explains, if ideology is the 'act of discerning some higher Necessity in a contingent occurrence', it can also be 'the opposite procedure of failing to . . . discern the hidden necessity in what appears as mere contingency'.[43] Žižek reminds us in this passage that ideology may manifest itself just as much in what I have called false contingency as it does in false necessity. It follows that the critique of ideology demands enquiry into both.

42 T Eagleton, *The English Novel* (Blackwell: Oxford, 2005) 311.
43 S Žižek, 'Introduction' in S Žižek (ed.), *Mapping Ideology* (Verso: London, 1994) 4.

What false contingency puts on our agenda, then, is above all this question of how necessity gets rewritten as contingency. As with false necessity, we are confronted with a process that can take many different forms. To begin with one characteristic mode, things may be addressed in such a way that determination becomes difficult or impossible to discern. Thus, for instance, the angle of vision may be too narrow, or the time-frame too short, so that patterns and logics cannot appear. Systemic factors may also be removed from view insofar as the focus is on issues conceived as monadic and autonomous, rather than relational and interactive. Alternatively, to mention another mode, analysis may be framed by assumptions, or may start from premises, that rule out in advance the idea that necessary factors could exist. Here necessity is not so much unnoticed as repudiated. This takes us back to my earlier comments about the elision of determination with determinism, and determinism with Marxism, for most commonly the assumptions and premises that discredit the consideration of necessity or place it beyond respectable scrutiny rest on just those elisions (and just that anti-Marxism—I will return to that aspect later). Or yet, to refer to one final mode, explanatory ambitions may be disavowed, so that the existence or non-existence of determining factors becomes a matter of indifference in the discussion at hand. Rather than being unnoticed or repudiated, necessity becomes simply irrelevant. This, of course, is common practice in legal scholarship; we tend to be deeply interested in 'how' questions (not to mention 'what', 'where', 'when' and some 'who' and 'whom' questions), but distinctly reserved when it comes to 'why' questions. Hence indeed my own preference, indicated earlier, for using determination as a guiding concept, rather than causation. On the other hand, Carr has an important message, and not only for professional historians. This is that if we don't ask why, and insistently so, the argument is stacked in favour of voluntarism; it is the investigation of causal relations that pushes open the compass and exposes to analysis the full range of (intentional and non-intentional) factors affecting social processes.

Falsity as a Critical Concept

In elaborating the concept of false contingency, I have dwelled at some length on the idea of contingency and on the neighbouring or related ideas of necessity, false necessity, determinism and determination. But I have not yet said very much about the other element that goes to make up the concept of false contingency: the idea of falsity. In what sense is false contingency false? According to the familiar scholastic notion of truth, a statement is true if it accurately represents the way things are, and false if it does not. Truth is the correspondence of reality and thought. That account no doubt remains useful for many purposes, but, as is well known, it has come under severe strain in recent decades, at least among philosophers. As Alex Callinicos explains, '[i]f truth is the correspondence of reality and thought, then we could only conclusively establish the truth of a sentence by comparing discourse to the world, which presumes the existence of some Archimedean point outside discourse'.[44] Yet there is no such point. Reality is out there, of course, but thought has no unmediated access to it; knowledge has to be recognized as 'propositional', rather than 'immediate'. From this perspective, returning to my question, false contingency cannot be a straightforward error or failure accurately to represent the state of the world. It cannot simply mean that necessity matches empirical reality while contingency does not. So what can it mean?

We can get help with this by revisiting the overlapping concept of ideology I touched on earlier, as a similar issue has arisen in debates about what it might mean to characterize ideology as false consciousness. Some theorists of ideology, Callinicos among them, have concluded from the abandonment of the idea of immediate knowledge that we should reject the conception of ideology as false consciousness altogether.[45] Instead, according to him, ideology should be viewed in pragmatic or political terms as referring to the symbolic terrain of social struggle, and epistemological issues—questions of truth and falsity—should be dismissed as 'beside the point'.[46] For other theorists of ideology, however, we can hold onto the idea that ideology involves falsehood. After all, the propositional notion of truth still allows for truth and falsity; it just entails that truth claims are propositions that are answerable not to reality itself but rather to other propositions, in the shape of verifying criteria. Terry Eagleton is among those who consider that falsehood remains relevant in this context, but he shows that some care is needed in capturing it. As he characterizes the

[44] A Callinicos, *Marxism and Philosophy* (Oxford University Press: Oxford, 1983) 126.
[45] Ibid, 134–5. [46] Ibid, 135.

situation, ideological statements are often true at one level and false at another: 'true in what they affirm but false in what they exclude', or true in their surface meaning, but false in their subtext and implications.[47] To use a different vocabulary, such statements are often true if we confine ourselves to the 'constative' dimension—the description of facts—but false if we consider also the 'performative' dimension—what the words enact and the effects they produce. Viewed in this light, ideology is not false because it is erroneous, whether under the correspondence theory or the propositional approach. Rather, it is false because it is misleading: it skews understanding, stunts enquiry and dazzles analysis. And since in each case it does so in ways that contribute to the stabilization of prevailing power, whatever illusion is involved is very much a part of reality—as much a part of reality as that otherwise fragile power itself.

Taking Eagleton's lead, we can begin to make out the sense in which false contingency can be said to be false. The point is not that necessity matches reality while contingency does not. It is that discussion is structured in such a way that necessity gets obscured. False contingency is generally true *so far it goes*, but false as to what it excludes; true in what it says but false in what it leaves unsaid, in its unarticulated assumptions, implications and effects. Thus, to return to my examples, it really is the case that the meaning of democracy is less self-evident than debates over the norm of democratic governance might have led us to believe. And it really is the case that international human rights initiatives are less universally beneficial than the international human rights movement generally admits. But to stop the discussion there is in each case silently to signal that these phenomena are isolated problems, unrelated to wider processes, tendencies and dynamics at work in the world, and that is false. Indeed, it is not only false; in leaving those processes, tendencies and dynamics unacknowledged and unexplored, we also occlude awareness of what it will take to effect change. To show how things that are necessary may be made to seem contingent is, then, to show how the assertion of contingency, whatever its validity, overwhelms the investigation of necessity, and how in the process mutability becomes an abstract claim, only tenuously related to real, historical possibilities.

There is another aspect to this. The idea of ideology as false consciousness has been controversial not only for reasons having to do with

[47] T Eagleton, *Ideology* (Verso: London, 1991) 16.

the nature of truth. It has also been controversial because of the apparent implication that an enlightened few have privileged knowledge of the truth while the rest of humanity languishes in darkness and delusion. That is plainly an arrogant and patronizing idea, but, more importantly, it is entirely implausible. Most people are unlikely to be deluded most of the time. In the case of false contingency, this could scarcely be clearer. It seems a safe bet that almost no-one actually believes that contingency is all: Williams is surely correct that when he writes that to believe that would be 'in real terms a kind of madness'. At any rate, to refer again to my earlier examples, David Kennedy and I are both, I hope, quite rational, and were certainly aware at the time we wrote those texts that phenomena in the social world are not purely random or arbitrary. We were aware of that, but it was not reflected in what we did. One is reminded here of Peter Sloterdijk's concept of 'cynical reason' or 'enlightened false consciousness'.[48] These are Sloterdijk's phrases for the experience of being 'without illusions' and yet, as he puts it, 'dragged down by the "power of things"'.[49] In his words, 'enlightened false consciousness' is that 'modernized, unhappy consciousness, on which enlightenment has labored both successfully and in vain'[50]—successfully in that lessons have been learnt, but in vain in that those lessons have not been put into practice; perhaps, in some measure, they cannot be put into practice. Linked to that, 'this consciousness no longer feels affected by any critique of ideology; its [ideology's] falseness is already reflexively buffered.' Thus, we act, not in ignorance, but 'against better knowledge'.[51] Does this put paid to notion of false consciousness, and hence false contingency? Slavoj Žižek, in his psychoanalytically inspired work on the concept of ideology, argues that it does not.[52] He agrees with Sloterdijk that ideology is often, perhaps always, reflexively buffered to various degrees: the idea of ideology critique as a form of symptomatic reading designed to confront representations with their repressed truth cannot be accepted. But what if the illusion is not on the side of knowledge, but rather on the side of action? While we may know that contingency is not all, what we may still fail to recognize are the effects of acting as if it is; we may fail to see how this impacts upon lived reality. For Žižek, it

[48] P Sloterdijk, *The Critique of Cynical Reason* (University of Minnesota Press: Minneapolis, Minn, 1988). [49] Ibid, 6.
[50] Ibid, 5. [51] Ibid
[52] S Žižek, 'How Did Marx Invent the Symptom?' in S Žižek (ed), *Mapping Ideology* (Verso: London, 1994) 296, especially at 314–6.

is this failure to recognize the way ideology is 'structuring our real, effective relation to reality'[53] that constitutes the basis of false consciousness. This then clarifies another facet of the sense in which false contingency is false. Just as it cannot be equated with simple error, so too it cannot be equated with simple delusion. You may well know that history is not simply a matter of chance and will, but what counts is that you act as if it is.

Allow me to mention one final matter related to this question of falsity as a critical concept. I have so far touched only obliquely on the 'psychology' of false contingency, so to speak. By this I mean, in particular, the issue of whether it should be regarded as deliberate, or whether instead we are talking about something which is normally unconscious. The drift of most of what I have said is that it is normally unconscious. In addition to the discussion just now of ideology, recall, for instance, my reference at the beginning to Carr's insistence that any adequate theory of history has to take into account that people's actions often have results they do not intend or even desire. With this in mind, GA Cohen has remarked that the charge of 'conspiracy theory', so often levelled at those who dwell on the dimension of necessity, is a canard.[54] The point is not to expose some elite plot, but to understand the way the world around us works, in all its complexity, subtlety and contradictoriness. On the other hand, Cohen also suggests that too much sensitivity about the charge of conspiracy may be misplaced. In his words, '[t]here is more collective design in history than an inflexible rejection of "conspiracy theories" would allow'.[55] This statement can be interpreted, of course, in a variety of ways, but on one interpretation Cohen is reminding us that the psychology of false contingency is no less complex than the rest of social reality. What begins as naiveté may end up as hypocrisy, and what emerges as self-deception may get mixed up with manipulation. Assuredly, unconscious factors play a part, but they cannot be held to exclude conscious ones. For, to quote Cohen once more, '[c]onspiracy is a natural effect when men of like insight into the requirements of continued class domination get together, and such men do get together'.[56]

[53] Ibid, 316.

[54] GA Cohen, *Karl Marx's Theory of History* (2nd edn, Oxford University Press: Oxford, 2000) 289–91.

[55] Ibid, 290.

[56] Ibid

Concluding Reflections

I should now sum up and conclude. Beginning with Marx's study of the history of post-1848 France, I have highlighted his insight that men and women make their own history, but they do not do so just as they please in circumstances they choose for themselves; they do so in present circumstances, given and inherited. The transformation of Louis Bonaparte from elected president into self-proclaimed emperor was not inevitable. But nor was it purely fortuitious. Rather, it was determined historically by a variety of factors which Marx explores in this study. I have suggested that, as scholars of law, we tend to give considerable attention to vindicating the contingency of history, but rather less attention to its necessary, or determined, aspects. As a result, a form of 'false contingency', as I have called it, is left unchallenged, according to which the injustices of the present order are made to appear as though they were random, accidental and arbitrary. And if they are random, accidental and arbitrary, then the prospects of changing them become every bit as remote as if they were fated. The category of possibility—not just abstract possibility, but real, historical possibility—drops out of sight.

What are the implications of this argument? Just as Roberto Unger's concept of false necessity prompts enquiry into the processes by which necessity is produced, so the concept of false contingency prompts enquiry into the processes by which contingency is produced. The operation of these processes can only adequately be grasped in particular contexts, but we can identify some general, or preliminary, lessons. First, the concept of false contingency urges an approach that considers phenomena not in discrete, monadic or free-floating terms, like Eagleton's swirl of vivid odds and ends, but relationally, as elements with larger social systems. Secondly, the concept of false contingency encourages explanatory ambitions. At any rate, it highlights that fighting shy of explanation constitutes a stake in the politics of knowledge. Finally, the concept of false contingency invites us to get over our debilitating fear of determinism, and begin to engage more fully with the quite distinct issue posed by its non-doctrinal cousin, determination.

I have suggested that the fear of determinism is also, in some sense, a fear of Marxism, and with that in mind, let me end now with one further thought. It will not have escaped your notice that many of authors I have cited in this paper are people closely associated with

Marxism: at the outset Karl Marx himself, of course, but then EH Carr, Raymond Williams, Louis Althusser, Ellen Wood, Terry Eagleton, Alex Callinicos, G.A. Cohen—and perhaps even Slavoj Žižek falls in that category. Clearly, one subtext of the paper is that there is much inspiration and instruction to be drawn from the Marxist tradition, and we neglect it to our detriment.[57] So is the argument of false contingency ultimately a call for the renewal of Marxist legal analysis? Within international legal scholarship there is indeed at present something of a renaissance of Marxist analysis, led by Bill Bowring, BS Chimni and China Miéville, and their work has challenged received understandings in immensely productive ways.[58] But no, the argument of false contingency is not made on behalf of Marxism. If it is made on behalf of any 'ism', it is anti-anti-Marxism,[59] along the lines of the anti-anti-communism (as distinct from communism) that emerged and helped to energize resistance during the McCarthy years in the United States.

[57] See further the essays collected in S Marks (ed), *International Law on the Left* (Cambridge University Press: Cambridge, 2008).

[58] See especially BS Chimni, *International Law and World Order* (Sage: New Delhi, 1993) and 'An Outline of a Marxist Course on Public International Law' in S Marks (ed), *International Law on the Left* (Cambridge University Press: Cambridge, 2008) 53; C Miéville, *Between Equal Rights* (Brill: Leiden, 2004); and B Bowring, *The Degradation of the International Legal Order?* (Routledge-Cavendish: London, 2008).

[59] I believe this term has been used by, or in connection with, Edward Said. See S. Howe, 'Edward Said and Marxism: Anxieties of Influence' 67 *Cultural Critique* (2007) 50, at 79. (Howe's article contains the sole reference to the phrase 'anti-anti-Marxism' I have found.)

Abstraction and Equality

*William Lucy**

> It is not easy—perhaps not even desirable—to judge other people by a consistent standard. Conduct obnoxious, even unbearable, in one person may be readily tolerated in another; apparently indispensable principles of behaviour are in practice relaxed—not always with impunity—in the interests of those whose nature seems to demand an exceptional measure.
>
> A Powell, *A Question of Upbringing*[1]

Two Ways of Being Judged

When called to account by our nearest and dearest, it is normal to expect their judgement to be tempered not just with mercy but also by knowledge: not only of the conduct in question and its context, but knowledge of our character. We expect to be judged by those closest to us in all our particularity. We hope they know us and thus show a greater understanding of our deeds because of their knowledge of our characters or 'selves'. We are not strangers but intimates, with a history. Thus it is that those who know me best know that I am often tardy and, although they are rightly beyond excusing this inexcusable behaviour, they now plan with it in mind. I am told, for example, to arrive for meetings earlier than they are actually scheduled to start. In addition, their judgement of this aspect of my conduct is in some sense mitigated or restrained by their knowledge of me; what they would invariably

* Professor of Law, Law School, University of Manchester. Some work on this paper was carried out at the John Fleming Centre for the Advancement of Legal Research, College of Law, Australian National University. Thanks to Michael Coper, Dean of the College of Law, and Peter Cane, Director of the Centre, for their hospitality. Versions of this paper were read by Dora Kostakopoulou, Richard Mullender and John Murphy and presented at the 2008 SLS annual conference and as a CLP lecture at UCL: I'm grateful to them and the audiences at both presentations for all the comments received.

[1] A Powell, *A Question of Upbringing* (Arrow: London, 2005) 52.

regard as inexcusable in others in most contexts, they sometimes find acceptable in me in some contexts. My nearest and dearest clearly do not judge me by standards generally applicable to the rest of humankind.

The law does. Or, at least, it purports to judge me in the same way as it judges all its addressees. This is because bourgeois law's judgement is abstract. That is to say: it judges us (i) not in all our particularity but as identical *abstract beings*; (ii) by reference to *general and objective standards equally* applicable to all such beings; (iii) the application of these standards being mitigated only by a *limited range of exculpatory claims*.[2] It follows from these three components of law's abstract judgement (hereinafter 'the three components' or 'the components') that one cannot, in absence of a recognized exculpatory claim, resist or deflect the law's judgement by claiming, for example, that one lacks the fortitude or capacity to adhere to its standards. It would also seem to follow that one should not be able to demand a level of legal protection tailored to one's extraordinary sensitivities rather than those of an ordinary (or reasonable or abstract) person.

Law's abstract judgement is the focus of what follows. Although that label is used hereinafter principally as a shorthand way of referring to the three components just identified, this usage does not imply that the three components are necessary and sufficient conditions of law's abstract judgement. The possibility that law's abstract judgement has other components is not therefore foreclosed.

The fact that law's abstract judgement is obvious and commonplace to lawyers, invoked each and every day, cannot shield it from critical attention nor reduce the need for justification. The latter need arises not just because state power operates through the medium of law's abstract judgement. It also arises because this form of judgement seems, *prima facie*, morally problematic. Yet law's abstract judgement may also be a morally and politically significant historical development. Historically informed lawyers will see in its emphasis on generality and

[2] It is tempting to say these features show that law's judgement is also objective and there is at least one credible sense of 'objective' in which this is right (see M Kramer, *Objectivity and the Rule of Law* (Cambridge University Press: Cambridge, 2007) pp 38–45). However, the notion of objectivity when applied to law can have many other senses (all of which are dealt with in Kramer, ibid, and in K Greenawalt, *Law and Objectivity* (Oxford University Press: New York, 1992) and is undoubtedly complex. Although some significant points about law's abstract judgement can be made using various senses of that term (see Greenawalt, ibid, chs 6–8), this runs the risk of unnecessary complication.

abstraction a distinction between feudal and bourgeois law. If the former was made up of different legal incidences tied to a variety of fairly rigid roles, one's rights and obligations being determined by those roles, then the latter seems distinctive in its lack of such rigidity and because all citizens are legally formally equal. Law's abstract judgement seemingly embodies the latter idea and this could plausibly be regarded as a constitutive characteristic of bourgeois law. Being apparently both morally worrisome and morally significant ensures that law's abstract judgement is worthy of our attention.

What follows has two parts. The first sketches in a little more depth the elements of law's abstract judgement and highlights why it might be thought morally problematic. The second, and longer part, considers what might be said in favour of law's abstract judgement.

Law's Abstract Judgement

Before sketching the three alleged components of bourgeois law's abstract judgement, two preliminary points need be noted. The first is that law's abstract judgement, insofar as a 'pure' version of it exists, is found in most current legal systems—common law, civilian or 'mixed'—and functions in both private and criminal law. While the latter two areas are indeed very different, the differences do not obviously impact upon the abstract nature of law's judgement, save perhaps to explain its possibly more limited role in criminal as compared to private law.[3] The second point is that the purest form of law's abstract judgement is found at the liability stage in private law and the conviction stage in criminal law. The selection, details and quantum of the remedy in private law and the sentence in criminal law are quite often (although certainly not always) tailored to the situation of the particular claimant and defendant in the former, and the precise circumstances of the accused, his conduct and its affect upon the victim, in the latter. Why the role of law's abstract judgement is limited in this way is an interesting question, but not one tackled here.

[3] Insofar as liability judgements in the criminal law are also regarded as moral judgements, it might be thought that law's abstract judgement and its components, like reasonableness standards, are inappropriate. This, however, assumes a somewhat dubious picture of moral judgement, as will be noted below, as well as assuming an exaggerated distinction between private law judgements and moral judgements.

The Three Components

The third component of law's abstract judgement is best examined first, since this is the least complex and (perhaps) least interesting of the three. It can be labelled the *limited avoidability* component. That the law, be it private or criminal, recognizes only a limited number of exculpatory claims is not news.[4] Nor is it particularly informative to highlight that these exculpatory claims are not easily available, being constrained by a variety of requirements. Almost as trite is the observation that some think the law's 'progress' from barbarism is marked by greater permissiveness and flexibility in its recognition of excusing conditions. The salient point, for current purposes, is that far fewer exculpatory claims are currently legally recognized than would be if defendants were judged by reference to all the detail of their context and particular attributes. If each defendant's conduct was judged not just against the law's general standards, but also through a fine-grained assessment of her particular capacities on this particular occasion, in these precise circumstances, then the grounds for excusing her conduct could multiply. To know the details of this particular defendant's character and situation at the time of, for example, a traffic accident, might be to know that in some sense she could not have avoided it. And this, some assume, should generate either a complete or partial excuse. But, while such factors may be taken into account at the sentencing stage in the criminal law, they are almost completely irrelevant at the conviction stage and at the liability stage in private law.

That, when accepting exculpatory claims, the law rarely delves into the particularities of the defendant's context or character is reinforced by something else: such exculpatory claims are usually valid only if reasonable. Reasonableness requirements are the principal means by which the law treats those before it as abstract beings rather than as the beings they actually are. The third component of law's abstract judgement thus takes us to the core of the other two. All three are functionally connected since, both alone and combined, they serve to lead law's judgement away from particularity and toward abstraction.

[4] In speaking of 'exculpatory claims' I do not intend to elide or even take a position on the plausibility of the oft-drawn distinction between justification and excuse. For some of the themes here see J Horder, *Excusing Crime* (Clarendon Press: Oxford, 2004) ch 1 and 99–103.

The functional connection between the first two components becomes apparent as soon as we attempt to unpack them. The first, remember, is that the law regards those called before it as abstract beings. Let us name this the *presumptive identity* component. What does it entail? At the least this: that the law sees neither claimant nor defendant, neither accused nor victim, as the actual human beings they truly are, in all their detail and specificity. The law does not often see or even notice the specific set of abilities or experiences those being judged have, nor does it usually notice their different social, cultural, economic or ethnic backgrounds. The law's judgement is supposedly blind to these differences, treating Duke and pauper, man and woman, Christian and non-Christian, homo- and heterosexual, aesthete and philistine alike. The law most obviously treats those brought before it alike, as the same, in that it regards all its addressees as having the same bundle of formal legal rights.

Another way in which those judged by the law are treated as being both abstract and alike, is that all are usually held to the same general standards of conduct. This is the second limb of law's abstract judgement; it can be dubbed the *uniformity component.* The standards are general in the sense that their content is the same and they apply to all those whom they address, applying whether or not particular addressees can actually live up to their requirements. Lack of interest in the specific capacities of particular individuals is, of course, the essence of reasonableness standards. The pass mark for examinations or driving tests is almost never set with a view of the abilities of particular candidates in mind. It is, rather, set with a view to marking basic standards of competence anyone must achieve in order to succeed, provided it is possible for some to succeed. Whether or not specific candidates succeed, given their background, abilities and circumstances at the time of attempt, is irrelevant unless an exculpatory claim is triggered. This situation is obviously echoed in the law. Insofar as the law assumes all citizens can achieve the same standards of (usually reasonable) conduct, or embody the same standards of (usually reasonable) fortitude, it ignores obvious differences between them which actually determine whether they can or cannot achieve these standards on particular occasions. Holding addressees of the law to the same general standards is therefore a means of treating them as abstract beings rather than as actual beings in all their particularity.

Most current legal systems contain standards for the assessment of a *defendant's* conduct or character that explicitly disregard the particularities of that individual, the context of their conduct, or both. Perhaps the most obvious private law example is the reasonable care standard in negligence and its cognates. In English and Scots law a defendant's conduct must be of the same standard as that of a reasonable person engaged in that kind of activity, a reasonable person being—by definition—reasonably competent. That the defendant cannot actually reach that standard is usually irrelevant.[5] There, are, however, some exceptional instances in which a judgement of negligence is influenced by the specific circumstances or particularities of the defendant. Child defendants are treated somewhat differently when determining the duty of care they owe to others.[6] There are also *dicta* in English negligence and nuisance cases to suggest that the level of a defendant's wealth will make a difference in the assessment of whether or not her conduct was reasonable.[7] Furthermore, in some jurisdictions it has been recognized that what is reasonably foreseeable for the purposes of establishing a duty of care in negligence can differ according to the ethnic and religious context of both claimant and defendant.[8]

If the standard of reasonable care in negligence and the abstraction it involves set a demanding standard, then the default standard of performance in contract law is even more stringent. It is not enough in many contracts for a defendant to have used reasonable endeavours to perform, since the standard of compliance is strict.[9] Thus not only those unable to achieve a reasonable standard of performance are judged by a standard that is beyond them; so, too, are those capable of a reasonable level of performance. Both reasonableness and strict standards ignore the particularities and context of the individual being judged; both are therefore manifestations of law's abstract judgement.

[5] See *Nettleship v Weston* [1971] 2 QB 691 (UKCA); *Wilsher v Essex Area Health Authority* [1988] AC 1074 (HL); *Imbree v McNeilly* [2008] HCA 40.

[6] *McHale v Watson* (1966) 115 CLR 199 (HCAus); *Mullin v Richards and another* [1998] 1 All ER 920 (CA). Perhaps the first sustained analysis of the particular physical, psychological and other features of claimants and defendants regarded as salient by the US courts in determining tort liability was G Calabresi, *Ideals, Beliefs, Attitudes, and the Law* (Syracuse University Press: Syracuse NY, 1985), chs 2–4. Do not assume that the differential treatment of child defendants by the courts is unimpeachable: M Moran, *Rethinking the Reasonable Person* (Clarendon Press: Oxford, 2003), chs 2 and 3.

[7] *Knight v Home Office* [1990] 3 All ER 237 (HC); *East Suffolk Rivers Catchment Board v Kent* [1941] AC 74 (HL); *Goldman v Hargreave* [1967] 1 AC 645 (PC).

[8] See *Kavanagh v Aktar* (1998) NSWCA 779 (NSW, Aus.); *Mustapha v Culligan of Canada Ltd* [2005] 138 ACWS 3rd 767 (Ontario, Can).

[9] *Rainieri v Miles* [1981] AC 1050, 1086 (HL). See also G Treitel, *The Law of Contract* (11th edn, Sweet and Maxwell: London, 2003) 838–40 and S Smith, *Contract Theory* (Clarendon Press: Oxford, 2004) ch 10.

A number of defences in English criminal law also rest upon assessments of reasonableness. The most problematic defence in recent years has been the partial defence of provocation. To invoke this defence an accused must, *inter alia*, establish that the alleged provocation was such as to lead any reasonable person to lose their self-control. There are a number of problems with this defence, both in terms of its rationale and its practical consequences. But one issue has proved pre-eminently problematic: the determination of what a reasonable person is and how such a person behaves in specific contexts. Particularly fraught has been the question of which physical features, character traits or habits of the accused should be regarded as pertinent to the alleged provocation.[10] The circumstances of the cases are usually such that endowing the reasonable person with one or other of these features makes the putative provocation more rather than less salient. A substance abuser whose perception of the world is addled by abuse could well regard as provocation conduct that in the eyes of others would be worthy of nothing more than laughter or a raised eyebrow. Of course, the greater the degree to which the reasonable person in provocation cases is endowed with the character, traits and habits of the accused, and situated as the accused was situated at the time, the less weight the reasonable person standard carries. The thrust of some recent decisions in England and elsewhere has been the virtual obliteration of the distinction between a reasonable person standard and a subjective standard tailor-made for the particular accused.[11]

A less prominent but equally interesting emerging issue in the criminal law is that of so-called 'cultural defences'.[12] While quite different in doctrinal terms, this issue has some resonance with recent developments in the provocation defence. This is found in the fact that cultural defences—whatever their particular form or detail—claim that the accused's conduct is either justified, excused or mitigated by the fact that

[10] Three vivid (from many) examples in a number of jurisdictions are *R v Morhall* [1996] AC 90 (HL); *Stingel v R* (1991) 171 CLR 312 (HCAus); *R v Thibert* [1996] 1 SCR 37 (SCCan).

[11] See *R v Smith* (*Morgan*) [2000] 4 All ER 289 (HL); *Luc Thiet Thuan v R* [1997] AC 131 (PC); *Jersey v Holley* [2005] 2 AC 580 (PC) and *R v Van Dongen* [2005] EWCA Crim 1728. Despite its status, *Smith* is now apparently overruled.

[12] An interesting introductory discussion is A Phillips, 'When Culture Means Gender: Issues of Cultural Defence in the English Courts' (2003) 66 Modern Law Review 510–31. Much more comprehensive is AD Renteln, *The Cultural Defense* (Oxford University Press: New York, 2004). One of the most vivid cases is *People v Kimura* No A-091133 (Sup Ct, LA County, 24 April 1985), on which see Renteln, ibid, at 25.

it is right, reasonable or normal within a specific cultural group. The general claim by proponents of such defences is clear. It is that once account is taken of the accused's background and beliefs (and, perhaps, other features of their cultural context), then their conduct, which would ordinarily be contrary to the criminal law, is either justified or excused.

Does private law treat *claimants* in the same way as it often treats defendants, namely, as abstract beings? Some doctrines suggest so. The law of contract, for example, only rarely awards damages for what can be called subjective losses which, on one view, are understood as those that arise from the specific non-market valuation claimants put upon performance.[13] Although different from one another in detail, the remoteness rules for damages in contract and tort seemingly ensure that claimants cannot claim for injury that results from their particular sensitivities. Insofar as such injury and the losses that result from it are not foreseeable by a reasonable person, they go uncompensated. While unlikely to be a goal of the remoteness rules, one of their practical effects is therefore to treat claimants as abstract rather than actual beings. This effect is, however, almost completely negated with respect to some physical and psychological features of the claimant by the eggshell skull rule in the law of negligence.[14] If the claimant has an unusual sensitivity to a particular process or form of treatment inflicted by the defendant in breach of a duty of care, the consequence being that the claimant is affected far more seriously than others would be, then the defendant cannot escape liability for the claimant's commensurately greater losses.[15] Much the same rule holds in the criminal law.[16]

By insisting tortfeasors and accused take their victims as they find them, the law is recognizing some particularities of the actual claimant or victim before the court. There are other areas of private law—defamation, for example—in which the courts should in principle be willing to take seriously the claimant's cultural or religious context. It is surely right that a statement which clearly does not defame a non-Muslim can be defamatory when made about a Muslim. Yet, alongside these instances in which the law recognizes some aspects of a victim's

[13] See *Ruxley Electronics and Construction Ltd v Forsyth* [1996] AC 344 (HL) and *Farley v Skinner* [2002] 2 AC 732 (HL).

[14] The relevant psychological features, in the US cases, usually relate to matters of belief rather than psychological fortitude: see Calabresi, n 6 above, chs 3 and 4.

[15] A masterly treatment, although now slightly outdated, is HLA Hart and T Honoré, *Causation in the Law* (2nd edn, Clarendon Press: Oxford, 1985) 172–6.

[16] See *R v Blaue* [1975] 3 All ER 446 (CA) and the discussion in Hart and Honoré, ibid, 360–2.

particularity, there are doctrines which suppress other such aspects. In the tort and crime of battery, for instance, victims must display reasonable fortitude in light of the touching, buffeting and other non-consensual contact of everyday life.[17] The criminal law also rules out consent as a defence to some crimes whether or not the particular 'victim' consented, the animating notion of this prohibition being in part the idea that reasonable people will never agree to some forms of treatment by others.[18]

Three Points

The first point is that the preceding sketch of law's abstract judgement shows that it is not ubiquitous. It is more deeply embedded in some areas of legal doctrine than in others and a more expansive survey would surely disclose areas in which it has little influence.[19] Judged across entire legal systems, the abstract nature of law's abstract judgement is thus a matter of degree, of more or less. There is, moreover, undoubtedly a constant process of mediation between more and less abstract forms of judgement within areas of legal doctrine—like negligence and the defence of provocation—where law's abstract judgement is entrenched. This mixed picture might suggest that law's abstract judgement is actually in tension with a model of pure particularistic judgement, rather than being in tension with less abstract versions of itself. The question of that with which law's abstract judgement can and must be contrasted is the second point worthy of note here. A number of considerations suggest that the tension cannot be understood as one between abstract judgement, on the one hand, and pure particularistic judgement, on the other.

First among these is that law surely is, in some significant sense, a matter of subjecting human conduct to *general* rules. And general rules are themselves unavoidably a matter of abstraction, a means of setting aside or ignoring particularity. The rule 'drive on the right' applies to all drivers whatever their context or particular capabilities: it means drive on the right *regardless* of such matters. Some might deny that law

[17] See *Re F* [1990] 2 AC 1 (HL) 72–3 (Lord Goff).

[18] See, for example, *R v Brown* [1994] 1 AC 212 (HL).

[19] Two obvious examples are the sentencing stage in criminal law and the 'best interests of the child' principle in family law. Note that the latter ostensibly particularistic form of judgement is usually deployed not in relation to either claimant or defendant but rather to their offspring or ward.

and legal judgement must invoke general rules. Frederick Schauer, for example, holds that 'disputes could . . . be *resolved* largely without reference to . . . rules imposing substantive constraint on the content of decisions. Having been empowered to resolve a dispute, the adjudicator would be authorised . . . to come to a conclusion as open-endedly as appropriate in the circumstances'.[20] While this is undoubtedly possible—an adjudicator could be empowered to resolve disputes however she likes, deciding one by flipping a coin, another by the reference to the height of the disputants etc.—it is important to see that general rules are nevertheless still in play here. First, as Schauer himself notes, 'empowering rules create the institutions of dispute resolution and empower certain officials to resolve certain sorts of disputes'.[21] These rules must surely be general to some extent if they are to perform their task. Secondly, the dispute here must, if genuine, have a subject-matter, a basis, and what else could that be except some or other standard of conduct for the disputants? If the dispute is not about whether one or other disputant did or refrained from doing something required or otherwise appropriate, then what could it conceivably be about? The dispute must revolve around either a standard of conduct, in which case the standard is likely to be general, or a contested matter of fact. A standard of conduct need not be general as a matter of necessity, since it is possible that a bespoke standard be created for and applied to no one but the disputants in question. Although conceivable, such a limited standard would be rare in a developed legal system. Furthermore, such a standard might, by virtue of its specificity, come into tension with some components of the rule of law ideal in such a legal system.

A second consideration showing it is implausible to regard law's abstract judgement as being in tension with pure particularistic judgement is both banal and true. It is that the idea of pure particularistic judgement is *prima facie* senseless. If this is judgement based upon all the specificities, physical and mental, of those being judged, and responsive to the context and all the relevant circumstances of their conduct, without recourse to any general rule or standard, then it is hard to see how anything is being judged. If the reply here is: 'the person before us' then it invites this question: 'against what standard?'

[20] F Schauer, *Playing by the Rules* (Clarendon Press: Oxford, 1991) 10 (emphasis added). It will be clear to anyone familiar with this book that the conception of rules in play in the picture of law's abstract judgement developed in this essay is much the same as Schauer's conception of rules as entrenched generalizations: ibid, chs 2–5.

[21] ibid

If we allow (as we surely must) that judgement assumes a standard against which conduct or character or both are assessed, then this problem of intelligibility disappears, but we face another difficulty. This is that extremely fine-grained responsiveness to the character and context of those whose conduct is being judged can undermine the power of the standard against which they are assessed.

Suppose, for example, that the pass mark for an examination is 40 per cent. If, in assessing whether a candidate has failed, we have recourse to much more than the bare figure of their examination performance, taking into account and allowing marks for all the aspects of the candidate's character and context that affected their preparation for and performance in the examination, then the pass mark itself plays a relatively minor role in judging performance. Indeed, as the range of factors taken into account to explain and mitigate a 'failed' performance expands, so the weight of the standard embodied in the pass mark declines. While its weight cannot diminish to zero, provided the standard is still in force, it can get close to that if a massive number of factors can serve to turn a mark of less than 40 into a mark of 40. The rule that the pass mark is 40 persists, but the ways of getting 40 far exceed what was once the primary way of achieving that mark, namely, by answering a sufficient number of questions at or above the pass level.

That law's abstract judgement must be contrasted with less abstract (but not pure particularistic) judgement prefigures another and related warning. It is that law's abstract judgement should not be flippantly contrasted with moral or ethical judgement. This is a mistake because there is no *a priori* reason why the models in play in one domain should not be similar or even exactly the same as those in another. Moreover, if the contrast is motivated by the thought that morality's judgement is always and ever particular, then that is assuredly questionable.[22] Morality's judgement is sometimes abstract and sometimes less abstract (or particular), at least as a matter of moral practice. We accept that, generally speaking, an important characteristic of some moral judgements is their generality and abstraction: we think, for instance, that some moral duties are owed by all human beings as human beings to all human beings as human beings. Of course, this is a euphemistic way of referring to such duties for, although agent-neutral in the sense that they are owed by all human beings regardless of their conduct or projects, they are almost never unspecific in terms of their subjects and

[22] Schauer's reading of act-utilitarianism comes close to this: see n 20 above.

objects. Thus the agent-neutral duty to aid those in mortal peril is defined by the situation of those to whom it is owed. The duty is thus not one actually owed to 'all human beings' but only to 'all human beings in mortal peril'. This does not, however, entail that the judgement which gives rise to the duty is in any but the most trivial sense particularistic.

In addition to fairly broad, agent-neutral duties, our moral lives also contain agent-relative duties rooted in our past conduct or arising from our context.[23] The judgements that give rise to these duties—the judgement that, for example, some of my duties to my children are more demanding than some of my duties to the children of strangers—are obviously more particular or less abstract than some of those that generate agent-neutral duties. Yet it is far from clear that one kind of duty and judgement clearly dominates the other: agent-neutral and agent-relative duties, and the more and less abstract judgements that generate them, are undoubtedly both significant parts of the moral landscape. This relatively complex view of moral practice might be contested at the level of moral philosophy. Some moral philosophers might, indeed, argue that it embodies a flagrant contradiction. Arguments to that end, interestingly, can come from two completely differently directions: that ordinary moral practice is contradictory either because all moral duties, and the reasons that support them, are general and invariable, or because all moral duties and their supporting reasons are in fact variable and context-sensitive.[24] Each claim resonates with a broader position about the place of general principles in moral reasoning, and each can imply a view of the role of reason and impartiality in morality and moral deliberation.[25] The complexities here are sidestepped in what follows, the essay's only commitment on this topic being that moral practice, like law, embodies both more and less abstract models of judgement.

The third and, for present purposes, most important point worthy of note here is raised by this question: 'what is wrong with law's abstract judgement?' Even a brief survey of the many discussions of law's

[23] See D Parfit, *Reasons and Persons* (Clarendon Press: Oxford, 1984) 143 and T Nagel, *The View from Nowhere* (Oxford University Press: New York, 1986) 152–4.

[24] The eye of this current intellectual storm is the dispute between moral particularists and their opponents. For an introduction to one version of particularism, see J Dancy, 'The Particularist's Progress' in B Hooker and M Little (eds) *Moral Particularism* (Clarendon Press: Oxford, 2000) ch 6 and J Dancy, *Ethics Without Principles* (Clarendon Press: Oxford, 2004).

[25] On which see L Blum, 'Against Deriving Particularity' in Hooker and Little, ibid, ch 9.

abstract judgement and its cognate ideas suggests that the answer must be: a very great deal. The charge sheet includes *inter alia* the indictment that it is an historical anachronism, that it is not gender-neutral, that it suppresses the law's ability to respect difference, that it is a morally insensitive means of assessing culpability, and that it is a bearer of normal but discriminatory standards for the assessment of conduct.[26] Although a harrowing list for any defender of law's abstract judgement, this still does not contain the two most obvious indictments. The first is that law's abstract judgement, while a means of treating people equally, is simultaneously a means of treating them unequally. Treating different people as if they were the same, or treating different people in exactly the same way, is in effect a form of unequal treatment.[27] Law's abstract judgement functions in just this way and it seems, at least at an intuitive level, to raise a problem of fairness.

Fairness is also the crux of the second obvious indictment, which is probably closer to the surface of common sense than the first. Keeping defendants rather than claimants in mind, it appears intuitively unfair

[26] If western legal systems are indeed caught in a transition from autonomous to reflexive law (as sketched, albeit somewhat speculatively, in P Nonet and P Selznick, *Law and Society in Transition* (Transaction Publishers: New Jersey, 2005 (originally published in 1978)), or in a shift from legal order to post-liberal legal order (as noted in R Unger, *Law in Modern Society* (Free Press: New York, 1976)), then law's abstract judgement does indeed seem to be historically doomed. See, for a related discussion, E Pashukanis, *Law and Marxism: A General Theory* (Pluto Press: London, 1983), Introduction and chs 2–4. N Lacey, *Unspeakable Subjects* (Hart Publishing: Oxford, 1998) chs 6 and 7, provides an overview of the ways in which contemporary feminism engages legal doctrine and theory. For a discussion of the links between feminism, deconstruction and law's abstraction see N Lacey, 'Violence, Ethics and Law: Feminist Reflections on a Familiar Dilemma' in S James and S Palmer (eds), *Visible Women* (Hart Publishing: Oxford, 2002) ch 5. D Cornell, *Philosophy of the Limit* (Routledge: New York, 1992) chs 4–6, outlines some of the challenges some versions of deconstruction present to law's abstract judgement (and many other dimensions of law as well). A similar task, more critically conducted, is the burden in J Balkin, 'Deconstruction's Legal Career' (2005) 27 *Cardozo Law Review* 719. A nuanced and admirably clear general treatment of the some of the problems of abstraction (and categorization) is M Minow, *Making All the Difference* (Cornell University Press: Ithaca, NY, 1990) Introduction and chs 1–3. The abstraction and universality of human rights law, itself a manifestation of law's abstract judgement, has been impugned in Hegel's name by C Douzinas, *The End of Human Rights* (Hart Publishing: Oxford, 2000) chs 10 and 12. On the ethical bluntness of the criminal law's means of assessing culpability see A Norrie, *Punishment, Responsibility and Justice* (Clarendon Press: Oxford, 2000) chs 1–2 and 9; for the discriminatory impact of reasonableness standards in tort see Moran, n 6 above.

[27] The classic statement of the point is K Marx, 'Critique of the Gotha Programme', *Marx-Engels Collected Works*, 1874–1883, Volume 24 (Lawrence and Wishart: London, 1989) pp 86–7.

that the law holds them to standards of behaviour which they cannot achieve. If those standards are reasonableness or strict standards, then a group of defendants—including the accident-prone and clumsy, the dim-witted, the bad-tempered, the easily distracted and the hasty, the absent-minded and the over-selfish—are almost always going to be short-comers when judged against them.[28] This situation would be troubling enough in our non-legal lives, but the fact that state power is brought to bear against short-comers seemingly compounds the problem.

To elucidate this intuition is not necessarily to commend it. And, indeed, with only a slight widening of focus, the intuition can appear less robust. If we keep claimants rather than short-comer defendants in mind, matters are less clear cut. Imagine a blameless claimant is damaged by the conduct of a short-comer. The question of the fairness of leaving that loss where it falls must surely arise. That the short-comer could not have achieved that standard of conduct, breach of which has given rise to the claimant's damage, is not a compelling answer to that question. For we are still left with a baleful situation: a blameless claimant has suffered damage and that damage was undoubtedly caused by the short-comer defendant. Are the moral merits here obviously in favour of the latter? It seems not, at least in purely legal terms, since defendants feel the force of law's abstract judgement more than claimants. Generally speaking, legal doctrine is less accommodating towards the particularities and context of defendants than claimants (think again of the egg-shell skull rule). This may well represent an explicit higher valuation of claimants' interests as against those of defendants and, if so, it is not completely without moral foundation. At least, that is so if (i) we are just as—or more—troubled by the situation of the blameless claimant as that of the short-comer defendant; and (ii) there are respectable moral reasons for that.

Abstraction and Equality

What might be said in favour of bourgeois law's abstract judgement? In answering this question, let us suppose a pure form of law's abstract judgement is in play—all three components are in play to the maximal

[28] The term 'shortcomer' belongs to T Honoré: see *Responsibility and Fault* (Hart Publishing: Oxford, 1999) 16.

degree. This form excludes much. It ignores character, particularity and context. Its positive aspects appear to be generality, equality of treatment and impartiality. Although a pure form of law's abstract judgement is not ubiquitous, it is still probably rightly regarded as the focal meaning, or paradigmatic instance, of bourgeois law's judgement.[29] For, despite the many doctrinal departures from a pure and unyielding form of abstract judgement, the latter remains intact and central just because the former are usually regarded as exceptions. That they are seen as abnormal, as in need of justification, attests to the power the pure form law's abstract judgement has over swathes of juristic thought.[30]

The following discussion is narrowly focused: only one broad type of argument that might support law's abstract judgement is examined. The type is arguments from equality and only two examples are considered, one of which proceeds directly from a conception of equality, the other of which moves indirectly, beginning with an account of the wrongs entailed by particular forms of inequality. Arguments of this type are an obvious and promising starting point here because law's abstract judgement undoubtedly embodies forms of equality of treatment. Law's abstract judgement might therefore be supported by broader, compelling conceptions of equality or by the considerations (not themselves necessarily egalitarian) that support such conceptions. It should be noted that the two equality-based arguments examined below are drawn from a limited intellectual palette, namely, the existing resources of contemporary liberal political and legal philosophy. Furthermore, the discussion is also completely unoriginal, offering no new argument for, or account of the nature of, equality. It can, however, claim to be original in another sense, for it seeks to test contemporary liberal political and legal philosophy by reference to its ability to support law's abstract judgement, an obvious feature of existing legal institutional design.[31] More will be said about whether or not this is an

[29] On focal meaning, see J Finnis *Natural Law and Natural Rights* (Clarendon Press: Oxford, 1980) 9–18 and 277–81.

[30] Evidence in support of this claim can be garnered from the critical response to cases such as *Morhall, Stingel* and *Thibert*, n 10 above and *Smith*, n 11 above. Much the same responses are provoked by cases varying the standard of the duty in negligence.

[31] Features of legal institutional design are, for the purposes of this essay, aspects of legal systems broader than particular legal doctrines, rules and principles but sometimes embodied in such doctrines, rules and principles. Jurists are reminded of the importance of both features and principles of general institutional design in, *inter alia*, Lon L Fuller, *The Principles of Social Order* (KI Winston ed) (Duke University Press: Durham NC, 1981).

appropriate way of testing and evaluating normative theories below. The discussion also considers whether or not the normative over-determination of aspects of legal institutional design is a problem.

Narrowness of focus means much is ignored. For example, non-normative arguments are left untouched, even though they are likely to do some work in supporting law's abstract judgement.[32] Moreover, at least two other plausible sources of normative support for law's abstract judgement are set aside. One is the argument from responsibility, which is primarily a response to an alleged source of unfairness in law's abstract judgement, namely, that arising from holding agents to standards of conduct they cannot achieve. At least one conception of responsibility provides an immediate challenge to this view, although it is not discussed here.[33] Another principally normative argument (or, more accurately, family of arguments) also left untouched is that from the rule of law.[34]

Finally, note that the equality-based arguments considered below respond directly only to one of the already noted objections to law's abstract judgement. Responding to each of these objections in the depth required would far exceed the boundaries of even a lengthy essay. The discussion draws the sting from the indictment which holds that law's abstract judgement is simultaneously a form of equal and unequal treatment, suggesting that this charge is not, ultimately, troubling. Rather than rebutting each of the other specific indictments against law's abstract judgement, the aim is instead to counterbalance them by illuminating some considerations weighing in favour of law's abstract judgement.

Dimensions of Equality

A pure form of law's abstract judgement ensures equality of treatment in a number of different ways. Its *uniformity component* usually holds all

[32] Two apparently non-normative arguments that could well justify law's abstract judgement are therefore overlooked. These are (i) arguments from some or other conception of efficiency and (ii) arguments from convention. Standard introductions to the former are R Posner, *Economic Analysis of Law* (7th edn, Aspen Publishers: New York, 2007); S Shavell, *Foundations of Economic Analysis of Law* (Harvard University Press: Cambridge Mass, 2004). On the latter, helpful treatments are Finnis, n 29 above, 284–9 and E Ullman-Margalit and S Morgenbesser, 'Picking and Choosing' (1977) 44 *Social Research* 757–85.

[33] See Honore, n 28 above, ch 2.

[34] But see W Lucy, 'Abstraction and the Rule of Law' (2009) 29(3) OJLS, 481–509. I am grateful to the editor of that journal for permission to reproduce section II of that essay here.

addressees of the law to the same general standards. The content of those standards is the same for all of those to whom they apply, and the standards are applied to all addressees alike, whether or not they are capable of compliance. The form of equality of treatment that this component embodies is therefore something like equality *under* the law, understood as requiring, at the very minimum, that all are governed by the same laws. The *presumptive identity component* is a means of ensuring equality *before* the law, since it regards all the law's addressees as the same: as abstract beings with formally equal bundles of legal rights and duties, rather than the real human beings they truly are, in all their particularity, specificity and difference. The *limited avoidability* component functions in much the same way as the other two, operating to allow excuses and defences only when reasonableness standards are satisfied, whether or not particular defendants can actually satisfy those standards. It thus regards those judged by the law as the same—as having the same capabilities and levels of fortitude—and holds them to the same standards. It is therefore a manifestation of equality before and under the law.

In a very clear sense law's abstract judgement, and the forms of equality of treatment it embodies, is a matter of exclusion. Each component illustrates what the law does not (or should not) see when judging its addressees, at least not explicitly and not at the conviction or liability stage. The law does not usually see the obvious differences in wealth, status and class that exist between its addressees; nor does it usually see differences in education or upbringing that often accompany these other differences. It is also rare for the law to register other equally or more obvious differences between its addressees: its judgement does not and, it is often assumed, should not differ in accordance with the gender, religion, ethnicity or sexuality of those before it, except when such tempering is unavoidable. Law's judgements, furthermore, are usually made without reference to the particular differences in aptitude, temperament, character or attitudes of those before it.

Some Wrong Turnings

Are there any arguments from broader conceptions of equality that can support the forms of equal treatment embodied in law's abstract judgement? It is helpful, at the outset, to know where *not* to look for guidance when seeking an answer to this question. The thinnest and most formal account of equality available to us, which insists that like cases be treated alike and different cases differently, is unhelpful because its most important constituents are left unspecified. And, since the process of specifying criteria of likeness and difference usually serves to elide the distinction between this supposedly 'formal' account of equality and its more substantive competitors, there seems little point in according it separate attention.[35] It also seems plain, as some jurists have already realized, that some contemporary philosophical accounts of equality have little relevance to our questions or to questions about juristic equality more generally.[36] These accounts constitute that strand of contemporary political philosophy best labelled 'luck egalitarianism'.[37] This strand of thought originated as an engagement with John Rawls's *A Theory of Justice*, and is distinctive at least because it appears to take much more seriously than Rawls the outcomes of both natural and social lotteries.[38]

Luck egalitarians' efforts to either cancel out or mitigate the consequences of the natural and social lotteries have led them to a vast number of proposals seemingly unlimited in their jurisdictional range. There is thus apparently no realm, or very few realms, of social life immune to the force of luck egalitarian principles. They supposedly extend not only to Rawlsian primary goods but to the distribution of temperament and marriage partners.[39] They do not, however, explicitly touch features of (legal) institutional design like law's abstract judgement. This might be because luck egalitarianism is not in any genuine sense a 'political' conception of equality, being unconcerned with the political structure of a society and the opportunities for power and

[35] See HLA Hart, *The Concept of Law* (2nd edn, Clarendon Press: Oxford, 1994) 159–60 and D Lyons, *Moral Aspects of Legal Theory* (Cambridge University Press: Cambridge, 1993) ch 2. For an optimistic treatment of the notion of formal justice and some of its constituents, see C Perelman, *The Idea of Justice and the Problem of Argument* (Routledge and Kegan Paul: London, 1963) ch I.

[36] See S Moreau, 'The Wrongs of Unequal Treatment' (2004) 54 University of Toronto Law Journal 291, 291–4.

[37] The term was coined in Elizabeth Anderson, 'What's the Point of Equality?' (1999) 109 *Ethics* 287, 289. See also S Scheffler, 'What is Egalitarianism?' (2003) 31 *Philosophy and Public Affairs* 5.

[38] J Rawls, *A Theory of Justice* (revised edn, Clarendon Press: Oxford, 1999) 62–5. For discussion see Scheffler, ibid, 8–12 and 24–31.

[39] Anderson, n 37 above, 287–8 (citing GA Cohen, 'On the Currency of Egalitarian Justice' (1989) 99 *Ethics* 906–44, 922–3 and 930–1; P Van Parijs, *Real Freedom for All* (Clarendon Press: Oxford, 1995) 127).

advantage it contains.[40] Yet rather than excusing luck egalitarian accounts of equality, this surely serves to indict them. For, without claiming that a society's political structure is the most important determinant of the life chances of its citizens, it is surely one of a number of such determinants. It is thus not unreasonable to expect it to loom large in theories of equality.[41]

The apparently paradoxical combination of lack of institutional impact and unlimited jurisdictional range in luck egalitarianism is often conjoined with the dubious assumption that equality is solely or principally a distributive and quantitative notion. On this view equality is concerned with the appropriate distribution of some divisible 'thing' or 'things' in proper amounts.[42] This contrasts with the understanding in play in most juristic formulations of equality. These formulations include that class of equality provisions found in many legal systems, either in constitutional documents or in ordinary legislative provisions such as, *inter alia*, Amendment XIV of the US Constitution; sections 15 and 28 of the Canadian Charter of Rights and Freedoms; Article 14 of the European Convention of Human Rights; sections 1–4 and schedule 1 of the Human Rights Act 1998; and section 8 of the ACT Human Rights Act 2004. The idea of equality in these sources is principally qualitative, a matter of 'forms' of treatment—no person shall be denied equal protection of the law—rather than a matter of distributing amounts of treatment (of the laws?) or other things. Being principally qualitative, the subject matter of these equality provisions is not easily 'distributed' in any obvious sense, which is not to say that some distributions of some things cannot provide evidence of unequal treatment under these provisions.

It might be thought that, since these provisions invoke a more limited, primarily qualitative, institutionally focused and institutionally

[40] This is clearly not true of Dworkin whose account of equality, while in some respects rightly dubbed luck egalitarian, also engages with the political structure: see *Sovereign Virtue* (Harvard University Press: Cambridge Mass, 2000) chs 3 and 4 and 'Equality, Luck and Hierarchy' (2003) 31 *Philosophy and Public Affairs* 190–8.

[41] The near absence of an obviously political conception of equality in luck egalitarianism has been noted by Anderson, n 37 above, 312–37. Scheffler, n 37 above, 34–9 makes a similar general point.

[42] Thus it is that 'outcomes' (which usually imply a distribution some or other measurable 'thing' or set of 'things') are of primary interest to many philosophers of equality. See L Temkin, *Inequality* (Oxford University Press: New York, 1993) 11–12. Temkin notes that some notions of equality might not be illuminated by distributive-cum-quantitative (and thus outcome obsessed!) conceptions: ibid at 16.

embedded idea of equality, they will be a more fruitful source of support for law's abstract judgement than luck egalitarianism. These juristic statements of equality are not, however, as useful as they might seem. This is mainly because these provisions, in and of themselves, provide relatively little guidance as to the nature of equality and inequality. For, although some instances of official behaviour are now clearly invalid under these provisions (such as, for example, the enactment of a legal provision explicitly favouring Caucasians and disadvantaging non-Caucasians),[43] there is nevertheless a large range of behaviour about which it is hard to be certain. This, at least, is so if we have reference to nothing more than the wording of these provisions themselves. Thus it is unclear from the wording of Amendment XIV of the US Constitution, for example, that the University of Michigan Law School's admission procedures, which in some instances prioritize factors over and beyond academic merit, deny some citizens equal protection of the laws. It is similarly far from obvious whether equivalent broad equality provisions in other jurisdictions permit, for instance, differential access to public spaces, schooling, legal advice or differential levels of social security benefits.[44]

In all but the most blatant cases, then, the courts must necessarily go beyond the literal wording of most juristic equality provisions, in part because of the distance between these general statements about equality ('every individual is equal before and under the law') and specific legal questions (is it discriminatory for the province of Quebec to pay the young unemployed less in benefit than their unemployed elders?). Since the words of this and similar equality provisions give relatively little guidance as to what or how they should be applied in the specific circumstances of particular cases, something more is therefore necessary than the bare text. But what is this 'more' and, further, what informs the search for it and gives it traction?

[43] The key word in the first clause of this sentence is 'now', particularly if we have the history of the XIV amendment in mind: see W Nelson, *The Fourteenth Amendment: From Political Principle to Judicial Doctrine* (Harvard University Press: Cambridge Mass, 1988) chs I, VII and VIII and A Bickel, 'The Original Understanding and the Segregation Decision' (1955) 69 Harvard Law Review 1.

[44] A smattering of the vast number of cases must include: *Grutter v Bollinger* 539 US 306 (2003) (US Sup Ct)—access to law school and the XIVth Amendment; *Gosselin v Quebec (AG)* [2002] 4 SCR 429 (SC Can)—differential welfare benefits and s 15 of the Canadian Charter; *Baczkowski and others v Poland*, App No 1543/06, ECtHR 2007—Article 14 (*inter alia*) of ECHR and permission for public gathering.

If the provision in question has been litigated before, then the precedents will obviously provide some guidance. So, too, might the legislative history of the provision, but there is no guarantee that it will include anything salient. Furthermore, even textual sources like precedents and legislative history will rarely rationally compel a particular interpretation of an equality provision in a specific case. This is because this additional textual evidence must itself usually be subject to a process of elaboration or interpretation. Consider, for example, what courts usually do with precedents cited to them as a guide to the meaning of some or other equality provision. Whether or not such precedents are factually close, they are usually examined (i) with a view to the light they cast upon the meaning of the provision; and (ii) with a view to their implications, were they to be applied in the case at bar. Particular precedents might be found satisfactory or unsatisfactory on one or both dimensions. This process is clearly anything but automatic and almost never determined solely by the precedent(s) cited. If the precedents were indeed determinative in this 'self-interpreting' way, then the case would assuredly not be 'hard' and thus unlikely ever to be litigated.[45]

Moreover, when 'the meaning of the provision' is sought, either in precedents if there are any, or in other textual sources if there are none, what exactly is being sought? The words of the provision are there in the text, so how can its 'meaning' reside elsewhere? And when the implications of applying a precedent to the case at bar are determined to be either good or bad, how is that judgement arrived at? The answer is that the meaning sought, and the basis for judging implications to be good, bad or indifferent is found, as many lawyers would say, in 'a theory' of the provision in question, by which they mean an account of its point, purpose or value.[46] The process of elaboration in the interpretation of

[45] On what makes a hard case hard, see the slightly different views in N MacCormick, *Legal Reasoning and Legal Theory* (revised edn, Clarendon Press,: Oxford, 1994) 65–72 and chs VI–VIII and R Dworkin, *Taking Rights Seriously* (Duckworth: London, 1977) 81. MacCormick's original view has been supplemented in his *Rhetoric and the Rule of Law* (Clarendon Press: Oxford, 2005) 49–52.

[46] Although this process is described in somewhat different ways by jurists in various jurisdictions, its substance is at root the same. Interesting characterizations of the process with regard to the XIVth Amendment of the US constitution include J Trusman and J ten Brook, 'The Equal Protection of the Laws' (1949) 37 California Law Review 341–81; O Fiss, 'Groups and the Equal Protection Clause' (1976) 5 *Philosophy and Public Affairs* 107–77; and L Tribe, *American Constitutional Law* (2nd edn, Foundation Press: New York, 1988) vol II, ch 16. For the interpretation of equality provisions in the Canadian Charter and elsewhere, see A Brudner, *Constitutional Goods* (Clarendon Press: Oxford,

juridical equality provisions is thus one that involves both descent, moving from the general provision to the particular case, and ascent, moving from the general provision to an account of its point, purpose or value. Both aspects of this process are connected in that 'the theory' of the provision indicates the interpretative pathways along which to proceed in particular cases. Note, though, that such theories are not rightly viewed as more abstract than the provisions they theorize. Rather, they usually serve to make those provisions more specific, both in terms of their point, purpose or value and in terms of what that account of point, purpose or value requires in particular cases. Such a theory gives the provision 'depth' or 'body', showing us how to go on applying it, and is thus not best regarded as being solely abstract.[47]

The relative emptiness of juridical equality provisions, and the process of elaboration involved when the courts apply them in all but the simplest of cases, warrant the claim that these provisions cannot explicitly support law's abstract judgement. The distance from these provisions to law's abstract judgement is just as far, and just as contestable and problematic, as that from such provisions to, for example, a decision about the legitimacy of differential welfare payments. Furthermore, the fact that law's abstract judgement is not ubiquitous in legal systems shows it is unlikely that general equality provisions can implicitly support law's abstract judgement. If such provisions did indeed *require* law's abstract judgement, then the doctrinal instances in those legal systems in which the law's judgement is not abstract—some segments of the criminal law, for example—would surely already have come under challenge. That they have not does not entail the conclusion that these provisions cannot support law's abstract judgement; it does, however, make it unlikely that they do.

If general juridical equality provisions are unlikely to provide much support for law's abstract judgement, how should we proceed? More attention could be given to the theories said to provide an account of the point of these provisions and their constitutive value or values.

2004) 131–42; D Beatty, *The Ultimate Rule of Law* (Oxford University Press: New York, 2004) ch 3; and R Sharpe and others, *The Charter of Rights and Freedoms* (3rd edn, Irwin Law: Toronto, 2005), ch. 15. An interesting treatment of the interpretative pathways of the European Court of Human Rights is G Letsas, *A Theory of Interpretation of the European Convention on Human Rights* (Clarendon Press: Oxford, 2007) chs 3 and 5.

[47] The idea of 'knowing how to go on' and its many complications and ramifications (all of which are ignored above) was, of course, a preoccupation of the later Wittgenstein: see L Wittgenstein, *Philosophical Investigations* (2nd edn, Blackwell: Oxford, 1958) I, §143-§242.

For, while the actual provisions may not explicitly support law's abstract judgement, the theories said to inform such provisions might. Viewed in direct light, rather than through the prism of general equality provisions, the content of these theories should become more explicit and tractable. This way of proceeding is, however, potentially rich with distractions and our examination must, therefore, be doubly limited. First, our interest is only in those theories of general equality provisions that invoke, either directly or indirectly, an account of equality. Equality can function here either as a single and significant value in and of itself or as a bearer and protector of other interests and values. Secondly, our interest is in whether or not law's abstract judgement can be supported by some of these theories; we are not ultimately concerned with whether or not the accounts of equality examined below do or can provide plausible theories of the general equality provisions. General equality provisions are on our agenda, remember, only because they—or the broader theories that animate them—might be capable of supporting law's abstract judgement.

The Right to Equal Concern and Respect

The first candidate potentially well equipped to both animate general equality provisions and support law's abstract judgement is Ronald Dworkin's right to equal concern and respect.[48] The right holds that:

> [g]overnment must treat those whom it governs with concern, that is, as human beings who are capable of suffering and frustration, and with respect, that is, as human beings who are capable of forming and acting on intelligent conceptions of how their lives should be lived. Government must not only treat people with concern and respect, but with equal concern and respect. It must not distribute goods or opportunities unequally on the ground that some citizens are entitled to more because they are worthy of more concern. It must not constrain liberty on the ground that one citizen's conception of the good life of one group is nobler or superior to another's.[49]

[48] By singling out this right for attention, I do not assert that it is the only possible foundation in Dworkin's work that might support law's abstract judgement. In both *Law's Empire* (Hart Publishing: Oxford, 1998) 184–5 and *Justice in Robes* (Harvard University Press, Cambridge Mass, 2006) 176–8, Dworkin suggests an understanding of integrity that includes a form of equality before the law. There could be support here for law's abstract judgement, but this pathway is not further examined, principally because in each instance the argument is made only in passing and is somewhat inchoate. Dworkin's general statement on integrity is found in *Law's Empire*, ibid, chs 6 and 7.

[49] Dworkin, n 45 above, 272–3.

Thus 'individuals have a right to equal concern and respect in the design and administration of the political institutions that govern them'.[50] They should be 'treated with the same respect and concern as anyone else'.[51]

The right to equal concern and respect is far more limited than the injunctions of luck egalitarianism, applying only to the conduct of 'government' and, presumably, some of its outcomes or consequences. Nor is there any legitimate sense in which the right is exclusively concerned with the quantitative distribution of some 'thing', be that resources, welfare or some hybrid of the two.[52] For, in addition to sometimes having distributive implications, the right always entails that certain interests of all citizens must be treated in the same way.[53] The right is also clearly more specific than the general equality provisions just mentioned, principally because it sketches reasonably precisely what must be valued—citizens' ability to formulate and pursue conceptions of the good life as well as their capacities for suffering and frustration. Furthermore, the right tells us how this 'bundle' of interests, which presumably all citizens have, must be treated by government, namely, with both equal concern and equal respect. It is therefore an exaggeration to claim that this right 'does not have sufficient content to explain the precise nature of the wrongs that are done to people who are not treated with equal concern and respect.'[54] The wrong done by breach of this right is some combination of: (i) curtailment, partial or complete, of some citizens' ability to pursue or formulate conceptions of a good life; (ii) the undervaluing or ignoring of some such conceptions; (iii) the undervaluing or ignoring of the suffering and frustration caused to citizens by either (i) or (ii). Although not compendious, the wrong here is sufficiently clear and substantial to show that the right to equal concern and respect is not empty. That much becomes even more obvious on switching from the negative to the positive mode for, if instead of cataloguing the wrongs done by breach of the right we think instead of the capacities it upholds, it is

[50] Ibid, 180. [51] Ibid, 227.

[52] In the remainder of this subsection I will speak of 'the right to equal concern and respect', 'the right' and 'this right' indiscriminately.

[53] Dworkin, n 45 above, 227.

[54] Moreau, n 36 above, 296. Note that Moreau thinks the right to equal concern and respect is but part of a more general conception of human dignity. It may be that she regards the latter as vague but not the former, although the text suggests that she thinks both suffer the same ailment.

clear that at the very least the values of autonomy and freedom must loom large.

The right to equal concern and respect does a good deal of intellectual and practical work for Dworkin. It was invoked in his early work as a means of making sense of the principal theoretical components of Rawls's account of justice. It played another equally important role, along with the distinction between personal and external preferences, in Dworkin's defence of reverse discrimination, and appeared to be *the* (or one) basis of the normative power of the rights thesis, the most distinctive component of Dworkin's account of hard case adjudication.[55] In his mid-period work, Dworkin argued that the right was the core of any coherent and meaningful liberal political philosophy.[56] His more recent work on the nature and content of distributive justice also appears to rely upon a variant of this right.[57]

But what, exactly, might this right entail or support? It is probably too demanding to expect a strict entailment between this very general right and a particular concrete feature of institutional design such as law's abstract judgement. We will therefore content ourselves with examining less rigorous forms of support, if any, that this right might provide for the latter. There is certainly no bar to the right supporting a policy or form of treatment (like law's abstract judgement) that is not itself obviously a right. For, although Dworkin regards the right to equal concern and respect as abstract and fundamental, and therefore a good basis from which to derive other rights,[58] he also claims that the right can support collective welfare claims. Thus he holds 'that particular political rights, *and* the idea of collective welfare, *and* the idea that these function as antagonists at the level of political debate, are all consequences of the fundamental ideal of a political community as a community of equals'.[59] It is this kind of claim that marks Dworkin as a hedgehog in political theory rather than a fox.

[55] Dworkin, n 45 above, chs 6, 9 and 12. The right to equal concern and respect 'appeared' to support the rights thesis because there is no explicit claim to this effect in Dworkin, n 45 above, ch 4 (although the right does appear in passing). Rather, there is a medley of statements that seemingly license this conclusion: see Dworkin, n 45 above, 101 in conjunction with xii and xv.

[56] *A Matter of Principle* (Oxford University Press: New York, 1985) ch 8.

[57] In Dworkin, *Law's Empire*, n 48 above, 222 and ch 8, and in Dworkin, *Sovereign Virtue*, n 40 above, 1–3, 128, 131 and 184 the right to equal concern and respect becomes (just) the right to equal concern or equality of concern.

[58] Dworkin, n 45 above, xiv-xv.

[59] Ibid, 368: emphasis in original.

Since the right *can* in principle support law's abstract judgement, it remains to determine whether it actually *does* support it. One way in which it surely does so is this: taking the right to equal concern and respect seriously ensures a form of equality before the law, namely, that citizens cannot be discriminated against or favoured because of their status, conception of a good life, or overall 'worthiness'. Interestingly, law's abstract judgement also ensures a similar kind of equality before the law by prohibiting judicial reference to many of the considerations that the right to equal concern and respect also embargoes. Like the right to equal concern and respect, law's abstract judgement is a way of not seeing many of the differences between citizens. Law's abstract judgement does not register, except when legal doctrine demands, whether a claimant's style of life is worthy or base, or whether she is patrician or plebeian, aesthete or philistine. Citizens are treated as if they were the same by law's abstract judgement and, if it is genuinely successful in doing this, it therefore functions in much the same way as the right to equal concern and respect. If we value the right to equal concern and respect, in part because of the function it fulfils, must we therefore also value law's abstract judgement because it fulfils the same function?

There are two immediate objections to an affirmative answer. One holds that similarity of function (between law's abstract judgement and the right to equal concern and respect) cannot justify. Suppose X (the lawful interrogation of those suspected of crime) functions so as to bring about, or bring us closer to, Y (unearthing the truth). The fact that X is justified tells us nothing about Z, which also functions so as to bring us closer to Y. Unless X and Z are ultimately identical, there is simply no warrant for concluding that the justification for the former extends to the latter, even though both have the same function. This is apparent if Z in this example were torture. Torture may well have the same goal as lawful interrogation, but the considerations which justify the latter are unlikely, in most circumstances, to extend to the former. Furthermore, it might also be the case that whatever value is realized by some particular institution or institutional feature is best realized only in one context or only in a specified amount. It is then possible that the realization of this value, or an increase in its amount, brought about by another institution or institutional feature, is a bad thing. Thus the fact that the right to equal concern and respect embodies some or other value warrants neither the conclusion that that value is always and ever valuable, nor that its realization by other means or in ever greater amounts is always and ever valuable.

It is tempting, in the face of this objection, to try to unearth the considerations that justify or support the right to equal concern and respect. It could then be determined whether or not these considerations can also support law's abstract judgement. If they can, then there is not only unity of function here but unity of justification. This line of thought, however, serves to reinforce the first objection and in fact constitutes the second objection. The problem is that the search for deeper considerations supporting the right to equal concern and respect is virtually fruitless.[60] The right's abstract and fundamental status—the principal factor in its favour for Dworkin is its ability to support and make sense of many other principles of political morality—means that attempting to find considerations to support it is hard and, perhaps, pointless. That the main argument in favour of this right is its power to link together and illuminate other important values and concerns clearly suggests it is non-derivative. If it is, then it is assuredly silly to look for considerations supporting it.

What, then, remains to be said about the way in which the right to equal concern and respect can support law's abstract judgement? Principally that the conclusion just reached does not close off all the available justificatory space. It could still be maintained that the values instantiated or realized by the right to equal concern and respect are, as a purely contingent matter, also realized by law's abstract judgement. It could also be added that this situation was in itself a desirable one. At least, the latter could be maintained pending a demonstration that the values realized by the right to equal concern and respect were confined to certain contexts only, or had an optimum distribution or quantity.

[60] 'Virtually fruitless' because the right could well be supported by the abstract egalitarian principle sketched in R Dworkin, 'Comment on Narveson' (1983) 1 *Social Philosophy and Policy* 24–40, 31–5 (a seemingly related version of which Dworkin invokes in *Sovereign Virtue*, n 39 above, pp 128–9)). However, Dworkin offers no positive argument in favour of this principle, thinking it 'too fundamental . . . to admit of any defence in the usual form' (Comment, ibid, 31). He contents himself with showing how hard it is to reject the principle. This approach does not persuade Narveson: J Narveson, 'Reply to Dworkin', ibid, pp 41–4. The right might also gain support from the value of integrity, for discussion of which see Dworkin, *Law's Empire*, n 49 above. Of course, a non-Dworkinian justification for the right to equal concern and respect is presumably possible (it might, for example, be derived from a conception of autonomy or public reason or from the type of consideration Narveson himself highlights (ibid, 44)), but this would simply extend further the seemingly endless search for justifications (this time, for the conception of autonomy or public reason or other considerations invoked to support the right). For an example, see Moreau's effort to root the right in a conception of human dignity: Moreau, n 36 above, 295–6.

If it is morally important that government conduct is not based upon judgements about the worth of different citizens' lives, then law's abstract judgement is presumptively just as important as the right to equal concern and respect. This claim need not hold that similarity of function always and ever justifies, but only that similarity of function justifies in this particular context (*cateris paribus*).

Some critics of the right to equal concern and respect are, however, sure to be dissatisfied with this argument, primarily because they think that the right itself is a fundamentally flawed idea. One objection they make should be dismissed at the outset. The objection denies that the right can entail any genuine form of equality, principally because it is alleged that the invocation of 'equal' in the right is empty. Herbert Hart claimed that what is wrong when the right to equal concern and respect is breached by, for instance, legislation denying freedom of worship is the straightforward restriction of liberty. It is 'fantastic' to suppose that victims of this legislation should complain about not being treated with equal concern and respect.[61] Hart clearly does not accept that the denial of freedom of religion to one group is a form of unequal treatment, in the sense that they are denied a liberty that other groups enjoy. But the ground for his refusal is unclear. For, since it does not seem in any way unnatural to characterize this situation as one of unequal treatment, why should we refrain from such a characterization? Hart says that 'equal' in this characterization is playing an empty role, but he buttresses the point by changing the example. Were a tyrant to ban *all* forms of religious worship, he says, citizens could not complain that their right to equal concern and respect had been breached, since all have been treated in the same (objectionable) way.[62] In part, that is surely true. But this example simply raises a different issue from that in which some citizens are allowed freedom of worship and some are not. It should not, therefore, guide what we would say in the latter case. Furthermore, the blanket ban on religious worship could indeed be challenged, in normal circumstances, by the right to equal concern and respect. This is because it would surely be unusual for such a ban ultimately to be based upon anything other than a judgement of the

[61] HLA Hart, *Essays in Jurisprudence and Philosophy* (Clarendon Press: Oxford, 1983) Essay 9, 220. A related version of this objection, which rather mysteriously insists that 'equal' in the right does not flow 'from a conception of equality but from the fact that . . . [the right refers] to a group with equal claim to have the right', is offered by J Raz, 'Professor Dworkin's Theory of Rights' XXVI *Political Studies* 123, 130.

[62] Hart, ibid, 221.

unworthiness of a life informed by religious observance. While the wrong here is non-comparative (because all citizens are treated in the same way), it is still plausibly a breach of the right to equal concern and respect: the ban accords no concern and no respect to this aspect of citizens' lives.

Two related objections might still be tabled by critics. One holds that the right to equal concern and respect cannot reliably entail or support anything because it is internally contradictory. The contradiction arises from the conflict between the right's two key components, respect and concern. The other objection, by contrast, concedes that the right to equal concern and respect may well support law's abstract judgement in the limited, functional way just noted, but affirms that the right also supports models of judgement incompatible with law's abstract judgement.

The argument that the right to equal concern and respect is internally contradictory is at best inchoate; certainly it has never been explicitly unpacked. The point is usually made in passing and consists only of noting a possible and plausible difference between respect and concern, namely, that the latter is consistent with paternalism while the former is not.[63] This clearly falls far short of demonstrating that these two notions (and the right they constitute) cannot be combined because they are contradictory. This would require a demonstration that in every, most or many instances in which the right is in play, its different components pull in opposite directions. That this is not the case in a number of instances is clearly affirmed by Dworkin's own invocations of the right in such different contexts as reverse discrimination, civil disobedience and euthanasia.[64] While it must be conceded to these critics that the right to equal concern and respect is certainly complex, that does not show it to be contradictory.

For the second objection to succeed, it would have to establish that the opposite to law's abstract judgement—a form of purely particularistic judgement—fulfils the same function as the right to equal concern and respect. It seems unlikely that such a case can be made. This is

[63] Raz, n 61 above, 130. A closely related version of this objection, briefly but judiciously stated (there is 'on the face of it' a conflict between these two components) is offered by R Sartorius in his essay in M Cohen (ed), *Ronald Dworkin and Contemporary Jurisprudence* (Duckworth: London, 1983) 208–9. Dworkin's subsequent use of the bare 'equal concern' formulation, in which respect drops out of the picture (see n 56 above for references), could be explained as a recognition of the power of this objection.

[64] See Dworkin, n 45 above, chs 8 and 9 and R Dworkin, *Life's Dominion* (Vintage Books: New York, 1993) ch 7.

principally because forms of particularistic judgement give free reign to considerations excluded from judicial and other government decisions by the right to equal concern and respect. On what grounds, for instance, would a form of particularistic judgement exclude a defendant's view of his own superiority as a good reason for risky conduct? Since for this defendant the interests of others are plainly less significant than his own, and since this belief informs his conduct, how can it be excluded as a relevant factor in determining his liability? Similarly a defendant who accepts the belief, rife in her community, that it is right to kill her children and herself in the face of marital infidelity would seem, on a particularistic model of judgement, to have grounds for a defence. If such considerations —presumably deeply held and in some sense constitutive of the defendant's identity—are excluded, then the form of judgement in play cannot be exclusively particularistic. The right to equal concern and respect is a tempting and serviceable basis upon which to exclude such considerations, although it is clearly not the only possible basis. Yet the mere fact that the right functions in this way serves to show its incompatibility with models of particularistic judgement.

The Wrongs of Unequal Treatment

Some jurists and philosophers analyse the notion of equality indirectly, focusing not upon equality itself but rather elucidating the various wrongs unequal treatment can entail. When used to generate an account of the point, purpose or value of juridical equality provisions, this approach generates results more piecemeal or incremental than those yielded by general statements of what equality entails.[65] There are at least two reasons behind this approach: one consists of an attempt to place the value of equality in the context of our other moral and political values. Thomas Scanlon undertakes this task and concludes that, rather than being as deep or fundamental a value as is sometimes thought, the substantive notion of equality does relatively little work in explaining what is wrong with many forms of unequal treatment.[66] Values other than equality are often in play here,

[65] Which is not a criticism. An excellent illustration of the value of this approach is Moreau, n 36 above.

[66] T Scanlon, 'The Diversity of Objections to Inequality' in *The Difficulty of Tolerance* (Cambridge University Press: Cambridge, 2003) 202. A substantive idea of equality holds 'that it is morally important that people's lives or fates should be equal in some substantive way: equal in income, for example, or in overall welfare' (ibid, 202).

according to Scanlon. These values highlight a set of discrete wrongs, each one of which may be brought about by particular instances of unequal treatment. Another reason motivating this approach is found in the alleged vagueness and abstraction of general political-philosophical accounts of equality, particularly when used to illuminate the meaning of various conceptions of juridical equality. So, for example, Sophia Moreau alleges that the right to equal concern and respect is too vague to do much work with regard to juristic equality provisions, but that it can perhaps be operationalized, or its content further specified, by considering the wrongs brought about by breaches of those provisions.[67]

Neither reason for adopting this approach can be accepted without cavil. Scanlon's examination of the wrongs of unequal treatment seems premised upon this assumption: what he calls a non-substantive idea of equality cannot make direct good sense of all the wrongs unequal treatment entails or brings about. But there is reason to doubt this move, if the conceptual cartography of the relationship between equality and inequality is that of different sides of the same coin. We often take the notions of justice and injustice to be connected in this way, knowledge of what the former looks like being quickly translatable into knowledge of what the latter looks like by way of simple opposition. If equality and inequality are similarly connected, then a non-substantive account of the former should serve to generate an account of the latter and, additionally, its constitutive wrongs. Moreau's reason for exploring the wrongs of inequality is also questionable, for reasons already noted: it exaggerates the vagueness or abstraction of the right to equal concern and respect.

Despite these reservations, the accounts of the wrongs of unequal treatment offered by Scanlon and Moreau are certainly worth exploring. They might, for instance, serve to make even more concrete and precise the wrongs that flow from breach of the right to equal concern and respect; in addition, they could also highlight wrongs other than those that flow from breach of this right. A demonstration of the latter serves to show either that the right to equal concern and respect does not exhaust the concept of equality in play here or that that concept is not unitary and thus includes different and possibly conflicting components. A demonstration of the former serves to further illuminate the function of law's abstract judgement: if the right to equal concern and

[67] Moreau, n 36 above, 293–6.

respect protects against certain wrongs then it is likely, given their functional equivalence, that law's abstract judgement does the same job. What, then, are the wrongs of unequal treatment?

For Scanlon there are five such wrongs; for Moreau, four. They agree, in broad terms, on three: (i) that unequal treatment can perpetrate suffering or severe deprivation or deny access to basic goods; (ii) that it can perpetrate stigmatizing differences in status or be based upon prejudice or stereotyping; (iii) that it can perpetrate oppressive power relations.[68] Moreau highlights another allegedly free-standing wrong, traces of which appear within Scanlon's statement of other types of wrong.[69] This is the wrong of diminution of individual self-worth which, for Moreau, is rarely 'sufficient to render . . . treatment unfair'.[70] It is thus not, after all, a free-standing wrong and is therefore set aside hereinafter. That leaves outstanding the two additional wrongs which Scanlon thinks can be brought about by unequal treatment.

One of these is the wrong of undermining equality of starting points, which, as Scanlon notes, overlaps with the wrong in (iii). Scanlon puts the issue thus: '[s]ome forms of equality are essential preconditions for the fairness of certain processes, and the aim of making or keeping those processes fair may therefore give us a reason to oppose inequalities [of power and control]'.[71] One way in which some can come to exercise and maintain power over others is by denying them access to particular goods or sources of power. If in one political community citizens of group A, for example, ensure that citizens of group B are unable to vote in elections because necessary administrative procedures have not been completed, then this is a double wrong. It is wrong, first, because it excludes some from a process in which all are equally entitled to participate and, secondly, because it undermines the legitimacy or fairness of that process. Both wrongs can clearly serve to perpetrate oppressive power relations but this is not, as Scanlon notes, a necessary truth. Thus denial of the equality that is an essential

[68] Moreau characterizes the three wrongs as (i) based upon prejudice or stereotyping (n 36 above, 297–303); (ii) perpetuating oppressive power relations (ibid, 303–07); or (iii) leaving some individuals without access to basic goods (ibid, 307–12). For Scanlon, the three wrongs are characterized thus: (i) causing suffering or severe deprivation; or (ii) perpetuating stigmatizing differences in status; and (iii) the exercise of unacceptable forms of power or domination (n 66 above, 207). I do not affirm that these two lists are identical. Rather, I treat them as more or less the same for the purposes of this essay in the belief that the differences that exist are not sufficiently salient to effect the arguments in the text.

[69] Scanlon, n 66 above, 212–18.

[70] Moreau, n 36 above, 313.

[71] Scanlon, n 66 above, 205.

precondition of the fairness of the election result must be baleful for reasons other than the perpetration of domination. But whatever these reasons may be—and they must not, *ex hypothesi*, be reducible to those identified in (i) to (iii)—it is hard as a practical matter to envisage a denial of equal rights to some group of citizens being anything other than an exercise of domination by another group. Even if group A's restricting group B's access to the democratic process were based upon laudable or altruistic reasons, that would surely still be an illegitimate exercise of power. For this reason, the distinction Scanlon attempts to draw between the third and fourth wrong of unequal treatment is ignored in what follows; they are regarded as synonymous.

Scanlon's fifth potential wrong is, for present purposes, irrelevant. He says 'the idea of a fair procedure can . . . provide another kind of reason for insisting on equality of outcomes. (This is my fifth reason for objecting to inequalities.)'.[72] This claim is unpacked by reference to two others: that of a group in which all have equal claim to some benefit and that of a procedure for distributing that benefit. He holds that '[i]f a distributive procedure is supposed to be responsive to these claims, then it will be unfair if (absent some special reason) it gives some of these people a higher level of benefit than others'.[73] This seems plausible, but is salient only within a more general understanding of the propriety of an equal distribution of benefits and of the appropriate means for achieving such a distribution. Societies as a whole, or particular segments thereof, might be understood in this way, but without such a prior understanding—without, that is, a full-blown political theory—this wrong is inchoate at best.[74] It is henceforth set aside.

The question which must now be answered is clear: does law's abstract judgement protect against wrongs (i) to (iii)? The wrong in (i) is a composite, made up of the perpetuation of suffering or severe deprivation and denial of access to basic goods. For Moreau, denying some access to basic goods is, unlike other forms of unequal treatment, a non-comparative wrong.[75] The wrong is the denial, plain and simple. If government denies some citizens access to basic goods there is no need, in order to see what is wrong here, to determine how other groups are, or have been, treated. Because he thinks it rests on a 'moral

[72] Ibid, 205–6. [73] Ibid, 206.

[74] Scanlon is not ignorant of the point; he sketches two different political theories of the state, each of which has different distributive implications: ibid, 206-7.

[75] Moreau, n 36 above, 312.

idea[. . .] that . . . [is] not fundamentally egalitarian',[76] it seems likely that Scanlon would also accept that the infliction or perpetration of suffering and severe deprivation is a non-comparative wrong. The wrong here is objectionable regardless of the treatment of others. This much is clear from that fact that an effort by the wrong-doer to point to the even greater deprivation or suffering they have inflicted on others would have no exculpatory or ameliorative effect. The wrong to one person or group stands regardless of the wrong (and its magnitude) done to another person or group.

Is law's abstract judgement complicit in perpetrating or maintaining this wrong? For those who think that law's judgement should be more ethically sensitive, a move from more to less abstract forms opens the way for the admission of factors—like, for instance, the claimant's or defendant's relative economic deprivation—that should be salient in liability judgements. But these factors are normally excluded by law's abstract judgement: it stands as a bulwark against them, thereby contributing to the perpetration of deprivation and suffering and/or the denial of access to basic goods. Some attempt might be made to weaken this point. It is, obviously, true only if claimant or defendant is actually a member of a deprived group or a group denied access to basic goods. Furthermore, even in that case, the denial is perpetrated or maintained only in an incremental or piecemeal way, within the context of a decision in a particular case. Neither of these deflationary claims is, however, particularly weighty. The latter claim is misleading because decisions in particular cases are, in a system of precedent, usually generalized. The denial in a particular case can thus quite quickly become general. And the former claim is simply a statement of the obvious. Law's abstract judgement thus seems quite capable of perpetrating or maintaining this wrong. Is there any way of softening that blow?

Perhaps, since law's abstract judgement can also serve as a bulwark against this composite wrong. If law's judgement were less rather than more abstract, then space is created not only for judgements based upon the allegedly appropriate factors just noted, but for judgements based upon entirely inappropriate generalizations. Such generalizations can begin, for example, from factors such as character traits allegedly unique to a particular defendant or claimant. It must surely be the case that, on a non-abstract model of law's judgement, all facets of a particular defendant's or claimant's character are potentially relevant to

[76] Scanlon, n 66 above, 207.

determining liability. While this might be considered an ethical advance within the context of deciding liability in a particular case, this process has more troubling ethical implications once generalized. In the particular case, the defendant's fecklessness or feeble-mindedness, for example, could be regarded as conclusive to the question of liability. So far, so good. Yet, while fecklessness or feeble-mindedness might indeed be genuine facets of this particular defendant's character, their recognition in him can be inappropriately generalized so that, for instance, all members of the gender, ethnic, religious, socio-economic or national group of which he is a member are regarded as sharing this character trait. Insofar as members of such groups are already economically or otherwise deprived, or denied access to basic goods, then a more particular form of law's abstract judgement might function so as to maintain or increase that baleful situation. A more abstract form of law's judgement restricts, more or less stringently, recourse to the particular character or other traits of those being judged (either as individuals or as members of a class).

Although plausible, this argument is not unproblematic. It does not actually show that law's abstract judgement protects against the wrong in (i). Or, rather, it does so only by collapsing the distinction between that wrong and the wrong in (ii). The latter wrong has two limbs: first, the perpetuation of stigmatizing differences in status and, secondly, the utilization of (presumably illegitimate) prejudices and stereotypes. And, as the substance of the discussion of the previous paragraph makes clear, it is surely the latter limb of this wrong against which law's abstract judgement protects when it impedes improper generalization. Could law's abstract judgement serve to perpetrate or maintain suffering and deprivation, or deny access to basic goods, without invoking dubious generalizations? It is not clear how it could do this directly without excluding some from the judgement of the law entirely. But agents can only be beyond the law's judgement because the law fails to confer upon them any legal status and thus any legal rights. And this lack of recognition is plainly not a consequence of law's abstract judgement as such, but a function of the statuses and rights upheld by the legal system as a whole. Law's abstract judgement operates within, and does not itself establish, the distribution of rights and statuses recognized by the legal system as a whole.

Insofar as law's abstract judgement treats all citizens as if they were the same, the generalizations it licenses about them are limited: the generalizations must presumptively be about *all* citizens. The presumptive universality of law's abstract judgement is not, of course, always realized in each and every legal system. How could it be, if the picture offered in the second part of this essay is correct, namely, that a pure form of law's abstract judgement is incompletely realized in many legal systems with which we are familiar? The inchoate realization of law's abstract judgement allows room for false or improper generalization—generalization without reference to the whole class or generalization arbitrarily limited—and that is undoubtedly troubling. Furthermore, even properly universal generalizations can still be morally troubling in other ways: the law might, for example, regard all citizens as either stupid or as having the fortitude of saints. That neither generalization is accurate is just one aspect of the problem here. Another and more obvious problem of fairness arises from the legal consequences that flow from reliance on such unfounded generalizations. It seems bad enough that the generalization in question is wrong, but insult is added to injury when the application of the inaccurate generalization has legal consequences.

The moral qualms raised by the use of generalizations should, however, give us pause: what, if anything, is law's abstract judgement if not a conglomeration of generalizations? Furthermore, if there are objections to generalizations, they might be compounded if generalizations also partake of the objectionable features of stereotypes. What, then, is wrong with generalizations and stereotypes? As to the former, the problems just noted are perhaps best labelled thus: the problem of simple inaccuracy (all citizens are stupid) and the problems of over-inclusivity (generalization without reference to the whole class) and under-inclusivity (where the generalization is arbitrarily limited). Henceforth, generalizations that manifest one or other of these problems (and note that the last two can be true of one and the same generalizations) are dubbed 'incomplete'. When incorporated into, or used as the basis, for rules, incomplete generalizations are often troubling. Take, for example, the generalization 'dogs are disruptive'.[77] This is clearly not universally true, since we know that some dogs are not disruptive: the generalization is thus over-inclusive. It is also under-inclusive because it identifies only one class of disruptive agent, namely, dogs.

[77] The example and the discussion that follows draws upon Schauer's excellent treatment of the issues: see n 20 above, chs 2–5. Schauer has tackled closely related issues in *Profiles, Probabilities, and Stereotypes* (Harvard University Press: Cambridge Mass, 2003).

This generalization can quite obviously be incorporated or provide the justification for a rule such as, for example, that prohibiting dogs from restaurants. And, insofar as it is so incorporated, the generalization's over- and under-inclusiveness infects the rule: prohibiting dogs from restaurants because they are disruptive is mildly troubling if (i) not all dogs are disruptive and (ii) not all disruption is caused by dogs.

Incomplete generalizations can clearly also inform legal rules and the problem of fairness they pose is much more troubling here. Law's abstract judgement holds citizens to the same standards of conduct. So, for example, all citizens have a duty to treat others and their interests with reasonable care, and all must react to threats and provocation with reasonable fortitude. One generalization behind these two rules is surely that all citizens are indeed capable of achieving these standards and this is clearly over-inclusive: some citizens are certainly unable to satisfy them. What incomplete generalizations of this type and the rules that arise upon them do is this: they replace an unimpeachable probabilistic causal connection—some dogs are disruptive, some citizens can achieve these standards—with a dubious universal causal connection embracing, respectively, *all* dogs and *all* citizens.[78] When rules based upon incomplete generalizations are applied to citizens they raise the same moral problem of fairness as does law's abstract judgement. The problem with rule- and decision-making based upon incomplete generalization, and with law's abstract judgement itself, is that the rules and standards in play, and the decisions they inform, do not take proper account of the capacities or context of those to whom they apply. This moral qualm might be reduced if reliance upon incomplete generalizations and law's abstract judgement were otherwise morally acceptable. One potential moral advantage of law's abstract judgement is that it has egalitarian credentials, since it functions in the same way as does the right to equal concern and respect. Some have also noted that rules based upon incomplete generalizations have other, non-egalitarian pragmatic advantages.[79] It is, however, unclear whether either consideration is sufficiently weighty to displace the moral qualm.

[78] Schauer, n 20 above, 31–4.

[79] Schauer, n 20 above, ch 7. It is perhaps unfair to Schauer to hold that the advantages he identifies (reliance, efficiency, minimization of the risk of mistakes, stability, clear allocation of power and community) are solely pragmatic, since a case could be made that they have some moral content. The point, though, is *that a case must be made*; the advantages are thus not pre-eminently or obviously morally valuable.

What of rule- and decision-making by stereotype rather than generalization? For Moreau, a stereotype is 'simply any generalisation or classification that one group of people treats as though it captured an essential feature of certain other individuals, and which this [former] group takes to render unnecessary any individualised consideration of their characteristics or circumstances'.[80] Furthermore, stereotypes need not carry negative connotations for Moreau, but they must be adopted by one group as a description of another group without being derived from that other group's own attempt at self-definition.[81] It is not immediately clear how stereotypes can be distinguished from generalizations on this account since Moreau rules out a tempting version of the distinction in which the former carry negative connotations while the latter do not. The distinction might reside in the fact that stereotypes, for Moreau, purport to capture an essential feature of another person or group, but it is unclear why generalizations cannot do the same.

What is clear are Moreau's reasons for regarding rules or decisions based upon stereotypes as objectionable. One extends or deepens the moral qualm about incomplete generalizations already noted: when stereotypes do not fit the group or person to which they are applied, that person or group can be denied a benefit or incur a burden on apparently arbitrary and irrelevant grounds.[82] It is also the case, according to Moreau, that in some circumstances this process undermines the autonomy of those subject to it. Rather than defining 'himself and his circumstances as he understands them, he has been presented in the manner of another's choosing . . . this will lessen his autonomy . . . it will limit his power to define and direct his life in important ways'.[83] Since law's abstract judgement is a conglomeration of often incomplete generalizations, the latter raising much the same worries as rules and decisions based on stereotypes, it seems likely that the ills of the latter are shared by the former. Thus law's abstract judgement may well exacerbate rather than avoid the second limb of the second wrong.

What of the first limb? The perpetuation of stigmatizing differences in status does not necessarily follow from decisions and rules based upon incomplete generalizations and stereotypes, although it may often do so. Indeed, law's abstract judgement can stand as a barrier against such stigmatizing differences simply because it regards all citizens as in some

[80] Moreau, n 36 above, 298. [81] Ibid [82] Ibid, 298.
[83] Ibid, 299.

respects the same. The fact that law's abstract judgement eliminates considerations of the relative worth of claimant and defendant as possible bases for judicial decisions, except when legal doctrine explicitly requires it, makes stigmatizing differences in status more difficult to uphold than they otherwise might be. That law's abstract judgement seems unlikely to function as an explicit creator of stigmatizing differences in status does not, of course, rule out the possibility that such differences will flow from the utilization of stereotypes and generalizations. Indeed, if rules and decisions based upon stereotypes and (incomplete) generalizations serve to undermine the autonomy of those subject to them, it seems quite plausible in some circumstances that that reduction of autonomy could in the long-term culminate in stigmatizing differences. Thus, while they cannot be a primary goal of law's abstract judgement, such differences could be one of its long-term effects.

Finally, we must turn to the third wrong of unequal treatment: the perpetuation of oppressive power relations. The wrong here is that of 'further entrenching or reinforcing power imbalances that are unacceptably large and that leave individuals without sufficient social or political influence'.[84] Thus described, it might be thought that this wrong is otiose, because always reducible to, or always a consequence of, the other two. Hence to the extent that law's abstract judgement can function, however limitedly, to prevent the first and second wrongs of unequal treatment, then it can surely stand as a bulwark against the third. Making the first and second wrongs harder or perhaps even impossible to perpetrate reduces the chances of bringing about the third. That, at least, is so if oppressive power relations are always a consequence or cause of (i) the invocation of (derogatory) stereotypes, or of (ii) exclusion from basic goods and/or of (iii) the perpetration of suffering and deprivation. Similarly, to the degree that law's abstract judgement serves to perpetrate or maintain the first and second wrongs—and, as we have seen, it can undoubtedly be complicit in the second—it can also thereby perpetrate and maintain the third.

What, then, is the connection between the third wrong and the first and second? While accepting that there will often be a link between the three, Moreau holds that it is contingent rather than necessary.[85] She therefore holds that oppressive power relations could in some instances be maintained or created without recourse to the other two wrongs of unequal treatment. The conceptual independence of the third wrong

[84] Ibid, 304. [85] Ibid, 304–5.

from the others therefore requires that we consider those instances in which this wrong is unrelated to the other two: can law's abstract judgement prevent it or is it complicit in its perpetration? The example Moreau uses to show the conceptual independence of the third wrong draws upon the case of *Vriend v Alberta*.[86] The example does not, however, succeed in its aim. Mr Vriend was unable to bring an action for discrimination on the basis of sexual orientation against his employer because this type of discrimination was not included in the Alberta Individual Rights Protection Act (IRPA). The Supreme Court of Canada held that the exclusion of sexual orientation as a ground for discrimination in the Alberta IRPA was an unjustified infringement of section 15(1) of the Charter of Rights and Freedoms.

Moreau thinks it implausible to hold that the lacuna in the Alberta IPRA was based upon stereotypes held by Alberta's legislators, but she offers no reason for thinking this. Instead, she points to another possible explanation of the gap: 'it seems more likely that they [Alberta's legislators] simply made a judgement about which decision would yield most popular support'.[87] Yet no grounds are adduced in support of this assessment of the reasons of Alberta's legislators and this explanation is therefore no more salient than other more sceptical explanations. It would indeed be more encouraging if Alberta's legislators were moved solely by the reason Moreau highlights, but one need not be a great sceptic about politics to think that objectionable prejudice and stereotypes could have informed the deliberations of some. Moreover, it seems at least arguable that the lacuna in the IPRA could be instrumental in the perpetuation of suffering and deprivation of the kind covered by the first wrong. Although this judgement is speculative, and could be supported or denied by testimony from Mr Vriend, it is not wildly implausible to think that the suffering, pain and annoyance of being discriminated against on the basis of sexual orientation drove him to pursue a legal remedy.

A variation in Vriend—Vriend_2—is perhaps conceivable, on which there is no recourse to stereotypes and in which the suffering is insufficient to trigger the first wrong. In *Vriend*$_2$, then, the claimant has no legal recourse for discrimination and this presumably perpetuates oppressive power relations (manifest in the denial of a legal remedy to all those who suffer sexual orientation discrimination). Can law's abstract judgement serve to protect against this kind of wrong?

[86] [1998] 1 SCR 493 (SCCan); ibid, 305–6.

[87] See n 85 above, 305.

Probably only to the extent that it protects against the other two wrongs. For a *Vriend*-type legislative gap will not be made impossible by law's abstract judgement, nor even challenged by it, unless the gap turns on objectionable stereotypes. And, even in that case, there is no guarantee that the said stereotype will run up against law's abstract judgement. Law's abstract judgement does not therefore directly prevent the third type of wrong.

Some Objections and a Generalization

The principal question of this essay has been what, if anything, might be said in favour of law's abstract judgement? The answer offered was limited, drawn from a narrow range of raw materials found in contemporary liberal legal and political philosophy: an argument from Dworkin's early work and a more recent argument derived primarily from Scanlon. These two arguments tell us that law's abstract judgement can be supported (i) by the fact that it functions in much the same way as the right to equal concern and respect; and (ii) by virtue of its role as a bulwark against some of the wrongs of unequal treatment. While it could be claimed, somewhat portentously, that there is a 'discovery' here, namely, that law's abstract judgement is not completely without normative support, it could also be said that this discovery was hardly worth unearthing. This is because the two arguments are either too weak, when taken separately, or incoherent when combined.

The first limb of this charge could turn out to be well founded. It is not, however, an *a priori* truth that each of the arguments elucidated above is insufficiently weighty. That could only be established by a thorough evaluation of each. This task must surely be undertaken at some stage, since law's abstract judgement is undeniably both a significant feature of most contemporary legal systems and to some degree morally vexing. While part of this essay made some effort to counterbalance the morally troubling nature of law's abstract judgement it serves, at most, as preamble to a more robust and extensive evaluation of all the arguments that might support law's abstract judgement.

That the two arguments supporting law's abstract judgement do not amount to a coherent whole is also not an *a priori* truth. It needs to be shown that they are genuinely incompatible. Pending such a demonstration, it must be noted that there is textual evidence to support this alleged incompatibility. It consists of Scanlon's view that equality is not as fundamental a value as we often think and Dworkin's view that equality is a crucially important—sovereign—political virtue.[88] Both views cannot be true and about the same idea. Nor is it plausible to suggest that, while Dworkin undoubtedly has a political notion of equality in mind, Scanlon has a purely moral conception in view. For, although this claim repeats a truth about Dworkin's view, it is false to Scanlon's arguments.[89] If Dworkin and Scanlon are indeed speaking about the same thing, how can their views be reconciled?

A closer look at the textual evidence yields one suggestion, while an examination of the substance of Dworkin's and Scanlon's arguments yields another. Scanlon says that '[t]he idea that equality is, in itself, a fundamental moral value turns out to play a surprisingly limited role in my reasons for thinking that many of the forms of inequality which we see around us should be eliminated'.[90] In saying this, he has 'in mind an idea of substantive equality—that it is morally important that people's lives or fates should be equal in some substantive way'.[91] This he contrasts with 'a merely formal notion of equal consideration, as stated in, for example, the principle that the comparable claims of each person deserve equal respect and should be given equal weight. This is an important principle. Its general acceptance represents an important moral advance'.[92] Thus Scanlon undoubtedly thinks that substantive equality is less important than it is often thought to be, and that equality understood as equal consideration or equal respect is important, although 'taken by itself . . . [the latter] is too abstract to exercise much force in the direction of substantive equality'.[93]

Do Dworkin and Scanlon actually disagree about the relative importance of equality? No. This is principally because Dworkin's right to equal concern and respect is not, as he takes pains to emphasize, a right to equal treatment.[94] It is not therefore a substantive conception of equality in Scanlon's terms. Since Dworkin is not necessarily committed to such a conception by virtue of his commitment to the right to equal concern and respect, there is space in which he and Scanlon can agree on the relative importance of substantive equality. Both could agree that it is less important than often thought, while still maintaining that non-substantive conceptions of equality are very important indeed. The only genuine disagreement between Dworkin and Scanlon highlighted by the

[88] Scanlon, n 66 above, 202; Dworkin, ibid. [89] See n 66 above, 208–18.
[90] Ibid, 202. [91] Ibid [92] Ibid [93] Ibid
[94] Dworkin, n 45 above, 227.

textual evidence is one about the alleged depth and utility of the idea of equal respect and consideration. Scanlon thinks principles of this type morally important but also 'formal' and 'abstract'. This, remember, is the exact objection made against the right to equal concern and respect by Moreau. Some effort was made to neutralize it in the discussion above. The argument was that this charge against the right to equal concern and respect is, at best, not proven.

The reconciliation suggested by the textual evidence is backed up by that which arises from consideration of the substance of Dworkin's and Scanlon's arguments. Focusing upon the content of their non-substantive conceptions of equality shows that their positions are in many ways perfectly compatible. To see this, recall the composite wrong against which the right to equal concern and respect protects. As noted above, the wrong occasioned by breach of this right is some combination of: (i) government curtailment, partial or complete, of some citizens' ability to pursue or formulate conceptions of a good life; (ii) the undervaluing or ignoring of some such conceptions by government; and (iii) the undervaluing or ignoring, by government, of the suffering and frustration caused to citizens by either (i) or (ii). Each element of this wrong can also bring about one or more of the three wrongs of unequal treatment identified by Scanlon and Moreau. Thus, a denial or infringement of one's right to equal concern and respect can clearly: (i) perpetrate suffering, severe deprivation and/or serve to deny access to basic goods; (ii) perpetrate stigmatizing differences in status or invoke objectionable prejudices or generalizations; and (iii) perpetrate oppressive power relations.

Clearly the consequences of a denial or infringement of the right to equal concern and respect are not necessarily limited to these three possibilities, since it is conceivable that in some (albeit unlikely) circumstances the right may be breached without causing any of these three wrongs. As a practical matter, however, most breaches of the right will bring about at least one of these wrongs. Consider again some of the most commonplace types of exclusion familiar from the relatively recent history of the West. Think, for example, of the denial of some group's right to religious worship: what plausible basis could this limitation have, if not some or other objectionable prejudices or generalizations? Furthermore, what would have to be true for this prohibition *not* to perpetrate stigmatizing differences in status? Suppose also that some ethnic, gender or sexual-orientation group is forbidden access to law schools at public universities. How, in practical terms, could such a prohibition scrupulously avoid perpetrating oppressive power relations and/or stigmatizing differences in status and/or objectionable prejudices or generalizations? And, even if it did, could it also avoid the perpetration of suffering and/or deprivation, not to mention serving to deny access to some basic goods?

While not perhaps substantively incompatible, it might nevertheless be maintained that the two arguments are structurally unstable. Since they are not hierarchically ordered, the two cannot be combined in a stable way: if neither argument is ranked as more important than the other, each can in some instances serve to cancel out the other. So, for instance, what prevents, in the possibly rare but conceivable case of a breach of the right to equal concern and respect not bringing about one or other wrong of unequal treatment, the inference that there is 'therefore' no wrong here? What, in other words, stops the argument from the wrongs of unequal treatment 'trumping' the argument from equal concern and respect?

If the right to equal concern and respect does indeed identify wrongs over and above those said by Scanlon and Moreau to flow from unequal treatment, then it is clearly broader than the argument from the wrongs of unequal treatment. While not of itself sufficient to establish the priority of the former over the latter, this is a step toward that goal. If it can additionally be shown that the composite wrong protected by the right to equal concern and respect is a genuine wrong even when unnoticed by the argument from the wrongs of inequality, then there is greater progress towards that goal. Since the argument from the wrongs of inequality would not identify all the wrongs against which we expect a conception of equality to protect, it is reasonable to supplement it. The right to equal concern and respect can play exactly that role and this provides a basis upon which to rank these two arguments. The argument from the right to equal concern and respect dominates the argument from the wrongs of inequality because it identifies more of what we regard as vexing about unequal treatment.

This riposte is unlikely to be effective against an objection slightly broader than the charge of instability. This objection holds that it is simply misconceived to even attempt to marry the two different accounts (and the two different approaches) to equality found in the work of Dworkin and Scanlon. This is because both general moral and political theories, on the one hand, and the more specific moral and political analyses of particular concepts derived from them, on the other, are intended to have unlimited logical range. They are intended, even if pluralistic, to exhaust all the available logical space and therefore cannot be combined because they divide or classify that space in plainly incompatible ways. Think, for example, of Rawls's account of distributive justice and that of Robert Nozick.[95] Each account provides an answer to the question about the nature of distributive justice strictly incompatible with the other: Rawls's two principles of justice simply cannot be coherently combined with the three principles of Nozick's historical entitlement theory. Now, if all moral and political theories and the more specific analyses derived from them are, so to speak, incompatible *ab initio* in this sense, then it is indeed foolish to seek to combine them with one another. But even if (as seems unlikely) this were generally true, the point is surely irrelevant to one of this essay's central concerns, namely, that of determining what, if anything, might be said in favour of law's abstract judgement.

The way in which that concern has been addressed is clear: through the medium (albeit a very small segment) of recent political and moral philosophy. This concern is certainly not accurately described as that of determining the general compatibility of two different views of and approaches to equality. Rather, the task was the lower level one of seeking normative support for an obvious feature of legal institutional design. That these sources of normative support might ultimately be incompatible with one another need not undermine either the interest or the validity of elucidating them and that for which they provide support. Indeed, the fact that some or other aspect of institutional design might be supported by a range of broader and possibly incompatible moral or political theories, or analyses derived therefrom, is suggestive of a deeper possible truth. It is a truth about both those broader theories and the analyses derived from them, on the one hand, and aspects of (legal) institutional design, on the other.

Imagine a spectrum. At one end we have general moral and political theories and their analyses of specific moral and political concepts, at the other various features or perhaps just one feature of institutional design. One obvious way in which the two points on the spectrum can be brought into contact is by asking whether or not one can throw light upon the other. The light we have searched for is normative light and, although we have focused only upon one feature of legal institutional design, we have examined two moral-cum-political accounts of equality

[95] See Rawls, n 38 above, and compare with R Nozick, *Anarchy, State and Utopia* (Blackwell: Oxford, 1974).

(many other accounts could have been considered instead).[96] That law's abstract judgement draws support from arguments as different as that from the right to equal concern and respect, and that from the wrongs of inequality, is interesting whether or not those broader analyses of equality are incompatible one with another. Indeed, if they are actually incompatible that might serve to make the fact of law's abstract judgement drawing support from them even more interesting. Why?

Because it suggests that this aspect of legal institutional design is normatively over-determined as well as being theoretically 'blunt' and that this might also be true of many other aspects of legal institutional design. Some such features—certainly particular doctrinal rules such as, for example, the rule about past consideration in English contract law—appear neither explicable by a single general normative-cum-explanatory theory, nor do they entail only one such theory.[97] Rather, some doctrinal rules and related features of legal institutional design seem compatible with—and thus capable of being supported by—more than one such theory and are in this sense normatively over-determined. That some such rules and institutional features rarely seem to entail any single normative-cum-explanatory theory is the flip-side of this coin and illustrates their theoretical bluntness.[98] Some legal doctrines and institutional features simply do not make one explanatory or normative theory any more salient than another; they are compatible with many such theories. The discussion so far provides limited grounds for thinking that law's abstract judgement is normatively over-determined and therefore theoretically blunt. Is this a problem? It seems less of a problem provided the supporting considerations are ultimately consistent or hierarchically ordered. But even if they are not, the *prima facie* paradoxical situation in which incompatible normative theories or analyses support some institutional feature or aspect of doctrine still illuminates something significant about some of our normative theories and some features of the social world.

[96] One of the most interesting being A Ripstein, *Equality, Responsibility, and the Law* (Cambridge University Press: Cambridge, 1999).

[97] It does not follow that such features and doctrines are therefore necessarily conventional, having the same rational and normative status as rules about which side of the road to drive on, although they might sometimes have that status.

[98] On bluntness see NE Simmonds, 'Bluntness and Bricolage' in H Gross and R Harrsion (eds), *Jurisprudence: Cambridge Essays* (Clarendon Press: Oxford, 1992) ch 1 and W Lucy, 'Method and Fit: Two Problems for Contemporary Philosophies of Tort Law' (2007) 52 McGill LJ 605–56, 643–7.

It is eminently possible for there to be different views about the exact significance of what is illuminated here. One view is that widespread normative over-determination of legal doctrine, on the one hand, and aspects of legal institutional design, on the other, prefigures a different approach to understanding law than is common in much current legal-theoretical work. This alternative approach is one which works out from some or other feature of law towards broader normative or other theoretical accounts. Taken as an approach to legal philosophy, this would have as its rallying call something as mundane as 'law first, then theory' (if it were true that law itself is in no meaningful sense already theorized). Moving the other way, from some or other theory to an understanding of law or some of its features, risks distorting the phenomenon in order to fit the selected normative or explanatory theory; it can become something of a Procrustean procedure. Law's normative over-determination also implies that law's normative landscape is both diverse and plural. This need not imply anything at all about the ultimate status of values, but it certainly supports a more theoretically modest approach to understanding law than is currently common. By 'theoretical modesty' I have in mind the obviously rebuttable assumption that no single normative theory, be it a particular account of moral right and wrong or an account of economic efficiency, has the explanatory power to reach all aspects of law.

This view of what the normative over-determination of aspects of law might imply for the way in which we should go about understanding law, and doing legal philosophy, has no appeal for jurists enamoured of intellectual generality and tidiness. A penchant for generality and tidiness is often the symptom of a deeper commitment, holding that law's many doctrinal segments and related institutional features simply must be explained by a single, unified general theory. Faced with the putative fact of normative over-determination, such committed generalists would presumably insist upon an intellectual war of attrition between the competing normative (or other) theories which support some or other feature of legal institutional design or doctrine. The position arrived at in this essay would thus be regarded as only the end of the beginning of the jurisprudential task. While there is no obviously compelling ground upon which to reject this approach, it can be noted that the candidates suggested by jurists for the role of unified general theory of law (or some segment thereof) have not been conspicuously successful. The candidates include, amongst many others, economic analysis of law, some examples of critical legal studies, and some instances of 'orthodox' legal philosophy.[99] A crucial difficulty for many such theories is that of combining explanatory generality and unity with an accurate and reasonably fine-grained understanding of features of the law, be they aspects of doctrine or institutional design. Thus most versions of economic analysis of tort law struggle to explain the bilateral nature of private law adjudication in terms which show this feature to be anything more than a second-best historical accident, while some non-economic theories are forced to disregard or 'reinterpret' significant swathes of settled doctrine.[100] The point is that theories which aim at the broadest level of explanatory and normative generality should not be assumed to be *ipso facto* virtuous. Theoretical generality is sometimes a virtue, sometimes not.

Finally, a generalization. There might be a broader notion of equality of which law's abstract judgement is part. This broader notion could be labelled 'juridical equality', its referent being the various instantiations of equality within the law. These instantiations include not just the ideas of equality before and under the law, but also legal equality provisions with a broader scope, law's abstract judgement, and the various procedural manifestations of equality (such as equality of standing before the court, equal access to legal knowledge and advice, and the judges' obligation of actual and apparent impartiality). While the propriety of subsuming all these instances under one rubric may be questioned, it is surely permissible to search for links between these instances and to examine in what ways, if any, such links (if found) are significant and informative. That research programme cannot be ruled out without argument, but nor can it be claimed that great progress has been made upon it here. Yet one tentative point, pending the results of a more complete study of the alleged instances of juridical equality, can be made. It is that the recognition of a broad notion of juridical equality, combining the many instances of equality in the law, suggests this notion is both complex and capable of being supported by a range of diverse arguments and considerations. Complexity does not entail a diversity of justificatory considerations in all cases; these two features can, indeed, be quite separate. But in this instance they surely go side

[99] See Posner and Shavell, n 32 above; RM Unger, *What Should Legal Analysis Become?* (Verso: London, 1996) and *The Critical Legal Studies Movement* (Harvard University Press: Cambridge Mass, 1986); E Weinrib, *The Idea of Private Law* (Harvard University Press: Cambridge Mass, 1995).

[100] See S Shavell, *Economic Analysis of Accident Law* (Harvard University Press: Cambridge Mass, 1987), 265–70; and Weinrib, ibid, ch 7.

by side, the various aspects of the complex notion of juridical equality quite possibly requiring different types of normative and other support.

To conclude, it is worth reminding ourselves again that law's abstract judgement is currently subject to a degree of both doctrinal and theoretical contestation. The specific charges against it might, in the end, be compelling. Law's abstract judgement in its current form could thence rightly be discarded on the rubbish heap of history. The suggestion here is that we pause before doing this and consider if there is a positive case for law's abstract judgement. Only when such a case has been considered shall we know if anything of significance will be lost by excising this familiar feature of familiar legal systems.

The Human Face of the Rule of Law

*Sean Coyle**

This essay will offer some thoughts on the relationship between two different sets of ideas concerning the nature of law. On the one hand, the legal order may be viewed as a system of technical rules and doctrines, concepts and distinctions. On the other, it takes the form of an organized body of ideas defined and given expression through processes of systematic contemplation. Legal scholarship is to some extent a process of familiarizing oneself with the operation of a complex body of rules. Yet such familiarity is not in itself legal scholarship, much less legal practice. For in order to use the rules as lawyers use them, the rules must be contemplated and considered, and the relationship between the different rules must be understood. Because the intellectual processes involved in handling the rules exhibit a high degree of sophistication, those intellectual processes may themselves become the subject matter of philosophical argument. Thus we may regard jurisprudential theories as embodying differing understandings of the processes of handling legal rules; and we may conceive of legal theory as the attempt to grasp the significance of rules as a foundation for social order.

It is possible to think of the dichotomy of rules and systematic contemplative processes as reflecting a distinction between the humanly-created aspect of legal order and its principled, rational character. For whereas the statutory and doctrinal rules are the product of conscious decision, the structure of a system of rights is thought to be determined by tracing out underlying conceptions of justice which are not the outcome of deliberate choice. My aim in the essay will be to question the relevance of this dichotomy, and of the notions of

* Professor of Jurisprudence, School of Law, University of Exeter. Previously Reader in Jurisprudence, University College London. I would like to thank Ross Harrison, Lucinda Miller, Amanda Perreau-Saussine, Joanne Scott and Fiona Smith for their very helpful and insightful comments on an earlier draft.

legality which it invites. I shall argue that it is, in fact, in the law's systematic and rational nature that the human face of law is most fully comprehended.

Rational Coherence and Rule-based Authority

Understanding of the nature of law hinges to an extent on an appreciation of the human context in which the law operates. A line might be drawn which divides the political thought of the classical and medieval worlds, in which politics was thought to play a constitutive role in bringing about the human good, from that of modernity which has centred upon the role of politics in the creation of a stable framework of rules and entitlements within a world of disagreement about the nature of the good. Modernity engenders an important shift in understandings: we ask not, how law may foster conditions conducive to the living of excellent and virtuous lives, but how political stability and legal order are possible in a context where our very individuality threatens to erode the common sympathies and understandings which underpin our social survival. The relevant intellectual framework for jurisprudential reflection is thus thought to be one in which legal rules and lawyerly processes of contemplation provide a necessary matrix of binding standards against which individuals may formulate and pursue their own private conceptions of the good.

It is this intellectual framework which structures our understanding of the modern legal order: both of its existence and functioning, and of the problems and questions that can be raised in relation to that functioning. Within this intellectual framework, we can think of the dichotomy of rules (on the one hand) and the processes of contemplation (on the other) as pointing to two distinct aspects of the legal order. An obvious dimension of legality consists in the creation and maintenance of a variable body of rules as a means of pursuing a variety of social goals. Rules are intrinsic to legality in that the subjection of human conduct to regular governance is the principal means by which rationality and intelligibility are manifested in human affairs. Human societies tend to act both as a locus for collective human achievement and as a permanent source of tensions and conflicts of interest, in which the presence of opposing ideas of virtuous or worthwhile activity have a randomizing effect on human choice and action. Such disagreements reduce the effectiveness of moral considerations in creating orderly and secure patterns of interaction necessary for purposeful activity. A stable body of rules is thus required in order to bring about the conditions necessary for a rational human existence, by demarcating complementary domains of optional conduct and of obligation.[1]

The creation of domains of liberty and obligation might be deemed an intrinsic dimension of legality, for a central function of the law consists in the establishment of areas of protected autonomy in which one is not subject to the will of others.[2] Outside the context of such stable domains, the force of moral considerations is felt unevenly so that our comprehension of what may be required for a peaceful coexistence will vary contingently upon the specific circumstances and strength of the conflicting dispositions. Here, the restoration of good relations would depend upon a structure of specific compromises or deals, of a kind incapable of giving direction to the activities of others; for each person would lack the knowledge of how to orientate their behaviour within a body of general considerations so as to avoid future conflicts and ensure the retention of benefits brought about by their purposive activity. The existence of legal relations is thus inevitably a function of general rules or considerations which operate in place of particular decisions.

A quite different dimension of legality is revealed if we reflect upon the necessity of handling rules as general grounds of decision. Areas of liberty constitute important enclaves for the structuring of individual human action over time. The purposive quality of such action derives not from the presence of bare instances of freedom so much as from the existence of continuous blocks of freedom understood as according a degree of protection or recognition to certain kinds of action which might be deemed as valuable or worthwhile. In the same way, specific obligations imposed by the law tend not to take effect in splendid isolation from one another, but rather combine together to form intelligible regulatory regimes: the various possible grounds of liability in tort, for example, impose restraints upon conduct not as self-standing and unrelated obligations but as elements of a wider duty to perform actions with due care. The existence of legal obligations and entitlements therefore seldom correlates with the existence of specific

[1] See L Fuller, *The Morality of Law* (New Haven, 1969) 9. Fuller speaks of the legal system as in part constituting 'a complex of rules designed to rescue man from the blind play of chance and to put him on the road to purposeful and creative activity.'

[2] Grotius, *De Iure Praedae Commentarius* [1604] (Oxford, 1950) 18.

rules which create them. More usually, their existence and scope must be inferred from a body of laws which operate systematically to define and demarcate areas of permissive or protected conduct in the light of numerous opposing considerations. Rights to resist trespassers are defined not against a fixed and determinate set of rules, but in the context of general principles of ownership, adverse possession, theft, assault, etc.

The nature of law is such that it operates not simply as a set of imposed rules, but also as a general body of ideas requiring systematic contemplation. For (to return to my earlier assertion) in order to use the rules as lawyers use them, the rules must be applied within a context of reflection on the purpose of a body of laws, taken as manifesting some form of internal organization and rational coherence. A set of imposed rules is naturally looked upon as embodying the conscious choices of the polity in pursuit of deliberately chosen goals, whereas the search for rational coherence involves those dimensions of legality which are not the product of deliberate choice. Rules, on this view, embody the humanly-created aspect of law, whereas the processes of contemplation reflect the law's principled, systematic character. The central question for legal theory might then be said to concern the relationship between these two distinct elements.

The processes of systematic contemplation occupy a mysterious place in legal thought, for although they do not represent products of conscious decision or human will, they are nevertheless creatures of human thought and intellect. What, then, is the status of such ideas? Much of the jurisprudential thought of modernity has taken the form of an inquiry into the truth of 'legal positivism', understood as a debate concerning the presence or absence of 'necessary connections' between law and morality. Here, the humanly-created rules define the category of 'law', whilst systematic contemplation embodies the category of 'moral' contemplation. We might then ask whether the idea of law *necessarily* includes the idea of moral contemplation. One aim of this essay is to demonstrate the irrelevance of this debate to juridical thought. The intellectual oppositions arising from this debate have in the main been explored in the context of adjudication, but we can better perceive the unimportance of the issue if we consider the question as one closely concerning the nature of legal doctrine.

Having isolated the systematic and coherent character of law from its status as an authoritative body of rules and decisions, it lies open to us to describe the nature of the common law in two distinct ways.

On the one hand, the common law might be presented as a fixed body of precedents which establish, by authority, a system of posited rules: the rational coherence of law being explicable as a function of the repeated resort to the rules, and convergent interpretations of their purported significance. On the other hand, the precedents may be viewed as mere evidence for rational principles which underpin and structure the positive rules; a view evident in Lord Mansfield's famous judgment in *Rust v Cooper*: 'Law does not consist in particular cases, but in general principles which run through the cases and govern the decision of them.'[3]

Any complex body of laws is likely to require some form of systematic exposition: for we are liable to regard the conditions of intelligibility of law as depending upon the assumption that vast bodies of statutory laws and judicial decisions may be organized into more specific categories or doctrines according to their underlying purpose. For example, the law relating to theft invites exposition in terms of concepts and ideas of property which also relate to the explanation of forms of ownership; and those ideas will in turn inform any attempt to make systematic sense of the law of trusts. Such explanations inevitably 'go beyond' the reporting of authoritative rules and decisions, and (because they seem inevitable) contribute to the sense of doctrinal science as occupying a mysterious place in the modern legal order. For, in reaching beyond the reporting of established rules, how can the doctrinal scholar's propositions claim to possess authority as statements of law?

Among those to confront this question was the young Jeremy Bentham. Bentham had set about describing the common law as a series of particular decisions, rather than a body of general doctrinal rules. For 'to give [judicial decisions] any sort of connection with one another and with the rest of the matter of which law is made a set of general rules must be abstracted from them and worked up into the form of a treatise. . .'[4] Yet the treatise is not law, but the seamless blending of expository matter with the author's subjective impressions concerning the interests or purposes to which such rules are related as ends. In this way, Bentham believed, we are led into the error of supposing the existence of rights, interests and obligations of which the authoritative

[3] *Rust v Cooper* [1774] Cowper's Reports of Cases in the Court of King's Bench 632.

[4] J Bentham, *Introduction to the Principles of Morals of Legislation* [1789] JH Burns and HLA Hart (eds), (London, 1982) 188.

rules and decisions are mere partial expressions. A rigorous separation of the expository matter from the censorial would thus reveal the law's nature as a body of discrete imperatives by dismissing the 'underlying principles' celebrated by Lord Mansfield, as mere phantoms.

Yet Bentham himself could hardly eliminate altogether the need for systematic exposition of the law. Systematic explanations of large bodies of particular rules and decisions are an intrinsic part of understanding the policies or purposes such rules are designed to serve. Law was not to be construed as a product of 'reason', but as a body of discrete rules which, taken together, are capable of systematic expression in different ways for different purposes: in terms of the interests protected, or policies pursued. If the censor's role was to explain the utilitarian basis of legal propositions, the expositor was charged with organizing the corpus of legal materials into a structure which reveals their utilitarian character. The activity of doctrinal reasoning became, as Milsom observed, the 'business [of arranging] yesterday's results in whatever way will be most convenient for those working on today's problems.'[5] The processes of legal contemplation therefore remained an intrinsic part of legal scholarship; but Bentham equally insisted that those processes were not *themselves* part of the law. The need for some form of systematic scholarship should not make us lose sight of the law's character as a body of imperatives and commands, rather than a body of general rules.

Bentham's account of these intellectual processes testifies to the problematic status of doctrinal scholarship within modern jurisprudential thought. The activities of the expositor are *neither* those of the censor, *nor* those of a mere reporter: to what status do the expositor's systematic reconstructions then aspire? In categorizing the common law as a body of particular, unconnected decisions, Bentham sought to expel general doctrinal rules to the confines of the unauthoritative treatise. But as such general rules and understandings are an integral part of legal understanding, what exactly does this definitional move accomplish? Whether the doctrinal writer's propositions are regarded as 'unauthoritative' or not matters little to the issue of their theoretical importance in legal thought, for it is through such propositions that law is initially learned and understood; and it is through the same forms of argument that legal issues are debated in practical

[5] SFC Milsom, 'The Nature of Blackstone's Achievement' (1981) 1 Oxford Journal of Legal Studies 1.

contexts as much as academic ones. If legal understandings depend upon the systematic reconstruction of 'general rules' from the scattered particulars, to what does the adjective 'unauthoritative' serve to draw attention, if something other than the status of such rules as merely 'contentious' or 'defeasible'?

Legal practice, thus, in the end depends upon the presence of systematic understandings which incorporate some idea of the point or purpose served by authoritative rules and decisions. Understandings of this kind are inevitably moral understandings, for even where the rules are thought to serve prudential or pragmatic ends, the characterization of some collective project as 'pragmatic' rather than 'moral' itself identifies an ethical judgment concerning the nature and limits of moral significance.

I hope these remarks demonstrate that the question of 'necessary connections' between law and morality does not provide the ideal intellectual context for reflection upon the nature of law. Reflective insight into the nature of legality is best advanced not by the drawing of categorical divisions, but by contemplation of the form of moral reasoning manifested in legal thought. The prevalence of arguments concerning the validity of such divisions has operated to blind jurisprudential writers to an obvious truth: that moral understandings can only be present within legal understandings (or embody obligations and ideas which diverge from legal understandings) if morality itself takes a juridical form.[6] I want to suggest, therefore, that the intellectual framework of modernity which functions as the unexamined background to legal thought, is in fact sustained by a series of metaphysical assumptions that are shared both by positivism and its immediate rivals. Thus, if we seek a more enlightened understanding of the significance of our own legal thought, rather than participating in that narrow framework, might we not seek to *challenge* the presumptions on which it rests?

Historicism and Legality

If law can *embody* moral understandings, then morality must itself resemble a law-like set of standards capable of being understood

[6] See NE Simmonds, *The Decline of Juridical Reason* (Manchester, 1984) 39; and JB Schneewind, *The Invention of Autonomy* (New York, 1998) ch 7.

systematically and in abstraction from particular cases and facts. Such a conception of morality may well define the modern ethical consciousness: for in possessing such a form, morality appears on the intellectual landscape as a detached and autonomous outlook on the world, deriving from an intellectual source outside that of historical experience. The development of an ethical consciousness is thought to require the ability to impose an interpretation upon the human practices which make up the social world. In this way, moral judgment is not seen as something which is dependent upon the form of one's experience, but upon the adoption of an 'interpretative attitude' in relation to that experience. These ideas have brought about an intellectual environment in which reflection upon shared historical attachments is not considered as relevant to the generation or refinement of moral insights; the adoption of a consciously interpretative attitude standing in opposition to that of adherence to customary forms. Rather, moral insight requires the orientation of one's thinking within a set of abstract values which then inform one's judgment of specific institutions.

This has led to a belief that the historical form of human institutions is irrelevant to an understanding of their moral character. Human institutions can possess moral significance, it is thought, just because moral insights embody ideas which are not historically bounded in the way that human practices surely are. The resultant framework of thought is essentially Protestant, in that one's moral understandings represent an autonomous mode of personal engagement with the public world: a world in which 'legality' does not form an independently constituted source of moral understanding, but in which each person must instead interpret the law in the light of his or her own conception of the demands of legality.

Within a Protestant framework of juridical thought, legality will inevitably assume a downward trajectory. That is, in a world characterized by disagreement over the nature of the good, we are bound to regard law as establishing some necessary set of shared standards by which conduct might be regulated. Arising from a context of disagreement, such a body of standards cannot be thought to *reflect* shared understandings, but is rather to be conceived as an imposed order of rules for regulating understandings. The bases of social order are thus not to be found in the historical attachments of those whose actions it regulates and coordinates, but in authoritative standards which are imposed upon civil life, as it were, from above.

The emergence of a shared set of reasonably determinate standards must either represent points of convergence between rival moral understandings, or else it must impose some reasonable ordering upon the conflicting interests identified by those understandings. A descending conception of legality may thus be traced out in two distinct ways. On the one hand, the legal order may be viewed as a neutral framework of rules establishing reasonable limits within which individuals are free to pursue their own, private conceptions of the good. We might refer to this view as the 'liberal neutrality' conception of legality. On the other hand, the law may be regarded as itself embodying an elevated moral ideal structured around notions of justice and equality. This approach to the nature of legality might be termed 'liberal idealism'. The jurisprudential thought of the modern day can be understood as a long-running debate between these two opposing perspectives.

By approaching the problem in this way, the relevance of historical reflection to jurisprudential thought can be perceived more clearly. The modern jurisprudential writer often regards his task as that of describing the conditions which make legal practice possible and intelligible. Such conditions, it is thought, cannot be internal to the forms of social order investigated by the theorist, for they concern the conceptual divisions whereby social institutions count as manifestations of *law*. Because a notion of legality is necessary to clarify one's understanding of social institutions, historical reflection upon the nature of those institutions cannot serve to ground one's appreciation of legality.

Before the analysis of legal institutions is possible, on the prevalent view, one must take the prior step of clarifying the concept of 'law'. Thus in his 'Postscript' to *The Concept of Law*, HLA Hart observes that the legal theory put forward in that work '. . . is not tied to any particular legal system or legal culture, but seeks to give an explanatory and clarifying account of law as a complex social and political institution . . .'[7] In a similar vein, Raz states that:

> [I]t is easy to explain in what sense legal philosophy is universal. Its theses, if true, apply universally, that is, they speak of all law, of all legal systems; of

[7] HLA Hart, *The Concept of Law* (2nd edn, Oxford, 1994) 239. See also J Raz, *The Authority of Law* (Oxford, 1979) 44. For some discussion of these claims, see S Perry, 'Hart's Methodological Positivism' (1998) 4 Legal Theory 427–67, and S Coyle, 'Two Concepts of Legal Analysis' in S Coyle and G Pavlakos (eds) *Jurisprudence or Legal Science?* (Oxford, 2004) 16–32.

those that exist or will exist, and even of those that can exist or never will. Moreover, its theses are advanced as necessarily universal.[8]

This form of conceptual archaeology occupies a rather curious place in the intellectual landscape. On the one hand, such activities purport to ascertain the necessary or 'essential' conditions for the existence of a legal system; but on the other, the identification of *those* conditions (in place of some other list) serves to articulate a sociological judgment about the instances of legal order that actually exist. It is tempting to say, in such contexts, that our understanding of 'law' is guided by our identification of the 'central instances' of the concept; other, marginal examples qualifying as instances to the extent that achieve some threshold of fulfilment or resemblance of the criteria which constitute the central case. But it is unclear what is to be gained from pointing to the marginal nature of such judgments; for the recognition of an instance of legal order as a marginal rather than a clear one is premised purely on the adoption of the criteria which form the supposed central case. The status of the philosopher's 'necessary conditions' thus hovers uneasily between a stipulative definition and a sociological claim that a certain form of regulatory framework is *in fact* most prevalent among existing forms of social order.

We will thus regard certain concepts or distinctions as clarifications or illuminations *of law* only on the basis of some tacit set of assumptions about which forms of social practice are to count as 'law.' The notions of clarity, illumination, elucidation, etc, can play no constitutive role in the making of such assumptions, since it is precisely in relation to the latter set of ideas that the former are rendered meaningful: any set of conceptual distinctions and ideas will have the effect of highlighting certain questions or features of the legal order as problematic or central, whilst dissolving or marginalizing others. The features of juristic practice that we regard as standing in most need of clarification will in turn depend upon the historical entrenchment of certain basic premises or ideas, which form an implicit and unproblematic background to our understanding, and the assumption of others as problematic or confused.

It might have been expected that critics of the dominant position would have drawn attention to the need for sensitive historical reflection upon actual manifestations of social regulation. For our judgment

[8] J Raz 'On the Nature of Law' (1996) *Archiv fur Rechts und Sozialphilosophie* 1–25, at 1–2.

in relation to forms of social practice is more naturally explained by reference to the perceived point or purpose of those practices within a particular way of life.[9] Yet the main alternative to analytical jurisprudence has in fact served to entrench further the perception of deep divisions between jurisprudential insight and historical reflection. Having grasped the point that the character of human practices depends upon their meaning, we are encouraged to think of human practices as features of the world which do not possess intrinsic meaning and significance, but rather function as abstract bearers of meaning which take on varying significance in the light of animating interpretations. This essentially Protestant view reflects the moral character of juridical thought; but in presenting interpretative reasoning as a necessary framework for moral reflection, it blinds us to the historical character of our own moral life. For Protestant political theory presupposes its own metaphysical picture of the world: a picture in which divergent conceptions of the good derive, not from immersion within a historical form of association, but from personal reflection upon one's own nature independently of shared associations.

An interpretative conception of juridical thought shares with an analytical, or positivist, view a number of metaphysical assumptions which although taken largely for granted, are nonetheless contestable. The classical conception of ethics had centred first and foremost upon the notion of the excellent or worthwhile life, and the constitutive role played by social institutions in realizing conditions conducive to the pursuit of excellent lives. Such a life was thought possible only within the fabric of a shared social existence, for it required each individual to align her conduct with forms of human flourishing that can be realized only in common. Alignment within the forms of flourishing might take place in a number of different ways; but the essentially social nature of human wellbeing was formed against the background of a finally unified conception of the good. Requiring an established matrix of social institutions to foster and sustain it, the nature of that good was thought

[9] See J Finnis, *Natural Law and Natural Rights* (Oxford, 1980) 3–4: '[Law] is constituted by human actions, practices, habits, dispositions and by human discourse . . . But the actions, practices, etc., can be fully understood only by understanding their point, that is to say their objective, their value, their significance or importance, as conceived by the people who performed them, engaged in them, etc. And these conceptions of point, value, significance, and importance will be reflected in the discourse of those same people, in the conceptual distinctions they draw and fail or refuse to draw.'

to be reflected in the historical nexus of institutions which nurture forms of human association. Thus, moral understanding demanded sensitive reflection upon one's own way of life, as reflected in established social institutions such as the family, the market, the law, etc. Law, as the most articulate of these institutions, therefore provided a particularly potent source of insight into the nature of morality and the human condition. We might, therefore, think of the legal order as that social institution in which the human face of the polity is most clearly and directly reflected.

Modernity, by contrast, presents a context of reflection in which most of these ideas have been suppressed or eliminated: for it addresses an idea of the human condition informed not by a single, unified conception of the good, but by fragmented conceptions of the good which vie and compete with one another in the social world. Against such a background of thought, morality no longer concerns the fostering of personal excellences but rather seeks to define the interpersonal relationships which maintain social bonds in the context of competing projects and ideals. To the extent that the rule of law embodies a moral ideal, it is then revealed to be deeply *impersonal* in character: the vision offered by liberal neutrality viewing laws as occupying areas of overlap or convergence *between* personal conceptions of virtue, and that of liberal idealism regarding the law as embodying lofty ideals of 'equality' and 'agency' at some high level of abstraction from the embodied characteristics and choices of concrete persons.

Protestant moral thought in both its 'liberal neutrality' and its 'liberal idealist' guises embodies a form of moral voluntarism that regards choices and values as products not of ethical understanding, but of the will. The absence of a single unifying conception of the good brings to an end the search for moral insight and understanding within the practices and institutions which define our shared experience. Moral knowledge could not derive from consideration of historical facts, it was thought, unless those facts were contemplated in relation to general moral laws: 'That reason should be able to discover any morality in the actions of a man without reference to a law', wrote Pufendorf, 'is as impossible as for a man born blind to choose between colours.'[10]

[10] Pufendorf, *De Iure Naturae et Gentium* (London, 1749) I.2.6. Again: moral entities, standing apart from the causal nexis, 'do not arise out of the intrinsic nature of the physical properties of things, but they are superadded, at the will of intelligent entities, to things already existent and physically complete.' (Ibid, I.1.5–6).

This law-like conception of morality entailed a fundamental shift in the metaphysical basis of ethical thought. No longer was morality a matter of contemplating human purposes and ends as embedded within a rational, universal order that is open to the human intellect. Rather, moral knowledge became a matter of sensitivity and obedience to moral *laws*. One must then seek to establish 'reflective equilibrium' between the various different sources which generate our intuitions: our intuitions of variable facts, and of general moral principles which exist in detachment from those facts.

The metaphysical assumptions which underpin the Protestant view of the world thus firmly entrenched within jurisprudential thought two mutually reinforcing intellectual dogmas. On the one hand, classical ethical thought was deemed to involve a curious inattention to the dichotomy between facts and values, and to the impossibility of deriving moral propositions from facts. On the other, the metaphysical basis of morality was located within the intellectual life of the agent, understood overwhelmingly in terms of will. These developments gave impetus to a perspective from which metaphysics was itself deemed to be irrelevant to an understanding of morality. For the law-like character of morality seemed to exclude the possibility of *understanding* the source of moral laws. The ultimate source of morality had traditionally resided in God. Yet once moral ideas are viewed as *laws*, the only theological source for such laws could be God's will; for the premise of divine omnipotence rendered impossible the suggestion that such a will could be governed by anything external to itself.[11] As the Divine Will must remain incomprehensible to the human mind, human knowledge of the moral law too was thought to be located in the will:

> Since it is only the will of God which can be ascertained in the relation between God and man, man cannot possibly give his response to God through an act of thinking or perceiving, but only by his being obedient or disobedient, that is to say by his will.[12]

[11] Thus Luther was to observe that '[W]hat God wills is not right because He ought, or was bound, so to will; on the contrary, what takes place must be right, because he so wills it.' See M Luther, 'The Bondage of the Will' in J Dillenberger (ed), *Martin Luther: Selections From His Writings* (New York, 1961) 196. See also J Calvin, *Institutes of the Christian Religion*, III.xxiii.2: 'For if [God's will] has any cause, something must precede it, to which it is, as it were, bound; this is unlawful to imagine. For God's will is so much the highest rule of righteousness that whatever he wills, by the very act that he wills it, must be considered righteous.' See Schneewind, *Moral Philosophy from Montaigne to Kant* (New York, 2003) 8.

[12] A Dilhe, *The Theory of Will in Classical Antiquity* (Berkeley, 1982) 15.

Protestant political thought in this way contained within itself the means by which its own metaphysical underpinnings could be eventually suppressed. For it began to appear to early-modern jurists that, if the Divine Will surpassed human understanding, then the intellectual force of moral propositions could not in the end derive from a theological framework. The desired underpinning could instead be provided by the premise of human agency and autonomy. Thus, Kant had argued that morality is that which 'can rise above the emotional impulses of human nature through the purifying processes of choice:' a choice which is 'free' in that it 'involves an act of independent will rather than a mere acquiescence in a goal set by nature . . . Reason paradoxically becomes practical by subjecting every maxim to the purely formal test of whether it can be redescribed as a universal law.'[13] The intellectual force of moral propositions is thus a function of their immediacy in relation to human will and choice.

It is no accident that the notion of reason associated with Protestant thought should be viewed as giving rise to paradox. For if morality addresses, not a unified human good but the relations between individuals with opposing ideas of the good, then how is agreement to be reached upon the 'universal' laws which govern those relations? The disagreement cannot be resolved by reference to the 'rational' nature of such laws, since moral disagreement is in that sense a disagreement about what is rational. Is not the selection of universal laws then simply to oppose one, privileged, conception of the good to the rest? Viewed from this perspective, the areas of convergence between rival moral positions (on the 'liberal neutrality' conception) could emerge only as a contingent feature of moral experience, and as is familiar to those who work within the law, the meaning of any fixed body of rules which might be thought to embody 'neutral' positions tend to fragment and erode as they are applied in a range of specific cases. Similarly, the conceptions of equality or right which inform a liberal idealist interpretation of the legal order are easily revealed as themselves depending upon contentious theories of justice or the good, and which have thus to some degree to be imposed upon individuals contrary to their own

[13] TJ Hochstrasser, *Natural Law Theories in the Early Enlightenment* (Cambridge, 2000) 198. See also Kant, *Groundwork of the Metaphysics of Morals*, HJ Paton (translator) (New York, 1964) 80: 'Everything in nature works in accordance with laws. Only a rational being has the power to act in accordance with his idea of laws . . . and only so has he a will. Since *reason* is required to derive actions from laws, the will is nothing but practical reason.'

interpretations and moral understandings. The universality of a moral ideal depends upon the rationality of the judgment which underlies it, and so the 'correct' interpretation of the legal order (that which most clearly reveals the dimensions of 'equality' and 'right' that inform the ideal of legality) might be one which differs from the judgments of those subject to it. Yet it is by no means easy to see how each person's 'Protestant' interpretation of the legal order should lead to a convergence in understandings as to what constitutes a 'rational' judgment, or ideal.

The theological framework of Protestantism had provided a context within which the apparent rationality of the autonomous agent could be reconciled with the existence of a transcendent body of moral laws binding on all: for the agent's choices could be conceived as private determinations about the correct means of participating in and achieving a basic good (entry into the kingdom of Heaven) presupposed as an ultimate end. Thus private 'conceptions of the good' functioned in reality as mere constituents of a unified, but complex ethical ideal. As morality became increasingly separated from moral theology, under the pressure of Protestant ideas, a secular concern with the individual began to emerge for which the capacity for autonomous reflection signalled genuinely distinct forms of the good. For we can think of each person's understanding of the means of achieving salvation as the adoption of a 'form of life'. It then becomes possible to view such understandings not simply as causal mechanisms for the realization of some postponed good, but also as constituents of a good life in their own right. Protestantism thus allows scope for fundamental conflict amongst these differing forms of the good. The central problem for moral Protestantism is thus an explanation of how such essentially subjective acts of autonomous willing can produce collective insights into virtue and the moral good. The detachment of that theory from its underlying, sustaining metaphysical framework leaves entirely mysterious the means by which this intellectual gap is to be bridged.

The Impersonal Face of the Rule of Law

The jurisprudential thought of the modern day is the heir to these Protestant forms of thought. As such, our understandings of the legal and political realms remain mired in a moral voluntarism which detaches the ethical significance of social institutions from their historical character as a body of human practices. This has served to obscure the human face of the rule of law by instead emphasizing its depersonalizing quality. We might explain this as follows.

Law represents both an aspirational moral ideal, and a set of variable, human arrangements. The variability of those arrangements, and their tendency to embody divergent or ambivalent ideas, has led to the suggestion that legal practices may be represented in different ways, as expressing differing ideals: the law of tort may be viewed as embodying ideals of economic efficiency *or* corrective justice precisely because the practice of tort lawyers variously reflects concerns with *both* sets of ideals. Instead of seeking to uncover the sources of tension or fragmentation within shared practices, modern legal philosophers have adopted the voluntarist belief that human practices are therefore 'mere conventions' awaiting an 'interpretation' with which to invest them with moral significance. Legal reasoning, at an abstract level, then involves an evaluative choice between rival interpretations.

The choices presented by this embedded notion of interpretation are somewhat limiting. On the one hand, we might regard the set of concrete arrangements (the rules and doctrines, and so forth) as supplying a fixed and stable framework of 'brute' facts in which to construct our Protestant interpretations. We will then think of legal practice as engendering a firm distinction between the rules and doctrines, on the one hand, and the processes whereby such rules are interpreted and applied, on the other. Lawyerly practices of argument and analysis are accordingly thought to be sustained by an implicit background of moral and political thought which lawyers do not consciously address in their arguments. Such background theories are then the stuff of 'normative jurisprudence', a pursuit of legal philosophers to be carefully distinguished from the technical practices of lawyers. On the other hand, we may treat the statement of rules and doctrines as inseparable from the background theories, such theories forming the basis for idealistic visions in which moral and political values constitute 'the general part of adjudication' and (where not raised explicitly in legal judgment) the 'silent prologue to any decision at law.'[14]

[14] R Dworkin, *Law's Empire* (London, 1986) 90. Legal positivists would, of course, deny these last two claims. But they would not, I think, dissent from the basic idea involved, that (having described the 'valid' rules of a legal order) normative jurisprudence consists in the application to law of specific moral or political theories: see eg Raz, 'Interpretation Without Retrieval' in A Marmor (ed), *Law and Interpretation* (Oxford, 1995) 155; also the essays in L Alexander (ed), *Constitutionalism: Philosophical Foundations* (Cambridge, 1998). The activities of Bentham's 'Censor' also constitute a good example: see earlier.

Legal thought, on either of these views, consists not in a distinctive process of moral reflection, wherein our intellectual grasp of a set of ideas is continually deepened and refined as they are applied in particular situations, but in the general interpretation of a body of laws according to an abstract scheme of justice. Such theories of justice centre on dimensions of moral or political concern that form obligations purporting to regulate competition between deeply divergent goods, and which have in consequence no essential connection with the good of the person thus obligated. The source of such demands therefore lies in abstract principles which have no basis in a rich understanding of the moral nature of the human person. Law and morality instead come to centre upon the general social conditions and lines of connection governing the interaction between morally equal 'agents'. Once the relevant moral unit becomes not the person but the *agent*, there is little to be gained from sustained reflection upon the concrete attachments which constitute personal identities: each such concrete instantiation will reflect merely the series of choices, or interaction between choices, exercised by otherwise morally equal agents.

This line of thought is particularly seductive, but also most destructive of genuine insight, where the aspirational ideals at work within the law are thought to embody a deep commitment to a liberal conception of justice centred upon 'the individual'. Here, the law is viewed as an instrument through which individuals with diverse interests and agendas might be orientated within a normative framework wherein they relate to one another as juridical equals. Such equality must, it is thought, seek to establish dimensions of parity between persons without regard to the particular identities or characteristics which render us distinct from one another (for to do otherwise is to elevate accidental features of the human person to the status of privileged constituents of a theory of the 'good' which is then reflected in the law). The juridical ideals at work in the law are thus thought to concern only certain theorized conceptions of personhood (such as agency), shorn of present characteristics and attachments. Thus in Rawls's influential book *A Theory of Justice*, our understanding of 'justice' is said to emerge from a hypothetical social agreement conducted under certain idealized conditions in which 'agents' determine the form of social arrangements from behind a 'veil of ignorance'. The content of justice is then thought to be fully revealed only when expunged of all knowledge of the concrete identities and present institutional attachments of those to whom it applies.[15]

Despite the philosopher's propensity to regard generalized, theorized strata as embodying deep or fundamental aspects of the human person, it is clear that such a form of moral thought can address only a superficial concept of the person, understood in abstraction from the very capacities and inequalities which constitute separate personal identities.[16] By mistaking abstract and general categories for essential truth, Protestant theories of law and justice actually operate to subvert the supposedly liberal foundations on which justice is said to rest.

Consider the theory of liberal neutrality. Liberal rights require a context of stable institutions and shared practices which nurture the social freedoms on which they are based. Maintenance of social institutions and practices is thus thought to depend upon the creation of a framework of rules which regulate competition between diverging notions of the good, whilst remaining neutral as between conceptions of the good. Yet we cannot for long sustain the belief that a body of rules can fulfil this function on the basis of *neutral* interventions in the political controversies which would otherwise undermine the basis of social order. For the application of legal rules will normally depend upon an understanding of their aim or purpose. But legal rules are designed to apply generally and prospectively, and so cannot be said to exist in a realm of clearly envisaged purposes and modes of application. Functional or purposive explanations of the rules will hence tend to fragment and conflict when applied in differing contexts, rather than establishing areas of convergence or neutral understanding.

Considered this way, the idea of neutrality is readily transformable into a more direct concern with human equality and democratic respect. A liberal polity may then itself mutate into an idealistic politics of principles in which law represents, not an instrument of policy, but the articulate search for an elevated moral perspective through which liberal rights may be related to, or derived from, fundamental principles of justice. Given the obvious ability of idealism to resonate with prevalent political attitudes and aspirations, it is not, perhaps, the vision of 'liberal neutrality' which presents the greatest potential for distortion and erosion of liberal understandings, but the starry-eyed idealist's.

[15] See J Rawls, *A Theory of Justice* (Cambridge, 1971). Also see the valuable discussion in R Geuss, *Outside Ethics* (Princeton, 2005) ch. 2.

[16] See GWF Hegel, *Phenomenology of Spirit*, AV Miller (translator) (Oxford, 1977) para 44. See also E Craig, *The Mind of God and the Works of Man* (Oxford, 1987).

By diminishing experience from a rich source of moral insight into an arena of contingencies to which more permanent moral insights are applied, idealism embodies an ethical vision only tenuously anchored in the mundane realities which supply the ordinary context of motive and action. For those mundane realities are produced and sustained by human practices which reflect diversity and pluralism, but also tolerance. In transforming social practices and institutions into an ideal embodiment of public virtues, the pursuit of consistency will encourage the development of overriding perspectives which inevitably treat certain aspects of a fragmented vision as having more centrality or importance than others, reducing the capacity for the expression of liberal tolerance.

Such imperialistic visions might thus hope to sustain themselves by feeding off those aspects of social life which nurture the beliefs that gave rise to them.[17] Liberalism is best thought of not as a particular body of beliefs, however, but as a historical tradition: as such it may be expected to contain within itself the numerous contradictory impulses felt by the diverse participants who think of themselves as 'liberals.' A liberal understanding of the rule of law is thus revealed not by 'fitting' abstract theories to partially described practices, but through the sensitive exploration of overlapping modes of thought which might coexist within a body of practices only in complex patterns of tension. The difference in approaches I am suggesting bears some similarity to that identified by Michael Walzer, in the following passage:

> One way to begin the philosophical enterprise—perhaps the original way—is to walk out of the cave, leave the city, climb the mountain, to fashion for oneself . . . an objective and universal standpoint. Then one describes the terrain of everyday life from far away, so that it loses its particular contours and takes on a general shape. But I mean to stand in the cave, in the city, on the ground. Another way of doing philosophy is to interpret to one's fellow citizens the world of meanings that we share. Justice and equality can be conceivably worked out as philosophical artefacts, but a just or egalitarian society cannot be. If such a society isn't already here—hidden, as it were, in our concepts and categories—we shall never know it concretely or realise it in fact.[18]

[17] See eg JL Austin, 'Three Ways of Spilling Ink' in *Philosophical Papers* (Oxford, 1969) 285, which talks of the 'freedom in the "structuring" of history . . . by means of words'.

[18] M Walzer, *Spheres of Justice* (Oxford, 1983) xvi. See also Walzer, *On Toleration* (New York, 1997) ch 1, especially 1–5; R Plant, *Politics, Theology and History* (Cambridge, 2001) 116.

The idealist may be motivated by the desire to reconcile the existence of pluralism with the need for unconditional standpoints from which to engage in moral contemplation. Yet morality is universal, not in the sense that particulars must be related to detached and unconditioned universals, but in that particulars contain the universal, as part of their intelligibility: for, in this way, particulars are a prism in which aspects of the human condition are reflected (sometimes obscurely). Morality may thus be said to concern universal ideas without issuing in standpoints that avoid immersion in 'conditions'.

Idealism, by nature, tends to underestimate the importance of the mundane forms of rule-application with which the ordinary lawyer is familiar. Because the idealist views rules as 'mere conventions', in themselves devoid of moral significance, it must then seem as if ordinary rule-applying processes hide or suppress a more fundamental dimension to legal thought of which the practising lawyer is largely unaware. Operating at the 'surface' level of adjudication, lawyers are inevitably portrayed by the idealist as a pretty unreflective bunch, operating within a complex structure of deeply principled ideas of which they may catch no more than the odd fleeting glimpse.[19] This view has obvious comforts for the legal philosopher, whose job is then to enlighten his legal brothers to the existence of that elevated moral perspective. It is the obvious fact that specifically legal modes of argument and conflict-resolution exclude moral or political reasons which may otherwise have a bearing on decision that makes idealism such a splendidly adaptable thesis: for any attempt to 'go beyond' or restate the settled rules and established doctrines will appear to embody underdeveloped forms of philosophical idealism, awaiting a deeper and more general justification by the philosopher. Employing the distinction between 'surface' conventions and 'deep' or underpinning principles, the philosopher may point with relative ease to the common law's 'inadequately theorized' and 'insufficiently systematized' state as the product of a lawyerly failure to 'think in terms of overarching principles' or develop a fully reflective 'rights consciousness.'[20]

The common law mode of reasoning is one in which judges modify existing doctrines and standards as they apply them. It takes no great familiarity with case-law, moreover, to comprehend the fact that there

[19] Cf Dworkin's suggestion that jurisprudence is the '*silent* prologue to any decision at law': see Dworkin, *Law's Empire*, n 14 above.

[20] J Wright, *Tort Law and Human Rights* (Oxford, 2001) 5–7.

is, in the context of juridical thought and judgment, no clear distinction between those two intellectual processes: the lack of a fixed verbal form indicates the operation of ideas which depend for their form upon the precise manner of their articulation in each case. Because such meanings may be formulated with greater or lesser degrees of reflective insight, it becomes impossible to separate a 'surface' meaning for rules and doctrines from a deeper, philosophical level of meaning. Legal thought is thus more closely depicted as involving the gradual deepening of a reflective understanding, rather than the application of abstract theoretical insights to floating sets of 'givens'.

Juridical argument thus constitutes a form of thought which becomes increasingly distorted as it is systematized. For the pursuit of theoretical coherence demands the isolation of a manageably small set of considerations (conceptions of justice or fairness, etc) through which currently diverse particulars are to be classified. Yet the complex concerns which make up the law of contract, of tort, property, etc, are identifiable with no finite set of considerations running through every case, or informing decision at every point. Common law precedents can be developed along various differing trajectories, and often contain many possible lines of development. Doctrinal rules thus tend to be subject to complex exceptions, distinctions and rationalizations both general and highly specific. Being shot through with competing concerns and overlaid by regulatory regimes, legal rules represent complex jurisprudential ideas reflecting a heady mixture of ends and purposes. Such richness is not easily reflected where legal thought is alleged to serve a limited number of interpretative ideals. For to impose a framework of abstract ideals upon legal thought is to solidify the form and possible meanings to be given to doctrinal ideas: we must see them as (perhaps unconsciously or unreflectively) serving *these* ends, at a suitable level of abstraction.

Such general interpretative principles would doubtless necessitate the creation of complex exceptions to mitigate potential injustices in particular cases; yet any attempt at formulating a principled basis for such departures would either itself embody abstract ideals subject to open-ended exceptions and modifications, or lead to massive injustices and distortions in its application to specific cases which may, though similar, be viewed as morally unalike.

Raymond Geuss has drawn attention to a liberal society's capacity for self-delusion: as society swings to the right economically and politically, it increasingly seeks solace in theories of social justice as a kind of 'compensatory fantasy', much as Feuerbach suggested the image of God as the necessary personification of those strengths and virtues of which humans, lacking them, must construct as ideals.[21] Such theories provide the comforting vision that utopia resembles the basic structure and features of the society of the present, only slight changes in direction or attitude being needed to advance towards the ideal. The effect of such intellectual tendencies is to elevate the social and political forms of the day to the status of historical inevitabilities: the conjunction of liberalism, democracy, human rights and the free-market being celebrated as the final form of enlightened human society.[22] We may, thereby, effectively disguise, even from ourselves, the obvious truth that *every* political system has its ideal form: communism, aristocracy, anarchy, as much as liberalism. Yet it is not the ideal forms (which do not emerge as genuine possibilities in the real world), but the historical record of the real political movements in the world which carry the name of such systems, that reveal most clearly the 'essence' of the political philosophies they claim to instantiate.

The relationship between opposing packages of ideals and the social objects theorized by them, is never likely to be straightforward. This is particularly so in the case of highly articulate objects such as the law, which are in part constituted by those ideals. We may expect such objects to act as a prism through which the constituent ideals and other, mundane and pragmatic realities may be confusingly and distortingly refracted. The legal order of the British polity is a complex historical object created in part by the divergent traditions of liberal neutrality and idealism. Yet its central processes of moral reflection belong to a tradition of ethical thought lying wholly outside the philosophical world which those major traditions inhabit. It thus reflects an aspect of human social nature which is both enormously complex, fragmented and possibly incoherent. The moral nature of law lies ultimately neither in positivist-inspired liberal 'neutrality', nor in idealistic reflections upon encompassing systems of rights; but rather in an intellectual world beyond both sets of ideals.

Legality and Civility

I began this essay with the suggestion that an understanding of the nature of law requires an understanding of the human context within

[21] See R Geuss, n 15 above, 34–5; L Feuerbach, *The Essence of Christianity* (New York, 1957). I borrow the ideas of the argument of this paragraph from Geuss, *Outside Ethics*, ch 2: see n 15 above.

[22] See F Fukuyama, *The End of History and the Last Man* (Harmondsworth, 1993).

which the law operates. We might then think of the law as embodying the moral consciousness of the people to whom it applies. By focusing upon the notion of the Protestant 'agent', legality will seem to involve the establishment and interpretation of a coherent body of rights, within which agency may be freely exercised. In this way, law will appear to give expression to a comprehensive theory of liberal justice. But we must also keep in mind the importance of the social framework in which such phenomena exist and function, and of the law's role in maintaining that framework. (Indeed, it may be more apposite to speak of a number of distinct yet overlapping frameworks of social order and governance, and of the centrality of the legal order in securing the smooth interaction of the various frameworks.) Notions of justice may play a significant part in relation to some areas of this framework, but they are unlikely to be omnipresent within it: for much of social life consists in sporadic interaction between strangers of whom we know relatively little, on the basis of informal social rules rather than well-understood conventions that are capable of being fully articulated by the relevant participants. Governance often consists not in the deliberate redistribution of powers or resources in relation to such modes of interaction, but in the provision of an orderly basis on which the interaction can continue. In this way, a major project of governance (and of law) might be seen as attempting to give transparency and structure to otherwise shifting and ambiguous aspects of everyday life.

The factors which guide decisions in a large number of cases are not deliberately chosen elements of a theory of justice, but doctrinal considerations of a broadly conventional nature which seek to give greater definition to the content of informal understandings on which the majority of social relationships are based. The rules of contract, or the definition of a gift, say, are of this kind in that much of their understanding finds its root in somewhat amorphous social conventions, whilst at the same time seeking to restructure such conventions by assigning clear meanings to doubtful aspects of established practice and resolving ambiguities which hinder their operation. In such cases, the process is one of gradual refinement and adjustment, not the selection of distributive or aggregative ideals.

We find in these ideas a reflection of the human face of the rule of law. For legality is to be thought of, not as a descending structure of rules or principles imposed upon an otherwise formless social void, but rather as an articulate embodiment of a tradition of civility. Embodying such a tradition, it is not immediately clear that legal order should represent an intellectual artefact transparent to theoretical understanding. For given the complex and non-linear nature of English social history and politics, we might instead have expected the law to comprise successive layers of meaning that have become superimposed to form an elusive cultural and historical object. In such a case, we could give univocal expression to our traditions of legality only if we are willing to embrace a certain level of distortion and intellectual blinkeredness in our theoretical explanations. At the same time, we might think, law does not simply *personify* the traditions of thought and practice upon which our civility depends; it also alters and creates forms of social interaction in pursuit of objectives that go beyond the desire merely to sustain present conceptions of social order. If we think of a tradition of civility as embodying certain moral ideals, then it is the case that law not only personifies certain ideals, but in many cases shapes its own ideals in the course of its daily existence. Any attempt to relate the mundane, everyday manifestations of legal practice to those ideals must, of necessity, exhibit a considerable degree of complexity.

To embrace such a conception of legality is to embrace a form of moral reasoning that is rooted in the particular, rather than in general principles which exist in abstraction from particular situations to which they apply. Acceptance of such a position is often thought to involve adherence to an unsustainable intellectual dogma known as 'particularism'.

Some degree of generality in moral thinking is, of course, an inescapable feature of moral wisdom. The character of that generalization is often thought to demand recognition of a form of thought in which the relevant intellectual processes involve endeavours of 'constructive interpretation' or reflective equilibrium. But it may also be suggestive of a quite different set of intellectual processes, in which emphasis lies not upon the guiding of particular decisions by general rules or hypotheses, but instead upon the sensitive exploration of the particular through careful attention to the moral features of individual situations. Particulars can be apprehended by the intellect only when viewed in combination, as part of a structured whole; but they are never understood through abstract rules or principles. The moral knowledge sought would then represent a body of ideas incapable of being fully grasped or articulated in abstraction from particular judgments and decisions which are perceived more clearly and immediately by the moral understanding: a mode of thought in which particulars are related to a general framework in which, rather than *by* which, they are understood.

The need for sensitive and careful reflection upon particulars as a condition for moral understanding ought to have alerted us to the fact that experience itself (when understood as a conjunction of such particulars) is an object of the understanding, rather than a set of 'givens' which are simply perceived. As such, the established features of legal and social practices constitute a source of moral understanding, and cannot operate merely as 'constraints' upon an otherwise freely floating interpretative will.[23]

We would have approached, in this way, something akin to Aristotle's position:

> Since it seems that there is nothing outside and separate in existence from sensible spatial magnitudes, the objects of thought are in the sensible forms, namely, both the abstract objects and all the states and affections of sensible things. Hence, no one can learn or understand anything in the absence of sense. . .[24]

For Aristotle, the universal does not exist in separation from particulars; rather the particular is the perceptible or intelligible form of the universal. He is thus able to say that although we perceive particulars, *perception* is of universals, or rather of the universal-in-the-particular.[25] In the same way, morality transcends particular or momentary concerns, but moral understanding proceeds from the contemplation of particular situations that are either actually confronted or envisaged. Such understanding is manifested by the ability to give sensitive and careful expression to the dimensions of a situation which mark it out from others before the moral imagination, or which (in a legal context) require intervention of some sort. Moral knowledge does not exist in a manner which allows for understanding in advance of its application or specification in individual cases, for moral ideas are not independent of the contexts in which moral judgments are given specific formulation. The relevant image is thus not one in which a body of a contextually determinate propositions *applies* to actual or hypothetical cases, but one of a deepening sense of the moral flowing from immersion within, and treatment of, particular situations.

[23] As Nigel Simmonds has observed, 'Shared understandings may be eroded, but they never become "constraints" within which the interpreter may move freely. Precisely in being understandings, they inform and guide interpretation at every point.' See Simmonds, 'Between Positivism and Idealism' (1991) 50 CLJ (1991) 326.

[24] See Aristotle, *De Anima*, III 8, 432a3–8.

[25] Aristotle, *Posterior Analytics*, I 31, 87b28–30.

Hart famously characterized shared juridical reasons as resting upon an agreement in judgments. These reflections, I believe, help us to understand how the presence of diversity within cultural backgrounds and interests does not prevent broad agreement upon the judgment of particular cases, even where there is sharp divergence between individual reasons for accepting those judgments.[26] For they indicate that moral knowledge might be fundamentally particular, in manner of intelligibility. Furthermore, the above reflections explain the nature of that particularity without the need for problematic distinctions between two sources or levels of moral understanding, or of the existence of 'objective' versus 'subjective' understandings: the understanding of the subject proceeds from reflection upon the meaning of present attachments and concerns as they relate to a universal order in which they participate. The particularity of moral understandings should not, therefore, be taken to imply that the relevant knowledge is to be found in an endless series of discontinuities which may only be related or combined by will. Discontinuity can only be comprehended within the context of broader continuities between the human person and the external order she inhabits.[27] Such continuities are composed of aspects of human existence that combine to form coherent projects and ordered capacities, for human beings relate to the social forms and institutions which surround them not simply as a disconnected series of moments or occasions of choice, but as integrated personalities defined by interconnecting plans and projects of medium-to-long-term range. Only insofar as the social environment exhibits purpose and continuity can human life and experience be said to manifest intelligibility.

Moral reflections are thus to an extent reflections upon how individuals simultaneously construct and are constructed by the social environment.[28] Such moral deliberations might be directed with profit to the consideration of private law. For it is here that the frontier between the individual and a shared environment is most clearly defined and articulated. Propositions of private law cannot without distortion be taken to represent a set of general rules established by authority and imposed

[26] See AR Jonsen and S Toulmin, *The Abuse of Casuistry* (Los Angeles, 1989).

[27] See J Porter, *Nature as Reason* (Portland, Or, 2005) 116. The notion of 'universal order' need not be conceived in theological terms (though it must depend upon metaphysical assumptions as profound as a theological world-view): it may be taken to ground a tradition of civility, or a form of life, in Wittgenstein's sense.

[28] See M Gibson, 'The Historical Nature of Human Nature' (1975) 72 *Journal of Philosophy* 604–11.

upon the civil polity. Many of the forms and concepts of private law exist not to restrict or govern conduct, but to facilitate ordinary transactions by creating determinate meanings for informal understandings. The traditional emphasis within private law has thus not centred upon the identification and eventual elimination of instances of fragmentation or inequality within social life, but rather upon the enunciation of a set of rules which allow for the possibility of a peaceful and meaningful coexistence in the presence of fragmentation. Law's embodiment of a moral ideal does not betoken the attempt to give direct expression to a general theory of justice, in the idealist's sense. Rather, it suggests a gradual refinement and deepening of one's grasp of a body of ideas as those ideas are applied in endlessly differing contexts.

Legality, Civility and *Geist*

To the Protestant thought of the modern day, such ideas will seem to depend upon unsustainable metaphysical assumptions. For if each person possesses the capacity to formulate and pursue genuinely distinct conceptions of the good, a society aware of its own complexity will then perceive the need for a political process to mediate between plural visions of the good. Law may then embody civility only in the diminished sense of a hypothetically consensual body of rules which establish certain boundaries and conditions in which the joint pursuit of divergent conceptions of the good is possible. It will then seem that a philosophical account of law's nature cannot be illuminated by the notion of a *tradition* of civility, but must instead be directed towards the abstract possibilities presented by systems of moral principles in relation to the conditions of agency. Whilst this view is implicit in most legal and moral philosophy at the current day, I believe it is wholly wrong.

The resistance of modern philosophy to the idea of civility might be thought to hinge upon the impossibility of centring upon a unified object of practical contemplation ('the good') presupposed as an end in human nature and reality. For might not social reality embody wickedness and injustice, rather than virtue and enlightenment? How, then, can history or experience act as a source of moral insight into the nature of the good?

I wish to suggest that both the 'Protestant' *and* the classical Aristotelian modes of ethical thought ultimately depend upon the manifestation in human affairs of some form of *Geist* (or 'benign guiding spirit') as the means by which the ideal of the good life is rendered intelligible and coherent. In the medieval world, Christian theology supplied the obvious framework through which individuals could abstract their reason from the harsh realities and injustices of earthly politics, and approach the divine. The schisms and internal conflicts which characterized the European Reformation rendered that framework itself the subject of disagreement, but insofar as entry into the Kingdom of Heaven remained central to ethical belief, the emergence of Protestantism signalled a breakdown in consensus about the means by which the ultimate good for man is to be realized, whilst leaving the intrinsic nature of the good intact. With the decline of religious belief as a central constituent of moral and political reflection, however, disagreement about the means of achieving the good readily transforms into recognition of plural forms of the good which exist in mutual tension. In such circumstances, belief in the rationality *and* autonomy of Protestant wills (ie convergence between transcendent rationality and Protestant autonomy) must be motivated and sustained by a set of beliefs which are of at least equivalent weight and significance as an underpinning theological perspective. Without such beliefs, there exists no reason for supposing that autonomy can be reconciled with rationality.

Although it does not exhibit the same tension between autonomy and rationality, the classical alignment of moral wisdom and experience also depends upon the assumption that the good is realized in ordinary life to some degree. But this basic assumption is more easily and fully integrated into the framework of Aristotelian thought, for in claiming that practical wisdom involves knowledge of the good through its realization, Aristotle is addressing his remarks to those already possessed of good character and noble dispositions. Those who exhibit *akrasia*, or weakness of will, Artistotle says, require the imposition of rules to instil benevolent patterns of conduct.[29] The element of *Geist* in classical ethical thought is therefore a much clearer and more integrated part of the metaphysics of morals than is the case where facts and values are taken to denote separate logical or natural kinds. For, having provided an extensive psychological underpinning for human nature as essentially benign,[30] Aristotle is then in a position to treat the

[29] See Aristotle, *Nicomachean Ethics*, 1152a6–7.
[30] See, *inter alia*, Aristotle, *De Anima*.

human practices and forms of association which embody that nature as themselves providing a central source of insight into the nature of the good.

Do we find, in Protestant political thought, a similarly fully integrated and worked-out understanding of human nature? On the whole, we do not: for such theories tend to replace detailed investigations of the psychology of human nature with broad and general categories of autonomy, rationality, self-interest and freedom, etc, as the basis of an account of moral thinking. As moral thinking becomes progressively detached from its foundation in the human character (and thus divorced from prudence and wellbeing),[31] abstract principles of reason are forced to supply the necessary element of *Geist* in leading those of suitable bearing towards the ultimate good. Such a manifestation of *Geist* inevitably operates in a much more detached and free-floating way in respect to human wills than is conceivable within classical ethical thought. For, being separated from both human *telos* and the supposition of external imposition by a divine will, the rational convergence of human wills upon common standards of justice and right becomes a matter of diffuse optimism concerning the 'objectivity' of moral values, and the ability of human minds to apprehend them.

An understanding of the law's moral nature thus does not derive from an abstract structure of ratiocination (in the form of 'interpretations' of legal concepts) but constitutes an immanent form of reflective speculation upon the values for which present forms of human ordering exist. Modern philosophy has, by and large, directed attention to the definition of a complex object (comprised by norms of justice) and has sought to understand personal interests and the relations between them in the light of that objective perspective. Such a strategy, I have argued, is deeply mistaken about the relationship between civility and plural forms of the good. For human preferences and interests are not self-standing objects of the will which operate within normative interstices, but rather they take their form from factors within the social environment which are thus external to the 'agent'. Insofar as human action manifests rationality, human actors do not develop preferences or formulate coherent medium- or long-term projects that are incapable of fulfilment within the immediately available conditions. This relates as much to the social as to the natural conditions of life: our bases for

[31] If there exist diverse forms of the good, but a unique set of moral rules is necessary as the ground of social order and stability, it follows that morality may conflict with that which is good for a person.

action are premised not upon the assumption of a greatly increased lifespan, nor the absence of social norms which structure human interaction, but upon the matrix of social, legal and moral understandings within which each person operates. Forms of jurisprudential thinking which perceive society as being governed by a descending conception of justice thus tend to foster imperialistic, rather than liberal, understandings of pluralism.

The central question for jurisprudence is how plural visions of the good combine within a tradition of civility. Civility is not a theoretical structure which exists in detachment from plural visions of the good, for (in being civilized) such visions partly constitute the structure within which they move. It follows that the notion of 'the good' is not an ethical category that stands fully apart and in abstraction from ordinary experience. Social ordering, in constituting part of that experience, is thus not a mere *framework* within which pursuit of the good is possible, but forms part of the good that is being pursued. It is for this reason that secular Protestantism is not the most suitable intellectual standpoint from which to pursue a rich jurisprudential understanding. The standpoint required is that of Hegel: one in which plural or fragmented understandings are comprehended within a complex and unified object that embraces their combination. Such a standpoint on the nature of the good, as a finally unified object of understanding, might be worked out within the intellectual structures of a theological or a humanistic (though not secular) world-view.[32] Insofar as one's ethical commitments depend upon attachment to such fundamental metaphysical world-views, philosophical understandings of the moral nature of law and society are products ultimately not of will, but of faith.

The value of legality within the British polity is thus not separable from national spirit, conceived (as in early-modern philosophy and 19th century literature) as an essentially benign force in the world. The main characteristics of this national spirit are a reverence for liberty[33] and the avoidance of extremes, and a deep attachment to the ordinary

[32] A reminder is in order here that in seeking to illuminate the general form of the British polity, one confronts a tradition of civility formed (in at least its 'modern' manifestation) by predominantly Judeo-Christian ethical ideas.

[33] The idea of liberty was not in this traditional sense a political notion but a social condition of Englishness (being the birthright of every free Englishman): see eg Jerome K Jerome, *Three Men in a Boat* [1889] (various editions) ch 11.

moral experience of the 'middling sort.'[34] Moral thinking of this kind is seldom capable of abstract or fully general formulation as a set of principles. Thus, the conception of legality through which an understanding of the law proceeds is one rooted in the value, not of fixed rules or of abstract principles, but of informal understandings and of sensitive and careful reflection upon specific features of each case. The English spirit is captured most eloquently by George Eliot:

> All people of broad, strong sense have an instinctive repugnance to the men of maxims; because such people early discern that the mysterious complexity of our life is not to be embraced by maxims, and that to lace ourselves up in formulas of that sort is to repress all the divine promptings and inspirations that spring from growing insight and sympathy. And the man of maxims is the popular representative of the minds that are guided in their moral judgment solely by general rules, thinking that these will lead them to justice by a ready-made patent method, without the trouble of exerting patience, discrimination, impartiality – without any care to assure themselves whether they have the insight that comes from a hardly-earned estimate of temptation, or from a life vivid and intense enough to have created a wide fellow-feeling with all that is human.[35]

The tenor of such remarks reveals the deep affinity between the English moral sense and that of Aristotelian moral wisdom, manifested in experience but incapable of full articulation. The English legal consciousness involves the direction of legal attention to aspects of this fabric of shared characteristics and understandings as part of a constant process of social self-consciousness and reflection. It is upon such understandings and thought-processes that jurisprudence must seek to cast illumination, if it is to reveal the human face of the rule of law.

[34] eg, see the profusion of texts in the 'common sense' tradition of moral philosophy in the 18th century, such as Thomas Paine's *Common Sense* [1776] and Francis Hutcheson's *On the Nature and Conduct of the Passions* [1742]. The common law provides an obvious example of thinking in this tradition.

[35] Eliot, *The Mill on the Floss*, Book 7, ch 2.

Constitutional Review, the Courts, and Democratic Scepticism

*Aileen Kavanagh**

Introduction

In the UK, there is a long intellectual tradition of opposing any enhancement of judicial power in the name of protecting rights. Jeremy Bentham was a hugely influential figure in forging that tradition. He was deeply sceptical of canonical and abstract statements of rights, which he famously castigated as 'nonsense upon stilts'.[1] Bentham denounced the 1791 Declaration of the Rights of Man as 'a perpetual vein of nonsense, flowing from a perpetual abuse of words'[2] and dismissed the rights contained in the Declaration as:

> . . . sentimental conceits, as trite as they are unmeaning . . . frippery ornament compared to the majestic simplicity of good sound sense—and the acts of the senate loaded and disfigured by the tinsel of the playhouse.[3]

Bentham's invective was not just focused on rights. It was also directed at the courts and judges. A firm believer in the value and importance of strong parliamentary government, Bentham was deeply sceptical about the desirability (and indeed, ability) of judges to supervise or limit what parliament decides to do. His concerns about the legitimacy of giving the courts powers to enforce rights are encapsulated in the following stark warning:

> Give the judges the power of annulling [Parliament's] acts; and you transfer a portion of the supreme power from an assembly which the people have had

* Reader in Law and Fellow of St Edmund Hall, University of Oxford. I am grateful to Trevor Allan, Nicholas Bamforth, Nick Barber, Eric Barendt, Lizzie Barmes, Costas Douzinas, Colm O'Cinneide, Matthew Robinson and Lord Sedley for helpful discussion of the ideas presented in this chapter.

[1] J Bowring (ed), *The Works of Jeremy Bentham* (Tait: Edinburgh, 1843) 501.

[2] J Bentham, 'Anarchical Fallacies', in *The Works of Jeremy Bentham*, ibid, Vol II, 491–524.

[3] Ibid 497.

some share, at least, in choosing, to a set of men in the choice of whom they have not had the least imaginable share.[4]

The sceptical battle waged by Bentham in the 19th century is still being fought with unmitigated fervour in the 20th and 21st centuries.[5] In fact, David Dyzenhaus suggests that we are experiencing a:

> neo-Benthamite revival . . . [which is] part of an attempt in legal and constitutional theory to focus attention on legislatures rather than the courts . . . The revival claims that Parliaments in vigorous democracies protect human rights better than courts and that trust in judges to resolve political disputes results in the capture of our political processes by elites and thus in 'democratic debilitation'.[6]

Contemporary scepticism about judicial power is aptly described as 'neo-Benthamite' because it echoes both the positive and negative dimension of Bentham's views.[7] The positive dimension celebrates the value of democracy and the supreme importance of strong parliamentary government, in whose decision-making all citizens can participate to some degree. The negative dimension is contained in a deep-seated scepticism about judges and judicial power. I will refer to critics who support these two dimensions as *democratic sceptics*—'democratic' because their arguments are firmly rooted in democratic concerns and 'sceptics' because this captures nicely their disposition towards judicial power.[8]

[4] *Fragment on Government* (Cambridge, 1988) ch IV, para 32. For further discussion of Bentham's scepticism both in relation to rights and the courts, see Lord Hoffmann, 'Bentham and Human Rights' (2001) 54 CLP 61.

[5] eg, see J Griffith, *The Politics of the Judiciary* (Fontana, 1997); T Campbell, K Ewing and A Tomkins (eds) *Sceptical Essays on Human Rights* (Oxford Univeristy Press: Oxford, 2001).

[6] D Dyzenhaus, 'The Genealogy of Legal Positivism' (2004) 24 OJLS 39, 62. For the term 'democratic debilitation', see M Tushnet, 'Policy Distortion and Democratic Debilitation: Comparative Illumination of the Counter Majoritarian Difficulty' (1995) 94 Michigan Law Review 245.

[7] See Dyzenhaus, 'The Left and the Question of Law' (2004) 17 Canadian Journal of Law and Jurisprudence 7, at 10–11.

[8] For use of this label, see also T Campbell, 'Incorporation through Interpretation' in Campbell, Ewing & Tomkins (eds) *Sceptical Essays on Human Rights*, n 5 above, 79, 88; S Fredman, 'Scepticism under Scrutiny: Labour Law and Human Rights'in Campbell, Ewing & Tomkins (eds) *Sceptical Essays on Human Rights*, n 5 above, 213; A Kavanagh, 'Judging the Judges under the Human Rights Act 1998: Deference, Disillusionment and the 'War on Terror' (2009) Public Law 287–304.

The subject-matter of this chapter is the contemporary sceptical challenge to constitutional review in the UK.[9] I will not attempt to address, still less refute, the full array of challenging arguments advanced by democratic sceptics against constitutional review.[10] My aim here is much more modest. It is simply to reflect on the nature and form of the central arguments advanced by sceptics and to explore their underlying motivations. In the first part of the chapter, I will show that democratic sceptics tend to rely on a combination of two types of arguments: one moral, the other empirical. I argue that the moral argument fails to undermine the legitimacy of constitutional review. In fact, I claim that the legitimacy of constitutional review cannot hinge on this type of argument alone. Rather, the justification for constitutional review must depend ultimately on empirical assumptions about the likelihood that courts will succeed in protecting rights. This brings us to the empirical argument, which I believe is fundamental to the sceptical tradition in British public law scholarship. In the penultimate section, I discuss the problems associated with providing a meaningful and sufficiently comprehensive assessment of the empirical record of judging under the Human Rights Act 1998 ('HRA'). I conclude with the suggestion that judicial decision-making has changed for the better in the last 20 years and examine the challenge this poses for democratic scepticism.

A number of preliminary clarifications should be made before embarking on these tasks. First, democratic scepticism is a label I have given to an admittedly diverse body of public law scholarship in the UK. Whilst its proponents are generally Left-leaning scholars who adopt a critical stance towards judicial power,[11] they are not all

[9] The debate between democratic sceptics and supporters of constitutional review under the HRA has been the subject-matter of many recent CLP lectures, see C O'Cinneide, 'Democracy, Rights and the Constitution – New Directions in the Human Rights Era' (2004) 57 CLP 175; G Phillipson, 'Deference, Discretion, and Democracy in the Human Rights Act Era' (2007) 60 CLP 40; S Fredman, 'Judging Democracy: The Role of the Judiciary under the HRA 1998' (2000) 53 CLP 99.

[10] This task is undertaken in A Kavanagh, *Constitutional Review under the UK Human Rights Act* (Cambridge University Press: Cambridge, 2009) ch 13.

[11] For an historical survey of the 'radical, dissenting tradition' at the LSE (from which democratic scepticism partly stems), see R Rawlings, 'Distinction and Diversity: Law and the LSE', in R Rawlings (ed) *Law, Society and Economy: Centenary Essays for the London School of Economics and Political Science 1895-1995* (Oxford: Clarendon Press, 1997) at 18ff. Hugh Collins argues that the sceptical strand within UK public law scholarship has intellectual affinities with the type of scepticism which underpins American legal realism, see H Collins, 'Law as Politics: Progressive American Perspectives', in J Penner, D Schiff & R Nobles (eds) *Jurisprudence and Legal Theory: Commentary and materials* (Butterworth, London, 2002) 285–286.

sceptical about the same things. Nor are they equally sceptical.[12] However, considerable agreement nonetheless collects around the positive and negative propositions noted above. For example, in an edited collection entitled *Sceptical Essays on the Human Rights Act* published in 2001, some 21 sceptical authors signed a mission statement voicing 'very considerable doubts about the wisdom of [the HRA] within the British democratic tradition'[13] and lamenting what they described as 'the extensive shift of political authority to the judiciary which is involved in the HRA'.[14] Thus, a positive belief in the value of democracy and a concomitant scepticism about judicial power is a strong theme running through the writings of most democratic sceptics.

Secondly, whilst many democratic sceptics share Bentham's reservations about the appropriateness of letting judges make decisions on matters of high constitutional principle, the contemporary torchbearers of this school of thought nonetheless tend to endorse unequivocally 'the importance of human rights within any democratic system of government'.[15] Naturally, rights and rights-talk are not without their academic detractors,[16] but this is now perceived to be something of an 'outlier'[17] position within the mainstream of democratic scepticism in UK public law theory. Contemporary democratic sceptics are not opposed to rights, but only to making judges their guardians. Thus, whilst they share with supporters of constitutional review the view that rights are valuable, the main bone of contention concerns the institutional question of *how* we should go about protecting rights and, crucially, *who* should be given power to enforce them.

Thirdly, democratic sceptics are not just sceptical in the etymological sense of being an inquirer, a seeker after truth. All scholars should

[12] A Tomkins, 'Introduction: On Being Sceptical About Human Rights' in *Sceptical Essays on Human Rights*, n 5 above, 8. [13] Ibid, 2.

[14] Ibid, 2.

[15] Tomkins, ibid, 2; J Waldron, 'A Right-Based Critique of Constitutional Rights' (1993) 13 OJLS 18; K Ewing, 'Human Rights, Social Democracy and Constitutional Reform' in C Gearty & A Tomkins (eds) *Understanding Human Rights* (Mansell: London, 1996) 45; see also Ewing and Gearty 'Rocky Foundations for Labour's New Rights' (1997) European Human Rights Law Review 146, 150 who claim that it is 'self-evidently true' that those who believe in the virtues of democracy will also believe in the values of civil liberties and human rights.

[16] eg, see C Douzinas, *The End of Human Rights: Critical Legal Thought at the Turn of the Century* (Hart Publishing: Oxford, 2000).

[17] J Waldron, 'The Core of the Case Against Judicial Review' (2006) 115 Yale Law Journal 1346, 1365

be sceptics in this sense. Rather, democratic sceptics tend to approach the object of their scepticism (in this case, the courts) in a spirit of 'caution, concern, and doubt'.[18] Thus, in the Introduction to *Sceptical Essays on the Human Rights Act*, Adam Tomkins describes democratic sceptics as being 'dubious, mistrustful, and questioning as to the likely effects of the HRA'.[19] As will become clearer later in the chapter, this attitude of distrust is crucial to the democratic sceptics' critique.

Finally, one of the primary targets of the contemporary sceptical critique of judges in the UK is the Human Rights Act 1998 and the judicial record in upholding it. I will refer to the judicial powers under the HRA to review primary legislation for compliance with Convention rights as 'constitutional review'.[20] This distinguishes it from traditional 'judicial review' in administrative law and brings into focus the fact that, under the HRA, the courts are, for the first time, empowered to review primary legislation for compliance with a codified set of fundamental rights. It also emphasizes the constitutional character of the courts' supervisory powers over primary legislation under the 1998 Act.[21]

The Form of the Argument Against Constitutional Review

Democratic sceptics tend to rely on two main types of argument against constitutional review. The first is the *moral argument* that constitutional review is democratically illegitimate, because it allows unelected judges

[18] A Tomkins, 'Introduction: On Being Sceptical About Human Rights' in *Sceptical Essays on Human Rights*, n 5 above, 3. [19] Ibid, 3.

[20] For use of this term with reference to adjudication under the HRA, see J Jowell, 'Beyond the Rule of Law: Towards Constitutional Judicial Review' (2000) PL 669; D Oliver, *Constitutional Reform in the UK* (Oxford University Press: Oxford, 2003). It should be noted that the idea of 'constitutional review' at work here does not necessarily include a judicial power to invalidate primary legislation if it is found to violate constitutional rights. Such a definition was proposed by Paul Craig, see P Craig, 'Constitutional and Non-Constitutional Review' (2001) 54 CLP 147, 147–8. However, Craig acknowledges that the line between 'constitutional review *stricto sensu*' (which he defines as review leading to invalidation of the offending legislative provision) and what he terms 'non-constitutional review' is often blurred in UK public law since 'courts may constrain the exercise of the primary legislative power very significantly in ways which stop short of formal invalidation'. Craig instances review of primary legislation under the HRA as an example of such a borderline case.

[21] For a more detailed elaboration of the constitutional nature of the judicial powers under the Human Rights Act vis-a-vis primary legislation, see Kavanagh, *Constitutional Review under the UK Human Rights Act*, n 10 above, 277–81. Rodney Austin has argued that in the last two decades, a new constitutional dimension to judicial review has developed, see Austin, 'The New Constitutionalism, Terrorism and Torture' (2007) 60 CLP 79.

to constrain and sometimes override decisions made by our elected representatives. Jeremy Waldron encapsulates the nerve of this argument in the following vivid terms:

> By privileging majority voting among a small number of unelected and unaccountable judges, [constitutional review] disenfranchises ordinary citizens and brushes aside cherished principles of representation and political equality in the final resolution of issues about rights.[22]

The second is the *empirical argument* that judges do not do a very good job of protecting rights. Put simply, if our destination is the optimal protection of rights constitutional review is not the best way to get there. Responding to what they perceive as the dismal judicial record in protecting rights, many democratic sceptics argue that we are more likely to get good outcomes for rights, if we leave legislatures free to enact legislation as they wish, unfettered by meddling judges.

The empirical argument has been the animating force behind democratic scepticism in the UK throughout the 20th century. The classic example of this type of scholarship is John Griffiths' *The Politics of the Judiciary*.[23] First published in the 1970's at a time when industrial relations dominated the political agenda, Griffith highlighted and excoriated the notoriously illiberal decisions handed down by the courts in this period. Those decisions did little to inspire confidence that we should entrust the judiciary with the task of protecting civil liberties.[24] For many democrats sceptical of the role of the courts, the empirical evidence from this period made a deep and lasting impression. As Keith Ewing observed, scepticism about giving the courts the power to enforce rights 'was based on a distrust of the judges. This distrust was built upon empirical evidence and came out of the experience of frustration about judicial intervention in the social sphere over many years.'[25]

[22] Waldron, n 17 above, 1353.

[23] See also K Ewing and C Gearty, *The Struggle for Civil Liberties: Political Freedom and the Rule of Law in Britain 1914–1945* (Oxford University Press: Oxford, 2000) which argues that parliament did a consistently better job of protecting civil liberties over this period than judges and, moreover, that judges were often bent on denying the protection of civil liberties to individuals who belonged to groups which the judges considered politically dangerous. Gearty and Ewing's conclusion was that we should restore parliament to a central place in public life, rather than place our trust in judges.

[24] See J Griffith, 'Judges and the Constitution' in R Rawlings (ed) *Law, Society and Economy: Centenary Essays for the London School of Economics and Political Science 1895-1995* (Clarendon Press: Oxford, 1997) 294–5.

[25] K Ewing, 'The Futility of the Human Rights Act – A Long Footnote' (2005) 37 Bracton Law Journal 41.

Many democratic sceptics avail of both the moral and empirical arguments, running them together as a two-pronged attack against constitutional review. Thus, they castigate constitutional review as an inherently undemocratic and illegitimate practice, but also argue that even if we overcame our moral and democratic qualms, the empirical evidence shows that judges will not deliver enhanced rights-protection in any case. There may be nothing wrong with appropriating both types of argument to secure the conclusion that we should reject constitutional review. However, it raises interesting questions about whether the moral argument can, on its own, be a knock-down argument against constitutional review or, alternatively, whether the merits or demerits of constitutional review rest ultimately on empirical claims. This is an immensely important question, because if the moral argument holds sway, then this will impugn constitutional review for all time and for all jurisdictions 'quite apart from the outcomes it generates'.[26] However, if the justification for constitutional review hinges (even in part) on empirical claims, then it will be contingent on the judicial record at a particular time and place. Thus, if the facts change, then this may warrant a shift in position about the practice of constitutional review itself.[27]

It should be noted at the outset that the moral argument against constitutional review is often couched in timeless language. It is presented as if it were a knock-down argument, which is not temporally or politically contingent on the judicial record.[28] The alleged democratic illegitimacy of constitutional review is said to contaminate it for all time. The best and most sophisticated example of this type of argument is provided by Jeremy Waldron. In seeking to present an argument 'uncluttered by discussion of individual judicial decisions'[29], Waldron opposes constitutional review on the basis that it denies (or at least curtails) citizens' 'right to democratic participation', namely, the right to 'participate on equal terms in social decisions on issues of high principle and not just interstitial matters of social and economic

[26] Waldron, n 17 above, 1346. [27] See also Ewing, n 25 above, 41.

[28] Note that this is also true of many arguments made in favour of constitutional review, ie that its virtues are often presented as necessary and not temporally or politically contingent facts about judges and court-structures, see further F Schauer, 'Neutrality and Judicial Review', (2003) 22 Law and Philosophy 217, 237ff.

[29] Waldron talks about making a general case against constitutional review in a way that is '*uncluttered* by discussions of particular [judicial] decisions', n 17 above, 1346 (emphasis added).

policy.'[30] For Waldron, this is nothing less than the 'right of rights', so-called because its exercise 'seems peculiarly appropriate in situations where reasonable right-bearers disagree about what rights they have'.[31] Echoing Bentham, Waldron argues that by taking decisions about rights away from participatory-majoritarian institutions and placing them in the hands of the courts, constitutional review involves an unjustifiable 'disempowerment of ordinary citizens on matters of the highest moral and political importance'.[32]

Waldron explicitly eschews what he calls a 'rights-instrumentalist' approach to the justification of constitutional review.[33] For him, the right to participate is not one value to be included in a balance with others. Rather, participation is *fundamental*: a participatory-majoritarian resolution of political disputes should be adopted, even if this would lead to worse outcomes than any other decision-making mechanism.[34] Thus, the likelihood that constitutional review might offer better protection to human rights than participatory majoritarianism, is insufficient justification to restrict or limit the right to participation. The reason Waldron gives for this is as follows:

> If a process is democratic and comes up with the correct result, it does no injustice to anyone. But if the process is non-democratic, it inherently and necessarily does an injustice, in its operation, to the participatory aspirations of the ordinary citizen. And it does this injustice, tyrannises in this way, whether it comes up with the correct result or not.[35]

Waldron thus assigns a special status to the right of participation that makes it inappropriate to limit it for the sake of protecting other rights or furthering other principles of political morality. As Larry Alexander observed, Waldron's right to participation is 'a moral right the violation of which cannot be traded off against minimizing violations of other rights'.[36]

In making this argument, Waldron seems to commit himself to the view that the hypothetical good consequences of constitutional review will have no normative relevance to the justification of constitutional review. This is rooted in his more general aversion to instrumental

[30] Waldron, *Law and Disagreement* (Oxford University Press: Oxford, 1999) 213.
[31] Ibid, 232. [32] Waldron, n 15 above, 45.
[33] Ibid 36; see Waldron, n 10 above, 242.
[34] See further A Kavanagh, 'Participation and Judicial Review: A Reply to Jeremy Waldron' (2003) 22 Law and Philosophy 451, 456ff.
[35] Waldron, n 15 above, 50, 38.
[36] L Alexander, 'Is Judicial Review Democratic? A Comment on Harel' (2003) 22 Law and Philosophy 277, 279.

theories of political authority, ie theories based on the instrumental value of certain institutional structures to the furtherance of certain goals or ideals such as the protection of human rights. Waldron opposes the very idea that one can justify a form of political authority on the basis of the results they may deliver for the simple reason that the goals of political morality are subject to widespread disagreement:

> Rights-instrumentalism seems to face the difficulty that it presupposes our possession of the truth about rights in designing an authoritative procedure whose point it is to settle that very issue.[37]

Since we are never going to be able to agree on what these rights are, the reasons supporting a majoritarian decision procedure operate as exclusionary reasons;[38] they are not to be balanced against the controversial reasons in the first-order debate, because they are on a different normative level.[39] Rather, they exclude the first-order reasons altogether.

When the argument against constitutional review takes this exclusionary form, it encounters a number of problems. Before outlining what those problems are, I should concede that the moral argument based on the right of all citizens to participate equally in the decision-making of their polity, carries enormous rhetorical force. By trading on a cluster of seemingly incontrovertible ideas (such as, for example, egalitarianism, individual empowerment and inclusion) it loads the discursive dice in favour of democratic scepticism. The language of egalitarian respect for ordinary people gives a sort of moral immunity to the right to participate which exposes supporters of constitutional review to the charge of being elitist and anti-democratic. At first glance, the rhetorical potency gives credence to the idea that the right to participate should override or even exclude consideration of other values. But when we strip this argument of its undeniable rhetorical force, it becomes less compelling than may at first appear. Despite its intuitive appeal, the right to participate does not warrant the fundamental or exclusionary status accorded to it by Jeremy Waldron.

Let me begin by noting some common ground. I fully accept that popular participation in public decision-making is of undoubted

[37] Waldron, n 30 above, 253, 243.

[38] On exclusionary reasons, see J Raz, *The Authority of Law* (Clarendon Press: Oxford, 1979) Part I.

[39] Waldron, n 30 above, 248: 'the problem is not about weighting and balancing; the problem is that we disagree in these cases about what exactly rights require', 248; see further D Enoch, 'Taking Disagreement Seriously: On Jeremy Waldron's *Law and Disagreement* ', (39) Israel Law Review 25.

importance and is intrinsically valuable precisely for the reasons offered by democratic sceptics, namely, that it gives people the opportunity of contributing to the public life of their country and exerting popular control and influence over their representatives.[40] This is what Ronald Dworkin has described as the dignity value of participation, namely, the dignity of being included and having an influence in political decisions.[41] Thus, the intrinsic desirability of democracy as offering a means of participating in the public life of one's community, is not in doubt here.

But even if we acknowledge the intrinsic value of democratic participation, it does not necessarily follow that we must value it to the exclusion of all else or that it is never justifiable to limit it to some degree. Whilst we certainly care about political participation and the right to vote, this is by no means all we care about. It seems to me that what matters most are the substantive outcomes of the democratic process, rather than the procedure alone. Those outcomes include whether people have a job; whether they are subject to a fair tax regime; whether they have access to good local schools and medical facilities; whether crime is being tackled, etc. When we descend from the lofty resonance of the so-called equal democratic right to participate, we can see that other values gain pride of place. Put simply, democratic decision-making procedures, whilst certainly important, are not the be all and end all of political morality. And if that is correct, it is by no means a foregone conclusion that we are not prepared to countenance some limitation on the right to participate, if to do so would enhance the protection of other values.

In more realistic moments, democratic sceptics acknowledge that political participation is not all we care about, still less our most important or cherished value. Adam Tomkins has given the following blunt assessment of the role of the right to participate in our lives:

> Most of us, of course, could not be bothered [with participation in political affairs]. We really could not care less. Even the meagre act of voting is just too much effort for many these days.[42]

[40] See further Kavanagh, n 34 above, 458ff.

[41] R Dworkin, 'What is Equality? Part 4: Political Equality' (1987) 22 University of San Francisco Law Review 4-5, 19-23; A Phillips, *The Politics of Presence* (Clarendon Press: Oxford, 1995); J Hyland, *Democratic Theory: The Philosophical Foundations* (Manchester University Press: Manchester, 1995), 189.

[42] Tomkins, 'In Defence of the Political Constitution' (2002) 22 OJLS 157, 175. Tomkins made this statement prior to the US election in November 2008 where Barack Obama was elected President. For that election, there was a high voter turnout and a palpable sense that voting mattered a great deal to millions of Americans—so much so, that many were prepared to forego their salary for that day in order to vote. Apart from

Of course, contemporary disillusionment with voting in the UK does not undermine the normative argument that we *ought* to cherish political participation, but it casts considerable doubt on the empirical claim that we do in fact cherish it in anything like the way suggested by the writings of democratic sceptics. But my aim here is not to deny or minimize the importance of political participation. It is to make the more modest claim that participation is not the only important value in political decision-making and, indeed, that the participatory dimension of democratic decision-making does not *exclude* consideration of those other values. On the contrary, the goal of securing popular participation must be *balanced* against other valuable goals. In some cases, we will be prepared to accept a partial compromise in other values if necessary to secure the goal of participation. In others, we will be willing to accept a partial compromise in participation in order to achieve other valuable goals, such as, for example, the promotion of human rights.[43] This is a common way of justifying constitutional review. Such a justification proceeds not by denying the importance of participation, but by showing that the normative weight of the right to participate does not always override other considerations.[44] Thus, if we believe in the value of protecting human rights, then there may be situations where we are willing to accept some shortfall in the right to participate in order to further this goal.

Four points need to be emphasized here. The first is that we are only justified in using democratic decision-making procedures to give people the opportunity of participating in the public life of their country, if it leads, by and large, to good outcomes. This is what Joseph Raz has referred to as 'the instrumentalist condition of good government', where good government includes the realization of other valuable goals such as, for example, the protection of human rights.[45] A community's political institutions should be designed so that they are

the fact that the 2008 election was remarkable precisely because it was exceptional in contemporary times, I will just make two brief points. The first is to emphasize that I am not denying the significance and importance of the right to vote. The second is that the reason why Americans came out in such large numbers to vote in that election was their belief that Barack Obama would make a difference and change life in the US for the better. In other words, they exercised their right to vote primarily for instrumental reasons of hoping to achieve good government, see further Kavanagh, n 34 above, 463–4.

[43] For a similar argument against a 'pre-emptive role for democratic decision making' and in favour of the idea that 'democratic reasons are to be weighed in the balance against other reasons', see T Christiano, 'Waldron on Law and Disagreement' (2000) 19 Law & Philosophy 524, 538.

[44] eg, see Kavanagh, n 34 above.

[45] Raz, *Ethics in the Public Domain* (Oxford University Press: Oxford, 2004) 117.

likely to make good political decisions. The design that is most likely to yield good decisions is most justified. Secondly, the intrinsic value of participation does not undercut the central role of the instrumentalist condition of good government. The issue is whether one can limit the right to participate to some degree in order to secure other valuable goals. Thirdly, by supporting the idea that the justification of political authority must rest ultimately on its instrumental value to 'good government', I do not want to give the impression that effective rights-protection is the touchstone for legitimate political authority across the board. Rights are only one small part of the concerns and values to which governments must respond. However, since rights-protection is one of the main tasks given to judges under constitutional review, their success in realizing this goal is central to the justification of constitutional review. Finally, my support for the centrality of the 'instrumentalist condition of good government' does not entail a straightforward prioritization of rights over democracy. Nor do I wish to deny that effective rights-protection can support and strengthen democratic institutions. All I wish to show here is that although the right to participate is important (*both* intrinsically *and* instrumentally), it is not the 'right of rights'. Both rights and democratic procedures are important in various ways. Indeed, the intrinsic importance of participation means that no system of political authority is justified unless it secures the goal of participation to some meaningful degree.

The centrality of the instrumentalist condition for the justification of political authority is widely supported by many legal and political theorists, despite their disagreement on other issues.[46] Thus, John Rawls noted: 'the fundamental criterion for judging any procedure is the justice of its likely results . . . the test of constitutional arrangements is always the overall balance of justice'.[47] This view also accords with the common belief that it is the duty of democratic governments to rule in the interests of the governed or for the common good. After all, democracy is not just decision making 'by the people', but also 'for the people', ie in their best interests. Government decisions on behalf of the governed are frequently assessed on the basis of whether they made the right/just/fair decision. In fact, democratic political decisions tend to

[46] R Dworkin, *Law's Empire* (Harvard University Press: Cambridge, Mass, 1986) 376; L Alexander, n 36 above, 283; J Rawls, *A Theory of Justice* (Harvard University Press: Cambridge, Mass, 1971) 230–1; Raz, *The Morality of Freedom* (Oxford University Press, 1996) ch 4; T Christiano n 43 above, 542.

[47] Rawls, ibid, 230–1.

be justified not merely on the basis that they were made by elected officials, but also that they tend to be the right decisions.

There is another point worth bearing in mind here. This relates to the statement that constitutional review entails a *partial* limit on the democratic right to participate. Democratic sceptics sometimes suggest that the justification of constitutional review hinges on an all-or-nothing view of the importance of democracy. *Either* one is a supporter of democratic government *or* one favours a 'juristocracy'[48] or 'judicial aristocracy'[49] in its place. But this is a false contrast. It gives the misleading impression that constitutional review is a complete system of political authority in the same way as, say, democracy, aristocracy or monarchy. However, constitutional review relates to a much more limited range of decisions (and indeed a more limited type of decision-making) than the term 'juristocracy' suggests.

For one thing, in political systems which possess judicial powers of constitutional review, most political decisions, (including important policy-making issues), are left to the democratic process, accountable to the citizen-body. Nor is it even the case that all matters related to constitutional rights are allocated to the courts under constitutional review. Much of the detailed regulation of rights is carried out by the legislature in the course of their policy-making decisions, not all of which will be in response to judicial decisions.[50] Moreover, as is well known, judges do not get to choose which areas of the law to adjudicate since they are largely responsive to the vagaries of litigation. Only a very small proportion of the statute book ever comes before the courts through litigation. Constitutional review does not give the courts the power to make primary political decisions, but merely the power to *review* the exercise of primary decision-making authority possessed by the legislature and executive for compliance with a set of legal norms. The task of review is therefore secondary to the primary law-making powers of parliament and is only activated in relatively rare circumstances. This highlights the fact that unlike, say, democracy, monarchy or aristocracy, constitutional review is not a complete theory of political authority. It is a decision-making procedure designed to deal with a limited range of issues, and in a limited way. As such, it should not be posed as an alternative to

[48] Ewing, 'The Futility of the Human Rights Act' (2004) PL 829, 831; Tomkins, *Our Republican Constitution* (Hart Publishing: Oxford, 2005) 7.

[49] Waldron, n 30 above, 248.

[50] Kavanagh, n 10 above.

democratic government, but rather (if at all) as one element within that government.

It is worth noting that although almost all western democracies endow the courts with special responsibilities for the protection of fundamental rights, no-one seriously suggests that these countries therefore fail to be democracies. In fact, in general, all democratic regimes contain some political decision-making processes which are not directly accountable to the electorate. In the UK, the immensely powerful civil service, who are unelected and largely unaccountable to 'the people', is just one local example of this more general phenomenon.[51]

It follows that the question raised by constitutional review is not an all or nothing matter of whether we favour democratic rule or not. It is a question of the extent and scope of majoritarian decision-making, ie whether democratic decision-making should be extended to *all* decisions made in the community, or whether there is a case for restricting its scope in matters related to constitutional rights.[52] It is fully accepted here that for democratic government to exist, there must at least be an electoral mechanism in place which allows citizens to influence the choice of legislation by participating periodically in the choice of legislators. No system which debars citizens from playing a part in the decision-making process can be deemed legitimate from a democratic point of view, and no conception of democracy that excludes such a role is tenable. But the exact *kind* or *degree* of participation that is desirable, is subject to debate. It is not axiomatic given the value of participation.[53] Since there are a variety of institutional arrangements which could satisfy the participatory requirement of democracy to a

[51] Indeed, it is sometimes argued that the major role played by non-elected civil servants in governmental decision-making constitutes a 'dilution of democracy', see Darrow & Alston, 'Bills of Rights in Comparative Perspective', in P Alston (ed) *Promoting Human Rights through Bills of Rights: Comparative Perspectives* (Oxford University Press: Oxford, 1999) 465, 502.

[52] For this way of framing the debate between those who advocate and oppose judicial review in a democracy, see Robert A Dahl, *Democracy and Its Critics* (Yale University Press: New Haven, 1989) p 163; see also Albert Weale, 'The Limits of Democracy' in A Hamlin and P Pettit (eds) *The Good Polity: Normative Analysis of the State* (Basil Blackwell: Oxford, 1989) 2.

[53] Thus, Tim Scanlon claims that political philosophy can tell us little about what kinds of participatory and/or representative institutions will satisfy the requirement of effective and equal participation, see TM Scanlon, 'Due Process' in R Pennock and J Chapman (eds) *Nomos XVIII: Due Process* (New York University Press: New York, 1977) 98; see also C Beitz, 'Procedural Equality in Democratic Theory: A Preliminary Examination' in *Nomos XXV: Liberal Democracy* (New York University Press: New York, 1977) 69–70.

greater or lesser degree, the chosen one must bear a burden of justification.[54] This burden reflects the fact that we care about participation. But, as one commentator has observed:

> once we assign representative institutions a share of government power above a rough threshold, there is nothing wrong with distributing the rest of government power, including supervisory functions, to nonelected organs to a reasonable scheme of division of labour. In fact, we do this all the time.[55]

There is one further point about the way in which democratic sceptics articulate the moral argument, which warrants mention here. This is that they tend to present constitutional review as an elitist form of decision-making made by unelected and unaccountable judges, and contrast this with an egalitarian and inclusive form of decision-making made by 'ordinary men and women'.[56] Of course, no one would deny that one of the values of democratic decision-making is that people are given some say in political affairs. Moreover, since judicial decision-making is not directly responsive to the electorate, constitutional review can be described as elitist in the sense that it is removed from direct popular input and control. However, this point needs careful handling in order to avoid succumbing to an unrealistic picture of what is involved in democratic decision-making.

The first point to note is that by using language which refers to decisions made 'by all citizens' or 'by ordinary men and women', democratic sceptics give the misleading impression that democracy is somehow direct, with citizens voting directly on substantive issues. However, in modern democracies like the UK, it is almost invariably the case that political decisions are made by public representatives, rather than directly by ordinary men and women. So the question about constitutional review is not whether 'the people themselves'[57] should make decisions about rights or hand them over to elitist judges, it is about who should make decisions about rights on behalf of the people—elected representatives alone or elected representatives combined with constitutional review by judges.

The second point concerns the nature of democratic participation and the vaunted egalitarianism on which it supposedly rests. Some democratic sceptics present the right to participate as 'the democratic

[54] Kavanagh, n 34 above, 459; Beitz, ibid, 79.
[55] D Kyritsis, 'Representation and Waldron's Objection to Judicial Review' (2006) 26 OJLS 733.
[56] Waldron, n 15 above, 49.
[57] Waldron, n 17 above, 1349.

right of the citizens of the UK to determine the basic principles on which their society is to be governed and to have an equal say in how these principles are to be embodied in binding rules'.[58] Many readers will find this statement deeply unrealistic, either as a general characterization of the way democratic majoritarian politics works or, more particularly, as an accurate characterization of the nature of democratic participation in the UK. When we exercise our right to vote at a general election, we are not given the opportunity to determine directly the basic principles on which we are governed. All we have is the opportunity to choose one elected representative in our own constituency, from an extremely limited range of political parties once every four or five years. Moreover, 'a vote at a general election is scarcely an opportunity to participate in decisions *about human rights*'.[59] As Sandra Fredman has pointed out:

> under the current system, the right of citizens to participate in decisions about rights is so attenuated as to be almost fictional, largely because of the weakness of Parliament relative to an all-powerful executive.[60]

The effective dominance of parliament by the executive, combined with the first-past-the-post electoral system and strong party discipline, means that, in effect, policy decisions (including the fundamental rules by which we are all governed) are made by a small group of politicians, backed up by an influential and anonymous civil service. The element of elitism inherent in democratic decision-making is often unacknowledged by democratic sceptics and is obscured by the mesmerizing rhetoric of the equal right to participate.[61] Similarly, the extent to which constitutional review can empower the marginalized in our society to get their voice heard in a public forum and exert a meaningful influence over political decisions, is often underplayed. This is highlighted by the fact that some of the most prominent litigants under the HRA (eg destitute asylum seekers, non-British terrorist suspects

[58] T Campbell, 'Incorporation through Interpretation' in *Sceptical Essays on Human Rights*, n 5 above, 99.

[59] Fredman, n 8 above, 199.

[60] Fredman, ibid, 208.

[61] Kyritsis argues that legislative decision-making involves an aristocratic element analogous to that which exists in judicial decision-making: see n 55 above, 750. Perhaps one of the reasons why the elitism inherent in democratic decision-making is so firmly resisted and overlooked is that anti-elitism is a cornerstone of the contemporary public and political culture. As Carol Harlow points out, 'the climate of public opinion is relentlessly anti-elitist', see 'Public Law and Popular Justice' (2002) 65 MLR 1, 16. Needless to say, if elitism is a feature of our public and political culture, we would do better to openly acknowledge it.

imprisoned without trial, prisoners, mental patients, immigrants, etc), come from the worst-off and most unpopular groups in society. It is difficult to see how they would have succeeded in vindicating their rights through the normal channels of parliamentary politics. Many of these litigants (namely, prisoners, mental patients and immigrants) do not possess the right to vote in any case, so are also excluded formally from the primary method of democratic participation.[62] For many ordinary men and women, participation through litigation offers a much better chance of getting grievances addressed, than pursuing a case through the normal channels of democratic politics.

Let us summarize the points made thus far:

(1) The right to participate does not have the fundamental status attributed to it by democratic sceptics such as Jeremy Waldron. It does not *exclude* consideration of other values. Nor does it necessarily *override* them. Democratic decision-making procedures, though certainly important, are not all we care about in politics.

(2) Participation in political affairs is intrinsically valuable. Therefore, a political system which denied it altogether would be illegitimate. But partial curtailment of the right to participate may be justified, if it would lead to better government overall. One can balance the loss in participation against other values. That constitutional review is carried out by unelected public officials is not a knock-down argument against it.

(3) The intrinsic importance of participation does not undermine the centrality of the instrumentalist condition of good government. The participatory aspect of democratic decision-making may well 'transcend'[63] issues of outcome but it does not supplant them. This means that when assessing the justification for constitutional review the empirical judicial record in upholding rights matters a great deal. The factors which influence that empirical assessment, including the problems which afflict it, will be considered in the next section.

[62] See the Representation of the People Act 1983, ss 1(1) (children under 18), 3(1) (prisoners), and 7(1) (mental patients). For the argument that litigation based on a Bill of Rights has been successfully and widely used by hitherto marginalized persons or groups to counter injustice see, eg, O'Cinneide, n 9 above, 188; B McLachlin, 'The Canadian Charter and the Democratic Process' in Gearty and Tomkins (eds), *Understanding Human Rights* (Mansell: London, 1996) 28; see further Kavanagh, n 10 above, 339–44.

[63] Waldron, n 15 above, 38.

There is one final point to be made about the instrumentalist justification for constitutional review. I presented Jeremy Waldron as the strongest advocate of the procedural justification of constitutional review and the strongest opponent of the instrumentalist justification. However, despite Waldron's fervent opposition to instrumentalist justifications of political authority, he also avails of an instrumentalist justification to support the primacy of the right to participate. Thus, even in his early writings, he claimed that by participating in majoritarian politics, citizens have a better chance of protecting their rights than if this protection is left to others:

> We value participation not just as an end in itself, but also because we think that this is one way to ensure that each person gets what is hers by right.[64] . . . Participation is also valued as a mode of self-protection: each individual acts, to some extent, as a voice for those of her own interests that ought to be taken seriously in politics.[65]

Elsewhere, I have tried to show that the justification for participatory democracy based on its instrumental value for individual self-determination is misguided.[66] The merits of this argument are not my concern in this chapter. What matters here is its form or structure. The very fact that Waldron falls back on an instrumentalist argument for the right to participate, may serve to bolster the claim that it is implausible to justify political authority in a way which is completely detached from the outcomes it produces. At the very least, it suggests that there is an ambivalence in Waldron's writings about the claim that the right to participate should have primacy, irrespective of the outcomes that it delivers.

This ambivalence is even more evident in his most recent contribution to the debate about constitutional review[67] where he argues

[64] Waldron, n 15 above, 37. [65] Ibid, 37.

[66] Kavanagh, n 34 above, 479–82.

[67] Waldron, n 17 above. Another ambivalence which comes to light in Waldron's recent writings concerns the issue of the legitimacy of constitutional review when judicial decisions can be overturned by democratically-elected decision makers, see n 17 above, 1346ff. When Parliament has the power to override a judicial determination about the constitutionality of legislation, then it seems as if Waldron's objections lose some of their force. Jeffrey Goldsworthy argues that it is not at all clear that democratic sceptics should oppose the constitutionalization of human rights in situations where parliament has the final authority to override the judges, see Goldsworthy, 'Judicial Review, Legislative Override and Democracy' in T Campbell, J Goldsworthy and A Stone (eds) *Protecting Human Rights: Instruments and Institutions* (Oxford University Press: Oxford, 2003).

that the justification of constitutional review is conditional on certain empirical assumptions of modern liberal democracies being in place, for example, that the society in question has good working democratic institutions and that most of its citizens take rights seriously. If these assumptions do not apply, then some powers of constitutional review may be justified, if the judiciary could offer 'hope of ameliorating a particular situation'.[68] For example, if it could be shown that, in a particular society, prejudice against minorities might hamper the operation of ordinary political processes to protect minority rights, then those minorities 'may need special care that only non-elective institutions can provide – special care to protect their rights and special care . . . to repair the political system and facilitate their representation'.[69] In making this argument, Waldron seems to have softened his position on constitutional review by acknowledging that when the political decision-making processes fail to protect rights for whatever reason, some type of constitutional review may be justified.[70] This is a common way of justifying constitutional review. We must now turn to consider the empirical evaluations on which such justification is based.

The Empirical Argument

Thus far, we have established that whilst the democratic legitimacy of the decision-making procedure is important, what matters most is

[68] Waldron, n 17 above, 1402.

[69] Ibid, 1403, JH Ely, *Democracy and Distrust: A Theory of Judicial Review* (Harvard University Press: Cambridge, Mass, 1980) 135–79. It is also worth noting that in Waldron's recent writing on constitutional review, it seems that he only opposes what he calls 'strong form judicial review' (ie judicial review on the US model including a judicial strike-down power, with no legislative override provision such as obtains in Canada.) This means that he may not object to constitutional review under the UK HRA. For further discussion of Waldron's distinction between strong-form and weak-form review, see Kavanagh, n 10 above, 416–20.

[70] Thus, David Enoch queries whether Waldron 'no longer believes (if he ever did) that other values and reasons are excluded by whatever normative considerations support a majoritarian decision-making procedure. Is it now Waldron's official view that we are entitled to balance the loss in participation against other things that are of value even if they are controversially so?': n 39 above, 26. It is certainly the case that whilst in earlier writings Waldron tended to stress that the question of whether we support participatory majoritarianism, even if it leads to more rights-violations overall, was 'not about weighing and balancing' he now seems to accept the possibility that 'outcome-related' and 'process-related' reasons may be weighed against each other: see Waldron, n 17 above, 1375.

whether that procedure is conducive to good results. This means that the justification of constitutional review hinges, to a large extent, on its instrumental benefits and the extent to which it succeeds in enhancing the protection of human rights. If this is correct, then the justification of constitutional review is a contingent question, which may have different answers for different societies and, indeed, different answers for the same society over time. So, the question then becomes: have the courts enhanced the protection of fundamental rights post-HRA?

Unsurprisingly, public law scholars in the UK offer radically different answers to this question. For some, the judicial record in upholding rights since 1998 has been so dismal that we should reject the HRA as futile.[71] For others, the judiciary have done a reasonably good job in upholding rights under the Act.[72] This is not the place to get embroiled in a case-by-case evaluation of the first decade of constitutional review under the HRA. However, I nonetheless wish to highlight some of the general difficulties which beset the empirical analysis.

The first difficulty is noted by Colm O'Cinneide, namely, that there is a tendency to assess the instrumental benefits of constitutional review using highly selective case examples.[73] What ensues is a 'war of examples, where sceptics cite various allegedly retrogressive judicial decisions, while enthusiasts produce specimens of rights review striking down abusive denials of equality or liberty'.[74] Rather than presenting an overview of the case-law which takes the good with the bad, the debate about the merits of constitutional review seems to degenerate into a winner takes all form of combat with isolated emblematic cases used as lethal weapons.[75] Thus, in the American context, *Lochner*[76] and *Korematsu*[77] are pitted against *Brown v Board of Education*[78] and in the UK, *Liversidge v Anderson*[79] is pitted against the *Belmarsh Prison* case.[80]

Needless to say, when the 'debate' about constitutional review is conducted in these terms it tends not be productive. Since the opposing camps rely on different examples from the judicial record, they tend to talk past each other. Moreover, the highly-charged nature of the issues

[71] K Ewing, 'The Futility of the Human Rights Act' (2004) PL 829.

[72] B Dickson, 'Safe in Their Hands—The Law Lords and Human Rights' (2006) 26 LS 329–46; Kavanagh, n 10 above, ch 13.

[73] O'Cinneide, n 9 above, 180.

[74] O'Cinneide, n 9 above, 180.

[75] See also Phillipson, n 9 above, 57.

[76] *Lochner v New York* 198 US 45.

[77] *Korematsu v US* 323 US 214.

[78] *Brown v Board of Education of Topeka* 347 US 483.

[79] *Liversidge v Anderson* [1942] AC 206.

[80] *A v Secretary of State for the Home Department* [2005] 2 WLR 87.

decided in those cases only serves to further entrench and polarize positions. Thus, in the UK, rights enthusiasts may seize upon the *Belmarsh Prison* case as definitive proof that judges can step in to protect rights when the executive fails to do so. But by the same token, democratic sceptics who fear that *Belmarsh* might be used 'as a compelling case to disarm [them]'[81] rush to criticize it, stressing only its shortcomings. There is a danger of hyperbole on both sides. Moreover, when the battle of examples is fought to the death, a fundamental point is lost in the crossfire, namely, that one single case cannot win the war either way.[82]

This raises another fundamental question relating to the assessment of the empirical record, namely, the appropriate *standard* by which we should assess the judicial record in upholding rights. Elsewhere, I have argued that there is a tendency amongst some democratic sceptics to assess the judicial record with reference to an absolutist standard.[83] As HLA Hart pointed out, sceptics are sometimes 'disappointed absolutists'[84]—they expect everything and when it does not materialize, they are thrown into a state of 'abject disappointment and growing disillusionment'.[85] Thus, if the HRA cannot achieve the 'bald elimination'[86] of all human rights violations and provide an absolute barrier to the relentless 'war on terror' waged by an almighty executive, then it must be condemned as an utterly futile measure. In my view, the appropriate standard by which to assess the judicial record in protecting rights is one of success in some measure, not absolute success. The question is whether the courts do a sufficiently good job overall—sufficiently good, that is, to outweigh the costs.[87] Thus, when considering which political decision-procedure should be entrusted with the task of enforcing fundamental rights, the question is: in the circumstances of the time and place under consideration, which institution is most likely to enforce them well, with fewest adverse side effects?[88] Are the instrumental benefits sufficient to outweigh the costs?

This standard of assessment has a number of advantages. For one thing, it emphasizes that an evaluation of the empirical record is a

[81] Ewing, n 25 above, 41. [82] See also Gavin Phillipson, n 9 above, 4.

[83] Kavanagh, 'Judging the Judges under the Human Rights Act 1998: Deference, Disillusionment and the "War on Terror"' (2009) PL 287–304.

[84] HLA Hart, *The Concept of Law* (Clarendon Press: Oxford, 1961) at 135 (discussing 'rule-sceptics' in particular). [85] Ewing, n 71 above, 852.

[86] Gearty, n 8 above, at 21. [87] Enoch, n 39 above, 23.

[88] J Raz, 'Disagreement in Politics' (1998) 43 *American Journal of Jurisprudence* 25, 45.

matter of seeing the judicial record in the round, balancing the strengths and weaknesses of various judicial decisions, whilst bearing in mind the constraints under which judges labour when handing down those decisions. This means that an advocate of constitutional review need not resort to an unduly idealistic picture of either judges or judicial decision-making. They can openly acknowledge and accept that there may be some bad judicial decisions, or even that there are some bad periods in the history of the court decisions. Similarly, it is open to democratic sceptics to argue against the legitimacy of constitutional review, whilst nonetheless accepting that, at particular times and places, constitutional review has given us some good decisions.

In fact, this standard of reasonable rather than absolute success is appropriate for the assessment of all political institutions. It is only to be expected that all political institutions will have a fair share of both advantages and disadvantages. As Dimitrios Kyritsis has pointed out:

> We design institutions with a certain main preoccupations in mind and on the basis of predictions of how things are likely to evolve. But we cannot make them perfect. They serve as well just in case they respond adequately to the primary tasks we have assigned them.[89]

The standard of 'adequate' discharge of the tasks given to the courts curbs the temptation to rely on either a utopian or dystopian vision of judicial decision-making. Like all other political institutions, the courts are staffed by fallible human beings. There is no political institution and no political decision-making procedure which will deliver perfect decisions across the board.[90] We should not expect the judicial record to be completely without blemish. There are better and worse judges, there are good judges on a bad day and there are bad decisions for other reasons.

Thus far, I have suggested that an evaluation of the empirical record should ideally be based on a representative sample from the case-law, rather than relying on one or two high-profile decisions. Moreover, the task of evaluating the judicial record must be carried out with a certain amount of realism about what judges can and should achieve. But the centrality of outcomes to the justification of constitutional review means that support for, or indeed opposition to, judicial enforcement of fundamental rights will be 'a sometime thing',[91] with scholars

[89] Kyritsis, n 55 above, 747. [90] Rawls, n 46 above, 83.

[91] Charles Black, *A New Birth of Freedom: Human Rights, Named and Unnamed* (Yale University Press: New Haven, CN, 1997) 109 cited in Waldron, n 17 above, 1351.

supporting it when it delivers outcomes they favour and opposing it when it delivers outcomes they deplore.

An example of such a shift in position is provided by Professor Conor Gearty's defection from the ranks of democratic sceptics since the HRA. Whilst not reneging entirely on his democratic and sceptical roots, Gearty became a supporter of the HRA, in part because it seemed to give parliament/government the so-called 'last word' on human rights, thus giving the judiciary a reassuringly subordinate role.[92] But as time went on (and especially post-9/11), Gearty was swayed by what he saw as a change in the empirical evidence, namely, that under the HRA judges were doing a better job than they had before in upholding civil liberties.[93] From Gearty's point of view, this change was particularly acute in the area of national security where the courts were ameliorating the worst excesses of the draconian legislation enacted by the Labour government post-9/11 as part of the so-called 'war on terror'.[94] In light of this evidence, Gearty called on his former comrades to 'swallow whatever suspicions they might have had of the judges (right-wing, reactionary, illiberal) and recognize that . . . judges have found themselves in the front line in the defence of freedom'.[95] Scepticism about the judiciary was an intellectual luxury we could ill-afford in the post-9/11 climate, where the rush to enact repressive legislation was unabashed.[96]

If I am right about the temporal and political contingency of the justification for constitutional review, then it is perfectly rational for scholars such as Gearty to change their views about constitutional review, in light of changes in the empirical evidence.[97] In fact, if my

[92] Gearty, *Principles of Human Rights Adjudication* (Oxford University Press: Oxford, 2001). For a critique of the idea that the HRA gives parliament or government the so-called 'last word' on issues of rights, see Kavanagh, n 10 above, 322–4 and 408–11.

[93] For discussion of similar shifts by some American scholars when the outcomes delivered by the US Supreme Court changed from liberal to conservative or vice versa, see Schauer, n 28 above, 236ff.

[94] Gearty, '11 September 2001, Counter-Terrorism and the Human Rights Act' (2005) 32 Journal of Law and Society 18.

[95] Gearty, 'Rethinking Civil Liberties in a Counter-Terrorism World' (2007) EHRLR 115.

[96] Ibid.

[97] Thus, Schauer queries whether 'there is a whiff of opportunism or hypocrisy in the recent conversion of left-leaning American constitutionalists who had celebrated the virtues of judicial review when Earl Warren was Chief Justice but seem to have reversed course now that the Supreme Court is populated differently', n 28 above, 236. Schauer seems to support an instrumental justification of constitutional review and this would suggest that 'there is no inconsistency in urging a change in the shape and nature of judicial review as the time and people change', n 28 above, 238.

argument is correct, we might expect scholars to do so more routinely. But Gearty is the exception, not the rule. In general, scholars of whatever persuasion tend to stick to their positions irrespective of changes in the judicial and political record. There are a number of factors which account for the fact that scholarly u-turns are relatively infrequent, without undercutting my general point that the justification of constitutional review hinges crucially on its conduciveness to producing good outcomes for human rights.[98]

The first point limiting the nature and frequency of scholarly changes of mind is the fact that when evaluating political institutions, it is appropriate to take a medium or long-term view of their value and performance. Given the value of having a stable decision-making procedure which is operated over time and bearing in mind the institutional cost involved in reviewing and changing decision-making procedures, it is appropriate to be cautious when responding to flaws in the outcomes it delivers. Institutions created at one time cannot be changed quickly, or without cost, when the political winds change. There is also the danger of not being able to foresee the consequences of radical institutional change. When one adds to this the fact that one of the purposes of constitutional law is to provide a stable backbone on which the details of the legal system is based, this creates a bias in favour of caution and conservatism when approaching constitutional design and reform. Given the value of stability in constitutional structures, we should not rush to change them on the basis of a few bad decisions. Quite rightly, this leads public law scholars to be hesitant before changing their general views about a practice such as constitutional review, even if there is a period where judicial decision-making changes.

The second point limiting the extent to which we are likely to change our general views about constitutional review concerns the *evaluative* nature of the assessment of the judicial record. Let us return

[98] Apart from the three factors enumerated above, one more mundane reason why scholars may be reluctant to change their views on issues such as constitutional review, may simply be that it may seem like an admission that one got it wrong. As mentioned above, the justification (or indeed critique) of constitutional review is often couched in timeless (rather than temporally or politically contingent) language. As Frederick Schauer has observed, if constitutional review is applauded (or indeed castigated) in these terms, then one may be accused of inconsistency or disingenuousness if one changes one's mind, n 28 above, 237. However, if the argument of my chapter is correct, there is no necessary inconsistency in supporting constitutional review when it delivers good outcomes and criticizing it when it does not.

to the point made by Keith Ewing that opposition to constitutional review in the UK was based on a visceral distrust of judges which was 'built upon empirical evidence and came out of the experience of frustration about judicial intervention in the social sphere over many years.'[99] The problem is that once this attitude of distrust takes hold and becomes deeply rooted, it may be difficult to overcome, even when the empirical evidence changes for the better. Similarly, if one has a sanguine or trustful attitude towards the judiciary in general, then one may be forgiving of mistakes even if the empirical evidence changes for the worse. Building up trust (either in individuals or institutions) takes time, and once it exists, it enables us to give the benefit of the doubt, to view mistakes as aberrations rather than pervasive flaws, and to believe that even if some mistakes are made, the longer-term picture will be better. Similarly, if one has had reason to be distrustful, then in all likelihood, isolated mistakes will be viewed in a much more damning light. The issue of trust and distrust of the judiciary is foundational in the debate about constitutional review. Although trust or distrust may be 'built upon' the empirical evidence, these attitudes also influence and feed into the way in which that empirical evidence is evaluated.

The final factor limiting the extent to which it might be appropriate for us to change our views about constitutional review concerns the way in which general institutional features can influence decision-making and give us confidence that decisions will be made in a certain way. Thus, one common way of justifying constitutional review is to argue that since judges are relatively immune from electoral pressures, they are more likely than elected politicians to make decisions which protect human rights, even when those decisions are unpopular with the electorate.[100] Or take, for example, the argument that judicial review provides a much more effective constraint on government than, say, review of executive decisions by a committee of lower civil servants.[101] It is not my concern here to establish the merits or demerits of either of these arguments. My purpose is simply to highlight an important point about their nature, namely, that they do not rest on any detailed knowledge about how specific judges decide cases or indeed how specific legislators or civil servants carry out their functions. Nor, might I add, do they rest on any preconception about the inherent moral virtues of judges or anyone else. Rather, if we assume that all officials

[99] Ewing, n 25 above, 41.
[100] Kavanagh, n 10 above.
[101] Kyritsis, n 55 above, 747.

(judges, legislators, or civil servants) will carry out their respective roles in good faith and with a reasonable level of competence, we may still have an institutional reason to favour judges over, say, civil servants, simply on the basis that judges are less vulnerable than civil servants to pressure by the executive.[102] Similarly, the argument that judges may be able to withstand electoral or popular pressure to a greater degree than politicians, is not based on the idea that judges are inherently more enlightened or more courageous than the typical legislator. The point is simply that politicians and judges make their decisions in different institutional contexts, such that it is easier for judges to withstand popular pressure.[103] Given that their institutional design makes them relatively immune from popular pressure, this gives us a reason to favour constitutional review as a reviewing procedure to ensure protection of human rights, especially when such protection may be deeply unpopular.[104]

Certainly, this is far from a conclusive argument in favour of constitutional review. It may be that this institutional advantage is, in the circumstances of a particular time and place, overshadowed by other disadvantages. The only point I am making here is that when evaluating an institution like constitutional review, one focuses not just on particular outcomes in particular decisions, but also on the general institutional and constitutional structures in which officials make decisions. Given that these general structures remain relatively constant over time, this accounts (in part) for the fact that scholars are less likely to change their general view about the justification of constitutional review on the basis of changes in the judicial record at a particular time and place. Evaluating the 'empirical evidence' on judicial decision-making is not only a matter of working out judges' politics and assessing their individual decisions, but also considering the pros and cons of the institutional structures within which they make their decisions.

[102] Ibid, 747.

[103] W Waluchow, *A Common Law Theory of Judicial Review: The Living Tree* (Cambridge University Press: New York, 2007) 163, 255ff.

[104] Phillipson notes that in the area of national security, not only is there no electoral gain involved in protecting rights, there is in fact a significant electoral cost, n 9 above; see also TRS Allan, 'Parliament's Will and the Justice of the Common Law: The Human Rights Act in Constitutional Perspective' (2006) 59 CLP 27, 30. This kind of empirical speculation can be used to mount an argument in favour of a non-elective decision-making procedure with respect to the enforcement of those rights, see Kavanagh, n 10 above.

Democratic Scepticism and the Changing Facts

So, have the facts pertinent to the role of the judiciary in our political system changed to any significant degree? Many commentators believe that there has been a significant shift in judicial attitudes and performance in the UK in the last 20 years. In the early part of the 20th century, left-wing public law scholars in the UK became confident that the 'forces of democratic politics had become allied with the forces of social progress'.[105] However, this optimism evaporated in the Thatcher era when legislation was 'wielded as a sledgehammer to dismantle much of the achievement of the social state'.[106] Responding to the poor civil liberties record of governments during the Thatcher years, Keith Ewing and Conor Gearty suggested that the traditional political checks on government were insufficiently effective as a method of curbing the power of a determined and illiberal governing party: 'Mrs Thatcher has merely utilized to the full the scope for untrammelled power latent in the British constitution but obscured by the hesitancy and scruples of previous consensus-based political leaders'.[107] But this seemingly untrammelled power was eventually met with some resistance in the courts. The growth of judicial review in the 1990s even leads John Griffith to acknowledge that 'judges since 1990 have become far more willing to strike down ministerial exercise of power than during the 1980s.'[108] He accepted that the attitude of the senior judiciary had changed for the better.[109]

However, despite the growth of judicial review in the 1990s, democratic sceptics still believed that if the UK had a Bill of Rights, the courts would use it 'to quash or limit the extent of socially progressive

[105] Dyzenhaus, n 7 above, 11.

[106] Ibid, 12. That the historical belief in the ability of the elected branches of government to protect civil liberties was put under severe strain during the Thatcher years was noted by Ewing and Gearty *Freedom under Thatcher: Civil Liberties in Modern Britain* (Clarendon Press: Oxford,1990) 7; H Fenwick *Civil Liberties and Human Rights* (Routledge-Cavendish: Oxford, 2007) 159. In fact, the dissatisfaction with the civil liberties record during this time led Helen Fenwick to describe the HRA as 'Thatcher's legacy', see H Fenwick *Civil Rights: New Labour, Freedom and the Human Rights Act* (Pearson Education Ltd: Essex, 2000) 9.

[107] Ewing & Gearty, ibid, 7; D Feldman, 'The Human Rights Act 1998 and Constitutional Principles' (1999) 19 LS 165, 166.

[108] J Griffith, 'Judges and the Constitution', n 24 above, 296.

[109] J Griffith, *Judicial Politics since 1920: A Chronicle* (Wiley Blackwell: London, 1993) 190–1. Though for a more equivocal evaluation of the recent empirical evidence, see J Griffith, 'The Common Law and the Political Constitution' (2001) 117 LQR 42, 66.

legislation'.[110] Has this prediction been borne out, post-HRA? Although the views of democratic sceptics have remained largely unchanged post-HRA, many have been dismayed to discover that 'precious little socially progressive legislation has been passed under the new Labour government of Tony Blair and Gordon Brown'.[111] Whilst acknowledging 'some surprisingly welcome and progressive [judicial] decisions',[112] sceptics have tended to suggest that post-HRA, 'the old, illiberal conservatism of the courts has been depressingly repeated'.[113]

Keith Ewing has been the most damning and uncompromising critic of the HRA and the judicial record in upholding it.[114] However, he has nonetheless pointed out that many of the empirical facts pertinent to the role of judges in upholding rights have changed in the HRA era: 'if the world has not exactly turned upside down, it has certainly changed in a number of crucial respects relevant to the human rights debate'.[115] In the period immediately following the House of Lords decision in the *Belmarsh Prison* case, Ewing enumerated five such changes:[116]

(1) Social democracy is now in retreat such that 'there is no prospect of great waves of redistribution, or of progressive policies by national or local government'.[117]

(2) 'We no longer live in an era when the juristocracy is a relatively conservative bloc, especially at its highest levels . . . the present generation is perhaps the first of whom it can be said that the juristocracy is as liberal as the political class'.[118]

(3) Statutory bills of rights such as the HRA 'do not necessarily adopt the antidemocratic extremism of the US Bill of Rights, designed as a restraint on big government'.[119]

[110] A Tomkins, 'The Rule of Law in Blair's Britain' (2008) University of Queensland Law Review 24.
[111] Ibid, 25.
[112] Ibid, 25.
[113] Ibid, 25.
[114] eg, see Ewing, n 48 above.
[115] Ewing, n 25 above, 41. John Griffith has also pointed out that it is the *recent* empirical evidence which matters in terms of assessing whether it is justified to give enhanced power to the courts to adjudicate rights, see 'The Common Law and the Political Constitution' (2001) 117 LQR 42, 66.
[116] This article was written after the House of Lords decision in the *Belmarsh Prison* case but before the House of Lords handed down the three control order decisions: *Secretary of State for the Home Department v JJ* [2007] UKHL 45; *Secretary of State for the Home Department v MB and AF* [2007] UKHL 46; *Secretary of State for the Home Department v E* [2007] UKHL 47. For discussion of the control order decisions see Ewing, n 25 above, 41.
[117] Ibid, 41.
[118] Ibid. 41
[119] Ibid, 41.

(4) There is 'the growing formal power which has been extended to the Executive by parliament'.[120]

(5) Finally, the hope that a left-wing government would protect civil liberties in the context of a threat to national security seems unfounded:

> The debates surrounding the Prevention of Terrorism Act 2005 have confounded even more historical certainties. It was assumed in the past that it was the Labour Party and not the Conservative party that would be 'strong' on civil liberties and 'soft' on national security . . . it was also assumed in the past that the more conservative House of Lords would be similarly robust in its defence of national security at the expense of civil liberties should a challenge between the two arise.[121]

So, what consequences do these changes have for democratic scepticism? If judges are just as liberal as the political class and left-wing governments are not producing any socially progressive legislation, then this goes to the heart of the democratic-sceptical tradition in British public law scholarship. The idea that we should oppose constitutional review on the basis that it will lead inexorably to retrogressive judicial interference with progressive legislation, becomes very difficult to sustain in contemporary times. At the very least, the presupposition of this position, namely, that judges will be 'disposed by their class membership to undermine the redistributive programmes of the welfare state',[122] begins to sound dated.[123] Whilst it may have been true of the

[120] Ibid, 42.

[121] Ibid, 42. Though the assumption that the Labour party would be strong on civil liberties in the national security context is not borne out by history see, eg, D Bonner, 'Responding to Crisis: Legislating Against Terrorism' (2006) 112 LQR 602, especially 613, 620, and 621; see generally D Bonner, *Executive Measures, Terrorism and National Security* (Ashgate: Aldershot, 2008). The empirical shift in judicial attitudes described by Ewing may well be reflective of wider trends which have created a different society to the one which formed the background to Griffith's work. Though undoubtedly relevant an examination of these broader societal developments lies outside the scope of this chapter.

[122] Dyzenhaus offers this statement as a partial characterization of the 'functionalist school of thought associated with the London School of Economics, a school often associated with the work of John Griffith', see *The Constitution of Law* (Cambridge University Press: Cambridge, 2008) 123; for further discussion of the 'LSE functionalist' school, see Tomkins, *The Republican Constitution* (Hart Publishing: Oxford, 2003) 35ff.

[123] Thomas Poole has pointed out that Griffith's portrayal of the political background against which his critique of the judiciary was set, now sounds hopelessly dated, see T Poole, 'Tilting at Windmills? Truth and Illusion in 'The Political Constitution' (2007) 70(2) MLR 250 at 250, citing as an example the following statement: 'no one nowadays doubts that the Conservative party exists to promote the interests of private capital and the Labour Party the interests of organised labour', see Griffith, 'A Political Constitution' (1979) 42 MLR 1 at 16.

judiciary in the 1970s and 80s, this does not capture the political reality today—at least not to the same extent. If 'the events of our time determine our philosophy'[124], as John Griffith claimed, then an increased judicial willingness to stand up to the executive to protect rights must surely influence our evaluation of the role and value of constitutional review.

One of the burning political issues of our time concerns the political and legal response to terrorism post-9/11. More than any other factor, the legislative and executive response to terrorism post-9/11 must make uncomfortable reading for those who urge us to place our faith in parliamentary politics as a sure way of protecting rights in times of crisis. Now is not the best time to be celebrating the wonders of parliamentary democracy. As democratic sceptics remind us, 'the torrent of restrictive legislation continues apace'.[125] It is widely agreed that the anti-terrorist legislation enacted post-9/11 has left a lot to be desired, both in terms of democratic procedure and in terms of substantive outcome concerning individual liberty. The draconian legislation passed in this short period reminds us that governments under pressure to respond quickly and effectively to a perceived security threat, and eager to pacify a fearful public, are all too prone to hasty and populist decisions which pay scant regard for the human rights of marginalized groups and indeed pay less than diligent attention to the values of accountability and parliamentary scrutiny which are said to underpin parliamentary democracy.

The most notorious example of this is the Anti-Terrorism, Crime and Security Act 2001 which, despite its staggering length, breadth and draconian implications, was rushed through parliament in a matter of days.[126] This is not a wonderful example of the allegedly participatory, democratic decision-making procedures so prized by democratic sceptics. It is one (albeit a particularly notorious and egregious) example of what Adam Tomkins described as the 'well-established tradition of rushing terrorist legislation through Parliament'.[127] As Tomkins rightly observes, in the field of national security 'parliamentary scrutiny continues to be meagre'.[128]

[124] Griffith, n 24 above, 290. [125] Ewing, n 25 above, 46

[126] See Tomkins, 'Legislating against Terror: The Antiterrorism, Crime and Security Act 2001' (2002) PL 205, 205 who points out that the government only allowed 16 hours of debate on this Bill in the Commons and it received 9 days in the House of Lords; see also Gearty, '11 September, Counter-terrorism and the Human Rights Act 1998', n 94 above, 22ff. [127] Tomkins, ibid, 205.

[128] Tomkins, 'Defining and Delimiting National Security' (2002) 118 LQR 200, 203.

Set against the backdrop of the draconian counter-terrorist legislation, Conor Gearty has urged his fellow democratic sceptics to rethink their traditional opposition to judicial enforcement of fundamental rights. In Gearty's view:

> . . . news on the judicial front is not at all as bad as is sometimes supposed by those of us who are dyed-in-the-wool critics of judicial conservatism . . . the 'war on terror' has made liberals of us all. When the executive and legislative branches have been won back to the civil libertarian side we can go back to arguments about how judges are holding up social progress, but now is not the time for such luxurious disputes.[129]

Whilst many democratic sceptics have criticized the courts for failing to stop the government's 'war on terror',[130] they have nonetheless accepted that the courts have mitigated the worst excesses of the draconian counter-terrorist legislation enacted by the Labour government post-9/11. The *Belmarsh Prison* case is perhaps the most high-profile instance of this phenomenon. It is a remarkable case 'not only for the fact that the House of Lords stood up so convincingly to the Executive but also for their manner of doing so'.[131] Although the control order regime enacted to replace indefinite detention has attracted much criticism,[132] even Keith Ewing accepts that the judges have 'shaved the worst features of the control order regime.[133] By their decisions in a number of cases, the courts have revealed that they are unquestionably a major irritant that the government in a number of fields'.[134] For Ewing, these are 'only marginal gains in the wider cause of protecting human rights'.[135] Ewing would like to see the courts do much more. He concludes that 'if the rule

[129] Gearty, 'Rethinking Civil Liberties in a Counter-Terrorism World', n 95 above, 115–16.

[130] eg, see Ewing, n 71 above. The characterization of the government's response to terrorism post-9/11 as a 'war on terror' (in particular, its implication that the primary response should be military) has been questioned by the Foreign Secretary (David Miliband MP) at <http://www.guardian.co.uk/commentisfree/2009/jan/15/david-miliband-war-terror>. For further reservations about the appropriateness of this terminology see D Bonner, *Executive Measures, Terrorism and National Security: Have the Rules of the Game Changed?* (Ashgate: Aldershot, 2007).

[131] Ewing, n 25 above, 42.

[132] For discussion of the control order regime, see L Zedner, 'Preventive Justice or Pre-Punishment? The Case of Control Orders' (2007) 60 CLP 174; E Bates, 'Anti-terrorism Control Orders: Liberty and Security Still in the Balance' (2009) 29 LS 99–126.

[133] Ewing, 'The Continuing Futility of the Human Rights Act' (2008) PL 688.

[134] Ibid, 691. [135] Ibid, 690.

of law is to be a fairly 'weak reed' in this 'dismal swamp', it makes sense to focus attention on parliament rather than the courts as a source of restraint on the executive'.[136]

But does it make sense in the current climate? At first glance, it is at least open to doubt. The structure of the democratic sceptics' argument seems to be as follows:

(1) There is a 'torrent of restrictive legislation' enacted by parliament.
(2) The courts do not stop the flow of this torrent completely, though they sometimes prevent its worst excesses.
(3) Therefore, we should give unfettered decision-making powers to parliament unconstrained by the courts.

As democratic sceptics often acknowledge, step 3 only makes sense if we can find ways of *improving* parliamentary scrutiny of the executive. As it currently stands, parliamentary scrutiny of counter-terrorist legislation is 'meagre'[137] and the outcomes for individual liberty worrying to say the least. As Keith Ewing tellingly puts it, democratic sceptics must work out 'how to *create* powerful representative institutions'[138] Given that parliament is effectively dominated by the tiny political elite constituted by the government, and given the draconian legislation proposed by the government post-9/11, it is difficult to argue that we should give unfettered power to the government to regulate such areas of the law. Many observers of the current political and legal landscape concerning national security and civil liberties will conclude that it is better to have 'marginal gains' for civil liberties than none at all.

The challenge for democratic sceptics is to show why we should abolish constitutional review, despite the fact that, at least in the current climate, it enhances the protection of civil liberties of unpopular minorities and vulnerable groups to some degree. Why should we favour parliamentary supremacy unfettered by constitutional review, if that would give us worse outcomes in terms of human rights? Gavin Phillipson had no hesitation in arguing that we should support constitutional review under the HRA because of its instrumental benefits for rights-protection.[139] In the current political climate, he believes that

[136] Ibid, 693.

[137] Tomkins, 'Defining and Delimiting National Security' (2002) 118 LQR 200, 203.

[138] Ewing, n 131 above, 693.

[139] Phillipson, n 9 above.

prioritizing a democratic/participatory decision-making procedure for issues of rights led to worse outcomes for rights:

> [Sceptics] must be prepared to live with the fact that proposed electoral accountability for violation of civil liberties is largely a fiction, as is the notion of effective protection by the Commons . . . sceptics should be honest enough to accept that a reduction in judicial power to protect rights will mean worse treatment of terrorist suspects, asylum seekers, paedophiles.[140]

If the argument of this chapter is correct, democratic sceptics cannot simply respond to this challenge by saying that it is the democratic decision-making procedure which matters most. The ultimate standard by which we judge political institutions is their likelihood of achieving good substantive outcomes.

Conclusion

All scholars should be sceptical in the etymological sense of being a seeker after truth, an inquirer who has not yet arrived at definite conclusions. In subjecting judicial decisions to critical scrutiny, we contribute to the task of holding judges to account. Even if we believe that judges are doing a relatively good job of enforcing human rights, we should not be sanguine about the powers they exercise. Judges are part of the political elite and they need to be reminded that their decisions will be assessed with a critical eye.

Democratic sceptics pursue this scrutinizing task with a vengeance. Much of their scholarship is a valuable 'counsel against complacency'.[141] They seek to debunk and demystify judicial decision-making and are relentless in their urge to question judicial authority and legitimacy.[142] Of course, judges are not the only object of the democratic sceptics' critique. Also in the firing line are 'those in the mainstream of public law who are rule of law enthusiasts and strong proponents of a vigorous role for judges'.[143] The debate between enthusiasts and sceptics of judicial power in the UK might be described as the battle between 'constitutional review lovers' and 'constitutional

[140] Ibid, 51–2. [141] Poole, n 121 above, 261.

[142] In fact, Thomas Poole argues that a 'relentless questioning of those in authority' is one of the hallmarks of Griffith's writings, see n 121 above, 275–6.

[143] Dyzenhaus, n 7 above, 9.

review haters'.[144] Characterizing the rival positions in public law scholarship in terms of love and hate is not as fanciful as may at first appear. For one thing, it captures the fervent and highly-charged nature of the debate. Public law scholars care deeply about the role of judges in human rights adjudication, because it is a locus for broader moral and political beliefs about the nature of the society in which we live, whether public decision-making is elitist or inclusive and, at its most basic, whether we have good or bad government. If there is a war on this issue amongst public law scholars, then it is a war of hearts and minds. Also relevant is the well-known fact that strong emotions influence our judgment. When we love someone, we may be blind to their flaws. Even when we see their flaws, we may be disposed to underplay them or make excuses for them. Similarly, when we are in the grip of hatred, we are reluctant to accept that those we hate may possess good and laudable character traits. Indeed, we may be reluctant to give them credit even when it can be shown that they have changed.

In this chapter, I have argued that no matter what side one takes, the empirical record of judicial decision-making (together with the political context in which it operates) is central to the justification of constitutional review. The political and legal landscape which gave democratic scepticism its animus and target in the 1970s was marked by retrogressive judicial interference with progressive legislation. But the times have changed. The challenge for democratic sceptics is to respond to the changing facts. Otherwise, their sceptical stance will become a cynical one.

[144] This characterization is adapted from Dimitrios Kyritsis, 'Principles, Policies and the Power of Court' (2007) XX *Canadian Journal of Law and Jurisprudence* 1 at 1.

English Lessons: A Comparative Analysis of UK and US Responses to Terrorism

*David Cole**

Introduction

In August 2006, the United Kingdom arrested 25 suspects in what was described as a plot to explode passenger airlines flying from London's Heathrow Airport to North American destinations. It held them without criminal charges for up to 28 days under an anti-terrorism preventive detention law that had been expanded in the wake of the 7 July 2005 London subway and bus suicide bombings. United States Attorney General Alberto Gonzales promptly announced that the US should examine the United Kingdom's approach to anti-terrorism, and that he would send a team of lawyers to do so. In particular, Gonzales seemed interested in the power to lock up suspects without charges for up to 28 days.

One month later, the Senate Subcommittee on Homeland Security held a hearing entitled 'Catching Terrorists: The British System Versus the US System' featuring Judge Richard Posner and Professor John Yoo, two of the country's leading conservative legal scholars on fighting terrorism. Judge Posner and Professor Yoo, like Attorney General Gonzales, were particularly taken with the ability of the

* Professor of Law, Georgetown Law Center. I have given versions of this chapter as talks at the University of California at Berkeley Law School; the Center for Transnational Legal Studies in London; a criminology symposium at All Souls College, Oxford; and at University College London. The chapter has benefited from many comments from scholars, practitioners, and students, including Andrew Ashworth, Laura Donohue, Conor Gearty, David Kris, Colm O'Cinneide, Nina Pillard, Philippe Sands, Muthucumaraswamy Sornarajah, Paul Schwartz, Ben Ward, John Yoo, Lucia Zedner, and Lorenzo Zucca. A shorter version of this essay was previously published as D Cole, 'The Brits Do It Better', *New York Review of Books*, vol 55, no 10, 12 June 2008.

British government to detain suspects for 28 days without charges. More generally, both stressed the limitations of the American law enforcement model in combating terrorism, and urged instead an aggressive preventive approach, including the use of military force. Subcommittee chairman Senator Judd Gregg welcomed these views and eagerly joined in their criticism of the FBI for its 'reactive' law enforcement mindset.

Given the subject matter, the Senators apparently felt obliged to invite someone from the United Kingdom as well—former British counter-terrorism official Tom Parker. While his tone was conciliatory—he followed Posner and Yoo by saying that he found himself 'in the position of an echo to an echo'—his message was in fact quite at odds with the conventional wisdom in the room. He insisted that the most important thing about the British approach to fighting terrorism was its determination to treat terrorism as crime—*not* as an extraordinary military threat. And he argued that Scotland Yard's relative success in disrupting several apparently serious terrorist plots and bringing the perpetrators to justice turned in large measure on *not* intervening preventively, but maintaining surveillance without arrest as long as possible, until it could develop a strong case that would then support a criminal prosecution.

Parker noted that the British government had tried the more military and pre-emptive approach in the 1970s in Northern Ireland—sending in troops, interning large numbers of suspects without trial, and employing coercive interrogation tactics to gather intelligence. But, Parker explained, those approaches backfired, serving only to inspire further support for the Irish Republican Army and to unite the Nationalist community against the British security forces. The principal lesson we should learn, insisted the only British subject in the room, was not the poverty of the law enforcement model as a response to terrorism but the absolute necessity of that model. Needless to say, this was not the message that advocates of the Bush administration's 'war on terror' wanted to hear.

What lessons can be learned by comparing the UK's and the US's experiences fighting terrorism? One might expect that, in view of the two countries' legal systems and political and demographic circumstances, the UK would be at best an example of what *not* to do. At the same time, the widespread international and domestic criticism of the United States' response to the terrorist attacks of 11 September 2001 suggests that the US would have little to offer the UK in the way of positive lessons. Yet the picture, as always, is more complicated than it may first appear. Each jurisdiction has been far too willing to sacrifice principled commitments to individual rights in the face of terrorist threats. But each country has also shown residual sensitivity to rights concerns in some areas. As a general matter, the UK has been more restrained in terms of liberty and interrogation, while the US has been more restrained in terms of privacy. These differences tell us something about the role of history, culture, and legal struggle in the ongoing effort to find a legitimate democratic response to terrorism. Each country has learned from its own past mistakes, but not from the mistakes of the other. The comparative enterprise is, at least in part, an effort to facilitate learning across borders.

Overview

There are many reasons to believe that the United Kingdom would be considerably less protective of privacy and civil liberties than the United States. Some of the world's most important human rights judicial decisions condemn the United Kingdom for its treatment of IRA suspects. While it is customary for commentators to warn about what will happen in the United States after 'the next attack,' the UK has already been the victim of a long, bloody, and quite relentless series of terrorist attacks, as a result of its 30-year struggle with the IRA. Over the course of 30 years the IRA killed 1800 persons and injured 20,000, in a country with only one-fifth the population of the US.

The regular use of violence in that struggle has, thankfully, ended. But terrorism from other quarters remains a serious issue. According to British intelligence the UK is now Al-Qaeda's prime target, in part because the UK's Muslim immigrant community has such strong ties to Pakistan, where Al-Qaeda is reported to have reconstituted itself. As the 'homegrown' attacks of 7/7 and several other plots illustrate, the UK appears to have a much more serious problem with its domestic Arab and Muslim populations than the United States does. In particular, the Arab and Muslim communities in England are, as a general matter, poorer, less educated, more alienated, and thus more vulnerable to radicalization than the Arab and Muslim populations in the United States, where Arabs and Muslims are, on average, more highly educated, more likely to be professionals, and wealthier than non-Arab and non-Muslim Americans.[1]

The UK fortunately has not suffered any single attack on the scale of 9/11. But the British have suffered the suicide bombings of 7/7, the attack on Glasgow International Airport in 2007, and the attempted car bombing in London at the same time. Meanwhile, Scotland Yard has arrested, tried and convicted numerous individuals with substantial caches of arms and seemingly well-developed plans to carry out terrorist attacks. In the United States, by contrast, most of the post-9/11 'terrorism' prosecutions have been for the provision, or attempted provision, of 'material support' to terrorist groups, not for conspiracies or attempts to undertake actual terrorist acts, and many of the 'plots' disrupted have been instigated by FBI undercover agents or informants, not by the defendants themselves.[2] So the UK appears to face at least as great, if not a greater, terrorist threat than the US.

At the same time, structural safeguards of liberty and privacy would seem to be much stronger in the US than in the UK. The UK has no written Constitution, and so no exact counterpart to the document in the US system designed to protect individual rights and liberties from political passions and government repression. UK courts have never had the power to declare national legislation invalid, a power that in the United States dates to *Marbury v Madison*, and has established a primary role for the Supreme Court in the protection of individual rights. Separation of powers, a structural safeguard of liberty under the American Constitution, is substantially less robust in the UK, where the executive is chosen by the majority party in the legislature, and where parliamentary supremacy is the rule.

Yet with respect to two important counter-terrorism measures—detention and interrogation—the UK has been more restrained and rights-sensitive in the post-9/11 era than the US. Moreover, the debate about security and liberty in the UK after 9/11 featured more prominent voices of moderation than in the US. At the same time, when it comes to issues of privacy, the picture seems reversed: the US has shown more sensitivity to privacy rights, even where

[1] This is not to suggest that terrorism is limited to the poor and uneducated. As many have pointed out, many of the 9/11 terrorists were middle-class and well-educated. However, the absence of fulfilling or rewarding alternatives is certainly one factor that can lead to the resort to violence.

[2] See D Cole and J Lobel, *Less Safe, Less Free: Why America is Losing the War on* Terror (New Press, 2007) 109–22.

terrorism is at issue, than the UK. Any effort to compare UK and US counter-terrorism initiatives is hindered by the fact that both countries have cloaked much of what they have done in secrecy. We do not know, for example, the full extent of the electronic surveillance conducted by the National Security Agency ('NSA'); many of the details regarding the US extraordinary rendition program; or the extent of UK complicity in torture inflicted on terror suspects by other countries. Still, comparing UK and US responses with respect to three key counter-terrorism enforcement policies—detention, interrogation, and surveillance—suggests that democracies can learn from their own historical mistakes but may find it difficult to learn from the mistakes of other nations.

Detention

Both nations dramatically expanded their use of detention in response to the increased threat of terrorism since 9/11. The UK, however, has been considerably more restrained in both the assertion and exercise of detention power than the United States. As has been well rehearsed elsewhere, within two years of 11 September 2001, the Bush administration rounded up over 5,000 Arab and Muslim immigrants within the United States, often without any basis other than their ethnic or religious identity; detained citizens and foreign nationals as 'enemy combatants' on the military's say-so, initially without any hearings whatsoever, and subsequently with patently unfair hearings; 'disappeared' about 100 suspects into secret prisons run by the CIA, where they were held incommunicado for months or years, without access even to the International Committee of the Red Cross; and rendered other suspects to third countries such as Syria and Egypt for detention without charge and interrogation by security services infamous for their use of torture.[3]

By contrast, the UK's anti-terrorism detention measures have been modest. Its most extreme detention measure was a 2001 law that authorized indefinite detention without trial of foreigners subject to deportation orders and suspected of terrorism but who could not in fact be deported (usually because they faced a risk of being tortured if returned to their country of origin). The law required an emergency

[3] See generally, ibid, 23–69.

'derogation' from the obligations of the European Convention on Human Rights, and engendered substantial debate in parliament, the bar, and the press. But in 2004, the Law Lords declared it incompatible with the European Convention on Human Rights notwithstanding the UK's derogation, because it impermissibly discriminated between foreign nationals and British nationals.[4] Under the law, a *British* terror suspect could not be detained indefinitely without trial, even if he or she posed the same danger as a foreign terror suspect. Since parliament felt it unnecessary to detain British nationals under such circumstances, the Law Lords reasoned, it was not necessary to detain foreigners either. Shortly thereafter, parliament let the law lapse. In February 2009, the Grand Chamber of the European Court of Human Rights effectively affirmed the Law Lords' judgment that the indefinite detention provision violated the European Convention.[5]

Parliament subsequently enacted a more limited 'control order' regime, applicable to British citizens and foreign nationals alike.[6] Under this regime, the government may subject persons reasonably suspected of involvement in terrorism-related activities to a range of restrictions on their freedom of movement and association where necessary to protect the public from a risk of terrorism. Control orders contain a variety of obligations, and vary from individual to individual, but the most common ones restrict where an individual may live, worship, and work, and with whom he may associate or communicate. They often include confinement to one's home for most of the day, with strict limits on who may visit and on Internet and phone access.[7] The legality of the control order regime has been subject to judicial challenge since its enactment. The courts have held that orders confining individuals to their homes for 18 hours constitute an impermissible deprivation of liberty in violation of the European Convention on Human Rights, and that while control orders may be based on confidential evidence, a person subject to a control order must be provided sufficient details about the evidence

[4] *A and ors v Secretary of State for the Home Department* [2004] UKHL 56.

[5] *A and ors v United Kingdom* (2009) ECHR 3455/05, 19 February 2009.

[6] Prevention of Terrorism Act 2005.

[7] For a good general overview of control orders, see Lord Carlile of Berriew QC, *Fourth Report of the Independent Review Pursuant to Section 14(3) of the Prevention of Terrorism Act 2005*, 3 February 2009; see also L Zedner, 'Preventive Justice or Pre-Punishment? The Case of Control Orders' (2007) 60 *Current Legal Problems* 174–203.

against him so that he can instruct his lawyer meaningfully in his defence.[8] As of February 2009, 38 individuals had been subject to control orders.[9]

The other detention measure the UK has relied upon for counter-terrorism purposes is pre-charge detention. The Terrorism Act 2006 authorized the government, subject to judicial approval, to detain an individual without charges for a maximum of 28 days. To do so the government must persuade a judge that there are 'reasonable grounds to believe' that further detention is necessary to obtain or to preserve evidence relevant to a criminal investigation, and that the investigation is being conducted diligently and expeditiously. Prime Minister Tony Blair initially sought authority to arrest and detain suspects for 90 days without charges. That measure was defeated, however, in the House of Lords, as a number of Labour party members broke from their party to side with Conservatives, Liberal Democrats, and independents to force the government to strip back the authority to a maximum of 28 days. When Prime Minister Gordon Brown, in 2009, advocated extending the 28 day period to 42 days, Ken MacDonald, the Director of Public Prosecutions, stated publicly that there was no need to extend the period beyond 28 days, and other current and former senior law enforcement officials concurred. The proposal was again defeated.

Both countries have looked for ways to effectuate detention outside the traditional criminal justice approach. On the whole, however, the UK's measures have been significantly more limited than the detention authority asserted and exercised by the United States. Even so, the British measures have prompted considerable debate and controversy within the UK. By contrast, the Bush administration exerted almost boundless authority to detain anyone it asserted was an 'enemy combatant', a category it unilaterally defined as including anyone who had ever provided any support to Al-Qaeda or the Taliban, even if the support was unknowing. (It infamously told one court that it could detain even a 'little old lady in Switzerland who writes checks to what she thinks is a charity that helps orphans in Afghanistan but really is a front to finance

[8] *Secretary of State for the Home Department v AF* [2009] UKHL 28 (holding that the controlee must be provided with sufficient information about the evidence against him to enable him to meaningfully instruct his lawyer in his defence); *Secretary of State for the Home Department v JJ* [2007] UKHL 45 (holding that the imposition of a curfew of 18 hours on a detainee constituted a violation of the right to liberty protected by Article 5 of the ECHR).

[9] Carlile Report, n 7 above.

Al-Qaeda activities'[10]). It has detained approximately 775 men at Guantanamo under that authority, approximately 100 in CIA black sites, and hundreds more at Bagram Air Force Base in Afghanistan. While the authority has been challenged, courts have only in the last year or so started to order individuals released who were held as 'enemy combatants.'[11]

Moreover, when the United States adopted a power to detain almost identical to the UK authority at issue in the *Belmarsh Prison* case,[12] it sparked little attention and no controversy. In November 2001, the US Justice Department issued a regulation giving itself precisely the power that the Law Lords later deemed a violation of fundamental human rights in the *Belmarsh Prison* decision.[13] The regulation authorizes indefinite detention of foreign nationals subject to deportation if they cannot be deported and are suspected of terrorism. While the UK law generated substantial debate and was ultimately invalidated, the US regulation received almost no attention, and was arguably invited by a US Supreme Court decision.[14]

The UK also seems to have employed its detention measures more surgically. In the first two years after 9/11 US authorities locked up more than 5,000 foreign nationals in anti-terrorism preventive detention, virtually all of them Arab or Muslim. Today, not one of the 5,000 stands convicted of any terrorist offence.[15] Most were affirmatively cleared by the FBI of any terrorist connections—but not before they spent days, weeks, or in some cases months in jail, often without any showing that they posed any danger to the community or risk of flight (the showing constitutionally required to justify preventive detention). By contrast, in the United Kingdom, less than 20 foreign nationals were placed in indefinite detention under the Anti-terrorism, Crime and Security Act 2001 and fewer than 40 have been subjected to 'control orders.'

Interrogation

The UK and the US have also taken different approaches to interrogation—although recent disclosures about UK policy suggest that the

[10] A Liptak, 'In Terrorism Cases, Administration Sets Own Rules' *New York Times*, 27 November 2005, 1 (quoting transcript of oral argument in the case of *In re Guantánamo Detainee Cases*, 355 F Supp 2d 443, 475 (DDC 2005)) .

[11] eg, see C Lee, 'Their Own Private Guatánamo' New York Times, 22 July 2009.

[12] *A v Secretary of State for the Home Department* [2004] UKHL 56.

[13] 66 Fed Reg 56979, 14 November 2001 (codified at 8 CFR 241.14).

[14] *Zadvydas v Davis*, 533 US 678 (2001) (limiting detention of foreign nationals who cannot be deported, but stating in *dicta* that detention of suspected terrorists might pose a different question).

[15] See Cole and Lobel, n 2 above, 107.

differences may be less clear-cut than initially appeared. After 9/11, US officials authorized both the CIA and military interrogators to use coercive interrogation tactics, including sleep deprivation, stripping suspects naked, dousing them with water, subjecting them to stress positions, slamming them into walls, slapping them in the face and abdomen, and waterboarding. Secret memos, some of which have since been disclosed and disclaimed, defined torture and cruel, inhuman and degrading treatment extremely narrowly, with the evident purpose of freeing up CIA and military interrogators to use coercive tactics that had previously been forbidden.[16]

In addition, the Bush administration authorized and carried out 'extraordinary renditions,' in which US officials abducted suspects and delivered them to security services in countries such as Egypt and Syria, with long records of torture, so that these security services could conduct interrogations. Many individuals found themselves tortured after being delivered on US jets to foreign countries. In one case, Maher Arar, a Canadian citizen born in Syria, was stopped by US officials while he was changing planes at JFK Airport, on his way home to Canada from Europe, and sent on a federally chartered jet to Syria, where he was tortured while being asked a set of questions virtually identical to those federal officials had asked him at JFK.[17]

The US government has aggressively employed secrecy to hide its authorization of these tactics and to frustrate accountability. It authorized the tactics through a kind of secret law, set forth in classified memos. Even as the law seemed to tighten in response to revelations about the abuses, the Justice Department continued to assure the CIA in secret memos that it could continue to employ its coercive tactics.[18] The CIA kept videotapes of its interrogations, but destroyed them when ongoing judicial proceedings threatened to reveal them.

[16] See D Cole (ed), *The Torture Memos: Rationalizing the Unthinkable* (Oneworld Press, 2009) (reproducing six memos from the US Justice Department's Office of Legal Counsel giving a green light to coercive interrogation tactics by the CIA, including waterboarding); see also P Sands, *Torture Team* (2009 revised paperback edn, Penguin) (detailing how Defense Secretary Donald Rumsfeld authorized military interrogators to use coercive interrogation techniques at Guantanamo).

[17] The US District Court and the Court of Appeals for the Second Circuit accepted the government's argument that adjudicating Arar's claims would impermissibly interfere with national security and foreign relations, and dismissed his case: see *Arar v Ashcroft* 2009 US App LEXIS 23988 (2d Cir November 2, 2009) (en banc).

[18] See David Cole (ed), *The Torture Memos: Rationalizing the Unthinkable* (The New Press, 2009).

The Bush administration declared its interrogation tactics a secret, and forbade even the victims' lawyers from disclosing publicly the abuse that their clients had suffered. And in the *Arar* case and several others, the government asserted the 'state secrets' privilege to frustrate attempts to obtain judicial determinations of responsibility.

By the end of President Bush's administration, the US military had banned its interrogators from using such tactics but the CIA was not subject to the military rules. One of President Obama's first acts was to prohibit all use of such tactics by the CIA. His administration disclosed many details about the CIA interrogation programme, and in August 2009 launched a preliminary criminal investigation into some of the worst abuses. Still, to date, no high-level official has been held accountable for the policies that encouraged abuse of prisoners by the CIA and the military.

The extent to which the UK has relied on torture tactics in the wake of 9/11 is still a matter of dispute. In two contexts the UK government argued unsuccessfully that other countries' torture practices should not bar the UK from pursuing measures to protect itself from persons thought to pose a national security threat. It contended that evidence obtained through another government's torture should be admissible in a UK administrative proceeding: where British authorities played no part in the wrongdoing; where the evidence could be shown to be otherwise reliable; and where the proceeding was administrative, not criminal. In December 2005, however, the Law Lords unanimously rejected that position. Lord Bingham, the Chief Justice, wrote: 'I am startled, even a little dismayed, at the suggestion (and the acceptance by the Court of Appeal majority) that this deeply-rooted tradition and an international obligation solemnly and explicitly undertaken can be overridden.'

Similarly, in 2007, the UK asked the European Court of Human Rights to overturn a prior ruling that barred deportation of foreign nationals to countries where they face a risk of 'cruel, inhuman, or degrading treatment.'[19] The British government argued that where no risk of actual torture was present, and where the foreign national's continued presence in the UK posed a risk to British security, the risk that the individual might face cruel, inhuman, or degrading treatment abroad should be 'balanced' against the UK's security risk. In some cases it maintained that the national security risk at home might justify

[19] *Chahal v UK* (1996) 23 EHRR 413.

deportation. The European Court of Human Rights rejected the UK's argument, and held fast to its earlier position.[20]

The differences between these initiatives and those of the United States are significant. First, where the UK sought to free itself to deport an individual *despite* the *risk* of cruel treatment, the US rendition policy seems to have been designed to send people to particular third countries *for the purpose* of having them tortured. Secondly, while the United States adopted and implemented its policy covertly and outside the law, the British transparently pursued a legal avenue to seek a change in the legal standard. And there is no indication that the UK has not abided by either of the decisions that ruled against it.

More recent evidence suggests, however, that the differences between the UK and the US on torture are less sharp. Evidence has emerged that UK authorities turned a blind eye to torture committed by other countries' security services, and to varying degrees collaborated with those services in order to obtain information that was tainted by torture. In particular, the UK is alleged to have provided questions to pose to Binyam Mohammed after he was abducted by US authorities and rendered to Morocco, where he claims he was brutally tortured. Similarly, the UK allegedly informed Pakistani authorities that two individuals suspected of terrorism were returning to Pakistan, and then interrogated the men in detention there both before and after the Pakistanis tortured them.[21]

Depending on what the facts ultimately show, these practices may be uncomfortably close to the US practice of extraordinary rendition. While the UK has not been accused of affirmatively abducting individuals and delivering them to known torturers, knowing complicity in others' torture comes very close, and is also illegal.[22] On the other

[20] *Saadi v UK* (2008) 47 EHRR 17. Both the US and the UK have sought to use 'diplomatic assurances' as a way of returning individuals to countries where, absent the assurances, they would face a risk of torture. Reliance on such assurances has been widely criticized, in part on the ground that if a country engages in systemic torture (after having committed itself, as all of these countries have, to adhere to the provisions of the Convention Against Torture), why should anyone trust its promise not to do what it has already promised not to do and nevertheless done, repeatedly.

[21] I Cobain, 'The Truth About Torture: Britain's Catalogue of Shame' *The Guardian*, 8 July 2009, available at <http://www.guardian.co.uk/politics/2009/jul/08/mi5-mi6-acccused-of-torture>.

[22] P Sands, 'Complicity with Cruelty' *The Guardian*, 18 June 2009, available at <http://www.guardian.co.uk/commentisfree/2009/jun/18/torture-intelligence-abuse>; P Sands, 'The International Rule of Law: Extraordinary Rendition, Complicity and its Consequences' (2006) 4 European Human Rights Law Review 408.

hand, if the practice turns out to consist of paying insufficient attention to the possibility of torture, it might be seen as less morally (and possibly legally) reprehensible than the US's rendition policy. No one has even alleged that the UK authorized its own agents to use the kinds of brutal tactics that the CIA or the US military employed, and in that important respect, at least, the UK's approach has been more measured. (As we will see later, the UK did issue roughly analagous authorizations in the context of interrogating IRA suspects in the 1970s, but has not done so since).

From the standpoint of detention and interrogation, then, the United Kingdom's response, while hardly exemplary, seems to have been more measured, nuanced, and carefully tailored than that of the United States. The UK has not detained people without trial as 'enemy combatants,' rounded up thousands of foreign nationals in its own country, or authorized its agents to engage in disappearances, coercive interrogations, or renditions. There are undoubtedly areas in which UK law goes further than US law, and that is probably what appealed to Attorney General Gonzales in 2006, but, on the whole, the UK seems to have invoked fewer and less extreme exceptions to the norm; hewed more closely to a criminal law enforcement model; and sought to maintain a more calibrated balance between liberty and security.

Some might point to the fact that the UK has suffered two terrorist attacks since 9/11 to suggest that its approach has not worked as well as the US's more aggressive stance. However, given the multitude of factors that might conceivably affect the level of terrorist threat that a nation faces and the effectiveness of its containment policies, one cannot infer much of anything from this difference. More telling, perhaps, is the fact that Scotland Yard appears to have disrupted and brought to justice more would-be perpetrators of terrorist acts than the US since 9/11. In fact, three of the most apparently serious terror plots to have been disrupted since 9/11 appear to have been disrupted by the UK, not the US. On 30 March 2004, British authorities arrested eight Britons of Pakistani origin in the UK in a series of pre-dawn raids.[23] Police seized 1,300 pounds of ammonium nitrate fertilizer in the raids.[24] Scotland Yard had been keeping the group under surveillance

[23] S Fidler, M Huband and F Tiesenhausen, 'Bomb-making Material Discovered in London Warehouse Following 24 Dawn Raides by Five Forces and MI5 Officers' *Financial Times (London)*, 31March 2004, 1.

[24] D Van Natta Jr and S Grey, 'Investigators Are Clear Who Carried Bombs, But Have Far to Go to Explain More' *New York Times*, 18 July 2005, A8.

for some time and, following the Madrid train bombings, the British authorities decided to arrest the men.[25] Similarly, in August 2004, British authorities arrested eight men for conspiring to detonate a radiological 'dirty bomb' in London.[26] The men's goal was allegedly to set off a big bomb at a prestigious target. The bombers reportedly specifically considered Heathrow Airport, the Houses of Parliament, and Westminster Abbey.[27] Here, too, the arrests followed a year-long surveillance operation.[28] In August 2006, British authorities disrupted yet another terrorist plot. This one allegedly targeted international flights from Heathrow Airport to the United States, and was to use liquid explosives in carry-on luggage. Again, the individuals had been under extended British surveillance before they were arrested.[29] Thus, while the UK has managed to disrupt serious plots, it has done so not by using rendition, torture, disappearances, or indefinite detention without trial, but through good, old-fashioned police work.

Privacy and Surveillance

In at least one important arena, however, UK counter-terrorism policy seems less rights-sensitive than that of the US: privacy and surveillance. Here, as elsewhere, the differences are a matter of degree, not of kind. In 2007, the UK-based Privacy International and the US-based Electronic Privacy Information Center characterized both countries in a report on privacy worldwide as 'endemic surveillance societies,' ranking them with Russia, China, and Malaysia.[30] Still, the US seems to have

[25] PE Tyler, 'Europe Trying To Act First Against Terrorist Networks' *New York Times*, 7 April 2004, A12.

[26] n 25 above.

[27] M Isikoff, 'Terror Watch: The Real Target?' *Newsweek*, 17 November 2004.

[28] A Zagorin and E Shannon, 'London's Dirty-Bomb Plot', 11 October 2004, 22.

[29] A Cowell, 'Britain Charges 11 in Plane Case: Bomb Gear Cited' *New York Times*, 22 August 2006, A1. In September 2009, three men were convicted of conspiracy to murder by bombing aircraft in flight, and a fourth man was convicted of a lesser charge of conspiracy to commit murder. The jury deadlocked on three other men, and acquitted one on all charges. A Faiola and K Adam, 'Britain Convicts Three in Plot to Rival 9/11' *Washington Post*, 8 September 2009, A4. Reportedly, US authorities pressed the British to arrest the men pre-emptively, while the British sought to keep them under surveillance to make sure that they could gather sufficient evidence to convict. Ibid.

[30] Privacy International, *The 2007 International Privacy Ranking*, available at <http://www.privacyinternational.org>. This judgment may be biased by the fact that these groups, based in the UK and the US respectively, may well choose to emphasize the problems within their own countries.

greater protections than the UK for privacy, at least on the books including when it come to counter-terrorism measures.

As a general matter, UK authorities appear to be considerably less constrained with regard to intrusive investigatory tools than are US authorities, although given how much secrecy surrounds surveillance in both countries, all such judgments are subject to the caveat that we do not know what we do not know (including, within the United States, such important questions as the scope of the National Security Agency's warrantless wiretapping programme and the implementation of the Foreign Intelligence Surveillance Act, or within the United Kingdom, the rigour of the executive oversight process for electronic surveillance). Nonetheless, as a formal matter there is no question that US law offers its citizens greater privacy protections.

The Fourth Amendment, for example, requires that, absent certain (broad) categorical exceptions, judges must issue warrants based on probable cause of criminal activity or evidence in order to justify searches of homes and wiretaps of phones. Any evidence obtained in violation of Fourth Amendment requirements generally may not be used to prosecute the individual whose rights were violated. The exceptions are many but the system presumptively requires probable cause and judicial supervision for searches of homes, persons, and effects. On a lower standard of 'reasonable suspicion' that crime is afoot the police may temporarily stop a citizen in order to question him to confirm or dispel their suspicion, but searches for evidence on 'reasonable suspicion' are not permissible. If, and only if, police have reasonable suspicion that the individual is armed, they are permitted to frisk him for weapons—but that search is limited to a pat-down of outer clothing, and may not constitute a search for evidence of criminal conduct, but only for weapons.

By contrast, the UK has no Fourth Amendment. It regulates searches and electronic surveillance by statute. Subject to exceptions, a search of premises requires a warrant issued by a justice of the peace, but the standard for issuance may be lower than the US standard of probable cause. The Police and Criminal Evidence Act 1984 ('PACE') requires only 'reasonable grounds' for believing that evidence of a crime will be found and that the search is necessary to obtain that evidence.[31] Another provision of the same statute authorizes stops and searches on the basis of a similar 'reasonable grounds for believing' that evidence

[31] Police and Criminal Evidence Act 1984, c 60 (hereinafter 'PACE') s 8.

relevant to an indictable offence will be found on a person.[32] As one treatise puts it, the standard for suspicion under PACE is 'at a fairly low level. Certainly there is clear authority for saying that nothing in the nature of a prima facie case is required.'[33]

In the UK, there is also no judicial involvement in authorizing electronic surveillance. The entire process is carried out within the executive branch. At the insistence of the security services, wiretap evidence is not admissible in court, thus ensuring that the process is largely immune from judicial review even after the fact. Until 1985, electronic surveillance in the UK was not even governed by statute. In 1984, the European Court of Human Rights ruled that wiretapping without statutory guidelines or limits violated the right of privacy protected by the European Convention,[34] and that ruling prompted parliament to enact the Interception of Communications Act of 1985. In 1997, the European Court ruled that this law was also insufficient,[35] and parliament responded by enacting the Regulation of Investigatory Powers Act of 2000 ('RIPA'). That law generally requires the Secretary of State, not a court, to issue a warrant in order to authorize wiretapping. The standard for issuance is much more expansive than in the United States—warrants may be issued wherever the Secretary deems them necessary for national security, to detect or prevent serious crime, to safeguard the UK economy, or to implement any international mutual assistance agreement regarding serious crime.[36] By contrast, in the United States, all wiretapping must be approved by a judge, and must be predicated either on probable cause that it will reveal evidence of criminal activity, or on probable cause that the target is an agent of a foreign power.

In enacting RIPA, parliament did create alternative checks. The Interception of Communications Commissioner inspects intercepting agencies and communications service providers; reviews warrants; and issues an annual report detailing the number of interceptions and violations of the statute.[37] However, while his reports identify the

[32] Ibid, ss 1(2), 1(3), 1(7), and 1(8).

[33] R Stone, *The Law of Entry, Search, and Seizure* (4th edn, Oxford University Press, 2004) 22.

[34] *Malone v United Kingdom* (1984) 7 EHRR 14.

[35] *Halford v United Kingdom* (1997) 24 EHRR 523, 536.

[36] RIPA, ss. 5(2)-(3).

[37] eg, see *Report of the Interception of Communications Commissioner for 2005-06*, HC 315, 19 February 2007, available at <http://www.official-documents.gov.uk/document/hc0607/hc03/0315/0315.pdf>

number of errors found they generally do not provide the public with any details about the errors, and instead address those details only in a confidential annex.[38]

RIPA also established an Investigatory Powers Tribunal, to adjudicate and provide remedies for alleged violations of the wiretapping laws. However, that tribunal has ruled for the complainant and against the government only once, in February 2007. A predecessor tribunal, established under the Security Services Act of 1989 heard 338 cases over 10 years, from 1989 to 1999, and never found a violation of law.[39] It is certainly possible that the mere existence of such tribunals and commissioners exerts a checking influence on law enforcement authorities but because so much is kept under wraps one cannot tell—and the raw numbers certainly do not give much ground for optimism on this score.

The UK is also less protective of privacy with respect to temporary stops and searches both for general criminal law and counter-terrorism purposes. As in the US, British officers may temporarily stop and search a person or vehicle where they have reasonable suspicion that he may be carrying contraband.[40] However, while the 'frisk' authorized in the US is limited to a pat down for weapons and only where there is reasonable suspicion that the individual is armed, British officers may search for contraband as well. The Home Office found that 87 per cent of stops and searches do not result in arrests,[41] suggesting that police officers' standard for suspicion appears to be quite low.

The Terrorism Act of 2000 went further, authorizing the police to designate certain geographical areas in which officers may stop and search any pedestrian or vehicle without any suspicion whatsoever.[42] The search is limited to items connected with terrorism. Area designations must be made by a supervisory police officer, are subject to review by the Secretary of State, and must be renewed every 28 days. Nonetheless, the entire metropolitan area of London has been subject to such a designation ever since the Terrorism Act of 2000 came into force in February 2001.[43] The Law Lords have upheld this authority

[38] See L Donohue, *The Cost of Counterterrorism: Power, Politics and Liberty* (Cambridge University Press, 2008) 197–9. [39] Ibid, 199.

[40] PACE, ss 1(2), 1(3), 1(7), and 1(8).

[41] S Uglow, *Criminal Justice* (2nd edn, Sweet & Maxwell, 2002) 120.

[42] Terrorism Act 2000, ss 44, 45.

[43] R Stone, *The Law of Entry, Search, and Seizure* (4th edn, Oxford University Press, 2004) 266; *R (Gillan) v Commissioner of Police for the Metropolis and anor* [2005] QB 388, 397 (rejecting a challenge to the continual designation of London for stops and searches without suspicion).

against legal challenge.[44] Thus, all Londoners are subject to stops and searches without suspicion in the name of fighting terrorism.

In addition, the UK has a domestic intelligence service, MI5, devoted to gathering intelligence at home. Several US commentators, most prominently Judge Richard Posner, have advocated that the US follow in Britain's footsteps in this regard.[45] They contend that, as a law enforcement agency, the FBI is ill-suited to gathering intelligence and that the US should therefore create a separate domestic intelligence unit along the lines of MI5. Civil liberties advocates have long opposed the creation of such an entity and have insisted on strict limits on what the CIA, the US foreign intelligence agency, may do with respect to domestic matters. Given the secrecy surrounding MI5 and its operations it is difficult to assess precisely how intrusive it is on the private lives of British residents but the mere fact that the UK has such an agency and the US has long rejected that option underscores the latter's greater sensitivity to privacy.

The UK may well appear to be the world leader in the proliferation of closed circuit television cameras, or CCTV, for crime prevention and detection purposes. The cameras are ubiquitous in London.[46] There has been little conclusive evidence that the cameras actually reduce crime but the cameras have proven useful in some settings, such as in identifying violators of traffic regulations and in conducting investigations after crimes have occurred.

One area in which UK citizens may have greater privacy protections than US citizens is government access to data about individuals held by third parties. In the modern era, virtually every transaction in which we engage, whether it be surfing the net, purchasing a cup of coffee with a credit card, checking out a book from the library, or emailing or telephoning friends, creates a computer trace of information held by banks, credit card companies, telecommunications companies, and Internet service providers. In the US, the Supreme Court has ruled that the Fourth Amendment does not protect this information from

[44] *R (Gillan) v Commissioner of Police for the Metropolis* [2006] UKHL 12.

[45] R Posner, 'We Need Our Own MI5' *Washington Post*, 15 August 2006, A 13.

[46] See 'Privacy vs. Security: Electronic Surveillance in the Nation's Capital: Hearing Before the Subcomm. On the District of Columbia of the Comm. On Government Reform', 107th Congress (2002) (statement of Rep Constance A Morella, Chairman); see also 'One Crime Solved for Every 1,000 CCTV Cameras Senior Officers Claim' *Telegraph.co.uk*, 24 October 2009, available at <http://www.telegraph.co.uk>,

government acquisition because individuals have no 'expectation of privacy' in information they have shared with another, at least vis-à-vis the government obtaining that information from the third party.[47] A patchwork of statutes protects some of this information from government acquisition, but these protections were weakened considerably after 9/11 by the USA Patriot Act.[48]

Europe appears to impose much more substantial restrictions on access to and processing of commercial data even by the private corporations that collect it in the first place. The UK is subject to those protections. Corporations are restricted in what they may do with personal information by the European Union Data Protection Directive.[49] However, RIPA expansively authorizes UK government officials to gather communications data for purposes of national security, detecting or preventing crime, promoting public health, or protecting the UK's economic well-being. These purposes are so expansive that they might conceivably justify the collection of vast amounts of data. At the end of the day, it is impossible to assess precisely the relative degrees of privacy in the US and the UK with respect to commercial data, as the legal protections are ambiguous, and neither government has revealed the extent to which it is in fact collecting and processing such data.

Accordingly, it seems fair to say that, data protection aside, privacy rights within the US are significantly greater than in the UK. Many of these differences are not specific to terrorism, but apply across the board. That is, UK residents generally have less privacy protections, regardless of whether the state's interest is traffic enforcement or counter-terrorism. Moreover, as noted above, there is much that we do not know, from the extent of the NSA warrantless wiretapping programme's intrusion on US phone and email communications, to the extent of data mining in both countries, to the practical working standards for suspicion actually employed in each country. Still, from what we can know, the UK authorizes intrusions on privacy on lower bases of suspicion and with fewer safeguards than does the US. And because it has no exclusionary rule, the UK also provides less effective enforcement of the laws that do purport to restrict surveillance.

[47] *California v Greenwood*, 486 US 35 (1988).

[48] See D Cole and J Dempsey, *Terrorism and the Constitution: Sacrificing Civil Liberties in the Name of National Security* (New Press, 2002) 107–76.

[49] Donohue, *The Cost of Counterterrorism*, n 40 above, 206–08.

Accounting for Differences

What might account for these differences in the UK's and the US's approaches to terrorism? Attributing causation for differences between nations is always a risky endeavour. There are so many possible factors at play that it is very likely impossible to specify with any certainty what accounts for the differences. Nonetheless, it may be enlightening to speculate about some possible explanations.

Experience

Virtually every British lawyer or scholar I asked about what might account for the character of their nation's response to terrorism cited the UK's lengthy experience in fighting the IRA. Yale Law Professor Bruce Ackerman has speculated that a series of terrorist attacks would create a spiralling effect of increasingly repressive security measures in the US.[50] In the UK's case, however, an extended experience with terrorism seems to have rendered the populace and their leaders less susceptible to panic and more able to respond in a calibrated way to terrorist threats.

In part, a long experience with terrorism may adjust public expectations. The British have seen that one cannot simply strong-arm one's way out of the problem; no defence shield is impermeable, particularly in an open society, and committed terrorists will find a way to strike. A lengthy terrorist and counter-terrorist campaign underscores the reality that while the risk of terrorism can be managed and reduced, it cannot be eliminated. In the US, politicians acknowledge this reality at their peril, as Democratic presidential candidate John Kerry learned when he was derided for suggesting during the 2004 campaign that Americans need to learn to live with the risk of terrorism.[51] Unrealistic demands that terrorism be eliminated may push government officials to take more extreme measures than are otherwise justified. Some British experts have suggested that their relevant national experience in this regard goes back to World War II, when London was bombed on a regular basis. Many of the country's elder statesmen lived through those bombing raids, and all of the nation's leaders lived through part or all

[50] B Ackerman, *Before the Next Attack: Preserving Civil Liberties in an Age of Terrorism: Emergency Powers in an Age of Terrorism* (Yale University Press, 2006).

[51] See M Bai 'Kerry's Undeclared War', *New York Times*, 10 October 2004, available at <http://www.nytimes.com/2004/10/10/magazine/10KERRY.html>.

of the ensuing IRA struggle. The US, by contrast, has been relatively free of bombings and attacks, terrorist or military, on domestic soil, and therefore may have been less well prepared to respond in a measured way when the attacks came on 9/11.

More importantly, however, UK officials of all stripes emphasize that the primary lesson of the IRA experience was that overly repressive responses are very often counterproductive.[52] The UK's initial responses to IRA terror were strikingly similar to the US responses to Al-Qaeda thirty years later—they deployed the military, interned large numbers of loosely-labelled suspects without trial, and used coercive interrogation tactics, which they claimed fell short of torture, to compel suspects to talk. Over time the UK learned that these methods backfired. A military approach played into the IRA's hands; they wanted to be treated as warriors, not criminals.[53] Internment and coercive interrogation led to the identification of few actual terrorists yet radicalized the Nationalist community, encouraging some to join the IRA, and many others to support its actions covertly.[54]

Indeed, as Professor Conor Gearty, Former Director of the Centre for the Study of Human Rights at the London School of Economics, told me, the struggle with the IRA may be 'the defining event in the political and legal education of many of the UK's leaders today.' Many of the UK's elite lawyers and politicians grew up in the cauldron of that long struggle, and were on the front lines of those criticizing government overreactions to the IRA as both a violation of human rights values and counterproductive. They now hold the reins of power, and while that experience does not entirely eliminate the temptation to overreact, it appears to have left the British elite more open to arguments about the importance of restraint.[55]

[52] See generally the analysis of the impact of the Northern Ireland experience in L Richardson, *What Terrorists Want: Understanding the Enemy* (Random House, 2006).

[53] Ibid.

[54] Ibid. See also M O'Connor and C Rumann, 'Into the Fire: How to Avoid Getting Burned by the Same Mistakes Made Fighting Terrorism in Northern to Ireland' (2005) *Cardozo Law Review* 24, 1662; C Campbell and I Connolly, 'Making War on Terror? Global Lessons From Northern Ireland' (2006) *Modern Law Review* 69, 935–57.

[55] The fact that a Labour government was in power when the terrorist attacks of 9/11 and 7/7 occurred, while a Republican administration was in the White House, may also account for some of the differences. Before the terrorist attacks, the Labour government, after all, spearheaded the campaign to incorporate the European Convention on Human Rights into UK domestic law, and that government has historically been closer to the stance traditionally adopted by the Democratic Party in the US on issues of rights and liberties. The Bush administration, by contrast, was not known for its commitment to

Experience may also explain the US's apparently greater sensitivity to rights of privacy. The principal example of government overreaction to a security threat in US history prior to 9/11 was the FBI's extensive surveillance and harassment of liberal and progressive organizations and individuals in the 1950s, 1960s and 1970s. In the name of identifying Communists, the FBI infiltrated, surveilled, and conducted a range of 'dirty tricks' against civil rights activists and groups (including Dr Martin Luther King, Jr, whose hotel room the FBI bugged), anti-war demonstrators, environmentalists, and many others. These abuses were revealed in detail in a series of public congressional hearings conducted by Senator Frank Church in the 1970s. Those hearings, covered extensively in the press, showed Americans in very dramatic fashion that intelligence and surveillance in the name of national security could easily become a tool for targeting lawful, non- violent, and legitimate dissent. In response to that experience, Congress and the executive both imposed a variety of safeguards on surveillance and intelligence gathering, all designed to forestall such abuses in the future.

Thus, while the formative experience of overreaction for today's British leaders was the administrative detention and coercive interrogation of IRA suspects, the formative experience for today's American leaders was the political spying scandal exposed by the Church Commission. Rights protections and consciousness often arise in reaction to evidence of abuse, and the distinct experiences of abuse in the two countries may account for some of the differences outlined above. It is still too early to tell, but it may well be that the Bush administration's 'war on terror' may provide important lessons for Americans in the dangers of administrative detention and coercive interrogation, leading to more sensible and rights-regarding security policies in these areas in the future.

International Law Oversight

Another possible explanation for the different UK and US approaches to counter-terrorism may lie in the two countries' very different relations to international law. Many of the most significant reforms in UK counter-terrorism strategy have come about in substantial part because of international law. For 50 years, the UK has been subject to a

civil rights or liberties even before 9/11. At the same time, this explanation is plainly too simple. Some of the strongest proponents of civil liberties in the UK have been members of the Conservative Party.

meaningful, enforceable international human rights regime under the European Convention on Human Rights ('ECHR')[56]. The UK signed and ratified the Convention in 1951, the first country to do so. In 1966, it recognized the right of individuals to challenge British laws and executive actions before the European Commission and Court of Human Rights. The existence of an international judicial check is particularly important where national security concerns are at stake, because it requires the UK to justify its actions not only to members of its own government, but to judges from other nations who, because they are outside the UK, are likely to be able to assess the situation more objectively. Thus, it was the European Court of Human Rights, not any domestic British court, that declared invalid, as a violation of the European Convention on Human Rights, Britain's use of 'moderate physical pressure' to interrogate IRA suspects;[57] its attempt to deport suspected terrorists to countries where they face a risk of torture;[58] and its unregulated use of wiretapping.[59] In each area, the UK responded by reforming its laws.

Critics of international law and tribunals often criticize them for their 'democratic deficit,' by which they mean the fact that they are not in any direct way held accountable to an electorate. But this distance from democracy may in fact be a good thing, in much the way that life tenure for Article III judges in the United States is thought to be beneficial. It provides an institutional oversight mechanism that, precisely because it is less susceptible to the political exigencies of a particular national system, may be able to offer the benefit of the long view. The flipside, of course, is that an international court may not be as attuned to the specific conditions of, or challenges faced by, particular nations. The European Court of Human Rights employs what it calls a 'margin of appreciation' in order to reflect just that fact; the result is that a degree of diversity in different nations' approaches to common problems is tolerated.[60] But as the UK cases cited above well demonstrate, the 'margin of appreciation' does not mean complete deference.

[56] Convention for the Protection of Human Rights and Fundamental Freedoms (4 November 1950) 213 UNTS 222; 312 ETS 5, entered into force 3 September 1953.

[57] *Ireland v United Kingdom* (1978) 2 EHRR 25.

[58] *Chahal v United Kingdom* (1996) 23 EHRR 413.

[59] *Malone v United Kingdom* (1984) 7 EHRR 14.

[60] See the analysis in O Gross and F Ní Aoláin, 'From Discretion to Scrutiny: Revisiting the Application of the Margin of Appreciation Doctrine in the Context of Article 15 of the European Convention on Human Rights' (2001) 23 *Human Rights Quarterly* 625.

The legitimacy of the ECHR in the UK, despite its so-called 'democratic deficits,' was dramatically underscored by the UK's decision in 1998 to make the European Convention directly enforceable by its own courts. This decision to 'bring rights home,' as the campaign slogan put it, suggests that at some level, despite its many losses before the European Court, the British public accepted the legitimate role that an international human rights enforcement mechanism had to play. Adopting the Human Rights Act was no mean feat in a nation that has never had a written Constitution and that maintains a strong fidelity to parliamentary supremacy. For the first time, the law gave British courts the power to adjudicate claims that British executive actions and laws conflict with the European Convention. Prior to its enactment, aggrieved citizens were unable to pursue such claims domestically, and instead had to wait and take their case to Strasbourg—a time-consuming and expensive process that was not feasible for many. Under the HRA, British courts may declare executive action invalid for violating the ECHR. But the Act required an ingenious compromise in order to accommodate the new role that the Act gave the courts with the supremacy traditionally accorded parliament. Courts may not declare legislation invalid under the ECHR; rather, the Act directs courts to interpret statutes as far as possible to render them consistent with ECHR demands, and gives them the power only to declare a statute 'incompatible' with the ECHR. Such a declaration has no legal effect of its own force; it is up to parliament to choose how to respond.

This compromise, necessitated by the unwillingness to abandon parliamentary supremacy, might appear to be a fatal flaw from an American perspective, where federal courts have long exercised the power to invalidate federal statutes that they deem unconstitutional. But the compromise has thus far worked very effectively. The Law Lords have declared laws incompatible with the European Convention about 15 times—and each time parliament has responded by abandoning or revising the provision called into question.[61] Such responses

[61] As of 23 May 2007, 24 declarations of incompatibility had been made by domestic courts under the HRA. Of these, 6 had been subsequently overturned on appeal and 1 at the time remained subject to appeal: however, 11 had been addressed and remedied by new primary legislation or remedial orders; 1 was in the course of being addressed by a Bill before parliament at that time; and the government was considering how to remedy 5 more declarations of incompatibility. In no case had the government refused to respond to a declaration of incompatibility. See *Monitoring the Government's Response to Court Judgments Finding Breaches of Human Rights*, Joint Committee on Human Rights, 16th Report, Session 2006–07, HL 128/HC 728, 18 June 2007, para 109.

may not be entirely voluntary, as parliament surely knows that if it fails to comply the case will go to the European Court of Human Rights, which is likely to back the view of the British courts as to what the European Convention demands of the British. Still, the fact that as a formal matter parliament need not comply and that the declaration of incompatibility does not invalidate any statutory provision means that each time parliament does comply it lends further legitimacy to the Law Lords' ruling—and to the Convention itself. At the same time, it may be that because a declaration of incompatibility is less drastic medicine than an outright invalidation, decisions upholding the Convention and calling statutes into question may be easier for the Law Lords to issue.

The Law Lords' decision declaring indefinite detention of foreign nationals incompatible with the European Convention illustrates another critical feature of the UK's embrace of the Convention as it relates to counter-terrorism initiatives. Nations in crisis often seek to enhance security by selectively sacrificing the rights of the most vulnerable people, especially foreign nationals.[62] That is an easy way to cheat on the trade-offs between rights and security, as foreign nationals typically lack a voice in the political process.

In the indefinite detention case, the Law Lords proclaimed such a double standard a violation of the European Convention. A similar ruling would be extremely unlikely from the US Supreme Court under the US Constitution, at least as it is currently understood. Indeed, in 2003, the Supreme Court stated that 'Congress may make rules as to aliens that would be unacceptable if applied to citizens,' expressly invoking a double standard to uphold a statute that authorized preventive detention of certain foreign nationals without an individualized determination that they posed any risk of flight or danger to others.[63]

An *international* human rights treaty is far less likely to tolerate distinctions based on citizenship, because its foundation is built on a universalist conception of human dignity, and because the document itself is transnational. If a nation is precluded from selectively imposing burdens on foreign nationals, and must instead treat foreign nationals and its own citizens alike, the political process is likely to ensure that its initiatives are more measured and more sensitive to rights concerns. Given the temptation, especially in counter-terrorism law and policy,

[62] D Cole, *Enemy Aliens: Double Standards and Constitutional Freedoms in the War on Terror* (revised edn 2005).

[63] *Demore v Hyung Joon Kim*, 538 US 510, 522 (2003).

to exploit double standards based on citizenship, this non-discrimination principle is likely to be an especially important check on abuse in the name of security.

In any event, it is clear that the ECHR and, in particular, its incorporation into domestic law via the Human Rights Act, have helped transform the role of the legal profession and courts in the UK. Lawyers suddenly have entirely new legal claims that they can pursue on behalf of individual rights. And courts have newfound power to protect individual rights. In some instances, the effects are direct, as when the Law Lords declared the 2001 indefinite detention law incompatible with the European Convention. In other cases, the effect is more indirect, as the courts increasingly interpret British law to conform to Convention principles, as the Law Lords did in ruling that British common law barred the admission of torture evidence even in non-criminal cases. But either way, the ECHR and the HRA have brought welcome international oversight to the UK legal system that may help reduce the extent to which the UK overreacts to new terrorist threats. The US, by contrast, remains largely immune to meaningful international oversight.

Extrajudicial Protections of Rights

American constitutional scholars, frustrated with the conservative direction of the current US Supreme Court, have increasingly looked to alternative forms of constitutional protection, and have argued that we need to encourage forms of 'extrajudicial constitutionalism'—which means constitutional decision-making by the political branches, and even by the people themselves. I am sceptical of such arguments to the extent that they reduce the courts' obligation to protect constitutional rights. Political actors are likely to advance or protect constitutional rights only where the rights are sufficiently popular to not need to be constitutionalized. Those most in need of protection—the criminally accused, members of minority groups, and foreign nationals—are generally unlikely to receive the attention, much less the protection, of Congress or the executive. Thus it may be a mistake to vest much hope in extra-judicial constitutionalism.

In the UK, however, perhaps because constitutional protections as the US understands them do not exist, alternative ways to check abuses of power have developed. Consider Lord Alex Carlile of Berriew, appointed in 2001 as the 'independent reviewer' of terrorism legislation. A barrister, former Deputy High Court Judge, and Liberal Democratic member of the House of Lords, as independent reviewer Lord Carlile investigates and reports to the public on the application and enforcement of anti-terrorism legislation. He appears to act in a truly independent fashion sometimes siding with the government and differing from the human rights community, as on the subject of 'control orders,' and sometimes siding with human rights advocates and against the government, as when he was critical of the 2001 indefinite detention law before the Law Lords declared it incompatible with the European Convention.

Similar watchdog roles have been assigned to commissioners who oversee the implementation of laws governing surveillance as discussed above. Such commissioners are generally given inspection powers and full access to government records and files. They act both by bringing pressure to bear within the government, and by issuing reports and public statements.

In addition, parliament's Joint Committee on Human Rights, comprised of members of both the House of Lords and the House of Commons, has played a significant role in providing independent and rigorous 'scrutiny' of pending terrorism bills with respect to their implications for, and compatibility with, the European Convention on Human Rights. The Committee's views are taken very seriously, and its careful, well-reasoned, and timely reports play an important role in shaping parliamentary debates on such bills.[64]

In the US, congressional committees sometimes perform such oversight roles but they generally have a lot of other work on their plate, and their principal focus is on legislation, not implementation. Most US executive branch departments have inspectors general, and the Department of Homeland Security has both a Privacy Officer and a Civil Rights Officer, but these officials are all part of the executive branch, often come from the same party as the executive and rarely issue public reports calling the executive to task for violation of individual rights.[65]

[64] For an analysis of the impact of the JCHR on parliamentary processes in the UK, see J Hiebert, 'Parliament and the Human Rights Act: Can the JCHR Help Facilitate a Culture of Rights?' (2006) 4(1) International Journal of Constitutional Law 1–38.

[65] The Justice Department's Inspector General has been a welcome exception to the rule since 9/11, publishing important critical reports on such issues as the abuse of immigration powers to round up foreign nationals in the year following 9/11, and on the exploding and often illegal use of 'national security letters,' a form of administrative subpoena, after the USA PATRIOT Act vastly expanded the sorts of information that could be obtained with such letters.

Privacy and Liberty Trade-offs?

As we have seen, the UK has been more restrained on issues of detention and interrogation, while the US seems to have been more restrained on issues of privacy and surveillance. Might these respective differences be related? Could it be that the gross over-reaching that characterized the US response to 9/11 was in part attributable to the disastrous state of US intelligence about Al-Qaeda and that US ignorance about Al-Qaeda was in turn a function of privacy protections? As former attorney-general John Ashcroft admits in his memoir of his time at the Justice Department, the government felt great pressure after 9/11 to prevent the next attack, but 'we didn't yet know who the terrorists were, or where we could find them.' Accordingly, he writes, 'we had to buy time.'[66] Sweeping blindly, the US government detained over 5,000 foreign nationals in the United States in the first two years after 9/11, none of whom stands convicted of terrorism today. It brought approximately 775 persons to Guantanamo, more than 500 of whom have subsequently been released, suggesting that they may not have been the 'worst of the worst' after all. And once it had pre-emptively rounded up thousands of 'suspects'—here and abroad—there were no longer many ways to gather intelligence about them other than interrogation, leading the authorities to authorize harshly coercive interrogation tactics. As Sir David Omand said at a counter-terrorism conference in London in 2006, 'without good intelligence, you're driven to use a bludgeon rather than a rapier.' In the wake of 9/11, the US generally used a bludgeon, and it is at least possible that it did so because its intelligence was so flimsy.

By contrast, if the state has a good idea about where the threat lies, it need not sweep so widely or intervene so pre-emptively. It can instead conduct surveillance, attempt to infiltrate the suspect group, and undertake further investigation. If the government has identified a potentially dangerous individual, and that individual does not know that the government is watching him, he may reveal much more reliable information about what he plans to do and with whom he plans to do it than he would under direct interrogation. Police can observe who an unaware suspect calls, where he goes, and what he does, and in

[66] J Ashcroft, *Never Again: Securing America and Restoring Justice* (Center Street, 2006).

so doing can acquire admissible evidence that can then be used to bring the individual—and his accomplices—to justice once he is arrested. In all three instances discussed above in which the UK disrupted serious terrorist plots, British authorities had the perpetrators under extended surveillance long before they were arrested, and only arrested them when they had developed evidence of wrongdoing and felt that they could wait no longer. In all three instances, probably because police had done the old-fashioned detective work first, the suspects were caught in possession of substantial incriminating evidence.

The Scotland Yard approach also suggests that with good intelligence, the post-9/11 conventional wisdom that law enforcement is necessarily reactive and backward-looking, and therefore ill-suited to preventing terrorism, is wrong. In fact, traditional police work may be more effective at disrupting plots than precipitate interventions that may ensnare innocents, foreclose intelligence gathering, and make it more difficult to hold suspects accountable. Constitutional and human rights law both recognize the validity of surveillance, searches, informants, and interrogation, not only to investigate past crimes, but also to disrupt ongoing plots and conspiracies. And the law of 'attempt' and conspiracy means that individuals may be arrested and held accountable for initial steps toward uncompleted crimes; officers need not wait until the proverbial bomb goes off before they can investigate, arrest, or even prosecute. But to do so effectively requires good intelligence.

In some sense, the speculation that limits on privacy may reduce the need for other sacrifices in human rights is the flipside of Michel Foucault's insight that the modern state exercises power not so much through harsh punishment as through the close observation and regulation of day-to-day activity by a variety of state institutions.[67] Foucault famously invoked as a metaphor Jeremy Bentham's Panopticon, an architectural design that enables prison guards to observe prisoners efficiently without letting the prisoners know that they are under observation. In Foucault's telling, as state power evolves into a less harshly punitive but more closely insinuated regulatory form the state exercises greater and greater disciplinary control over the body politic and freedom is insidiously diminished. But what if giving the state more expansive ability to observe its residents' private activities contributed to a more measured approach with respect to

[67] M Foucault, *Discipline & Punish: The Birth of the Prison* (Vintage Books: New York, 1995) translated from the French by Alan Sheridan (original publication 1975).

other liberties, such as the freedoms from detention, disappearance, and torture?

At the same time, broader intelligence powers and less robust privacy protections may not necessarily yield less extreme intrusion on other rights. What Sir David Omand said was that 'good intelligence' allows the state to use a rapier rather than a bludgeon—but good intelligence does not necessarily equate with reduced privacy protections. Intelligence gathering can be improved in a variety of ways fully consistent with maintaining privacy protections. According to the 9/11 Commission and most commentators inside and outside of government, the principal problems that US intelligence and law enforcement apparatuses faced before 9/11 were not that they lacked the legal authority to gather intelligence about Al-Qaeda, but that they had failed to focus sufficient resources on Al-Qaeda; had ignored certain warning signs that at least in retrospect stick out like red flags; had far too few Arabic speakers as employees, agents, and analysts; were reluctant to share information across agencies; and had failed to prioritize analysis of the voluminous data they did have. All of these problems may be solved—and intelligence improved—without reducing protections for privacy.

Indeed, constitutional privacy safeguards may make intelligence and law enforcement more efficient. By requiring the state to justify intrusive surveillance by pointing to objective evidence of wrongdoing, rising to the level of either reasonable suspicion or probable cause, the Constitution discourages wild goose chases and sweeping collections of evidence that are likely to waste resources and drown intelligence analysts in static. If the problem before 9/11 was a failure to 'connect the dots,' reducing the standards for surveillance is likely to generate still more dots, and because the standard for surveillance would be lower, the vast majority of the dots would likely involve no terrorist activity whatsoever. The result is as likely to obfuscate the line between the dots as it is to help bring it into focus.

There is, however, another sense in which privacy and liberty may be in tension. One of the striking features of domestic American politics of security since 9/11 is that proposed and actual invasions of privacy have tended to provoke more widespread political resistance than seemingly more extreme measures, including preventive detention, Guantanamo, torture, disappearances, and rendition. The USA Patriot Act provisions that generated the most attention were search provisions—such as those authorizing roving wiretaps, 'sneak-and-peek' searches, national security letters, and demands for the production of third-party records.

Other Patriot Act provisions were arguably more egregious but received little attention, including one that authorized preventive detention of foreign nationals suspected of terrorist ties, and another that authorized the Treasury Department to freeze an organization's assets and effectively shut it down without finding any violation of law, on the basis of secret evidence never disclosed to the affected group.

Similarly, the first three post-9/11 security initiatives by the executive to prompt Congressional action in favour of civil rights all involved intrusions on privacy: a proposal to study national identity cards; Total Information Awareness (a data mining programme run out of the Pentagon); and Operation TIPS (a Justice Department plan to recruit millions of citizens to spy on their neighbours and report suspicious activities to the FBI). Congress expressly barred the expenditure of funds on all three programmes.

By contrast, Congress took no action on Guantanamo or the issue of detaining 'enemy combatants' until the Supreme Court declared the president's military tribunals illegal. When Congress did eventually act, it largely ratified what President Bush had been doing previously in violation of the law, with only minor modifications. Congress took no action to condemn or close down the secret CIA prisons into which suspects were 'disappeared' for years, to challenge rendition, or to demand fair proceedings for enemy combatants. Congress did reject the Bush administration's view that the international prohibition on cruel, inhuman, and degrading treatment was categorically inapplicable to foreign nationals held outside US borders, but it provided no enforcement mechanism in the event that the administration continued to engage in such abuse.

The American public, it seems, has been much more sensitive to incursions on privacy rights than on rights of liberty, dignity, and autonomy. The US may therefore have adopted more extreme detention and interrogation measures because it was less costly in political terms than infringing on privacy.

Inside/Outside

The final explanation for the differences between the counter-terrorism policies of the UK and the US looks to the nature of the attacks each nation has suffered, and the nature of the threats each nation faces.[68] In

[68] I am indebted to David Omand for making this suggestion to me in conversation in 2006.

the US, the attacks came from outside, and the threat is predominantly external. In the UK, the attacks and plots have largely been the work of British nationals, and the threat is significantly internal. This explanation may help make sense of the particular difference this chapter has identified, namely between surveillance on the one hand and detention and interrogation on the other. When one is attacked from without, the natural reaction is to fight back—and to quickly divide the world into 'us' and 'them' in doing so. That dynamic makes overreaction almost inevitable. In addition, when one is attacked from without, one is likely to emphasize methods that incapacitate the 'enemy,' in particular detention. And when one is fighting an external foe, one is especially likely to demonize and dehumanize, thus making possible the kinds of inhuman treatment of detainees authorized by the Bush administration.

By contrast, when one is attacked from within, one searches for a cure, not a fight. One's response is likely to be more measured, but also more watchful. If the source of the threat is within, a nation is likely to emphasize surveillance. Just as a patient who is ill willingly surrenders his privacy to the doctor who seeks to cure him, so a nation that perceives itself as under attack from within may be more likely to accept sacrifices in privacy. And where the threat comes from one's own population, it will be more difficult to separate neatly 'us' and 'them,' and resort to double standards may be less acceptable.

The difference between attacks from within and without also helps to explain what is perhaps the most striking disagreement between the US and the UK (and indeed all of Europe); namely, whether it was appropriate for the US to respond to the 9/11 attacks by declaring a 'war on terror.' One of the most common refrains in the UK and Europe contends that the proper way to address terrorism is through the criminal justice (and administrative) system of ordinary law, not by declaring war and employing the military. There is certainly much to be said for this position. As Louise Richardson has argued, labelling terrorists 'warriors' may be just what they want, and may in the long run be self-defeating.[69] But it is of course much easier to advocate a criminal over a military response where the threat is internal rather than external. States are loath to admit that an opposition force within their borders is 'at war' with them, but have far less compunction when the

[69] L Richardson, *What Terrorists Want: Understanding the Enemy* (Random House, 2006).

threat comes from outside. And the criminal process may be much more difficult to employ against overseas threats.

Conclusion

The US and the UK have now each had significant experience with the perils of terrorism and, equally importantly, with the perils of fighting terrorism. Both have been susceptible to unprincipled overreaction, abandoning basic commitments to individual rights in times of fear. The UK's experience, however, suggests that it is possible for nations to learn from their prior mistakes. Its response to Islamic terrorism today seems, at least in part, to be tempered by the lessons it learned in fighting the IRA. An irreversible downward spiral in rights protections is not inevitable. The learning process must of course be an ongoing one, and does not by any means guarantee that mistakes will not be repeated. But it helps. Such a learning process may now be underway in the United States, where the Obama administration has sought to strike a very different tone from that of its predecessor.[70] As globalization brings nations closer together and facilitates the transnational exchange of experiences and information, comparative inquiry may prove more and more fruitful in helping nations learn, not only from their own mistakes, but from the mistakes of others. There is of course no universal 'right' way to respond to terrorism, but there may well be 'wrong' ways to go about it. The goal of comparative investigation should not be simply to identify powers employed by one country that are not available in the other (as former Attorney-General Gonzales seemed to think), but to develop a deeper understanding of the nature of the challenge that terrorism poses to democracy, and a more nuanced sense of how different circumstances may contribute to different policy outcomes.

[70] Compare President Obama's first major speech on national security given the same day that former vice-president Dick Cheney gave a speech defending the Bush administration's approach at the American Enterprise Institute. 'Remarks by the President on National Security', The White House, 21 May 2009 available at <http://www.whitehouse.gov/the_press_office/Remarks-by-the-President-On-National-Security-5-21-09/>; 'Remarks by Richard B Cheney', American Enterprise Institute, 21 May 2009 available at <http://www.aei.org/speech/100050>.

Art, Law, and Creativity

*Sarah Worthington**

We all think we know something about art. Indeed, many of us have a passionate part-time interest in it. And as lawyers we surely know something about law. This chapter begins with those two strands, and takes the perspective of an outsider looking in, asking whether the legal regime around art (more narrowly, paintings) is one that assists in delivering incentives for 'creativity' amongst artists and increasing the chances of the public having greater access to works of art. This tension between private incentives and public benefit is familiar in the workings of the law.

This chapter was something of a summer frolic since I am not an expert in art law or intellectual property law. On the other hand, it is not completely unfamiliar territory. One of my areas of interest as a lawyer is personal property. Normally I focus on debts and derivatives rather than cars and bicycles, and look at the ways the law goes about protecting those particular intangible, non-physical, forms of wealth. So at one level this digression into art is simply a rather predictable transition to investigate how intellectual property—or rights somehow related to creative ideas—fits into that property spectrum. I wanted to know what, if anything, the law does or can do to ensure that we continue to have the benefits of a public domain of creative works. If we really understand why art is special and who it is special to (a challenge which is well beyond the reach of this chapter), then we are in a better position to decide what structures, strategies and protections the law could put in place to protect this special value. This is the role of law—to protect interests in such a way as to allow societies to function and to facilitate development of the things we value.

* Professor of Law, London School of Economics and Political Science.

Is Art Especially Valuable?

Value is hard to measure. People certainly seem to be increasingly interested in art. As Thornton notes in her recent popular book:[1]

> The art market is booming. Museum attendances are surging. More people than ever call themselves artists. Contemporary art has become a mass entertainment, a luxury good, a job description and a kind of alternative religion for atheists. Art receives the sort of breathless media attention once reserved for celebrities and royals.

And this is despite the fact that, as she adds, 'the art world is still opaque to outsiders.'[2]

Opaque or not, people are certainly prepared to pay a lot for art. Recall the eye-watering prices paid for Damian Hirst pieces at a Sotheby auction just the evening before Lehman Brothers collapsed: over £110 million was spent in an evening. Or consider the advertisements in any weekend *Financial Times*. A recent special section on collecting[3] included a Sotheby's advertisements for a Lucian Freud painting (a mere £10–15 million), and an Edvard Munch painting (this one an 'estimate on request', that cryptic indication of a stratospheric sum).

Clearly these prices are not for materials and labour. They reflect the financial uplift that creativity can add to the raw ingredients of canvas plus paint. Viewed through that sort of lens, the financial multiplier delivered by artist and art dealer makes the financial sector's sub-prime industry look naive. And, counter-intuitively, art dealers have typically defined themselves as anti-commercial, 'disinterested promoters and patrons rather than merchants and marketers of art.'[4] Despite this, they still manage to transform goods which lack any direct utilitarian value into some of the most highly priced commodities of modern retail markets, and, more strikingly still, to do that when these works are 'hardly meaningful, intelligible or valuable to people outside of the art world'.[5]

But these prices are not entirely and extravagantly fantastic; they reflect an added value we attach to art. We do not put art, even art investments, in quite the same category as financial investments; we think there is something quite different in paying £25 million for a

[1] S Thornton, *Seven Days in the Art World* (Granta Publications, 2008) ix.
[2] Ibid [3] *Financial Times*, 11 October 2008.
[4] O Velthuis, *Talking Prices: Symbolic Meaning of Prices on the Market for Contemporary Art* (Princeton University Press, 2005) 21. [5] Ibid, 23.

painting compared with £25 million for a collateralized debt instrument. That leads to the common assertion that we are purchasing or protecting something more emotional and fundamentally societal. This is reinforced when we appreciate that it is not simply odd (or even oddly rich) individuals who are so moved. Countries fight for their art and their cultural property. The Elgin Marbles in the British Museum provide a very public example of contested possession. So too do nationwide bids for funds to prevent the export of national treasures to rich buyers overseas, as happened in the UK to save one version of Canova's Three Graces[6] for the nation.

Foreign states are no different. The 2008 Royal Academy exhibition, 'From Russia: French and Russian Master Paintings 1870–1925' is a contemporary illustration. The Russian authorities refused to release the 120 paintings for the exhibition until something formal was done to address their very real fears that the paintings might be seized. In the end, the UK Culture Secretary, James Purnell, saved the exhibition by bringing forward the enactment of a provision of the Tribunals, Courts and Enforcement Act 2007. The issue was seen as important in meeting public interest—millions viewed the exhibition—and perhaps even in easing tensions between Russia and the UK following the Litvinenko incident.[7]

Clearly art (or at least some art) is of interest and of value, financial and otherwise, to individuals and to the public. We may not be quite sure what counts as art, and indeed the popularity and financial value of art changes, but art is commonly regarded not simply as property which is the subject of individual and private ownership, but also property of value to the public (or to 'the commons', as it is described in the US).

Putting this more specifically, and focusing on artwork by painters, the common conclusion is that to deliver these goals we need legal rules that protect the artists ' creativity, autonomy, labour, and the product of their efforts, and provide for better public engagement by delivering more and better art into the public domain.

[6] This version is shared between the Victoria and Albert Museum and the National Galleries of Scotland. Another, earlier, version is in the Hermitage.

[7] The masterpieces included paintings by renowned artists such as Cezanne, van Gogh and Picasso, as well as by prominent Russian artists. The paintings were all owned by Russia's most prestigious museums, but the Russian Federal Agency of Culture and Cinematography claimed that British law did not protect the paintings from seizure as a result of law suits or court decisions.

This easy assertion is, however, worth brief pause for thought. We take this approach for granted when talking about art and artists, and indeed all intellectual property. Private interests and public good are held in delicate balance so as to deliver the greatest good for the greatest number. But precisely the opposite is true of other forms of personal property. There, private rights dominate, and *exclusion* of the public is the order of the day. What permits the agreed pursuit of such different ends with art? What justifies this quite different special social goals to 'special legal rules' translation? Clearly this is too big a question for this chapter, but it merits at least a limited digression.

Creative ideas are widely recognized as valuable. They are clearly a good thing for society. The modern expression, the knowledge economy, simply puts a new label on that old idea. And just as the knowledge economy is not a new idea, neither is the almost universal recognition that generating a source of ideas for the benefit of society requires some form of protection for the creators of those ideas, so that they have some incentive to create. But in the UK at least, that incentive is carefully balanced against the goals of ensuring delivery of any general good that might be derived from the ideas if they are widely exposed. This idea of a balanced and carefully negotiated social contract exposes a rationale that appears to lie behind all property rights. In dealing with commercial property, the typical answer to the social contract question is to deliver maximum benefits by favouring the values of individual autonomy and public (or market) certainty. Art puts the goalposts in a different place because art has a value that is more than commercial. It is worth asking whether the current positioning of the legal goalposts is effective in delivering the twin goals of increased incentives to artists and increased accessibility by the public.

Incentives that Promote Creativity

Legal regimes work by giving rights to certain groups, and ensuring those rights are respected because of a carefully defended and robust adherence to the rule of law. The issue here is what sort of rights should be given to which groups in order to promote artistic (and other forms of) creativity for public benefit. There are four principal theoretical justifications for legal models that are designed to promote artistic (and other forms of) creativity for public benefit.[8]

[8] S Stokes, *Art and Copyright* (Hart Publishing, 2003) 10ff, describes the first three.

Moral Arguments

The first argument is that artists have intrinsic moral rights to their creative efforts.[9] This analysis is typically sourced to Locke or, on a slightly different basis, to Kant and Hegel. John Locke bases his analysis on the idea of a 'just reward' for labour.[10] As Fisher describes it:

> . . . a person who labours upon resources that are either unowned or 'held in common' has a natural property right to the fruits of his or her efforts – and that the state has a duty to respect and enforce that natural right. These ideas, originating in the writings of John Locke, are widely thought to be especially applicable to the field of intellectual property, where the pertinent raw materials (facts and concepts) do seem in some sense to be 'held in common' and where labour seems to contribute so importantly to the value of finished products . . .[11]

The analysis put forward by Kant and Hegel is, by contrast, grounded in the value of individual personhood, from which flows the idea that under natural law artists (and other creators) have an exclusive right of property in their labours. As described again by Fisher, this analysis proposes:

> . . .that private property rights are crucial to the satisfaction of some fundamental human needs; policymakers should thus strive to create and allocate entitlements to resources in the fashion that best enables people to fulfil those needs. From this standpoint, intellectual property rights may be justified either on the ground that they shield from appropriation or modification artefacts through which authors and artists have expressed their 'wills' (an activity thought central to 'personhood') or on the ground that they create social and economic conditions conducive to creative intellectual activity, which in turn is important to human flourishing . . .[12]

These arguments, based on the moral and just treatment of persons, support artists' ownership not just of the tangible creations they produce, but also ownership of the intellectual property behind their

[9] Stokes, n 8 above, 12; similarly L Bently and B Sherman, *Intellectual Property Law* (2nd edn, Oxford University Press, 2001) 33–4.

[10] J Locke, *Second Treatise on Government* (1690) discussed in GB Ramello, 'Intellectual Property and the Markets of Ideas' in JG Backhaus (ed), *The Elgar Companion to Law and Economics* (2nd edn, Edward Elgar, 2005) 127–44 at 128.

[11] W Fisher, 'Theories of Intellectual Property', in SR Munzer (ed), *New Essays in the Legal and Political Theory of Property* (Cambridge University Press, 2001) 168–200, also available at <http://www.law.harvard.edu/faculty/tfisher/iptheory.html>, from which this extract is taken.

[12] Ibid

endeavours. In effect, intellectual property rights are justified in the same way as all personal property rights, and are merely added to the panoply of those rights. The public benefit angle is recognized, if at all, simply as an inevitable and desirable side-benefit of the private rights that artists are justly granted. In short, there is no judicious weighing to determine some prudent division between private and public rights, with a decision to limit one in favour of expanding the other.

Economic Arguments

The second, and more modern, argument is based on economic analysis, and is overtly far more attuned to balancing private and public interests. At root, the economic argument is that copyright ensures that artists profit from their creative efforts (the static element); this in turn provides the necessary incentive for artists to create, and for intermediate parties (dealers, publishers, etc) to invest in exploiting their efforts (the dynamic element).[13]

The economic theory of property provides one explanation of why these assertions make sense.[14] This economic/property rationale was accepted by Adam Smith almost 250 years ago, admittedly in a rather lukewarm fashion. The idea was then developed by Jeremy Bentham into a more robust utilitarian theory of 'an incentive to create'. Bentham recognized that 'he who has no hope that he will reap, will not take the trouble to sow.'[15] He also recognized what we now term the problem of free-riding: that, without legal protection, artists (and other creators) are exposed to the risk that others will appropriate their innovations without bearing the creative cost, and will then be able to 'reap where they have not sown' by selling at more competitive lower prices.[16] Rousseau, too, adopted a similar line.[17]

These economic arguments recognize that the value of this form of proprietary protection is not simply the benefit created for the artist, but also the benefit for society as a whole; it plays to the perceived centrality

[13] Stokes, n 8 above, 10–11.

[14] WM Landes and RA Posner, *The Economic Structure of Intellectual Property Law* (Harvard University Press, 2003) ch 1. For criticisms of this approach, see, eg D Campbell and S Piccottio, 'The Acceptable Face of Intervention: Intellectual Property in Posnerian Law and Economics' (2006) 15 *Social & Legal Studies* 435–52.

[15] Cited in GB Ramello, n 10 above, 127–44 at 129. [16] Ramello, ibid, 129.

[17] M Davies, *Property: Meanings, Histories, Theories* (Routledge-Cavendish, 2007) 137–8.

of innovative activity in any developing economy,[18] and implicitly credits intellectual property rights as having a crucial role in this.

These economic arguments also explain why the initially desirable monopoly ownership rights must be time-limited. Two competing economic propositions are in tension here. The first is that, so far as possible, all valuable resources should be owned by someone so as to create incentives for their efficient exploitation and to prevent over-use (congestion problems). The second is that copyright should be of limited duration because otherwise the social costs of the artists' right are too high. Buyers spend too long tracing copyright owners; new inventors pay too much to use good copyright material; intellectual property is a public good and copyright costs increase the incentives to use lower quality substitutes or waste social and economic capital creating substitutes; and, finally, the empirical observation that incentives to create new intellectual property would not be lost simply because the terms are made shorter.[19]

The current time-limited terms (the artist's life plus 70 years in the UK) are often conceded to be appropriately timed on purely pragmatic grounds: extension of copyright beyond this period is not generally warranted because the artworks are not sufficiently valuable. Take two illustrations from literature and music, since both have been examined in far more detail than art in this context. First, of the 10,000 or more books published in the US in 1930, only 174 (or 1.7 per cent) were still in print in 2001 (ie more than 70 years later). Secondly, of *all* the composers over time, eight alone account for almost 50 per cent of all current classical recordings.[20] On the other hand, where copyright is financially valuable beyond this limited time, owners and dealers have instigated passionate and sustained campaigns to have the term extended: see the recent 'Disney' extension in the US, so labelled because of the prime beneficiary.[21]

But this sort of justification focuses exclusively on the position of the artist, not on the public interest. In effect, the argument is that longer

[18] J Schumpeter, *Capitalism, Socialism and Democracy* (Unwin, 1943) cited in Ramello, n 10 above, at 130.

[19] Landes and Posner, n 14 above, 213.

[20] Ibid, 212 and 230, fn 30 respectively.

[21] Sonny Bono Copyright Term Extension Act 1998, giving a 20-year extension (ie to 95 yrs) to copyright in the US. Only 2% of works where copyright was effectively extended by the Bono Act (ie those works released between 1923–43) have any commercial value, according to Lawrence Lessig: see P Choate, *Hot Property: The Stealing of Ideas in an Age of Globalisation* (Random House, 2005) 277–82.

copyright terms are not needed because *most* artists could not make economic use of longer terms. But the facts rather show that most artists would not be affected if the terms were far shorter and if the relevant intellectual property were then simply freely accessible to the public. Indeed, Landes and Posner suggest an approach that might suit both ordinary and extraordinary artists. They suggest that copyright terms should be very substantially reduced from their present rather lengthy term, but that there should be a right to renewal for a fee—ie the regime should be modelled on that for trademarks.

The end result, they suggest, would be an increase in the volume of intellectual property in the public domain because of the high percentage of likely non-renewals. Admittedly, this also means there would be a decrease in the average *quality* of that public intellectual property pool, because all the economically valuable copyrights would be renewed rather than released. This would not be too high a price, however, according to Landes and Posner, because an indefinite copyright for valuable works brings its own social benefits in that it increases incentives and optimizes use, while also preventing over-use.[22] These ideas are revisited later in this chapter.

Public Good Arguments

The third argument is robustly utilitarian, focused on the greater good of society. It is generally regarded as being for the public good that artists and others should be encouraged to create so as to ensure as wide a dissemination of knowledge and culture as possible.[23] The goal is maximization of net social welfare. In the context of creative endeavours, that requires striking an optimal balance between the rights of the artist (these rights must be sufficiently strong to stimulate the creation of works of art) and the public good (the rights of the artist must not be so strong that they curtail widespread public enjoyment of those creations by making enjoyment too expensive).[24]

The legal regime that might be supported by this sort of analysis is unlikely to be significantly different from that suggested by an economic analysis, although any balancing of relative rights would perhaps be predisposed to prefer the public good over private rights. This

[22] Landes and Posner, n 14 above, 221.

[23] Stokes, n 8 above, 12.

[24] See Fisher, n 11 above.

might, for example, suggest a preference for shorter copyright terms. Again, these ideas feed into the arguments later in this chapter.

Promoting Public Dissemination

This final argument has only been proposed more recently, and suggests that what is needed is not an incentive to *create*, but incentive to make further investments and improvements in the creative outputs.[25] Behind this refocusing is a more recent appreciation that, although we do not understand precisely what *does* motivate artists, strong legal protections are unlikely to be the primary driver. We would still have art and artists with or without these rules. On the other hand, if we want the general public to have greater access to these artistic works, then we do need strong legal rules to protect the necessary investment in dissemination. We can see this is especially true in the context of easily disseminated forms of art, such as music, film, computer programmes, and even books, where an absence of protective rules may promote excessive free-riding and lead to a 'tragedy of the commons' in which the new ideas will be overused. The current fascination with effective knowledge transfer is likely to bring these arguments even further to the fore, and to give good cause to review the effectiveness of current legal structures.

These, in brief, are the four theoretical arguments most often called upon to support the creation of an appropriate legal regime that balances private and public rights so as to promote the creation of, and public access to, art more effectively. All these various theories are united, however, in their underlying assumption that a robust legal regime (ie tight central control) is necessary to produce the most efficient outcome; simple market choice will not deliver.[26] The obvious next issue, then, is what legal rules do these theories suggest we should put in place to protect artists and promote public access?

Designing an Effective Legal Regime

All of these theories suggest that artists need legal protection, and that property rights deliver the right incentives, but that the interests of the

[25] MA Lemley, 'Ex Ante Versus Ex Post Justifications for Intellectual Property' (2004) 71(1) University of Chicago Law Review 129–49, also available in the Berkeley Public Law and Legal Theory Research Paper Series, University of California, Paper no 144; accessed at SSRN <http://ssrn.com/abstract=494424>.

[26] Ibid

public need to be weighed in the balance in defining the elements of these property rights. Although the legal philosophers worked on exactly this balance, the economists now seem to have stolen the analytical high ground. The economists' rationale for any rights, and property rights in particular, is efficient maximization of value. They argue that non-ownership, or common ownership (the difference is immaterial in this regard), of assets leads to 'the tragedy of the commons'.[27] It is worth noting, however, that the lawyers' assumption that these 'ownership benefits' must be delivered by orthodox legal property rules may not be accurate. To an economist, anything of value is an asset, and furthermore all assets are property—they do not have the lawyers' nice debates over what is and is not property.[28]

The economic theory of property[29] provides one explanation of why property is such an effective mechanism for providing legal protection to valuable rights, realizing that rights are valuable only when they are scarce (recall Adam Smith's illustration of the contrast between diamonds and water, although water is certainly more valuable now than it was in the 18th century). According to economists, the type of protection given is the minimum necessary to extract value, so property rights are only awarded where there are too many potential users and the transactions with each of them would be uneconomic. The rights that property gives are excludability and transferability, and the benefits of these are both static and dynamic: static, in that the rights reduce transaction costs and crowding, and dynamic in that they create incentives to make improvements because owners know they can reap where they sow.

Even on this simple basis, the theory suggests that the artists should at the very least be the first legal owners of their physical creations.[30] The familiar legal rules of contract and tort as they relate to tangible personal property will then govern many of the relationships between the artist and most third parties, be they purchasers, dealers, auctioneers, valuers, heirs, and so on.

[27] G Hardin, 'The Tragedy of the Commons' (1968) 162 *Science* 1243–8, in his now paradigmatic example of a 'pasture open to all' with many villagers using it to pasture their cattle.

[28] S Worthington, 'The Disappearing Divide Between Property and Obligation: The Impact of Aligning Legal Analysis and Commercial Expectation', in S Degeling and J Edelman (eds), *Equity and Commercial Law* (Thomson Lawbook Co, 2005) ch 5 (reprinted with minor amendments in (2007) 42 *Texas International Law Journal* 917–39).

[29] Landes and Posner, n 14 above, ch 1.

[30] See below for some of the unexpected complications that arise from this theory.

On the other hand, what really needs protection in the context of art has rather less to do with the physical asset—the canvas or the sculpture—and much more to do with the creative element that led to the work being in that particular form. It is not so many metres of canvas and litres of paint, or so many kilograms of marble, but the precise form of their presentation. If creators are not given this extra protection, then the risk of imitation and free-riding is enormous, and the consequences dire: the economic incentive to create is lost; the economic incentive to copy is promoted.

Clearly additional protective rules are needed. Again, the economists put it very simply, and again they resorted to rules and explanations based on property. This time the property is intellectual property, with different types of intellectual property seen as meriting different forms of protection in order to deliver the most efficient use of resources.

Modern analysis typically attributes these protective ideas to economists, as in the paragraphs above, but legal philosophers in fact got there first.[31] At least three centuries ago, legal philosophers (and no doubt many commercial parties too) argued for property rights in just these circumstances. The Crown eventually provided the necessary legal framework. Initially the Crown itself assumed the royal prerogative of granting licences to printers. The motivation was undoubtedly self-interested: these licences were not only highly profitable for the King; they also facilitated tight central control over the dissemination of seditious material.[32] Only later were these commercial and control rights given to the artist as the author of the work. This change was delivered by means of the first real copyright statute in the UK, which dates back to the Statute of Anne in 1709. Since then, increasingly protective versions (protective of the artist) have emerged in the 19th and 20th centuries.

These copyright statutes are by no means the only form of protection for intellectual property rights. But, whatever their form, all these statutes ascribe to the creative expression some of the attributes of property and give artists a monopoly over those rights for a limited period.

[31] See below.

[32] The Rt Hon Sir Robin Jacob, D. Alexander and L Lane, *A Guidebook to Intellectual Property* (5th edn, Thomson/Sweet & Maxwell, 2004) 150.

On these early arguments, the grant of monopoly rights to artists was clearly designed to generate a public benefit, not simply to enhance the position of artists. In a sense, the monopoly rights were simply the incentive necessary to generate the desired public benefit. In balancing the incentives of monopoly rights against the public benefits of access, it was from the outset accepted that copyright terms should be time-limited. This is the public benefit *quid pro quo*. On the other hand, no serious empirical analysis lies behind the chosen timescales. Despite this, the limitation period for copyright has increased substantially over the past three centuries since such rights were first articulated.[33] This increasingly protective trend (protective of the artist) takes copyright in the same direction as some other areas of intellectual property protection. For example, trademarks are not time-limited; they are indefinite, subject only to failure to renew, loss by abandonment, laches or becoming a generic name. Although the trends are in the same direction, it is not clear what useful analogies the copyright regime could have drawn from the trademark regime (or vice versa) to support the similar developments. Trademark protections are difficult if not impossible to analyse in terms of the tragedy of the commons, and there is not the same demand to satisfy the protection of private creativity with the provision of a public benefit. Indeed, for copyright, the analogy with patents is probably a stronger one, and there the protection is very much shorter (20 years, subject to payment of an annual renewal fee).

In summary, giving the artist ownership of both the tangible asset and the right to permit the copying of that creative expression (ownership of the copyright) have been seen for centuries as the efficient protective regimes necessary to create incentives for artists to deliver works that will also be of benefit to the larger public. It is worth spending some time assessing whether these assumptions are true. If we dig deeper into ownership and copyright rules, do they either effectively protect artists *or* benefit the public?

Ownership of the Tangible Asset

Artwork is a chattel. Ownership of such tangible personal property brings with it the right to exclude others from the physical asset, and to alienate

[33] See below.

(ie sell) the asset. The rights of exclusion can be pursued by relying on tort law (conversion) or criminal law (theft). There is, however, no right to prevent others viewing the spectacle of the artwork provided no other wrong is committed in doing so,[34] nor (absent copyright law) to prevent others reproducing the work, nor (even with the protection of copyright law) to prevent others copying the idea if this can be done without reproducing the work in a way that breaches copyright.

All of this seems very simple and straightforward, but each aspect of the rights associated with ownership raises its own complications. Indeed, ownership of the artwork itself is sometimes a problem.

The basic rule is that ownership is determined by the agreement of any relevant parties. Nice questions can therefore arise where works are commissioned but then not completed and handed over by the artist, or are fully completed but not paid for by the commissioner. In this context, questions about the terms of the agreement are typically not directed at damages,[35] but at ownership of the artwork itself.

Still more complicated questions arise where there is *no* agreement. If the artist paints with her own paints on her own canvas, then no one can doubt that she owns the painting. But what of paintings done on, and with, materials that belong to others? For example, paintings produced at school or at work, or using materials supplied by a commissioner? Absent contractual agreement to determine the ownership of the product, the common law is not well placed to determine the outcome. English authority is very slim, and not very persuasively reasoned. It asserts reliance on Roman law rules, and these differ markedly depending upon how the problem is categorized.

In cases of manufacture, where the original products cease to be identifiable, the assumption is that the provider of labour—the artist—is the owner, but that is based on slim and fragile authority.[36] This certainly suits the artist. But other potentially more appropriate categorizations deliver the opposite result. For example, the problem may be better classified as one of accession, not manufacture, since the

[34] *Victoria Park Racing and Recreation Co v Taylor* (1937) 58 CLR 479 (denying tort protection).

[35] But see, in the case of authorship, *Planché v Colburn* (1831) 8 Bing 14, 5 C & P 58, where modern commentators have argued about the inability to justify the outcome on either contract or unjust enrichment grounds. See D Harris, D Campbell and R Halson, *Remedies in Contract and Tort* (2nd edn, Butterworths, 2002) 235–41.

[36] S Worthington, *Proprietary Interests in Commercial Transactions* (Oxford University Press, 1996) 141–3, especially 143; *Thorogood v Robinson* (1845) 6 QB 769, 115 ER 290.

original goods do not lose their identity even though they cannot be separated without serious damage or destruction of the components. In this category, the Roman rule is quite different. Then ownership stays with the owner of the dominant—not necessarily the most valuable—chattel, here likely to be the canvas.[37]

To add to these uncertainties, the outcomes in decided cases do not always follow these identified Roman rules. In the circumstances, it is a relief to know that some form of inferred agreement between the respective parties is almost invariably found. Otherwise the argument can proceed further into nice debates on whether the Roman and English rules determine ownership, or only rights to possession, in the absence of agreement.[38]

If ownership is settled, there are other generic shortcomings in the law related to chattels. Two or three are worth mentioning. They certainly make non-lawyers wonder whether the goals of private law are being delivered.

The first is the idiosyncratic rule that does not give owners of chattels the right to insist on return of their goods. The English remedy for conversion requires the defendant to pay the claimant damages equal to the value of the goods rather than returning the goods.[39] Return of the goods is available only at the discretion of the court.[40] In the context of conversion of valuable artworks, the problem is thankfully theoretical rather than practical. It is inconceivable that a court would not order return of the artwork to the real owner. Nevertheless, at a theoretical level the distinction stands as an example of poor protection of property by English law.

[37] Ibid, 136–8, which also notes the cases where co-ownership has been ordered, although these all seem to be cases of inferred agreements. [38] Ibid, 143–4.

[39] As the law stands at the moment, copyright, as an intangible property right, cannot be converted. However, see the dissenting judgments in *OBG Ltd v Allan* [2007] UKHL 21. Receivers had been appointed under an invalid floating charge. The claimants brought proceedings for various wrongs, including conversion of their debts and contractual rights. Lords Hoffmann, Walker and Brown decided conversion was not available; Lord Nicholls and Baroness Hale thought that the old rule should no longer apply, and that conversion should be available. As Sarah Green notes, this would have recognized that 'the problem with the receivers' behaviour lay not in its nature but in its effect; their actions were not bad, but they were wrongful, and conversion recognizes the nicety of that distinction. See S Green, 'To Have and to Hold? Conversion and intangible property' (2008) 71 MLR 114–31, 114.

[40] Torts (Interference with Goods) Act 1977, s 3. Also see N Curwen, 'The Remedy in Conversion: Confusing property and obligation' (2006) 26 Legal Studies 570-583; contrast S Worthington, *Equity* (2nd edn, Oxford University Press, 2006) 168–74.

Moreover, conversion is a tort with strict liability, so an innocent auctioneer who sells another's property may be liable for its full value to the owner, of whom he was not aware, and although he gained nothing from the sale but his commission.[41] These rules favour commerce: security of receipt is valued over security of ownership. Although this certainly oils the wheels of genuine commerce, it creates problems in cases of theft, as described below.

Theft is a crime. Title to goods does not pass to the thief, and even a *bona fide* purchaser from the thief does not get good title. This is the *nemo dat* rule. In the art world, this *nemo dat* rule strikes hardest at the intermediate purchasers and handlers of art, not the artists themselves. Museums, galleries and large auction houses are mindful of the consequences of broken title claims. The titles to chattels have to be traced, and the more valuable the asset the more likely is it that disputes as to ownership will arise. Ordinary thefts are not unheard of; thefts in times of war are more common. Indeed, disputes over rightful ownership can escalate to a national or international scale. The Elgin Marbles in the British Museum and the Lindisfarne Gospels in the British Library are well known examples.[42] The common law rules of ownership are enhanced by EU law, treaties and agreements relating to cultural assets.[43] This is a fascinating subject, but well beyond the scope of this chapter.

The inevitable conclusion from all of this is that legal ownership of the tangible asset does not always adequately protect the artist. This is not, however, where energies are focused. The real protection for artists comes from the copyright regime that affords protection to the intellectual property rights in the artwork.

[41] SFC Milsom, *Historical Foundations of the Common Law* (2nd edn, Butterworths, 1981) 379.

[42] These Gospels illustrate that disputes are not necessarily between states. The Gospels are at present in the British Library, but 'belong' (this is disputed) to the British Museum. Chris Tighe complains, rather forcefully, that, 'Almost five centuries since Henry VIII's thugs looted Durham Cathedral and stole the Lindisfarne Gospels, hopes are rising that this stunning work of art may return to its spiritual home.' If they return to Durham, however, they will be on loan; there is no acknowledgement of ownership being with Durham Cathedral or any related entity: *Financial Times*, 28–9 June 2008.

[43] For example, the Royal Academy exhibition of French and Russian paintings in London earlier this year ('From Russia: French and Russian Master Paintings 1870–1925') was apparently threatened by the possibility of seizure of paintings whose ownership was contested, as previously discussed above. The exhibition went ahead as a result of an agreement concluded between the Russian and UK governments, with the UK government agreeing to rush legislation through parliament to protect the paintings against seizure.

Copyright

Since the Statute of Anne in 1709, copyright protection has been based on the unproven intuition that artists (and others) will not make their works available to the public unless they can prevent copying, at least for a limited time.[44] This protection is described as necessarily delivered via property,[45] not contract, because of the transaction costs: this is the only way to ensure practical enforcement of the right to exclude others.[46] This form of artists' rights to prevent copying is created by statute via 'copyright'.[47]

Copyright provides protection to literary, dramatic, musical and artistic works, and does so by way of a monopoly, for a fixed term, allowing the artist to prevent anyone who does not have consent from making copies, or adapting the artwork into other formats or other media.[48] While the monopoly subsists, a copyright is treated as personal property: it can be bought and sold, inherited, used as security, claimed by creditors to pay off overdue debts, and used to grant licences to others to use the artwork. In the UK, the current rules are set out in

[44] The *public's* interest in intellectual property (and therefore the citizens' rights in art), as opposed to the artist's, is viewed differently in different jurisdictions. See JC Ginsburg, 'A Tale of Two Copyrights' (1990) Tulane Law Review 991, 992–3: 'A leading French copyright scholar states that one of the "fundamental ideas" of the revolutionary copyright laws is the principle that "an exclusive right is conferred on authors because their property is the most justified since it flows from their intellectual creation." By contrast, the US Constitution's copyright clause, echoing the English Statute of Anne, makes the public's interest equal, if not superior, to the author's. This clause authorizes the establishment of exclusive rights of authors as a means to maximize production of and access to intellectual creations.' From the above logic it follows that Anglo-American copyright laws afford authors no more control than is strictly necessary to induce an author to perform his or her part of the social exchange.

[45] The whole basis is built on foundations that presume that what is being regulated by law is property, but property that somehow needs to be treated in a way that benefits both the creator (the artist) and the community (the commons). But there is another view emerging, that the artist is a supplier of services, not a creator of property. This is a critical question in deciding the applicable WTO agreement (GATT or GATS): see I Bernier, 'Trade and Culture' in FJ Macrory, AF Appleton, and MG Plummer (eds), *The World Trade Organization: Legal, Economic and Political Analysis* (Springer, 2005) 747–93.

[46] Copyright is not the only form of intellectual property, although it and patents are the best known. Others are trademarks, trade names, design rights, and plant breeder rights. These are all monopoly rights protected by the law for a limited time (or unlimited in the case of renewed trademarks and maintained trade secrets).

[47] For the history in the UK, see The Rt Hon Sir Robin Jacob, D Alexander and L Lane, n 32 above, 150–1.

[48] Although see Ibid. 226–9 on the EU rules on free movement and competition, and their impact on intellectual property rights.

the Copyright Designs and Patents Act 1988 ('CDPA'), which prevents the unauthorized duplication of the art work subject to certain limited exceptions.[49]

Copyright is not applied for[50] and copyrights are not registered. Moreover, copyright only protects the *form* in which an idea is expressed, not the idea itself. This can only be protected, if at all, by patent and trade secret law.[51]

These rights (like other forms of intellectual property rights) provide protection that extends only to the borders of the state's jurisdiction. This is less than ideal, and for well over a century international conventions have striven to make copyright genuinely international, so that work produced in one state will enjoy protection in all states that are signatories to the convention. This of course raises the issue of different states granting protection according to different rules.[52] This issue is seen most dramatically in the extension of copyright protection to computer programmes and databases.

Copyright is clearly intangible property, but is quite different from other forms of intangible property such as debts. A debt gives its holder the right to require someone to do something—ie pay money. Copyright, by contrast, and along with other forms of intellectual property, is much more like tangible property in that it gives the holder the right to require others *not* to do something, and make them pay compensation if they do.[53] Copyright (and other intellectual property rights) thus provide 'the grit in the wheels of industry'.[54]

[49] If a work qualifies for copyright protection, two distinct categories of rights arise: economic rights and moral rights (the latter are discussed below). Economic rights (as set out for the UK in ss 16–21 of the CDPA cover: the right to copy the work (reproduction right); the right to issue copies of the work to the public (distribution right); the right to rent or lend the work to the public (rental or lending right); the right to perform, show or play the work in public (public performance right); the right to communicate the work to the public; the right to make an adaptation of the work, or do any of the above acts in relation to an adaptation (right of adaptation); and the right to authorize others to carry out any of these activities.

[50] It vests automatically in the artist when the work is created, and lasts for the artist's lifetime plus 70 years (in the UK).

[51] See below for some of the difficulties in this area.

[52] Much standardization has occurred under the aegis of the World Intellectual Property Organization (an arm of the UN) and the World Trade Organization, and through EU Directives and Regulations. The WTO has also produced a standardization of the trade-related aspects of intellectual property (TRIPS). But none of this is of immediate concern here.

[53] FH Lawson and B Rudden, *The Law of Property* (3rd edn, Oxford University Press, 2002) 38–43 for a general description.

[54] The Rt Hon Sir Robin Jacob, D Alexander and L Lane, n 32 above, 4.

This is all the more so because, subject to some specific defences,[55] all the rights in the CDPA are based on a notion of strict liability. As such, it does not matter whether a defendant knew that the work was protected by copyright or that the claimant owned the work; nor does it matter that the defendant mistakenly believed that there was permission to copy the work. All that matters is that the defendant copied the artist's work. Indeed, a breach is committed not just by the actual copier, but also by anyone who authorizes the infringing copying (section 16(2) of the CDPA). The only concession to innocent infringement is in potentially reducing or negating a damages award.

Copyright is, in economists' terms, a costly right compared with tangible property rights. It is easy enough to sell a physical asset—the painting itself—or lend it, or offer it as security; there the transaction costs are low.[56] But to transfer the right to make copies (the copyright), or some subset of those rights, is more costly simply because these rights are more difficult to define, and their transfer requires greater formality. Even more importantly, it is far more costly to police infringements of copyright compared with infringements of tangible property rights. For a start, use of intellectual property by an infringer can go unnoticed. This is because it does not have the same immediate physical impact as theft of a car; often it does not take anything away from the owner—there is no 'crowding' effect; in addition, even if there is an identified suspected infringement, it is necessary to decide whether something that looks very much like the original picture is in fact an infringing copy or is, instead, a legitimate independent creation that merely resembles the original.

When considering the totality of an artist's rights, copyright protection needs to be analyzed quite separately from ownership rights in the work of art itself. The sale, or even the commissioning, of a work of art will not necessarily transfer the copyright in the artwork to the buyer/commissioner. This is engagingly reiterated in the common assertion that if you own a book you may do anything with it *except copy it*: you own the copy, not the right to copy.[57] The latter is likely to be held by either the author or, more likely these days, the publisher.

[55] The defences for copyright infringement include fair dealing, review, criticism, news reporting, and non-commercial educational purposes.

[56] That said, some nice questions arise in relation to lost, stolen and abandoned works of art: see Landes and Posner, n 14 above, 27–35.

[57] FH Lawson and B Rudden, *The Law of Property* (3rd edn, Oxford University Press, 2002) 39.

Is the Legal Regime Effective?

Does the artist's legal ownership of the artwork and the copyright, as just described, ensure delivery of the desired public goals? This is the big question. We need to know whether these legal rules, specifically designed to create incentives for artists and also allow greater access by the public, do indeed deliver those ends. Has there been an effective translation from social goals to legal rules?

There are certainly those who think the balance has been achieved successfully. For example, Netanel says[58]:

> Copyright, in sum, is a state measure that uses market institutions to enhance the democratic character of civil society. Copyright law accords a limited proprietary entitlement that underwrites democratic culture and citizenship in three ways. First, it promotes the creation and distribution of information and educational resources. In supporting a market for creative expression, copyright aims to increase and make widely available the store of knowledge required for effective citizenship and civic association. Second, it enhances civil society's participatory character. Through economic incentives and a careful balance between exclusivity and access, copyright seeks to foster widespread citizen participation in public deliberation. Third, it supports the plurality, independence, and vitality of civil society's communicative sphere. By according authors a carefully tailored proprietary entitlement, copyright frees them from reliance on patronage and cultural hierarchy, while opposing market-based hierarchy and encouraging transformative uses of existing works. In that way copyright law hopes to generate diverse and autonomous contributions to our common discourse. . . .Too thin a copyright would diminish the incentive for autonomous creative contribution, but a copyright of bloated scope, and one that would treat creative expression as simply another commodity, would stifle expressive diversity and undermine copyright's potential for furthering citizen participation in democratic self-rule.

But the voices to the contrary can look rather persuasive, even though the sceptics would say their various arguments, and even the factual support for them, often pull in opposite directions. These arguments variously suggest that, in the area of art, the copyright rules are either unnecessary or, alternatively, dysfunctional; that copyright for artists is not needed because it does not give any, or any appropriate, or any comprehensive incentive to the creative impulse; and, worse still, that

[58] NW Netanel, 'Copyright and a Democratic Civil Society' (1996) 106 *Yale Law Journal* 283, 363.

copyright does nothing to increase the benefit to the public. Each of these assertions is worth considering in more detail.

Copyright is Unnecessary or Dysfunctional

The first argument is simply that the law itself is ineffective, and therefore pointless. There are too many cases of copying that the existing copyright rules do not catch, so if prevention of copying is a necessary goal, then the current copyright rules do not help.

An alternative argument starts from a different base, but leads to the same conclusion that copyright rules are not needed. Copyright rules are not needed, so this argument goes, where there are few incentives to copy, as is the case where any copy would inevitably be of inferior quality even when executed by the best copiers.[59] This is true of most art reproductions. Copyright rules may also not be needed where increased copying is an *advantage* to the artist. This is so when copying is likely to increase the market value of the original, as when museums produce posters, postcards and other products. It is also true when the pecuniary and non-pecuniary benefits of wider dissemination (reputation, prestige, secondary commissions, etc) are of more value to the artist than the royalties generated by copyright licences.[60]

Coase would argue that the market can resolve the issue behind this second argument very easily. According to the Coase theorem, the government simply has to assign property rights to *someone*, and the markets will work out the rest.[61] This may sound simple, but the realities often ruin the economic model. In the case of art, the problem comes from the unrealistic assumption that transaction costs are zero when in fact they are very high. High transaction costs arise whenever there are either too many parties or too few (especially so few as to create a bilateral monopoly). This is often the case with artwork. Transaction costs are also high whenever there are serious wealth effects (ie the 'stickiness' produced because there is a need for wealth every time someone wants to buy, but not when they want to sell).[62]

[59] For this, and other circumstances that are of less importance in the art world, see Landes and Posner, n 14 above, 41–9.

[60] Ibid, 46.

[61] But see GB Ramello, n 10 above, 127–44 at 132: the ever-increasing duration of copyright over the decades—now life plus 70 years, or in the US 95 years in the case of a company owning a copyright—means that now the duration of copyright has become infinite at least for the purposes of modern economic analysis and decision-making.

[62] L Harrison and J Theeuwes, *Law and Economics* (WW Norton & Co, 2008) 87–94.

In short, the markets cannot necessarily deal effectively with 'unnecessary' or 'ineffective' property rights.

Copyright does not Create the Desired Incentives

The next class of anti-copyright arguments, in the art context, suggests that the rules do not provide the desired incentives to artists.[63] In particular, the rules either do not deliver any incentive benefits *at all*; or (against this), the rules *do* create incentives, but this is bad because it either prompts the creation of too much (poor) art, or art of only a particular sort (the sort valued by the copyright rules, which do not protect all art as that description is understood in lay terms).

Some argue that copyright does not provide the assumed incentive to create new works, and that the contrary view, on which all copyright rules rest, remains an unproven intuition.[64] These detractors point to the high level of creative activity and its public dissemination before legal copyright rules took root, and suggest that levels have changed little. Behavioural scientists, too, have assessed the motivations of artists, and concluded that economic benefit is only one of the drivers and perhaps not the most significant. These conclusions support the intuitively compelling assumption that artists are perhaps the least likely of all of us to behave as rational economic actors. It follows that economic incentives may not work in the artistic context as they do elsewhere. In the end, however, the arguments either way remain inconclusive in the absence of reliable data.

Other arguments go in the opposite direction and insist that copyright *does* create incentives, but this carries with it too high a social cost. Arnold Plant[65] and his successors lead on this view.[66] Plant summarizes the arguments by saying that property rights manage scarcity, whereas intellectual property rights create scarcity. Because incentives are favoured over public access, *too much* intellectual property is produced: artists and authors rent-seek because the copyright monopolies prevent competition. Copyright monopolies increase the cost of the intellectual

[63] See B Frank, 'On an Art Without Copyright' (1996) 49 *Kyklos* 3.

[64] See the references cited by R Towse, 'Copyright and Artists: A View from Cultural Economics' in M McAleer and L Oxley (eds), *Economic and Legal Issues in Intellectual Property* (Blackwells, 2007) 96 –7, 99.

[65] A Plant, 'The Economic Aspects of Copyright in Books' in A Plant, *Selected Economic Essays and Addresses* 57 (Routledge and Kegan Paul, 1974).

[66] See Landes and Posner, n 14 above, 20–4.

property to the public, so decreasing access and reducing public benefit.[67] This is too high a social cost. (Note how this argument has parallels in other spheres of endeavour where competition is seen as the cornerstone of efficient markets.)

They dismiss the contrary argument, that *without* copyright we would have *too little* intellectual property. They say that copyright protection is not the real incentive for creation of intellectual property;[68] that even if it were, intellectual property would be sufficiently protected by existing alternative legal means; and that even were that not the case, levels of duplication would not be unacceptably high because the high costs of duplication provide a practical barrier to free-riding. This last may have been true when Plant was writing in the early 20th century, but it is unlikely to be the case now.

The next argument is that copyright's incentives impede the full development of different artistic genres. Copyright prohibits creative imitation and developments built on the work of others. Instead, it creates incentives for every artist to produce 'original' work (or more ephemeral works that are difficult to copy). This distorts the market by limiting certain areas of supply and re-focusing efforts in other directions. Here there may be an argument worth our attention. History tells a rather convincing tale: look at authors, including those of the calibre of Shakespeare, who copied much more than the mere styles or stories of others; or artists such as Manet, who copied extensively and unmistakeably from the earlier works of Raphael, Titian, Courbet and others.[69]

A further take on this argument is that copyright is not sufficiently comprehensive, so its incentives are far too narrowly focused on particular types of art. This means that large swathes of work that the public might value are ignored by the copyright regime and its associated incentive scheme. Take a simple example: does copyright law protect aboriginal art; is this classed as (original) art, or is it simply conveying culture? Only original artworks can be copyrighted,

[67] Copyright carries with it the problems of monopoly pricing, which is why there is pressure not to expand copyright beyond the minimum necessary to provide authors with an incentive to produce: NW Netanel, 'Copyright and a Democratic Civil Society' (1996) 106 *Yale Law Journal* 283, 308.

[68] See n 64 above, especially the references cited at 99.

[69] Landes and Posner, n 14 above, 57–68. Also see M Fried, *Manet's Modernism - Or, The Face of Painting in the 1860s* (University of Chicago Press, 1996) 150–4, cited Ibid at 68.

although the work need not be especially creative. The 1989 case of *Bulan Bulan v Nejlam Pty Ltd*[70] concerned an aborigine suing for breach of copyright in reproducing his art. The case roused serious academic discussion, with the issue being whether tribal or primitive art could be 'original', or was merely reproducing traditional truths in a well defined and customary way without the necessary exercise of creativity. Perhaps unfortunately, the court did not decide the matter; it simply assumed originality. This means we are left with the academic debates, which (perhaps predictably) go both ways.

In addition, and of far greater impact, is the limitation in the CDPA and other equivalent statutory regimes that they do not protect ideas; they only protect the form of their expression.[71] Copyright's job is simply to protect against reproduction.[72] This is a serious limitation since artists have few means, other than copyright, for protecting their 'genius'. Contractual protection is unworkable; tort protection is limited;[73] and according to the common law this aspect of the artist's work is not property.[74] As Latham CJ, an Australian High Court judge, put it when refusing to treat a transfer of information as a transfer of property: having a richly stored mind does not make one a man of property.[75]

[70] (1989) Federal Court, unreported, discussed in J Anderson, 'The Making of Indigenous Knowledge in Intellectual Property Law in Australia' (2005) 12 *International Journal of Cultural Property* 347– 73, 359ff.

[71] So, 'copyright. . . does not extend to ideas, or schemes, or systems, or methods; it is confined to their expression; and if their expression is not copied the copyright is not infringed': *Hollinrake v Truswell* (1894) 3 Ch 420, although the dichotomy between ideas and expression is frequently a cause for disagreement between scholars.

[72] According to Tim Harford, this makes it especially difficult to protect certain types of creative ideas, such as magicians' tricks and chefs' recipes: *Financial Times Magazine*, 13–14 October 2007.

[73] See below.

[74] In other words, information and ideas are not property. On information: P Kohler and N Palmer, 'Information as Property', in N Palmer and E McKendrick (eds), *Interests in Goods* (2nd edn, LLP, 1998); *Victoria Park Racing and Recreation Co v Taylor* 1937) 58 CLR 479 (denying tort protection); *Douglas v Hello! Ltd* [2001] 2 All ER 289. True, some cases have described information as property: see Lord Radcliffe in a tax case treating know-how as a form of intangible property in the way goodwill is, *Rolls Royce Ltd v Jeffrey* [1962] 1 All ER 801, 805; Lord Shaw describing trade secrets as property in a restraint of trade case, *Herbert Morris Ltd v Saxelby* [1916] 1 AC 688, 714; *Boardman v Phipps* [1967] 2 AC 46 (Lords Hodson and Guest and Viscount Dilhorne, but contrast Lord Upjohn, 127–8, whose views are now regarded as accepted); and Browne-Wilkinson VC in *AG v Guardian Newspapers Ltd* [1987] 1 WLR 1248, 1264. All these are noted in M Bridge, *Personal Property Law* (3rd edn, Oxford University Press, 2002) 5–6.

[75] *Federal Commissioner of Taxation v United Aircraft Corporation* 1944) 68 CLR 525, 535 (Latham CJ), cited in Bridge, n 74 above, 6.

Surprisingly, this dividing line between the idea and its form has arisen in very particular forms for modern artists.[76] Although we readily assume that all art is copyrightable, several post-modern movements illustrate that this protection can be relatively weak.[77] For example, late Abstract Expressionism and Pop Art (of the Andy Warhol genre) illustrate styles where the primary importance is in the conceptual approach, not in the technique or craftsmanship. The concept —or idea—behind these paintings is not copyrightable. This means that although the artists do, of course, have copyright in their original works, an attempt to 'copy' a Jackson Pollock is unlikely to breach copyright law; nor will an attempt to exhibit an ordinary consumer item (such as cans of Heinz beans).

Another art movement, that of super-realism, illustrates a similar problem. Super-realists aim to produce paintings that are so realistic that they look like photographs—there were quite a few of them in the 2008 BP Portrait Award exhibition at the National Portrait Gallery in London. Here the emphasis is on technique, not concept, but technique, too, is not copyrightable. It follows that protection of this form of art suffers from the same problem as protection of copyright in photographs. Although the artworks are protected by copyright (as are photographs) arguments that this copyright has been breached are difficult, although not impossible, unless the scene and setting are copied, not merely the artistic technique.[78]

Finally, Appropriation Art is another difficult category. This is where artists deliberately and publicly borrow from one or more earlier artists but use these borrowings to make their own original and unique work. Courts then have to decide whether the appropriation art is itself in breach of copyright and, later, whether any derivative works are simply copying the technique or the idea rather than the artwork itself.[79]

Putting all this together, there is a lot of 'art' that is left unprotected—or largely unprotected—by the copyright regime. If the regime is helpful at all, then its help is not comprehensive, and this in itself is a failing.[80]

[76] Landes and Posner, n 14 above, 254–9.

[77] Post-modernists depart radically from the classical modernists, such as Picasso, Matisse, Mondrian and Kandinsky, and pursue the direction of 'post-modern' thought.

[78] The Rt Hon Sir Robin Jacob, D Alexander and L Lane, n 32 above, 148, 152, 159, 173.

[79] Landes and Posner, n 14 above, 266–9.

[80] Of course, this rather damning conclusion is not one that applies generally. The core copyright industries are not art, but music and book publishing, radio and TV broadcasting, cable TV, newspapers and periodicals, records and tapes, movies, theatrical productions, advertising, computer software, and data processing. This is because

Copyright does not Benefit the Public

Other criticisms centre on the complaint that the copyright rules do not deliver appropriate benefits to the public. Over the past 300 years of legal development, so the argument goes, the artist has been overly favoured. There has been a clear and increasing tendency to enhance the scope of intellectual property rights in various ways: in how long the coverage persists, what form of creative endeavour is covered, and how comprehensive the degree of protection from duplication is. These expansions deliver a corresponding diminution in the rights of the public.

For example, the duration of copyright has increased from 28 years under the 1709 Statute of Anne, to the present life plus 70 years. The range of protectable subject matter has expanded from literary and artistic works in the 18th century, to photographs in the 19th century, to cinematographic works then sound recordings, broadcasts and computer programs in the mid-20th century, and now database protection. Finally, the scope of protection has been expanded so that copyright in a single work can be used to control the production and distribution of all other derivative forms of the work (other than those expressly excluded by the statute), including communicating, distributing, renting and lending the work.[81]

On the other hand, other commentators suggest that all this expansion has not produced significantly greater benefits for *artists*, but rather for the people in the middle, the facilitators (the art dealers and book publishers). These are the people in the 'creative industries'.[82] The economic value of Britain's creative industries is now estimated to be broadly comparable to the financial services sector.[83] But this, too, if

the main source of an artist's income (notwithstanding *droit de suite*—see below) comes from sale of the original. This is also true of art intermediaries such as dealers. This stands in stark contrast to authors, film directors, musicians and computer programmers, for example, whose main source of income is precisely from regulated copies of the book, movies, musical scores and CDs, software, etc. This means that for artists, copying is a much smaller threat to their ability to recover their fixed costs. Indeed, copies, or derivatives, whether authorized or not, may only serve to enhance the profile and reputation of the artist. See P Choate, *Hot Property: the Stealing of Ideas in an Age of Globalisation* (Random House, 2005) 92.

[81] See U Suthersanen, 'Technology, Time and Market forces: The Stakeholders in the Kazaa Era', in MP Pugatch (ed), *The Intellectual Property Debate: Perspectives from Law, Economics and Political Economy* (Edward Elgar, 2006) 244 –7 and the references cited therein.

[82] Ibid, 240–4.

[83] The Work Foundation, 'Staying Ahead: The Economic Performance of the UK's Creative Industries' (June 2007) available at <http://www.theworkfoundation.com/assets/docs/publications/176_stayingahead.pdf>.

it is true, does not necessarily assist the public. If the benefits of current copyright regimes are overwhelming in favour of the distributors (dealers and publishers) rather than the artists, then these classes will have incentives to create their own monopolies to maximize still further their own economic advantages. The risk then is that there will only be a relatively small number of large distributors, and this is likely to restrict the diversity of the creative products on offer, so reducing the public benefit.[84]

All of this reinforces the powerlessness of the public in this set up. If copyright is to deliver a public benefit, it is one that comes without any public *rights*. There is nothing in copyright statutes that *requires* the copyright author (the artist) to create, use, publish or sell the product that is protected by copyright.[85] This has led to the assertion that the public interest in the protection of artworks is not adequately safeguarded, even though the legal basis for such protection arguably exists, at least in some parts of the US.[86]

Arguments have therefore been advanced for a public right, and a correlative duty imposed on the guardians of public art.[87] But these suggestions do not meet the full force of the problem. They do little more than impose duties on the curators of artwork that has *already* been put in the public domain,[88] either by sale, loan or outright donation to museums or galleries. What is, or should be, of greater concern is the effectiveness of incentives to put the artwork in the public domain in the first place, for the greater public benefit.

The rather depressing conclusion at the end of all of this is that the public is probably not much better off as a result of copyright rules. It has no *rights* to access, and if copyright does not provide much

[84] Ibid. Note especially the 7th and 3rd of the eight drivers of success for the creative economy.

[85] Note that in this respect the law on patents is different. A patented invention that is not used can be recognized as an abuse of the monopoly rights involved, and the Patents Office may grant a compulsory licence to some other applicant to use the breakthrough (eg a patented cure for a disease), paying the patent owner reasonable compensation.

[86] eg California Art Preservation Act, California Civil Code §987 (1979): 'The Legislature hereby finds and declares. . .[that there is] a public interest in preserving the integrity of cultural and artistic creations. . .'; and Historic Sites, Buildings and Antiquities Act, 16 USC §461 (1976): '. . .[it is a] national policy to preserve for public use. . . objects of national significance.'

[87] See Note, 'Protecting the Public Interest in Art' (1981) 91 Yale Law Journal 121.

[88] It seems this is done by way of implied agreements creating trusts for public benefit and imposing fiduciary duties of care, not obligations of strict liability.

incentive, but creates monopolies, then there is likely to be little increase in the quality or the volume of art produced, and even that may indeed be coupled with increased cost and reduced access. This issue is revisited later.

Surely the law has struck on alternative mechanisms that are more effective in creating incentives for artists and delivering the benefits of access to the public? The next sections consider some of the tested options.

Moral Rights

Copyright is regarded as a commercial or economic right. Artists also have 'moral rights'.[89] These are not property rights, but personal rights which protect an author's non-pecuniary interests.[90] These moral rights can be waived (in the UK), but they cannot be alienated, so they remain with the artist regardless of who owns the copyright in a work. They include the right to be identified as the artist, and to object to any derogatory treatment or false attributions of the work. Whether the moral rights of the artist include the right to prevent a subsequent owner destroying the piece has always been controversial, with most thinking it does not.[91] In the UK, these moral rights must be specifically asserted.[92] This is commonly seen in books, but perhaps not often enough with artworks.[93] The outcome can seem most unfair, especially when commercial use is made of art without any recognition of the artist.[94]

[89] See G Dworkin, 'Moral Rights and the Common Law Countries' [1994] Australian Intellectual Property Journal 28.

[90] Under the CDPA, moral rights consist of right of attribution; right to object to a false attribution; and right of integrity (protecting against defacing and damaging the artwork, for example).

[91] See Stokes, n 8 above, 68 and the references cited there. Also see the engaging illustrations in H Lydiate, 'Moral Rights: The Right to Destroy Artwork' (2001) on Artlaw website at <http://www.artquest.org.uk/artlaw/moral-rights/the-right-to-destroy-artwork.htm>.

[92] CDPA, s 78.

[93] Although there is a special provision dealing with the public exhibition of artistic works; the name of the author on the artwork is usually sufficient to assert the right: CDPA, s 78. also see Stokes, n 8 above, 69 and the references cited there.

[94] J Anderson, 'The Making of Indigenous Knowledge in Intellectual Property Law in Australia' (2005) 12 *International Journal of Cultural Property* 347–73, 354, describing the plight in 1976 of Wandjuk Marika who found his art reproduced on tea towels without his permission.

Economists do not favour moral rights. They see them as reducing the economic return to the artist, and providing no protection that is not already provided by other legal routes.[95] Even Hansmann and Santilli,[96] who consider both equity and efficiency arguments for the right and on balance find in favour of such rights on the basis that they preserve 'reputation' in an oeuvre, not just in one single work of art, will not go so far as to suggest that they are efficient.

According to economists, the reason that artists themselves favour moral rights—and they do—is that the rhetoric and the prestige of the people supporting these rights is a signal to the community at large that art is a valuable social enterprise. This, in turn, improves the environment for artists. But, as the economists are quick to point out, this more favourable environment may not bring financial rewards; it may simply attract more artists, thus increasing their competition for buyers.[97]

Breach of Confidence and Passing off

Even where a work of art is not protected at all by copyright, or where the alleged infringing activity does not involve a substantial reproduction of the protected work, other forms of legal protection *may* be available. These include breach of confidence and passing off. Indeed, breach of confidence, where available, has the added value that it can sometimes protect ideas as well as their expression.[98] On the other hand, it is obviously rare that a work of art, disclosed to the public, will involve a breach of confidence but not an infringement of copyright.[99]

The same overlap is less apparent between copyright and passing off, and indeed both claims are often pleaded concurrently when weak copyright cases go to court. The law of passing off protects artists whose work is being passed off as someone else's. This claim is in addition to any moral right claim, for example for false attribution of authorship,

[95] Landes and Posner, n 14 above, ch 10.

[96] H Hansmann and M Santilli, 'Authors' and Artists' Moral Rights: A Comparative Legal and Economic Analysis' (1997) 26 Journal of Legal Studies 95.

[97] Landes and Posner, n 14 above, 291.

[98] See the wide remedy awarded in *Prince Albert v Strange* (1849) 2 De Gex & Sim 652, 1 McN & G 2, 41 ER 1171.

[99] Of course, there *are* examples, as in the case of the assembly of objects for the Oasis album cover in *Creation Records Ltd v News Group Newspapers Ltd* [1997] EMLR 444.

or any claim of copyright infringement, and extends beyond the artist to successor owners or their copyright holders.[100] On the other hand, misrepresentation of authorship lies at the core of a passing off claim, so artists can rely on this right only in very particular circumstances. The claim will not, for example, protect against imitation of style unless that leads to confusion about authorship. So, again, this right provides little real additional protection for artists.

Other Support for Artists

All of this suggests that ownership, copyright and moral rights are not much help, and breach of confidence and passing off are of even less use. The real problem in supporting the creative endeavour of artists is that artists make most of their money from the initial sale of their works. Few artists retain copyright. This means that the real commercial benefits of the artist's work, especially an artist with a growing reputation, are likely to accrue almost exclusively to the subsequent purchasers and any intermediate dealers. This division of benefits is likely to leave artists poorly remunerated for their efforts, with little financial incentive (or means) to produce more.

The law, if it wants to help, must do it in other ways. It does. So does the public. Beyond primary sales, the financial incentives to artists generally take two forms. The first is granted by law (*droit de suite*), the second is discretionary (public and private patronage).

Droit de Suite

Since early 2006, under the influence of EU law,[101] UK artists have a new right, the *droit de suite*.[102] This gives artists the legal right to a royalty each time one of their works is resold in a sale involving an art market professional. The right is based on a philosophical approach to intellectual property that follows Hegel's emphasis on possession of property as the mark of the free man. From this it has been suggested

[100] Stokes, n 8 above, 163 –5.

[101] In 1996, the EU Commission proposed and then adopted (in 2001) a Directive requiring all member states to introduce a resale royalty right into their domestic laws by 2006: Directive 2001/84/EC. The UK rules became effective on 14 February 2006.

[102] The details that follow are from the Intellectual Property Office website at <http://www.ipo.gov.uk/pro-types/pro-copy/c-policy/c-policy-artist.htm>.

that perhaps intellectual property should be inalienable, in the same way that freedom itself is inalienable (ie one cannot sell oneself into slavery). *Droit de suite* rules pursue that approach, although in a rather modified form.[103]

The 'royalty right' only applies to sales for €1,000 or more, and is calculated on a sliding scale (see table below). The maximum royalty payable on any single sale is €12,500. This royalty is subject to compulsory collective management, so artists cannot claim their royalty independently but must receive it through a collecting society. In the UK the right currently only applies to sales of works by living authors, but from 2010 (or perhaps some later date if the government decides to delay this proposed change) the right could be extended to cover sales of all works that are still copyright (ie all those where the artist has been dead for less than 70 years).

Driot de Suite Royalty Rates

Royalty	For the portion of the resale Price (in EUR)
4%	Up to 50,000
3%	Between 50,000.01 and 200,000
1%	Between 200,000.01 and 35,000
0.5%	Between 350,000.01 and 500,000
0.25%	In excess of 500,000

Perhaps surprisingly, economic analysis suggests that the *droit de suite* *reduces* the incentive to create intellectual property. This is for four reasons. First, because this right is not alienable, it does not allow the artist to negotiate in a way that shifts risks back to the dealer. Secondly, it affects pricing because it is no longer possible to sell the full rights associated with copyright. Thirdly, to the extent that the right applies to all artwork rather than simply artwork created after the law came into force, it favours established artists at the expense of newer ones because it gives them an unexpected windfall return on earlier paintings and reduces the price that collectors are willing to pay for new works.[104] Finally, it is suggested that the right is likely to act as a disincentive to dealers to promote an artist's work.[105]

[103] Landes and Posner, n 14 above, 4.

[104] See Landes and Posner, n 14 above, 38.

[105] R Towse, n 64 above, 89.

There are some obvious logical flaws in each of the criticisms of the *droit de suite* but, even ignoring them all, the arguments do not seem to amount to proof that *artists* (as opposed to buyers or dealers) will be *disadvantaged* by the *droit de suite*. More pragmatically, however, the very low cap on *droit de suite* ensures that artists can only ever be paid a tiny percentage of the price of any secondary art sales, even though these prices are likely to escalate as the artist's reputation grows. This is readily illustrated. Recall the sorts of prices that have been paid for various pieces of art in public auctions in Europe over the past 12 months. At the top end, Roman Abramovitch, the Russian minerals tycoon (and owner of Chelsea Football Club) was the buyer of two of the three most expensive paintings sold at the Sotheby's May 2008 sale in New York.[106] He paid approximately €26 million for Lucian Freud's 'Benefits Supervisor Sleeping'. This is reportedly the highest price ever paid in public auction for a work by a living artist. Under the *droit de suite* rules, Freud would collect €12,500 on the €26 million sale (ie a little under 0.05%). Abramovitch also paid approximately €65 million for Francis Bacon's 'Triptych, 1976'. Since Bacon is dead (he died in 1992), no *droit de suite* applies at all, although it will to sales from 2010 (or some later date if the government decides to delay this proposed change). It would seem from these figures that the real winners from an artist's creative endeavours are the sellers and the auction houses, perhaps especially the latter since they not only collect commission from the seller but also from the buyer.

Even if the financial returns are relatively low, the *droit de suite* stands out as a truly exceptional right. No other property right entitles a first owner to capture a share of the current market value of the property on any future resale. The logic behind this unique reward is rather opaque. If the right is intended as a fair compensation to artists for any third-party trading on their (growing) reputations, personality or personhood, then it seems odd that the *droit de suite* is not calculated on the *increase* in value between each successive sale. In the same way, if the right is designed to provide an incentive to artists to produce *better* artwork, then it is strange that the *droit de suite* is not restricted to a percentage of the *increasing* value of the artwork rather than applying whatever the sale price.

[106] These paintings were allegedly for an art gallery in Moscow being set up by his partner. The Qataris, too, are building art museums, and Sheik Saud al-Thani has emerged as one of the biggest collectors in the world: *Financial Times* 28–9 June 2008.

In short, the *droit de suite* does not seem to provide the necessary incentives or necessary rights to either the artist or the public. It is of limited application, delivers limited reward, and may indeed decrease the prices for artworks by young artists.

Given all these problems, some have suggested that a 'display right' would be preferable (much like a royalty on sales of books). This would clearly have far higher tracing costs than the *droit de suite*, and may for that reason be practically unworkable.[107] It may also benefit only a small proportion of artists. Nevertheless, given the inadequacies of the existing law, the potential advantages of such a display right probably deserve further and more detailed examination.

Public and Private Patronage

Another way of supporting artists is by patronage,[108] prizes and awards.[109] A good deal of art was produced in the past without the benefit of copyright, supported instead by private patronage. That source of support has dwindled.

Indeed, the level of private patronage of the arts as a whole is very low.[110] In the UK, the richest 20 per cent of the population give only 0.7 per cent of their household income to charity; the poorest 20 per cent give at four times that rate, although the total sums are very much less. Not all—or even most—of that goes to the arts, much less to the artists themselves. Only 4 per cent of charitable donations go to cultural institutions. That translates to 0.028 per cent of the household income of the richest 20 per cent, or £28 per year from someone earning £100,000 per annum. That said, an Arts and Business survey showed investment in the arts by the private sector grew by 11 per cent in 2007, to nearly £600 million, the increase coming from individuals (£298 million), with corporate giving remaining static (£172 million) even though in the last five years before the survey corporate profits had soared (from a 2009 perspective, those fortunes have taken rather a tumble).

107 Ibid, 90; H Hansmann and M Santilli, n 96 above.

108 See P David, 'Does the New Economy Need All the Old IPR Institutions and More?', in L Soete and B ter Weel (eds), *The Economics of the Digital Society* (Edward Elgar, 2005) 113–51.

109 Note that these different forms involve quite different assessments of where support should be directed: patronage is *ex ante* and prizes *ex post*.

110 For the statistics that follow, see *Evening Standard*, 30 January 2008.

Public support for the arts is also relatively meagre and, again, generally directed at museums and art galleries, not the artists themselves. For example, Arts Council England has announced that from 2008–11 it will 'invest in excess of £1.6 billion of public money from the government and the National Lottery to create . . . experiences [of great art] for as many people as possible across the country.'[111] The amount may seem large, but it is only about £30 per person in the UK.

Whether publicly funded grants and subsidies provide a better stimulation for creativity remains moot. Towse notes that these are *ex ante* payments rather than *ex post* copyright payments, and suffer not only from the problem that they too may cause over-production in the same way that some suggest copyright does, but also from the public finance aspect that they tax all for the benefit of the few, those few being principally high income users of high-end art (opera, etc).[112]

And again, the rewards seem to go to dealers, gallery owners and secondary purchasers. The richest collectors are as celebrated as the artists they support, although this is a relatively young development, as noted by the *Financial Times*:

> The world's greatest museums—the Louvre, Hermitage, Prado—began as lavish civilisation-is-power statements by monarchs and emperors; private individuals did not emerge as significant museum patrons before the 19th century. . . . [..and the likes of Tate and Tretyakov were] democratic visionaries who paid for buildings and donated core collections to kick-start evolving national, state-run institutions. [113]

By contrast, modern museum builders are dedicated to far more personal projects, with a more individualistic flavour.[114] This is not an unrivalled good. Of course it does mean more art on display for more people to see; but these entrepreneurs dilute quality, and their wealth enables them to have a dramatic, and not always beneficial, influence in driving the market for particular styles of art.[115]

[111] See <http://www.artscouncil.org.uk/funding>.

[112] See the references cited in R Towse, n 64 above, 86–7.

[113] *Financial Times*, 11 October 2008.

[114] Prime examples are Dasha Zhukova's museum of contemporary art in Moscow (the Garage), and Guy and Miriam Ullens' contemporary art museum in Beijing: *Financial Times*, 11 October 2008.

[115] Although there are exceptions: Saatchi's collection of Chinese art in his new museum in Chelsea ('The Revolution Continues') is apparently one the Tate would 'kill for': *Financial Times*, 11 October 2008.

Conclusion

It is difficult to draw definitive conclusions in this area, but the tentative conclusions do not look encouraging. *If* (and this can be legitimately contested) the goal of private law in this and other areas is to provide a public benefit, and to do so in this context by creating an incentive for artists to deliver more and better art, and to have that art exposed to public scrutiny,[116] then it is doubtful that the current legal rules succeed. None of these rules—from basic ownership through to *droit de suite*—seem to be effective in increasing the incentives for artists *or* the supply of a diverse diet of creative art for the public. Nor do any of the typical modern non-legal interventions.

This is not for lack of focused thought. There is no shortage of theory supporting every possible regulatory stance, although there is little empirical behavioural research to help selection. Intuition rather than evidence suggests that copyright is unlikely ever to be the vehicle that provides real creative stimulus to artists or ensures great financial rewards. Equally, looking to the other side of the equation, copyright is unlikely ever to provide an effective lever to the public to enforce, or even encourage, greater creativity or more and better public dissemination of art.

Moreover, the inability to deliver these public benefits is not because copyright law favours a competing interest, in that it prefers protection of the individual artists over promotion of a public benefit. Copyright, as described above, provides only limited practical protection for artists' creative endeavours.[117]

The rather depressing conclusion, then, is that copyright is of little practical relevance in protecting artists, *or* in promoting creativity and its public enjoyment in the sphere of art. It is not the balance of protections that is at fault; the regime is simply not best suited for either purpose. On a more positive note, however, we seem in little practical danger of a public shortage of art, whatever the shortcomings of these rules of law.

[116] See the (non-legal) aspiration expressed on the Arts Council England website: 'Great art inspires us, brings us together and teaches us about ourselves and the world around us': <http://www.artscouncil.org.uk/aboutus/index.php>

[117] This assertion is not true generally: copyright law *is* effective in protecting artists and intermediaries in many other forms of artistic endeavour, but not, it seems, painters and sculptors. See n 80 above.

'A Normal Man . . . Hardly Exists': Law, Narrative, the Psyche, and the Normal Man

*Melanie Williams**

Introduction

This chapter sets out to explore the discourses and narratives linking orthodoxies of law and the sciences of the psyche, in a quest to reveal the extent to which professional narratives engage the 'truth' of those subject to, and coming to the notice of, the law. In current terms, the enquiry may be understood by reference to the large numbers of prison inmates reportedly suffering from mental disorder whose moral responsibility for action is thus in doubt, as well as those notionally 'normal' persons, driven to extreme behaviour but failed by the lacunae of doctrine. Tied into this is a concern that orthodox psychiatry is limited in its capacity to pay recognition to the forces of the unconscious, albeit that such forces may be the most profound influence and stimulus to action. More generally, this quest for truth derives from a realization that the 'truths' of individuals spring from complex internal narratives which may not correlate readily to the doctrines of medicine and law, either in relation to the boundary of mental responsibility as mental health, or as agency. The professions too relate to themselves, to one another and to their subjects with complex hegemonic narrative discourses and assertions which may prove frail when subject to scrutiny. For individuals, the pursuit of coherence may translate as silence or as being inauthentic, though for subjects such narrative accounts—their testimonies—may reflect profound beliefs and truths. At the

* Professor of Law, School of Law, University of Exeter. This chapter was first delivered as a public lecture in the Current Legal Problems series at the Faculty of Laws, University College London in October 2008.

deepest level, rigorous practitioner psychoanalytic commentary may offer the most cogent and compelling interrogation of state of mind. Though this realization may not always change the broad practical solutions imposed by the law, it may alter some fundamental attitudes towards those subject to the law. At the very least, such struggle should invoke a degree of compassion for the subject labouring under the burden of belief; a scepticism towards the evidential standing accorded to the 'master narratives' of medicine and law; and an openness to the further insights gained by less lionized fields of psychological enquiry.

Disturbing incidents, appearing all too frequently in news reports around the world, contribute to the perennial toll of inscrutable tragedies permeating community life. In August 2008, Christopher Foster shot his wife and daughter and the family animals and then set fire to the family estate. In September 2008, David Cass smothered his two little girls to death then killed himself. Brian Philcox, who killed his two children and himself on Father's Day, was remembered as 'a brilliant dad who loved his kids'.[1] Given the suicide accompanying these killings, the law is prevented from adjudicating the state of mind and degree of mental responsibility accompanying these acts. All presented with clear evidence of premeditation. Christopher Foster, for example, went to great lengths to ensure the efficiency of the conflagration of his home. Yet this was the same man who had, even in the face of financial difficulties, bought his daughter the very best ponies and showered his family with luxuries.

Evidence of premeditation, of planning in the execution of the events, naturally steers opinion towards believing that the perpetrator was entirely in control of his or her faculties. Thus, the story informing popular opinion (and, had he lived, the trial) of Christopher Foster, might well have characterized him as a calculating and controlling individual who, when he could no longer control his 'empire' destroyed it in preference to allowing his creditors to recoup their losses, his destruction of his wife and child and annihilation of his 'property' as cold-blooded as that of his home, dogs and horses. A contrasting reading of his state of mind could theorize that, having protected the 'princesses' in his life from the baser aspects of ordinary existence and from the economic failures of the business underpinning that protection, his premeditation simply signalled a bizarre and misplaced belief

[1] Kate Hilpern, 'Ending it All', G2 Cover, *The Guardian*, 24 Wednesday September 2008.

that he must spare them the horrors of what was to come once his empire collapsed. On this account, Foster could be characterized as a man tragically upholding a distorted but, in his view thoroughly loyal and loving, protective integrity towards his family, although the cold-blooded, prolonged and detailed planning of the events make this reading difficult.

Suicide presents the world with lips forever closed upon the questions we would wish to ask, of which 'story' best accounts for these appalling events; of the character and motivations to be ascribed to these apparently 'normal' citizens. One recent case *did* leave us with a 'live' perpetrator—that of Joanne Hill, recently convicted of the murder of her small daughter, who was drowned in her bath in November 2007.[2] In Hill's case, there was overt evidence of a long history of mental disorder though with little room for a narrative concerning protective instincts or displaced integrity. Hill's husband gave evidence for the prosecution that he sometimes returned from work to find his wife the worse for alcohol and that she was 'ashamed' of their daughter's mild disabilities. This account clearly fuelled the view of Joanne Hill as an unnatural mother, coldly judging and finding her daughter wanting for being less than perfect. Though commentary and expert testimony during and subsequent to the case highlighted Hill's history of mental illness, dating back to her teens and including two suicide attempts, chronic anxiety and a 'hypermanic' episode, the jury nevertheless satisfied themselves that Hill was in command of her faculties when the event took place. Yet one might speculate as to the difficulties of inhabiting a psyche imposing an entrenched and dramatically distorting impact upon day-to-day life and consider whether this implies such mental abnormality as to mitigate, or negate her responsibility for the act.

Common to all the cases, though apparently most strenuous on the part of Hill, was the attempt on the part of each of the perpetrators to present and function with a 'normal' persona, yet unable to articulate in words the magnitude and power of the chaos unfolding within them. Whilst a rich fabric of surmise—popular and professional—settles around such cases, the narrative of the subject themselves resists exposure. For both legal and psychiatric interpretation in all these cases, evidence of premeditation situates the forensic accounts of agency whilst at the same time narrative informs this situational approach to

[2] Helen Pidd, 'The mental strife behind tragedy of a child's death', *The Guardian*, 27 Saturday September 2008.

the characterization of the legal subject. Yet, in the drive to demonstrate the forensic proficiency and impartiality of its practices, the law is much concerned with 'doctrine' and 'principle', subsuming recognition of its own rhetorical and narrative gloss. *Some* academic recognition has occurred—Bernard Jackson undertakes an extensive exploration of the links between 'law, fact and narrative coherence' in the book of that name[3] explaining that 'narrative structures inform not only the content but also the manner in which stories are told', and acknowledges that 'neither the Common Law of evidence nor the strategies of Anglo-American pleaders necessarily challenge our conventional presuppositions regarding language, truth and reality'.[4] Jackson also notes the importance of notions of 'narrative coherence', citing MacCormick's discussion of narrative coherence as:

> A test of truth or probability in questions of fact and evidence upon which direct proof by immediate observation is unavailable . . . [ultimately] MacCormick is not satisfied by the common-sensical status of narrative coherence; he seeks, at the least, to validate narrative coherence through recourse to a more scientific form of justificatory discourse.[5]

It may be argued, however, that a measure of disquiet should arise from the realization that this delicate interchange, between narrative apprehensions of fact and evidence and a 'more scientific form of justificatory discourse' is an elusive conception; the implications for the reliability of evidence profound.

Narrative is at the heart not only of legal practice, it is also central to legal theory and to the epistemologies of specialist forms of knowledge generally upon which the law relies—to the stories specialisms tell, not only of those subject to their gaze, but of themselves, of their locus in making such statements. Of course, potentially such thoughts have major implications as to the very identity of the law itself, of the standing of authoritative disciplines to make pronouncements. This chapter simply sets out to explore a 'subset' of issues, concerned with how we orientate our pronouncements on the 'normal' and how that links into the disciplines concerned with analysis of the human psyche. In particular, the discussion touches upon the challenge posed by the 'discovery' that is the unconscious and of the possible impact this entity holds for the orthodoxies of forensic psychiatry. And since the idea of

[3] Bernard S Jackson, *Law, Fact and Narrative Coherence* (Deborah Charles Publications: Liverpool, 1988).

[4] Ibid, 11–12.

[5] Ibid, 18–19.

narrative is intrinsic to our engagement with the world, whether as individuals or as practitioners, it may be helpful to think of the relevance of narrative to these issues—and of the interplay between discourses as authority and as premise. 'Narrative', Prince tells us, is a particular mode of knowledge communication which:[6]

> Does not merely reflect what happens; it discovers and invents what can happen. It does not simply record events, it constitutes and interprets them as meaningful parts of meaningful wholes, whether the latter are situations, practices, persons, or societies . . . By showing that disparate situations and events compose one signifying structure (or vice versa) and, more specifically, by giving its own form of order and coherence to a possible reality, narrative supplies models for that reality's transformation or redescription and mediates between the law of what is and the human desire for what may be.

As others have observed, law may be regarded as a 'master' or 'meta' narrative, a narrative in which various conceptual artefacts sustain one another by association. In 'The Postmodern Condition', Lyotard defines the postmodern[7] simply as 'incredulity toward metanarratives': certainly there is scope if not for incredulity, then for scepticism, towards the metanarratives of the reasonable and the normal in law and in medicine and such scepticism may extend to the critiques of those metanarratives since critiques are always situationally positioned. Thus, doctrinal critiques of the law and of the relationship between law and its expert advisors tend to be incremental, whilst radical critiques may be absorbed by the political or aesthetic dis/location of their own new voice. The justice available to the legal subject is enmeshed and sometimes submerged within these turbulent intellectual realms.

Narrative analysis of authoritative discursive sources may yield very different insights to those permitted by purely doctrinal constraint. The hegemonies of medicine as well as law drive particular visions of reality and these impact dramatically upon their practitioners and end-subjects.[8] Yet, one can see the relevance of Prince's account not only to

[6] Gerald Prince, 'On Narratology (Past, Present, Future)' in Martin McQuillan (ed) *The Narrative Reader* (Routledge: London, 2000) 129. Prince identifies that the word narrative relates to the Latin *gnarus*—'knowing', 'expert', 'acquainted with'—which itself derives from the Indo-European root *gna* 'to know'.

[7] Jean-Francois Lyotard, 'The Postmodern Condition' in Julie Rivkin and Michael Ryan (eds) *Literary Theory, An Anthology* (Wiley Blackwell: Oxford, 2004) 356.

[8] Patricia Ewick and Susan Silbey, 'Subversive Stories and Hegemonic Tales: Toward a Sociology of Narrative', (1995) 29(2) Law and Society Review 197–226 at 212:

constructions of reality in such different spheres, but to the law in particular, which 'constitutes and interprets' events most profoundly.[9] Everyday life too presents individual persons with the need to construct narrative accounts: negotiating everyday life involves an endless process of judgment, where personal encounters, diverse information sources and belief systems must all be interpreted for *their* integrity (as reliability and as veracity) in line with the existing experiences and persona

'Narratives do more than simply reflect or express existing ideologies. Through their telling, our stories come to constitute the hegemony that in turn shapes social lives and conduct . . . hegemony (Silberstein 1988:127) has "a protean nature in which dominant relations are preserved while their manifestations remain highly flexible".' Ewick and Silbey (at 201) also refer to Bruner's distinction between narrative and 'non-narrative' forms of discourse: 'Bruner describes two "modes of cognitive functioning, two modes of thought, each providing distinctive ways of ordering experience, by constructing reality". One mode he calls logico-scientific, or paradigmatic. This mode includes arguments that make truth claims which are falsifiable through either formal logic or empirical evidence. The second mode of cognition, Bruner identifies as *stories* or *narratives*. Rather than truth, narratives seek lifelikeness and verisimilitude. In the worlds of law and medicine it may be argued, the distinction between the two is less clear than this definition suggests.'

[9] Indeed, free of the hegemonic constraints of professional corroboration and endorsement, of taxonomic adherence and legitimation, literary sources by comparison have long presaged developments later acknowledged by formal doctrine. For example, Dostoyevsky's *Crime and Punishment* (published in 1866, years before the true formulation of psychiatric medicine and psychoanalytic insights) is recognized as a leading work of the realist genre and a profound reflection upon the relationship between aberrant behaviour and state of mind. Specifically, the text holds a truly radical approach to such issues through the perspectives both of omniscient narrator and protagonist. The main character in the book, Raskolnikov, is a law student who commits a murder; intelligent and tortured, he experiences a range of mental states. Clearly premeditated, full mental responsibility for his action is nevertheless arguable. Though *Crime and Punishment* may be said, in simple terms, to portray the life of a criminal—from the emergence of his criminal intent, through the perpetration of the crime, the agonies of mind in relation to concealing and revealing his role, his exposure, punishment and eventual remorse—analysis of the text highlights the chaotic and antic background to this chronicle. For the influences governing the access to truth are themselves dominated by utterly disorienting psychological landscapes, from the idiosyncratically personal to the ideological. Ideologically driven action is a central theme in *Crime and Punishment* and the text can be read as an early discussion of politically motivated crime, of the 'freedom fighter' or 'terrorist', who believes himself 'superior', the source of heightened vision and insights. Both themes of course remain profoundly relevant to current local and global debates in politics and criminology. Such direct manifestations of terrorist type activity, though pressing, are not the main theme of this chapter. They are however, tangentially relevant to the discussion of the relationship between constructions of integrity—as personal 'wholeness' and verisimilitude—and of reality, of the engagement with the material world as perceived. In addition, Dostoyevsky's explorations of fabulating mental landscapes, waking dream states and liminal states of consciousness are prescient portrayals given current concerns in a range of disciplines, from neurology to psychology and philosophy.

of the judging subject.[10] In building individual identity, the subject must exercise judgment as to which values and beliefs require allegiance, and this exercise of judgment requires both analytical and emotive intellectual engagement, culminating in the approach towards narrative coherence informing both identity and agency.[11]

Cases and Issues in Law and Psychiatry

Just as the legal subject must engage with the narrative processes available to her, extrapolating those most relevant to personal and cultural values and beliefs, so too practitioners of law and of medicine are locked into particular narrative drives. In law, this is nowhere more apparent than in the assessments and doctrines concerned with reasonableness and normality.[12] Certainly there is wide appreciation of the fact that analyses of reasonable conduct in various extreme circumstances and responses to such circumstances, of long-term provocation and self-defence, for example, are not simply the products of 'common sense' perspectives, but of cultural beliefs and of professional assertions too and are therefore vulnerable to criticism. Where such assessments

[10] For example see Daniel Kahneman, 'Judgment and Decision Making: A Personal View' (2006) 2(3) *Psychological Science* 142–5; Wolfgang Blankenburg, 'First Steps Towards a Psychopathology of Common Sense' (2001) 8(4) *Philosophy, Psychiatry, and Psychology* 303–15.

[11] Discussion of this axis is particularly developed in philosophical terms amongst normative philosophers such as Christine Korsgaard; the reflective values described however tend to represent deeply considered processes of abstraction—see, eg, Eric Watkins and William Fitzpatrick, 'O'Neill and Korsgaard on the Construction of Normativity' (2002) 36 *The Journal of Value Inquiry* 349–67.

[12] Though the 'reasonable man' should not, according to legal principle, be confused with the 'normal' or 'average' man, as AP Herbert so famously satirized, the logic of the distinction is questionable. JR Lucas, 'The Philosophy of the Reasonable Man' (1963) 13(51) *The Philosophical Quarterly* 97–106, 103 speaks of the 'fallibility of the reasonable man' and asserts that it is this very fallibility that is responsible for the *dialectical* quality of much of our thinking (emphasis added). See also Tatjana Hornle, 'Social Expectations in the Criminal Law: The "Reasonable Person" in a Comparative Perspective' (2008) 11(1) New Criminal Law Review 1–32. In juristic discourse, the characteristics of normality are usually only identified by contrast with the qualities in question, for example in *R v Bowen* [1996] 2 Cr App Rep 157 the court considered that the principles available from the authorities on the issue included the observation (in relation to duress) that if the accused is more 'pliable, vulnerable, timid or susceptible to threats than the normal person—these are not characteristics with which the reasonable/ordinary man is to be invested'. Certain 'characteristics' have of course been accorded special status in doctrinal formulae, such as that pertaining to provocation; the provision of such status may however be open to debate on many fronts, as is demonstrated by the vicissitudes of common law decisions.

collide with assertions concerning the psychological robustness of the legal subject and the possible boundary of mental health and well-being, the territory becomes troubled indeed. In some cases, this issue of the boundaries of mental health is a direct diagnostic challenge—for example where specialists are called upon to identify whether the legal subject is mentally ill.[13] In addition, for the law in recent years, such debates have been particularly exercised in the discussion of 'provocation doctrine', of the strange nexus between 'common sense' understandings of what a person might do under extreme circumstances, and what psychiatric assessments assert to be normal, rational reactions to such circumstances, with the cases and debates challenged still further by the impact of gender.[14] In England and Wales, the legal

[13] As legal academics know, the frameworks concerned with assessing mental status are complex. The M'Naghten Rules direct the (very rarely used) finding of insanity, requiring identification of a 'disease of the mind', causing a 'defect of reason' such that either a) the defendant does not understand the nature and quality of his act or b) does not know that it is wrong. The Draft Criminal Code Bill (Law Commission Report No 177, clauses 34–5) suggests revision to include reference to 'severe mental illness' or arrested development or a state of automatism for example. States such as automatism have given rise to debates as to whether the condition is caused by an 'internal' or 'external' factor, and liability will be affected by whether the condition was 'self inflicted'. A successful plea of automatism provides a complete defence. The pleas of insanity and automatism are rare. More generally, the mitigating issues of provocation and diminished responsibility may be raised. Provocation is defined by the Homicide Act 1957, s 3 which states '[W]here on a charge of murder there is evidence on which the jury can find that the person charged was provoked (whether by things done or by things said or by both together) to lose his self-control, the question whether the provocation was enough to make a reasonable man do as he did shall be left to be determined by the jury; and in determining that question the jury shall take into account everything both done and said according to the effect which, in their opinion, it would have on a reasonable man'. The case law on provocation demonstrates the difficulties arising from notions of 'self control', of 'sudden and temporary' and of 'reasonableness', especially in relation to the kind of characteristics pertinent to such an assessment. The resultant doctrine is not coherent. In addition it should be noted that, although in recent years psychiatric evidence has been deployed to explore these questions, the definition does not require proof of psychiatric disturbance in order to make out the plea. This contrasts with the plea of diminished responsibility (Homicide Act 1957, s 2) which requires proof of an abnormality of mind leading to a substantial impairment of responsibility. Clause 56 of the Law Commission's proposals would amend this to read 'if, at the time of his act, he is suffering from such mental abnormality as is a substantial enough reason to reduce his offence to manslaughter'. 'Mental abnormality' is defined as 'mental illness, arrested or incomplete development of mind, psychopathic disorder, and any other disorder or disability of mind except intoxication'. As will be seen, arguably, defining 'mental abnormality' in these terms simply compounds one doubtful term with another.

[14] eg, see Bernardette McSherry, 'Criminal Responsibility, "Fleeting" States of Mental Impairment and the Power of Self-control' (2004) 27(5) *International Journal of Law and Psychiatry* 445–57.

convolutions around such debates have become so troubled that the Law Commission Consultation Paper *A New Homicide Act for England and Wales* (published in 2005 and currently revisited) concluded that the law of homicide is 'a mess'.[15]

When one comes to examine current trends in the scholarship of the psyche and in the links between law and the psyche, the epistemological and disciplinary strands are notably separate—so, for example, the languages, narratives and debates held by and within forensic psychiatry differ from those in psychology.[16] Though there is some recognition that uncertainties in the relationship between these strands taint the court process, in the criminal realm, there is a predominant acceptance of entrenched convention which, whilst no doubt generally defensible on pragmatic grounds, appears somewhat complacent. Forensic psychiatry, that branch of theorizing the psyche most concerned with providing evidence and rationales for legal use, struggles heroically with the plethora of jurisprudential and nosological issues arising in the courtroom and, as the advising profession, is obliged to assume a mantle of diagnostic certainty in the pyramidal process that is evidence.

The sciences of the psyche have real limitations in this regard. In truth, forensic psychiatry has little certainty when identifying the borders of conditions. In current medical classifications relevant to criminal law and mental health law, much reliance is placed upon the formal listing of psychiatric conditions within the ICD–10, the International Classification of Diseases,[17] so that identification of mental capacity and therefore criminal responsibility may rest upon location

[15] Law Commission, *A New Homicide Act for England and Wales*, Consultation Paper No 177.

[16] For the last several years (as indicated in the article referred to atn 8 above) debate in psychiatry has been very much dominated by the 'dangerousness' debate—by the suggestion that potentially dangerous individuals be incarcerated pre-emptively and that legislative and institutional structures be shaped in support of this. This polarizing issue tends, somewhat simplistically to pitch the 'civil liberties/human rights' camp against the state-orientated theorists of a claimed collective welfare. A linked, and arguably equally pressing issue is that of the very dependability of psychiatry itself. Where there may be questions regarding the diagnostic limitations of psychiatry in these mental health debates, so too questions arise in relation to the expert role of forensic psychiatry in the criminal law, with its enquiry into rationality and responsibility. At heart, this is not simply a diagnostic or pragmatic question, but a philosophical and epistemological one.

[17] World Health Organisation, *International Statistical Classification of Diseases and Related Health Problems* (10th edn, 2007) available at <http://www.who.int/classifications/apps/icd/icd10online>. The independent American system is the DSM, the *Diagnostic and Statistical Manual of Mental Disorders*.

within this index. Indeed, the very existence of such an index supports the assertion that psychiatry holds a scientifically reliable diagnostic key to capacity and foresight. Yet examination of the ICD itself reveals a number of taxonomic residues, suggesting a wide degree of diagnostic licence or, to put it more bluntly, forensic uncertainty masked as nosological genera.[18] This uncertainty is clearly evident, for example, in relation to the bundle of characteristics labelled 'personality disorders'.[19] Such profiles, which, according to the ICD–10 range from paranoid to schizoid, anxious, dependent, anankastic, histrionic, emotionally unstable/impulsive, and dissocial types to borderline types, chart a wide range of human personality characteristics; the classification system suggests that 'mental illness' can be readily identified as an entity separate from these disordered types. Disordered persons of the psychopathic type are, it is said, recognizably common amongst the criminal population[20] and 'the differential diagnosis of personality disorder includes deterioration in personality and social functioning and/or disinheriting of behaviour due to *severe mental illness*'.[21] The fact that the term 'mental illness' is not defined for legal purposes must be a matter of some disquiet, given its central role in legal assessment.[22]

The narrative structures and rationales of the law and of medicine appear to provide a seamless collaboration of authoritative discourses. Diagnostic uncertainty around the context of an otherwise functional, indeed premeditating and apparently rational individual, leans towards

[18] Even where conditions do attain status through inclusion, the jurisprudential standing accorded to the index remains questionable given the forensic uncertainties dominating this branch of psychiatry, evidenced most dramatically in the residue of generic, nosologically 'overspill' conditions—the ICD 10 listing of mental and behavioural disorders includes 'F99—unspecified mental disorder' and this is typical of many sub-categories. See <http://www.who.int/classifications/apps/icd/icd10online/>.

[19] eg, see M Marlow and P Sugarman, 'ABC of Mental Health: Disorders of Personality' (1997) 315(7101) *BMJ* 176–9 available at <http://www.bmj.com/cgi/content/full/315/7101/176>.

[20] See Puri, Laking and Treasaden, *Textbook of Psychiatry* (2nd edn, Churchill Livingstone: London, 2002) at 307.

[21] Ibid. The emphasis appears in the original text.

[22] In the Mental Health Act 1983, no definition of 'mental illness' was given and indeed no official legal definition exists, although numerous attempts to define it have been made through the years. On the 3 November 2008, the successive statute, the Mental Health Act 2007 was amended to excise the classification of mental disorder into four categories—'mental illness', 'psychopathic disorder', 'mental impairment' and 'severe mental impairment', replacing these with a single, wider reference to 'mental disorder' accommodating 'any disorder or disability of the mind'. The likely impact of this alteration upon medico-legal prognostications is unclear; in the meantime, the term 'mental illness' continues to be used in case law as a common term.

the presumption of capacity and, it may be argued, in so doing reflects a falsely reductive position.[23] Two issues in particular form a backdrop to the categorization process. The belief in the metaphysical phenomenon of 'evil' supports the separation of the 'mad' from the 'bad'—the phenomenon is, though an artefact of disputable philosophical status, of significantly religious origins.[24] Evidence of premeditation, in particular, feeds into belief in a ready separation of those who have rational control from those who have not.[25] In addition, conventional psychiatry is incapable of paying recognition to the power of the unconscious and to liminal states of mind in their capacity to direct an apparently autonomous individual.[26] Though psychological and neurological studies provide evidence of radical challenges to conventional views of the relationship between mind and brain, between dreams and waking perception and apperception,[27] such findings remain at the periphery of established medico-legal doctrinal formulations. In the courtroom, psychiatrists continue to assert their powers of divination to distinguish the responsible from the deranged, whilst at the same time, offenders take up residence in an apparently lucid identity which, while presenting characteristics of responsibility for action—of a capable

[23] Barratt and Felthouse argue that the convergence of scientific advances in cognitive neuroscience holds promise for greater diagnostic certainty in this regard—see Ernest Barratt and Alan Felthouse, 'Impulsive Versus Premeditated Aggression: Implications for *Mens Rea* Decisions' (2003) 21(5) *Behavioural Sciences and the Law* 619–30. This may however reflect an overweening confidence in the capabilities of the science.

[24] See the somewhat naïve references to the identification of 'evil' in William Tucker, 'The "Mad" Versus the "Bad" Revisited: Managing Predatory Behavior' (1999) 70(3) *Psychiatric Quarterly* 221–30.

[25] This in particular presents a barometer of agency utilized both by medical and legal commentators, yet it may be to some degree the product of cultural impositions and therefore of doubtful status—see Lena Jayyusi, 'Premeditation and Happenstance: The Social Construction of Intention, Action and Knowledge' (1993) 16(4) *Human Studies* 435–54.

[26] Tentative forays have occurred in American courts—see Susan Schmeiser, 'Punishing Guilt' (2007) 94(30) *American Imago* 317–37.

[27] See Mark Mahowald, 'Understanding Consciousness: Implications and Consequences' (2003) 46(2) *Perspectives in Biology and Medicine* 297–304; see also Terrence Chorvat and Kevin McCabe, 'The Brain and the Law' (2004) 359(1451) *Philosophical Transactions of the Royal Society: Biological Sciences*, 29 November 2004, 1727–36. The article identifies five areas of neuroscience research of particular application to law—the resolution of moral dilemma, the 'ultimatum game', 'trust games' the interplay between rejection and other forms of enforcement and 'automation'—all exploring the impact of culture upon cognition and behaviour. Research into the boundaries of sleep and consciousness suggest new perspectives—for example in 'Lack of Sleep is a Lot like Mental Illness', *New Scientist*, 26 October 2007, it was reported that brain activity associated with psychiatric illness was observed in healthy people who had missed a single night's sleep.

persona or calculating premeditation, for example—may well be truly deserving of psychiatric (and philosophical) notice.

Yet the narrative processes of law and medicine, as well as those of the individual, may converge to produce a seamless account which appears to fulfill the requirements of narrative unity required by the rules of evidence[28] and law and apparently in conformity with the burden of proof.[29] Consider for example two recent murder appeal cases in the United Kingdom. The first arguably is a case of psychiatric illness poorly served by medical opinion, the second deals essentially with an individual of psychiatric *health* poorly served by the doctrinal maelstrom of medico-legal narrative—indeed one could characterize the controversial aspects of the cases as issues of narrative and evidential dubiety at least as forcibly as those of forensics.

In the case of *R v Stewart Michael Diamond*,[30] Diamond had murdered a 17 year old youth and disposed of the body. Diamond denied being the perpetrator, but was convicted on the basis of strong forensic evidence. He was sentenced to life imprisonment and, with a long history of violent behaviour already behind him, was later diagnosed as suffering from the mental illness of paranoid schizophrenia. Diamond's legal team appealed (permission to appeal having first been refused) to the Criminal Cases Review Commission in 2005, and in 2006 his conviction was referred to the court by the Commission on the basis that:

(1) he had admitted to killing the victim;
(2) there was strong evidence that his responsibility for the killing was substantially impaired by an abnormality of mind;

[28] It is only relatively recently that forensic evidence as to *physical* phenomena has come under scrutiny, with the incidence of cases such as that of Sally Clark and Angela Cannings—see Alex Wade, 'Science on Trial', *The Guardian*, 18 September 2004 available at <http://www.guardian.co.uk/world/2004/sep/28/law.features11>. Yet psychiatric phenomena are even more disputable. Once expert evidence is deployed, excessive deference seems to attach to it, suspending the usual stringency of examination attaching to other forms of evidence. Although it is recognized that forensic evidence of 'material' issues should be subject to more extensive scrutiny (for example chemical traces)—see Gary Edmond, 'Constructing Miscarriages of Justice: Misunderstanding Scientific Evidence in High Profile Criminal Appeals' (2002) 22(1) Oxford Journal of Legal Studies 53–89, this concern does not appear to extend to forensic psychiatry.

[29] This narrative collaboration may arise as a result of a positive rapport in the doctor-patient relationship—see Rita Charon, 'Narrative Medicine: Attention, Representation, Affiliation' (2005) 13(3) *Narrative* 261–70; the incidence referred to above is less patient-centred and potentially more damaging—a narrative collaboration which may corroborate assertions of capacity or agency.

[30] [2008] EWCA Crim 923; 2008 WL 1867197.

(3) that his mental capacity was significantly impaired by his mental illness at the time he gave his instructions to his defence team; and
(4) that the court should substitute a verdict of manslaughter for that of murder.

The Court of Appeal rejected the plea understandably, and in large part because, it did not feel inclined to prefer later psychiatric assessments over those made nearer to the time of the killing. For our purposes two issues are of interest. First, and the reason for ground (2) of the referral to the Court of Appeal, Diamond persisted in instructing his Counsel that he was not willing to undergo psychiatric assessment for the purposes of pleading that at the time of the killing he was suffering diminished responsibility, maintaining instead the line that he was not responsible for the death of the victim and that he would plead not guilty on that basis. The difficulty here is that the initial not guilty plea, trial and conviction for murder and subsequent unsuccessful appeal, originated in part in an attribution of choice of plea to the accused when that choice may well have reflected his delusional state of mind yet, because he was presented as capable of understanding the nature of the charge and the options open to him, his choice was indulged and drove the subsequent process. Secondly (and this is a factor contributing to the indulgence above) the nosological certainty asserted by psychiatric assessment over the years and relied upon by the Appeal judges was arguable. For some years prior to the killing as well as the period afterwards, Diamond had been subject to a number of psychiatric assessments, all of which, alongside a history of extremely violent behaviour, indicated the presence of a seriously disordered mind. The combination of a somewhat integrated, nominally 'normal' assertive personality with violence and delusional traits presented a challenge to psychiatric interpretation, but this did not prevent practitioners from returning an expert opinion which determined mental responsibility for the purposes of law. Nevertheless, the instability of that opinion is apparent. For example, after stabbing another youth in 1996, the consultant forensic psychiatrist reported in 1997 that the appellant suffered:

> a personality disorder which amounted to a psychopathic disorder within the meaning of the Mental Health Act 1983; she could not recommend a medical disposal as he was not motivated to undergo treatment, but stated that he had significant personality problems and the risk of him offending violently in the future was extremely high. She found no evidence of mental illness.[31]

[31] 2008 WL 1867197, 9 at ix.

After the killing, he was again assessed and it was:[32]

> concluded that there was no doubt that the appellant was unusual and he probably had personality difficulties which might amount to a personality disorder and he might in addition have a mental illness [but] concluded that he was fit to plead in accordance with the legal requirement for fitness to plead.

The first report quoted above, referring to a 'personality disorder' amounting to a 'psychopathic disorder' with 'no evidence of mental illness' amounts to an edifice of liminal assertions.[33] Most significantly, 'mental illness' has no legal or pathological status, though this is the crucial diagnostic assertion as far as the ascription of legal responsibility is concerned. The frailty of the diagnostic edifice becomes more acute in the subsequent assessment, where 'probable' 'personality difficulties' 'might' amount to a 'personality disorder' and 'might' in addition amount to a 'mental illness' though the subject is judged 'fit to plead'. In narratological, as well as diagnostic terms, the assertion clearly lacks coherence. Almost an admission of the inadequacy of the nosological process, this statement is nevertheless accepted as sufficiently reliable by the legal process.

R v Williams, Stephanie[34] is very different in that the perpetrator has no history of mental illness and no significant history of violence or criminality, yet the case provides an additional and similarly troubled example regarding the role of psychiatric assessment. In 2002 appellant Williams killed her partner of three years, John Lamont, with a steak knife during a row in a restaurant. The single wound proved fatal and Williams was tried and convicted of murder. The prosecution case was that Williams murdered Lamont in a rage. The defence was self-

[32] Ibid, 10 at ix.

[33] 'Personality disorder' remains controversial in diagnostic terms whilst the ICD–10 and its American counterpart, the DSM–IV stake diagnostic territory by sub-classifying the paranoid, schizoid, dissocial and histrionic types for example, yet these categories and sub-categories are delicate structures. 'Dissocial' personality disorder is, according to the ICD–10, the diagnostic category established for psychopathy, so presumably this feeds into the confirmation of 'psychopathic disorder'. For a discussion of psychopathic personality disorder, see Puri, Laking and Treasaden, n 20 above, 306 citing Henderson's classification system, which includes 'creative psychopaths, who have high ability combined with their severe personality disorder, such as Lawrence of Arabia and the Renaissance sculptor Cellini'.

[34] [2007] EWCA Crim 2264; 2007 WL 2817884. In July 2008, Williams was granted leave to appeal for a reduction in her sentence in light of new evidence as to the severity of the violence suffered by her and the extent of her progress towards rehabilitation in prison: *Liverpool Echo*, 15 July 2008).

defence. The issues left by the judge to the jury were self defence and provocation.

A summary of the background to the case may be helpful at this point. For much of the three years of their relationship, John Lamont had been serving a prison sentence. There was evidence that he was a highly volatile personality. The relationship was highly charged—Lamont was verbally abusive as well as physically violent and affectionate in turn. Williams presented a generally stable persona. She had, it transpired, suffered sexual abuse as a child; she was described[35] as a woman who had on occasion 'shown aggression' to others, (though not of the order of that meted out to her—she had been the victim of several assaults at the hands of the deceased and others but had no history of physical violence herself) and was generally resourceful, loving, a person who stood up for herself, verbally though not physically, to Lamont.

On his release from prison, Lamont returned to the home of Williams and despite his recent imprisonment and against her wishes, again started dealing drugs. On the 19 February 2002, Lamont and Williams went out to dinner at a restaurant. After the first course, Lamont disappeared for a considerable length of time. Williams believed that his absence was due to a drug dealing arrangement and, on his return, a loud argument ensued to the consternation of other diners. Williams gave evidence that she tried to leave and that Lamont stood up to restrain her, in the struggle Williams picked up a knife from the table and stabbed him once, causing the fatal blow. Whilst counsel for the defence felt that female relatives and friends (capable of attesting to the abuse suffered by Williams at the hands of Lamont) might be somewhat unsuitable and inept in the witness box,[36] diners gave evidence for the prosecution at her trial—no doubt, to lay onlookers, a violent argument between two strangers culminating in a fatal stabbing

[35] Lord Justice Auld [2007] EWCA Crim 2264, para 3.

[36] They were: (i) Michelle Williams, a cousin of the appellant, who referred to having seen the appellant many years before with bad injuries said to have been caused by a previous boyfriend, and of an incident three years before when Lamont had grabbed the appellant by the hair and ripped off her dress. Michelle Williams' statement about the dress incident conflicted with the account of the appellant. Her statement also referred to Lamont's almost paranoid suspicion and jealousy over any contact by the appellant with others; (ii) Angela Hornby, a close friend of the appellant. In her witness statement she referred to an incident in which she had seen Lamont throw the contents of a glass of beer over the appellant and threaten to kill her. Her statement, too, differed in material respects from that of the appellant's account of the same incident; and

presented a 'cut and dried' case.[37] Arguably, the legal strategies adopted responded to evidential and doctrinal drives which constrained the opportunity to represent the most cogent account. The legal narrative could have highlighted a vision of a person of fairly ordinary, perhaps even relatively robust, stability, who nevertheless succumbs to a more 'classical' response to provocation. The defence case could have recounted the dedication, hours, years, emotional and financial sacrifice and willingness to risk domestic stability endured by the accused, in addition to the clear history of psychological and physical cruelty. Instead it would appear to be the case that the narrative was driven first by perceived constraints in doctrinal choices and, thereafter, by an increasingly problematic, pathologizing account.

In July 2007 Williams was unsuccessful in her appeal against conviction and therefore remains imprisoned for murder. The appeal

(iii) Patricia Williams, a sister of the appellant. In her witness statement she referred to the same beer throwing incident, and also to an incident when Lamont had threatened to 'batter' the appellant, of many arguments between them, and of seeing bruises and other signs of violence upon her. Finally, there was a written statement from one of the appellant's previous boyfriends, confirming her account of his violence to her, including the incident in which he seemingly broke her jaw and in respect of which he was convicted of causing her grievous bodily harm.

[37] It is likely that the court was influenced by proximity, by the fact that the injury was inflicted with a close and direct movement not from, say, the other side of the room, nevertheless this factor is not alone compelling in the construction of intention. Several successful appeals and much scholarship have been dedicated to considering the knotty difficulty of identifying the existence and meaning of intention for murder. The key precedents on the construction of intention for murder (*R* v *Moloney* [1985] 1 AC 905; *R* v *Hancock and Shankland* [1986] 2 WLR 257; *R* v *Woollin* (1998) 4 All ER 103) succeeded in being reduced to manslaughter on appeal because of objections raised as to the appropriate judicial direction on the point, and resultant doubt as to whether the presence of intention had been proved, as well as to judicial management of the question, was significant to such reductions. From a technical and critical point of view, two significant articles appeared subsequent to this line of cases. Kaveny (CM Kaveny, 'Inferring Intention from Foresight' (2004) Law Quarterly Review 120) points out the difficulty created by the confusions of doctrine, in distinguishing between morally distinct scenarios: it may be argued that though heinous in her sudden act, there is significant doubt as to whether Williams ever formed a 'murderous purpose'. The facts of *Moloney* and of *Woollin* are relevant here—in both cases, the perpetrator killed from a more or less 'point blank' physical proximity (thus a jury in the first instance might have been more likely to 'assume' an intention to kill or cause GBH was present) but the circumstances of the killings—the 'contest' between stepfather and stepson; their less than controlled state against a background of their clear affection for one another in the one case and the father experiencing a moment of exasperation in the other—gave context to the doubt at appeal as to judicial direction in the trial at first instance. Kaveny's citing of Duff's counterfactual test is also significant to this point—Kaveny refers to the counterfactual test/Duff's 'test of failure'—which asks, essentially, if the defendant had not succeeded in creating the event risk, would they have failed to achieve their purpose?

related to a request that the court consider fresh medical evidence and its impact upon the relevance of pleas of provocation or diminished responsibility.[38] It should be noted however that these pleas had not been mounted by counsel in the original trial—indeed, provocation was mentioned only belatedly, by the judge. The concatenation of arguments, doctrinal and medical, both at original trial, and at appeal, creates a complex edifice of doubtful equity in the adjudication of the case.

In purely doctrinal, as well as narratological terms, the case is disturbing given the questionable issue of specific intention. Scholarship points to the inconsistent reasoning underlying the line of precedents concerned with intention to kill or cause serious bodily harm, a field which again may be understood as a narrative concerned with normality and norms. The circumstances of the killing in *Williams*—of a violent argument breaking out during a special dinner date in a restaurant, following significant provocative and violent behaviour by the victim—when set against the context of a sometimes loving though volatile relationship and somewhat misplaced protectiveness towards the victim by the accused, militates against a suggestion of premeditation or the formation of intention for murder.[39] The fact of a direct knife wound might be construed as providing evidence of direct intention, nevertheless the contextual circumstances point away from that conclusion, as was the subtext to the appeal case for example in the case of *R v Moloney*.[40] The defence should have provided a spirited account querying the formation of intention yet such a critique cannot find a ready conduit through the doctrinal routes of the law on the point. Though we must 'prove' an intention to kill or cause serious bodily harm, the caution, indicated by the complexity of judicial direction, arguably does not readily transmit effectively to juries—the

[38] Lord Justice Auld summarizes the argument in his concluding judgment (para 42): 'Having received or having considered whether to receive, pursuant to section 23 of the 1968 Act, "new" psychiatric evidence, coupled if necessary with "new" factual evidence on which it is purportedly based, a court may allow an appeal against a conviction for murder as unsafe on the ground that, if that evidence had been before the trial jury, they might have acquitted the appellant on one or other of the defences of diminished responsibility, or provocation where applicable, or self-defence. Such evidence may, in a conviction of a woman for murder of her husband or partner, go to a defence, whether or not run at trial, based on evidence of "battered woman syndrome" in support of a defence of provocation, as in *R v Thornton* [1996] 2 Cr App R 108, and/or of diminished responsibility. . .'

[39] It also epitomizes the kind of case arguably envisioned by the prospective reforms to the law of homicide.

[40] [1985] 2 WLR 648.

attempt to create a lucid narrative thread becomes 'lost in translation', diverted into complex doctrinal by-ways.[41]

Here again, psychiatric assessment was critical to the outcome of the case, and again the accused, both at first instance and on appeal, presented a persona which 'steered' the finding that she was fully competent at the time of the offence[42]. It should be recalled here that classical provocation doctrine did not require a psychiatric account of state of mind, nor would a calm and stable persona some time after the event—say in the classic male perpetrator—necessarily have undermined a finding of a momentary loss of self-control at the time of the offence. Williams seemed equable when visited in her cell; she refused to allow submission of evidence that she had been sexually abused as a child although this history would have been germane to her subsequent pattern in entering a series of violent and abusive relationships—a damaging background which may well have been a significant precursor to the state of mind leading to the fatal act. Yet the psychiatric assessment not only adjudged Williams to be not suffering from mental instability at the time of the killing (which again may be arguable once one takes account of the possibility that Williams, like Diamond, may simply have been able to present a persuasive 'overlay' of a coping, assertive, and capable persona) but in doing so, perhaps also influenced the confirmation of premeditation. A Dr Boyd was called by the appellant's solicitors, somewhat belatedly, to make an assessment of her mental condition. At a later stage a Dr Johns also contributed an opinion on behalf of the defence. At appeal, Dr Boyd—for the defence —we are told[43]

> . . .also took issue with Dr Johns' conclusions some years after the event that the appellant had moderately severe depression or any clinical mood disorder.

[41] Duff and ors explore changes in the trial culture contributing to these difficulties —see Anthony Duff, Lindsay Farmer, Sandra Marshall, and Victor Tadros, *The Trial on Trial* (Hart Publishing: Oxford, 2007) 53.

[42] Williams was subject of a number of psychiatric reports—the first provided for the Crown Prosecution Service in 2002 (by a Dr Noblett) with a hasty commissioning of a defence report just a few days before the trial, written by Dr Boyd. A Dr Johns reported in 2005 as part of the preparation for the appeal case, and again in 2006; Dr Boyd added comments in a letter of 2007 and oral submissions were made too. This complex expert evidential chronology indicates the troubled management of doctrinal strategies, with defence evidence called belatedly and then, at appeal, suffering inroads upon its credibility both from legal attempts to direct it to create doctrinal 'fit' and from medical disagreement as to the finer points of nosological and narratological status.

[43] 2007 WL 2817884, para 31, quoting letter from Dr Boyd dated April 2007.

He asserted that such 'features' of post-traumatic stress disorder, if any, were not 'more severe than those one would normally expect to find in someone who has experienced episodes of violence'. He confirmed his earlier diagnosis of no depressive disorder or any 'elements that would constitute an inherent cause' or anything in her mental state that would have supported a defence of diminished responsibility. He concluded with the following inconclusive reference to a possible defence of provocation and to the sort of issues that it might throw up, on which Mr Bennathan placed some reliance. He said: 'I do not believe that at the time of the index offence [the appellant] had post-traumatic stress disorder, any depressive order, or any elements that would constitute an inherent cause. As such I do not consider that [the appellant] had any abnormality of mind that could be considered to have substantially impaired her mental responsibility at the time in question. I do not therefore feel that a defence of diminished responsibility is relevant in this case . . . In my original report I did suggest that if [the appellant] had been abused by John Lamont one could understand how she would have felt particularly threatened in the situation she claimed at the time in question and her response in hitting out at him may be understandable and possibly not unreasonable. One could propound that there was a loss of self-control influenced by a history of violence and the threatening situation at the time. This is where the degree of previous violence could be an issue in relation to the level of [the appellant's] response to her perception of the situation, and may be a factor that the jury at the time did not fully consider. The fact that [the appellant] had picked up a knife before hitting out at John Lamont does bring into question her intent at the time, how much self-control she had and whether the degree of her response to the perceived threat was proportionate. There would appear to be issue concerning a possible plea of provocation.'

Narratologically, this commentary reveals a series of movements which 'locate' the author in relation to his professional colleague in a complex chronicle of self-justification. The entire passage reveals a disturbing combination of medical conjecture, doctrinal speculation and legal muddle which, were it not for the arcane standing of expert evidence and the semiotic power of the legal context and report, would clearly attract queries as to its credibility. The last comment is particularly bizarre. Dr Boyd—an expert for the defence—effectively *points out* to the court that picking up the knife may have implications regarding the formation of intention. Asked to give a medical opinion, he strays into the doctrinal legal narrative concerning the formation of intention, signalling the fact that the act of picking up the implement indicates a high degree of premeditative association between mind and body. The apparent neutrality of his statement, that it does 'bring into question' her intent is undermined by the clear signal towards decisive action.

The subsequent addition of the comment regarding the potential relevance of provocation doctrine is therefore undermined. Strangely discordant with the role of medical expert called on behalf of the defence, the opinion is significant for its ambivalence bordering upon hostility. Dr Boyd begins by attacking the finding of mood disorder, and feels able to distinguish the response of the subject to trauma as '*not more severe than one would normally expect to find in someone who has experienced episodes of violence*' (italics added). Claiming such certainty in identifying pathologically non-significant, as opposed to significant, responses to the troubled territory traversed in the experience of episodes of violence is odd—certainty as to the presence of pathology is one thing, asserting its absence is altogether strange.[44] Even the most expert medical witness can only speculate as to the likely impact of such a long-term trauma, especially given the subtle interaction between psychological reaction to trauma and the endless intangibles concerning the robustness of personalities.

Not only is critique of such cases significant from the professional evidential point of view—raising questions about the hegemonic status ascribed to psychiatric prognostications—it can also liberate a kind of narrative perspective too. Narratologically, the key actors in these cases, perpetrators and professionals, become caught in the compelling 'scripts' of their cultures. The legal team in *Diamond* must acknowledge his capacity to direct the approach to the case—and structure their doctrinal approaches accordingly—so long as the medical experts advise that he is not suffering from a 'mental illness'. The medical experts themselves must advise that he has this adequate capacity since his profile does not 'fit' within the (clearly unreliable) forensic constraints of pathological prognostication. Yet asserting that personality disorder of such severity does not amount to 'mental illness' is deeply questionable and ultimately somewhat circular—as already mentioned, 'mental illness' itself is not readily defined.

In *Williams*, the intelligible narrative of a 'last straw' reaction to an extreme build up of pressures in the context of threats and violence becomes caught in the strategic narratives of medico-legal dogmas, whilst the somewhat inappropriate (in light of her dire circumstances) composure of the perpetrator may well form the irresistible 'script' of

[44] It also shows ignorance of the symptoms of 'affect' as a result of trauma—one of which is a shocked, calm competent externality such as the accused showed at the time of and after the event (I am grateful to Eleanor Creed-Miles, Consultant Psychotherapist, for making this point).

her background. Without wishing to glorify or excuse her failings, one cannot help feeling that, at the heart of this case is a woman whose own potentially viable claim to a juristically relevant history of trauma is undermined by her propensity for survival, still a somewhat unfeminine trait, exacerbated by a persona not crafted to adduce juristic sympathy. From such tough socio-economic backgrounds individuals, even when victims themselves, frequently take pride in maintaining an aura of self-sufficiency and defiance.[45] 'Feisty' and at times foul-mouthed, a seeming 'match' for her aggressors, Williams did nothing to help herself. Other traits—of honesty (Williams surrendered herself and was not willing to draw upon the abuse she had suffered formerly to ameliorate her position), and of misplaced loyalty (to Lamont, with her bungled attempts to help him, and to her abusing stepfather) gained her no credit. They indeed worked directly against her, where a less frank persona might indeed have 'worked' the circumstances, teasing justice from the maelstrom of tragedy produced by the collision of these two young lives. Medical assessments of status are vulnerable to such coping mechanisms and cannot in truth vouch the security of their pronouncements, hence the reliance, medical and legal, upon the word 'opinion'. Yet these assessments drive subsequent doctrinal legal strategy. In *Williams* in particular, with a weak initial selection of self-defence as the main defence strategy, which neglected the potential for provocation and diminished responsibility doctrine, and a somewhat chaotic appeal strategy in which the conflict in medical and legal

[45] This of course implicates an additional debate about free will and determinism—for a discussion of the links between philosophical notions of free will and determinism and neurological findings, see Joshua Greene and Jonathan Cohen, 'For the Law, Neuroscience Changes Nothing and Everything' (2004) 359(1451) *Philosophical Transactions of the Royal Society: Biological Sciences*, 29 November 2004, 1775–85 at 1776–84: 'The law *says* that it presupposes nothing more than a metaphysically modest notion of free will that is perfectly compatible with determinism. However, we argue that the law's intuitive support is ultimately grounded in a metaphysically over-ambitious, libertarian notion of free will that is threatened by determinism and, more pointedly, by forthcoming cognitive neuroscience . . . Neuroscience is unlikely to tell us anything that will challenge the law's stated assumptions. However, we maintain that advances in neuroscience are likely to change the way people think about human action and criminal responsibility by vividly illustrating lessons that some people appreciated long ago. Free will as we ordinarily understand it is an illusion generated by our cognitive architecture. Retributivist notions of criminal responsibility ultimately depend on this illusion, and, if we are lucky, they will give way to consequentialist ones, thus radically transforming our approach to criminal justice'. For a report—and caution as to the potential contribution of neuroscientific findings, see Linda Geddes, 'Could brain scans ever be evidence?' *New Scientist*, 4 October 2008, 8–9, considering the potential use of fMRI brain scanning as a form of lie detection.

approaches combines to further undermine the credibility of the appellant, it could be argued that the whole case, from initial first instance trial through the process of appeal, evidences little more than a catalogue of narratives competing for hegemonic supremacy, leaving Williams herself displaced by uncertain doctrinal and medical taxonomies.[46] It would seem that her legal team were diverted initially from pleading provocation (so that the judge felt compelled to mention it belatedly in summing up) due to a perceived lack of 'fit' in the case with the already diluted diversion of doctrine into the 'slow burn' of the female victim turned perpetrator. Given that self-defence is an absolute defence, its chances of success in such circumstances would always have been in doubt. It is possible that fear was a dominant factor in that fatal split-second act, and this could have informed a more potent argument from provocation as well as that for self-defence. The emotional territory in these extreme circumstances is truly complex. Law Commission discussions acknowledge this.[47] Holton and Shute acknowledge

[46] The confusion is no doubt compounded by the pressure to identify a sensitizing pathology, so justifying the adduction of expert opinion. Roderick Munday points out the principle that '[T]he expert's opinion must relate to something outside the ordinary ken of the average juror. . .*Turner* [1975] QB 834 is one of a number of cases that betray a certain reserve regarding the evidence of medical witnesses who specialize in the workings of the human mind. . .If the court is dealing with someone who is not normal, then the testimony of experts will be admitted. . .in *Gilfoyle* [2001] 2 Cr App R 57, a murder case. . .the court stated, *inter alia* that a jury did not need a psychologist to inform them how ordinary people were likely to react to the stresses and strains of life. This principle assumes a somewhat extensive juror sensibility as well as a reliable system for calibrating the normal and the abnormal. Rarely, courts have allowed psychological or psychiatric evidence of an accuser's disposition, eg where a judgment must be made as to the relative credibility of competing co-defendant accounts'. See R Munday, *Evidence* (Oxford University Press: Oxford, 2007) 358–61.

[47] The Consultation Paper theorizes a logical correlation between circumstances pertaining to provocation and those relating to self-defence, a discussion of direct relevance to the circumstances of the *Williams* case. At paras 4.36 and 4.37 it is argued: '[S]elf-defence if successfully pleaded is a defence to murder resulting in a complete acquittal. However, for the defendant successfully to raise the defence, he or she must have used no more than reasonable force. If a jury finds that the force used was unreasonable the defence fails and the defendant is guilty of murder. There is no legal "halfway house" for those who overreact, even if they do so in the face of serious unlawful violence. This emphasizes the lack of coherence in the law. If a plea of provocation can reduce murder to manslaughter, it ought to be possible to reach this result when a jury decides that there has been an excessive reaction to a threat of serious unlawful violence. In our report Partial Defences to Murder we recommended that the partial defence of provocation should be reshaped to include cases where the offender acted in response to fear of serious violence to him or herself or another.' *A New Homicide Act for England and Wales*, Law Commission Consultation Paper No 177, 4.37.

Horder's view that someone who acts from fear rather than anger should be able to avail herself of the defence of provocation:

> Fear, too can undermine self-control, and, as Horder points out, is a more likely response to provocation in cases where the provoker is the more powerful. Legal opinion is turning to recognize this. In *Smith*, Lord Hoffman indicated that there are cases where fear may now provide a sufficient basis for invoking the provocation defence: 'the law now recognizes that the emotions which may cause loss of self-control are not confined to anger but may include fear and despair'.[48]

As mentioned heretofore, Williams has been permitted an appeal as to sentence, sought by her legal team on the basis of 'new' evidence as to the extent of the threats and mental cruelty to which she was subjected—having failed in the appeal court as to doctrinal location, only the less technically troubled locus of sentencing policies remain. Yet one might argue that this is a poor recompense following upon the failure of poor original defence strategies. The 'new' evidence appears in the form of letters written by the deceased to the appellant from prison, promising death to her should she alter her position to him—and what greater statement of love might such a woman have come to expect than a man's dedicated expression of desire to kill her?

Forensic psychiatry is of necessity somewhat embattled because, at its nosological and taxonomic boundaries lie the big questions of human being—of the relationship between mind and brain; of the meaning of mental disorder; of the relationship between good and evil, capacity and madness.[49] The sciences of the psyche themselves hold countless philosophical mysteries, buried in the assertions of their 'master narratives'. Thus forensic psychiatry claims a dramatic territory of Shakespearean proportions, of privileged access to the inner truths of the mind, of absolutes of sanity and madness, good and evil, and rallies such pronouncements to a legal process dispensing a practical day's work.[50] In his exploration of the unconscious, Freud famously recognized the

[48] Richard Holton, Stephen Shute, 'Self-control in the Modern Provocation Defence' (2007) *Oxford Journal of Legal Studies* 49–73, at 72.

[49] Some psychiatrists attempt to chart these waters—for example exploring distinctions between 'psychopaths' and 'evil narcissists' through a 'cognitive-affective neuroscience'—see Dan Stein, 'The Philosophy of Evil' (2005) 12(3) *Philosophy, Psychiatry and Psychology* 261–3.

[50] Yet the great writers of the classical tradition, from the ancient tragedies and philosophies to Shakespeare and modern classical creations from Dickens to Dostoyevsky, recognize that such reductive accounts are wholly misleading.

relevance of classical archetypes, from Narcissus to Oedipus, but though trained in conventional medicine and psychiatry in addition to exploring the realms of the unconscious, he was notably wary of the medico-legal evidential circuit, similarly recognizing the false footing of presumptive nosology. Indeed, the silent yet pervasive influence of the unconscious is subversive of readily tangible accounts. Freud, reflecting upon Dostoyevsky's *Crime and Punishment* once famously stated that Dostoevsky 'could have been mankind's liberator–but instead, he chose to be its jailer', disappointed at Dostoevsky's turn to religion and the philosophy of redemption as his answer to the effects of political injustice upon the human psyche. Yet Nietzsche acknowledged Dostoevsky as 'the only psychologist I have anything to learn from' and this statement more accurately reflects the dramatic and presciently rendered interplay of conscious and unconscious drives in the creation of agency—something Freud might have acknowledged with more generosity.[51]

Once one even begins to accept the existence and influence of the unconscious as a force, orthodox psychiatry is clearly lacking, since unconscious drives are beyond its taxonomic capacity. Only psychoanalysis has attempted seriously to chart the realms and influence—the narrative drives—of the unconscious, yet, in the soundings permitted by the hierarchies of the professions, psychoanalytic accounts are not consulted. Lacan, Freud's professional descendant, was deeply conscious of the territorial significance of the divide. Though himself qualified in conventional psychiatry as well as psychoanalysis, Lacan refused to take part in expert evidential contributions to legal cases, recognizing that such contributions simply reified the location of the already dominant 'master narrative' of forensic psychiatry. Yet psychoanalytic theory, though developed long after the writing of key classical texts, provides perceptive touchstones relevant to the issues raised by them—of fabulation; of dream-like states of consciousness; of the links to liminal states of normative judgment and mind; and of the crucial role of narrative in all of these phenomena.[52] In the quest to

[51] For both quotations, see the 'Afterword' to *Crime and Punishment* in the 2006 Penguin USA edition (Penguin: New York, 2006).

[52] Indeed if one were to focus upon a psychoanalytic critique of *Crime and Punishment*, a number of psychoanalytic sources might be adduced in support of a 'psychoanalytic' reading of the text. Some of these points are notably topical—Lacan's interest in creative writing as a conduit for psychopathic impulses is referable to Raskolnikov, who only discovers after he has committed murder that his article on the relationship between crime and power has been published. The absence of a father in the life of

identify more cogent sources of insight into the mystery that is the human psyche and the journey from 'normal' to 'abnormal' behaviour, recent writings in psychoanalysis not only provide more coherent and unifying accounts of agency, but also of the fundamental need to appreciate the role of narrative in the troubled axis between psyche and agency.

Law, the Psyche, and History

As we have seen, the links between the worlds of law and medicine are philosophically and evidentially complex. Epistemological histories form part of this evidential story. Debates concerning the relative credibility and merit of psychiatric and psychological nosology in particular have an intriguing history. Carolyn Dean[53] has traced the particular sensitivity to the issue in France, where:[54]

> . . . determining a criminal's actual responsibility for his or her crime had been a controversial issue within the psychiatric profession since 1907, when psychiatrists were asked to take a greater role in judicial decision making—to translate complex medical terminology into a comprehensible legal vocabulary—at the same time that medical indecision had created what Robert Nye has called a 'crisis' in public and judicial confidence in expert medical testimony . . . by the early twentieth century, psychiatric nosology had become so complex that psychiatrists were required to clarify its categories for juries. . ..at the same time that this very complexity was overwhelming psychiatrists themselves . . .

In addition to this strictly nosological issue, some commentators were aware of the fact that the uncertainty posed radical implications for jurisprudence. As Dean recounts:[55]

> Henri Claude, for example, wrote in 1932 that more and more psychiatrists were having trouble deciding who was lucid at the moment of a crime and who was not. Without a relatively clear definition of normality, of what kind of

Raskolnikov is no doubt deliberate, given the extensive management of plot undertaken by Dostoyevsky, and it may be that he divined the potential impact of this absence, of a literal father, as well as nodding towards the failure of institutional law and affective political environment that is the loss of the Lacanian 'Name-of-the-Father'. Most dramatically however, Dostoyevsky portrayed the complex interplay between states of mind, identity and agency, effective even now in raising questions for criminal jurisprudence.

[53] Carolyn Dean, 'Law and Sacrifice: Bataille, Lacan and the Critique of the Subject' (1986) 13 *Representations* 42–62.

[54] Ibid, 44.

[55] Ibid, 46–7.

behaviour could be expected within a given context, it was impossible to judge to what extent the criminal could be held responsible for the crime committed. Along these lines another psychiatrist, Paul Courbon, sought to redefine the concept of mental lucidity [in reference to the criminal act] as mental 'validity' [*validite*] since, according to him, lucidity was always only the appearance of validity [i.e. the ability to reason]. He claimed that there often existed a discrepancy between a criminal's words and acts. . .In a plea for the creation of psychiatric annexes, Rene Charpentier, an eminent psychiatrist, claimed that, given the much more nuanced understanding of psychopathology by modern psychiatry, the conception of criminal responsibility as defined by the penal code had become obsolete.

Moreover, though clearly of contentious standing, the field of psychoanalysis, with its route into the difficult realm beyond the reach of psychiatry—that of the unconscious—held clear explanatory potential. Dean indicates an article, considering the provenance of 'unmotivated' murder, written by Paul Giuraud in 1931 in which Giuraud admits 'while conserving my entire independence from orthodox psychoanalysis, I think in cases of this type it is necessary to admit the possibility of unconscious motivating factors'. This caution towards the field of psychoanalysis was, and remains, extensive. In 1939, Healy had warned of the 'distinct tendency to overvaluation of psychoanalytic concepts as alone providing workable solutions for a large share of individual and social ills'.[56] Nevertheless, Healy is keen to indicate:

. . . the vastly important dynamic quality of the unconscious portion of mental activity. So-called 'voluntary behaviour' is often directly related to the activities of the unconscious. Indeed, the keystone of the valid structure of psychoanalysis is the fact of repression. Utilizing the structural organisation—the mechanism, as it were, of our minds—there are active mental processes which not only allow us to forget infinitely more than we consciously remember but which also forcefully hold down in the unconscious such kinds of material as are obnoxious to or even disavowed by our conscious selves. And the holding-down creates turmoils and stresses which seek outlets, and hence in one form or another find expression in ideas or behaviour, the causation of which we are unaware.

Whilst wishing to maintain a degree of caution towards wholesale adoption of psychoanalytic approaches to understanding criminal

[56] William Healy, 'Psychoanalytic Contributions to the Understanding and Treatment of Behavior Problems' (1939) 45(3) *The American Journal of Sociology* 418–25, 419–20.

behaviour, Healy and his colleagues invested considerable energies in the investigation of the link between crime and the unconscious, concluding that 'the hope in this field is for a closer rapprochement between psychiatry—with its newer understandings derived from psychoanalysis—and sociology.'[57] A plea for 'rapprochement between psychiatry and sociology, informed by the understandings of psychoanalysis (perhaps today we might refer to cultural, economic and social conditions rather than 'sociology') remains apposite, especially bearing in mind the failings of the master narratives of law and medicine.

The most cogent correlation to Dostoyevsky's vision of the alternative reality that is the aberrant landscape of the psyche, no doubt informed by his experience of his co-prisoners, is found in the work of psychoanalytic practitioners working with already convicted criminals, for whom narrative, fabulation, dream states, and the displaced realities of dissociation forge an entire and radical perspective.[58] Bearing in mind the prevalence of mental disorder (often combined with traumatic backgrounds) in the histories of perpetrators this vision should be given attention. Abby Stein describes how, in the 1990's, she observed overwhelming patterns in the convicts she worked with, where:

> A nightmarish childhood both shadowed and illuminated each man's polyglot narrative of destruction and redemption . . . The question was: to what degree is [a multiple][59] whose 'alter personality' commits a crime to be held accountable for his or her extralegal activities? It was the wrong question . . . by the end of the 90's I had come across a body of thought that I believed superseded a medicolegal inquiry into the topic and forced a new kind of question. Informed by mounting clinical evidence of the ubiquity of dissociative rejoinders to threat, many psychoanalysts were reinvigorating a theory of mind that named dissociation, rather than repression, as the critical defensive operation.[60]

[57] Ibid, 425.

[58] The early theories of 'repression' and the damaging press surrounding the idea of 'recovered memory' did little to recommend psychoanalytic theory. Nevertheless, psychoanalysis offers potentially the most instructive explanation of state of mind, moving towards 'dissociative' theory as a central theme, where criminal behaviour reflects a response to an unbearable tension created by earlier traumas.

[59] Although Stein at this point refers to those regarded as suffering from 'multiple personality disorder', the discussion radiates out to a discussion of the broad class of perpetrators whose actions reflect a skewed narrative springing from dissociation.

[60] Abby Stein, *Prologue to Violence* (The Analytic Press: London, New Jersey 2007) xv–xvi.

In psychology as well as psychiatry, dissociation refers to a perceived detachment of the 'mind' from the emotional state or even from the body, 'characterized by a sense of the world as a dreamlike or unreal place'.[61] Essentially, dissociation involves the interposition of a new or fragmented narrative, displacing the elements of self too traumatic to be faced. Incidentally, this dissociative pattern may not only affect the intimately traumatized victim-turned-perpetrator, or the socially traumatized 'ideological' perpetrator, but may be relevant too in less overt form, to the 'ordinary' person. As Stein explains, contemporaneous with this stream of thought, laboratory research increasingly:

> . . . point[ed] toward a novel model of the mind that envisions waking, sleeping and dreaming as distinct neurodynamic states that lie along a continuum and are separated by imperfect, sometimes porous, boundaries. States can get 'dissociated,' or mixed together in the way script from one program can hang up in another when you're shifting between the windows of a buggy computer . . .[62]

Again, this underscores the prescience, evident throughout his work, of Dostoyevksy's characterization of the psyche. As the quotation demonstrates in its reference to 'scripts', psychoanalysts are keenly aware of the crucial role of narrative in the construction of realities, and it is thus in the most modern accounts that we find compelling correlations to the insights of Dostoyevsky concerning liminal states of mind. Stein refers to the work of Meltzer, who describes the characteristic patient as:[63]

> . . . man imprisoned in his mind, with no affective linkages, convinced of, and therefore authoring, his own fraudulence, communicating only in rehearsed lies and transparent evasions. When emotion, known only by its physiological correlates, threatens, 'confabulations are constructed to forestall thought'. The narratives are representations, symbols presented by culture and appropriated to substitute for created, personally meaningful ones . . . These are the social suits of the antisocial person, what Cleckley [1941] called their 'masks.' Of course they are not much different from the operational facades that most people adopt to protect their psychic boundaries: the mask is just more so—more rigid, more opaque, and wrapping something more lurid.

Such findings do more than point to the role of narrative in the construction of reality: they challenge the moral basis of attributing guilt:

[61] eg, see the definition given by an online medical dictionary at <http://www.medterms.com/script/main/art.asp?articlekey=38857>.

[62] Stein, n 60 above, xvi.

[63] Ibid, 127.

the relationship between subliminal causative forces, formal doctrinal processes and analyses of 'normality' in English law becomes even more acute. Madden, writing in 1957, begins by asserting that:

> Psychoanalysis, moralists generally have come to see, does not reinforce traditional determinism. The psychoanalyst's point is that much less behaviour than anyone ever dreamed possible is free or responsible in the ordinary sense that it is consciously and reasonably shaped.[64]

Here, the compulsive nature of the hold of the unconscious over the conscious mind has powerful implications for the notion of responsibility for action, whilst at the same time allowing the subject to appear 'functional' (as indeed was the case in the cases discussed *ante*, of Diamond and Williams) in normative terms.[65] As a result, the doctrinal approach to mental status is wholly incongruous. As Madden suggests:[66]

> One can disallow the presence of mens rea, or mitigate it, or simply defeat the allegation of responsibility, only if he can present defenses [sic] or exceptions like duress, provocation, infancy, or insanity. However, since the neurotic person meets the requirement of knowing consequences, etc., and is not under duress, or provoked, or insane, he cannot be judged otherwise by the court than as legally and morally responsible for his acts. The McNaghten Rule, it should be noted at the outset, not only prevents the psychiatrist from making a case for the non-responsibility of a neurotic individual but even

[64] Edward Madden, 'Psychoanalysis and Moral Judgeability' (1957) 18(1) *Philosophy and Phenomenological Research* 68–79, 68.

[65] Another characteristic documented by Dostoyevsky is also recounted by Stein—the strange tension between evading and courting capture after the crime. Though on the one hand Raskolnikov goes to some lengths to outwit his interrogators, he experiences an appalled fascination with his own situation, daring his own identification. Though outwardly resistant he suffers internal conflict over his crime and, ultimately, embraces his punishment. This accords perfectly with modern psychoanalytic observation. Stein recounts (see Stein, n 60 above, 40–1): '. . . the covert [and not so covert] ways offenders telegraph evidence of an extant conscience, however disengaged or disorganized it might be. . . .those who break the law often seek containment. . .these observations comport with much in both classical and contemporary psychoanalytic theory. They stand however, in opposition to the beliefs of several influential clinicians and law enforcement agents who believe that many, if at most, violent, repetitive criminals perform their acts without conscience and with fully conscious intent. . . . Leaving clues to one's identity at the crime scene furthers four goals: recognition, punishment, containment, and restoration . . . Finally, being punished perversely equates with love [Freud, 1919]. Obedience to authority holds out the hope of salvation and resurrection; identity can be reconstituted without one's having to acknowledge the true source of anxiety or conflict as resting with distant others, more seminal and significant.'

[66] Madden, n 64 above, 71.

makes it extremely difficult for him to establish the non-responsibility of the psychotic. . .[67]

Flowing from any acceptance of these psychoanalytic insights must be the inevitable conclusion that we are incarcerating as criminals those whose behaviour cannot correspond to classical notions of free will. The law therefore compounds an already entrenched problem, adding its own distorting lens rather than providing opportunities for therapeutic repositioning. On this view, the presumption of capacity and free will, tied into a very particular vision of the human psyche and designed to safeguard the liberty to exercise choice and responsibility (as well as mark normative failure) contributes to the administration of injustice, too crude to respond to the spectrum of human apperception.

Current Scholarship

And what of current legal scholarship on these issues? Several strands may be identified, each with discrete conceptual and narratological profiles. In 'mainstream' law and psychiatry, central assertions concerning the tests of capacity and responsibility, continue to be raised and endorsed, as the cases referred to herein confirm.[68] Studies in 'law

[67] Ibid, at 72: 'The McNaughten type rule is psychologically unrealistic because the criminal's consideration of consequences, even when it is present, which is usually not the case, is impotent to prevent his acting out his wishes because of the compulsive nature of some motivation . . . The most important "disorder of emotion" is the flattening or dulling of the emotional tone of a person or its complete absence; this disorder is important because it is the one least understood empathically and so misunderstood as mere callousness'.

[68] See discussion of *R v Diamond* and *R v Williams, Stephanie*, above. Understandably, this 'contest' of psychiatric opinion often forms the core issue—see the differing views reflected by expert opinion: 'Killer is psychopath says expert', *BBC News*, 13 May 2005 available at <http://news.bbc.co.uk/1/hi/world/europe/jersey/4544901.stm>. In the USA, psychiatrists do debate the philosophical issues in a spirit of full enquiry, though still tend to affirm their own diagnostic power as satisfactory in this regard—eg, see Alec Buchanan, 'Commentary—Freedom and Function' (2008) 36(1) *Journal of the American Academy of Psychiatry and the Law* 25–6, the abstract for which reads: '[W]hile the question of whether our actions are determined or are the result of free will is a deep one in philosophy, it does not need to be answered for forensic psychiatrists to give evidence in court. As Stephen Morse has pointed out, the absence of free will is not named as an excusing condition. The insanity defense, for instance, requires proof of functional impairment, to which psychiatrists can usefully testify. Of the approaches available to determinism, my own preference is that of Herbert Hart: until we know that determinism is true, we will continue to prefer a system that requires persons to have made proper choices to act as they did before we hold them responsible.

and psychology', as evidenced by the *Current Legal Issues: Law and Psychology* collection, are open to the possibility of new approaches, the closest being Winick's conception of 'therapeutic jurisprudence'.[69] Law, Winick argues:

> . . . is a system of applied psychology and in our increasingly law-dominated societies, law is an important determinant of human behaviour. The borders between law and psychology therefore must be open, allowing the free passage of ideas. To function effectively as members of each discipline, we must increasingly understand the language and culture of the other. Both professions must be expanded to allow a greater degree of interdisciplinary exchange.

Here, Winick is arguing for a more effective rapprochement between an existing master narrative—law—and the cautiously received discipline of psychology; 'therapeutic jurisprudence' aims to improve the way overall practices and policies impact upon the legal subject—he does not presume to interfere with the fundamental psychiatric or doctrinal principles. Overall, the *Current Legal Issues* collection demonstrates an openness to recognizing, in particular, the policy orientated convergences between law and psychology. Elsewhere, a number of papers on law and neurology question foundational psychiatric assertions in the light of various neurological findings and resultant speculations about the nature of agency—the relationship of 'mind' to 'brain'—though such neurological findings tend not to find their way into the bastions of forensic psychiatry for the purposes of law.[70] In the field of 'critical criminology', writers such as Arrigo, discussing the issues with particular reference to American criminal law and mental health phenomena, provide powerful challenges to the status quo: the very title of a key text by Arrigo, *Punishing the Mentally Ill* points at the depth of the challenge.[71] Arrigo's approach, however,

This seems to resemble Dr. Felthous' preferred option that mentally responsible choices are choices made in the presence of a relatively natural ability to have decided otherwise'. In the UK, Jenny McEwan discusses the uncertainties of these complex psychological realms, noting that 'syndrome evidence' has not met with universal approval and describing the vagaries of evidential rules which allow judges to be effective 'gatekeepers' and experts to become 'more partisan than the parties': Jenny McEwan, *The Verdict of the Court* (Hart Publishing: Oxford, 2003) 18–8.

[69] See Bruce J Winick, 'Therapeutic Jurisprudence: Enhancing the Relationship between Law and Psychology' in B Brooks-Gordon and M Freeman (eds) *Current Legal Issues: Law and Psychology* (Oxford University Press: Oxford, 2006) 30–48, 31.

[70] eg, see Phiroze Hanzotia, 'A Neurologist Looks at Mind and Brain: "The Enchanted Loom"' (2003) 1(4) *Clinical Medicine and Research* 327–32.

[71] Bruce Arrigo, *Punishing the Mentally Ill* (State University of New York Press: New York, 2002).

derives from a strongly Lacanian perspective and embeds therefore in a richly rhetorical, rather than doctrinally intelligible account.[72] In the context of academic debate amongst critical legal scholars in Europe and the UK, the debate most closely aligned with recognizing the issues raised above for British consumption settles into a kind of art form. The dramatization of cases such as that of the Papin sisters,[73] conveyed through the literary-philosophical style of Lacan, contributes to the creation of what might be termed an 'aesthetic' jurisprudence—meditations in homage to the unfathomable and unknowable links between postmodern apprehensions of 'otherness' and the depths of the psyche. (Indeed, psychoanalytic discourse provides a natural exemplar for postmodern theory, since it may be characterized as the place of unknowable boundaries and disrupted realities). The focus of such scholarship is upon melodramatic, violent and inexplicable cases, pointing up the mystique of the absent narrative and of the quest for punishment. Thus, Salecl provides a useful and lyrically compelling exposition of Lacan's typology of crimes into those of Ego, Self and SuperEgo, with the sub categories leading to the 'passage a l'acte'.[74] This characterization of crime as the locus for resolving unbearable tensions does have direct significance to the themes recurrent in cases of extreme psychopathic behaviour recounted by psychoanalysts reviewing criminal mindsets. Indeed, Stein dedicates an entire chapter—entitled 'Conversing with Mutes'—to the phenomenon, well known to analysts working with offenders, linking the explosion of violent behaviour to the *absence* of narrative. Stein, commenting on this absence, references Bucci:

The more severe the dissociation, the more difficult the problem of learning to symbolize. In some cases the threat embodied in the dreaded schemas is experienced as so extreme that the individual turns against the symbolizing

[72] He does however chime strongly with the conception and caution towards professional metanarrative—see Arrigo, ibid, 182.

[73] The case of the Papin sisters (referred to hereafter by Salecl) is well known to psychoanalysts. Christine and Lea Papin were two French houseservants who murdered their employer's wife and daughter in Le Mans, France in 1933. The extreme violence employed in the attacks (the victims were said to be unrecognisable, injuries included the gouging of eyes) was wholly at variance with the quiet demeanour of the two perpetrators. The event has been referred to by French intellectuals such as Jean Genet, Jean-Paul Sartre and Jacques Lacan, giving rise to literary and cultural as well as psychoanalytic commentaries.

[74] Renata Salecl, 'Crime as a Mode of Subjectivisation: Lacan and the Law' (1993) 4(1) *Law and Critique* 3–20.

process itself in a more pervasive way[75]. . . The recitation of potent events appears in a surrealistically offhanded manner, sometimes in language that is regressed or in word inventories that are urged from the staccato narrator. As Bucci points out, alexithymia, a poverty of descriptive capacity, is best understood as a 'crisis' of symbolization . . .

Reflecting upon the high incidence of damaged childhood histories in such cases, Stein suggests that such histories are literally unspeakable, that the reality of 'toxic interactions with caregivers' 'defies articulation' and concludes that dissociation reflects a psychically unassimilated victimacy which:

. . . cannot be seamlessly woven into expressive discourse. Rageful impotence intersects myriad, seemingly minor, everyday degradations of the soul. Each experience is a split-off happening, not seen in moral relationship to other happenings, because no language exists to bridge them. Instead, the comforting pulse of gesture replaces voice. The criminal signature, so repetitive, is signed in silence.

Nevertheless, the directly applicable elements of such discussions are somewhat buried within the aesthetic of postmodern language and perspective. For example Salecl, writing of the Papin sisters, points out that psychoanalysis can emphasize[76] 'that the delirium of the two sisters was a part of some meaningful universe. As Lacan says, delirium does not isolate the subject from the outer world, on the contrary, delirium is that which enables the subject to enter the domain of intersubjectivity'.
This indicates the existence of a dissociative realm between encounters with the material world and with the subjective, 'inner' world. An insight of potential use in reconsidering current instances of psychopathy, this hint becomes absorbed into the more ambitious, antic and arguably, less practicable conceptual framework associated with Lacan.[77] As was indicated at the beginning of this paper, relative silence may be a marker of internal conflict, where lack of narrative capability informs the drive into destructive agency. *Lack* of narrative thus becomes the powerful text—a profound insight indeed for professions so committed to the excavation of meaning and reality via the narrative gloss.

[75] Stein, n 60 above, 22–5. [76] Salecl, n 74 above, 7.

[77] This is not intended to challenge the intellectual quality and challenge presented by such work. Rather, it is a recognition of the fact that the thrust of such work is to convey the Lacanian vision of the psychic landscape rather than to engage with the practice of law in relation to the psyche. Salecl notes that Lacan writes 'if the Other as the upholder of the law—the one which is called the Name-of-the-Father—establishes

Conclusion

The fabric of narrative issues facing the pursuit of truth and justice is complex indeed—from the 'liminal' narratives of legal subjects to the narratives of doctrine to those master narratives of authoritative discourse. A 'missing' narrative would no doubt present the most problematic phenomenon for jurisprudential management; 'found' narrative strands which create cogent realities for the legal subject but do not comply with doctrinal conventions also present a philosophical as well as practical challenge. Law and Medicine have worked to break free of prejudicial responses and cultivate the highest standards of disinterested practice. Yet the mysteries of the human mind cannot be addressed in purely disinterested terms and hypotheses are at least in part the inevitable products of belief and perspective, of subliminal 'stories' about who we are. Though in denial as to their underlying narrative drives, the forensic processes of law and medicine, (to recall the words of Prince)[78] do not 'simply record events', but constitute and interpret them as 'meaningful parts of meaningful wholes, whether the latter are situations, practices, persons, or societies'. Implicating the word 'narrative' into a discussion of legal or medical analysis is arguably an awkward juxtaposition, though hopefully a meaningful one. As Kreiswirth comments:

> When scholars in the human sciences present, theorize, endorse, or even deprecate storied knowledge, it is not always easy to determine what part of the story they are telling and where they are putting the emphasis, particularly in cases where an effect of the story is a truth claim. Do, for example, courtroom narratives concern the causal coherence-making operations of witnesses' accounts, or the referential correspondence of their narrativisations, or both? In the psychoanalytic dialogue, what relationships are established between the analysand's tellings, the analyst's retellings, and the told - or what Donald Spence. . .calls the 'narrative truth'?[79]

and legalizes desire in the phallic framework, the Other of jouissance partially escapes this law. This Other who escapes does not 'exist' because of the lack of the signifier of jouissance. . . The law as social order is a system of subjectivization . . . The legal system thus takes on the role of the symbolic, dead father who submits the subject to the law. But most importantly this law steps in against the subject's Super Ego: its role is to limit the subject's jouissance or unbearable enjoyment and not, as utilitarians say, to make it more possible': see Salecl, n 74 above, 17–18.

[78] Gerald Prince, 'On Narratology (Past, Present, Future)' in Martin McQuillan (ed) *The Narrative Reader* (Routledge: London, 2000) 129 (quotation cited above).

[79] Martin Kreiswirth, 'Merely Telling Stories? Narrative and Knowledge in the Human Sciences' (2000) 21(2) *Poetics Today* 302–18 at 303.

Such too could be the caution concerning the 'received notions' passing between the discourses of law and psychiatry. Although the pursuit of knowledge and truth must resist giving way to an entirely unreliable 'narrative hegemony',[80] recognition of its omnipresence in human discourse should give pause for thought. Where 'findings' as to human 'nature', norms or characteristics are concerned this is particularly pertinent, given the fact that the apparently reliable and expert findings of human sciences, as well as popular interpretations and beliefs, stand upon 'folk psychology'—the subjective foundations of conjecture as to 'human nature'.[81]

Clearly, criminal jurisprudence cannot readily dispense with doctrinal formulae designed to locate issues of responsibility for action, nor can it easily accommodate uncertainties concerning the sciences of the mind—the pragmatic drives of legal practice must adhere to some framework in the ascription of responsibility. Yet the professions should be conscious of their own limitations, of the profound impact their artefacts have one upon the other and of the deeply tenuous issues of truth and narrative at the heart of everyday practice.[82] There is a real danger that, whilst less rarefied evidential material is routinely subject to extensive juristic scrutiny, 'expert' evidence is all too readily accepted as a source of fact rather than opinion.[83] Yet evidence itself is the product of discourse and narrative as well as of empirical findings.[84] As Bernard Jackson has

[80] Ibid, 311.

[81] See David Herman, 'Narrative Theory and the Intentional Stance' (2008) 6(2) *Partial Answers* 233–60 at 238 ff: 'Philosophers of mind refer to . . . *folk psychology*. At issue is people's everyday understanding of how thinking works, the rough-and-ready heuristics to which they resort in thinking about thinking itself. We use these heuristics to impute motives or goals to others, to evaluate the bases of our own conduct, and to make predictions about future reactions to events'.

[82] As suggested by A Duff, L Farmer, S Marshall and V Tadros, *The Trial on Trial: Towards a Normative Theory of the Criminal Trial* (Hart Publishing: Oxford, 2007) at 61–2: '. . . the trial process fundamentally seeks a 'deep' notion of truth: The role of truth in the trial, or as an aim of the trial, is more complex than [a] simple instrumentalist account suggests . . . First, the truth at which the trial purports to aim has an intrinsic, not merely an instrumental, importance among the aims of a criminal justice system. Secondly, the truth that is sought is not merely a factual or non-normative truth about whether the defendant's conduct satisfied the law's definition of a criminal offence, but a richer, normative truth about whether the defendant is guilty of a wrong for which he is to be condemned. Thirdly, that what is sought is not merely truth, but something like knowledge.'

[83] Despite the fact that there are guidelines on the use of expert evidence (see n 46 above).

[84] John D Jackson, 'Towards a Dialectic Theory of Proof for Legal Procedure' (1991) 154 (1) *Journal of the Royal Statistical Society* 107–9 notes that the evaluation of evidence involves subjective feeling and imagination as much as reason and logic and that 'creative thought is also important in another aspect of fact reasoning which the rationalist tradition

observed, the semiotic power of the expert witness is potent.[85] Though formally the professions assert structures borne of the sciences of the mind, whether they be the logics of doctrinal jurisprudence or those of medical jurisprudence, at heart they function as frail semiotic systems, an exchange of totems. Doctrinal choices (for example, the calculation, no doubt driving many cases similar to that of *Williams*, that provocation is a tenuous ground for female perpetrators, resulting in a drive to identify suitable pathological profiles to fulfil either provocation or diminished responsibility doctrine, or indeed the initial decision to avoid both provocation and diminished responsibility arguments in favour of a weak 'self defence' account) may well result from strategic appreciation of failures in similar fact cases, yet run the risk of compromizing justice in a more fundamental way. The resultant narrative becomes fragmented and common sense, workaday hypotheses become buried in a plethora of medical and legal artefacts—a failed marriage of master narratives. The appearance of clemency and equity represented by the admission of a current appeal as to sentence mounted on behalf of Stephanie Williams could be regarded as a mask, or masque, disguising the underlying injustice of the original process. For subjects such as Diamond, professional views as to the presence or absence of mental illness are deeply conjectural. The high incidence of mental disorder recorded in prison inmates indicates the existence of a flaw in our professional assessment strategies which is certainly not addressed by current taxonomies.

and traditional theories of probability have tended to ignore, namely the use that can be made of narrative stories in thinking about evidence'. As Jackson and Doran express it: 'the rationalist tradition assumed that it is possible to start with certain basic items of evidence which correspond with reality and then reason from these towards a probability judgment of a past event. But some of the new evidence scholars are now arguing that we do not collect bits of evidence as one might collect shells from the sand. Instead evidence is gathered according to the relevance of the investigation in hand and this involves considering and testing hypotheses from the beginning. Furthermore, it is highly questionable whether we will all reach the same conclusion on the presentation of the same evidence. When we test evidence we do not test it against a universally available stock of knowledge about the common course of events but, according to certain cognitive scientists, by reference to particular schemas or stories that form the basis of our knowledge structures. It is questionable how far these ideas question the rationalist tradition.' See John Jackson and Sean Doran, 'Evidence' in D Patterson (ed) *A Companion to Philosophy of Law and Legal Theory* (Blackwell: Oxford, 2005) 172–83, 178 (references omitted).

[85] See Bernard Jackson, *Making Sense in Law* (Deborah Charles: Liverpool, 1995) 417: 'Since the scientific character of the evidence precludes any real narrativization of the semantics of the evidence, the narrativization of the pragmatics of expert testimony – whether the expert appears to be behaving and talking like an expert in court – must predominate. . . Sometimes, moreover, even the authority of the expert is assumed rather than investigated.'

This essay could have set out to pursue a direct critique of the relationship between law, psychiatry and psychoanalysis, of the doubt that can clearly be cast upon the entire framework of nosological evidence deployed so crucially in the adjudication of cases. Further discussion might also have focused upon the problems of hermeneutics where there are variant strands of discourse springing from common roots (as with psychiatry and psychoanalysis) but where standing *as* the authoritative discourse precludes the one from acknowledging the other and precludes the other from wishing to claim the doubtful authority, inheritance and associates of the 'master narrative'. The accounts provided within each discrete discourse maintain their own separate claims to coherence and integrity, yet these stakes in coherence limit the potential to create discursive links from one to the other, since they arise from radically different cultural and epistemological traditions. Though it is possible to juxtapose the findings of psychoanalysts working with offenders alongside the postulations of forensic psychiatry and, in so doing, highlight contradictions and failings, this essentially forms a contest between one already highly entrenched authoritative discourse and another self-evidently radical and problematic discourse. Yet the exploration of issues pertaining to the psyche and normality through the concept of competing and intersecting 'narratives' not only points up the central issue of competing realities in the noumenal domains of professional knowledge as well as subjective experience, it also highlights the tenuousness of the separation between the evidential, the philosophical and the fictive. Indeed the free narrative associations created by writers such as Dostoyevsky correlate closely to the findings of analysts working with offenders, at the same time highlighting the fact that the 'fabulating' capabilities of we 'ordinary' persons excuse us from paying full recognition to the moral imperatives of our everyday lives.[86] As Stein expresses the point, juxtaposing her own work with offenders alongside a rebuke to us law-abiding citizens:[87]

> The rest of us demonstrate similar contradictions and projections, in lesser forms, during the daily exercise of moral relativism. . .such situational pathologizing has not gone unnoticed: Geoffrey White has suggested the inclusion in the Diagnostic and Statistical Manual of 'political apathy disorder,' defined as the lack of social conscience. Like psychopaths, sufferers

[86] Indeed the 'conscientous' element of Raskolnikov's behaviour—his anxiety concerning social inequity and political injustice—indicates the moral heart of radicalism as a rebuke to the laissez-faire liberal.

[87] Stein, n 60 above, 58.

of the disorder have no subjective distress. Their actions are characterized by a pervasive pattern of failing to help those in need [e.g. the poor, the oppressed, the underprivileged] combined with over-consumption of the world's limited resources.

Nor are such questions of internal logic purely philosophical:[88] they are critical to psychological and psychiatric medicine too. The broad framework created by conventional psychiatry no doubt provides useful guidance in the identification of clear cases of incapacity to stand trial, for example. At times it can only be guidance: the implication that the range of mental states can be calibrated with any degree of certainty is wholly misleading and serves simply to reify the putative authority of the 'master narrative' of forensic psychiatry. The psychoanalytic portrayal of the individual and collective life of the psyche, beset with the need to formulate new narrative coherence whether as a result of impossible tensions, ideological seduction, dream states or fabulations, is a radical statement upon the human mind and agency. The implications of such phenomena for the law were especially apprehended by psychoanalytic practitioners in the early and mid decades of the 20th century, their history a telling source of critical commentary. More recent scholarship in law and psychoanalysis, albeit still relatively rare, can be found in the 'critical legal' sphere of jurisprudence: however this fascinating scholarship is delivered as a wholly allusive art form, rather than resource of utility for practitioners, lyrically directed by the aesthetic discourse of Lacan.[89] Fuelled by a revival of interest in Freud through Lacan, most critical jurisprudence on the subject has focused upon dramatic instances of crime notorious for their sensational mix of taboo-breaching and mystery—the bizarre case of the Papin sisters, for

[88] Indeed, for Althusser they are ideological first and foremost: see the extract from 'Althusser and Psychoanalysis: Subjectivity as Mistaken Identity' in J Penner, D Schiff and R Nobles (eds..) *Jurisprudence and Legal Theory*, (Oxford University Press: Oxford, 2005) 1086.

[89] The troubled relationship between Lacanian theory and mainstream psychiatry is discussed by Bruce Arrigo in particular, who notes the resistance of conventional psychiatry—of the 'master narrative'—to the 'truths' of psychoanalytic insight, yet Arrigo himself remains somewhat abstruse in his presentation of argument conducted through Lacanian theory and its linkage to postmodern theory. So, for example, Arrigo speaks of Lacan's 'effort to locate and define the discordant and mellifluous voices of the Other seeking recognition in the act of speech production. . .for Lacan, the effect of these coordinated language systems was the reconstitution and re-legitimation of entrenched ideologies, knowledges and truths along with the perpetuation and reaffirmation of personal alienation, repression and marginalization': see Bruce Arrigo, *Punishing the Mentally Ill* (State University of New York Press: New York, 2002) 227.

example.[90] The risk is that valuable hints from psychoanalysis, when channelled through the aesthetic discourse of theorists such as Lacan, remain abstruse and contradictory, yet the critique of law offered by psychoanalytic practice presents a genuine case for concern in relation to more commonplace instances of murderous and other aberrant behaviours. Back in 1957, commentators such as Madden, reflecting upon the insights of criminal behaviour gained from psychoanalytic and therapeutic practice, were producing pointed commentary: 'Rules of the McNaghten type. . .are psychologically unrealistic and, in their effects, pernicious because they utilize formal, universal criteria where individual analysis and insight is needed.'[91]

Here, Madden is hinting at a radical reformulation of the landscape whereby formal justice would become wholly subject to the adaptive capabilities of individualized assessment and substantive judgment. It may be argued that this fails to acknowledge the forensically liminal and fluid locus of the unconscious, and the potentially deleterious effect such radical alteration would have upon the notion of a formally reliable, knowable and universally applicable justice. Nevertheless, his statement is an attempt to confront what to him is an absolute failure of law. For the insistence upon the ready division of agents capable of meditation and premeditation, and therefore responsible, from those clearly beyond such rational capacity, ignores the inconvenient view that persons are more readily positioned according to a spectrum of mental states, rather than a polarity and that premeditation does not guarantee meditative mastery.

Overall psychoanalysis provides a radical challenge to conventional psychiatry and law in our philosophical and practical understanding of the construction of reality. As Madden observes:

> Even though there are accepted techniques for distinguishing veridical and illusory perception, how can I prove, or [Descartes' evil genius?] how can I be sure, that the allegedly veridical ones are not illusory or hallucinatory beyond the range of the accepted techniques—a crucial step in the dialectic of the issue over our knowledge of the external world.[92]

The contribution of psychoanalysis to the critique of consciousness, informing a diversity of experience in constructions of reality and the positing of fabulating narratives and liminal states of mind, all speak to our modern mismanagement of questions of sanity and responsibility

[90] For a brief account of the Papin sisters case see n 73 above.

[91] Madden, 'Psychoanalysis and Moral Judgeability' (1957) 18(1) *Philosophy and Phenomenological Research* 68–79, 72.

[92] Madden, ibid, 69.

for action. The worlds of law, and of psychiatry, are intimately bound to the deep questions of philosophy—of human nature and moral responsibility, and of the relationship between identity and reality, narrative and hermeneutics. Whilst pragmatic considerations may encourage over-reliance upon classical conventions regarding free will and the psyche, the true role of the psyche, especially the power and influence of the unconscious in shaping realities and responsibilities, continues to throw doubt upon the daily deliberations of law and psychiatry. Our presumptions of normality and our willingness to pronounce on the basis of such frail frameworks present a rebuke to the professions. Of course, it may be argued, we 'must draw a line'. As Dostoyevksy's Doctor Zossimov concludes:

> . . .we are certainly all not infrequently like madmen, but with the slight difference that the deranged are somewhat madder, for we must draw a line. A normal man, it is true, hardly exists. Among dozens–perhaps hundreds of thousands–hardly one is to be met with.[93]

[93] Fyodor Dostoyevsky, *Crime and Punishment* (London: Dover Publications, 2001), at 180.

Beyond Safety? The Broadening Scope of Risk Regulation

*Maria Lee**

Introduction

This chapter sets out to examine a consistent mismatch between the rhetoric and practice of regulation. It argues that whilst the politics of regulation, that is the relevance of social, political and ethical considerations, are to all appearances now perfectly mainstream, acceptance of the broad nature of regulation rarely feeds through into decision-making. Whatever the rhetoric, when it comes to the crunch and a decision needs to be justified and explained, the instinct is to turn to technical expertise on 'safety' and 'risk', sidestepping more broadly conceptualized concerns about the social or ethical commitments embedded in a technology. This ambivalence, whilst sometimes acknowledged, is not generally pursued very far into regulatory practice, either in the academic literature, which continues to urge responsiveness to the broad nature of decisions, or in the policy literature, which behaves as if all is well now that the politics of regulation are understood. And yet the gap between what is said (the politics of regulation) and what is done (expert assessment of safety and risk) raises important normative issues for those of us interested in the regulation of areas of high technical complexity. Not only do risk and safety fail to capture all that is at stake, but the current approach brings with it great costs to accountability, as well as raising profound questions about how, and by whom, decisions should best be taken.

The rhetorical openness of regulators, coupled with their practical reluctance to move beyond risk, is examined here by looking closely at

* Professor of Law, University College London. Many thanks to Joanne Scott for her comments on a draft of this article, and for chairing the lecture on which it is based. I am also very grateful to Elen Stokes for comments on this article, and to Denise Leung for her research assistance.

national, EU and WTO approaches to regulating difficult technologies. Three case studies will be used: nuclear energy in the UK, nanotechnology in the EU, and GMOs in the WTO. At each of these three levels of governance, there is a rhetorical opening up of decision-making, but persistent legal and political constraints narrow down the reasons provided for the final decision. Of course, this is not a simple story. Decisions are untidy and unclear, and regulatory paths that started way into the past carry on far after the legally significant decision has been taken. But it is time to begin to explore what these observations might mean for those of us who study law and regulation.

The Risk Debate

The proper regulation of controversial technologies such as nuclear power, nanotechnology and biotechnology is complex and contested. Difficult questions about the safety of these technologies, for the environment and for human health, resonate at the highest political level. There is also however *another* politics of regulation: whilst environmental and human safety are important, complex and political, so may be, for example, the way a technology distributes risk and benefit; the social and political arrangements a technology might favour; and the real purposes of the technology.

Risk is complex and intellectually contested. For many theorists, risk is a reminder of the fragility of human responses to danger and the unknown. And yet in a practical regulatory context, risk is far more commonly a technique that promises control and action, notwithstanding those difficulties of prediction.[1] This promise of control has led to the intrusion of 'risk talk' into a range of unfamiliar areas,[2] including criminal justice and immigration, and financial services. This chapter is concerned with the regulation of technologies rather than with the expansion of risk in regulation more generally. Even in this core of regulation (although more so beyond), risk is both the *object* of regulation (and so the driver of standard setting), and the organizing idea for regulation, a technique of decision-making.[3]

[1] See J Steele, *Risks and Legal Theory* (Hart Publishing, 2004) for a discussion of these two very different understandings of risk.

[2] M Power, *The Risk Management of Everything* (Demos, 2004).

[3] J Black, 'The Emergence of Risk Based Regulation and the New Public Management in the UK' (2005) Public Law 512; H Rothstein, M Huber, G Gaskell, 'A Theory of Risk Colonisation: The Spiralling Regulatory Logics of Societal and Institutional Risk' (2006) 35 *Economy and Society* 91.

My focus here is not the technique of risk assessment or the science behind it, but regulation. It has long, possibly even always, been recognized that technical assessments of hazard and likelihood are not alone an adequate basis for regulatory decision-making. First, it is clear that the expert judgment does not determine the political question of how much risk is acceptable, how safe is safe enough. The catastrophic nature of a serious nuclear accident, for example, together with its very low likelihood, reminds us that there is no value-free way of resolving the 'acceptability' of risk. Some argue that the harm is so enormous that no level of risk is acceptable,[4] others that the likelihood is so low that it can be ignored. Similar low probability/high impact scenarios arise for self-replicating technologies, such as biotechnology and potentially in the future nanotechnology, for example the possibility that super-efficient manufactured material will multiply, outcompeting and so destroying life-supporting natural biodiversity.[5]

This question of risk acceptability also arises in far more mundane ways, and generally empowers political decision-makers. In many jurisdictions, including the UK (more or less explicitly depending on context) and the EU (very clearly since 2000), the primary response has been to separate the technical and the political elements of a decision. So risk assessment is the technical process carried on by appointed experts, and risk management is the political process carried out by more or less representative bodies.[6] This is progressive in its recognition of the complexity of the decision to be taken, and in most *descriptions* of the process, the politics is in charge. Nevertheless, the dichotomy between risk assessment and risk management is (like most dichotomies perhaps) problematic. It is simply not possible to draw clear lines between the objective and the subjective, between the technical and the political elements of the decision: both elements imply ethical commitments as well as matters of substance, and fact finding is

[4] See the discussion in Department for Business, Enterprise and Regulatory Reform, *The Future of Nuclear Power: Analysis of Consultation Results* (2008) 57. For a different context, see also J Peel, 'When (Scientific) Rationality Rules: (Mis)Application of the Precautionary Principle in Australian Mobile Phone Tower Cases' (2007) 19 *Journal of Environmental Law* 1.

[5] Drexler's famous 'grey goo' for example, KE Drexler *Engines of Creation* (Anchor Books, 1986). Even Bill Joy, of Sun Microsystems, has argued for limits to the search for knowledge in respect of self replicating materials, 'Why the future doesn't need us', *Wired*, Issue 8.04, April 2000.

[6] eg, see European Commission, *Communication on the Precautionary Principle* COM (2000) 1 final.

not inevitably prior to, and independent of, normative judgments.[7] Formalizing those illusory boundaries may simply enhance the apparent objectivity of risk assessment, so that in the search for a defensible decision, technical risk assessment becomes paradoxically more attractive the more profoundly political the decision really is.

There is more to the 'politics of risk' than risk acceptability. Much of it rests upon an occasional, but highly visible, mismatch between expert and public understandings of risk, a mismatch subjected to decades of work in the social sciences. We have at least rhetorically moved beyond a 'deficit' understanding of public perception of risk. This is a long standing, persistent, assumption that the public disagrees with the experts because the public misunderstands complex information and lacks scientific knowledge, or is irrational. This launched the very important public understanding of science movement, but also the conclusion that the scientifically illiterate or uneducated should be excluded from decisions. Whilst no one denies that there are sometimes deficits in understanding (but not only on the part of 'non'-experts), this 'deficit' model has been consistently and compellingly criticized over many years. The deficit model is sometimes criticized as a cynical attempt to marginalize public concerns by manufacturing an image of ignorance. But there are two other main lines of attack. First, scientific objectivity and inevitability is elusive; and secondly, the public response is not in fact characterized by ignorance or passivity, but by what has been called a 'richer rationality'[8] that takes the public beyond safety and risk. To be clear, this chapter is not concerned with fear, risk aversion or even risk perception, but with substantive alternative perspectives on what matters to regulation.

Those criticisms of the deficit model that identify the inevitable space for unspoken values and assumptions of the profession or individual to enter the process of scientific judgment see science as socially embedded,[9] making it difficult to argue that risk assessment is *uniquely*

[7] Expert Group on Science and Governance, *Taking European Knowledge Society Seriously* (European Commission, 2007).

[8] See CR Sunstein, *Risk and Reason: Safety, Law and the Environment* (Cambridge University Press, 2002). Note that Sunstein ultimately rejects the 'richer rationality' model.

[9] eg, see Sheila Jasanoff's work, including *The Fifth Branch: Science Advisers as Policymakers* (Harvard University Press, 1990); *Designs on Nature: Science and Democracy in Europe and the United States* (Princeton University Press, 2005).

placed to provide decisions on safety. Again, examples can be found in our case studies. The risk assessment of GMOs contains silent judgments about the possibility and desirability of controlling our environment. This is a normative not a technical position, and raises questions about the nature of that control: to what end, and by whom? We might note that the unequal distribution of information and expertise means that scientific risk assessment can frequently be dominated by the industry seeking to promote a technology. So for example, the applicant for authorization of a GMO provides information to the regulator, who then in effect scrutinizes the risk assessment provided by the applicant. Whilst this places responsibilities and costs on the industry, the concern (ameliorated by regulatory detail on process and multiple opportunities for scrutiny) that the applicant thus gets to set the agenda for the risk assessment is almost too obvious to state.[10]

Another simple and usually unspoken assumption is that social progress is achieved through technological development, via economic growth.[11] The great post industrial hope provided by the e-economy or bio-economy makes being left behind seem disastrous: restriction of a new technology needs to be justified, not the new technology itself. The link between progress and economic growth made by the government in its efforts to justify the move to nuclear energy ('the aim of government should be to continue to raise living standards and the quality of life by growing our economy'[12]) does not go without saying. The assumption that 'growing the economy' is the only way to 'raise living standards and the quality of life' is increasingly contentious,[13] as indeed is the idea that even a growing economy needs to be as energy intensive as in the past.

[10] See N Gunningham, 'Regulating Biotechnology: Lessons from Environmental Policy' in H Somsen (ed), *The Regulatory Challenge of Biotechnology: Human Genetics, Food and Patents* (Edward Elgar, 2007). Some interest groups have expressed concern about the sole responsibility of the consent holder for monitoring, European Commission, *Second Report on the Experience of Member States with GMOs Placed on the Market under Dir. 2001/18/EC on the Deliberate Release into the Environment of Genetically Modified Organisms* COM (2007) 81 final, 6.

[11] Expert Group on Science and Governance, n 7 above, ch 2, describes and criticizes a linear model in which science moves to technology and to social progress. For an early example of links between technology and progress, see K Tranter, 'The History of the Haste-Wagons: the Motor Car Act 1909, Emergent Technology and the Call for Law' (2005) 29 *Melbourne University Law Review* 26.

[12] Department for Business, Enterprise and Regulatory Reform, *Meeting the Energy Challenge: A White Paper on Nuclear Power* (2008) 24.

[13] See *Analysis of Consultation Results*, n 4 above, 245.

An emphasis on (supposed) technical objectivity can also make us forget that safety cannot be assessed along a single dimension. So, for example, to say, as the Health and Safety Executive does, that our nuclear power stations must be 'at least as safe' as a nuclear power station anywhere in the world is unobjectionable.[14] It is not though a simple technical question, because there may be tradeoffs, for example, between reduction of accident risk and worker exposure, between emissions of radionuclides and waste generation. Rather than a technical question, this is a political judgment that demands information on the size, type, costs, and certainty of harms.

Turning to the publics' possible 'richer rationality', we might say that just like the experts, publics incorporate value judgments into their assessments of technological developments. Some well-worn examples are to observe that whilst experts might look at numbers dead, others might be more worried by who dies (children?) and how (painfully?). Whilst risk assessors will object that they are perfectly able to take this into account, they are not *uniquely* equipped for this task by their expertise. At this point we move beyond 'risk', beyond questions of safety.

Distributional questions are key in each of our cases, including the distribution of risk, benefits, harm and costs. The distribution of 'bads' and benefits is the bread and butter of politics, and the silencing of distributional questions by risk should be resisted. We might want to know, for example, who controls nanotechnology and to what purpose. Agricultural biotechnology has also raised more specific questions about possible negative impacts on small and organic farmers in the EU, and possible negative impacts for developing countries. And of course, a focus on distribution will also raise explicitly the question of how much we are prepared to pay for the unwillingness of others to bear risk.

Related to distribution are questions about whether a particular technological development incentivizes particular types of social and institutional arrangements. There are concerns that the high capital investment costs of agricultural biotechnology might enhance corporate control of food and agriculture, as well as the intensification of agriculture and increase in monocultures. Nuclear power is said to demand (or at least to be highly compatible with) more rather than less authoritarian and unequal social structures.[15] This seems to have been

[14] Health and Safety Executive, *Safety Assessment in an International Context* (2008).

[15] See the discussion in L Winner, 'Do Artifacts Have Politics?' in L Winner, *The Whale and the Reactor: A Search for Limits in an Age of High Technology* (University of

displaced in the current debate about nuclear energy by the catastrophic results of the potential use of nuclear material by terrorists.[16] And some object to private ownership of nuclear power stations, because of 'the perception that this increases the likelihood of accidents'.[17] It may be that, as with nanotechnology and biotechnology, we have become as concerned about corporate as about state domination.[18]

Beyond distribution, both biotechnology and nanotechnology provoke ecocentric or religious concerns around the acceptability of human interference with nature. These are sometimes expressed hyperbolically in descriptions of 'frankenfood' or 'playing god', but can raise profound questions around the future of human (post human?) nature as well as the future of nature.[19] Such concerns are usually dismissed out of hand, partly because utilitarian assessments tend to dominate the mainstream ethical debate in this area and partly because no single technological step ever seems to be sufficiently distinct from what has gone before to justify a break with 'progress'.[20] Absolute religious or secular positions also fit very uncomfortably with political liberalism,[21] and the wrongs done in the name of what is 'natural' or 'godly' need not be rehearsed. But even if the saddening that results from living in an altered, 'unnatural' world is ultimately not considered an adequate basis for the rejection of an entire technology, it is not necessarily wholly irrelevant, especially if the benefits of change are trivial or regressively distributed.

A fixation on a narrow understanding of risk can hide these multiple value judgments, this richer rationality. It can also create an illusion of controllability and certainty. But other approaches to risk remind us of the fragility of expert authority, and the complexity and depth of uncertainties. Expert fallibility is of course highly visible from time to

Chicago Press, 1986). This has been called the 'containment culture' of secrecy and control, see WJ Kinsella, 'Nuclear Boundaries: Material and Discursive Containment at the Hanford Nuclear Reservation' (2001) 10 *Science as Culture* 163 (discussing weapons rather than civilian nuclear power).

[16] There is an oblique reference to worry that 'future planning may take place more behind closed doors due to increased security threats', *Analysis of Consultation Results*, n 4 above, 257.

[17] *Analysis of Consultation Results*, n 4 above, 84 and 116.

[18] See M Kearnes and ors, 'From Bio to Nano: Learning Lessons from the UK Agricultural Biotechnology Controversy' (2006) 15 *Science as Culture* 291.

[19] F Fukayama, *Our Posthuman Future: Consequences of the Biotechnology Revolution* (Profile Books, 2002); J Habermas, *The Future of Human Nature* (Polity, 2003).

[20] For both of these arguments see *Genetically Modified Crops: the Ethical and Social Issues* (Nuffield Council on Bioethics, 1999).

[21] eg, see J Rawls, 'The Idea of Public Reason Revisited' (1997) 64 *The University of Chicago Law Review* 765.

time, when mistakes are made or experts have a public disagreement about professional judgment. Regulation at all three levels of governance discussed here explicitly accepts that scientific expertise is not 'monolithic'[22] or 'linear',[23] and the legitimacy of preferring minority over majority scientific views is fairly well established.[24] But we need to go beyond that.

Data gaps and lack of information can be a real barrier to regulation. Nanomaterials, for example, may enter the environment, the human body, and different organs within the human body, in a variety of still unexplored ways, during manufacture, use, or disposal of a product. How they behave in the human body and the environment is not known. [25] Further research to fill some of the gaps in this area is now being given considerable attention,[26] but whilst improving the knowledge base is crucial it will never answer all of our questions. Brian Wynne's classification of uncertainties is useful in this respect.[27] So 'risk' usually implies that the odds of adverse effect are known, with some level of certainty; 'uncertainty' that the broad nature of the problem is understood, but the likelihood is currently unknown. But what Wynne calls 'ignorance', the 'we don't know what we don't know' question, looms especially large in respect of biotechnology and nanotechnology. Just as nobody thought for decades to investigate the impact of CFCs on stratospheric ozone, for example, there may be problems that are not even on the research agenda. 'Theoretical' or 'hypothetical' risk is not, however, as discussed below, a valid reason for a regulatory decision, and

[22] In the WTO, *EC-Measures Concerning Meat and Meat Products*, WT/DS26/AB/R, WT/DS48/AB/R, 16 January 1998, 194.

[23] In the EU, Case C-300/95 *Commission v United Kingdom* [1997] 3 CMLR 923.

[24] In the UK, see for example *Downs v Secretary of State for Environment, Food and Rural Affairs* [2008] EWHC 2666.

[25] Royal Commission on Environmental Pollution, Twenty-Seventh Report, *Novel Materials in the Environment: The Case of Nanotechnology* (2008): 'Currently it is extremely difficult to evaluate how safe or how dangerous nanomaterials are because of our complete ignorance about so many aspects of their fate and toxicology', 3.12. For the general safety issues, see ch 2.

[26] eg, see the opinions of the EU Scientific Committee on Emerging and Newly Identified Health Risks (SCENHIR) (most recently, SCENHIR, *Risk Assessment of Products of Nanotechnologies* (19 January 2009), which are far from complacent about the weakness of risk assessment on the basis of information as it stands.

[27] B Wynne, 'Uncertainty and Environmental Learning: Reconceiving Science and Policy in the Preventive Paradigm' (1992) *Global Environmental Change* 111. For an alternative framework of uncertainties, see V Walker, 'The Siren Songs of Science: Toward a Taxonomy of Scientific Uncertainty for Decisionmakers' (1991) *Connecticut Law Review* 567.

the search for 'zero risk' is much derided,[28] even whilst more generally our improved awareness of ignorance suggests that 'ignorance loses its innocence'.[29] The dismissal of ignorance within regulation is a crucial part of the retreat to risk in decision-making.

What we *do* know we don't know is the real problem for nuclear energy, including, for example, disputed data on cancer clusters, but especially what Wynne calls indeterminacy. Indeterminacy arises from the complex and (literally) unpredictable behaviour of ecological and social systems. One of the greatest indeterminacies in respect of nuclear energy is caused by time: radioactive waste needs to be isolated from human beings and the environment for many thousands of years, a regulation-defying period during which the physical and institutional structures that we expect to keep us safe will undergo unimaginable change. More prosaically, 'social system' indeterminacy can be found in what we might call the 'Homer Simpson' problem: 'concerns that health and safety regulations may be flouted by bored or irresponsible staff'. [30] And we see routine ecosystem indeterminacies with respect to GMOs: we test genetic modifications one by one or a few by a few, against one or a few components of ecosystems (impact on certain insects or soil bacteria, for example). Even field trials are unable properly to assess the impact of *many* modifications in *many* living organisms on *many*, varied and complex ecosystems.[31]

Neither ignorance nor indeterminacy is likely to be resolved by more or better science. These challenges to risk assessment as a source of authority or legitimacy are, again, not just about the limitations of expertise, but also about the more positive role of politics. The 'public' is often derided for demanding absolute safety, or not understanding the inevitability of uncertainty. Post-BSE, the instinct of government is no longer to deny uncertainty, but it is still to deny its relevance—asserting not that something is safe, but that uncertainties are so pervasive that only the very foolish refuse to tolerate them. But a refusal to accept ignorance or uncertainty does not necessarily mean that the risk is thought to be too high; the complaint may be about the unrealistic

[28] eg, see *Communication on the Precautionary Principle*, n 6 above. Note that the meaning of zero risk is not entirely clear, and reducing a scientifically evidenced risk to zero is acceptable.

[29] Steele, n 1 above, 33.

[30] *Analysis of Consultation Results*, n 4 above, 57. Apparently (worryingly!) examples are provided by respondents who have worked in the nuclear industry.

[31] On the limitations of case by case risk assessment of GMOs, see for example Kearnes and ors, n 18 above.

claims made for institutional knowledge,[32] and may include substantive alternative perspectives on what matters about a technology. The political question becomes why we are creating these uncertainties, and in whose interests. The least acceptable question in regulation of health and environmental protection often seems to be this 'why' question. Engaging with the purposes and objectives of a new technology is simply beyond the pale, but it is actually the central value question—why take these risks, why redistribute costs now and in this way? Inevitable uncertainties, if they are not to be either ignored or allowed to stifle innovation, emphasize the importance of engaging with the purposes and objectives of innovation.

This is a quick sketch of several decades of insight from the social sciences on the complexity of decision-making in areas of high technological complexity. And these observations are no longer radical or unusual. Of course it is messy,[33] and in particular the reception of these ideas in industry is patchy. But the potential to impoverish decision-making by failing to recognize the complexity of regulation is recognized in the mainstream of regulatory thinking at national,[34] EU[35] and WTO level.[36] If it ever was, risk (narrowly defined) and safety are no longer thought to be the only good reasons for a decision. That

[32] B Wynne, 'Creating Public Alienation: Expert Cultures of Risk and Ethics on GMOs' (2001) 10 *Science as Culture* 445.

[33] In some cases we see an open retreat, R Hagendijk and A Irwin, 'Public Deliberation and Governance: Engaging with Science and Technology in Contemporary Europe' (2006) 44 *Minerva* 167. 'Sound science' legislation and policy continues to be introduced all around the world with not a word on values other than safety (and possibly economic efficiency). Eg, see M Carolan, 'The Politics in Environmental Science: The Endangered Species Act and the Preble's Mouse Controversy' (2008) 17 *Environmental Politics* 449.

[34] eg, see *HL Select Committee on Science and Technology on Science and Society, 3rd Report* (HL Paper, 2000–01); *Royal Commission on Environmental Pollution on Setting Environmental Standards, 21st Report* (Cm 4053, 1998); A Irwin, 'The Politics of Talk: Coming to Terms with the "New" Scientific Governance' (2006) *Social Studies of Science* 299, reviews the 'official' literature.

[35] *Communication on the Precautionary Principle*, n 6 above; European Commission, *White Paper on European Governance* COM (2001) 428 final and associated papers, including European Commission, *Communication on the Collection and Use of Expertise by the Commission: Principles and Guidelines 'Improving The Knowledge Base For Better Policies'* COM (2002) 713 final. The real complexities of the ethical and social elements of science and technology should have been made clear to the institutions by the Expert Group on Science and Governance, n 7 above. Although this report may prove to have a gradual influence over a number of years, it does not yet seem to have been much used, and within the internal structure of the Commission, the Group sits in DG Research rather than in internal market, or even environment or health.

[36] See especially the Appellate Body decisions discussed below.

much is clear. The more interesting question is how we assess the meaning of this shift. It raises a number of important questions, not least in respect of the role of the public and experts in decision making; at the very least, public participation provides an opportunity to identify, explore and challenge a wider range of values. But also, the shift is decidedly ambivalent, so that selective quotation even from single policy documents would be misleading.[37] By examining the case studies in more detail we can see what happens to the recognition of the breadth of decision making when decisions are made.

The Case Studies

In an effort to pin down the changing approach to regulation, I will examine, necessarily briefly, three different case studies at three different levels of governance[38]: the WTO's approach to GMOs; the regulation of a particular application of nanotechnology by the EU; and UK high level policy-making on nuclear energy.

These case studies are very different. Nanotechnology and biotechnology both lead to traded products, and the strength of trade law has important effects on reason-giving at all levels. And whilst biotechnology and nanotechnology are fairly (although contentiously) described as 'new' technologies, nuclear technologies remind us that some technologies take many years to 'settle'. The levels of governance are also very different. Like the EU, the WTO exercises a profound influence over the public reasons offered by its members to explain regulation. But unlike the EU, it has no positive regulatory powers with which to mediate the reduction of national autonomy.[39] And the UK approach is much more diffuse than the EU and WTO. Although all three jurisdictions provide a mixture of general principles and individual regulatory approaches, the EU and WTO have more in the way of sweeping judicial and policy statements on risk and regulation.

These case studies allow us to look at regulatory frameworks and decisions rather than the rhetoric. My concern is with the explanatory

[37] Irwin, n 34 below.

[38] This is already, of course, a simplification, as there are many other locations for the regulation of health and environmental safety, private sector as well as public, through the general legal context provided by liability rules and intellectual property.

[39] See the discussion in J Scott, 'International Trade and Environmental Governance: Relating Rules (and Standards) in the EU and the WTO' (2004) 15 European Journal of International Law 307.

power of factors that go beyond risk, both in the overall policy stance to a technology and in the regulatory framing of individual decisions on a particular GM maize, particular food wrappings containing nano-particles, or a particular nuclear power plant. In each area there is a very clear recognition of the social, political and ethical complexity of the regulatory enterprise. In each case however, regulatory frameworks and decisions ultimately seek to explain through risk.

The national level

UK and English policy on risk has made a mainstream orthodoxy of the proposition that regulation is about a range of values in addition to safety, and also that public involvement is crucial for 'good' decision-making.[40] The difficulty of matching this rhetorical responsiveness to a full range of considerations with the actual practice of decision-making can be seen in many areas, but in this chapter we will use the example of nuclear power.

The UK government held an extensive and multi-faceted consultation process on nuclear energy, which resulted in a *White Paper on Nuclear Energy* in 2008.[41] The consultation process was somewhat fragmented[42] and it was instigated in the first place because of Greenpeace's successful judicial review of an earlier process.[43] The largest environmental interest groups dropped out, fearing that their presence was legitimizing a process already dedicated to encouraging new nuclear build.[44] The UK government had indeed reached a 'preliminary view'

[40] See n 34above. [41] *White Paper on Nuclear Power*, n 12 above.

[42] There are separate consultations on nuclear waste, see Defra, BERR and the Devolved Administrations, *Managing Radioactive Waste Safely: A Framework for Implementing Geological Disposal* (Cm 7386, 2008); the 'justification' process, see <http://www.berr.gov.uk/whatwedo/energy/sources/nuclear/consultations/open/page44523.html>; and the Strategic Siting Assessment, see Department for Business, Enterprise and Regulatory Reform, *Towards a Nuclear National Policy Statement: Consultation on the Strategic Siting Assessment Process and Siting Criteria for New Nuclear Power Stations in the UK* (2008). Statutory environmental assessments involving consultation are also necessary, see Directive (EC) 2001/42 on the assessment of the effects of certain plans and programmes on the environment [2001] OJ L197/30; Directive (EEC) 85/337 on the assessment of the effects of certain public and private projects on the environment [1985] OJ L175/40, as amended.

[43] *R (on the application of Greenpeace) v Secretary of State for Trade and Industry* [2007] Env LR29.

[44] The UK government described this as 'a source of regret' but was 'satisfied that the environmental arguments both for and against nuclear power were thoroughly explored

which consultation was supposed to 'test'.[45] The intention here is not to review the pros and cons of nuclear energy, but to identify the range of issues addressed by the consultation. Government, far from ignoring the purposes and commitments of nuclear energy, is ostensibly eager to engage with those purposes, and it is clear that government accepts the relevance of a wide range of issues extending beyond safety. The question is quite how that range of issues is employed in the explanation of the final decision.

The UK government focuses on climate change and energy security as reasons for proceeding to new nuclear build. Research suggests that the public is, albeit ambivalently, responsive to this new framing of nuclear power.[46] The prominence of the purposes of nuclear power in explanations of government decision-making is interesting and in principle positive, allowing claims about the benefits of nuclear power to be subject to the same critical scrutiny as claims about the problems inevitably are.

The role of nuclear in climate change policy is however controversial.[47] There is an empirical debate about the calculation of carbon emissions over the entire life cycle of a nuclear power station.[48] But a major objection to the climate change argument is captured in the *Analysis* of consultation responses carried out for the government: 'Some of those opposed to nuclear power express anger that the Government

during the consultation'. *White Paper on Nuclear Power*, n 12 above, 1.14. The *Analysis of Consultation Results*, n 4 above, however said that 'a more vigorous opposing view was only present in a very limited form', 1.74.

45 *White Paper on Nuclear Power*, n. 12 above, 1.7. Traditional Internet and written consultation, as well as smaller more deliberative events around the country, formed part of the process. The different strands of the main consultation were analysed by consultants before the 2008 *White Paper on Nuclear Power* was published, see *Analysis of Consultation Results*, n 4 above.

46 On climate change, see K. Bickerstaff and ors, 'Reframing Nuclear Power in the UK Energy Debate: Nuclear Power, Climate Change Mitigation and Radioactive Waste' (2008) 17 *Public Understanding of Science* 145. Note that the deliberative element of the nuclear consultation suggests that there is greater concern about energy security than climate change, see *Analysis of Consultation Results*, n 4 above, 104.

47 I will concentrate on the climate change rather than energy security. Energy security also raises complex non-safety issues. For example, supporters of nuclear power see the crucial energy security concern as 'a baseload supply using easily obtained and stockpiled fuel from stable sources that is relatively immune to fluctuations of supply and price'; opponents of nuclear power are more concerned about 'locally generated electricity based on fuel sources that cannot be intercepted in transit or denied to the United Kingdom by a foreign power or terrorist action' (*Analysis of Consultation Results*, n 4 above, 27. Presumably those suffering from fuel poverty have a different understanding still.

48 *Analysis of Consultation Results*, n 4 above, 45.

is posing a false dilemma'.[49] This is partly a question of trust, in particular a questioning of the institutional and commercial commitments of the proponents of nuclear power, including those demonstrated by areas of government policy where climate change is anything but an overriding consideration. The government does not engage with the anger, and does not properly acknowledge that this is a choice rather than a necessity.[50] Moreover, it somewhat undermines its characterization of climate change as a central justification for nuclear power, when it moves the debate very neatly from carbon to cost: 'the key point was not whether we can meet [emissions reduction] targets without nuclear power, but the extent to which it is possible to meet those targets in a practicable manner at low risk and at reasonable cost.'[51] The government's position that 'a range of different options', including nuclear, will be necessary for deep cuts in carbon emissions is certainly respectable, and government insists that nuclear will not divert attention from renewables, carbon capture and storage, or energy efficiency.[52] But by presenting nuclear energy and fossil fuel (plus climate change) as straight alternatives, it is able to present the turn to nuclear as a risk/risk trade-off, avoiding any serious discussion of whether changes in lifestyle are an ethically more appropriate response to climate change. The calculation of a risk/risk trade-off also seems to assume better knowledge than we have; it is far from clear how these fine judgments have been reached.

The safety concerns at the forefront of the current wave of opposition to civilian use of nuclear energy are complex, including the effects on human health and the environment of both chronic pollution and acute exposure through accidents. The primary government response to all of the safety concerns, including the very complex indeterminacies discussed earlier, is to refer to the regulation of the

[49] *Analysis of Consultation Results*, n 4 above, 67, written consultation. Note that after deliberation, fewer people agreed that nuclear power could make 'an important contribution to reducing the UK's CO_2 emissions'. The number agreeing fell from 65% to 60%, those who disagree increased from 8% to 21%, see *Analysis of Consultation Results*, n 4 above, 105.

[50] The Sustainable Development Commission also emphasizes that a turn to nuclear is a choice: Sustainable Development Commission, *The Role of Nuclear Power in a Low Carbon Economy* (2006) 3.3.

[51] *White Paper on Nuclear Power*, n 12 above, 2.71. The government estimates that without nuclear energy, current carbon emissions would be 5–12% higher, *White Paper*, [14]. The alternatives are discussed at Annex A.

[52] *White Paper on Nuclear Power*, n 12 above, 2.72.

nuclear industry[53]: 'we have an effective regulatory framework in place to ensure that these risks are effectively managed and minimized . . . There are risks, but we consider these are very low and that our regulatory arrangements address those risks'. [54] This paradigm of 'reassurance through regulation' is very common. But public concern is based on rich public experience of regulatory failures,[55] and amounts to a profound questioning of the level of confidence claimed by the regulators, 'public judgments of dominant scientific and policy institutions and their behaviours'. [56] The UK government simply does not engage with these more complex questions. There is a similar response to security questions of nuclear proliferation and terrorism. So for example on the 'safety and security' of transport, the government assures us that 'these risks are well understood', again with a reassuring reference to regulatory framework.[57]

The assumptions of progress and of control that are embedded in reassurance through regulation are most significantly challenged by the fact and persistence of nuclear waste. But the 2008 White Paper sees no real problem, asserting the 'belief, based on scientific consensus and experience from abroad, that geological disposal will provide a technically possible means of disposing of radioactive waste'.[58] The reference to scientific consensus and feasibility plays down significant debate about the long term safety and security of geological disposal of waste, and ignores the profound challenges of safeguarding waste many years into the future.[59] But the language of safety is carefully avoided, replaced with the language of 'technical possibility'. And this idea of 'technical possibility' is immensely loaded, a clear example of taking a question that is ethical and social (as well as technical), and addressing it as if it were a technical question of capacity. Technical possibility tells us little about the preferred course of action. The government does, however, accept that creating radioactive waste raises ethical issues.[60]

[53] *White Paper on Nuclear Power*, n 12 above, 2.87ff.

[54] *White Paper on Nuclear Power*, n 12 above, 37–8. There is even reference to the need for 'proportionate' regulation, presumably as reassurance for the emerging market.

[55] Respondents specifically raised the role of the Pirbright laboratory in spreading foot and mouth disease, *Analysis of Consultation Results*, n 4 above.

[56] Wynne, n 32 above, 445.

[57] *White Paper on Nuclear Power*, n 12 above, 40.

[58] *White Paper on Nuclear Power*, n 12 above, 16.

[59] The language of technical possibility also downplays the fact that there are currently no geological disposal sites. The government intends to rely on 'voluntarism and a partnership arrangements' to identify sites.

[60] For the discussion of waste see *White Paper on Nuclear Power*, n 12 above, 86ff.

In reaching its conclusions on waste, it relies heavily on the independent Committee on Radioactive Waste Management (CoRWM).[61] CoRWM is one of a new generation of advisory bodies, with a wide remit including ethical issues, and reliant on deep and broad public involvement for its decision-making. The contrast with the closed and secretive decision-making that preceded it in this area is stark. In 2006 it published recommendations that the UK proceed to geological disposal, with interim storage pending availability of disposal sites, which the UK government has accepted.

The difficulty with relying on this report is that CoRWM and the *White Paper* are not addressing the same ethical question. As briefly acknowledged by the government,[62] CoRWM addresses already existing 'legacy' waste and future waste generated from already existing power stations,[63] whilst the *White Paper* is dealing with the creation of new waste. CoRWM identified two overarching alternatives: either deal with waste now (the generation benefiting from nuclear power also takes responsibility for nuclear waste); or 'leave it until later' (future generations might have better ways of dealing with waste).[64] These two alternatives do not suffice in respect of the creation of new nuclear waste; the third option has to be not to create it. A 'least bad' solution is fine for waste we have inherited, but we might expect a better ethical and practical solution before we knowingly create new waste.[65]

The government quite rightly consulted again on new build nuclear waste.[66] Nevertheless, the use of CoRWM helps the government to separate the questions of how we deal with waste from the main decision on whether to have new nuclear power stations, side-stepping precisely the ethics and practicalities of knowingly *creating* radioactive waste. And when it does address the ethics of *new* nuclear waste head on, the government compares the ethical implications of nuclear waste for future generations with the ethical implications of climate change.[67]

[61] The existing approach to nuclear waste collapsed in late 1990s, see the discussion in *HL Science and Technology Select Committee on the Management of Nuclear Waste, 3rd Report* (1999).

[62] *White Paper on Nuclear Power*, n 12 above, 2.143.

[63] Indeed, CoRWM identified the fact that nuclear energy was 'in retreat' at the beginning of its remit as an opportunity for those with conflicting views to reach some sort of consensus, Committee on Radioactive Waste Management, *Managing our Radioactive Waste Safely: CoRWM's Recommendations to Government* (2006) 4.

[64] CoRWM, Ibid, ch 6.

[65] W Cragg in A Blowers (ed), *Ethics and Decision Making for Radioactive Waste* (CoRWM, 2006)

[66] *Managing Radioactive Waste Safely*, n 42 above.

[67] *White Paper on Nuclear Power*, n 12 above, 97–9.

The government's efforts to reassure through regulation turn our attention to the dense and complex legal framework that applies to nuclear energy. A new Generic Design Assessment process is designed to assess safety of design in a non-site specific (generic) context.[68] Whilst enormous strides of openness have been taken relative to the tradition of very closed decision-making, even at this very early stage, it seems that the public is to be reassured and protected, rather than involved, in this highly specialized and technical process.[69] Following design approval, the Health and Safety Executive must be approached for a site safety licence, and the Environment Agency for authorization of discharges under the Radioactive Substances Act 1993, as well as for authorization of non-nuclear environmental issues.

For current purposes, it suffices to say that non-safety questions find no clear space in this regime; reassurance through regulation only properly responds to those concerns that are suitable for risk assessment. There is, however, a 'justification' process, which requires that 'all new classes or types of practice resulting in exposure to ionizing radiation are justified in advance of being first adopted or first approved by their economic, social or other benefits in relation to the health detriment they may cause'.[70] Whilst this is an interesting (and highly unusual) regulatory demand for the 'why' factor to be considered, we might note that the only negative consideration to be placed in the balance against 'economic, social and other benefits' is health.

Nuclear power stations also require planning permission. Planning is not a system of risk regulation, and the history and context of decision-making far more easily embraces a range of different issues than other areas of regulation. Planning is not immune from the risk obsession however. We very often see the range of concerns about a particular development expressed and presented as monolithic 'public concern' or 'public perception of risk', which is likely to be pitched against an 'expert risk' framework, rather than as a number of

[68] They have produced preliminary assessment reports on four nuclear power station designs, available at <http://www.hse.gov.uk/nuclear/reactors/>.

[69] eg, see GDA Process Review Board, *The Civil Nuclear Reactor New Build Programme – The Generic Design Assessment – First Report* (2008).

[70] Directive (Euratom) 96/29 laying down basic safety standards for the protection of the health of workers and the general public against the dangers arising from ionizing radiation [1996] OJ L159/1, art 6. *White Paper on Nuclear Power*, n 12 above, Annex B. The government insists that this justification is not site specific, and is not about a comparison with other forms of electricity generation.

substantive issues.[71] And under the Planning Act 2008, any application for planning permission for a major infrastructure project, including a nuclear power station, will be decided by the new Infrastructure Planning Commission rather than, as in the past, the Secretary of State following a public inquiry. This Commission must decide in accordance with a National Policy Statement on nuclear power, drawn up by the secretary of state and subject to parliamentary scrutiny.[72] The hope of the government is to deal with all of the 'general' questions about nuclear power in this single high level debate, calling on the national (and indeed global) interest as a trump card. The Commission can, however, decline to follow a National Policy Statement if to do so would lead to a breach of legal obligations, or if the Commission 'is satisfied that the adverse impact of the proposed development would outweigh its benefits'.[73] The playing out of the new planning legislation is still uncertain. The question of adverse impacts, for example, is certainly not *intended* to allow a revisiting of issues already addressed in the National Policy Statement, and the precise timing and impact of statutory environmental assessments may be contentious.[74] Whether the expectation of political closure is realistic is open to question, but the intention of the government is explicitly to speed things up.[75]

[71] See the cases discussed in C Hilson, 'Planning Law and Public Perceptions of Risk: Evidence of Concern or Concern Based on Evidence?' (2004) *Journal of Planning Law* 1638.

[72] The National Policy Statement is subject to scrutiny by a Parliamentary Select Committee, and can be referred to the floor of the House.

[73] s 104 of the Planning Act 2008. The National Planning Statement will also flag particular things that will require local consideration.

[74] The wider environmental effects of the Strategic Siting Assessment will be considered in the Strategic Environmental Assessment, see *Strategic Siting Assessment*, n 42 above, 5. The National Policy Statement on nuclear power will be subject to Strategic Environmental Assessment under Directive (EC) 2001/42, n 42 above, and sustainability appraisal (under the Planning Act). The National Policy Statement will also be subject to assessment under Directive (EEC) 1992/43 on the conservation of natural habitats and of wild fauna and flora [1992] OJ L206/7, *Strategic Siting Assessment*, n 42 above, 21. There may be subsequent assessments of individual projects, ibid, 66. Environmental Impact Assessment will be the responsibility of the developer at the time of application for permission for a project, see ibid, 36. Given that the National Planning Statement sets the framework for the decision, and there are no *substantive* obligations in the EIA process (ie no minimum environmental standards), presumably unless general environmental issues are flagged in the NPS as a possible reason for turning down an application, the EIA can only feed into conditions for planning permission, or perhaps the 'adverse impact outweighs benefits' criterion. This pre-judging is at least not within the spirit of the Directive.

[75] Note that the government expects the planning process to take 18 months, *White Paper on Nuclear Power*, n 12 above, 36.

So when the government reassures through regulation, that regulation is very much safety focused. This paradigm of 'reassurance through regulation' is very familiar, and we see it in every area from mobile telephone masts[76] to GMOs.[77] It misses the point. The regulation in this case ignores the most profound dilemmas around the unpredictability of real life ecological and human systems over long time scales. Nor does such an exaggerated confidence in regulatory systems address any question as to whether risk assessment is even an appropriate tool when we are concerned with high impact, low probability risks.

Whatever one's views on nuclear power, this is a fruitful area in which to examine the range of issues that go into making a decision. And we do indeed see an extensive and inclusive debate and provision of reasons. All issues are legitimate, and there is no effort to dismiss entire positions as irrational or irrelevant, which we have often seen in the past. In this, then, we come closest to a decision-making process that reflects the 'beyond risk' rhetoric. Nevertheless, we see a constant return to reassurance through regulation. And regulation in turn emphasizes a narrow and controllable concept of safety. The real nature of the concerns, even in nuclear power, is side-stepped or marginalized.

The EU level

There has never been a denial of the regulatory relevance of non-scientific/non-safety issues in the EU regulatory framework. But, as elsewhere, the end of the 20th century brought a new self-consciousness to the governance of technical complexity. A wealth of policy and even legislative discussion now confirms that a broad range of issues are legitimately addressed in regulation. The example of regulation addressed here is nanotechnology.

Nanotechnology is the technology of the tiny, and nanomaterials are particles, fibres or tubes on the scale of a few billionths of a metre. The change of scale changes the properties and behaviour of the material. For example, gold in its ordinary form is famously inert, but at the nanoscale becomes highly reactive; carbon in its various nanoscale forms is physically strong with great chemical stability. The differences

[76] eg, see Planning Policy Guidance Note 8, *Telecommunications* (2001) especially 29 and 30.

[77] See the discussion in M Lee, *EU Regulation of GMOs: Law and Decision Making for a New Technology* (Edward Elgar, 2008) ch 2.

between the nanoscale and bulk materials are the source of nanotechnology's practical applications, applied in fields as diverse as energy generation, medical diagnosis and drug delivery, sunscreen and food wrappings.[78] They are also the source of concern about potential negative impacts.

I am concerned here with decision-making *at* EU level rather than EU governance of decision-making at the national or local level. The products and processes of nanotechnology are regulated at EU level by at least food law, chemicals regulation and medicines regulation. I concentrate on food applications of nanotechnology because EU food regulation is most open in its structure, and as a result the most challenging for my argument. Nanotechnology promises 'modifications of taste, texture, sensation, consistency, fat content and for enhanced nutrient absorption'[79]; nanomaterials could also unintentionally enter the food chain via environmental exposure. There is currently no known nano-food, but food wrappings do already contain nanomaterials, for example to maintain freshness or fizz.

We have more than adequate indications that EU decision-makers do not consider themselves coolly technocratic on nanotechnology. Nanotechnology is being self consciously and explicitly compared with biotechnology—the same utopian promises, similarly dystopian visions. Given the hiatus in commercialization of GMOs, this is seen as a commercial and economic threat, and draws attention to the ethical, political, and social aspects of nanotechnology, including pervasive and profound ignorance. These issues are raised in more or less every policy document.[80] But none of this tells us how easily these broader

[78] For detailed discussion of nanotechnology and its governance, see Royal Commission on Environmental Pollution, n 25 above.

[79] European Food Safety Authority, *The Potential Risks Arising from Nanoscience and Nanotechnologies on Food and Feed Safety* (Scientific Opinion of the Scientific Committee) (2009) 958 *The EFSA Journal* 1, summary. The House of Lords Science and Technology Committee launched an inquiry into the use of nanotechnologies in the food sector on 3 February 2009.

[80] eg, see European Commission, *Nanosciences and Nanotechnologies: An Action Plan for Europe 2005-2009* COM (2005) 243 final, containing an entire section 'Integrating Societal Dimensions: Addressing Expectations and Concerns'; the preparatory *Towards A European Strategy for Nanotechnology* COM (2003) 338 final, providing that 'Societal impacts need to be examined and taken into account', 3; European Commission, *Nanosciences and Nanotechnologies: An Action Plan for Europe 2005-2009 First Implementation Report* COM (2007) 505 final, stating that 'Societal acceptance is a key aspect of the development of nanotechnologies' and that 'there should also be public consensus on their overall impact. Their expected benefits, as well as potential risks and any required measures, must be fully and accurately presented and public debate must be

considerations might be heard in the regulatory framework. Even the policy documents themselves are ambivalent. Tellingly, the Commission's Review of the *Regulatory Aspects of Nanotechnology*, which contains the hardest thinking on policy implementation, focuses on 'possible health or environmental risks associated with nanotechnology', with some peripheral attention to consumer protection and worker protection.[81] The sense of an enormous economic opportunity missed pervades policy as a whole. The main objective seems often to be ensuring that social and ethical *impacts* do not derail the commercial trajectory of these technologies.[82] One policy document even explicitly refers to 'real risk' versus 'perceived risk' and says that 'Dialogue with the public is essential to focus attention on issues of real concern rather than "science fiction" scenarios',[83] assuming presumably that we can tell the difference.

The Commission asserts, with its customary confidence, that its 'integrated, safe and responsible approach' to nanotechnology has 'been agreed by stakeholders'.[84] A dense web of EU policy and legislation applies to nanomaterials in the food area: at least the General Food Law,[85] the proposed replacement Novel Foods Regulation (which explicitly refers to nanotechnology[86]) and the Regulation on materials intended to come into contact with food,[87] ie food wrappings. This

encouraged, to help people form an independent view', 7. See also European Commission, *European Activities in the field of Ethical, Legal, and Social Aspects (ELSA) and Governance of Nanotechnology* (2004).

[81] European Commission, *Regulatory Aspects of Nanomaterials* COM(2008) 366 final, 3.

[82] See the discussion in Kearnes and ors, n 18 above, although not in the context of EU nanotechnology policy.

[83] *Towards a European Strategy*, n 80 above, 1.3 and 3.

[84] *First Implementation Report*, n 80 above, 1.

[85] Regulation (EC) 178/2002 Laying Down the General Principles and Requirements of Food Law, Establishing the European Food Safety Authority and Laying Down Procedures in Matters of Food Safety [2002] OJ L31/1.

[86] *European Commission Proposal for a Regulation of the European Parliament and of the Council on Novel Foods and amending Regulation* (EC) COM (2007) 872, 'Novel food should therefore include foods derived from plants and animals, produced by nontraditional breeding techniques, and foods modified by new production processes, such as nanotechnology and nanoscience, which might have an impact on food', Recital 6. The proposal may change on its route through the legislative process; European Parliament's 1st reading was on 25 March 2009. Novel food is food (not enzymes or additives) that 'has not been used for human consumption to a significant degree within the Community before 15 May 1997', and it can only be marketed if placed on an EU list. The new legislation will replace Regulation (EC) 258/97 concerning novel foods and novel food ingredients [1997] OJ L43/1.

[87] Regulation (EC) 1935/2004 on materials and articles intended to come into contact with food and repealing Directives (EEC) 80/590 and 89/109 [2004] OJ L338/4.

legislation depends on risk analysis, the rather progressive framework for which is provided by the General Food Law. Most importantly, the General Food Law expressly recognizes that 'scientific risk assessment alone cannot, in some cases, provide all the information on which a risk management decision should be based', and so 'other factors relevant to the matter under consideration should legitimately be taken into account'.[88]

The General Food Law approach to 'risk analysis' is divided into scientific 'risk assessment' and political 'risk management'.[89] The European Food Safety Authority ('EFSA') is at the heart of risk assessment. It is 'an independent scientific point of reference in risk assessment',[90] and is tasked to provide scientific excellence, independently of political (including national) and industry influence. The EFSA provides an opinion on risk assessment which it passes to the Commission for the start of the political, risk management phase of the process. The Commission in turn draws up a draft decision, taking into account 'the results of risk assessment, and in particular, the opinions of the Authority', but also, crucially for current purposes, 'other factors legitimate to the matter under consideration'.[91] The final decision is made by the Commission and member states through comitology.

'Other legitimate factors' are potentially open ended. 'Societal, economic, traditional, ethical and environmental factors and the feasibility of controls' are explicitly within the reach of this formula.[92] There are opportunities for the public to make comments[93] and for consultation of the European Group on Ethics in Science and Technology,[94] and we might expect comments to be both wide-ranging and

Materials intentionally transferred into food by 'intelligent' or 'active' wrappings are treated as ingredients under Commission Directive (EC) 2001/101 amending Directive (EC) 2000/13 of the European Parliament and of the Council on the approximation of the laws of the Member States relating to the labelling, presentation and advertising of foodstuffs [2001] OJ L310/19.

[88] Regulation (EC) 178/2002, n 85 above, recital 19.

[89] Regulation (EC) 178/2002, n 85 above, art 3, 6.

[90] Regulation (EC) 178/2002, n 85 above, recital 34.

[91] Regulation (EC) 178/2002, n 85 above, art. 6(3). This approach carries into the Food Wrappings legislation, n 87 above, art 11(2)) and the Novel Foods Proposal, n 85 above, which relies on a 'common authorization procedure', Regulation (EC) 1331/2008 establishing a common authorization procedure for food additives, food enzymes and food flavourings [2008] OJ L354/1, art 7.

[92] Regulation (EC) 178/2002, n 85 above, recital 19.

[93] Regulation (EC) 178/2002, n 85 above, art 9; Regulation (EC) 1331/2008, n 91 above, recital 10 (and although the body of the Regulation refers only to consultation of the applicant, there is some emphasis on public transparency and information provision).

[94] COM (2007) 872, n 86 above, recital 24.

'legitimate'. Often, the role of other legitimate factors may be to allow certain foods, for example locally traditional foods such as unpasteurised cheese, to continue to be marketed notwithstanding safety concerns, but it might also be the case that other legitimate factors would lead to more cautious regulation. The legislative reference to 'other legitimate factors' may allow (although not require) the regulator to take account of, and explain a decision by reference to, the likely impacts of corporate control and industrialization of the food industry, for example, or the distribution of risk and benefit. It may even allow a regulator to base a decision on the scale of uncertainty and ignorance. Normally, forms of uncertainty not amenable to risk assessment cannot be a reason for a decision. The Courts have ruled out consideration of 'hypothetical' risk,[95] and policy-makers the search for 'zero' risk.[96] This is a response to a straw man version of the precautionary principle, where we are paralyzed with doubt, unable to make any decisions because we can do nothing without knowing the result.[97] Ignorance would indeed be paralyzing if it was always decisive, and we would be living in a far duller far poorer world if we had been stopped by unknowability. Probably in most cases ignorance should not even be weighty, but it is at least odd to rule out so categorically the possibility of ever considering ignorance. Sometimes the ignorance may be easy to avoid, or the countervailing benefits may be equally hypothetical, or they may be trivial or narrowly distributed. Ignorance would force us to address the purposes of a decision. 'Other legitimate factors' may provide a tiny regulatory space for perhaps the most profound concern about nanotechnology, the concern that we simply do not know enough.

The 'other legitimate factors' formula is very significant, an explicit legislative recognition of the complexity of risk regulation. It is not a complete newcomer to EU regulation—in *Fedesa*, famously, when faced with 'divergent appraisals by the national authorities', the

[95] Case T-13/99 *Pfizer Animal Health SA v Council* [2002] ECR II-3305.

[96] See *Communication on the Precautionary Principle*, n 6 above. Note that this *Communication* does not refer to 'other legitimate factors', but does refer to the relevance of 'all pertinent factors' in situations of scientific uncertainty. These 'pertinent factors' include 'eg socio-economic information, technological perspectives', 6.3.5. It also refers to the relevance of perception of risk, efficiency or social acceptability of action taken. Presumably, given the rejection of a search for 'zero risk' in this communication, the Commission does not think that pertinent factors might include ignorance.

[97] See CR Sunstein, 'Beyond the Precautionary Principle' (2003) 151 University of Pennsylvania Law Review 1003.

Council acted within the limits of its discretion in banning the use of certain hormones in cattle, 'and respond[ing] in that way to the concerns expressed by the European Parliament, the Economic and Social Committee and by several consumer organizations'[98]. Nevertheless, because of the legislative status of other legitimate factors, food is the area of EU regulation that seems most likely to provide a full account of the reasons for regulating nanomaterials. 'Other legitimate factors' are however set within a very specific legal context, which prefers, although not exclusively, a scientific and safety-focused understanding of regulation.

Legal context would, of course, always be significant in the interpretation of legislative wording. But context can be organized by reference to a case in which the UK challenged the validity of a regulation on smoke flavourings in food.[99] Responding to arguments about the vagueness of 'other legitimate factors', Advocate General Kokott said that 'What may legitimately be included under "factors" can be sufficiently delimited by reference to the general main aims of the present basic regulation, the aims of the legal basis in Article 95(1) EC, the criteria laid down and the regulatory context.'[100] The ECJ does not explicitly refer to 'other legitimate factors' in this case, but the context of the legislation is clearly relevant to the decision on whether the regulation contains 'the essential elements typifying a harmonization measure'.[101]

The Advocate General's first concern is with the objectives of food law. It is in any event not lawful to exercise powers for purposes other than those for which they were granted. The General Food Law has fairly broad 'aims': a 'high level of protection of human health and consumers' interest in relation to food, taking into account, in particular, the diversity in the supply of food including traditional products, whilst ensuring the effective functioning of the internal market.'[102] The express purposes of the Food Wrappings Regulation are 'to ensure the effective functioning of the internal market . . . whilst providing the basis for securing a high level of protection of human health and the interests of consumers.'[103] The Novel Foods Proposal similarly

[98] Case 331/88 *R v MAFF ex parte Fedesa* [1990] ECR I-4023, 9. More recent cases such as *Pfizer Animal Health SA v Council*, n 95 above, are less generous.

[99] Case C-66/04 *United Kingdom v European Parliament and Council* [2005] ECR I-10553; Regulation (EC) 2065/2003 on smoke flavourings used or intended for use in or on foods [2003] OJ L309/1.

[100] Ibid, 64.

[101] Ibid, 58.

[102] Regulation (EC) 178/2002, n 85 above, art 1.

[103] Regulation (EC) 1935/2004, n 87 above, art 1(1).

is concerned with 'ensuring a high level of human health and consumers' protection, whilst ensuring the effective functioning of the internal market.'[104] The main focus, other than internal market, is obviously on human health, taking us back to our risk assessment framework. But reference to consumer interests holds out the possibility of broader explanations for a decision, such as the long-term impact on consumers of reliance on a small number of patent holders. This would not be at all straightforward, however, given the rather specific consumer interests foreseen by the legislation (as discussed below, misleading consumers, nutritional disadvantages and safety). The most obvious justification for a decision is on safety grounds. If we follow the pattern of EU regulation of GMOs, conceptualizing non-safety issues as consumer issues means we are likely to see at most a debate about mandatory labelling.[105]

Legislative reference to 'other legitimate factors' only moves the debate on if the objectives of the legislation are also open ended. The relative narrowness of the context within which other legitimate factors affect a decision is reinforced by considering the conditions for authorization or listing within food law, which seems to be what the Advocate General means by 'criteria laid down'. The General Food Law does not set up an authorization process, but provides that 'food shall not be placed on the market if it is unsafe'; no other clear reasons are provided for denying a market to a food.[106] Listing of a novel food for marketing in the EU will be possible if the food does not, 'on the basis of the scientific evidence available, pose a safety concern to the health of the consumer', if it does not 'mislead the consumer, by the way it is presented or by its intended use' and, for food intended to replace another food, it is not 'nutritionally disadvantageous for the consumer'.[107] And food contact materials, should not 'endanger human health', 'bring about an unacceptable change in the composition of the food' or 'bring about a deterioration in the organoleptic characteristics thereof'.[108] Again, explaining a decision on safety ground seems most attractive.

[104] COM (2007) 872, n 86 above, art 1.

[105] See the discussion in Lee, n 77 above, ch 4.

[106] Regulation (EC) 178/2002, n 85 above, art 14 (1). 'Food shall be deemed to be unsafe if it is considered to be: (a) injurious to health; (b) unfit for human consumption' (art 14(2)). Art 14 is additional to more specific provisions applying to particular food stuffs, see arts 14(7) and 14 (8).

[107] COM (2007) 872, n 86 above, arts 6(a), 6(b) and 6(c).

[108] Regulation (EC) 1935/2004, n 87 above, art 3.

The aims of Article 95(1) are also raised by the Advocate General. The objective of measures passed under Article 95 is 'the establishment and functioning of the internal market'. Health, safety, environmental protection and consumer protection are not primary issues, although the level of their protection should be high. Famously, the provisions of Article 95 allowing member states to introduce or maintain national measures after harmonization are based on a narrow range of objectives (for new measures, protection of the environment or the working environment only), and are heavily constrained by the demand for scientific justification. All of this points us, not exclusively or overwhelmingly, but convincingly, towards human and environmental risk as a basis for decision-making, notwithstanding the express permission to base a decision on 'other legitimate factors'. This is reinforced by the preference of the courts for a scientific basis for decision making, the regulatory context referred to by the Advocate General. *Fedesa*, presaging the 'other legitimate factors' formula, provided that where there are 'divergent appraisals' of risk, there can be no expectation 'that a prohibition . . . could be based on scientific data alone', and public views were at least relevant in the final decision.[109] But whilst it would be an exaggeration to call *Fedesa* a one-off, the courts are now more willing to demand adequate scientific evidence for decision-making. So *Pfizer* and *Alpharma*, whilst confirming that 'scientific legitimacy is not a sufficient basis for the exercise of public authority', famously demand that when a Community institution departs from the opinion of a scientific committee, it must provide 'specific reasons for its findings', and moreover that the reasons 'must be of a scientific level at least commensurate with that of the opinion in question'.[110] And a decision in a complex technical area can be reached without seeking the opinion of a Community scientific body only in 'exceptional circumstances' and only where there are 'adequate guarantees of scientific objectivity' from another source.[111] The judicial preference for scientific explanations puts a premium on an explanation of a decision without reference to those 'other legitimate factors', complemented by the European judicial and political institutions' impoverished approach

[109] *Fedesa*, n 98 above, 10. As Christopher Hilson points out, these 'divergent appraisals' do not seem to have been supported by scientific evidence, or at least none that was presented to the Court: C Hilson, 'Beyond Rationality? Judicial Review and Public Concern in the EU and the WTO' (2005) 56 Northern Ireland Legal Quarterly 320.

[110] *Pfizer*, n. 95 above, 201, 199.

[111] *Pfizer*, n 95 above, 213.

to the precautionary principle, with its ever closer link between risk assessment and the precautionary principle.[112] The precautionary principle could take uncertainty and ignorance seriously, but its interpretation in the EU tends to maintain an illusory separation between 'values' and 'science'.[113]

So, to conclude, the policy around nanotechnology recognizes the regulatory importance of ethical and social questions. That recognition is, as ever, somewhat ambivalent, but nevertheless important. Crucially, there is an effort to follow this through in the wording of the legislation. But even with legislative intervention, the borders around an apparently highly evaluative, discretionary, flexible system are not clear. The legal context constrains the openness of policy-making and legislation, and limits the scope of 'other legitimate factors'.

The WTO Level

There is, in principle, very clear space in the WTO for members to pursue a broad range of ethical, social and political objectives in regulation, extending even to an open-ended 'legitimate objectives' provision and a rarely used morality exception.[114] My focus here is the WTO response to the regulation of GMOs, and although the regulation of GMOs raises many WTO issues, the famous *de facto* moratorium on new authorizations of GMOs in the EU has been the subject of a Panel decision.[115] That is a good place to work through the ways in which broad objectives are actually used in reasoning.

EC-Biotech addressed the moratorium entirely within the terms of the Sanitary and Phytosanitary ('SPS') Agreement, which (broadly) addresses measures designed to protect human, animal and plant life

[112] E Stokes, 'The EC Courts' Contribution to Refining the Parameters of Precaution' (2008) 11 *Journal of Risk Research* 491 examines the move to harder science in court decisions on the precautionary principle. E Fisher, *Risk: Regulation and Administrative Constitutionalism* (Hart Publishing, 2007) ch 6, identifies a change of approach following *Communication on the Precautionary Principle*, n 6 above.

[113] See the discussion in Expert Group, n 7 above.

[114] Agreement on Technical Barriers to Trade (the TBT Agreement) and the General Agreement on Tariffs and Trade (GATT), arts XX and XX, respectively.

[115] *EC–Measures Affecting the Approval and Marketing of Biotech Products*, DS 291, 292, 293, 29 September 2006. Between 1998 and 2004, no GMO received either a positive or a negative decision on authorization, and a number of member states also introduced measures barring national market access to GMOs that had already been authorized at EU level.

and health, as affected by particular risks (for example plant-borne disease or contaminated food).[116] Because the concern here is with regulatory objectives beyond safety, rather than how safety competes with trade, it might be objected that the SPS Agreement is the wrong study. However, one of the more worrying aspects of *EC-Biotech* is precisely its very expansive application of the SPS Agreement, [117] an 'SPS imperialism'[118] that is entirely consistent with the imperialism of risk in regulation more generally. The Appellate Body has not yet commented on the Panel's expansive interpretation of the SPS Agreement, and so we might hope for better to come; but the Panel's decontextualized, so-called 'plain meaning' method of interpretation is hardly unfamiliar to the Appellate Body.[119]

The language of both the SPS Agreement itself and the Appellate Body clearly recognize the complexity of regulation. This recognition is not always followed through in Panel decisions, *EC-Biotech*, as discussed below, being a prime offender. The Appellate Body's first *Hormones* decision in 1998, although ultimately finding the EU's ban on beef from cattle raised using certain hormones to be inconsistent with the SPS Agreement, is often seen as a high point in the WTO's recognition of the discretion allowed to WTO members in the context of WTO demands on risk regulation.[120] The Appellate Body's second *Beef Hormones* decision, in 2008, addressed the EU's response to this first finding.[121] Rather than allowing imports of North American beef to resume, the EU had commissioned research on the potential risks to human health from residues of the relevant hormones in beef, and used that research, along with reports from EU scientific committees, to

[116] See the definition of 'SPS measure' in Annex A; on the SPS Agreement, see J Scott, *The WTO Agreement on Sanitary and Phytosanitary Measures: A Commentary* (Oxford University Press, 2007)

[117] J Peel, 'A GMO by Any Other Name . . . Might be an SPS Risk!: Implications of Expanding the Scope of the WTO Sanitary and Phytosanitary Measures Agreement' (2007) 17 European Journal of International Law 1009; MA Young, 'The WTO's Use of Relevant Rules of International Law: An Analysis of the *Biotech* Case' (2007) 56 International and Comparative Law Quarterly 907; J Peel, R Nelson and L Godden, 'GMO Trade Wars: The Submissions in the EC-GMO Dispute in the WTO' (2005) 6 Melbourne Journal of International Law 141. Other parts of the WTO Agreements could undoubtedly apply to the regulation of GMOs, depending on how the relevant legislation and the claim are framed; for example the TBT Agreement would apply to non-safety consumer protection issues.

[118] Scott, n 116 above, 17.

[119] Peel, n 117 above, 1031.

[120] eg, see Fisher, n 112 above.

[121] See *Continued Suspension of Obligations in the EC – Hormones Dispute*, WT/DS/320/AB/R, WT/DS/321/AB/R, 16 October 2008

justify a new ban on one of the hormones and new provisional bans on the others.[122] The Appellate Body's second decision reiterated rather forcefully many of the more subtle and important aspects of *Hormones I*. So the narrow approach in *EC-Biotech* is to some degree overtaken by this decision. The full impact on Panels' ambivalence towards risk is, however unclear, because the Appellate Body lacked the necessary factual basis to reach a final conclusion on many of the pertinent issues itself.[123] Whilst the language of the decision is trenchant, my interest is in the mismatch between what the WTO says and what it does; the Appellate Body said, but did not do. Hence the continued significance of *EC-Biotech*.

Some of the main areas of flexibility in regulation can be stated briefly. Members enjoy a 'basic right' to take 'sanitary and phytosanitary measures necessary for the protection of human, animal or plant life or health',[124] which extends to autonomy in determining the level of protection appropriate to the member,[125] which may reflect tolerance or aversion to risk. Whatever the level of protection chosen, a measure has to be 'based on scientific principles'[126] and on 'an assessment . . . of the risks to human, animal and plant life and health'.[127] Evidence from the risk assessment does not, however, have to be 'monolithic', so that minority as well as mainstream scientific views can provide a basis for a decision,[128] and qualitative as well as quantitative risk assessment is permissible. If a risk assessment includes a divergent opinion from 'qualified and respected sources' (enjoying the 'scientific and methodological rigour to be considered reputable science'[129]), an SPS measure which reflects the divergent opinion can be said to be 'based on' the risk assessment.[130] The notion of 'risk assessment' is

[122] The US and the EU are now negotiating on beef imports, see 'EU and US Reach Provisional Agreement in Beef Dispute', DG Trade Press Release, 6 May 2009.

[123] Partly because the Appellate Body's decision that the appointment of experts who had served on certain international scientific committees breached the EC's due process rights undermined the factual basis provided in the Panel report; also because the Appellate Body's position on standard of review meant that the Panel had not asked itself (or the experts) the right questions.

[124] Art 2, heading and 2.1.

[125] Art 3.3 in respect of independence from international standards, art 4.1 in respect of the standards of other members.

[126] Art 2.2

[127] Art 5.1

[128] *Hormones*, n 22 above, 194; *Hormones II*, n 121 above, 529.

[129] *Hormones II*, n 121 above, 591. This part of *Hormones II* is clearly concerned with art 5.1, not just art 5.7, as the *EC-Biotech*, n 115 above, Panel appears to have thought.

[130] *EC-Biotech*, n 115 above, 7.3060. The Panel is concerned with minority views, or general caution, expressed within a risk assessment, and generally downplays the role of minority evidence.

interpreted broadly, not limited to purely laboratory studies, and not sharply distinguished from what the EU would call 'risk management', the political stage of decision-making.[131] A range of relevant factors can be considered, including the difficulty of control and of enforcement of good veterinary practice, and differing effects depending on social and environmental context, famously expressed in *Hormones 1* as the 'actual potential for adverse effects on human health in the real world where people live and work and die'.[132]

There are even some modest indications that the Appellate Body recognizes the importance of democratic responsiveness when scientific evidence is fragile, acknowledging that sometimes 'responsible and representative governments', rather than relying on majority scientific views, 'may act in good faith on the basis of what, at a given time, may be a divergent opinion coming from qualified and respected sources'.[133] And similarly, when deciding on the sufficiency of the scientific evidence, a Panel should bear in mind 'that responsible, representative governments commonly act from perspectives of prudence and precaution where risks of irreversible, e.g. life-terminating, damage to human health are concerned'.[134] And the mere fact of 'supposed multiple objectives' to legislation, including harmonization and consumer reassurance as well as safety, does not take a member out of the bounds of the SPS Agreement.[135]

When scientific evidence is 'insufficient' to perform a risk assessment, Members can take provisional measures based on 'available pertinent information', under Article 5.7 of the SPS Agreement. The precondition of 'insufficiency', whilst distinguished from uncertainty,[136] includes qualitative insufficiency.[137] New evidence that can render otherwise 'sufficient evidence' 'insufficient' need not amount to a 'paradigm shift', simply 'new evidence from a qualified and respected source'.[138] Moreover, the sufficiency of scientific evidence may depend on the level of protection pursued by a Member; the fact that

[131] *Hormones*, n 22 above, 181; *Hormones II*, n 121 above, 541–543.

[132] *Hormones*, n 22 above, 187; *Hormones II*, n 121 above, 527.

[133] *Hormones*, n 22 above, 194; *Hormones II*, n 121 above, 529.

[134] *Hormones*, n 22 above, 124.

[135] *Hormones*, n 22 above, 245.

[136] *Japan-Measures Affecting the Importation of Apples*, WT/DS245/AB/R, 26 November 2003, 184.

[137] *EC-Biotech*, n 115, especially Annex K.

[138] The Appellate Body identifies a spectrum of scientific evolution, with extremes of 'the incremental advance of science' and 'the more radical scientific changes that lead to a paradigm shift'. Scientific evidence 'at the margins' will not provide entry to art 5.7, *Hormones II*, n 121 above, 703.

international (*Hormones*) or EU (*EC-Biotech*) bodies considered that there was 'sufficient' scientific evidence to carry out a risk assessment, does not necessarily make that the case for a member choosing a higher standard of protection.[139] In this, the Appellate Body recognizes that risk assessment is not universally valid. If Article 5.7 does apply, it is not clear what 'counts' as 'available pertinent information' to justify measures under Article 5.7. The Appellate Body has not provided any enlightenment beyond requiring 'some evidentiary basis indicating the possible existence of a risk'.[140] There is scope for Article 5.7 to escape some of the more unwieldy demands of Article 5.1, and possibly also the bar on regulating 'theoretical uncertainty', 'the uncertainty that theoretically remains since science can never provide absolute certainty',[141] which raises the same questions as the EU bar on regulation of 'hypothetical risk', discussed above.

All of this is very encouraging. Failure to follow through in each respect can be seen in a number of Panel decisions, not least *EC-Biotech*. In *EC-Biotech* the Panel applied the SPS risk assessment requirements not to the EU-wide (non)decisions,[142] but to nine national safeguard measures by six member states who restricted the use in their territory of GMOs that had been authorized at EU level before the start of the moratorium. Whilst the language is expansive, none of the safeguard measures in *Biotech* complied with Article 5.1. Some of Austria's arguments can be used as examples.

Austria attempted to justify its measures by identifying problems with the 'risk assessment' on the basis of which GMOs had been authorized at EU level. The Panel held that whilst members are entitled to legislate on the basis of a disagreement with a risk assessment, they must provide their own study capable of meeting the definition of risk assessment: they must explain, 'how and why they assess the risks differently, and . . . provide their revised or supplemental assessment of the risks'.[143] Austria also argued that the relevant products had not been tested in realistic conditions and that monitoring was inadequate. It emphasized long-term effects, especially in environmentally sensitive areas, and argued that mountain eco-systems raised special issues.[144]

[139] *Hormones II*, n 121above, 685, 694. *EC-Biotech*, n 115 above, got this wrong.

[140] *Hormones II*, n 121 above, 678.

[141] *Hormones*, n 22 above, 186.

[142] This part of the moratorium, n 115 above, was dealt with under the provisions on delay in Annex B. Lack of space demands selectivity here; for more detail see Lee, n 77 above, ch 6.

[143] *EC-Biotech*, n 115 above, 7.3062.

[144] *EC-Biotech*, n 115 above, 7.2569.

The Panel's rejection of this argument reminds us that *indeterminacy* is recognized in the WTO only where that indeterminacy is nevertheless established by risk assessment. And yet, the unpredictable behaviour of living organisms in complex ecological and social systems is at the heart of doubts about the adequacy of risk assessment as a methodology to respond to GMOs.[145] These are doubts that find no space in the SPS Agreement. The welcome recognition of indeterminacy in the 'real world, where people live and work and die' did not help Austria any more than it had helped the EU in *Hormones*. In that case, the social indeterminacy regarding profligate use of hormones by farmers in the raising of beef cattle (the 'real world' risks) had not itself been subject to a specific risk assessment. [146] *EC-Biotech* moreover shows how this 'real world' proviso can cut both ways in an institution preoccupied by risk assessment. Austria's efforts to rely on laboratory studies of the effect of Bt maize on non-target insects were rejected by the Panel on the basis of scientific caution expressed in the studies themselves: 'No conclusions can be drawn at this point as to how results from . . . laboratory trials might translate in the field'.[147] The doubts expressed in this study, doubts that put a check on regulation, received very little scrutiny compared to doubts that might put a check on the import of goods, such as Austria's doubts about the quality of the risk assessment used to justify the cultivation of GMOs.

In addition, these laboratory studies were not 'sufficiently specific' to the risk at issue. In *Hormones*, whilst studies provided evidence that the hormones create a 'general risk of cancer', they were inadequate in their failure to focus specifically on the carcinogenic potential of residues those particular hormones, in meat, from cattle given hormones for growth promotion.[148] This very high degree of specificity[149] actually raises a significant barrier to the regulation of small and diffuse risks, which are more or less impossible to isolate with any precision. The

[145] Peel, n 117 above, suggests that it may be precisely because of our weak understanding of ecosystems, that ecosystem effects do not properly belong in the science based SPS Agreement, 1017. This is a strong point, although it is arguable that Peel overstates our understanding of human health in risk assessment terms.

[146] *Hormones*, n 22 above, 207–08; *Hormones II*, n 121 above, 559

[147] *EC-Biotech*, n 115 above, 7.3098, 7.3099.

[148] *Hormones*, n 22 above, 198 and fns.

[149] See AO Sykes, 'Domestic Regulation, Sovereignty and Scientific Evidence Requirements: A Pessimistic View' (2004) 3 Chicago Journal of International Law 353, 364; J Scott, 'On Kith and Kine: Trade and Environment in the EU and WTO' in JHH Weiler (ed), *The EU, WTO and NAFTA: Towards a Common Law of International Trade* (Oxford University Press, 2000).

incidence of cancer from, for example, meat from hormone treated cattle is likely to be impossible to establish, or even properly test for *specifically*, given the high background level of disease, the diffuse nature of the risk, the small additional numbers of disease and the other sources of these and other carcinogens. And yet, scientific understanding of the carcinogenic property of the hormones, together with knowledge of their presence in the meat might, reasonably it would seem, lead to a wish to regulate. Similarly, laboratory studies establishing that one form of Bt maize is capable of negative impacts on one non-target insect sounds like a good reason for regulating other forms of Bt maize that will provide food for similar insects. The possible legitimacy of regulating to protect from risks with a high background incidence on the basis of extrapolations from similar demonstrable risks is still an open question.

To conclude this brief discussion of the WTO, it is clear first of all that safety is not the only value that can compete with trade in the WTO framework. Independent social objectives can be found elsewhere in the WTO Agreement, but even within the SPS Agreement there is, in principle, considerable scope for a proper appreciation of the dilemmas associated with risk and risk assessment. Cases like *EC-Biotech* are however at best ambivalent, with professed respect for domestic autonomy and flexibility coupled with extraordinary confidence in the ability of science to arbitrate. It might be argued that *EC-Biotech*, unappealed and at least partly inconsistent with the spirit of the two *Hormones* decisions, is an irrelevance. Perhaps the most important element of *Hormones II* is the strong criticism of the Panel's standard of review. The Panel had wrongly 'reviewed the scientific experts' opinions and somewhat peremptorily decided what it considered to be the best science'.[150] The review power of a Panel is not to determine the correctness of a Member's risk assessment, 'but rather to determine whether that risk assessment is supported by coherent reasoning and respectable scientific evidence and is, in this sense, objectively justifiable'.[151] We might expect Panels to be more cautious in the future, and the renewed emphasis on minority science may raise doubts about elements of the *EC-Biotech* decision. *EC-Biotech* does, however, indicate very clearly how the fine words can slide away in a context that takes for granted the role of risk assessment as a neutral, objective way of finding a route through different views of the world. Moreover, of all

[150] *Hormones II*, n 121 above, 612.

[151] *Hormones II*, n 121 above, 589.

the failings of the *EC-Biotech* Panel decision, and they are many,[152] most significant for current purposes is its failure to acknowledge the 'social controversies',[153] including those around uncertainty, that led to the EU's difficulties. *Hormones II* does not deal with that gap.

What This Might Mean

The legal management of unsettled technologies is certainly not restricted to the regulation of safety, and is far from wholly technocratic. But this acceptance in principle of the broad nature of the regulation is very often overwhelmed by the more general legal and political context. Accounting for, and explaining, the difference between regulatory rhetoric and regulatory practice is not straightforward, and nor is it obvious what the next step should be. This section starts with a brief account of why the mismatch matters, before outlining some of the main pressures that restrict reasoning, and making some tentative suggestions about what this might mean for those of us interested in the regulation of areas of high technical complexity.

Why it Matters

Reason-giving is a basic requirement of fair regulatory processes, and the supposed purposes of reason-giving are well rehearsed.[154] Reasons allow for judicial and public scrutiny of a decision, as well as requiring

[152] For example: the length, repetition and technical obscurity of the report especially given the criticism of the WTO's lack of transparency and accountability; the dismissive and petulant tone towards 'groups and members of civil society' who dared to 'discuss and analyse' the leaked decision (see Annex K); the fragmenting effect on international law and selective approach to international sources (see Young, n 117 above); the Panel also avoids some of the most difficult issues, declining to assess the substantive validity of the EU's authorization process, and relying heavily on the EU material in finding the national safeguard measures to be in breach (see G Shaffer, 'A Structural Theory of WTO Dispute Settlement: Why Institutional Choice Lies at the Center of the GMO Case' (2008) New York Jounal of International Law and Politics available at http://works.bepress.com/gregory_shaffer/18/).

[153] See the EC's criticism of the complainants' case, *EC-Biotech*, n 115 above, 4.332.

[154] See G Richardson, 'The Duty to Give Reasons' [1988] Public Law 437; P.Craig, *EU Administrative Law* (Oxford University Press, 2006) especially 381 onwards. The main administrative law decision on 'reason giving' is *South Buckinghamshire DC v Porter (No 2)* [2004] 1 WLR 1953: reasons must deal with the substantial points that have been raised, but only have to go to principal important controversial issues.

decision-makers to reflect on their own decision. Reasons are a key mechanism for the various forms of rendering account and holding to account, and whilst neither necessary nor sufficient in every case, accountability is often a crucial element of legitimate decision-making.[155] The mismatch between rhetoric and practice raises two main concerns, partially contradictory, but fundamentally connected, and going to the root of the accountability of decision-making.

The first concern is that the depth and extent of the issues raised by a technology are unlikely to receive the full response that is promised if decisions are wholly framed by risk assessment. Although regulators claim to be listening, actually they seem not even to hear concerns beyond safety. This official emphasis on science silences uncertainty, and silences the economic and scientific values behind both decisions and opposition. I have avoided discussing 'public opinion', and my argument is not that public opinion should be followed, even if there were a monolithic public opinion to follow. My argument is that it should be possible at some point of the regulatory process to respond fully to the implications of a technology. This would also allow a more rigorous response to various strands of public opinion that are based on substantive considerations other than risk.

The second concern is almost the opposite: regulators may be highly aware of the political nature of the decision, but decisions reached on the basis of social, ethical and political commitments are presented as if they were decisions about risk. Minority science is, quite rightly, a legitimate basis for a decision at all levels, and light judicial scrutiny of the quality or nature of the science relied on[156] creates a real possibility that decision-makers will cast around for science to explain a political decision. Accountability falls apart. A proper explanation of reasons

[155] There is a great deal of legal and political science scholarship. See C Harlow, *Accountability in the European Union* (Oxford University Press, 2002) ch 1; B Morgan and K Yeung, *An Introduction to Law and Regulation* (Cambridge University Press, 2007). Colin Scott simply refers to 'the duty to give account for one's actions to some other persons or body', 'Accountability in the Regulatory State' (2000) 27 Journal of Law and Society 38. Julia Black discusses the obligation to render account as the constitution and presentation 'of a narrative of past events or actions', 'Constructing and Contesting Legitimacy and Accountability in Polycentric Regulatory Regimes' No 2 LSE Law, Society and Economy Working Papers (2008).

[156] V Heyvaert, 'Guidance Without Constraint: Assessing the Impact of the Precautionary Principle on the European Community's Chemicals Policy' (2006) 6 Yearbook of European Environmental Law 27. Recall also that the Appellate Body in *Hormones II*, n 121 above, emphasizes that Panels should not choose between science, reinforcing the role of minority scientific opinion.

allows those reasons to be challenged through the political or judicial process, and whichever way the decision goes, this is more important than ever in controversial and uncertain cases. The false accountability provided by risk might lead to premature closure of the political debate, encouraging a sometimes sterile debate on competing science. Good explanations are not going to lead to an eruption of consensus, but at least allow decisions to be properly assessed.

The Legal and Political Pressures on Decision-Making

The legal and regulatory pressures towards the explanation of decisions on the basis of safety are relatively clear in each of the case studies. Whilst there is no obligation to follow scientific advice, judicial and legislative preferences for risk assessment create a clear incentive for a particular framing of explanations.

But the role of legislative amendment in this process seems to be rather small. The authority of risk assessment has an informal, non-hierarchical impact as well as being represented by hard law. Risk offers an appearance of objectivity, control and organization,[157] responding to political pressure for explanations that show a decision-maker to be a rational, effective regulator. Its objective appearance creates a distance from politics and interests, paradoxically enhancing the appeal of risk in precisely those situations of high controversy in which it is least persuasive. Nor is it only the regulators who seem compelled to risk. The arguments of litigants and objectors are also structured around safety and risk, rather than explicitly exposing, for example, ignorance or the over-confidence of regulators.[158] The incentives to argue a case narrowly are the same as for regulators, and they are mutually reinforcing.

The need to justify at many levels (local, national, EU and WTO) and to varied publics and stakeholders, enhances both legal and political pressures to explain through risk.[159] As well as probably having to make some sense to the organization itself[160] and the multiple public(s)

[157] Steele, n 1 above.

[158] See Brian Wynne's discussion of Windscale in the 1970s, 'SSK's Identity Parade: Signing-Up, Off-and-On' (1996) 26 *Social Studies of Science* 357, but also consider elements of the EC's approach before the WTO in *EC-Biotech*, n 115 above.

[159] See Scott's discussion of 'extended accountability' and Black's idea of different legitimacy communities with their multiple claims, n 155 above.

[160] Black, n 155 above, citing JW Meyer and B Rowan, 'Institutionalized Organizations: Formal Structure as Myth and Ceremony' (1977) 83 *American Journal of Sociology* 340.

with which it engages, the explanation offered for a decision has to make sense to the partners in multi-level governance. The expert risk framework provides a useful response to these multiple pressures of accountability; an assertion of the 'facts' as a universal justification of action. GMOs provide an example. The WTO dispute is easy to re-present as a disagreement over approaches to regulation, science, social science, even democracy. The EU's arguments before the WTO Panel demonstrate a very sophisticated understanding of the complexity of risk, an approach rejected out of hand by the US. But a glance at the approach to similar disagreements *within* the EU (between the institutions, between member states, between the Commission and individual member states) shows a much more complicated picture. Here the Commission seems far more committed to using risk assessment as a trump card in disagreement. The language of risk allows the different levels of governance to *appear* to speak across their very different legislative and cultural contexts. In doing do they manage their own 'institutional' risk or 'secondary' risk,[161] but they fail to examine the real disagreement over the nature of risk and science. The problem is being defined by reference to a preferred methodology, rather than the other way around.[162]

In addition, the recognition of the importance of the social, ethical and political elements of regulation has only been allowed to affect the margins of decision-making—for example, adding 'other legitimate factors' to risk assessment without changing the purposes of the legislation. These marginal changes do not disrupt long standing institutional routines of decision-making and reason-giving.

Wynne argues that this is because whilst the 'political fact' of public opinion (including non-safety issues) is accepted as real and indeed legitimate, the 'intellectual substance' of what lies behind it, is not.[163] The consultation on nuclear energy provides an example: apparently, some people find it hard to 'emotionally relate' to nuclear as a 'green' source of energy.[164] The relevance of objections to nuclear energy is not denied, but the objections are seen as subjective feelings, rather than as substantive concerns about competing environmental goods. The

[161] See Rothstein and ors, n 3 above, and Power, n 2 above, although in very different contexts from those discussed here.

[162] See Frodeman's reference to the 'love affair with positivism', R Frodeman, 'Nanotechnology: the Visible and the Invisible' (2006) 15 *Science as Culture* 383, 383.

[163] Wynne, n 32 above, 457.

[164] *Analysis of Consultation Results*, n 4 above, 141.

'deficit model' is allowed to 'reconstitute' itself in various other ways, for example when failure to accept the benefits of biotechnology is characterized as a failure to understand.[165]

Decision-makers who both emphasize the legitimacy of broad reasons for a decision, and also seek shelter with experts and safety, are not necessarily cynical. No doubt the language of responsiveness is easily manipulated to disguise the narrow basis for decisions that will allow only physical harm to justify economic risks. And it is clear that social science can be used as strategically as risk assessment: again, consider the stark contrast between the Commission's sophisticated discussion of the social embedding of science when it defended itself at WTO level, and its quite glorious refusal to countenance anything but narrow scientific disciplines within the EU. And although I am concerned especially with ambivalence at the decision-making stage, this ambivalence in implementation is consistent with the policy documents that presaged a new age of broad decision-making.[166] Presumably in part the rhetoric is simply about decision-makers asserting their own freedom of action, to avoid being always and forever constrained by a particular type of expertise. But aside from any cynicism, this change is extremely difficult to pull off. It is not just about the practical difficulties of providing mechanisms to allow the exploration of broad concerns. Practically, representing at different levels of governance the complex and nuanced concerns such as emerged from a consultation exercise like the UK's *GM Nation* debate is hard to picture[167]; talking about safety is much easier.

Most fundamentally, it seems that the radicalism of these new ideas is not understood. The basic premise of change is accepted, but as if it were an incremental procedural change to decision-making structures. Integrating social and ethical perspectives into innovation and its regulation is actually rather daunting.[168]

What this Might Mean

Decision-makers must be held to account for the mismatch between what they say and what they do. That is clearly crucial, but it is not

[165] Kearnes and ors, n 18 above. [166] See Irwin, n 34 above.

[167] See the discussion in M Lee, 'Agricultural Biotechnology in the UK: Expanding the Scope of the Debate?' in M Everson and E Vos (eds), *Uncertain Risks Regulated* (Routledge, 2009).

[168] See Expert Group on Science and Governance, n 7 above.

terribly helpful. We have been talking about the first step, the recognition of the politics of risk, for a long time. That battle has been won now (although it might need to be won time and again). But any assumption of smooth progress into regulatory practice is clearly mistaken. The key question is no longer whether technologies are socially embedded, or whether political and social and ethical commitments are relevant in risk regulation. They are. The question is how to fix that recognition within regulatory decision-making. Even the best of the reports and consultation procedures discussed here tend to fall short at this stage.

The ethical and social elements of science and technology are generally thought to imply commitments to public participation. One possible response to the difficulties identified here would be to query whether the optimism about public contributions to technological decision-making is misplaced. Maybe it is just a bad idea to think about who benefits from a technology, and maybe the assumptions embedded in regulation, which have after all served many of us well and long, should remain unexposed. We do continue to see calls for the exclusion of the 'public' from 'issues and decisions they cannot understand'.[169] Similarly we see sometimes a point blank denial of the existence of ethical considerations in regulation, as (shockingly) in the nuclear consultation, where 'Almost as many people say there are no ethical decisions involved as say there are'.[170] Some suggest that inclusion actually *creates* 'new' areas of concern.[171] Although this seems unlikely often to be the case, concerns do become better articulated, and sometimes a wider public will become aware of otherwise hidden problems.

Those arguing for the exclusion of politics from regulation generally come from the industry perspective, seeking less regulation. There is also an attraction for those on the other side of the fence. It is so difficult for safety and environmental protection to compete with economic values that maybe it is self-defeating to introduce perspectives that might compete with safety. We have sometimes tried to isolate environmental and human health protection from countervailing

[169] *Analysis of Consultation Results*, n 4 above, 44. There is a more subtle argument in Sunstein, n 8 above: Sunstein 'celebrates technocracy', but does subject technocracy to 'deliberative democracy'.

[170] *Analysis of Consultation Results*, n 4 above, 68.

[171] See the discussion of such arguments in H Rothstein and ors, 'Regulatory Science, Europeanization, and the Control of Agrochemicals' (1999) 24 *Science, Technology & Human Values* 241, 106.

economic arguments, but when factors beyond risk do enter the regulatory process, they generally provide a process to *allow* dangers; a risk that would otherwise be unacceptable is permitted because of socio-economic benefits, for example.[172]

Tempting as it might be, a return to the bad old days is not realistic. We have learned too much about the politics of risk. The opposite response to this message of despair is the focus on how to achieve more, or better, public engagement processes. Regulatory consultation is often not particularly imaginative, and certainly we need to think harder about what public participation *is*, what it is *for*, and *who* our publics are. Moving public engagement 'upstream' [173] or 'continued "social intelligence" gathering'[174] rather than one-off events are ways of trying to address public and social commitments before institutional, scientific and commercial trajectories are set, shaping those trajectories, and recognizing that the *legally* significant decision is just one moment in a lengthy process. These are enormously complex endeavours,[175] and changing the institutional commitments at the heart of the problem will be extremely difficult. However early or persistent the consideration of social elements, the relationship between producers and public would almost certainly need some sort of regulation. This takes us back

[172] The main concerns of Regulation (EC) 1907/2006 concerning the Registration, Evaluation, Authorisation and Restriction of Chemicals (REACH), establishing a European Chemicals Agency [2006] OJ L396/1 for example are safety and the internal market. Even in the absence of the 'other legitimate factors' formula, however, REACH acknowledges that risk assessment alone does not provide all necessary information, and the European Chemicals Agency carries out socio-economic assessment of chemicals as well as risk assessment. But authorization requirements only *apply* to substances already deemed to be particularly troubling. The socio-economic criteria will mainly be used to *counter* the argument that because a chemical is persistent, bioaccumulative and toxic, it should not be used. See also the discussion of the 'politicisation' of science in the US: A Vermeule, 'The Parliament of the Experts' *Harvard Law School Programme on Risk Regulation*, Research Paper 09-1.

[173] J Wilsdon and R Willis, *See-through Science: Why Public Engagement Needs to Move Upstream* (Demos, 2004); Royal Society and Royal Academy of Engineering, *Nanoscience and Nanotechnologies: Opportunities and Uncertainties* (Royal Society, 2004); MacNaghten and ors, n 175 above.

[174] Royal Commission on Environmental Pollution, n 25 above, 4.95. Demos has recommended a commission on emerging technologies and society: see J Wilsdon, B Wynne and J. Stilgoe, *The Public Value of Science: Or How to Ensure that Science Really Matters* (Demos, 2005).

[175] P Macnaghten, M Kearnes and B Wynne, 'Nanotechnology, Governance, and Public Deliberation: What Role for the Social Sciences?' (2005) 27 *Science Communication* 268; Pierre-Benoit Joly and Alain Kaufmann, 'Lost in Translation? The Need for "Upstream Engagement" with Nanotechnology on Trial' (2008) 17 *Science as Culture* 225.

to the difficult question of integrating the non-risk issues into the decision.

Another way to try to take seriously the non-risk assessment elements of a decision is to render alternative forms of expertise. Scientific explanations of the dramatic human and environmental tragedies of climate change, for example, have been easily beaten as a justification for action by Stern's weighty economic analysis.[176] More mundane uses of economic expertise abound in the regulatory process. Expert ethical review is an increasingly common response to the recognition of the ethical implications of decisions. Those skilled in particular forms of discourse have something special to add to a decision, and the ethical or the multi-disciplinary expert group (like CoRWM for example) is potentially very valuable. But there is inevitably scepticism about the purpose of such expert groups (to delay, to isolate, to de-politicize, in the EU even to Europeanize an area where the EU's authority is contested),[177] and expert appropriation of ordinary politics, intensifying existing technocratic processes, would be problematic.[178] But just as it is not suggested that the public should be passing judgment on the safety or otherwise of nanotechnology, GMOs or nuclear power, so public preferences on distribution may not be ethically preferable.[179] In both respects, lay people can help to identify what is important in decision-making (not just safety and prosperity) and may have important insights into, for example, questions of distribution and ownership. So there should at least be a role for non experts in framing the questions and context for expert debate,[180] and an opportunity for scrutiny and review and *mutual* testing and challenging between experts and public.[181]

Most importantly, there needs to be real scrutiny of the ways in which expertise is used by decision-makers. Expertise in physics does not answer the ethical questions, but expertise in ethics may be problematic. The use of the CoRWM report is a particularly clear example of expertise being used to answer questions which it had not been

[176] N Stern, *The Economics of Climate Change: The Stern Review* (Cambridge University Press, 2007).

[177] See A Plomer, 'The European Group on Ethics: Law, Politics and the Limits of Moral Integration in Europe' (2008) 15 European Law Journal 639 for a discussion of the European Group on Ethics. This group has proven controversial at a number of levels, including the neutrality of the experts and the quality of its reports. See also Expert Group on Science and Governance, n 7 above.

[178] Jasanoff, n 9 above.

[179] Rawls in Blowers, n 65 above.

[180] The way that the public framed the questions for the Science Review in the UK *GM Nation?* debate is a nice example, see the discussion in Lee, n 167 above.

[181] Anna Vari's submission to CoRWM, see n 179 above.

asked. And the Nuffield Council on Bioethics' largely utilitarian approach to the ethical and social issues of GMOs not only allowed government to dismiss out of hand 'interference with nature' concerns, but also assumed an unrealistically high understanding of the impacts of GMOs.[182] Finally, the report of the European Group of Ethics on nanomedicine is regularly used as an example of EU engagement with the ethical questions around nanotechnology, when there are many other possible approaches.[183]

One final normative implication of this broadening of regulation is that it forces us to think very hard about the appropriate level of authoritative decision-making: not only how to regulate, but who should regulate. The less secure other sources of legitimacy (such as democratic processes), the more attractive the 'facts' as a source of legitimacy. The more globalized levels of decision-making have greater incentives to commit to risk assessment as a justification of decisions. They mistakenly see risk assessments as universal and objective, perhaps because they feel greatest pressure to speak to intense national diversity and because of limited political authority.[184] The national level is not only for the foreseeable future most closely subject to democratic pressures, in turn most connected to the broader issues and most sensitive to uncertainties. Because its legitimacy and democratic accountability is more firmly accepted by its constituents,[185] the national level is also most able to respond to these concerns. Greater autonomy for the national level to rely on the full range of reasons for a decision is then an important implication of the observations made here. So rather than, as currently, posing risk to human health or the environment as

[182] Nuffield Council on Bioethics, n 20 above.

[183] The European Group on Ethics in Science and New Technologies, *Opinion on the Ethical Aspects of Nanomedicine*, (2007). See, for example, *Regulatory Aspects*, n 81 above. The fairly bland Report focuses on safety and data gaps, on informed consent, and on fair distribution of the presumed benefits of nanotechnology; on public participation, but in a functional way, so that trusting publics will allow the presumed potential of nanotechnology to fulfilled.

[184] V Heyvaert, 'Facing the Consequences of the Precautionary Principle in European Community Law' (2006) 31 *European Law Review* 185, arguing that the courts are ambivalent between regulatory discretion and demands for expertise at least in part because of institutional questions.

[185] Which is not to dismiss arguments that obligations (including those that arise through WTO and EU obligations) to have regard to those beyond the jurisdiction have important legitimacy enhancing aspects. Scott, n 116 above, for example, discusses the impact in Kenya of EU regulations on freshwater fishing, 41–44. More generally on the borders of the political jurisdiction see, for example, IM Young, *Inclusion and Democracy* (Oxford University Press, 2000) especially ch 7.

more or less the only acceptable reason for derogating from EU legislation or interfering with global trade, other factors (perhaps 'other legitimate factors') should be available.

To indulge in understatement, this would be far from simple. The values of trade and market integration will be insisted on, and the type of evidence that would avoid the undermining of the 'other regarding' disciplines of trade law would be important. But to say that internal market or WTO law does not allow this sort of diversity forgets how challenging pushing through uniform systems of, for example, agriculture and food, would be to the authority and legitimacy of the EU and WTO. In fact, the meaning and depth of 'free trade' and the internal market is always, rightly, subject to political debate,[186] to which this argument contributes.

More challenging than trade law is the equal ambivalence at the national level to the developments in regulation. The UK has greater legal, economic and political autonomy in its consideration of nuclear power than in any other sector, and major decisions on nuclear new build are taken by government, rather than by more constrained independent agencies. And yet still, government calls on risk and regulation, with a confidence that is anachronistic, if not downright bewildering. National regulators want to talk across diversity and disagreement, and look like objective and rational decision-makers, just as much as their more globalized counterparts. So we cannot escape the need to scrutinize and expose the gap between regulatory rhetoric and regulatory decisions, to work through the challenges of a broader basis for decisions. Some form of elegant articulation of 'public concerns' within the regulatory process, some form of 'translation', for all of its difficulties, seems inevitable.[187] Resisting reversion to the deficit model is an ongoing endeavour.

Conclusion

This chapter is about the limitations of 'risk' as a way of making decisions in the regulation of unsettled technologies. It does not argue that we should not take risks or bear uncertainty, or even that we are

[186] eg, see A Lang, 'Reflecting on "Linkage": Cognitive and Institutional Change in the International Trading System' (2007) 70 Modern Law Review 523.

[187] See Mariano-Florentino Cuéllar's discussion of the ways in which a 'sophistication deficit' limits the incorporation of public concerns into regulatory decision making, 'Rethinking Regulatory Legitimacy' (2005) 57 *Administrative Law Review* 411; see also J Black, 'Regulation as Facilitation: Negotiating the Genetic Revolution' (1998) 61 *Modern Law Review* 621.

currently taking too many risks. But there is more at stake than can be grasped through the parameters of risk and safety. Regulatory decision-makers at all levels of governance now acknowledge, at least rhetorically, the relevance to regulation of the political issues inherent in the pursuit of technology. But regulatory frameworks and regulatory decisions are still framed in such a way as to provide almost no space for the debate on these political issues to feed through into decisions. Safety seems to be the only acceptable reason for raising barriers to economic and technological 'progress'.

The most urgent concern is the steadfast refusal to engage with the impact of ignorance and uncertainty. Everybody refers to the impossibility of guaranteeing safety, but as if that were a reason for ignoring ignorance, rather than engaging with it and acknowledging that it brings the other political questions centre stage. Beyond ignorance and uncertainty, but very tightly bound to them, are distributional questions that are too easily ignored. Regulatory failure to interrogate the nature and spread of benefits from a technology silences competing ideas of progress, even complementary ideas of progress. Many would no doubt approve, but the fact that it has served some of us very well tells us nothing about the way it might have served others, globally or within the jurisdiction. Nor does it tell us anything of the path never taken.

Whilst closely connected with the 21st century enthusiasm for public participation, it is not helpful to frame this debate as a 'public perception' problem, or a 'public opinion' problem. Objections to expertise or authority are not passive or based on fear, or risk aversion, or even a different perception of risk. They provide a different substantive perspective on what is interesting about a technology.

‘Fair Play to All Sides of the Truth’: Controlling Media Distortions

*Thomas Gibbons**

Our knowledge and understanding of the world is significantly influenced by news and current affairs reporting by the media. Yet the media can provide only a partial account of the truth, because they are not an infinite resource and selections have to be made about what can be published or broadcast. Editors have considerable discretion to choose what information should be disseminated, albeit constrained by considerations such as journalistic ethics, proprietorial objectives, and the economics of the production process. They may strive to provide at least as full an account of the truth as is possible. Alternatively, they may allow, or be indifferent to the possibility, that even partial truth will be distorted in the stories that they tell. JS Mill said that, ‘Truth, in the great practical concerns of life, is so much a question of the reconciling and combining of opposites’ that ‘correctness’ can only be discerned through the process of struggle between them. He continued, ‘. . . only through diversity of opinion is there, in the existing state of human intellect, a chance of fair play to all sides of the truth.’[1]

This chapter examines whether there should be limits imposed on editors’ discretion, and whether law or regulation have a role in determining those limits. It first considers the case for the media having a special role in truth-telling and then reviews the evidence about journalistic news practice. It is argued that, where distortions occur as a result of commercial and institutional pressures in the industry, there are no grounds for privileging the media on the grounds of their

* Halliwells Professor of Law, University of Manchester. An earlier version of this article was delivered as a lecture at University College London, 26 February 2009. I would like to thank Eric Barendt and an anonymous referee for their helpful comments.

[1] JS Mill, *On Liberty* (edited by G Himmelfarb) (Penguin Books: Harmondsworth, 1974) 110, 111.

freedom of speech. A number of regulatory options are considered as ways of minimizing distortion, the preferred approach being a system of 'enforced ethics.'

The Media's Claim to Truth-Telling

In assessing whether editors are likely to select material for publication in the interest of enhancing truth, the media's own aspirations and their social function are important considerations. There is a dominant viewpoint that newspapers and broadcasters may be seen as the 'fourth estate' of the constitution, reflecting what James Curran has described as the 'liberal theory' of the media.[2] It is represented by the practice of investigative reporting as the ideal to which journalists subscribe. The theory characterizes the media as having a democratic role to act as a check on the state, so as to 'monitor the full range of state activity, and fearlessly expose abuses of official authority'. It also sees the media as agents of information and debate, assisting informed choice, by channelling information between the government and the governed and providing a forum for debate. As Curran indicates, this requires that the media should be fully independent from the state, which implies that they should be located in the free market and should be subject to no, or minimal, state regulation. The theory features, at least implicitly, in political discussion, as a rationale for minimizing regulatory interference with media content.[3]

The theory also plays a prominent role in constitutional and legal thought. Although the idea of freedom of the media does not find support as an independent principle,[4] expression through the media is given special attention in free speech doctrine. There are many solemn declarations of the importance of the role of the media in court

[2] J Curran, 'Mediations of Democracy' in J Curran and M Gurevitch (eds) *Mass Media and Society* (4th edn, Hodder Arnold: London, 2005) 122–49. See also J Keane, *The Media and Democracy* (Polity Press: Cambridge, 1991); S Koss, *The Rise and Fall of the Political Press in Britain* (Fontana Press: London, 1990); L Gies, *Law and the Media: The Future of a Uneasy Relationship* (Routledge Cavendish: London, 2008) 92–4.

[3] In the United Kingdom, versions of the liberal theory have been advanced in countering attempts to increase legal and regulatory oversight of the press and in securing a gradual deregulation of the broadcasting industry. For an historical account, see J Curran and J Seaton, *Power without Responsibility: The Press, Broadcasting and New Media in Britain* (6th edn, Routledge: London, 2003) chs 7 and 15.

[4] E Barendt, *Freedom of Speech* (Oxford University Press: Oxford, 2005) ch XII; F Schauer, *Free Speech: A Philosophical Enquiry* (Cambridge University Press: Cambridge, 1982) 106–9.

decisions in the United Kingdom and at the European Court of Human Rights. For example, Lord Bingham observed in *McCartan Turkington Breen* that:

> the majority [of citizens] cannot participate in the public life of their society . . . if they are not alerted to and informed about matters which call or may call for consideration and action. It is very largely through the media, including of course the press, that they will be so alerted and informed. The proper functioning of a modern participatory democracy requires that the media be free, active, professional and inquiring. For this reason the courts, here and elsewhere, have recognised the cardinal importance of press freedom and the need for any restriction on that freedom to be proportionate and no more than is necessary to promote the legitimate object of the restriction.[5]

In the same case, Lord Steyn spoke of 'the importance of the press acting as the 'eyes and ears' of the public'.[6] In *Reynolds*, Lord Nicholls acknowledged that:

> It is through the mass media that most people today obtain their information on political matters. Without freedom of expression by the media, freedom of expression would be a hollow concept. The interest of a democratic society in ensuring a free press weighs heavily in the balance in deciding whether any curtailment of this freedom bears a reasonable relationship to the purpose of the curtailment. In this regard it should be kept in mind that one of the contemporary functions of the media is investigative journalism. This activity, as much as the traditional activities of reporting and commenting, is part of the vital role of the press and the media generally. . . . The press discharges vital functions as a bloodhound as well as a watchdog.[7]

Again, in *Loutchansky*, Lord Phillips noted the public interest, 'in a modern democracy in free expression and, more particularly, in the promotion of a free and vigorous press to keep the public informed'. He observed that, 'The corresponding duty on the journalist (and equally his editor) is to play his proper role in discharging that function. His task is to behave as a responsible journalist.'[8]

Similar sentiments have been expressed by the European Court of Human Rights and repeated in many judgments. The press is said to play an essential role in a democratic society. Although it must not

[5] *McCartan Turkington Breen (A Firm) v Times Newspapers Ltd* [2001] 2 AC 277, 291, in the course of holding that a press conference was a 'public meeting' for the purposes of statutory qualified privilege in defamation.

[6] Ibid, 298.

[7] *Reynolds* v *Times Newspapers*, [2001] 2 AC 127, 200, 205.

[8] *Loutchansky v Times Newspapers Ltd*) [2001] EWCA Civ 1805, [2002] QB 783, para 36.

overstep certain bounds, in particular in respect of the reputation and rights of others, its duty is nevertheless to impart—in a manner consistent with its obligations and responsibilities—information and ideas on all matters of public interest.[9] Not only does it have the task of imparting such information and ideas: the public also has a right to receive them. 'Were it otherwise, the press would be unable to play its vital role of "public watchdog".'[10]

Although these judicial comments contain empirical statements about the role of the media, their purpose is not to describe the reality of journalism but to impose normative standards on journalists' activities. Nevertheless, they serve to legitimize an empirical assumption that the media have the capacity and willingness to serve democratic goals and, so far as possible, should be left alone so that they can fulfil them. Furthermore, the liberal theory presupposes that the media provide a positive service for democratic debate because they will tell the story as it really is—the metaphor of the watchdog connotes the idea of being on guard against false or misleading information, and that of the bloodhound connotes the idea that relevant information is being concealed. The inference is that the media will provide an alternative account that is genuine and credible.

The Problem of Distortion in the Media

The liberal theory of the media appears to be influential, yet there is a countervailing view, supported by much evidence, that the media have a tendency to distort our understanding of the world. As Curran shows, the operation of media organizations in the marketplace is not an automatic guarantee of independence and effective scrutiny of power. The media devote a relatively small part of their content to public affairs, including official wrong-doing, preferring to emphasize entertainment more generally. They also devote little time to wider sources of power including economic power. Furthermore, news may be managed to serve the media's interests, whether they be the proprietor's or the company's more broadly.[11]

[9] *Castells v Spain* (1992) 14 EHRR 445; *Goodwin v United Kingdom* (1996) 22 EHRR 123; *De Haes and Gijsels v Belgium* (1997) 25 EHHR 1.

[10] *Bladet Tromsø and Stensaas v Norway* (2000) 29 EHRR 125.

[11] Curran, n 2 above, 129.

In addition, there is a tendency for commercially funded media to undermine intelligent and rational debate; rather, it emphasizes information that is 'simplified, personalized, decontextualized, with an emphasis on action rather than process, visualization rather than abstraction, stereotypicality rather than human complexity. . .'.[12] The media may not so much represent their readers and audiences in a democratic way as reflect their status as consumers of the information products which the media sells to them. So, even if the media do engage in some form of democratic scrutiny of the exercise of power, they will not necessarily provide accounts of the world that would provide authoritative alternatives to the versions offered by those in power.

If this view is taken to reflect faithfully some key characteristics of our media, it nevertheless describes them at an abstract level, in terms of the industry and its organization. To the extent that they are seen as creating problems for a free flow of information, their effects may be tempered by the belief that they are resisted by journalists. There are, indeed, notable exceptions to the general picture. Some newspapers do have honourable traditions of a more democratic style of journalism, and public service broadcasters are to an extent isolated from commercial pressures. More generally, there may be a sense that journalists subscribe to a different set of values and work hard, in difficult institutional and economic circumstances, to overcome the problems. However, the reality appears to be that journalism itself is structured by the organizations in which it takes place, and by the resources and budgets which are made available. These constraints have a critical effect on the ability of journalists to gather information and tell their stories.

Various studies[13] have shown that certain sources dominate the news. Journalists are attracted to sources which are close at hand, reliable, well-informed, and likely to be newsworthy. Government and established institutions dominate the sources of news. This is because they have greater resources, they command greater legitimacy and authority, and they are routine suppliers of material. Their sources are

[12] Ibid, 130.

[13] V Campbell, *Information Age Journalism: Journalism in an International Context* (Arnold: London, 2004) ch 4; Goldsmiths Media Group, 'Media Organisations in Society: Central Issues' in J Curran (ed), *Media Organisations in Society* (Arnold: London, 2000) 19–69, 34; P Schlesinger, *Putting 'Reality' Together* (Methuen: London, 1978).

supplemented by information from other professional information suppliers, such as pollsters, marketing agents, and public relations agencies. Furthermore, the evidence suggests that, once information has been obtained, the process of publication is equally slanted. The 'news values' of editors tend to favour stories which deal with the immediate, the topical, and matters of human interest. Furthermore, newspapers tend to reflect ideological biases and they may be willing to set news agendas to promote those viewpoints.

Recent evidence shows that these features of media practice continue to exist, and that they are endemic and systemic. The implication is that their deficiencies cannot be remedied by reliance on the ability and willingness of journalists to seek out and report the truth. It seems that the media are no longer assisting the functioning of a healthy democracy and may in fact be inhibiting it. In his book, *Flat Earth News*,[14] the journalist Nick Davies provides an insider's view of the news industry, showing how it is increasingly difficult, if not impossible, for the ideals of journalism to prevail. He notes the influences on journalists that are routinely mentioned—the influence of the proprietor and of advertising.[15] But he claims that there is a more basic problem, a failure of control over the gathering and testing of information.

What Davies describes as the 'news factory' is characterized by what has been called 'churnalism', the routine recycling of unchecked material. It is material that comes primarily from press agencies and from public relations operations; effectively, it is they who are choosing the material which is reproduced. Furthermore, that choice does not depend on any principles of significance. Instead, it is determined by commercial considerations of cost and convenience, against a background of low staffing and poor resources. The result is a highly selective diet of news which tends to reflect the interests of those who routinely supply it. It consists of relatively 'safe' ideas, and tends to give readers what they want to believe in. Just as significant is what is not reported as a result of this selection process. Davies emphasizes what has been a strong theme in related literature: that the greatest cause of distortion is omission.[16] Overall, he paints a depressing picture of a news industry that seems structurally incapable of challenging and

[14] N Davies, *Flat Earth News* (Vintage Books: London, 2009). The study also reports results from specially commissioned research conducted by the Cardiff School of Journalism.

[15] See B McNair, *News and Journalism in the UK* (4th edn, London: Routledge, 2003).

[16] Campbell, n 13 above, ch 5.

testing the information that it disseminates. The outcome is 'Flat Earth' news—news that is accepted as true because it appears so. What is interesting is that this phenomenon is not confined to the tabloid end of the market. According to Davies, only around 20 per cent of journalistic activity appears to involve traditional investigative techniques, and even the apparently 'quality' end of the market falls prey to churnalism from time to time.[17]

Other recent studies of the industry are consistent with Davies' view. The House of Lords Communications Select Committee reported on *The Ownership of the News* in 2008,[18] having gathered much evidence from the industry about the pressures of competing in a global 24 hour news world. It expressed particular disquiet at the potential for inaccuracy that the sheer speed of the 24 hour news cycle demands. From a different perspective, the Media Standards Trust has suggested a package of reforms to the system of self-regulation in the press[19] as a response to what it considers to be increasing public disquiet and lack of confidence about poor journalistic practice. It should be acknowledged, however, that the problem may not be so acute in broadcast journalism, where the requirement to report news with due accuracy and due impartiality[20] imposes a critical constraint on what is presented. However, broadcasting often follows the press when setting its own news agendas and it shares some dependence on information provided by press agencies and public relations firms.

Characterizing Distortion

This chapter explores the implications of this situation for law and regulation relating to the media. The basic problem is that we appear to have a media industry that is no longer capable of delivering the kind of service that we expect it to contribute to our democratic culture. Indeed, its practice appears to be moving in the opposite direction and

[17] Davies, n 15 above, 95 and ch 3 more generally. It is telling that Davies' study did not include tabloid newspapers.

[18] *HL Select Committee on Communication on The Ownership of the News, 1st Report* (HL Paper 122, 2007–08).

[19] Media Standards Trust, *A More Accountable Press. Part 1: The Need for Reform* (2009), available at <http://www.mediastandardstrust.org/resources/mediaresearch/selfregulationreview.aspx>.

[20] Communications Act 2003, ss 319, 320.

actually impeding the flow of information and exchange of ideas that we might think is necessary for a healthy society.

It is first necessary to examine in more detail what might be meant by 'distortion'. At a basic level, the reporting of facts may seem to be straightforward, but it is now long accepted that it is difficult to isolate 'pure' facts and that social reality is constructed and interpreted in the context of broader frameworks of meanings.[21] It is hard for one person's words to capture reality as another sees it, as the everyday practice of defamation law illustrates.[22] But even if there may be agreement about the reporting of what might be called 'events', any wider 'truths' that they represent will typically be dependent on the inferences to be drawn from them.[23] There is a continuum from simple facts that can be easily verified to abstract generalizations about the state of the world. In the middle, there are various nuances of complex situations, typically involving judgments about the relevance of sets of facts and their interrelationships, whose veracity may be contestable. Those judgments of relevance may be made from various kinds of perspective. In the academy, theoretical modelling is an essential way of simplifying the pattern of events in order to arrive at a deeper truth, whether it be scientific understanding or political ideology. Drama and the arts depend on fiction to provide deeper insights about our existence. Indeed, taking a view contrary to the picture that was provided above, David Hare recently lamented the management of the BBC for relying too much on journalism: 'Television has always been run by journalists. Journalists distrust the central claim of fiction: that by lying you get to truth'.[24]

These difficulties do not mean that truth is unobtainable but that it involves a process of discovery. As Lichtenberg has argued,[25] it is a 'regulative principle' an ideal for which we strive. Without it, we could

[21] See P Berger and T Luckmann, *The Social Construction of Reality* (Penguin Books: London, 1967).

[22] This is evidenced by the high volume of preliminary litigation on issues related to pleadings and the meanings of statements in issue.

[23] The law of defamation recognized this in the defence of justification, in particular, the distinction between specific and general facts: eg, see *Williams v Reason* [1988] 1 All ER 262; *Brookbinder v Tebbit* [1989] 1 All ER 1169.

[24] M Billington, 'The lame, the weak and the godawful' (*The Guardian* Interview with David Hare at the British Film Institute), *The Guardian*, 19 January 2009, available at <http://www.guardian.co.uk/stage/2009/jan/19/david-hare-television>.

[25] J Lichtenberg, 'In Defence of Objectivity Revisited' in J Curran and M Gurevitch (eds) *Mass Media and Society* (3rd edn, Arnold: London, 2000) 238–54, 249.

not make sense of grievances about news coverage that it is unfair, biased, sensational, misrepresents views or does not report impartially. They all 'imply the possibility of a contrast,' that particular claims are partial, distorted, or inadequate—that those who see things in one way are missing something important.[26] But that also provides an insight into the meaning of distortion. It occurs when the information needed for reflection on the meaning and significance of events is withheld or manipulated.

Here, the context is critical. Many factual questions can be resolved relatively simply, and distortions will typically amount to inaccuracy or lying. To establish more generalized and complex truths, sufficient information is required to resolve contestable interpretations of the circumstances. One kind of distortion is the partial truth, in which facts that are significant for understanding the fuller picture are omitted. For example, statistics about a firm's or government department's performance are reproduced in a story but without indicating that they are the claims of a one-sided press release. Another kind of distortion omits context. For example, a set of (factually correct) stories report that members of a social group (such as migrant workers, or an ethnic minority) have committed crimes, but do not mention that the behaviour is not representative. Again, a story about scientific findings does not reveal that they are based on a tiny sample, or the story emphasizes only a trivial result, or it fails to mention that the study does not reflect the weight of other research. Such omissions of significant pieces of information may be accompanied by exaggerated emphasis on others, perhaps encapsulated in the sensationalist headline.

In deciding whether to characterize 'less than complete' reporting as a distortion, some account must be taken of the real or implied motivation of the editor. If a newspaper decides to concentrate on a particular topic, for example, financial news, celebrity behaviour, or parliamentary politics, it would not regarded as distorting the news merely because it did not offer a different diet of information. Similarly, it may not be necessary to put every UK story in a world context. Media partisanship implies the editor's ability to choose the themes that will interest the readership or audience. However, a distinction may be drawn between choosing an issue and dealing with it appropriately. Distortion occurs when choices are not actually being made, because there is too much uncritical reliance on recycled information,

[26] Ibid, 242, 243.

or when the level of coverage is not adequate for the comprehensiveness of the reporting that is being implicitly represented to the readership or audience. A 'quality' newspaper may wish to offer pronouncements about the state of the nation and make judgments about the importance and significance of events, whereas a tabloid may wish only to cater for its readers' prurient interests. In each case, the editor's aspiration provides the standard by which the adequacy of reporting can be assessed.

A more ambiguous situation may arise, however, one which applies to all sectors of the media, when an editor possesses information but chooses to release it only selectively. This may be done for one or more reasons to attract readers and audiences, by whetting their appetite for more, or to cause embarrassment, or to score political points. Is this a case of distortion or acceptable partisanship? The answer may depend on whether the report is self-contained or whether it forms part of a larger story. While an editor cannot be required to publish what he or she does not want, once a decision is made to release a partial account, the effect will obviously be to distort the fuller picture.

Journalists are only too well aware of the difficulties of rendering an adequate account of the truth. They have relied on the idea of 'objectivity' as a way of dealing with them, a concept which has been described as 'a cornerstone of the professional ideology of journalists in liberal democracies'.[27] Objectivity connotes the reporting of facts at face value, providing an empirical view of the facts as given and recorded in a neutral way. There is a reliance on attributable sources, especially quotes, as a standpoint for veracity.[28] However, this makes reporting especially vulnerable to dependency on press agencies, which specialize in such basic material. For that reason, and because objectivity typically entails the balancing of conflicting claims, albeit without analyzing them, it has the ironic effect of itself contributing to media distortion. This is because it may leave the impression that unequal viewpoints are equally plausible. Nevertheless, the role of objectivity in journalism is not uncontested.[29] For example, Davies argues[30] that

[27] Lichtenberg, n 25 above, 238. See also A Edgar, 'Objectivity, Bias and Truth' in A Belsey and R Chadwick (eds), *Ethical Issues in Journalism and the Media* (Routledge: London, 1992) 112–29.

[28] V Campbell, n 13 above, ch 7.

[29] Ibid. See also M Schudson, 'Four Approaches to the Sociology of News' in J Curran and M Gurevitch (eds) *Mass Media and Society* (4th edn, Hodder Arnold: London, 2005) 172–97.

[30] Davies describes it as the 'great blockbuster myth', a Flat Earth tale in itself!

journalism requires judgments about what is important, provided that they are honest and sincere. This is a view that appears to be accepted by the European Court of Human Rights, which has accepted that 'journalists cannot be expected to act with total objectivity and must be allowed some degree of exaggeration or even provocation' and that a 'certain selectiveness of quotation' will not make a report inaccurate and unreliable.[31]

Intervening to Reduce Media Distortion

Although the nature of the problem of media distortion has been identified for some time, there has been little willingness to find ways of dealing with it. The complexity of the issue is no doubt one deterrent. But the principal objection is that any intervention would amount to an interference with freedom of the media or, at least, the media's freedom of expression. The objection rests on the ideas that media can claim some right to freedom of expression and that interference with their activities will be inconsistent with the justifications for giving special priority to the right—the familiar arguments based on truth, democracy and individual self-fulfilment.[32] The difficulty is that the remedy would be particularly intrusive because it would need to be directed at the very workings of the media organizations themselves, the editorial discretion. There is an understandable reluctance to use the state's power to constrain the freedom of owners and editors to choose what they wish to publish and how to present it.

This position is reflected in the current law. Liability for media expression is constrained by laws intended to protect a limited number of interests that may exceptionally override speech—reputation, privacy, national security, administration of justice. But the law does not go further in scrutinizing the scope of media expression. The regulation of accuracy and impartiality, currently found in broadcasting, is an exception. While there may be justifications for retaining it,[33] it is sometimes seen as an historical anomaly; it does not apply to the press (apart from limited self-regulation of 'inaccurate, misleading or

[31] *Selistö v Finland* (2006) 42 EHRR 8, para 63.
[32] Schauer, n 4 above; Barendt, n 4 above, ch I.
[33] See the discussion of impartiality and fairness, below.

distorted information' by the Press Complaints Commission[34]); and it is being resisted in development of new media.

The acknowledgement of the 'media freedom' objection means that the quality of news information is not a matter for law and regulation. Indeed, the courts have allowed journalists and editors much latitude in the way they choose to tell a story.[35] Their approach reflects more generally that of the European Court of Human Rights in holding that Article 10 of the European Convention on Human Rights protects not only the substance of the ideas and information expressed, but also the form in which they are conveyed.[36] Journalistic freedom in particular is regarded as including possible recourse to a degree of exaggeration, or even provocation.[37] If the media freedom objection is accepted, we appear to be left in the position that media distortions have to be accepted for the sake of the media's more important potential to contribute positively to society as a watchdog or democratic forum. It may seem that all that can be done, consistently with freedom of expression, is to exhort journalists and media organizations to act more professionally. Is there a way of breaking out of this moral and political stalemate, which amounts to a somewhat fatalistic resignation to the industry trends?

The starting point is to note that claims for a right to media freedom are weak. First, the relationship between the media and freedom of expression is merely contingent: sometimes they do advance free speech, but sometimes they do not. That fact provides the basis for a set of reasons for not giving a special constitutional or legal status to the media: the media are simply a specialized manifestation of individual freedom of speech and there are no grounds for giving them privileged status—at the most, they can claim some recognition for their instrumental contribution to speech.[38] In addition, there are significant

[34] Press Complaints Commission, *Code of Practice* (2007) Clauses 1(i) and 1(ii) available at <http://www.pcc.org.uk/assets/111/Code_Aug_2007.pdf>.

[35] Recent examples are: *Attorney-General's Reference No 3 of 1999: Application by the British Broadcasting Corporation to set aside or vary a Reporting Restriction Order* [2009] UKHL 34, para 25 per Lord Hope; *Jameel (Mohammed) v Wall Street Journal SPRL* [2006] UKHL 44; [2007] 1 AC359, para 33 per Lord Bingham and para 51 per Lord Hoffman. See also *A-G v English* [1983] 1 AC 116, 143 per Lord Diplock.

[36] *Oberschlick v Austria (No 1)* (1998) 25 EHRR 357.

[37] *Prager and Oberschlick v Austria* (1996) 21 EHRR 1. However, the recent decision in *Lindon, Otchakovsky-Laurens and July v France* (2008) 46 EHRR 5 insists on a minimum degree of moderation and propriety.

[38] E Barendt, *Freedom of Speech* (Oxford University Press: Oxford, 2005) 419ff.

practical problems involved, such as defining journalists or adjudicating between different loci of speech within the organization. But these considerations can be deployed equally to show that there should be no special exemption for media organizations, as media organizations, when their expression transgresses acceptable boundaries.

Secondly, we can note some distinctions between the characteristics of media organizations and of individuals in communicating information. A significant dimension is the scale, breadth, ubiquity, unrelenting presence, and sheer reach of media bodies.[39] Another is the systematic nature of their information processing. The wider question, therefore, is whether freedom of expression can, or should, be invoked to protect the power of institutionalized speech. As Onora O'Neill[40] has suggested, traditional theories of freedom of speech have been articulated with individuals, not institutions, in mind. The media are engaged in organized production. It is not for benefit of individual journalists, or indeed editors, but for those who control the organization. So we might look again more closely at the rationales for protecting speech and ask whether they apply with equal weight to organized media, compared with individuals, including journalists. To assist with this, the enquiry may well be sharpened up by reversing the typical burden of free speech discussion. Rather than examining whether there are any justifications for interference with media speech, it will be interesting to ask whether any arguments can successfully be deployed to show why media organizations should be allowed to disseminate distorted information.

Potential Arguments for Allowing Distortion

The enquiry is framed in this way because it is assumed that not only inaccuracy, but also distortion, are not desirable. The implications of not interfering with media distortions are that they are condoned, or regarded as inevitable, or regarded as too costly (whether socially, politically or economically) to regulate. On the face of it, distortions of information do not contribute to the values which justify the free speech principle, the aspirations of seeking truth, realizing democratic

[39] J Curran and J Seaton, *Power Without Responsibility: The Press, Broadcasting and New Media in Britain* (6th edn, Routledge: London, 2003) 323ff.

[40] O O'Neill, *A Question of Trust* (Cambridge University Press: Cambridge, 2002) 94.

government, or acknowledging the worth of individuals. More directly, they may be regarded as positively damaging, for reasons which are primarily concerned with the quality of democratic life. In particular, lies have been described as 'anti- democratic'[41] and it has been claimed that calculated falsehoods deny dignity and autonomy because they undermine audience choices, the reputation of victims, and the convictions of speakers.[42] As Lord Hobhouse observed, 'Misleading people and the purveying as facts statements which are not true is destructive of the democratic society and should form no part of such a society. There is no duty to publish what is not true: there is no interest in being misinformed'.[43]

However, these comments relate to deliberate falsehoods. It is hardly controversial to say that deliberate dishonesty in communication is regarded as wrong. Does the same principle apply to inadvertent falsehoods? According to Onora O'Neill, insofar as our society depends on trust for its effective functioning, both deliberate and careless distortions of the truth would seem to need strong discouragement.[44] But this is not only a matter of individual morality. The very process of democratic deliberation itself presupposes that distortions in information should be minimized. As Dryzek says, contestation is undemocratic if it is controlled by 'public relations experts, spin doctors and demagogues'.[45]

The apparent problem with the media industry is that it appears to be impeding the discovery of the truth in an organized and systemic manner. But in what circumstances can distortions be accepted, indeed justified? A number of possible answers need to be examined, with particular attention to the distinction between the individual and the media organization.

Distortion Assists the Discovery of Truth

One of the strongest arguments against interfering with media distortions is that there are positive benefits from disseminating them. This is

[41] *Garrison v Louisiana* 379 US 64 (1964) 75 per Brennan J.

[42] DAJ Richards, 'Free Speech as Toleration' in WJ Waluchow (ed), *Free Expression: Essays in Law and Philosophy* (Clarendon Press: Oxford, 1994).

[43] *Reynolds v Times Newspapers* [2001] 2 AC 127 at 238.

[44] O'Neill, n 41 above, 96. See also O O'Neill, 'Practices of Toleration' in J Lichtenberg (ed), *Democracy and the Mass Media* (Cambridge University Press: Cambridge, 1990) ch 5.

[45] JS Dryzek, *Deliberative Democracy and Beyond: Liberals, Critics, Contestations* (Oxford University Press: Oxford, 2000) 77.

the burden of the well known arguments for truth advocated by JS Mill. As Ten[46] has put it, there are three components to the argument: the 'avoidance of mistake' deals with the possibility that true facts and opinions may be suppressed when what is taken to be false is censored —we cannot completely be sure that what we suppress is false so it is better to let it be expressed. Here the emphasis is on the importance of true beliefs. The 'assumption of infallibility' component and the 'necessity of error' components deal with the importance of being confident that what we believe to be true is indeed true. To gain that confidence, freedom of expression is needed to be able to engage in discussion for the purpose of testing our beliefs. Furthermore, to know and appreciate the full grounds for our beliefs, we also need to expose them to testing against others' opinions.

This set of arguments is advanced in favour of individual free speech but it has been challenged on the grounds that its principal weakness is, as Barendt puts it, 'its questionable assumption that free discussion necessarily leads in a democratic society to the acceptance of truth . . .'[47] Assuming for the moment that it is possible to easily identify false information, the case for allowing it to circulate is not convincing. It is by no means clear that, if false claims of fact are disseminated, the true ones will rise above them. Nor is it likely that there will be widespread deliberation about contested facts, to enable the more plausible to be identified. In addition, rather like the economic concept of market contestability, the argument is essentially long-run, so necessarily ignores short-term harms to truth. It is even less convincing in the case of media information, given the media's influence on the very process of discussion that is anticipated to test factual plausibility. Furthermore, the argument cannot apply to the systemic ignoring of material—where again the effect of the system may be to prevent the possibility of the true facts from countering the false.

Of course, the question of what is indeed true is the point of the discussion. Mill was very much aware of the complexity of truths, the fuller understanding that comes from weighing facts and perspectives, rather than identifying either absolute truth or falsehood. The implication is that even distorted media half-truths should not be suppressed, although he did not go so far as to say that half-truths should actively be promoted, if only to give assurance to believers.

[46] CL Ten, *Mill on Liberty* (Clarendon Press: Oxford, 1980) ch 8.
[47] Barendt, n.4 above, 11.

In the absence of any critical weighing of countervailing versions of the truth, there seems to be no positive benefit from allowing the distortion that partial truth creates, and it may well be harmful if its impact is emotional or non-rational.[48] However, even if we allow that the utility of suppressing falsehood may be empirical and contingent (on a case by case basis, we may need to weigh the costs and benefits of allowing truth to emerge against the harm of falsehood),[49] the case of media distortion is different. The issue is not so much a wish to censor the half-truths that the media do publish as a concern with the media's omission to put other half-truths into the contest to allow them to be weighed. The difficulty with the media is one of distribution of information—the limited circulation of potentially relevant material. Even if the circulation of half-truths is considered to be generally beneficial, there seems to be no reason why media half-truths should be dominant.

This is not to suggest that democratic debate can only be conceived in purely rationalist terms.[50] There is what has been described as an informal political sphere of power, position and passion: 'There are too many valuable products of the human mind that would be suppressed if the egalitarian and public-spirited norms of the ideal deliberation were to characterize all areas of public communication'.[51] It may be said that media distortions are examples of the cut and thrust of debate, where sincerity and forcefulness of belief are demonstrated by the rhetoric and emotion of selecting material to persuade the listener. But, whilst acknowledging the importance of presentational style to democratic debate, which will rightly find its place in media coverage, it is important to recognize that the distorting effects on ultimate rational reflection have to be kept in proportion. If the effect of presenting one side of the truth through the media is to prevent it from being tested in a wider context, there will be no democratic benefit. This perspective does depend on the view that rational reflection is the ultimate arbiter of truth, even when dealing with rhetoric and persuasion.[52] If that is

[48] It has been suggested that 'the truth argument is most apposite to true statements of fact and to dogma or opinion. It works less well in the realm of false statements of fact.' See D Milo *Defamation and Freedom of Speech* (Oxford University Press: Oxford, 2008) 57. See also Schauer, n 4 above, 74–5.

[49] See Schauer, n 4 above, ch 6.

[50] As a Habermsian ideal speech situation might imply; see J Habermas, *Between Facts and Norms* (Polity Press: Cambridge, 1996), 107–11.

[51] See D Estlund, 'Democracy and the Real Speech Situation' in S Besson and JL Martí, *Deliberative Democracy and its Discontents* (Gower: Aldershot, 2006) 79.

[52] Dryzek, n 45 above. See also, S Chambers, *Reasonable Democracy: Jurgen Habermas and the Politics of Discourse* (Cornell University Press: London, 1996).

accepted, it seems to require constantly and actively checking for the rational, consistent with what Mill described as, 'the real morality of public discussion.'[53]

Distortion is a Price Worth Paying for the Media to Exist

A free media is considered to be one of the hallmarks of a liberal democratic society. But, for it to remain independent, it must be commercially viable. Is it too costly to the media to require them to eliminate all errors, including distortions? It is notorious that the traditional newspaper industry is in decline, with diminishing circulation resulting in much reduced income, especially from advertising. With the exception of public service broadcasting, which is relatively insulated from such pressures, it may be that distortion is necessary for the survival of the tabloids and is at least to be tolerated for other media? This view, that we need a press—however imperfect—rather than nothing at all, has found favour with some judges.[54] It is true that nobody forces the commercial media to exist and that their democratic role is a beneficial side-effect of their wider activities, which are indeed subject to global demands for more efficient news production. But the reality is also that commercial media do have a major influence on the sources and distribution of information. If the result of that is a negative impact on our understanding of the world, the onus may be on the media to demonstrate the net benefit of allowing that to continue.

One possible benefit is that, in telling distorted stories, the media are supplying readers and audiences with the information that they prefer. There may be, in economic terms, a 'market for bias'. Some readers and audiences may want reassurance and confirmation about the opinions that they already hold, and they may not want to have broader issues discussed. Would that justify an editorial policy of, for example, only covering (true) stories about members of a particular racial group if they are about law breaking? We might think not if the editor also has 'public' aspirations. But the motives of editors, and their readers or audiences, may be less significant than the quality of information that is being disseminated across the democratic spectrum of debate.

Are there more significant issues at stake here, however? An important free speech argument which may be relevant is one advanced by

[53] Mill, n 1 above, 118.

[54] *A v B*, [2002] EWCA Civ 337; [2003] QB 195, para 11(xii) per Lord Woolf CJ; *Campbell v MGN* [2004] 2 AC 457, para 143 per Baroness Hale.

Raz.[55] Derived from his broader defence of the value of pluralism, it maintains that 'bad' speech is worth tolerating because of the general signals that censorship sends about the value of styles or ways of life: '. . . public portrayal and expression of forms of life validate the styles of life portrayed, and . . . censoring expression normally expresses authoritative condemnation not merely of the views or opinions censored but of the whole style of life of which they are a part'.[56] Raz is concerned with a wide range of lifestyles, whether religious or cultural, but he also appears to include professional practice, noting that engaging in speech is a normal activity of 'economists, politicians, journalists or scientists' and that far reaching censorship can constitute their public condemnation. The social practice of free speech entails the possibility that some speech may be bad speech—'false, worthless, degrading, depraved, etc.'—but censoring those bad elements will undermine the wider benefits to pluralism of sustaining a tradition of speaking freely. Does this mean that media distortions cannot be criticized and must be tolerated? It partly depends on how far reaching the censorship is, but it also depends on the form in which the 'way of life' is conceptualized. Concerns about media distortion are not a condemnation of journalism. Rather, they lament the manner in which the organized media no longer appears to reflect the essence of the way of life that journalism represents.

Distortion is too Difficult to Identify for Regulatory Purposes

Even if it is accepted that some media distortions should be controlled, there is the problem of the censor. One of the most distinctive arguments in favour of giving special protection to free speech, and by implication, media speech, is a general distrust of government. It has been articulated most forcefully by Schauer,[57] and it has an important place in United States constitutional law.[58] The argument is not that the motives of government, politicians, and regulators cannot be presumed to be honourable, although that may be applicable, but that government tends to be incompetent. It cannot be trusted to make the necessary distinctions and determinations in terms of truth and falsity, or degrees of harm. It is better, therefore, to have minimal interference,

[55] J Raz, 'Free Expression and Personal Identification' (1991) 11 Oxford Journal of Legal Studies 303–24, 316.

[56] Ibid, 310.

[57] Schauer, n 4 above, 85.

[58] Barendt, n 4 above, 54.

because the consequence otherwise is likely to be a disproportionate suppression of justifiable speech.

This argument may be thought to be especially strong in relation to determinations about media distortion. As the earlier discussion indicated, there will be practical difficulties in making judgments about such a complex matter. However, the case is less convincing where those judgments are made, not by government, but by practitioners who are sensitive to the issues at stake. The argument does not provide support for allowing media distortions to take place but urges extreme caution in designing any regulatory scheme to deal with them.

In this context, the possible 'chilling effect' of regulation cannot be ignored; the uncertain prospect of being held liable may result in self-censorship, thereby denying a story to the public.[59] This has strong rhetorical appeal, implying that, if it were not for the law and regulation, the media would be running many more public interest stories. However, the evidence seems to be that they are not being inhibited by the law. It is the production process of the news 'factory' which is stopping investigative journalism from taking place.

Distortion Serves Interests More Important than Truth

For completeness, it may be acknowledged that, in some circumstances, there are overriding interests which may justify the reporting of distorted information. National security is an obvious example and, in areas of defence, the increasing practice of embedded journalism, and the continued use of the DA Notice system, testify to the advantages of managing information flows. The fact that these areas raise freedom of information questions for the media serves to demonstrate that they cannot provide support for allowing media distortion.

There is another area of interest, however, which may suggest that the moral status of distortion is more ambiguous than is supposed, and that it is unfair to apply stricter standards to the media. The interest in privacy is one that acknowledges the value of distorting information for the purposes of preserving dignity and preventing embarrassment. One of its dimensions is the maintenance of an image, and the point of privacy rights is to hold that we do not have to account for certain personal positions to the world at large. As a matter of personal

[59] See E Barendt and ors, *Libel and the Media: The Chilling Effect* (Clarendon Press: Oxford, 1997).

morality and integrity, this may entail some degree of hypocrisy, but the law will not criticize that in the absence of a wider public interest at stake.[60] However, such personal standards, whether or not ethical, do not provide the benchmark for judging the media contribution to democratic debate. Individuals' wishes to distort personal information do not justify the media's wish to disseminate distorted information to the world at large.

Options for Controlling Distortion

If it is accepted that there is no objection in principle to reducing media distortion, any attempt to control it will be justified primarily by the wish to improve the quality of discussion and activity in democratic life. The media are now such an integral part of our means of social communication that we cannot decline responsibility for their activities.[61] The liberal theory of the media, discussed at the beginning, offers some general standpoints for the media to assist citizens to monitor government and hold it to account. A prominent trend in recent democratic theory has been to examine the deliberative aspects of democratic participation[62] and that has clear implications for the media's role in providing information and enabling it to be evaluated and channelled into public expression and decision-making.

A media that supports a democratic way of life might be expected to provide conditions for adequate[63] reflection on the issues and choices that require deliberation. This implies that the media must be more than mere distributors of information, although it does not require that they should engage in active 'public journalism'.[64] Nor does it require that the media should become rationalist deliberative spaces in themselves. But neither would we want a media version of the mob, where legitimate emotion is not tempered by reflection, based on reasoning and explanation. This suggests that editors should adopt a principle of what might be termed 'open journalism,' being critical, reflective and

[60] *Mosley v News Group Newspapers* [2008] EWHC 1777.

[61] See R Silverstone, *Media and Morality: on the Rise of the Mediaopolis* (Polity Press: Cambridge, 2007).

[62] See Dryzek, n 45 above; Chambers, n 52 above; A Gutman and D Thompson, *Democracy and Disagreement* (Belknap Press, Cambridge, Mass, 1996).

[63] Amounting to what Dryzek describes as 'non-coercive' reflection, not influenced by structures of interpretation or of power.

[64] See J Rosen, *What are Journalists for?* (Yale University Press: New Haven, 1999).

enquiring about organizational and economic power over information and its interpretation. It is reasonable to assume that readers and audiences cannot do that for themselves or do not have the resources required. The public function of the media is, therefore, to assist in understanding the 'truth' in much of its subtlety, by at least offering 'fair play to all sides of the truth'.

It may be that these aspirations already have a place, at least implicitly, in systems of journalistic ethics.[65] However, the structure of the industry creates obstacles to their implementation and, in the absence of internal incentives to do so, some regulatory intervention may now be necessary. Bearing in mind the equally important need for sensitivity to concern about state censorship, a number of options may be considered.

Remedies for Falsehood

The law already provides remedies for falsehood—what could be conceived as an extreme form of distortion—notably in defamation. However, the recent development of the *Reynolds/Jameel* public interest privilege (responsible journalism) has moved in the opposite direction by effectively allowing a concession for certain kinds of faultless distortions.[66] There is a tension in the doctrine between allowing journalists to report without interference and not trusting them to make the correct judgments.

It is significant that the courts have not been willing to allow journalism itself to enforce good practice. While subscribing to the normative version of the liberal theory of the media, judges have expressed scepticism about the media's willingness or ability to embrace it. Lord Nicholls observed in *Reynolds* that:

> 'The defendant newspaper commends reliance upon the ethics of professional journalism. The decision should be left to the editor of the newspaper. Unfortunately, in the United Kingdom this would not generally be thought to provide a sufficient safeguard. In saying this I am not referring to mistaken decisions. From time to time mistakes are bound to occur, even in the best regulated circles. Making every allowance for this, the sad reality is that the

[65] eg, see International Federation of Journalists, 'Declaration of Principles on the Conduct of Journalists' (1986); and the UK's National Union of Journalists, 'Code of Conduct' (1998).

[66] *Jameel v Wall Street Journal Europe SPRL (No 3)* [2006] UKHL 44; [2007] EMLR 14.

overall handling of these matters by the national press, with its own commercial interests to serve, does not always command general confidence.'[67]

In the same case, Lord Cooke observed that:

'Although investigative reporting can be of public benefit, the commercial motivation of the press and other sections of the media can create a temptation, not always resisted, to exaggerate, distort or otherwise unfairly represent alleged facts in order to excite the interest of readers, viewers or listeners.'[68]

Nevertheless, in seeking to mitigate liability on the basis of responsibility, the impact of *Jameel* is to re-position the defence in a way that draws on a view of journalism as a profession which can offer a coherent set of standards to enforce. For example, Lord Bingham stated that:

'Lord Nicholls recognised (202–203), inevitably as I think, that it had to be a body other than the publisher, namely the court, which decided whether a publication was protected by qualified privilege. But this does not mean that the editorial decisions and judgments made at the time, without the knowledge of falsity which is a benefit of hindsight, are irrelevant. Weight should ordinarily be given to the professional judgment of an editor or journalist in the absence of some indication that it was made in a casual, cavalier, slipshod or careless manner.'[69]

Similarly, Lord Hoffmann said that:

'But whereas the question of whether the story as a whole was a matter of public interest must be decided by the judge without regard to what the editor's view may have been, the question of whether the defamatory statement should have been included is often a matter of how the story should have been presented. And on that question, allowance must be made for editorial judgment. If the article as a whole is in the public interest, opinions may reasonably differ over which details are needed to convey the general message. The fact that the judge, with the advantage of leisure and hindsight, might have made a different editorial decision should not destroy the defence. That would make the publication of articles which are, ex hypothesi, in the public interest, too risky and would discourage investigative reporting.'[70]

These remarks reflect a rather romantic view of journalism. First, journalism does not see itself as a profession but as a craft, so there is insufficient normative cohesion for ethical standards to be applied consistently across the industry. Secondly, there is an assumption that the court is only articulating, emphasizing and enforcing a set of norms

[67] Ibid, 202. [68] Ibid, 219. [69] Ibid, para 33. [70] Ibid, para 51.

that already reflect good practice. Thirdly, if some judges believe that the operation of the defence will improve journalism,[71] they fail to appreciate that the organizational pressures will not let it happen very often.

As a means of influencing a reduction in media distortions, however, the responsible journalism defence is of little assistance. Apart from being confined to defamation, since it is, precisely, a defence, it operates only in circumstances where journalists choose to engage in serious activity, behave responsibly, yet make a mistake. There is no requirement to conduct serious activity, so the media can still take a risk that they may be sued. But, more importantly, the law is not concerned about what selection choices are made, including decisions not to cover material at all. At the most, the law of defamation requires that journalists give serious consideration to the balance of evidence when drawing conclusions about the inferences it will support. However, it seems to show considerable deference to journalists' 'professional' judgments about the scope of enquiry.[72]

Impartiality and Fairness

As indicated previously, the problem of media distortion is rooted more in the press than in broadcasting. Ofcom's Broadcasting Code[73] imposes obligations of accuracy and due impartiality in reporting news and current affairs, and also requires the subjects of reporting to be treated fairly. The BBC positively embraces a set of journalistic values based on truth and accuracy; serving the public interest; impartiality and diversity of opinion; fairness; independence; and accountability.[74] A particular feature of impartiality, as it has been elaborated by broadcasters over many decades, is that it requires much more than a balancing of viewpoints. It requires material that is broadcast to be placed in a broader context in order to assist the audience's

[71] eg in *Jameel*, n 66 above, Baroness Hale stated that 'We need more such serious journalism in this country and our defamation law should encourage rather than discourage it,' 150.

[72] See *Charman v Orion Publishing Group* [2007] EWCA Civ 972.

[73] See *The Ofcom Broadcasting Code* (October 2008) available at <http://www.ofcom.org.uk/tv/ifi/codes/bcode/> s 5.

[74] See BBC, *Editorial Guidelines* available at <http://www.bbc.co.uk/guidelines/editorialguidelines/edguide/>. See also *The Neil Report* (BBC: London, 2004) available at <http://www.bbc.co.uk/info/policies/pdf/neil_report.pdf>.

understanding of the issues.[75] Impartiality goes some way, therefore, in dealing with distortion by seeking to minimize the incidence of partial truths. It does not necessarily cover the wider process of selection, involving the setting of the news agenda. However, in the area of public service broadcasting, especially represented by the BBC, it is clear that a broad diet of regional, national and international news and current affairs is a defining part of the remit.

Newspapers have not been willing to embrace obligations of impartiality, because it entails interference with editorial discretion. It is regarded by some theorists as interfering with freedom of speech because it prevents journalists from making a statement about their partisan viewpoint while at the same time attributing a different, 'neutral' viewpoint against the journalist's better judgment.[76] In a multi-channel broadcasting environment, there are increasing pressures to relax the obligation of impartiality for all but the public service providers and to allow partisan broadcasting news. Ofcom has stated, indeed, that it may be inappropriate to impose impartiality requirements in the new media marketplace. Partly, this appears to be because impartiality is associated with a 'public service' remit, and that should not be imposed on all content providers. Partly, it seems to be based on the belief that the marketplace will be filled with sufficient competing outlets so that the consumer will be able to judge the relative quality of different news providers' offerings. Ofcom has suggested that journalists should earn the trust and credibility of the audiences and users, who should be free to choose what news to obtain.[77] What Ofcom does not say is how those choices can be made in an informed manner.

There are certainly difficulties in making impartiality work in a practical way. Deciding the salience of information, and interpreting it for the audience, are matters which require critical reflection by editors and journalists. It also detracts from the ability of journalists to publish their own judgments about states of affairs. Furthermore, there may be a concern that impartial news coverage will be rather bland because its point—to provide a more rounded view of events—will necessarily

[75] See T Gibbons *Regulating the Media* (2nd edn, Sweet and Maxwell: London, 1998), pp.100-20.

[76] eg, see Schauer, n 4 above, 127; L Alexander, *Is There a Right to Freedom of Expression?* (Cambridge University Press: New York, 2005) 29ff.

[77] Ofcom, *New News, Future News: The Challenges for Television News After Digital Switch-over* (2007) available at <http://www.ofcom.org.uk/research/tv/reports/newnews/newnews.pdf>.

inhibit strong and passionately held viewpoints from being expressed. Within broadcasting practice itself, however, impartiality has always been recognized as not requiring crude balance, and there can be many opportunities for personal viewpoint programmes to be aired within a broader critical context.[78]

Nevertheless, it may not be appropriate to require it of all journalism because, in dealing with distortion of the truth, its aspirations are directed at providing the more abstract levels of understanding which, desirable as they may be, should be encouraged but not imposed on all kinds of reporting. However, in the absence of an impartiality requirement, there is a potential gap between information that is fully contextualized and information that is overtly biased. The concern is that the gap may be being filled by the selective dissemination of information that is not subject to critical examination and therefore distorts the readers' or audiences' otherwise fuller understandings.

Self-regulation

For the press, doubts about its ethical practice have been sought to be resolved through self-regulation. However, the current scheme, operated by the Press Complaints Commission ('PCC'),[79] does not deal with the kinds of distortion discussed in this chapter. The PCC's code does provide for general, but limited, obligations of accuracy and fair reporting, but it does not attempt to pronounce on the kinds of material that should be included in a story in the first place. More generally, the PCC's governance and effectiveness have been subject to forceful criticism.[80] There are strong reasons to doubt whether the press industry is really committed to improving journalistic practice and to enforcing acceptable standards. This is because the basic values of the media as an industry are not in tune with the values associated with journalistic ethics. Self-regulation can only be fully effective where the policy objectives which are required in the public interest are aligned with the economic objectives of the industry.[81]

[78] For a recent discussion of the problems see BBC Trust, *From Seesaw to Wagon-wheel: Safeguarding Impartiality in the 21st Century* (2007) available at <http://www.bbc.co.uk/bbctrust/our_work/other/century21.shtml>.

[79] Available at <http://www.pcc.org.uk/>.

[80] eg, see Media Standards Trust, n 19 above; G Robertson and A Nicol, *Media Law* (5th edn, Penguin: London, 2008) 757–96.

[81] Arguably, this is why the Advertising Standards Authority has been relatively successful in its self-regulation. For a general discussion of the issues see J Baldwin and

This is not to say that self-regulation cannot work in the press. A number of newspapers do have internal codes of practice.[82] They also have readers' editors or ombudsmen, which act not only as a channel for complaints from readers but also encourage continual monitoring of internal practice.[83] But other approaches appear to be motivated as much by the wish to engage with the readership as to develop principles for ethical practice. Schemes are more likely to be successful in encouraging the latter where the internal culture of the organization has a sense of open journalism rather than the running of stories that are calculated to maximize circulation.[84] But the underlying difficulties are that, not only are ombudsman schemes not found across the industry, they do not cater for the kinds of distortion being discussed here.

A System of 'Enforced Ethics'

It is no longer satisfactory to rely on self-regulation to deal with problems of distortion in the media. At the same time, although the arguments for not regulating in this area are fairly weak, there may be residual concerns about freedom of speech. To be more specific, the arguments for regulating the media as an industry are weak, but it is the threat to journalists' and other individuals' free speech that gives concern. Yet, decisions about reporting the state of the world are undeniably complex. Taken together, these point suggest that the preferred approach to minimizing distortion should be to encourage the industry to provide a solution to the problem.

This option will only be sketched out here, but it has two components, reflected in the phrase 'enforced ethics'. The underlying idea is to oblige the media industry actively to take steps to minimize inaccuracy and distortion, but for the interpretation of what that that means to be made

M Cave, *Understanding Regulation: Theory, Strategy and Practice* (Oxford University Press: Oxford, 1999) ch 10.

[82] eg, see *Guidelines: The Guardian's Editorial Code* (April 2007) available at <http://image.guardian.co.uk/sys-files/Guardian/documents/2007/06/14/EditorialCode2007.pdf>. There also exists an international association, the Organization of News Ombudsmen, which seeks to disseminate good practice: see the ONO website at <http://www.newsombudsmen.org/index.htm>.

[83] eg, see 'Readers' Editor Terms of Reference', *The Guardian*, 14 May 2009 available at <http://www.guardian.co.uk/theguardian/2009/may/14/readers-editor-terms-of-reference>.

[84] Without implying that its practice is necessarily exemplary, the corporate structure of The Guardian Media Group, directed by the Scott Trust's commitment to journalistic values, may be regarded as more likely to be successful in securing internal self-regulation. However, its structure is the exception.

by reference to a set of ethical standards that journalists are required to articulate and review. A weaker version would require media organizations to establish their own readers' editors/ombudsman schemes, with appropriate mechanisms for securing institutional independence, prominence and compliance. This version would be weak to the extent that news organizations treated the position as a presentational device rather than demonstrating commitment to better quality journalism.

A stronger version of enforced ethics would involve a duty not to distort, to be imposed on media organizations. It is important to note that it would not be imposed on journalism itself, but on the organized production process, the systemic side of distortion. Editorial freedom is no longer a sufficient guarantee.[85] It may have connoted a notional set of standards but it is no longer clear what they are or whether they are being followed. That may be indicated by the relative absence of voluntary internal self-regulation, possibly reflecting the relative priority being given to news production over quality. There is now a need for some institutional process to accompany a revived ethical discussion. It may appear a contradiction in terms, but a system of enforced ethics would be a way of requiring the industry to 'self-regulate' effectively, but by reference to its practitioners own ethical aspirations, whilst not involving direct governmental interference in the content of journalism.

A new institutional framework would need to be established to carry this out. It is that institution which would determine what counts as inaccuracy and distortion. It would deliberate in open discussion, with public consultation and input, adopting models of policy development already followed by Ofcom and the BBC. Its role would be to articulate guidelines for making editorial judgments about what should go into the news and how it should be presented. Membership would primarily be drawn from journalism, including academics, with members of the public and of media organizations. However, the latter would not be dominant and this would not be a revived version of the PCC's Editors' Code Committee.

This option differs from a system of enforced standards, such as those recommended in the Calcutt report.[86] While its scope is much

[85] cf T Gibbons, 'Freedom of the Press: Ownership and Editorial Values' [1992] Public Law 279–99.

[86] *Report of the Committee on Privacy and Related Matters* (Calcutt's Report) (Cm 1102, 1991).

broader and, of course, much more intrusive into everyday media activity, it would not impose standards by law. However, it does envisage that the duty not to distort would be imposed by law. The aim would be to enable the practice of journalism to have an impact within the industry it serves, enabling it to resist the countervailing economic and institutional forces that encourage distortion, by mandating media owners to take account of it. Such an approach would be consistent with various calls from within journalism to revive debates about its practice.[87] More broadly, it would be consistent with a deliberative approach to democracy.

The duty to minimize distortion is envisaged as applying to newspapers, broadcasters, press agencies and other forms of organized news production. It would not apply to ISPs nor to bloggers (who are assumed to be insufficiently organized). Magazines and propaganda sheets could be exempted from the duty in return for explicit and prominent statements of transparency about their standpoints and editorial interests.

The duty is envisaged as operating in two ways. First, it could be the basis for complaints about reporting. They would ideally be considered by a body which replaces the PCC. A more intrusive complaints mechanism would allow complaints about the substance of news reporting. Given the scope of 'distortion', however, it could well become overwhelmed with intractable disputes about detail, a problem that is evident in the operation of the BBC Trust's Editorial Standards Committee and that of Ofcom's Content Board.[88] A less intrusive mechanism would adopt a 'reviewing' model, examining the processes that the organization put in place to minimize distortion, but without requiring a definitive finding that distortion had occurred. It is a separate question but, under either mechanism, the complaints/reviewing body might well have the power to impose sanctions on the industry for non-compliance. To different degrees, both these approaches will be regarded by some as being too interfering,

[87] eg, see the evidence submitted to the *HC Select Committee on Culture Media and Sport on Self-Regulation of the Press, 7th Report* (HC Paper, 2006–07); see also the *HC Select Committee on Culture Media and Sport on Privacy and Media Intrusion, 5th Report* (HC Paper (2002–03) 458). There are also strong academic contributions to the debate, a notable focus being the Reuters Institute for the Study of Journalism at the University of Oxford.

[88] For an earlier analysis of the kinds of problem involved, see T Gibbons, 'The Role of the Broadcasting Complaints Commission: Current Practice and Future Prospects' (1995) 1 *Yearbook of Media and Entertainment Law* 129–59.

potentially cumbersome, and uncertain of success. There is also the possibility that the whole scheme could be hijacked by complainants who wish to use it as a platform to advance their own partisan viewpoints. But it is, nevertheless, removed from full-scale state regulation. It offers journalism an institutional structure for dealing with the difficult problems of distortion on its own terms, informed by its own internal dialogues, but sensitive to the media's wider role. In the absence of some such scheme, the news industry is likely to continue to produce the selective diet of information that currently characterizes so much media output.

The idea of enforced ethics could also operate in a different way and be used to assist the development of legal doctrine. It could elaborate the notion of professionalism that is being discussed in the law of defamation, and it could also form the basis for the appropriate code to be used in making privacy determinations under section 12 of the Human Rights Act 1998. But it would require a different attitude from the courts, entailing a more critical approach to journalists' and editors' claims for freedom to tell stories exactly as they want. In particular, it might support a distinction between the way the story is phrased, where no intervention might be appropriate, and the choice of sources used to validate its telling, where a stricter approach might be justified.

Conclusion

Media distortion has become a serious threat to the functioning of a healthy democracy. Yet there are understandable concerns about using law and regulation to interfere with editorial decisions, since a free media also have an undeniably positive effect on the circulation of information and opinion for democratic discussion. However, there appears to be cogent evidence that the internal functioning of the media is itself inhibiting the achievement of its more noble aspirations. A system of enforced ethics is suggested as a way to finesse the problem thereby created. Other options have been suggested to enhance the media's capacity to serve democratic interests. Improved transparency about media ownership, and therefore the editorial line, is one.[89] An integrated approach, with public service broadcasting at its core, is

[89] Gibbons, n 86 above; Barent, n 4 above, 106.

another.[90] However, those solutions are both narrower and wider than the particular difficulty with media distortions require. A minimal interference from the law, directed at the industry and not individuals, is required for progress to be made and to harness journalists' good will and expertise.

[90] See Curran, n 2 above; Keane, n 2 above. See also Barendt, n 4 above, mooting the idea of 'modest' public service requirements for national newspapers, 450.

Cohabitation: Current Legal Solutions

*Rebecca Probert**

To talk of solutions presupposes a problem, and one's perception of the problem will inevitably shape any proposed solution. For some, the growth in cohabitation in recent years is itself the problem that needs to be addressed, and the solution is to promote marriage as an attractive alternative. Thus the Social Justice Policy Group has suggested that initiatives such as transferable tax allowances would 'shore up marriage in its heartland' and send a signal 'to the lower deciles'.[1] Many reforms to family law over the course of the 20th century were driven, at least in part, by this perception of the need to facilitate marriage. Even when cohabitation was rare, those arguing for reform of the law of marriage or divorce often bolstered their case by suggesting that those who could not marry (because one or both were already married to a third party, or because they were within the then more extensive prohibited degrees of marriage) would simply cohabit.[2] The undesirability of this was taken for granted. This is most striking in the Law Commission's 1966 proposals for reform of the law of divorce: considerable weight was attached in the Report to the potential for 'illicit unions' to be regularized if long-dead marriages could be legally terminated,[3] perhaps because empirical research was beginning to indicate the rise in the extent of cohabitation outside marriage and because there was still

* School of Law, University of Warwick. I would like to thank Liam D'Arcy Brown, Jo Miles, Chris Barton and those who attended the CLP lecture for their helpful comments on an earlier version of this paper. Any errors remaining are of course my own.

[1] Social Justice Policy Group, *Breakthrough Britain: Ending the Costs of Social Breakdown. Vol 1: Family Breakdown* (London, 2007) 64.

[2] See Women's Co-Operative Guild, *Working Women and Divorce: An Account of Evidence Given on Behalf of the Women's Co-operative Guild Before the Royal Commission on Divorce* (London, 1911).

[3] Law Commission, *Reform of the Grounds of Divorce: The Field of Choice* (Cmnd 3123, 1966) 36.

optimism—which in the event proved to be misplaced—that those who could marry would do so.

For others, it is the fact that cohabiting couples are not accorded the same rights as married couples that is the problem, and their solution is, therefore, to confer those rights that married couples currently enjoy on those who are cohabiting. Critics of the current law often point to the sad case of *Burns v Burns*,[4] in which 'Mrs' Burns found that she was not entitled to any interest in the home that she had shared with Mr Burns for 17 years and where she had brought up their two children. Indeed, it is rare to find a critic who does not mention *Burns*. It should however be borne in mind that while *Burns* typifies the type of case in which the law of trusts does not provide an adequate solution, the demographic profile of cohabiting couples means that Mrs Burns is not necessarily typical of modern cohabiting women.[5] But examples of women experiencing the same result can of course be found,[6] and, as Lord Lester noted in the course of the second reading on the Cohabitation Bill currently before the House of Lords, 'many adults and their children are left in poverty at the end of a cohabiting relationship'.[7] Nor is this a problem confined to those who have been in a cohabiting relationship, since the burden of supporting such individuals will often, of necessity, fall upon the state and the taxpayer.[8]

That the current law is inconsistent and inadequate in its application to cohabiting couples is clear. That the solution is to confer on such couples the same rights as if they were married is less obvious, and the first part of this article suggests a number of reasons for caution. What, then, are the alternatives? Recent developments in the areas of contract, property and family law make it appropriate to re-evaluate their potential to meet the needs of cohabiting couples, viewed in the light of the demographic background.[9] In some cases, however, the potential is

4 [1984] Ch 317.

5 See R Probert, 'Trusts And The Modern Woman—Establishing An Interest In The Family Home' (2001) 13 Child and Family Law Quarterly 275.

6 See G Douglas, J Pearce and H Woodward, *A Failure of Trust: Resolving Property Disputes on Cohabitation Breakdown* (Cardiff, 2007) 138 available at <http://www.bris.ac.uk/law/research/centres-themes/cohabit/index.html>.

7 *Hansard* (HL), col 1413 (13 March 2009).

8 Ibid. See also Law Commission, *Cohabitation: The Financial Consequences of Relationship Breakdown* (Law Com No 307, 2007).

9 The need to define 'cohabitation' will of course vary according to the solution adopted: eligibility is self-defining in solutions based in contract and property law, in contrast to family law solutions that are rooted in the relationship rather than the actions of the parties. The focus here will be on unmarried couples of the same or opposite sex

limited, while in others it has not as yet been fully realized. The third part of this chapter accordingly suggests how the position of cohabiting couples could be improved, within the current legal framework, but also identifies the need for a more wide-ranging review of the legal treatment of marriage and cohabitation in order to balance the two perspectives identified here.

Reasons for Caution

Uncharted Waters

The first reason for caution lies in the fact that the current situation is unprecedented, in that the legal system has never before had to deal with cohabitation on such a scale as exists today. While it is, of course, possible to find examples of cohabiting couples from all periods of history, it is only recently that cohabitation began to emerge as a significant family form.

This of course runs counter to the suggestion that we are today seeing the revival of 'social marriage', a claim that has been made by a number of commentators.[10] While most concur in dating the emergence of modern cohabitation as a statistically significant family form to the 1970s,[11] there is also a widely-held belief that cohabitation had been popular in earlier centuries, in particular the late 18th and early 19th centuries.[12] These claims are dealt with in more detail

who are sharing a home, thus excluding those 'living apart together' (on which see J Haskey, 'Living arrangements in contemporary Britain: Having a partner who usually lives elsewhere and Living Apart Together (LAT)' (2005) 122 *Population Trends* 35), who do not have the same degree of interdependence.

[10] See S McRae, *Cohabiting Mothers* (London, 1993); A Barlow, S Duncan, G James and A Park, *Cohabitation, Marriage and the Law: Social Change and Legal Reform in the 21st Century* (Oxford, 2005) 53.

[11] See K Kiernan, H Land and J Lewis, *Lone Motherhood in Twentieth Century Britain* (Oxford, 1998) 40; M Murphy, 'The Evolution of Cohabitation in Britain, 1960-95' (2000) 54 *Population Studies* 43, 45; C Haste, *Rules of Desire: Sex in Britain: World War 1 to the Present* (London, 1992) 234. For empirical data see J Haskey, 'Cohabitational and Marital Histories of Adults in Great Britain' (1999) 96 *Population Trends* 13, and on the characteristics of cohabitants in the 1970s, see A Brown and K Kiernan, 'Cohabitation in Great Britain: evidence from the General Household Survey' (1981) 25 *Population Trends* 4.

[12] eg, see J Gillis, *For Better, For Worse: British Marriages 1600 to the Present* (Oxford, 1985); K O'Donovan, *Sexual Divisions in Law* (London, 1985) 46; S Parker, *Informal Marriage, Cohabitation and the Law, 1754-1989* (Basingstoke, 1990) 14–27; W Mansell, B Meteyard and A Thomson, *A Critical Introduction to Law* (3rd edn,

elsewhere;[13] for now, a single set of statistics will suffice to make the point that cohabitation was much rarer in the past than it is today. Despite the absence of national-level statistics, we can obtain a rough idea as to the popularity of cohabitation outside marriage by examining the proportion of children born outside marriage: after all, at a time when contraception was rudimentary, most cohabiting relationships would lead to the birth of children. Yet if one surveys the past 400 years, it is plain that the percentage of children born outside marriage did not rise above 10 per cent until the 1970s; while in the supposedly liberated 18th century it barely crept above 5 per cent and in the incontestably harsher Commonwealth period[14] it fell to as little as 2 per cent.[15] Such calculations provide a ceiling for any estimates of cohabiting relationships; in truth, such relationships accounted for only a small proportion of such births until relatively recently.[16]

Equally unfounded is the idea that cohabitants ever enjoyed the same rights as if they were married. The concept of 'common-law marriage' is in fact a 19th century American invention, based on a misinterpretation of English authorities;[17] the popular assumption that 'common-law marriage' existed in England before the Clandestine Marriages Act of 1753 is unfounded. In fact, at this time known cohabitants risked punishment by the ecclesiastical courts for fornication, or sometimes for the more specific but rarer charge of 'living

London, 2004); A Diduck and F Kaganas, *Family Law, Gender and the State: Text, Cases and Materials* (2nd edn, Oxford, 2005) 58–60.

[13] eg, see R Probert, 'Chinese Whispers and Welsh Weddings' (2005) 20 *Continuity and Change* 211; 'Common-law Marriage: Myths and Misunderstandings' (2008) 20 Child and Family Law Quarterly 1; and (with Liam D'Arcy Brown) 'The Impact of the Clandestine Marriages Act: Three Case-studies in Conformity' (2008) 23 *Continuity and Change* 309.

[14] On the laws that may have acted as a disincentive to extra-marital childbearing see, eg, S Roberts, 'Fornication and Bastardy in Mid-seventeenth Century Devon: how was the Act of 1650 enforced?' in J Rule (ed) *Outside the Law: Studies in Crime and Order 1650–1850* (Exeter, 1982).

[15] The figures used are those provided by P Laslett, 'Introduction: comparing illegitimacy over time and between cultures' in P Laslett, K Oosterveen and R Smith, *Bastardy and its Comparative History* (London, 1980) ch 1, for the period from 1600 to 1836; the figures from 1837 to the present derive from ONS, 'Live Births, Age of Mother Occurrence Within/outside Marriage and Sex' available at <http://www.statistics.gov.uk/STATBASE/xsdataset.asp?vlnk=4270>.

[16] eg, see GN Gandy, 'Illegitimacy in a Handloom Weaving Community: Fertility Patterns in Culcheth, Lancashire, 1781-1860' (unpublished dissertation, 1978) 21; J Robin, 'Illegitimacy in Colyton, 1851-1881' (1987) 2 *Continuity and Change* 307; G Frost, 'The Black Lamb of the Black Sheep: Illegitimacy in the English Working Class, 1850-1939' (2003) 37 *Journal of Social History* 293, 309.

[17] See further Probert, n 13, above.

scandalously and suspiciously without lawful marriage'.[18] The rule that a couple that had lived together and been reputed to be married would, in certain circumstances, be presumed to have married, needs to be understood in this context. In the ecclesiastical courts, which had jurisdiction over marriage, it was simply a presumption that could be applied where the evidence of the marriage was unavailable—for example where both parties had died and their descendants were unaware of the location of the marriage. In the common-law courts, which did not have jurisdiction over marriage, it was a way of resolving issues—for example a husband's liability for his wife's debts—without the need to refer the matter to the ecclesiastical courts. In both contexts the presumption rested on the twin assumptions that couples would not cohabit unless they were married, and certainly would not enjoy the reputation of married persons within the community unless there was good cause.[19] Far from equating cohabitation and marriage, the presumption in fact depended on there being a sharp distinction between the two.

It is clear, therefore, that reforms cannot be justified simply on the basis that the law would be returning to an earlier approach.[20] But, of course, the fact that a certain approach is unprecedented is not in itself a reason for dismissing it. The law must evolve to deal with changed circumstances. And the modern demographic picture is very different from that of the mid-18th century, or even the mid-20th century. While marriage remains the norm—according to the 2001 census there were 11.6 million married families, compared to 2.2 million cohabiting couple families[21]—it is facing increasing competition. Most couples now cohabit before they marry: in 2006, 80 per cent of brides and bridegrooms gave identical residential addresses,[22] while 50 years ago only 1 per cent did so.[23] In 2006, 22 per cent of single men and 27 per cent of single women under the age of 60 were in a cohabiting relationship, double the percentage 20 years earlier.[24] Twenty-five years ago the proportion of all women living in a cohabiting relationship was

[18] See further R Probert, *Marriage Law and Practice in the Long Eighteenth Century: A Reassessment* (Cambridge, 2009) ch. 3.

[19] Ibid

[20] cf Barlow and ors, n 10 above, 119.

[21] Office for National Statistics, *Social Trends No 38* (Basingstoke, 2008) 20.

[22] Office for National Statistics, *Marriage, Divorce and Adoption Statistics* (London, 2009) table 3.38. See also J Haskey, 'Spouses with Identical Residential Addresses before Marriage: An Indicator of Pre-Marital Cohabitation' (1997)89 *Population Trends* 13.

[23] K Dunnell, *Family Formation 1976* (London, 1979) para 2.4.

[24] Office for National Statistics, n 21 above, table 2.7.

as low as 3 per cent;[25] by the start of the 21st century cohabiting families accounted for 15 per cent of couple families.[26] Cohabitation has become the norm for first partnerships, and those who have been divorced are also more likely to cohabit with a new partner rather than to embark on marriage again.[27]

Such evidence is often presented as if it is self-evidently problematic.[28] For some, of course, living together outside marriage is simply regarded as wrong, being against their own moral or religious code. But the number of adherents to that view has diminished over the years. Even the Church of England no longer refers to living in sin. If it could be shown that the rise in cohabitation had created better, more equal, more satisfying and more durable relationships for such couples, in contrast to those of married couples, then it would be a cause for celebration rather than concern. But the evidence that this might not be the case leads on to the second reason for caution.

The Functions of Families

While the assumption that any increase in cohabitation is problematic needs to be tested against the evidence, it is equally true that the increase cannot automatically justify the extension of rights to cohabiting couples. But one argument that draws on demographic change is that family law should take a functional approach rather than attempting to channel behaviour into a certain form.[29] This is a powerful argument, but it requires a more considered application to the facts than it has received to date.The proposal that the law should adopt a functional approach and confer rights on cohabiting couples misses out a crucial stage of the necessary reasoning: what are the functions

[25] See A Brown and K Kiernan, 'Cohabitation in Great Britain: Evidence from the General Household Survey' (1981) 25 *Population Trends* 4.

[26] Office for National Statistics, n 21 above, 20.

[27] J Ermisch and M Francesconi, 'Patterns of Household and Family Formation' in R Berthoud and J Gershuny (eds), *Seven Years in the Lives of British Families* (Bristol, 2000).

[28] See K Gyngell, 'We can't let the family die', *Daily Telegraph*, 16 April 2009; S Doughty, 'How married couples will soon be outnumbered by people who have never wed', *Daily Mail*, 1 April 2009.

[29] eg, see A Barlow, S Duncan, G James and A Park, 'Just a Piece of Paper? Marriage and Cohabitation' in A Park, J Curtice, K Thomson, L Jarvis and C Bromley (eds) *British Social Attitudes: the 18th Report* (London, 2001) ch 2; J Millbank, 'The Role Of "Functional Family" In Same-Sex Family Recognition Trends' (2008) 20 *Child and Family Law Quarterly* 155.

that different types of relationships perform? Without considering this, the argument that cohabitants should enjoy legal rights is simply using relationship type as a proxy for function. It is also important to introduce a qualitative dimension: if one type of relationship performs certain functions better than others, then there is an argument for encouraging it over other family forms. Only if it could be shown that cohabiting relationships perform the same functions as effectively as marriage does would an equation of the two be justified by a functional approach.

At one level the argument that cohabiting relationships perform the same function as marriage would seem to be easily established. Cohabiting couples by definition live together, probably have sex, and presumably love each other:[30] they are clearly members of each other's family and the law has long recognized this. But to make these points is to go no further than identifying which couples could be described as cohabitants. Few would argue that the law should treat as married all couples who have shared a home, however fleeting their relationship. A truly functional approach requires us to probe further, to draw a distinction between the function of being a family and the functions that the family performs, and to identify why the law should recognize those particular functions.

One function of the family could be said to be to provide a stable environment for bringing up children, a crucial function in terms of the well-being of the next generation. In quantitative terms this is a function performed by a majority of married couples but only a minority of cohabiting ones, in that most cohabiting couples do not have children.[31] In qualitative terms the evidence is that married couples perform this function rather better than cohabiting couples. According to Kiernan, for example, fewer than 50 per cent of cohabiting parents were still together by their child's fifth birthday, in contrast to more than 90 per cent of married parents and approximately 75 per cent of parents who had married after the birth of the child.[32] This difference was significantly more marked in this jurisdiction than in the other countries studied. Ermisch has similarly suggested that 70 per cent of

[30] Although note Smart and Stevens' finding that a high proportion of cohabitants in their study could be characterized as being only 'contingently committed': C Smart and P Stevens, *Cohabitation Breakdown* (London, 2000).

[31] eg, see Office for National Statistics, *Social Trends 39* (Basingstoke, 200) table 2.6.

[32] K Kiernan, 'Unmarried Cohabitation and Parenthood in Britain and Europe' (2004) 26 *Law and Policy* 33.

children born to married couples will live their entire childhood with both natural parents, whereas this will only be the case for 35 per cent of children born to cohabiting couples.[33] While this may change over time—in contrast to earlier studies that found that cohabitants with children were more likely to separate than their childless counterparts,[34] a study of a more recent cohort found that having a child had a stabilizing effect on the union[35]—it is still a reason to be cautious in claiming that cohabiting unions fulfil exactly the same functions as marriage.

Providing a mutually supportive environment for the parties involved[36] could also be seen as a function of the family. And again, the evidence is that marriage performs this function rather better than cohabiting relationships do. There is an increasing body of evidence that marriage has a beneficial effect on the physical and psychological health of the parties; that such benefits are not shared to the same degree by cohabiting couples; and that the differences cannot simply be explained as a result of selection.[37] Domestic violence is just as likely to occur in a cohabiting relationship as in a married relationship,[38] and infidelity apparently more so, at least in the US.[39] Cohabiting relationships also tend to be shorter:[40] the average duration of a marriage that ends in divorce is 11.6 years;[41] the average duration of a cohabiting

[33] Ermisch and Francesconi, n 27, above.

[34] See J Ermisch and M Francesconi, 'Cohabitation in Great Britain: Not for Long but Here to Stay' (Colchester, 1999) 12.

[35] F Steele, H Joshi, C Kallis and H Goldstein, 'Changing Compatibility of Cohabitation and Childbearing Between Young British Women Born in 1958 and 1970' (2006) 60 *Population Studies* 137.

[36] And, possibly, for wider kin: see M Maclean and J Eekelaar, 'The Obligations and Expectations of Couples Within Families: Three Modes of Interaction' (2004) 26 *Journal of Social Welfare and Family* Law 117, who note that cohabitants are less likely than their married counterparts to see themselves as embedded in an extended family.

[37] For a review of the literature see CM Wilson and AJ Oswald, 'How Does Marriage Affect Physical and Psychological Health? A Survey of the Longitudinal Evidence' (2005) IZA Discussion Paper No 1619.

[38] See J Richardson, J Coid, A Petruckevitch, W Shan Chung, S Moorey and G Feder, 'Identifying Domestic Violence: Cross Sectional Study In Primary Care' (2002) 324 *British Medical Journal* 274.

[39] eg, see J Treas and D Giesen, 'Sexual Infidelity among Married and Cohabiting Americans' (2000) 62 *Journal of Marriage and the Family* 48. The topic does not appear to have attracted researchers in the UK.

[40] R Berthoud and J Gershuny, 'Seven Years in the Lives of British Families', in Berthoud and Gershuny, n 27 above, 236.

[41] 'Report: Divorces in England and Wales During 2006' (2007) 129 *Population Trends* 61.

relationship that has ended is 4.6 years.[42] Nor are cohabiting relationships necessarily more egalitarian: childless cohabiting couples and those cohabiting after a previous marriage are less likely than their married counterparts to pool their assets, which generally operates to the disadvantage of the party who earns less.[43]

A third function of the family might be said to be that of enabling role specialization without risk. There is in any household a certain minimum of tasks that need to be performed, and outgoings that need to be paid. Co-operation and sharing in such matters is one of the hallmarks of a family (in contrast to, for example, a student household in which exact accounting tends to prevail). Within an intact family the asymmetry that may be evident at any given time does not matter unduly as the enhanced earning power of one individual will also benefit the one who has taken responsibility for domestic work. The risk, of course, is that role specialization will often translate into inequality upon relationship breakdown if one party's earning power has been impaired. Thus Dnes suggests that the purpose of imposing obligations on divorcing couples may be to protect the economically weaker party 'from a form of exploitation that would reflect opportunistic behaviour emanating from an asymmetry in the life cycle of men compared with women';[44] however, on the evidence he is unconvinced that this argument applies to cohabiting couples. More evidence is needed as to the extent to which cohabitants render themselves vulnerable by taking on different roles, but some support for Dnes' contention is provided by economists Fisher and Low. Their calculations suggest that the income fall for women separating from cohabitation is less than those separating from marriage, and that they recover their level of income more quickly,[45] largely because they are less likely to

[42] A Barlow, C Burgoyne, E Clery and J Smithson, 'Cohabitation and the Law: Myths, Money and the Media' in A Park, J Curtice, K Thomson, M Phillips, M Johnson and E Clery (eds) *British Social Attitudes: the 24th Report* (London, 2008) 33. As the authors note, the duration of *current* cohabiting relationships is longer, but then so is the duration of current marriages, and it would thus be misleading to compare the duration of ongoing cohabiting relationships with that of marriages that had ended in divorce.

[43] C Vogler, 'Managing Money in Intimate Relationships: Similarities and Differences Between Cohabiting and Married Couples' in J Miles and R Probert, *Sharing Lives, Dividing Assets: An Inter-Disciplinary Study* (Oxford, 2009).

[44] A Dnes, 'Marriage, Cohabitation, and Same-Sex Marriage' (2007) 12 *The Independent Review* 85, 89.

[45] H Fisher and H Low, 'Who Wins, Who Loses and Who Recovers From Divorce?' in Miles and Probert, n 43 above.

have children. There is empirical evidence that childless cohabiting couples are more likely than their married counterparts to operate as separate economic units.[46] There is also evidence that some welcome the freedom from obligations that cohabiting currently brings. In McRae's study of cohabiting mothers, for example, almost 30 per cent of the cohabitants identified the lack of legal ties and greater freedom of cohabitation as an advantage.[47]

Such evidence should cause us to rethink the argument that a functional approach dictates treating cohabiting couples as if they were married. In so arguing, it is not intended to suggest that cohabiting relationships do not deserve legal recognition, or to denigrate in any way the loving, long-term committed relationships of many cohabiting couples, or to align with those who view cohabitation as a problem. But it is to suggest that the data so far suggests reasons for caution. It is perhaps worth stating that my own reaction to much of the data outlined above was initially one of scepticism, but the evidence was sufficient to convince me that there was a real issue here. Why marriage may have this effect has been debated: selection inevitably plays a part, but it has also been suggested that the very fact of making a promise, of incurring an obligation, has a stabilizing effect.[48] It may be an article of faith for some that cohabitation is a superior relationship to marriage—on the basis that it does not have the same history of discrimination and prescription[49]—but it needs to be recognized that marriage itself has changed and is now characterized by far greater equality.[50] Unless there is evidence to support the superiority of cohabitation, such beliefs should be accorded no more—and no less—respect than the equally strongly-held view that cohabitation itself is wrong.

In short, the answer to the question posed by Baroness Hale almost 30 years ago, that of 'whether the legal institution of marriage

[46] Vogler, n 43 above. [47] McRae, n 10 above.

[48] See S Fitzgibbon, 'Marriage and the Good of Obligation' (2002) 47 *American Journal of Jurisprudence* 41; J McGowan, 'Marriage Versus Living Together' in K Scott and M Warren, *Perspectives on Marriage: A Reader* (3rd edn Oxford, 2007) ch 6; RH Thaler and CR Sunstein, *Nudge: Improving Decisions About Health, Wealth and Happiness* (London, 2008).

[49] See R Auchmuty, 'What's So Special about Marriage? The impact of *Wilkinson v Kitzinger*' (2008) 20 Child and Family Law Quarterly 475. For a critical review of earlier attacks on marriage see R Fletcher, *The Abolitionists: The Family and Marriage Under Attack* (London, 1988).

[50] See B Hale, 'The Future of Marriage' in G Douglas and N Lowe (eds), *The Continuing Evolution of Family Law* (Bristol, 2009).

continues to serve any useful purpose',[51] may actually be 'yes'.[52] Marriage might well be, in Clive's terms, an unnecessary legal concept,[53] but it still continues to be a *convenient* legal concept in that almost all married couples are living together and most couples who live together are married. Clive suggested that it would become inconvenient and unjust to frame laws in terms of marriage if 50 per cent of married couples were not living together and 50 per cent of couples who were living together were not married, but we are a long way from this position. If marriage continues to perform a useful social function then there may be reasons for the law not only to retain it as a legal concept, but also to promote it as far as it is possible to do so. That marriage performs certain crucial functions better than other arrangements would suggest that a functional approach in fact justifies and indeed requires the law to encourage couples to marry by according at least some rights to married couples that are not extended to cohabiting couples.[54]

Views and Behaviour

It may, however, be objected that the law has very little role to play in determining whether people marry or cohabit, and so privileging marriage will have no effect on people's behaviour. Barlow has pointed out that the majority of cohabitants do in fact believe that there is such a thing as 'common-law marriage',[55] although the headline figure of 56 per cent covered those who 'definitely' believed this and those who thought that it was 'probably' true.[56] This may explain why, when they were questioned as to the specific rights that this might entail, far fewer believed that cohabitants had such rights.[57]

[51] B Hoggett, 'Ends and Means: The Utility of Marriage as a Legal Institution' in J Eekelaar and S Katz (eds) *Marriage and Cohabitation in Contemporary Societies: Areas of Legal, Social and Ethical Change* (London, 1980) 101.

[52] And note her recent suggestion that 'there is still a case for privileging the status of marriage': Hale, n 50 above.

[53] EM Clive, 'Marriage: An Unnecessary Legal Concept', in Eekelaar and Katz, n 51 above.

[54] eg, see C Roberts, *The Place of Marriage in a Changing Society* (London, 1996) 12; M Garrison, 'The Decline of Formal Marriage: Inevitable or Reversible?' (2007) 41 Family Law Quarterly 491; NR Burstein, 'Economic Influences on Marriage and Divorce' (2007) 26 *Journal of Policy Analysis and Management* 387.

[55] See also R Pickford, *Fathers, Marriage and the Law* (London, 1999) 26.

[56] Barlow and ors, n 29 above. In the latest survey this had fallen to 51 per cent: see Barlow and ors, n 42 above.

[57] Only 38% of respondents believed that a woman would have the same right to financial support after a 10-year cohabiting relationship as if she had been married; and

It is true that married and cohabiting couples do not tend to cite the law as a major influence on their decision whether or not to marry or cohabit.[58] One would hardly expect them to do so, especially given that legal differences in treatment generally only become acute at the time of relationship breakdown or other crisis. But a more subtle influence may be discerned. The legal rules contribute to the culture within which decisions are made: couples may articulate their decision to marry in terms of commitment and security[59] rather than legal ties and financial provision, but it is the latter rules that give meaning to the former.

In addition, responses to questions about the motivations for a particular course of action may reflect what the respondents think is acceptable. It is unsurprising that cohabitants present themselves as being as committed as if they were married; it would be surprising if they did not. The fact that a different story is told by the higher rates of dissolution and by interviews with *ex*-cohabitants tells us as much about the psychology of responding to questions as it does about the behaviour of cohabitants. Nor are the stories told by cohabitants necessarily a result of conscious suppression of information. As Regan has noted, '[i]ndividuals have the capacity to delude themselves in a variety of ways, and observers may have a clearer perspective on underlying grounds of action than persons directly involved in events'.[60] Support for this is provided by Dnes, who has pointed out that there are in fact observable links between legal changes and patterns of behaviour.[61] And it is perhaps significant that the increase in cohabitation in England and Wales occurred at the same time that the common-law marriage myth was being created.[62] Similarly, although some research would seem to suggest that there is no relationship between law reform benefiting cohabitants and marriage rates, this focused on the

37% that she had a right to the family home after her partner's death; 54% and 53% correctly stated that she did not: Barlow and ors, n 10 above.

[58] See M Hibbs, C Barton and J Beswick, 'Why Marry?—Perceptions of the Affianced' (2001) Family Law 197.

[59] eg, see McRae's study of cohabiting mothers, n 10 above, which found that those who had gone on to marry were three times as likely to identify the lack of commitment and security involved in cohabitation as a disadvantage than those who were still cohabiting; the main reasons given for marrying were to make a commitment and for the children's security.

[60] M Regan, *Alone Together: Law and the Meanings of Marriage* (Oxford, 1999) 79.

[61] Dnes, n 44 above. See also D Anderberg, 'Tax Credits, Income Support and Partnership Decisions' (2008) 15 *International Tax and Public Finance* 499.

[62] See further R Probert, 'Why Do Couples Still Believe in Common-law Marriage?' (2007) Family Law 403.

introduction of legislative reform, not the other, earlier legal changes that conferred rights on cohabiting couples.[63] Until we know much more about the relationship between the two, there is reason for caution.

Continuing to confer at least some exclusive legal privileges on marriage would also be consistent with the views of society more generally. Although there is now widespread acceptance of cohabitation, there is clear evidence that marriage is still valued more highly. A survey of 1,560 men and women aged between 20 and 35 found that 70 per cent of those who were not currently married wished to do so at some point in the future;[64] interestingly, among cohabitants this proportion rose to 79 per cent, with 10 per cent not expressing a view and only 11 per cent stating that they had no wish to marry.[65] This suggests that the vast majority of cohabitants see their relationship as a precursor, rather than as an alternative, to marriage. While cohabitation is now widely accepted, it is not necessarily celebrated: one small-scale study of wedding presents and those gifts made to cohabitants found that house-warming presents to the latter were 'fewer in number and . . . have less material and symbolic weight'.[66] In a similar vein, 54 per cent of respondents to the British Social Attitudes Survey agreed with the statement that '[e]ven though it might not work out for some people, marriage is still the best kind of relationship' while only 9 per cent agreed that 'there is no point in getting married—it's only a piece of paper'.[67] While Barlow's research did find considerable support for extending rights to cohabiting couples, it is significant that the questions postulated a 10-year cohabiting relationship (far longer than the average); and even then the proportion stating that a cohabitant should be able to claim financial support on relationship breakdown was significantly lower than the proportion endorsing remedies on death or relating to the father's rights during the relationship. When the period of cohabitation in the scenario was reduced to two years, only 38 per cent of respondents thought that a cohabitant should have a

[63] K Kiernan, A Barlow and R Merlo, 'Cohabitation Law Reform and its Impact on Marriage' (2006) Family Law 1074.

[64] A de Waal, *Second Thoughts on the Family* (London, 2008) 154.

[65] Ibid, 156.

[66] L Purbrick, *The Wedding Present: Domestic Life Beyond Consumption* (Aldershot, 2007) 176.

[67] Barlow and ors, n 42 above, table 2.2.

right to financial provision on separation, although this rose to 74 per cent for a cohabitant caring for the parties' child.[68]

So, if the solution is not to equate cohabiting relationships with marriage, how might the law develop to redress some of the problems faced by cohabitants?

Current Legel Solutions

Contract

The relevance of pre-marital contracts to cohabiting couples might not be immediately obvious, but their inclusion as a potential solution reflects the tension in the debates referred to at the outset. The strategy of changing the law of marriage and divorce to enable couples to marry has little to offer, partly because divorce is now readily available and the restrictions on who may marry whom have been reduced to a minimum, and partly because the ideas that underpinned those reforms also fuelled the increase in cohabitation in the 1970s. Yet it should be noted that the same period also saw fundamental changes to the legal consequences of marriage, as the courts acquired the power to reallocate assets between the parties: marriage may therefore have become less attractive to some at the same time that it became more available. Indeed, it could be said that while the trend in divorce law has been to make marriage more like cohabitation (in allowing freer exit), the trend in ancillary relief has been to underline the distinctiveness of marriage by enabling spouses to share in each other's wealth. So it is worth asking whether couples are rejecting marriage because of its legal consequences, and whether allowing them to determine those consequences for themselves might encourage couples (or rather, the party who has most to lose from marriage)[69] to marry.

The traditional objection to such contracts was that they were contrary to public policy, anticipating the end of the marriage before it had even begun. The modern counter-argument is that not upholding such contracts may make it more likely that some couples will cohabit rather than marry. Thus in *Supporting Families* in 1998 we find the suggestion that the security provided by pre-nuptial agreements 'could make it

[68] Barlow and ors, n 29 above; Barlow and ors, n 42 above.

[69] It was pointed out almost three decades ago that the terms of marriage have become less favourable to men: see Hoggett, n 51 above, 100.

more likely that some people might marry, rather than simply live together'.[70] A decade later the Law Commission noted, rather more tentatively, 'the view that the fact that pre-nuptial agreements are not currently binding may deter people from marrying or entering into civil partnerships in some cases'.[71]

In essence, the argument is that some individuals may choose to marry if marriage is made more like cohabitation. This raises two further questions. The first is an empirical one: are couples more likely to marry if there is the possibility of entering into a pre-nuptial agreement? In *MacLeod v MacLeod* Baroness Hale expressed doubt on this point, stating that '[i]t certainly cannot be demonstrated that the lack of enforceable ante-nuptial agreements in this country is depressing the marriage rate here as compared with other countries where such agreements can be made'.[72] The second is an evaluative one: what would be the benefits of doing so? Given that a pre-nuptial agreement may already be taken into account by the courts if it is deemed just to do so,[73] the issue about the enforceability of pre-nuptial agreements is really about the ability to enter into a contract that is *unfair* to one of the parties.

But is there anything to be gained from this? The copious evidence on the benefits of marriage was discussed above, but one might well ask whether the same benefits would accrue if one party's willingness to marry is dependent upon him or her being able to limit their obligations in the case of breakdown. If encouraging marriage is to be relied on as a reason for rendering pre-nuptial agreements binding, we need to know both whether it will have this effect and, if so, whether the resulting marriage is likely to be more durable than simple cohabitation would have been.

By contrast, cohabitation contracts could be seen as making cohabitation more like marriage, by creating legal obligations that will be enforceable on relationship breakdown. Three questions arise: will contracts made between cohabitants be legally enforceable contracts; are such contracts likely to provide a fair distribution on relationship breakdown; and will cohabitants actually make such agreements?

[70] Home Office, *Supporting Families* (1998) para 4.22.

[71] Law Commission, *10th Programme of Law Reform* (Law Com No 311, 2008) para 2.19.

[72] [2008] UKPC 64, para 33.

[73] eg, see *K v K (Ancillary Relief: Prenuptial Agreement)* [2003] 1 FLR 120; *Crossley v Crossley* [2007] EWCA Civ 1491; *NG v KR (Pre-nuptial contract)* [2008] EWHC 1532 (Fam).

The consensus is that cohabitation contracts are enforceable,[74] although the lack of any direct precedent led the Law Commission to suggest that 'for the avoidance of doubt' statute should clarify that a contract would not be regarded as contrary to public policy insofar as it governed the financial affairs of a cohabiting couple.[75] Cohabiting couples would still face the burden of establishing an intention to create legal relations, but the existence of a formal written agreement would easily satisfy that requirement. Similarly, in any modern cohabiting relationship the assumption of mutual obligations will satisfy the need for consideration.

It should not, however, be assumed that contract is the best solution to the current situation of cohabiting couples. There has, on occasion, been a tendency to idealize cohabiting relationships as more egalitarian than marriage; two persons coming together on an equal footing. But this is not necessarily the case: inequalities may exist within cohabiting relationships as within other types of relationship.[76] Contracts may be used positively—to confer rights where none existed before—but may also be used by one party to limit the other's claims in the event of separation (especially if that party mistakenly believes that the other will have a claim as a result of their 'common-law marriage'). Any express agreement that the other is to have a small share in the property would, for example, be conclusive evidence of a declaration of trust and would preclude the courts from finding that a larger share was merited on the basis of the other's contributions.

Nor is there much evidence of couples actually entering into cohabitation contracts. Lewis' survey found that contracts were regarded as 'cold', 'defeatist' and 'inflexible',[77] findings echoed in a survey of those who accessed the website of the 'Living Together Campaign'.[78] Indeed, even among those who had intended to take action in the wake of

[74] The very fact that the court enforces trusts based on an express or implied bargain between the parties suggests that an express contract would also be enforceable today: contrast the claim in *Diwell v Farnes* [1959] 2 All ER 379, 384, that any claim to the family home based on a joint venture would depend on a contract 'which, being founded on an immoral consideration, would not be enforceable'.

[75] Law Commission, n 8 above, para 5.8.

[76] See R Probert, 'From Lack of Status to Contract: Assessing the French *Pacte Civil de Solidarité*' (2001) 23 *Journal of Social Welfare and Family Law* 257.

[77] J Lewis, J Datta and S Sarre, *Individualism and Commitment in Marriage and Cohabitation* (London, 1999) 80.

[78] See A Barlow, C Burgoyne and J Smithson, *The Living Together Campaign: An Investigation of its Impact on Legally Aware Cohabitants* (Research Report to the Ministry of Justice, 2007) 7.

accessing the website, few had done so at the time of the follow-up survey.[79] The conclusion has to be that on the evidence available we cannot rely on contract law to provide either a solution to the problem of cohabitation or the problems faced by cohabitants, although a clear statutory provision that such contracts are binding and legally enforceable might encourage a few more couples to enter into such agreements.[80]

Property law

Property lawyers have a different take on whether cohabitation is a problem: some—with a certain amount of justification, it should be admitted—seem to view family relationships in general as posing a problem for the purity and logic of the law of property.[81] More seriously, it has long been recognized that the law of trusts poses certain problems for an ex-cohabitant seeking to establish an interest in the formerly-shared family home. Does it have the potential to provide a solution? After the retirement of Lord Denning it was a constant theme among judges hearing cases of this kind that the matter was one for parliament to address.[82] Parliament did not, however, show any willingness to act, and in 2002 the Law Commission suggested that development of the law of trusts could be achieved through judicial rather than legislative channels.[83] In *Stack v Dowden* the House of Lords rose to this challenge with Baroness Hale stating that the courts would have to be responsible for 'the evolution of the law of property to take account of changing social and economic circumstances'.[84] The majority rejected the orthodox view that the law of property should approach issues of ownership in the family context in the same way as in the commercial context.[85]

The key innovation in *Stack v Dowden* related to the principles to be applied where the home was in joint ownership. The starting point is, as it has always been, that equity follows the law; however, whereas in

[79] Ibid

[80] Ibid. The fact that a living together agreement might not be legally binding was identified as a reason for not entering into such an arrangement.

[81] See J Mee, *The Property Rights of Cohabitees* (Oxford, 1999).

[82] eg, see *Burns v Burns* [1984] FLR 216; *Drake v Whipp* [1996] 1 FLR 826.

[83] Law Commission, *Sharing Homes: A Discussion Paper* (Law Com No 278, 2002) 86.

[84] *Stack v Dowden* [2007] UKHL 17, para 46.

[85] Ibid, para 3 per Lord Hope; paras 14, 31 and 33 per Lord Walker; para 42 per Baroness Hale.

earlier cases this was a starting point that could be 'easily displaced',[86] there is now a 'considerable burden' on the party asserting an entitlement to a greater share.[87] As Baroness Hale put it, 'cases in which the joint legal owners are to be taken to have intended that their beneficial interests should be different from their legal interests will be very unusual'.[88]

Whether the law should infer such an intention has been questioned by some commentators;[89] more pertinent for current purposes is the question as to whether the decision indicates that the law of trusts might now provide a satisfactory legal framework for determining the rights of cohabiting couples. It has not necessarily introduced greater certainty into this area of the law. One difficulty with the actual decision in *Stack v Dowden* was that the proceeds of sale were not divided equally in that case, it being decided that Ms Dowden had succeeded in establishing that the parties had intended that their beneficial interests were to be unequal. Commentators have struggled to identify why *Stack v Dowden* was an unusual case: the fact that their finances were kept separate does not mark it out as such[90] (and empirical research has shown that couples may pool their assets in practice even if they keep separate accounts[91]), and the fact that they made unequal financial contributions is similarly unremarkable.[92] The case thus inevitably poses a challenge for those seeking to apply it.

A second concern is that the reasoning that benefited one higher-earning woman might work to the disadvantage of the majority of women who still, on average, earn less than their male partners.[93] To some extent this concern has been allayed by the decision in *Fowler v Barron*,[94] in which a female partner who made no direct financial contribution to the property was nonetheless entitled to half the equity of a property held in joint names at law. The male partner had paid the

[86] *McKenzie v McKenzie* [2003] 2 P & CR DG6, 65.

[87] *Stack v Dowden*, para 14.

[88] *Ibid*, para 69.

[89] See Douglas and ors, n 6 above. For evidence that buying a home in joint names was regarded as a commitment see Smart and Stevens, n 30 above, 47; J Lewis, *The End of Marriage?* (Cheltenham, 2001) ch 6.

[90] See Vogler, n 43 above.

[91] eg, see C Burgoyne and S Sonnenberg, 'Financial Practices in Cohabiting Heterosexual Couples: A Perspective from Economic Psychology' in Miles and Probert, n 43 above.

[92] eg, see RH George, 'Stack v Dowden – Do as we say, not as we do?' (2008) 30 Journal of Social Welfare and Family Law 49.

[93] eg, see J Scott and S Dex, 'Paid and Unpaid Work: Can Policy Improve Gender Inequalities?' in Miles and Probert, n 43 above.

[94] [2008] EWCA Civ 377.

deposit on the property and the mortgage instalments; he also paid the council tax and utilities bills, while the female partner paid for food, presents, holidays, clothes and special occasions. But the division as to who paid what was not regarded as a rigid separation of assets but rather as a pooling of assets, in practice if not in terms of strict title: 'The way that she used her own income indicates that the parties largely treated their incomes and assets as one pool from which household expenses will be paid'.[95] The inequality in their respective contributions was interpreted as evidence that they did not care how much each contributed: 'There was no prior agreement as to who would pay what. The inference from this, especially when taken with the evidence as to mutual wills referred to below, was that the parties simply did not care about the respective size of each other's contributions'.[96] The fact that the property had served as the family home for the couple and their children was also seen as an important factor in determining their common intention.[97]

However, a third and more serious problem with *Stack* in the current context is that it will have no impact on the majority of cohabiting couples, given that cohabiting couples are less likely than their married counterparts either to be owner-occupiers[98] or to own their home in joint names.[99] And the recent case of *James v Thomas*[100] provides an example of how the law may be applied harshly in a case of a home in sole ownership. Mr Thomas was already the owner of the property when Miss James moved in with him in 1989. From 1990 she worked with him in his business without remuneration. All household and living expenses were paid out of Mr Thomas' account, which was also the bank account for the business. From 1999 the business was carried

[95] *Ibid*, para 46. This is consistent with the empirical research which demonstrates that the lack of any specific joint bank account does not necessarily denote a lack of sharing in practice: see Burgoyne and Sonnenberg, n 91 above.

[96] *Fowler v Barron* [2008] EWCA Civ 377, para 41.

[97] Although all this could equally be said of the parties in *Stack*, and indeed was said by the judge at first instance, who noted that 'effectively they managed their affairs together' and 'both put their all into doing the best for themselves and their family', and who held that having regard to their relationship 'it is likely that there was some understanding between them' *Stack v Dowden* [2005] EWCA Civ 857, quoted at paras 32 and 34.

[98] Department for Communities and Local Government, *Housing by Marital Status*, 5 available at <http://www.communities.gov.uk/documents/housing/pdf/156984.pdf>

[99] J Haskey, 'Cohabiting Couples in Great Britain: Accommodation Sharing, Tenure and Property Ownership' (2001) 103 *Population Trends* 26, 33; S Arthur J Lewis, M Maclean, S Finch and R Fitzgerald, *Settling Up: Making Financial Arrangements After Separation* (London, 2002) 13.

[100] [2007] EWCA Civ 1212.

out as a partnership, and from 2002 the account was changed to a joint account. At the very least, one might think, Miss James could be credited with financial contributions made after 2002 from that bank account, and arguably from a much earlier date, however, the court approached this as a case of non-financial contributions and held that there was no common intention that she should have an interest in the property, nor any reliance on what were, it had to be admitted, rather ambiguous statements (such as 'this will benefit us both' and assurances that she would be well provided for in the event of his death). According to Chadwick LJ:

> The true position, as it seems to me, is that she worked in the business, and contributed her labour to the improvements to the property, because she and Mr Thomas were making their life together as man and wife. . . It is a mistake to think that the motives which lead parties in such a relationship to act as they do are necessarily attributable to pecuniary self-interest.[101]

It is interesting how the context of joint or sole ownership frames the courts' perceptions of the parties' intentions. In *Fowler v Barron* the parties were regarded as a couple, and the love and affection that underpinned their respective contributions—the willingness of one party to pay more, the willingness of the other to depend on the other —was taken as evidence of an intention to share everything equally. In *James v Thomas*, by contrast, the parties were regarded as two separate individuals, and love and affection was attributed solely to the claimant in a manner that defeated her claim.

Yet *James v Thomas* should not lead us to write off the potential of the law of trusts altogether. As noted above, it can be argued that Miss James should have been credited with having made a direct financial contribution; furthermore, account could have been taken of the explicit suggestion in *Stack v Dowden* that making improvements that added significant value to the property should be sufficient to generate an interest.[102] In addition, the House of Lords implicitly approved *Le Foe v Le Foe*,[103] which suggests that an indirect contribution to the purchase price—ie by paying household bills—should now be regarded as raising the inference of a common intention that the beneficial interest be shared. That no account was taken of this in *James v Thomas* highlights one of the problems with judicial law-making: judges are inevitably

[101] [2007] EWCA Civ 1212, para 36.
[102] *Stack v Dowden* [2007] UKHL 17, paras 12, 36, and 70.
[103] [2001] 2 FLR 970.

constrained by the case in front of them and any efforts to steer other aspects of the law in a different direction may be dismissed as merely *obiter dicta*. The conclusion thus has to be that although property law has the potential to provide an adequate solution to many of the problems facing cohabitants, that potential has not been fully realized.

Family Law

The same criticism could be made of the existing remedies under family law. Under Schedule 1 of the Children Act 1989 the court has the power to order periodical payments, a lump sum, the settlement of property, or a transfer of property, either directly to the child or to the applicant for the benefit of the child. This, one might think, would provide all the law needs to secure the financial well-being of the child—so far as parental resources allow—during that child's minority. One problem is that many cohabitants may not realize that any such provision exists. For this the media representation of 'common-law marriage' may be to blame. On the one hand there are frequent references to the term; on the other, there are intermittent articles pointing out that there is no such thing as common-law marriage and asserting that cohabitants have no legal rights.[104] As a consequence, the myth that there are *no* rights may be just as firmly embedded as the belief in common-law marriage.

A further problem is that those advising couples may not be familiar with this particular provision; one study of a small number of separating cohabitants found that, when they did seek legal advice, they were not advised about the possibility of an application under Schedule 1.[105] However, it is possible that this may have changed since that study was conducted, since the courts have developed the scope of Schedule 1 in recent years. It is now firmly established that a child is entitled to be brought up in circumstances that bear some relation to those of the non-resident parent,[106] and that an allowance for the child's carer may be included within periodical payments for the child.[107] True, most of

[104] See R Probert, 'Why Do Couples Still Believe in Common-law Marriage?' (2007) Family Law 403.

[105] Arthur and ors, n 99 above.

[106] *J v C (Child: Financial Provision)* [1999] 1 FLR 152; *Re C (A Child: Financial Provision)* [2007] Fam Law 101; *SW v RC* [2008] EWHC 73 (Fam).

[107] See *A v A (A Minor) (Financial Provision)* [1994] 1 FLR 657; *Re P (Child: Financial Provision)* [2003] 2 FLR 865; *F v G (Child: Financial Provision)* [2005] 1 FLR 261.

the reported cases have involved fathers who were 'fabulously wealthy'[108] but orders have also been made in cases where the assets are more modest (as in *Re R (a minor)*,[109] in which the father was a self-employed carpet-fitter earning £35,000[110]).

One limitation of Schedule 1 is the fact that its effect is confined to the minority of the child or children in question. The case-law is consistent in holding that any property settled on, or for the benefit of, the child, must revert to the settlor once the child attains the age of majority.[111] This was based on the approach taken in ancillary relief cases, and it is difficult to argue that children should be entitled to capital upon attaining their majority simply because their parents were not married. But does this necessarily preclude the parent who has been caring for the child retaining the property? One decision of the Court of Appeal hints that a transfer may be possible where a cohabiting relationship has broken down: Thorpe LJ in *Francis v Manning* contrasted the approach to be taken '[w]here a very rich man fathers a child on his mistress' with that appropriate:

> . . . where a family unit is created without marriage and where on the disintegration of the family the court has the opportunity to preserve the family home for the benefit of a child and for the parent who happens to assume the responsibility for primary care.[112]

The actual facts of the case do not, however, necessarily support an outright transfer, since the mother effectively bought out the father's share. While the words of Thorpe LJ would seem capable of a wider application, to date the potential of this has not been realized.

One possible argument that might be used to develop this interpretation is that it is for the benefit of children during their minority that the person responsible for their care should be freed from the necessity of seeking employment and that this requires that the carer should be entitled to retain at least some part of the property's value even after they have attained their majority—in short, that the potential benefit to the child requires a future benefit to the mother.

[108] See *Re P (Child: Financial Provision)* [2003] 2 FLR 865; *Re S (Unmarried Parents: Financial Provision)* [2006] 2 FLR 950.

[109] Unreported, Court of Appeal, 21 October 1999.

[110] Although he did own a Ferrari. However, this was described as 'a nearly disastrous' investment.

[111] eg, see *A v A (A Minor: Financial Provision)* [1994] 1 FLR 657; *Re P (Child: Financial Provision)* [2003] EWCA Civ 837; *MT v OT (Financial Provision: Costs)* [2007] EWHC 838 (Fam).

[112] [1997] EWCA 1231.

This interpretation may seem strained, but there are cases in which the courts have been generous in their assessment of what will benefit the child: in *N v D*, for example, the carer's allowance included the mother's needs 'to eat, clothe herself, maintain car expenses and take the child for holidays'. It was also held that it was reasonable to make provision for her medical costs on the basis that she 'must be sufficiently equipped and healthy in order to be able to care for S'.[113]

Even if possible, however, such an argument is likely to be of limited application: there are relatively few families that can afford the luxury of one parent remaining at home until the children leave school. In practice, the likelihood of a woman being in paid employment increases once the youngest child has reached the age of five and the employment rates for mothers whose youngest child is aged 16-18 are 76 per cent for lone mothers and 82 per cent for those living with a partner.[114] And the expectation of the government is clearly that mothers with school-age children will work: while until recently a lone parent with a child under the age of 16 was not expected to look for work, from October 2008 the age limit was lowered to 12 years and from 2010 those whose children have attained the age of 7 will be expected to look for work.[115] Such data may, of course, also suggest that the vulnerability of the child's carer when the settlement has come to an end is not as great as is sometimes portrayed.

By contrast, if the parties are living in rented accommodation—as almost half of cohabiting couples with children are—then the law does provide for a transfer of the tenancy.[116] The power to transfer tenancies is particularly valuable given that cohabiting couples are more likely than their married counterparts to be living in rented accommodation.[117] Unfortunately, as the Law Commission noted in its consultation paper, it is difficult to ascertain how much use is

[113] [2008] 1 FLR 1629, para 27.

[114] Office for National Statistics, n 31 above, table 4.3.

[115] Department for Work and Pensions, *In Work, Better Off* (Cm 7139, 2007).

[116] Family Law Act 1996, Sched 7.

[117] See J Miles, P Pleasence and N Balmer, 'The Experience of Relationship Breakdown And Civil Law Problems by People in Different Forms of Relationship' [2009] 21 Child and Family Law Quarterly 47, whose analysis of the 2004 English and Welsh Civil and Social Justice Survey found that 46.4% of cohabiting couples with children, and 32.6% of those without children, lived in rented accommodation. The equivalent figures for married couples were 13.3% and 13% respectively. See also Vogler, n 43 above.

made of this particular provision,[118] and what its impact and scope might be.

The deficiencies of the law have led to various proposals for reform being advanced. In 2002 the Law Society suggested that the wording in the Family Law (Scotland) Act 1985 provided 'a useful model for determining a claim'.[119] This stated that 'a fair account should be taken of any economic advantage derived by either party from contributions from the other, and of any economic disadvantages suffered by either party in the interests of the other party or of the family'.[120]

A more developed version of this basic principle was then put forward by the Law Commission in 2007. The basic elements of the scheme are that eligible cohabitants (defined as those who have had a child together, or have lived together for a specified minimum period) would be able to apply to a court for financial relief upon separation. The Law Commission recommended a two-pronged approach: that benefits conferred on one party as a result of qualifying contributions (which would include physical improvements to the property that improved its value, but not the payment of bills and other household expenses unless the other party could not otherwise have afforded to pay the mortgage) by the other be reversed, and that any economic disadvantage that the claimant will suffer as a result of contributions made during the relationship should be shared. However, the court would have a discretion in exercising its powers: it is to do so only 'insofar as that is reasonable and practicable' having regard to a list of discretionary factors, and, in the case of claims based on economic disadvantage, 'an economic equality ceiling'. The primary consideration, where any child of both parties is under the age of 18, is to be the welfare of the child. The financial needs, obligations, conduct and resources of both parties are also to be taken into account.

While attractive in its principled approach, the scheme might prove difficult to apply in practice. First, the very necessity of including eligibility criteria would inevitably create a layer of cases in which this was disputed, as parties who had been together for a period close to the specified minimum sought for inclusion or exclusion, depending on which would be of most benefit to them. Secondly, the concept of a

[118] Law Commission, *Cohabitation: The Financial Consequences of Relationship Breakdown: A Consultation Paper* (Law Com No 179, 2006) 59.

[119] The Law Society, *Cohabitation: The Case for Clear Law* (London, 2002) para 101.

[120] Family Law (Scotland) Act 1985, s 9(1)(b).

retained benefit offers little more to cohabiting couples than is currently available under property law, either in the contributions that are to be taken into account or the assets to which it is capable of applying, and might well result in the contributing party receiving less than they would do under the law of trusts.[121] Thirdly, although the principle of sharing any economic disadvantage from the relationship appeals to notions of justice, such disadvantage is difficult to predict, since it depends on choices as yet unmade as well as the actions of the past. The courts have exhibited reluctance to engage in a 'what if' exercise to determine compensation in the context of ancillary relief.[122] It is also open to question how far the disadvantage results from the relationship: the trigger might be rooted in the relationship, but the actual disadvantage will be affected by other factors (such as the availability of child care, whether the child's carer chooses to take up paid employment or not, or whether he or she enters into a new relationship). Even the relationship between the economic disadvantage and the eventual outcome would be difficult to discern, given that this would be mediated by the economic equality ceiling, as well as by the court's discretion.

A final problem with the scheme is its complexity. Litigation would be necessary to establish both the extent of any retained benefit or economic disadvantage and the extent to which it was practicable and appropriate to recognize these elements in the final award. Ideally, the law should be as simple as possible to understand and apply, not just for professional lawyers but also for the parties themselves. The same point could be made about the scheme set out in the Cohabitation Bill 2008, introduced into the House of Lords by Lord Lester in December 2008. The Bill provides that a court may make a 'financial settlement order' if the parties have separated and 'having regard to all the circumstances, the court considers that it is just and equitable to make an order'.[123] In the light of the courts' struggles to discern and apply

[121] See further R Probert, 'Review of *Cohabitation: The Financial Consequences of Relationship Breakdown* ' (2007) 41 Family Law Quarterly 521.

[122] 'Attempts under the rubric of Compensation to isolate and quantify the level of income or earning capacity sacrificed by a wife years after the event for the purpose of calculating a premium element on the award, constitutes a search for precision which is to be discouraged both on the grounds of policy and practicality': *VB v JP* [2008] EWHC 112 (Fam). See also *P v P* [2007] EWHC 779 (Fam), and note too the restrictive scope of the principle as interpreted in *NA v MA* [2006] EWHC 2900 (Fam); *H v H* [2007] EWHC 459 (Fam); *S v S (Non-Matrimonial Property: Conduct)* [2006] EWHC 2793 (Fam).

[123] Cohabitation Bill, cl 8(1)(b).

governing principles in the field of ancillary relief, the extension of a discretionary scheme to a new, large constituency does give cause for concern. While the Bill does draw a clear distinction between its proposed scheme and that applicable to divorcing spouses,[124] it provides more guidance on what the courts are *not* to do than on the principles underpinning potential awards.

Finding a Way Forward

On the assumption that neither of the Cohabitation Bills[125] nor the Law Commission's proposals will pass into law in the immediate future, are there ways of developing the potential of the current legal solutions reviewed above? In considering whether this patchwork of legal rights provides adequate coverage, attention must be paid to the characteristics of cohabiting couples. If the 44 per cent of cohabiting couples with dependent children[126] have a remedy under Schedule 1 of the Children Act; the 30 per cent of childless cohabitants in rented accommodation[127] can seek a remedy under the Family Law Act 1996; approximately half of the remaining owner-occupiers[128] will have registered their home in joint names and thus be presumed to own the home jointly in the wake of *Stack v Dowden*; and the majority of those living in a home registered in the name of the other party will be in a position to make financial contributions, then the number of cohabitants without any legal redress is far smaller than the headline figures would at first suggest.

Moreover, while it is possible to identify problematic aspects of each of these solutions, the potential for change has already been identified. Confirmation of the binding nature of cohabitation contracts and that indirect contributions and physical labour justify an inference that the

[124] For example, in requiring the courts to have regard to the 'nature of the commitment' between the parties, as well as the degree of dependency or interdependency (cl 9(b)), making it clear that 'there is to be no presumption that the applicant and the respondent should share equally in property belonging to either or both of them' (cl 8(2)(c)); and laying down the 'principle' that the parties should be self-supporting as soon as reasonably practicable (cl 8(3)(a)).

[125] A second bill dealing with cohabitation—the Cohabitation (No 2) Bill—was introduced in the House of Commons under the Ten Minute Rule on 25 March 2009, but failed to proceed to a second reading.

[126] Office for National Statistics, n 31 above, table 2.6.

[127] See Miles and ors, n 117 above.

[128] See Arthur and ors, n 99 above.

parties had a common intention to share the beneficial interest in the property would enhance these remedies.

It might be thought that one of the central problems with property law—the fact that certain contributions are ignored for the purposes of establishing a constructive trust—might be less susceptible to development in this way. But certain recent developments could point the way to a more flexible approach. First, the acceptance at the highest level that a distinct set of rules is appropriate when dealing with the family home and, building on this, a more relational approach in which it can be held that unequal contributions and a lack of articulated intentions actually meant that the parties 'simply did not care about the respective size of each other's contributions'.[129] Moreover, the logic of accepting that a common intention can be inferred from indirect contributions also points in favour of accepting domestic contributions as generating a common intention: in each case the ability of the legal owner to make the mortgage payments will often depend on the contributions of the other. Indeed, it might be thought that the argument is more compelling in the case where one member of the couple remains at home to care for a young child: the legal owner may well be able to afford to pay other bills in addition to the mortgage repayments, but were he or she to assume the responsibility for child care, then it would be necessary either to give up work or expend considerable sums on paid child care.[130] If domestic contributions could generate an interest in the shared home, this would also address the problem inherent in Schedule 1 of the Children Act that the carer risks being left without a home when the children attain their majority, since the carer would have an entitlement to property accrued during the relationship.

There is also much to be said for the approach to quantification adopted in *Fowler v Barron*. First, there is empirical evidence to suggest that there is rough parity between the contributions made within relationships: men work longer hours in paid employment (and are therefore in a better position to make a financial contribution), but women's paid work and unpaid work take up almost as much time.[131] Secondly, and perhaps more importantly, one can infer an acceptance by each party that each was content with the other's contribution from

[129] *Fowler v Barron* [2008] EWCA Civ 377, para 41.
[130] See Law Commission, n 118 above, 77, on the costs of childcare.
[131] See Scott and Dex, n 93 above. The available data unfortunately does not distinguish between married and cohabiting couples.

the continuance of the relationship. After all, what appear to an outsider to be unequal arrangements may not be experienced as such.[132] Unequal contributions may be, and often are, accepted in a relationship because of the love and affection between the parties; because each is contributing according to his or her means; or simply because the other party brings other skills and assets to the relationship on which it is difficult to put a price.[133]

There will, of course, be cases where the existing solutions, even if developed in line with the suggestions above, leave a cohabitant at a disadvantage compared to a spouse. But this should not by itself be regarded as problematic. First, it is not the place of the law to provide a remedy for every disadvantage. For example, if a couple had been dating, would we allow the one who had borne the brunt of the expenses to make a claim for compensation against the other when the relationship came to an end? Or for the one who was most in need to make a claim for support against the other? In order to make the link between the neediness of one person and a legal obligation on another, it has to be shown why the latter should be required to meet the needs of the other. Secondly, within a system that attempts to differentiate between marriage and cohabitation, it is an inevitable consequence that a claimant who is married will receive more generous treatment than one who is not. Thirdly, there is the risk that the result of attempting to devise a solution to meet the needs of all families will be either complexity (as under the original Child Support Act 1991) or uncertainty (as in the current law of ancillary relief). A good legal system is one that does not rely on litigation to establish entitlement. Indeed, it may be time to rethink the discretionary focus of family law in favour of more generally-applicable rules.[134]

But the conclusion that the current legal solutions may be developed to ensure better provision for cohabiting couples does not necessarily mean that no further action is necessary. What of the legal treatment of cohabitants in the context of pensions, tax, and social security? A review of the whole range of laws applicable to cohabiting couples was mooted by the Law Commission as long ago as the 1970s,[135] but to date no

[132] C Smart, *Personal Life: New Directions in Sociological Thinking* (Cambridge, 2007) 174.

[133] See Burgoyne and Sonnenberg, n 91 above, for a discussion of the way in which contributions are negotiated on an everyday basis.

[134] See Thaler and Sunstein, n 48 above.

[135] Law Commission, *Fourteenth Annual Report 1978-1979* (Law Com No 97, 1980) para 2.32.

such review has been carried out. The consultation paper issued by Resolution did include questions about the desirability of including provisions relating to tax, pensions and parental responsibility in its proposed Bill, but failed to offer any analysis in support of the suggestion that 'it is strongly arguable that they should be treated in the same way as married couples and civil partners',[136] an argument that was particularly problematic given that the main proposals in the consultation paper were premised on the basis that cohabiting couples should be treated *differently* to married couples.

There are two reasons for carrying out a review that examines the legal treatment of both marriage and cohabitation as a package, each reflecting one of the stances identified at the start. The first is to explore whether cohabitants are suffering particular legal disadvantages that the law should address (bearing in mind the point made earlier that not all disadvantages will merit a legal remedy); the second is to consider whether,[137] and, if so, how, the law can encourage and support the types of families that best fulfil the functions identified above, if necessary by promoting and privileging marriage.

The need for a specific review—rather than relying on judicial initiative—rests in part on the fact that judges often will not have available to them crucial evidence about the demographic and socio-economic background (which might inhibit the development of the law or lead to a development with unexpected legal consequences) or the power to make the necessary changes to the relevant legislation. But it is also motivated by the danger inherent in the incremental development of the law. The immediate needs of the individuals before the court may distort the questions asked. Viewed in isolation, any individual privilege accorded to marriage may appear anachronistic or unjustifiable. The argument that the 'protection of the traditional family' requires that a particular right be confined to certain types of relationships[138] can appear absurd. Those arguing for the extension of certain legal rights can demand rhetorically whether the 'traditional

[136] Resolution, *Reforming The Law For People Who Live Together: A Consultation Paper* (London, 2008) 20.

[137] This has been doubted: see HM Government: Policy Review, *Building on Progress: Families* (London, 2007); but cf de Waal, n 64 above.

[138] Note that in *Re P (Adoption: Unmarried Couple)* [2008] UKHL 38 the House of Lords took the view that the lack of marital status was a 'status' for the purposes of art 14, thus opening the way for claims of discrimination in the rights guaranteed by the Convention.

family' will really crumble if this one right is extended to others. In some cases the extension of legal rights will be justified. But the risk is that this mode of reasoning risks stripping the legal privileges away from marriage without ever thinking about how the law operates as a whole. If it then transpires that people do respond to legal change, it will be too late.

Lost in Translation? Towards a Theory of Economic Transplants

*Ioannis Lianos**

> *Film Director* [in Japanese, to the interpreter]: The translation is very important, O.K.? The translation.
>
> *Interpreter* [in Japanese, to the director]: Yes, of course. I understand.
>
> *Film Director* [in Japanese, to Bob]: Mr. Bob. You are sitting quietly in your study. And then there is a bottle of Suntory whiskey on top of the table. You understand, right? With wholehearted feeling, slowly, look at the camera, tenderly, and as if you are meeting old friends, say the words. As if you are Bogie in Casablanca, saying, 'Here's looking at you, kid,' –Suntory time!
>
> *Interpreter* [In English, to Bob]: He wants you to turn, look in camera. O.K.?
>
> *Bob*: Is that all he said?'
>
> Sofia Coppola, *Lost in Translation* (2003)

The interaction of law with economic theory has been an old story.[1] With some notable exceptions,[2] the first generation of scholarship interested in the interaction of law with economics focused on the understanding of the origin and transformation of legal rules and institutions through an analysis of the economic conditions and theories of the time.[3] The case law occasionally referred to economic theory[4] in its effort to uncover underlying principles of legal

* Reader in European and Competition Law, University College, London

[1] See J Walter Jones, *Historical Introduction to the Theory of Law* (Clarendon Press: Oxford, 1956) 235– 69; D Hughes Parry, 'Economic Theories in English Case Law' (1931) 47 *LQR* 183–202.

[2] HW Robinson, 'Law and Economics' (1939) 2(4) *MLR* 257–65.

[3] eg, see G Ripert, *Aspects Juridiques du Capitalisme Moderne* (*Libraire générale de droit et de jurisprudence*, 1946).

[4] See, for instance, CA Cooke 'Adam Smith and Jurisprudence' (1935) 61 *LQR* 326–32.

change.[5] Legal literature was predominately doctrinal but occasionally, in particular since the inception of the realist movement, it was taking some form of 'external' approach, examining the social, economic, and political landscape that was framing legal concepts and discourse.[6] The interaction of law with economics was a two-way traffic: legal concepts were also influential in framing economic discourse and lending content to economic concepts.[7] Law and institutions were a focal topic for economic analysis, which was largely following an inductive and empirical approach, based on a thorough analysis of the institutions that influenced the behavior of market actors in different industries.[8] The emergence of the discipline of 'economic law' epitomizes the need to take into account the dominant economic principles of the day, without however that leading to an abandonment of an internal doctrinal analysis. The integration of economic theories in legal analysis was followed by a normative and cognitive closure of the (legal) system once economic concepts were juridified.[9]

The second generation of scholarship on the interaction between law and economics did not limit itself to a simple doctrinal analysis. Explicitly adopting an 'external approach' the literature considered 'whether specific legal interventions are acceptable when assessed against external moral, ethical, or political principles'.[10] The law and economics scholarship advanced as a criterion the concept of economic efficiency, itself framed according to neoclassical economic theory and the idea of equilibrium, thus a principle entirely external and disconnected to the legal system. The interplay of law and economics acquired a normative interest as a research question, in the sense that economic concepts and methods have been directly influential in re- framing and enriching legal discourse. This evolution has led to an intense debate between the

[5] The laissez-faire theory in contract law for example: RA Epstein, 'Contracts Small and Contracts Large: Contract Law through the Lens of Laissez-Faire' in FH Buckley (ed) *The Fall and Rise of Freedom of Contract* (Duke University Press, 1999) 25–60

[6] C McCrudden, 'Legal Research and the Social Sciences' (2006) 122 *LQR* 632–50, 634.

[7] Jones, n 1 above, 238–45; CA Cooke, 'The Legal Content of the Profit Concept' (1936) 46 Yale Law Journal 436–46; A Leroux and A Marciano, *La Philosophie Economique* (Paris 1998) 15–18 on the notion of interest in economics.

[8] On the specificities of the old institutionalist school, see GM Hodgson, *The Evolution of Institutional Economics: Agency, Structure and Darwinism in American Institutionalism* (Routledge: London & New York, 2004).

[9] DJ Gerber, 'Constitutionalizing the Economy: German Neoliberalism, Competition Law, and the New Europe' (1994) 42 *American Journal of Comparative Law* 25–84.

[10] McCrudden, n 6 above, at 632.

defenders of this new paradigm and their opponents. At the same time, the Coase theorem led to a certain degree of indifference to legal institutions in economic analysis, one of the basic tenets of the theorem suggesting that when transaction costs are low efficiency can be achieved through bargaining, without any contribution from law.[11] The degree and the form of openness of the legal system to external sources determine the influence of the 'external approach' to legal change. In reality, there are two basic options of interaction between law and economic theory: law either defines itself 'through a specific object, approached in an interdisciplinary fashion' or it 'makes use of a hermeneutical and textual programme which is not [its] own'.[12]

The increasing influence of economic discourse was particularly felt in the area of competition law. Its main tenets and principles witnessed a profound transformation from a systematic recourse to neoclassical price theory as an external source of authority.[13] More than in any other field of law, except perhaps the related area of public utilities law, competition law is intrinsically linked with the discipline of economics, as is shown by the frequent references to economic concepts and methods in the decisional practice of the competition authorities; the case law of the courts; and the expanding soft law related to the interpretation of the competition law statutes.[14] A common feature of this transformation of competition law is the emphasis put on a, mostly synchronic, analysis of the welfare effects of the specific commercial practice on consumers or more broadly economic efficiency. This is the main thrust of the 'more economic', 'effects-based approach'[15] that gained momentum in European

[11] RH Coase, 'The Problem of Social Cost' (1960) 3 *Journal of Law and Economics* 1–44. This was not necessarily what R Coase himself had in mind, as he had recognized elsewhere the importance of institutions in economic theorizing. RH Coase, 'The Nature of the Firm' (1937) 4 *Economica* 386–405. One should wait the new institutional school of economics for institutions to be again the subject of mainstream economic theory: O Williamson, *Markets and Hierarchies: Analysis and Antitrust Implications* (The Free Press, 1975).

[12] G Samuel, 'Is Law Really a Social Science? A view from comparative law' (2008) 67(2) *CLJ* 288–321, 296, quoting J-M Berthelot, *Épistémologie des sciences sociales* (Presses Universitaires de France, 2001).

[13] I Lianos, *La Transformation du droit de la concurrence par le recours á l'analyse économique* (Bruylant/Sakkoulas, 2007).

[14] On the influence of economics on law more broadly, see WM Landes and RA Posner, 'The Influence of Economics on Law: A Quantitative Study' (1993) 36 *Journal of Law & Economics* 385–424.

[15] On this terminology and the opposition of 'effects-based' to 'form-based' approach see, 'Report by the EAGCP: on An Economic Approach to Article 82

competition law with the reform of merger control regulation, Article 81 EC and most recently Article 82 and State aids control. An important part of the evidence presented in competition law disputes is of an economic nature, such as consumer surveys, simulation techniques and economic models.

But economic theory is not only relevant for the adjudication of evidence in specific competition law disputes. It has also been increasingly relevant at the 'doctrinal stage' if one follows Ronald Dworkin's conceptualization of four stages in legal reasoning, to which it could be helpful to refer in order to define the scope of this chapter.[16] Dworkin distinguishes the semantic stage (which relates to the general assumptions and practices people share over the concept of law, for example, criterial, interpretive, natural), the jurisprudential stage (the development of a theory of law that is appropriate given the theorist's answer at the semantic stage, in other words, the development of the values justifying a specific legal practice), the doctrinal stage (where we construct an account of the truth conditions of propositions of law in the light of the values identified in the jurisprudential stage), and the adjudicative stage (where judges or decision-makers adopt propositions of law based on the conclusions reached at the doctrinal stage).

For example, the economic efficiency versus justice debate that permeates the question of the objectives of competition law belongs to the jurisprudential stage as it refers to the values (external in this case) that should provide content to the principle of coherence in legal interpretation. This important topic will be outside the scope of this chapter, which will instead attempt to focus on the implications of an external approach on the doctrinal stage. It will be claimed that an important implication of the second generation of interaction between law and economics is the emergence of economic transplants, that is, economic concepts that are 'translated' into the legal system at the doctrinal stage. These concepts also contribute to the influence of economics at the adjudicative stage. The claim is that the paradigm of translation is the most adequate explanatory framework for taking into account the dual nature of economic transplants in envisioning the interpretative strategy that should be employed. It can also serve, more

EC (July 2005) available at <http://europa.eu.int/comm/competition/publications/studies/eagcp_july_21_05.pdf> 2, 7.

[16] R Dworkin, *Justice in Robes* (Harvard University Press, 2006) 9–21.

broadly, to conceptualize the interaction of law with other social sciences. The first section of this chapter will introduce the paradigm of translation, which will set the broad theoretical framework of this study: a relation between law and economics marked by linguistic and conceptual hospitality. The second section will apply this framework to competition law by identifying the main characteristics of economic transplants and by distinguishing them from other forms of integration of economic concepts in law. The third section will discuss the interpretative techniques that preserve the specific characteristics of economic transplants and, more broadly, avoid any risk of hegemonic or deferent translation of economic concepts in law. The last section will conclude.

The 'Paradigm' of Translation

The term 'translation' characterizes the process of integration of economic concepts in law in the form of economic transplants. A prerequisite for translation is the existence of different languages.[17] One could follow Saussure and distinguish the terms language (*langue*) and discourse or use of the language (*parole*).[18] However, this study will assume that language and discourse are intrinsically linked to each other for reasons that will be exposed in the following section. If one takes this position, the concept of translation is an appropriate term to use for my purposes. I will first explore if law and economics are two separate languages (or discourses) before examining the concept of 'translation', as a form of communication between different systems of discourse.

Law and Economics Use Distinct Languages/Discourses

The term 'translation' should be understood as referring to a mode of external inter-linguistic communication. In his remarkable treatise *After Babel*, George Steiner adopts a wide definition of the term:

> . . . any model of communication is at the same time a model of translation, of a vertical or horizontal transfer of significance. No two historical epochs, no

[17] P Ricoeur, *On Translation* (translated by E Brennan) (Routledge, 2006) 2.
[18] F de Saussure, *Course in General Linguistics* (1915).

two social classes, no two localities use words and syntax to signify exactly the same things, to send identical signals of valuation and inference. Neither do two human beings.[19]

If a human being performs an act of 'translation', in the full sense of the word, when receiving a speech-message from any other human being, the concept has little interest for my purposes. I will therefore adopt a narrower definition of the term which will cover only *inter-lingual translation or translation proper.*[20] I employ the term 'inter-lingual' because what matters is the fact that the target language is a different language and/or discourse than the source language. It will be thus important to determine the relation of distinctness or strangeness (*alterité*) that exists between the separate languages/discourses of law and of economics.

One could determine the existence of two different languages/discourses by identifying two separate communities employing a distinct style of talk. One could identify a language community by the distinct techniques its members use from other communities. Economics has only relatively recently (since the end of the 18th century) been recognized as a different scientific discipline when it was gradually transformed from moral philosophy to political economy.[21] In his monumental *History of Economic Analysis*, Joseph Schumpeter famously asked 'is economics a science?', before answering that 'since economics uses techniques that are not in use among the general public, and since there are economists to cultivate them, economics is obviously a science within our meaning of the term'.[22] He identified these techniques as being essentially three: economic history, statistics and theory (explanatory hypothesis) to which he added in a later edition of his volume economic sociology, which form, what he calls, 'economic analysis'. These tools frame the style of talk that distinguishes the scientific economist from all other people who think, talk and write about the same (economic) topics.

This group has not always employed that specific style of talk. Schumpeter remarked that jurisprudence is relevant to a history of economic analysis first of all because, to a considerable extent,

[19] G Steiner, *After Babel* (Oxford University Press, 1975) 46.

[20] Following the typology of R Jacobson, 'On Linguistic Aspects of Translation' in R Brower (ed) *On Translation* (Harvard University Press, 2000) 232–9, 233.

[21] RA Backhouse, *The Ordinary Business of Life: A History of Economics from the Ancient World to the Twenty-First Century* (Princeton University Press, 2004) 132.

[22] J Schumpeter, *History of Economic Analysis* (Routledge, 1994) 10.

economists have been jurists 'who brought to bear the habits of the legal mind upon the analysis of economic phenomena'; He gave the example of the sociological and economic systems of the scholastic doctors of the 16th century which were 'primarily treatises on the political and economic law of the Catholic Church' and whose technique 'was derived primarily from the old Roman law as adapted to the conditions of the time'.[23] However, in many respects, the style of talk of this community of scholars evolved differently from that of those self-defined as jurists.

During the period Schumpeter wrote his treatise the tool of statistics was a language not employed by the community of lawyers, which made Schumpeter conclude that it was a distinguishing element. But is this still the case today? A more diachronic approach will indicate that statistics have now become a tool of legal scholarship (empirical legal studies). Can we therefore still claim that law and economics employ two different languages? Or, has the style of talk of economists, evolved so that the language of law and the language of economics still remain distinct from each other?

Schumpeter was telling only part of the story. Starting with the programme of 'social mathematics' of Condorcet,[24] (political) economists such as Canard, Cournot, Bertrand, Walras, Jevons, Edgeworth, Marshall and their followers, progressively recognized mathematics as the predominant style of talk of the community self-defined as economists.[25] Of course, the tool of mathematics has greatly evolved since the calculus used by Cournot to game theory and topography but the hypothetico-deductive system of mathematics forms the backbone of 'scientific' discourse in economics. In her seminal study of the 'rhetoric of economics', Deirde McCloskey observes that 'the economic conversation has heard much eloquent talk, but its most eloquent passages have been mathematical'.[26] Since the 1930s, economists have become enchanted by this 'scientific' way of thinking. The alliance of mathematical economics and neoclassical price theory in the 1950s, with the development of a mathematical proof of the general equilibrium

[23] Ibid, 24 fn 2.

[24] KM Baker, *Condorcet: From Natural Philosophy to Social Mathematics* (University of Chicago Press, 1975).

[25] See A Vazques, 'Marshall and the Mathematization of Economics' (1995) 17 *Journal of the History of Economic Thought* 247–65.

[26] D McCloskey, *The Rhetoric of Economics* (2nd edn, University of Wisconsin Press, 1998) 139.

theory, still dominates, in some respects, the field—at least economic theory applying in competition law.[27] The same trend towards mathematization can be observed in other social sciences during the same period, a by-product of the diffusion of game theory.[28]

Not everyone in economics agrees with this particular trend. Tony Lawson has in fact defined the '*nature of heterodox economics*' in opposition to economic orthodoxy or mainstream economics that he closely identified to the 'mathematising inclination' or the formalistic-deductive framework of mathematics.[29] One could distinguish, for reasons of conceptual clarity, the claim of mathematization and that of formalism of economic analysis.

Economic theory followed closely mathematical developments, starting 'with the elements of differential calculus and linear algebra and that gradually called on an ever broader array of powerful techniques and fundamental results offered by mathematics'.[30] In his seminal analysis of the evolution of Walrasian general equilibrium theory, Ali Khan observes the influence of the mathematical tools that were progressively integrated and have framed economic theory.[31] Khan notes that the evolution of economic theory was a function of the new tools that mathematics developed from differential calculus to convex analysis and non-smooth analysis.[32] The integration of convex analysis led to game theory and further developments in the field.[33] Debreu gives the example of non-standard analysis to claim that 'the lag between the date of a mathematical discovery and the date of its application to economic theory decreased over time'.[34] One could thus expect the evolution of economic theories, once new developments in mathematics are translated into the language of economics. Mathematics becomes the *Reine sprache* of economics and a means of dialectic interaction between the community of mathematicians and that of

[27] YP Yonay, *The Struggle over the Soul of Economics* (Princeton University Press, 1998) 187–190; G Debreu, 'Theoretic Models: Mathematical Form and Economic Content', (1986) 54(6) *Econometrica* 1259–70.

[28] AM O'Rand, 'Mathematizing Social Science in the 1950s: The Early Development and Diffusion of Game Theory' (1992) 24(Supplement) *History of Political Economy* 177–204.

[29] T Lawson, 'The Nature of Heterodox Economics' (2006) 30 *Cambridge Journal of Economics* 483–505, 488.

[30] G Debreu, 'The Mathematization of Economic Theory' (1991) 81 *American Economic Review* 1–7.

[31] M Ali Khan, 'The Irony in/of Economic Theory', (1993) 108(4) *Modern Language Notes* 659–803, at 784–85.

[32] Ibid, 778–81.

[33] Debreu, n 27 above, 1261.

[34] Debreu, n 30 above. 3.

mathematical economists,[35] the new guardians of the economics Temple. Mathematics ensures precision and openness to scrutiny for logical errors. It is *par essence* a universalistic language, closely related to the imaginary construction of 'economic physics' and its ideal of a 'unified science'.[36] It is allegedly ideology free.[37]

Yet, the translation of mathematics into economics is not without important implications on the content of economics. The translator moves from one linguistic medium to another. It serves two masters: the source language and the target language. There is a risk that the form of one language influences/deforms the content of the message transmitted by the other. It is impossible to avoid a tension between economic content and mathematical form. The only partial cure is the 'axiomatization' of the theory. Debreu explains that:

> (a)n axiomatized theory first selects its primitive concepts and represents each one of them by a mathematical object. [. . .] Next assumptions on the objects representing the primitive concepts are specified, and consequences are mathematically derived from them. The economic interpretation of the theorems so obtained is the last step of the analysis. According to this schema, an axiomatized theory has a mathematical form that is completely separated from its economic content. If one removes the economic interpretation of the primitive concepts, of the assumptions, and of the conclusions of the model, its bare mathematical structure must still stand.[38]

Indeed, the mathematical inclination of economics transposes itself to the use of models and formalization.[39] 'Theory means models and models mean ideas expressed in mathematical form (language)'.[40] Although one cannot deny that there are different discourses in economics (some of them declining the use of mathematics, such as the Austrian school) and that even in mainstream economic theory there is

[35] Debreu, n 27 above, 1263 explains: '(a)s new fields of mathematics were introduced into economic theory and solved some of its fundamental problems, a growth-generating cycle operated. The mathematical interest of the questions raised by economic theory attracted mathematicians who in turn made the subject mathematically more interesting'.

[36] BP Stigum, *Towards a Formal Science of Economics: the Axiomatic Method in Economics and Econometrics* (Cambridge University Press, 1990).

[37] Debreu, n 27 above. [38] Ibid. 1265.

[39] HKH Woo, *What's Wrong with Formalization in Economics: An epistemological critique* (Victoria Press, Newark, CA, 1986).

[40] D Strassmann, 'Feminist Thought and Economics; Or, What Do the Visigoths Know?' (1994) *American Economic Review, Papers and Proceedings* 153–158, 154 cited by Lawson, n 29 above, 490.

diversity of styles of talk, the mathematizing inclination is certainly a common feature of modern economics. Heterodox economics' slow integration to the mainstream paradigm follows the pace of their conversion to the mathematizing inclination.

This axiomatization may be understood as a response to the absence of 'a secure empirical base', which may have led economic theory to emphasize 'internal logical consistency', through 'methodological formalization'.[41] Formalism could in this case take the form of 'self-contained rule following', which would employ formal language and 'deductive systems that are independent of content'.[42] The recourse to the concept of equilibrium[43]; the divorce until recently of the study of economic behaviour from behavioural sciences' input[44]; or the 'narrowness of *homo economicus*'s concerns (the assumed separability of economics from politics and social philosophy, the absence of altruism, the lack of context) constitute the side effects of this axiomatization and formal logic.[45] Contrary to 'axiomatic reasoning', 'ordinary reasoning' authorizes 'several different starting points, each impinging on the subject from a different angle and bringing different knowledge to bear'.[46]

The fact that mathematics constitutes the language of economics has profound implications on the story of economics, that is, economic discourse. What is formalizable can be subject to economic inquiry; what is not, is excluded from the focus of the discipline. Debreu observed that as 'the very choice of the questions to which he (the theorist) tried to find answers is influenced by his mathematical background', 'the danger is ever present that, economics will become secondary, if not marginal, in that judgment'.[47] In other words, the

[41] RE Backhouse, 'If Mathematics is Informal, Then Perhaps We Should Accept that Economics Must Be Informal Too' (1998) 108 *The Economic Journal* 1848–58, 1857, building on Debreu, n 31 above, 2.

[42] V Chick, 'On Knowing One's Place: The role of formalism in economics' (1998) 108 *The Economic Journal* 1859–69, 1859.

[43] V Mosini (ed), *Equilibrium in Economics – Scope and Limits* (Routledge, 2006).

[44] For an interesting analysis see, D Wade Hands, 'Introspection, Revealed Preference and Neoclassical Economics: A Critical Response to Don Ross on the Robbins-Samuelson Argument Pattern' (2008) 30(4) *Journal of the History of Economic Thought* 453–78.

[45] Chick, n 42 above, 1862.

[46] Ibid

[47] Debreu, n 30 above, 4. This problem is not confined to economic theory but also extends to applied economics, econometrics, etc. See the discussion of statistical versus economic significance in D McCloskey and S Ziliak, *The Cult of Statistical Significance* (University of Michigan Press, 2007).

natural constraints of the language restrict the topics of conversation, its narrative. This is a profound consequence of modernist thought of which economics is a step-child. Modernism views science as axiomatic and mathematical. In the modernist view, considerations of efficiency and justice should be separated: 'they form churches with separate devotees: each can specialize in one kind of argument . . . But arguments do not cross: this year's GNP is one thing; an axiom of social choice is another; sympathy for the poor still another'.[48]

Modernist tradition is also present in legal discourse. How could one otherwise understand the fury with which arguments of economic efficiency were welcomed by some quarters in legal academia?[49] The value of economic efficiency was dismissed and ridiculed. Efficiency talk was wrong, a utilitarian blasphemy in the Temple of Justice.[50] The fact that this efficiency talk was coming from apostates, lawyers converted to economic discourse, who were suspected of ideological bias, their efficiency talk allegedly being a scientific masquerade of a profoundly libertarian political agenda, served to conceal the essence of the argument. To the rhetoric of numbers and optimization, lawyers responded by the rhetoric of values and morality, using their favorite weapons, those of hermeneutics.[51] But in essence, their argument had also a profound modernist taste: law is about justice, not about efficiency; these concepts should be separated. If efficiency was not to be a valuable consideration, it was probably because law did not have the adequate language to apprehend it without risking a profound reconsideration of its internal values and premises. These values are allegedly wider than those traditionally pursued by neoclassical economic theory. The increasing anxiety with which evidence law scholars reacted to the introduction of probability theory and methods of mathematical proof in evidence theory may also illustrate how issues of discourse and language are interrelated with each other.[52]

[48] D McCloskey, *The Rhetoric of Economics* (University of Wisconsin Press, 1985) 6.

[49] Efficiency was also criticized from the point of view of economics, notably from law and economics scholars members of the Austrian school which emphasizes dynamic process instead of a static approach: M Rizzo, 'The Mirage of Efficiency' (1980) 8 *Hofstra Law Review* 641–651.

[50] See the discussion in 'Symposium on Efficiency as a Legal Concern' (1980) 8 *Hofstra Law Review* 485– 770.

[51] eg, see R Dworkin, 'Why Efficiency?' (1980) 8 *Hofstra Law Review* 563–9; R Dworkin, 'Is Wealth a Value?' (1980) 9 *Journal of Legal Studies* 191–226.

[52] L Tribe, 'Trial by Mathematics' (1971) 84 *Harvard Law Review* 1329.

Deductive reasoning and abstraction is certainly not absent from legal discourse. The positivistic model of law aimed to transform the discipline to a proper scientific field. The search for coherence in law participated to this 'quest for natural science status'.[53] Geoffrey Samuel convincingly argues that 'the association of law with scientific rationality', a legacy of civilian legal history, 'marks an epistemological shift' and could be understood as a quest for a new source of authority, other than the authoritative texts of Roman law: '[. . .] for the jurists who succeeded the medieval doctors one part of the authority was to be found in the 'scientific' or systematic coherence of law because this rationality provided not just the deductively valid solutions but, in doing this and thus freeing judging from subjective bias, the very authority that gave law its validity'.[54] 'Law was a system, analogous to mathematics, consisting of axioms from which all other norms, together with the solutions to case law problems, could be logically deduced'.[55] Christopher McCrudden also notes how 'legal academics are constantly constructing explanatory "models" from the legal material at their disposal, models that they then test against that legal material'.[56] Nevertheless, the movement of axiomatization and formalism in law has never achieved the perfection and success it has achieved in economics. What some authors mocked as the 'Heaven of legal concepts'[57] where prediction, the cornerstone of scientific pretense, of how courts decide cases was finally possible through abstract analysis and deductive thinking, was quickly shattered by the challenge of *Interessenjuriprudenz*[58] and the functionalism of the realist movement.[59] Mathematics could never become the language of law.

The different techniques/styles of talk employed by the communities of lawyers and economists inevitably led to their perception as forming separate social sub-systems. This is a profoundly constructivist approach. The idea of social construction of reality is not also absent

[53] Samuel, n 12 above, 294. [54] Ibid. 295. [55] Ibid. 312.

[56] McCrudden, n 6 above, 634.

[57] R von Jhering, 'In the Heaven for Legal Concepts: A Fantasy' (translated by CL Levy) 58 *Temple Law Quarterly* 799–842 (first published as 'In Juristischen Begriffshimmel: ein Phantasienbild' in *Scherz und Ernst in der Jurisprudenz* (Leipzig, 1885).

[58] See O Jounjan, *Une histoire de la pensée juridique en Allemagne* (Presses Universitaires de France, 2005).

[59] W Twining, *Karl Llewellyn and the Realist Movement* (Fred B Rothman & Co: Hackensack, New Jersey, 1973); G Samuel, 'Can Legal Reasoning Be Demystified?' (2009) 29(2) *Legal Studies* 181–210, 205–6.

from systems theory or autopoietic theory,[60] Scientific knowledge, as any other knowledge is being shaped in a complex social process. It is, therefore, equally important to examine how scientific knowledge is actually constructed[61] and follow rigorously the historical development of theories[62], in order to convey the deep sense of the translated discourse than to adopt an approach purely internal to the discourse. The development of a discourse supposes the existence of a shared meaning and common beliefs in different communities forming different social sub-systems. One could indeed conceptualize the domains of law and economics as two distinct self-contained and self-referential autopoietic social systems or sub-systems (if one looks to their common origins in moral philosophy[63]), employing a distinct style of talk/rhetoric. For example, the concept of rationality could take a different form in the context of economic discourse than in legal discourse.[64] A characteristic of autopoietic systems is that communications occur mainly within the system itself, not with the outside world.[65] "Society is seen as fragmented into a multiplicity of closed communicative networks", each network constructing "a reality of its own".[66] One way to conceive this it is to think of the existence of different conversations going on at the same time within different groups of interlocutors. Once the conversations get started they have their own script, which participants of other groups that may occasionally participate in these conversations cannot alter.

Nevertheless, each sub-system does not ignore all others, nor is there always a situation of incommensurability between the two discourses.

[60] eg, see N Luhmann, *Law as a Social System* (Oxford University Press, 2004) ch 2 referring to the operative closure of the legal system.

[61] J Law, 'Theories and Methods in the Sociology of Science: An Interpretative Approach' (1976) 13 *Social Science Information* 163.

[62] eg, see A Pickering (ed), *Science as Practice and Culture* (University of Chicago Press, 1992).

[63] Adam Smith's economic thought was only a part of a broader moral philosophy project: see J Evensky, *Adam Smith's Moral Philosophy: A Historical and Contemporary Perspective on Markets, Law, Ethics, and Culture* (Cambridge University Press, 2005).

[64] Rationality is a product of 'situational analysis'. It is content-empty as it 'is merely the assumption that a person will act adequately or sensibly, given his or her goals and the situation': WA Gorton, *Karl Popper and the Social Sciences* (State University of New York Press, 2006) 8.

[65] See, the studies included in G Teubner (ed), *Autopoietic Law: A New Approach to Law and Society* (de Gruyter, 1988).

[66] G Teubner, 'How the Law Thinks: Towards a Constructivist Epistemology of Law' (1989) 23 *Law and Society Review* 727, 738.

Autopoietic social systems are cognitively open to their environment, despite being normatively closed.

More concretely, the self-containedness of autopoietic social systems means that foreign discourse cannot enter directly into the script/programme of another conversation. 'Each system reconstructs its own image of the external system within itself'.[67] This preserves the complexity of each environment but may also lead to incommensurability, because of different sets of normative values that operate within each system ('environment') that blur understanding and communication without the necessary coding. The development of some degree of incommensurability between the two discourses is inevitable. A normative closure and areas of untranslatability emerge.[68] However, interpenetration ensures that each system will be cognitively open: legal and economic discourses may mutually influence each other. As Deirdre Dwyer explains, 'this would mean that one believes that it is possible to agree on statements about the external world with people from another social group, but that statements about values cannot be directly translated'.[69]

It follows that the interaction between each system does not take only one direction, for example, economics influence law but that legal discourse should also influence the production and directions of economic discourse, as it is always the case for interpenetrating systems. Luhmann explains that, 'interpenetrating systems exist when this occurs reciprocally, that is when both systems enable each other by introducing their own already constituted complexity into each other'.[70] Interpenetration is of course a matter of degree and may follow specific cycles, for example, although early jurists played an important role in formulating the methods of different social sciences,[71] including political economy, this was followed by a period where each community of scholars evolved differently.

A possible explanation of this different direction could be the different 'paradigms', that is the 'epistemological orientation', 'kinds of reasoning'[72] or 'a body of attitudes or behaviour'[73] of the main actors

[67] D Dwyer, *The Judicial Assessment of Expert Evidence* (Cambridge University Press, 2008) 126.

[68] Ibid, 125.

[69] Ibid, 115.

[70] N Luhmann, *Social Systems* (Stanford University Press, 1995) 213.

[71] eg, see D Kelley, *The Human Measure: Social Thought in the Western Legal Tradition* (Harvard University Press, 1990).

[72] Samuel, 'Can Legal Reasoning Be Demystified?', n 59 above, 182.

[73] Ibid, 204.

of each discipline: social sciences allegedly follow a paradigm of inquiry that 'subjects research to means of validation' (or falsification if one follows Popper), while law embraces an 'authority paradigm', 'in which epistemological validity arises not from scientific inquiry but uniquely from authority'.[74] The sources of this authority have obviously changed and consist of the ideal of legal coherence based on some from of textual reference, *Grundnorm* or some principle of moral philosophy, even to the price of some distance from social reality.

However, even if one adheres to this broad description, it is clear that the principle of coherence is also of central importance to axiomatized modern economics. Empiricism and falsification are largely absent from economic theory. Much of economic theory is not based on empirical research but on 'a fairly abstract, sometimes unverifiable, and largely mathematically derived conclusions about human behaviour'.[75] The dominant paradigm in economic theory remains Friedman's instrumentalism, where the only validity test is the comparison of predictions with experience.[76] What counts is the theory's predictive adequacy and simplicity, not necessarily the correspondence of its assumptions with reality. The 'paradigm of authority' therefore plays a central role in economics as well. Furthermore, such a sharp dichotomy between the 'authority paradigm' and the 'paradigm of inquiry' ignores the fact that judges will also 'be sensitive to the consequences of any decision'.[77] The expectation exists that a court's decisions should be perceived not only as epistemologically true (ie as some sort of justified (true) belief) but also as persuasive, even to actors outside the legal sub-system.

In other words, what matters for a legal system's legitimacy is that those subject to the judicial decisions believe that the court adequately

[74] Ibid.

[75] H Hovenkamp, 'Economic Expertise in Antitrust Cases' in DL Faigman, DH Kaye, MJ Saks and J Sanders (ed) *Modern Scientific Evidence: The Law and Science of Expert Testimony* (2nd edn, West Group, 2002) 723.

[76] M Friedman, *Essays in Positive Economics* (University Chicago Press, 1953) 40, '[A] theory cannot be tested by comparing its "assumptions" directly with "reality". Indeed, there is no meaningful way in which this can be done. Complete "realism" is clearly unattainable, and the question whether a theory is realistic "enough" can be settled only by seeing whether it yields predictions that are good enough for the purpose in hand or that are better than predictions from alternative theories. Yet the belief that a theory can be tested by the realism of its assumptions independently of the accuracy of its predictions is widespread and the source of much of the perennial criticism of economic theory as unrealistic. Such criticism is largely irrelevant, and, in consequence, most attempts to reform economic theory that it has stimulated have been unsuccessful'.

[77] Samuel, n 59 above, 207.

explained its decision so that the losing party recognizes it as 'a valid', yet unfavourable, 'exercise of judicial authority'.[78] The accent is put more on the process of decision-making, rather than on the outcome, seen from the point of view of some external reality or principle. Outcomes certainly matter and the perception that a legal rule leads to unacceptable consequences, in terms of public policy, could eventually lead to its revision. However, the law's authority is not directly linked to the acceptability of such outcomes, from an external, to the discipline, for example public policy, perspective.

But legal reality cannot entirely 'immunize itself against conflicting realities produced by other discourses in society'.[79] This is the consequence of 'interference', the 'mutual diffusion of law and other social sciences'; As Teubner explains, '[. . .] juridical constructs are exposed to the constructs of other discourses in society [. . .] (t)hey are exposed to a test of "social coherence" that replaces the old fiction of a test of correspondence with outside reality'.[80] Indeed, 'legal discourse is supposed to incorporate social knowledge into its world constructions and permanently revise legal models of social reality according to the accumulation of knowledge in the social sciences'.[81]

One could advance a similar point with regard to economic theory, where outcomes outside the strict confines of the discipline do not matter. For example, one of the aims of the ordinalist revolution in economics was to clear economics from any reference to psychological assumptions: the concept of cardinal utility was abandoned and replaced by the concept of a scale of preferences.[82] This was linked to a shift in the acceptable methods of observation. In the words of Lionel Robbins, 'valuation is a subjective process. We cannot *observe* valuation. It is therefore out of place in a scientific explanation. Our theoretical constructions must assume observable data'.[83] The rejection of cardinal utility led also to the extrusion from economic analysis of behaviourist psychology, a 'queer cult'.[84] The question that economics should attempt to answer was, according to Robbins, 'choice under scarcity', scarcity being 'the scarcity of given means for the attainment of <u>given</u> ends'.[85] The agent's preferences are a 'given' which economists

[78] RB Katskee, 'Science, Intersubjective Validity, and Judicial Legitimacy' (2008) *Brooklyn Law Review* 857–77, 861. [79] Teubner, n 66 above, 745.

[80] Ibid. [81] Ibid, 747.

[82] P Baert, *Philosophy of the Social Sciences* (Polity, 2005) 150.

[83] L Robbins, *An Essay on the Nature and Significance of Economic Science* (2nd edn, London, 1945) 87. [84] Ibid

[85] Ibid, 46. Emphasis added.

have to identify in order to analyze consumer choice. The concept of revealed preferences further attempted to ground the theory of consumer behaviour on observable concepts and to suppress any reference to psychology and introspection.[86] The models established lacked, however, any correspondence to reality and were proved ultimately inapt (and illegitimate) for public policy prescription, an area where the role of economists was expanding.[87] This led contemporary economic theory to attach greater attention to inputs from psychology.[88] The psychological trend that is witnessed in many recent economic movements, such as behavioural law and economics; experimental economics; and neuro-economics transforms economics into a sort of cognitive science, where economic behaviour is reconceived on the basis of 'psychological facts' discovered with the method of experimental introspection. Economics and economists are in search of new sources of translation than mathematics and the more 'reality-proof' cognitive sciences constitute a popular candidate. The advanced hypothesis is that economics becomes more reactive to the pressure of reality the more it attempts to occupy the terrain of policy prescription and analysis and produces consequences to actors outside the specific sub-system. This pressure is not yet as strong as that generally faced by the legal system, but it may explain the importance attached by recent economic theory to more realistic assumptions.[89] In conclusion, the authority versus inquiry dichotomy does not take into account the broad social context of the evolution of social sciences.

One should also take into account the fact that the 'quest for truth' has a different purpose in science (social science included) than it has in the law and the courtroom[90], which might explain the different evolution of each separate sub-system. It is thought that the objective of

[86] For a criticism, see S Wong, *The Foundations of Paul Samuelson's Revealed Preference Theory: A study by the method of rational reconstruction* (Routledge, 1978).

[87] The expansion of economics as the main source of wisdom for competition law and consequently the role of economic consultants in competition policy analysis and prescription can be well illustrated with the rise of economic consultancies in competition law practice: see D Neven, 'Competition Economics and Antitrust in Europe' (2006) *Economic Policy* 741–56.

[88] For an overview see D Kahneman, 'A Psychological Perspective on Economics' (2003) 93 *American Economic Review* 162.

[89] eg, see GA Akerlof, 'The Missing Motivation in Macroeconomics' (2007) 97(1) *American Economic Review* 5–36.

[90] As the US Supreme Court noted in *Daubert v Merrell Dow Pharmaceuticals*, 509 US 579, 597 (1993), 'there are important differences between the quest for truth in the courtroom and the quest for truth in the laboratory'.

the scientific method is not to legitimate the power of scientists but to increase the stock of 'objective knowledge', in other words to discover more about the world. In contrast, the quest for 'truth' in the courtroom is to arrive at an ultimate, in the sense of persuasive, explanation, in terms of legitimate exercise of authority.[91] Ultimate explanations exist in the sense that they are defined by the courts.[92] This is not the case in the process of scientific discovery as 'every explanation may be further explained', in the sense that a known state of affairs may always be explained by an unknown state of affairs.[93] In other words, 'objectivity' and 'truth' may be the aim of both the scientific and the legal process but the nature of 'objectivity' or 'truth' that they aim to uncover is of a different kind.

Once we accept that law and economics form two distinct subsystems in interaction with each other, it is important to discover how interconnection and cognitive openness operate between them.

First, one could argue that when an autopoietic system of discourse is brought into being, it brings with it some of the elements of broader social discourse that it made use of before it became normatively and operationally closed. If we prefer this metaphor, it is possible to argue that all of us participate in different conversations or games at the same time. The participants to these different conversations (an individual can belong to more than one discipline) may bring to the conversation information acquired from other social sub-systems in which conversations they also participated.[94] This is how facts, concepts, methodologies and theories may spread over time from one specialist system into another or into society in general.[95] This establishes the ground rules of social communication between the different systems, a kind of

[91] As it is also recognized by the US Supreme Court in *Daubert v Merrell Dow Pharmaceuticals*, 597, '(s)cientific conclusions are subject to perpetual revision. Law, on the other hand, must resolve disputes finally and quickly. . . We recognize that in practice, a gatekeeping role for the judge, no matter how flexible, inevitably on occasion will prevent the jury from learning of authentic insights and innovations. That, nevertheless, is the balance that is struck by Rules of Evidence designed not for the exhaustive search for cosmic understanding but for the particularized resolution of legal disputes'.

[92] Katskee, n 78 above, 861.

[93] N Rescher, *The Limits of Science* (University of Pittsburgh Press, 1999) 136.

[94] F Ost and M Van de Kerchove, *Le Droit ou Les Paradoxes du Jeu* (Presses Universitaires de France, 1992).

[95] For a number of empirical studies documenting, among others, how facts and evidence claims travel between social sciences as well as over time, see the interdisciplinary project 'The Nature of Evidence: How Well Do 'Facts' Travel' available at <www.lse.ac.uk/collections/economicHistory/Research/facts/Default.htm>.

meta-language. The existence of a *tertium comparationis* or metalanguage is also a common feature of some theories of translation. Walter Benjamin defended the view that translation implies a pure language (*reine Sprache* or Mentalese) which will allow the passage from language A to language B by ensuring that both are equivalent to an expression in metalanguage C[96]. Chomsky's 'generative grammar'[97] derives from a similar intellectual tradition, what Ost perceptively titles '*Babel aboli: langues parfaites et autres langues imaginaires*'.[98] One could subject this view to criticism, as it is possible to argue that in order to decide if A and B are similar in meaning to a text in language C, one needs a new metalanguage D, etc . . . (the 'Third Man Argument').[99]

Secondly, some could argue that language and discourse are marked by the relations between power, hegemony and authority represented in the different sub-groups: translation is thus more than a simple technical exercise of transfer of meaning.[100] Some actors in several subsystems may acquire a specific status or power in the host system and they are then able to be perceived as the 'official' translators of cognitive signals coming from the exterior, and thus influence the choice of which source language to translate. Would antitrust have evolved differently if a sociologist or a behavioural social scientist was appointed Assistant Attorney General with responsibility for antitrust regulation instead of economist Donald Turner in 1965—Turner being instrumental in the inception and publication of the 1968 merger guidelines: the first systematic application of economic concepts in antitrust law enforcement? Laurence Sullivan once wondered about the existence of different sources of wisdom in antitrust than economics and has offered a possible alternative,[101] thus demonstrating that economics should not be the only source of (external) wisdom for competition law. As

[96] W Benjamin, 'The Task of the Translator' (1969) (translated by H Zohn) in L. Venuti (ed) *The Translation Studies Reader* (Routledge, 2000) 15–25, 21, 'a real translation is transparent; it does not cover the original, does not block its light, but allows the pure language as though reinforced by its own medium to shine upon the original all the more fully'.

[97] N Chomsky, *Aspects of the Theory of Syntax* (MIT Press, 1965) 3.

[98] F Ost, *Traduire—Défense et Illustration du Multilinguisme* (Fayard, 2009) 67–105.

[99] U Eco, *Experiences in Translation* (University of Toronto Press, 2001) 12.

[100] See, in particular, A Gramsci and MM Bahktin. For an analysis see P Ives, *Gramsci's Politics of Language: Engaging the Bakhtin Circle and the Frankfurt School* (University of Toronto Press, 2004) ch 2.

[101] L Sullivan, 'Economics and More Humanistic Disciplines: What Are the Sources of Wisdom for Antitrust? (1977) 125(6) *University of Pennsylvania Law Review* 1214–43.

Gunther Teubner observes, 'economic rationality does not have the privilege of society-wide institutionalization all to itself'.[102] The issue is not to eliminate 'moral-political monotheism, in favour of economic monotheism which law needs only to reflect' but 'to change from monotheism to polytheism, from the monotheism of modern rationality to a polytheism of the many discourses'.[103]

In conclusion, autopoietic theory brings attention to the separate beliefs that may animate the actors of the different sub-systems. These may be the consequence of the specific limitations of their language techniques and consequently the story and script of their conversation. One could, therefore, distinguish between legal and economic discourses: in the sense that the topics examined and the style of the conversation differs in each discipline. It follows that the meaning of a term/statement may be different if one takes it in isolation from the conversation to which it is integrated. I could give the example of polysemic concepts, such as 'property rights', which are present in the vocabulary of both disciplines but have a different meaning. This is more the object of the study of pragmatics (which examines the influence of context on the interpretation of an utterance) than of translation which, I should first hypothesize, emphasizes the transfer of meaning from one language/discourse to the other with the aim of equivalence in meaning (ie deep sense).

The Aim of Translation

If translation refers to a transfer of meaning/significance from a source language to a target language, its aim is to convey meaning, to express the deep sense of a *parole* (discourse). In that sense, the act of translation is a concept different from the act of communication or distorted communication, which does not necessarily involve the objective of the transfer of meaning or deep sense. No one shows this better than Lewis Carroll in *Alice Adventure's in Wonderland*. The beings inhabiting that country understand Alice's language, more or less, but the inhabitants of that place do not engage in meaningful (in terms of structured) exchanges with each other. Opposing this world to the paradigm of argumentation that he advances, Chaim Perelmann observes that

[102] G Teubner, '*Altera Pars Audiatur*: Law in the Collision of Discourses', in R Rawlings (ed), *Law, Society and Economy* (Oxford University Press, 1997) 149, 150.
[103] Ibid

'between Alice and the inhabitants of Wonderland, no hierarchy, precedence, or functions requires one to answer rather than another. Even those conversations that begin are apt to break off suddenly'.[104]

One could also distinguish translation from interpretation. Translation can be considered as a limited type, 'a species of interpretation governed by certain principles proper to translation'.[105] Interpretation involves a certain degree of correspondence to the original text, a constraint that is not faced by translation. In translation, there can be no correspondence between the two texts. George Steiner notes that:

> . . . the complete translation, the definitive insight and generalization of the way in which the translated language relates word to object would require a complete access to it from the translator. The latter would have to experience a total mental change'.[106]

It follows that there is no identity between the language source and the language target: there is rather some loose sort of equivalence of meaning. The translator is therefore free to change the story (content). She must decide what is the fundamental content conveyed. As Eco explains, 'in order to preserve a deep story, the translator will be entitled to change the surface one'.[107] Translation is a form of 'intersystemic interpretation with marked variations in the substance of the expression'.[108] Nothing better illustrates that than the translation of the title of Umberto Eco's book *Experiences in Translation* from Italian to French and to English. The title of the book in Italian is '*Dire quasi la stessa cosa, esperienze di traduzione*', which was translated in French '*Dire presque la même chose: Expériences de traduction*'. The first part of the title has disappeared in the English edition. This shows that translation is '*dire PRESQUE la même chose*' (Emphasis added). Translation involves a constant negotiation between different meanings without aiming to correspondence of meaning. Once one renounces to the 'very ideal of the perfect translation' the 'work of mourning' begins, that is exposing oneself to the 'test of the foreign'.[109]

But if translation does not aim to formal correspondence (in both form and content), what constitutes its aim? A possible option

[104] C Perlemann, *New Rhetoric* (University of Notre Dame Press, 1969) 15.

[105] Eco, n 99 above, 80: in the sense that translation is 'the outcome of an interpretative inference (a bet on the sense of a text) that can or cannot be shared by other readers (ibid, 16).

[106] Steiner, n 19 above, 309.

[107] Eco, n 99 above, 31.

[108] Ibid, at 106.

[109] Ricoeur, n 17 above, 23.

could be 'dynamic equivalence' that is, 'equivalence of response' or 'conformance' of the translation to the receptor language and culture as a whole'.[110] It is thus possible that the aim ('*skopos*') of the translator is to reach 'a set of addresses' in the target culture: 'the target text [. . .] is oriented towards the target culture, and it is this which ultimately defines its adequacy'. It follows that 'source and target texts may diverge from each other quite considerably, not only in the formulation and distribution of the content but also as regards the goals which are set for each, and in terms of which the arrangement of the content is in fact determined'.[111] Reflecting on our discussion of the interaction between law and economics, this indicates that the quest for correspondence/equivalence of the economic concept integrated in legal discourse with some ideal form of 'sound economics' is a futile exercise. The domestication of the foreign text is not without limits. The translator mediates between the author and the reader: 'to translate is to serve two masters: the foreigner with his work, the reader with his desire for appropriation'.[112] In some instances, the translation will maintain the foreign character of the translated message by indicating its linguistic and cultural differences from the culture of the target language (foreignizing translation).

In essence, the aim of the translation is to link two heterogeneous communities around the translated text. Its aim is to foster 'a community of readers who would otherwise be separated by cultural differences' but also to establish 'a community that includes foreign intelligibilities and interests, an understanding in common with another culture, another tradition'.[113] The objective of economic transplants is, therefore, to create this 'linguistic zone of contact between the foreign and translating cultures',[114] in our case between the rhetoric of law and the rhetoric of economics. A consensus has thus to be built between all discourse participants (lawyers and economists) in order to determine true from false statements.

110 E Nida, 'Principles of Correspondence' in L Venuti (ed), *The Translation Studies Reader* (Routledge, 2004) 153–67, 163.

111 HJ Vermeer, 'Skopos and Commission in Translational Action' in Venuti, n 96 above, 227–38, 229. Translation is not 'trans-coding', a procedure which is 'retrospectively oriented towards the source text, not prospectively towards the target culture' and thus 'diametrically opposed to the theory of translational action'.

112 Ricoeur, n 17 above, 4.

113 L Venuti, 'Translation, Community, Utopia' in Venuti, n 96 above, 482–502, 491.

114 Ibid.

The Emergence of Economic Transplants in Competition Law

Having defined the meaning of translation, this chapter will now analyze the interaction between legal and economic discourse in the area of competition law from the perspective of the paradigm of translation. This will begin with an examination of the different forms that may take the incorporation of economic discourse into legal discourse, before focusing on a specific form—economic transplants—which fits perfectly with the paradigm of translation that came to be exposed.

The Many Faces of Economic Analysis in Competition Law

The judge or legal decision-maker has different options in the incorporation of economic analysis into legal discourse.

He may choose to delegate the translation task to an 'expert', someone who is well versed into the economic discourse, who will attempt to provide an explanation of its deep meaning to the judge. The task of translation will be performed by an expert witness, a court-appointed expert, an assessor, or a single joint expert. The 'epistemic asymmetry'[115] that exists between the judge and the economic expert renders it necessary to delegate the translation task to the expert. The judge recognizes that the concept belongs to a different discourse, that of economics, and makes no effort to domesticate it within his own discourse. There are many reasons why a judge will decide to appeal to an 'expert' of economic discourse.

Economic discourse constitutes an importance source of inspiration and authority for the judge in enforcing competition law ('economic authority'). For example, one of the major implications of the evolution of competition law towards an economic approach has been the importance of normative economic arguments and theories for the interpretation of what constitutes a restriction of competition. The terms 'restriction of competition'; 'abuse of dominant position'; or 'significant impediment of effective competition' have no content on their own unless the interpreter has recourse to certain economic considerations, such as consumer welfare; economic efficiency; unilateral

[115] S Brewer, 'Scientific Expert Testimony and Intellectual Due Process' (1998) 107 *Yale Law Journal* 1535–681, 1586 (referring to the concept of 'epistemic deference').

effects; coordinated effects; collusion; etc. The judge needs, therefore, to have access to economic expertise, which will give this body of law its muscle.

It is clear that the judge will be influenced by economic authority as well as by legal precedent in enforcing the competition law provisions. This is particularly the case in situations where there is no consensus in the legal or in the economic community over the adequate competition law standard that will apply to a business practice. Chicago theories about economic efficiency gains; the post-Chicago theories of anticompetitive harm for vertical mergers and foreclosure, such as raising rivals costs theory; and theories about incentives to innovate are increasingly framing the debate over the adequate competition law standards for certain commercial practices. The Courts look implicitly or explicitly 'to economic authority in order to establish antitrust authority as a matter of law'.[116]

However, one should not conceive economic discourse as being marked by uniformity but as a discourse characterized by numerous sub-discourses, schools, theories etc. Often, these theories rest on first assumptions for which there is no consensus in the self-defined community of 'economists'. The choice of the expert will therefore have important implications on the act of translation. As indicated previously, each translation will be different as it is the outcome of an interpretative inference that can, or cannot, be shared by everyone. Each translator will inevitably emphasize different parts of the original discourse.

The recent US Supreme Court case in *Leegin* on the continuous validity of the per se interdiction rule for resale price maintenance may illustrate the variety of translations and therefore the difficulty of the task of the judge.[117] During the oral hearing, an interesting dialogue occurred between Theodore Olson, appearing for *Leegin*, and Justice Breyer. Olson claimed that it will only be in an economic context where retailers dispose of a strong market power that resale price maintenance will most likely lead to anticompetitive effects. He based his argument on the Chicago school's assumption that the interest of supplier and consumers are always aligned and on the need to preserve

[116] A Gavil, 'Competition Policy, Economics and Economists: Are We Expecting Too Much?' in B Hawk (ed), *1998 Fordham Corporate law Institute – International Antitrust Law and Policy* (1999) 575, 579.

[117] *Creative Leathers Products, Inc v PSKS, Inc*, 127 S Ct 2705 (2007).

a dealer's promotion efforts from free-riding. This assumption has been questioned by a number of other economists who claim that vertical restraints and, in particular, resale price maintenance, may lead to consumer harm.[118] Justice Breyer, a fine connoisseur of antitrust and regulatory economics, was quick to observe:

Breyer: 'Which economists? I know the Chicago school tends to want rule of reason and so forth. Professor Sherer is an economist, isn't he? Worked at the FTC for a long time? A good expert in the field . . . And his conclusion is, as in the uniform enforcement of resale price maintenance, the restraints can impose massive anti-consumer benefits. Massive . . .'

Olson: 'In the vast majority of the economist who have looked at this have come out to the opposite conclusion, Justice Breyer.'

Breyer: 'We're supposed to count economists? Is that how we decide it? (Laughter)'.[119]

One could understand the challenges of decision-making on the basis of conflicting economic expertise that follows different assumptions and different inferences. Because of the epistemic asymmetry problem, the judge is not able to assess, by her own, the 'loyalty' of the translation to the original. It is also not clear how the 'loyalty' of the translation will be examined, if it is not by another expert, which inevitably will raise the 'Third Man Argument' (for example, a third expert to verify the loyalty of the second expert's decision over the loyalty of the first one and so on). Loyalty may also matter a little, at the end, if one perceives the two discourses as separate, closed sub-systems. But we know that, in reality, this is not the case. The choice of a specific economic discourse by the legal system will have profound implications on the conversation that takes place between economists by conferring on some schools the authority and support of the legal apparatus and weakening others by rendering more difficult the recruitment of devotees to their church.

In other circumstances, the judge will not have to choose between different translations, as there is a broad consensus in economic discourse. This is particularly the case for 'economic facts': statistical data (firms' sales, turnover, sales in the industry, economies of scale, etc) or economic concepts widely used by the profession, such as opportunity

[118] See, WS Comanor, 'Vertical Price Fixing – Vertical Market Restrictions and the New Antitrust Policy' (1985) 98 *Harvard Law Review* 983–1002.

[119] US Supreme Court No 06/480 (26 March 2007). Oral argument transcript available at <http://www.supremecourtus.gov/oral_arguments/argument_transcripts/06-480.pdf> 7.

costs, variable costs, fixed costs, average avoidable costs, incremental costs, etc. These data are based on observations, which are ultimately theory laden.[120] There is, however, generally a broad consensus between economic experts on their meaning. This consensus does not include the inferences that are drawn from the data by the use of statistical methodology, in other words, the concept of economic facts includes descriptive statistics but excludes inferential statistics.[121] The involvement of the judge is limited in these cases to the decision to take into account this economic context in the qualification of the facts of the case. If the judge decides to take into account the economic context of the dispute, these economic facts will be established empirically by experts. The degree of epistemic asymmetry will reach its peak: the expert does not only have superior knowledge, in comparison with the judge, of the statistical methods that will be used to collect and to present the data but has also spent time in collecting and associating these specific data to the economic context of the particular dispute.

One could also identify circumstances where economic theories are universally accepted not only by the overwhelming community of economists but have been incorporated into the general social system: 'economic laws'.[122] The layman or non expert judge comprehends their meaning without any need for translation. These concepts form part of the common code of the legal and economic sub-systems. In the most extreme scenario, economic laws are well enshrined in all different forms of discourse and take the form of 'common sense'. For example, the idea that market power may produce allocative inefficiency is based on the perfect competition model, which could be conceived as a specific expression of the economic law of supply and demand. As Mark Blaug remarks in his *Methodology of Economics*, this is not a natural law, like the Universal Law of Gravitation, which can be tested (Blaug

[120] Observation is always informed by theory: E Beecher-Monas, *Evaluating Scientific Evidence* (Cambridge University Press, 2007) 37–9 (noting the social construction of scientific 'facts').

[121] Descriptive statistics describe the data (including concepts such as standard deviation, etc). Inferential statistics are used in drawing conclusions/inferences about the general population from a single study: ibid, 60.

[122] The distinction between economic 'facts' and 'laws' follows the pattern of the traditional 'fact/law' classification in legal thought: C Morris, 'Law and Fact' (1942) *Harvard Law Review* 1303, 1315, 'facts are transitory and particular', law is the opposite. This classification may be criticized, as facts relate to values and laws are not independent of facts (eg statistical laws). One should not thus consider that economic facts and laws are ultimately of a different kind.

adopts a Popperian perspective), but relies instead on hypothesis and assumptions such as the 'Invisible Hand', the rationality postulate, and constitutes a partial model of equilibrium. Economic laws may be subject to questioning by contrary empirical evidence. For example, recent advances in experimental economics demonstrate that real consumers are sometimes guided by their perceptions of fairness rather than by economic factors such as marginal utility, even when they make clear economic choices.[123]

However, despite these challenges, economic laws form part of general experience and there is no need for them to be established and explained by experts. Epistemic asymmetry between the judge and the expert is in this case minimal, almost non-existent. One could advance that these economic laws are integrated at the jurisprudential stage or, as Learned Hand called them, 'general truths derived from specialized experience'.[124] One could certainly question the universal validity of these general 'truths'. These economic laws form, however, an indistinguishable part of the legal and economic nexus. For example, theories that question the 'economic law' of supply and demand will have little chance of being accepted as valid economic authority in competition law. The judge will automatically exclude this type of economic expertise, based on her experience of the tensions that would exist between this economic testimony and the basic assumptions that lay the economic foundations of the legal system.

Economic Transplants in Competition Law

The task of translation may not be entirely delegated to an expert economist but part of it could be accomplished by the legal decision-maker/judge. This constitutes an important characteristic of economic transplants. Economic transplants also convey the decision to integrate explicitly economic analysis, not only at the adjudicative stage (as was the case with economic facts and economic authority) but also at the doctrinal phase, where they operate as guiding principles for all decisions adopted at the adjudicative stage. This chapter will now examine the emergence of economic transplants before analyzing the reasons

[123] M Rabin, 'Incorporating fairness into game theory and economics' (1993) 83(5) *American Economic Review* 1281–1302.

[124] L Hand, 'Historical and Practical Considerations Regarding Expert Testimony' (1901) 15 *Harvard Law Review* 40–58, 54.

that explain why the effort of translation has not been entirely delegated to experts.

The Emergence of Economic Transplants

The term 'economic transplants' refers to any concept of economic discourse that has been incorporated into legal discourse by an act of translation performed by an organ vested with the authority to adjudicate and capable, therefore, of producing an impact on the interpretation of legal norms. Economic transplants constitute, in most cases, analytical concepts (such as market power, barriers to entry, consumer welfare, efficiency gains) that are essential intermediary steps in the process of qualification of the facts of the case as constituting, for example, a restriction of competition, under Article 81 of the EC Treaty, or an abuse of a dominant position, under Article 82 of the EC Treaty. Economic transplants are most frequently incorporated in legal discourse by soft law instruments, such as guidelines. Eleanor Fox's aphorism 'the guidelines are when economists are kings' provides an adequate explanation for the role of soft law.[125] Economic transplants are not usually incorporated for the first time in hard law instruments, such as regulations, which employ instead descriptive, not analytic, concepts (such as market shares, the latter being proxies for the concept of market power).[126]

This situation should be distinguished from all those where expert economic evidence 'crystallizes into legal standards that are applied in subsequent cases'.[127] Barbier de la Serre and Sibony give the example of the concept of collective dominant position, framed progressively by the case law on the basis of economic evidence presented to the European Courts on the theory of tacit collusion. It is important to observe that the Courts did not adopt the economic concept of tacit collusion but preferred instead to develop a new legal concept, collective dominant position, thus breaking any link between this new concept and its economic underpinnings. This is not the case for economic transplants,

[125] E Fox, 'The 1982 Merger Guidelines: When Economists are Kings?'(1983) 71 *California Law Review* 281–302, 281.

[126] eg, see Commission Regulation (EC) 2790/1999 of 22 December 1999 on the application of Art 81(3) of the Treaty to categories of vertical agreements and concerted practices [1999] OJ L336/21; Commission Notice on Guidelines on Vertical Restraints [2000] OJ C291/1 (hereinafter 'Guidelines on Vertical Restraints').

[127] E Barbier de la Serre and A-L Sibony, 'Expert Evidence Before the EC Courts' (2008) *Common Market Law Review* 941–85, 969.

where the choice of an equivalent denomination to that employed in economic discourse emphasizes the economic origins and nature of the transplant. One could consider that this choice indicates a canon of interpretation addressed to the legal community—do not ignore that this concept also belongs to a separate discourse! The recent effort by the European Commission to integrate, as a substitute or complement to collective dominance, the economic concept of coordinated effects indicates that economic transplants are here to stay. This led to a dialogue between the European Commission and the European courts, which are less prompt to integrate economic discourse, most probably because of their composition by lawyers only. The Courts attempted to integrate the economic transplant of coordinated effects into their own legal concept of collective dominant position, without abandoning the later.

An interesting feature of economic transplants is that their interpretation is not always consistent with the exact meaning of the concept in economics. In that sense, they share a common characteristic with the concept of 'legal transplants'.

For Alan Watson, as legal systems develop, they are constantly borrowing concepts or approaches from other legal systems.[128] This possibility is denied by Pierre Legrand for whom legal rules may travel but legal meanings and cultures do not.[129] At best, these concepts take on a form and life of their own, as they are immersed into their receiving environments.[130] The concept of economic transplants refers to a borrowing of economic concepts through an act of translation. However, for any good translation, even if there is some degree of equivalence between the language *hospes* and the *hostis*, there may be important differences: as Umberto Eco illustrated *a propos* of the translation of his novel, *The Name of the Rose*, the same Italian text may be translated differently in Russian, German or French.[131] The economic transplant takes a different form as soon as it is translated: its content evolves separately than in its original setting, and it evolves in congruence with the context of its host language.

[128] A Watson, *Legal Transplants: An Approach to Comparative Law* (2nd edn, University of Georgia Press, 1993)

[129] P Legrand, 'The Impossibility of Legal Transplants' (1997) 4 *Maastricht Journal of European Comparative Law* 111–24.

[130] A Watson, *Law Out of Context* (University of Georgia Press, 2000); P Legrand and RJC Munday (ed), *Comparative Legal Studies: Traditions and Transitions* (Cambridge University Press, 2003).

[131] Eco, n 99 above, 28–9.

In competition law, economic transplants were predominantly integrated by instruments of soft law (Guidelines).[132] This followed the path of US antitrust law. Starting with the 1968 Guidelines on Merger Enforcement, US antitrust law integrated different economic concepts that became influential in framing antitrust law discourse in courts.[133]

Hillary Greene's important study on the institutionalization of US merger guidelines in antitrust discourse provides an excellent example of the integration of economic transplants through the instrument of guidelines.[134] Greene gives the example of concentration measures in merger control in order to illustrate the impact of the guidelines. Prior to, and shortly after, the 1968 US Guidelines on merger control, the Courts employed the four-firm ('CR4') concentration measure in merger analysis, representing the sum of the market shares for the four largest firms in the market.[135] In 1982, the Department of Justice revised its 1968 guidelines and introduced a new measure of concentration, the Herfindahl-Hirshman Index ('HHI'), which is the sum of the squares of the market shares of the firms present in that market.[136] Hillary Greene observes that the HHI index had been discussed in economic circles, since at least the early 1960s,[137] when George Stigler published his seminal work on oligopoly theory,[138] and that it 'became part of the mainstream legal literature' following the suggestions of the law professor, then judge, Richard Posner.[139] She observes, however, that the case law on section 7 of the Clayton Act[140] ignored the HHI index until the 1982 Guidelines were adopted.[141] Prior to that date, case law was written almost entirely in terms of CR4 or other

[132] P Areeda, 'Justice's Merger Guidelines: The General Theory' (1983) *California Law Review* 303–10.

[133] The 1968 Guidelines were the intellectual child of Donald Turner, the first PhD economist to be appointed Assistant Attorney General for Antitrust and a key figure in the reorientation of antitrust law in the US towards an economic approach in the 1960s. See O Williamson, 'The Merger Guidelines of the US Department of Justice—In Perspective' available at <http://www.usdoj.gov/atr/hmerger/11257.htm#N_1_>.

[134] H Greene, 'Guideline Institutionalization: The Role of Merger Guidelines in Antitrust Discourse' (2006) 48(3) *William & Mary Law Review* 771–857.

[135] US Department of Justice, 'Merger Guidelines: 1968' reprinted in (1968) 4 *CCH Trade Regulation Report*, 13, 101.

[136] US Department of Justice, 'Merger Guidelines: 1982', reprinted in (1982) 4 *CCH Trade Regulation Report* 13,102.

[137] Greene, n 134 above, 788.

[138] G Stigler, 'A Theory of Oligopoly' (1964) 72(1) *Journal of Political Economy* 44–61, 59.

[139] RA Posner, 'Oligopoly and the Antitrust Laws: A Suggested Approach' (1969) 21 (6) *Stanford Law Review* 1562–606, 1602–3.

[140] 15 USC § 12.

[141] Greene, n 134 above, 789.

concentration ratios. Immediately after the adoption of the 1982 Guidelines, a transition period started during which both CR4 and HHI concentration measures were relied on by the courts, although the later gained a progressively more important role.[142] She also notes the important increase in the rate of references to the Guidelines since the early 1970s. In conclusion, the adoption of a new version of the Guidelines profoundly influenced the direction of the case law (hard law). According to Greene:

> . . . from around 10–15% in the 1970s the reference rate increased to 15-20% in the late 1970s and early 1980s. In 1983 shortly after the adoption of the 1982 Guidelines were issued, the reference rate increased to above 50% and by the late 1980s the rate averaged 60% or higher. After the 1982 Guidelines were issued, merger guidelines quickly became the 'basic reference point' in section 7 Clayton Act rulings'.[143]

The Small but Significant Non Transitory Increase in Price test ('SSNIP') illustrates also the role of guidelines in transplanting an economic concept in legal discourse.[144] The test measures cross-price elasticity between two products through a speculative experiment postulating a hypothetical small but lasting change in relative prices (5–10 per cent) and evaluating the likely reactions of customers to that increase. The test was first developed by American economist Morris Adelman in an article published in a legal journal in 1959[145] and then reformulated by American economist FM Scherer in an expert testimony he presented at the Federal District Court for the Eastern District of Michigan during April 1972 before including this test in the 1980s edition of his industrial organization textbook.[146] The test found its way in official antitrust legal discourse when economist Lawrence White used it in the 1982 Department of Justice Merger Guidelines, in his capacity of chief economist of the Department of Justice Antitrust Division.[147] This proved extremely influential in US courts which, prior to the 1982 Guidelines, were employing in merger control the definition provided by the *Brown Shoe* case law of the Supreme Court, which emphasized

[142] Ibid, 790–1. [143] Ibid, 802–3. [144] Ibid, 796–8.

[145] MA Adelman, 'Economic Aspects of the Bethlehem Opinion' (1959) 45 *Virginia Law Review* 684–96, 688.

[146] FM Scherer, 'On the Paternity of a Market Delineation Approach' (2009) available at <http://ssrn.com/abstract=1337079>.

[147] L White, 'Present at the Beginning of a new Era for Antitrust: Reflections on 1982-1983' (1999) New York University Center for Law and Business, Working Paper No 99-005 available at <http://papers.ssrn.com/sol3/papers.cfm?abstract_id=167208>.

functional characteristics for market definition.[148] Since 1982, cross-price elasticity and the SSNIP test gradually acquired prominence in US merger control discourse before migrating to Europe.

The European Commission referred to cross-price elasticity in its *Eurofix-Bauco v Hilti* decision in 1987.[149] The decision was later reviewed by the European Court of Justice.[150] The Commission argued that its emphasis of cross-price elasticity was a 'synthesis of all the factors that determine whether or not two different products can properly be said to be in the same relevant market, according to the previous case law of the Court'.[151] The ECJ repeated its previous case law emphasizing product characteristics and interchangeability (a functional approach based on its *Continental Can* case law[152]) but found the Commission's decision 'sufficiently clear and convincing' to carry its belief.[153] The SSNIP test had been employed in other occasions by the Court,[154] before it was formally incorporated by soft law at a doctrinal stage in 1997,[155] as the first step of the 'modernization' effort of EC competition law: in other words, the attempt to put EC competition law in conformity with neoclassical price theory and economics, in the late 1990s.[156] The Courts' reaction was not initially very positive. In *Colin Arthurs Roberts*, the applicants argued that consumers distinguish between pubs and clubs based on the difference of the price of beer (the price of beer in bars is 82–3 per cent of the price of beer in clubs) which demonstrated, according to them, that consumers of beer in pubs will not switch to consume beer in clubs if there was an hypothetical increase of the price by 5–10 per cent.[157] The applicants relied on the Commission's Market Definition Notice. The Court rejected this argument and although it cited the Notice, it also considered the previous case law on market definition in the beer sector (the *Delimitis*

148 *Brown Shoe Company v United States*, 370 US 294 (1962).

149 Decision (EEC) 88/138, *Eurofix Bauco v Hilti* [1988] OJ L 65/19, para 73.

150 Case T-30/89, *Hilti AG v Commission* [1991] ECR II-1439.

151 Ibid, para 55.

152 Case 6/72 *Continental Can v Commission* [1973] ECR 215, para 32.

153 Case T-30/89, n 150 above, para 70.

154 eg, see Case T-83/91 *Tetra Pak International SA v Commission* [1994] ECR II-755, paras 67–8; Case C-333/94 *Tetra Pak International SA v Commission* [1996] ECR I-5951, para 16.

155 Commission Notice on the Definition of Relevant Market for the Purposes of Community Competition Law [1997] OJ C 372/5, para 17.

156 For a critical assessment see Lianos, n 13 above, 163–290.

157 Case T-25/99, *Arthur Roberts and Valérie Ann Roberts v Commission* [2001] ECR II-1881, para 20.

case) which emphasized structural factors.[158] For the Court, the applicants relied on the single criterion of price difference and disregarded a specific feature of the sale of beer, which is that 'consumption of beer in establishments selling it for consumption on the premises does not depend essentially on economic considerations' but is influenced 'primarily by their environment and atmosphere'.[159]

However, the Court has, in subsequent cases, explicitly and systematically cited the Commission's Notice, in particular in the merger area, but also beyond.[160] There are now an increasing number of cases where the Courts adopted the SSNIP definition (see Table 1) culminating in 2006–8 towards an institutionalization of the SSNIP test as the main test for market definition in the case law of the Court. The Commission has also incorporated in its Notice the so-called

Table 1: SSNIP test by competition law area

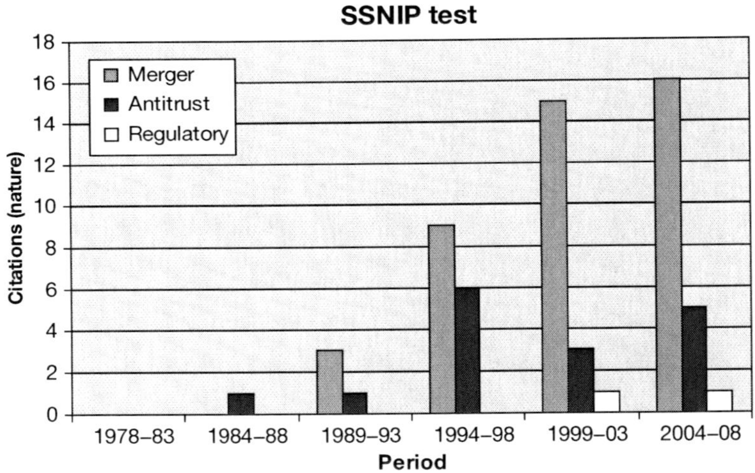

[158] Case C 234/89, *Stergios Delimitis v Henninger Brâu AG* [1991] ECR I-935.

[159] Case T-25/99, n 157 above, para 40.

[160] eg, see Case T-342/99, *Airtours plc v Commission* [2002] ECR II-2585, para 45; Case T-210/01, *General Electric Co v Commission* [2005] ECR II-5575, para 477; Case T-177/04 *Easyjet Airline Co Ltd v Commission* [2006] ECR II-1931; Case T-340/03, *France Télécom SA v Commission* [2007] ECR II-107, para 86; Case T-201/04, *Microsoft Corp v Commission* [2007] ECR II-3601, para 484.

'cellophane fallacy', which advises against employing an SSNIP test based on prevailing market prices for abuse of dominance cases, as 'the prevailing price has been determined in the absence of sufficient competition'.[161]

In conclusion, economic transplants should be distinguished from economic authority. One of their important features is that the legislator (an actor of the legal sub-system) defines their content and use, while at the same time the legislator notes the foreign character of the concept, by employing the same term as that employed in economics. This emphasizes their dual nature, in other words, their mutual appurtenance to the separate sub-systems of law and economics, which provides important guidance for the interpretation of these concepts. But, it may also explain how the same economic concept may take various forms when immersed in different legal systems. With regard to the SSNIP test, the European legislator defined the percentage of price increase that has been since employed for the hypothetical experiment

Table 2: SSNIP test in general

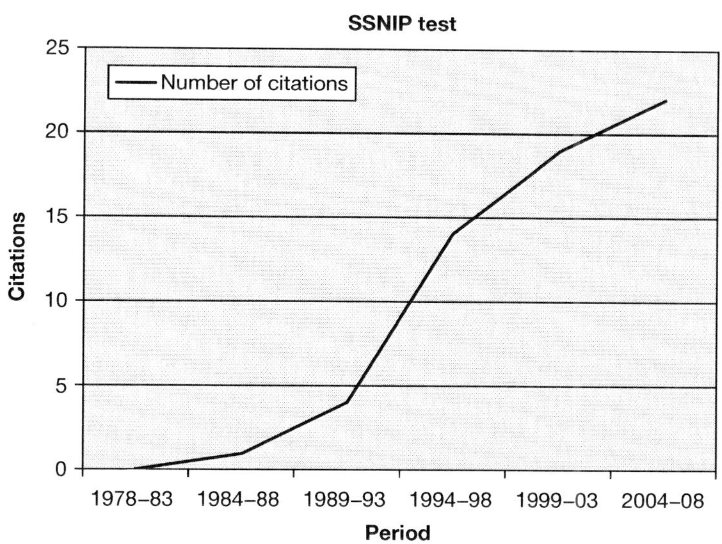

[161] Commission Notice on the definition of relevant market, n 155 above, para 19.

(5–10 per cent)[162] at a different level than that chosen by the US legislator (5 per cent),[163] although it is not clear if the SSNIP test requires a relative increase in the price of one, some or all of the products in the candidate market (aggregate diversion ratio) in the case of multi-product firms[164] and there is considerable variation of the emphasis given to supply or demand-side factors in practice.[165] These differences are often motivated by policy motives which are external to economic discourse. The policy-maker may aim to favour infra-marginal, instead of marginal, consumers thus adopting a lower threshold for market definition, generally, or in certain specific circumstances.[166]

But why doesn't the policy-maker or legal adjudicator delegate the task of translation to an external (to the legal system) expert, as is the case for economic authority?

Economic Transplants and the Translator's Aim

Economic transplants have a dual nature. They belong to both legal and economic discourses. This constitutes the principal motivation for their adoption: the aim is to build a bridge with a 'foreign' culture, a shared space between the distinct communities of lawyers and economists and inscribe the concept with the intelligibilities of both discourses. Establishing this shared understanding supposes a link between the legal process and the scientific process.

Sheila Jasanoff observes how the interaction between legal and scientific discourse does not take only one direction (for example, economics

[162] Ibid, para 17.

[163] US Department of Justice and Federal Trade Commission, 'Horizontal Merger Guidelines: 1992', reprinted in 4 *CCH Trade Regulation Report* 13,104, although it is also mentioned that 'what constitutes a 'small but significant and nontransitory' increase in price will depend on the nature of the industry, and the Agency at times may use a price increase that is larger or smaller than five percent'.

[164] For a discussion, see Ø Daljord, L Sørgard and Ø Thomassen, 'The SSNIP test and market definition with the aggregate diversion ratio: A reply to Katz and Shapiro'(2008) 4(2) *Journal of Competition Law and Economics* 263–70; A Ten Kate and G Niels, 'The Relevant Market: A Concept Still in Search of a Definition' (2008) 5(2) *Journal of Competition Law and Economics* 297–333.

[165] MB Coate and JH Fischer, 'A Practical Guide to the Hypothetical Monopolist Test for Market Definition' (2007) Potomac Papers in Law and Economics 06-01, available at <http://ssrn.com/abstract=940667>.

[166] See Competition Commission, *The Supply of Groceries in the UK Market Investigation*, available at <http://www.competition-commission.org.uk/rep_pub/reports/2008/fulltext/538.pdf>, 4.11, '(g)iven the importance of groceries expenditure in the household budget, we think that the appropriate price increase for assessing the relevant market for the supply of groceries is likely to be less than 5 per cent'.

influence law) but legal discourse or legal institutions also influence economic discourse.[167] She eloquently highlights how 'the law today not only interprets the social impacts of science' but also 'constructs' the very environment in which scientific discourse comes to have 'meaning, utility, and force'.[168] Research is conducted and interpreted to answer legal questions and the content of scientific knowledge is shaped in a complex social process, which includes the legal sub-system as well as the specific scientific discourse. Judicial decision-making exercises an important influence on the definitions of 'good science', therefore affecting at the same time the content and direction of economic doctrine.

An illustration of the profound interaction between legal and economic discourses is the emergence of economic 'schools of thought', a way to conceptualize and rationalize *ex post* legal doctrine and authority in the area of competition law. If explanatory features of economic discourse, such as schools of economic thought, become also explanatory features of legal discourse, this strongly illustrates the profound interaction and mutuality between these two forms of discourse in competition law. This approach of conceptualizing the evolution of competition law doctrine indicates that institutionalized 'schools' or 'networks' play an important role in antitrust law, if not always, during the process of formation of competition law doctrine, at least at the stage of the *ex post* conceptual rationalization of the case law and, therefore, its subsequent interpretation.

It follows that the decision by the legal decision-maker to maintain authority by incorporating the economic transplant into the legal discourse (and therefore not by delegating the authority to 'external' experts) is explained by a broader regulatory aim: impact as much as possible on the evolution of both legal and economic discourses. But what, more precisely, would be the regulatory aims followed by the legal translator?

First, with regard to the impact on legal discourse, the translator may attempt to distinguish the specific transplant from an existing economic transplant incorporated into the legal system of another jurisdiction. In other words, the aim of the translator is to render explicit the specific objectives followed by her legal system. This implies that, as for legal transplants, economic transplants do not have a similar

167 Sheila Jasanoff, *Science at the Bar* (Harvard University Press, 1997)
168 Ibid, 16.

content when incorporated in different legal systems, even if the economic concept from which they both originated is similar.

Secondly, with regard to the impact of the translation on economics, the translator may also wish to preserve the variety of economic discourse: in other words to preserve her legal system from the influence of a dominant trend in economics which, for different reasons, does not address or does not correspond to the objectives (preferences) of her legal system or, more broadly, is so dominant that it suppresses any other competing form of discourse within economics (in case the regulator values diversity and competition in economic theory)[169]. In this case, the regulatory intervention will aim to preserve variety in the marketplace of ideas.

The Impact of Economic Transplants on Legal Discourse

Economic transplants are often preferred to economic authority, as they enable the integration in economic discourse of the objectives of the specific legal system, in comparison with other legal systems. In this case, the definition of the content of the transplant, or even the form of integration, may indicate the specific nature of the economic transplant, in comparison to similar economic transplants integrated in other legal systems. The economic transplants of 'market power' and 'consumer welfare' exemplify this impact.

Market Power

The integration of the concept of market power in competition law is an illustration of the growing importance of economic transplants in competition law discourse. The following tables make more explicit the expansion of the concept of market power, measured by the total number of citations to 'market power' in court cases, Commission's decisions, guidelines and regulatory texts relevant to competition law (based on research conducted with Westlaw and LexisNexis).

The next table details these citations according to the area of competition law. The concept of market power plays a dominant role in the area of merger control. The reduction of the number of citations of the concept of market power in cases or documents related to antitrust

[169] On the risks of 'monoculture' in competition economics, see O. Budzinski, 'Monoculture Versus Diversity in Competition Economics' (2008) 32 *Cambridge Journal of Economics* 295–324.

Table 3: Market power

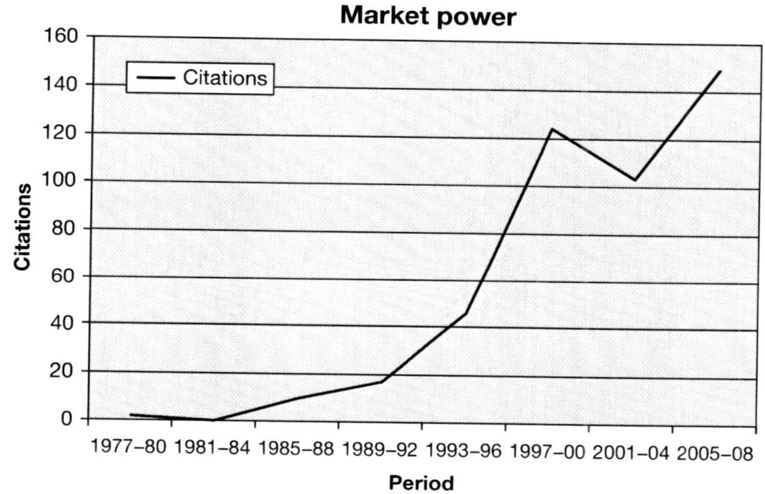

(Articles 81 and 82 of the EC Treaty) does not mean that the relative importance of the concept has decreased in this area. What has decreased is the number of total competition law cases based on Articles 81 and 82 of the EC Treaty brought by the European Commission during that period (in particular during the period 2002–4, probably as a result of the economic crisis following the dot-com bubble burst in 2001) and the decentralization of competition law enforcement during that period.

An interesting feature of economic transplants is that their interpretation is not always the exact same meaning of the concept in economics. A typical example of this asymmetry is the different conceptions of market power in competition law and in economics.[170]

The neoclassical definition of market power has always focused on the ability of a firm to raise prices profitably and to reduce output, based on the conception of competition as an efficient outcome,[171],

[170] For a further analysis see Lianos, n 13 above, 328–84.

[171] For an interesting comparison of the different original definitions of market/monopoly power in law and in economics, see E Mason, 'Monopoly in Law and Economics' (1937) 47 *Yale Law Journal* 34–49.

Table 4: Market power by area of competition law

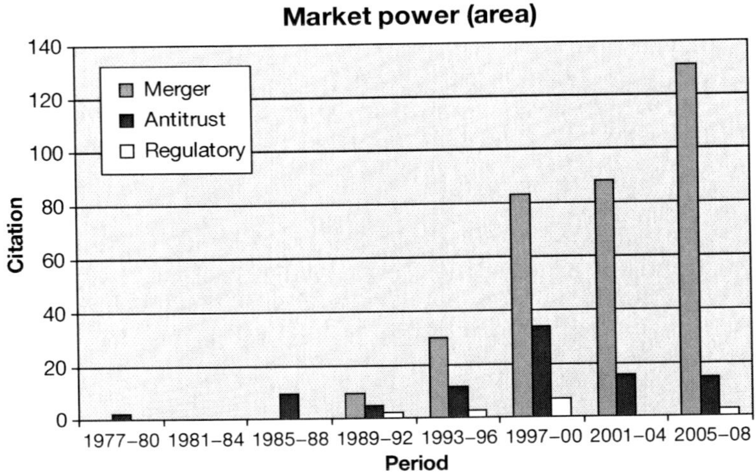

whereas the legal definition of market/monopoly power has always emphasized the ability of the firm to exclude competitors and to affect the competitive process, a definition that fits well with the competition as a process of rivalry paradigm.[172]

The concept of dominant position in EC competition law has been predominately inspired by the second approach, as it insists on the ability of the firm to maintain independent behaviour from the other actors of the market system rather than on market outcomes. The classic definition of the concept of dominant position within the

[172] See M Blaug, 'Competition as an End-State and Competition as a Process' in M Blaug (ed) *Not Only an Economist: Recent Essays by Mark Blaug* (Edward Elgar, 1997). One could also note that this definition of market power is also compatible with the emphasis given by the Structure-Conduct-Performance school, the dominant school of neoclassical economic analysis in competition policy during this period, to barriers to entry: see J Bain, *Barriers to New Competition* (Harvard University Press, 1956). The Chicago school's emphasis on allocative efficiency and the more restrictive definition of the concept of barriers to entry they adopted widened the distance between the legal and the economic conception of market power, see RH Coase, 'Industrial Organization: A Proposal for Research,' in V Fuchs (ed) *Policy Issues and Research Issues in Industrial Organization: Retrospect and Prospect* (National Bureau of Economic Research, 1972) 59–73.

meaning of Article 82 is found in the ECJ's judgment in the *United Brands* case, and refers to:

> . . . a position of economic strength enjoyed by an undertaking which enables it to prevent effective competition being maintained on the relevant market by giving it the power to behave to an appreciable extent independently of its competitors, customers and ultimately of consumers.[173]

The broad definition of dominant position as essentially an ability of independent behaviour enabled the Court to consider a variety of sources of economic power, including the power to exclude competitors (exclusionary economic power) or purely relational economic power because of the existence of a situation of economic dependence.[174]

The position of EC competition law has nevertheless evolved towards more convergence with an outcome based approach. Article 2 of the former EC Merger Regulation 4064/89 employed the concept of dominant position but linked it more directly than the previous case law on Article 82 of the EC Treaty to the concept of effective competition.[175] In order to define the existence of effective competition, one should look to indications of performance as well as of market structure. In other words, effects on the market count. Relying on this effects-based approach, subsequent case law broadened the concept of dominant position in order to cover situations of coordinated effects. It was not clear if the concept could, however, be extended to cover unilateral effects. This led to the implementation of a new substantive test in EC merger control, the significant impediment of effective competition test. According to Regulation 139/2004, the criterion of dominant position serves now as a simple indication of a significant impediment of effective competition and therefore of the existence of a potential harm to consumers.[176] A deeper understanding of this evolution will, however, advance that the alleged unilateral effects 'gap' was not the principal reason for the institution of the new substantive test in EU merger control;[177] the main motivation can be found in the need to

[173] Case 27/76, *United Brands v Commission* [1978] ECR 207. See also Case 85/76, *Hoffmann-La Roche v Commission* [1979] ECR 461.

[174] Lianos, n 13 above, 348–84.

[175] Council Regulation (EEC) No 4064/89 on the control of concentrations between undertakings [1989] OJ L395/1.

[176] Council Regulation (EC) No 139/2004 on the control of concentrations between undertakings (the EC Merger Regulation) [2004] OJ L24/1, art 2(2).

[177] For a critical assessment of the test see G Monti, 'The New Substantive Test in the EC Merger Regulation—Bridging the Gap between Economics and the Law' (2008)

provide tools to both the legal and economic communities to work together *de novo* in framing the content of the new substantive test, without being subject to the constraints of the previous case law on dominant position. In other words, the significant impediment of effective competition test recognizes the need for translation.

In its most recent documents, the Commission embraced this more economics- oriented definition of the concept of dominant position in areas other than EU merger control. The staff discussion paper on Article 82 illustrates this subtle evolution:

> [T]he definition of dominance consists of three elements, two of which are closely linked: (a) there must be a position of economic strength on a market which (b) enables the undertaking(s) in question to prevent effective competition being maintained on that market by (c) affording it the power to behave independently to an appreciable extent.[178]

Of particular importance here are the last two elements, which, according to the staff discussion paper, are intrinsically linked. The discussion paper reveals the nature of the relationship between these two elements of the dominant position, that is, the idea of independent behaviour and the concept of effective competition and brings this concept closer than ever to the economic conception of monopoly:

> The notion of independence, which is the special feature of dominance, is related to the level of competitive constraint facing the undertaking(s) in question.For dominance to exist the undertaking(s) concerned must not be subject to effective competitive constraints. In other words, it thus must have substantial market power.[179]

Market power, or substantial market power, is the missing thread that operates as the unifying concept for the application of Articles 81 and 82 of the EC Treaty and the introduction of a more economics-oriented approach in justifying antitrust intervention on the market-place. A capacity of independent behaviour with regard to the competitors and consumers is not a sufficient criterion for the finding of a dominant position. The discussion paper adopts, instead, an approach

LSE Legal Studies Working Paper available at <http://papers.ssrn.com/sol3/papers.cfm?abstract_id=1153661>; MB Coate, 'Did the European Union's market dominance policy have a gap? Evidence from enforcement in the United States' available at <http://ssrn.com/abstract=1410246>.

[178] DG Competition, 'Discussion Paper on the Application of Art 82 of the Treaty to Exclusionary Abuses' (2005) available at ec.europa.eu/comm/competition/antitrust/art82/discpaper2005.pdf, para 11.

[179] Ibid, 23.

that is closer to the definition of market power by neoclassical price theory (the ability to raise prices profitably and reduce output). The recent Commission Guidance on its Enforcement Priorities in Article 82 (hereinafter Commission Guidance) adopts an equivalent formulation but further emphasizes the link with neoclassical price theory:

> . . . [t]he Commission considers that an undertaking which is capable of profitably increasing prices above the competitive level for a significant period of time does not face sufficiently effective competitive constraints and can thus generally be regarded as dominant.[180]

The convergence of the economic and the legal definition of monopoly power or dominant position is not, however, complete. While the definition of the concept of market power adopted by the Commission Guidance as well as the recent non-horizontal merger guidelines presents similarities to the economic concept of market power, its scope is broader. In a similar formulation for Articles 81 and 82 of the EC Treaty and EC merger control purposes, the Commission defines market power as 'the ability of one or more firms to profitably increase prices, reduce output, choice or quality of goods and services, diminish innovation, or otherwise negatively influence parameters of competition'.[181] This broad definition accommodates the emphasis of EC competition law on the protection of the competitive process and consumer sovereignty. Although the ability to increase price stays the primary concern of competition law, in conformity with the neoclassical price theory approach, the emphasis on other parameters of competition than price, in particular consumer choice, epitomizes the broad definition of what constitutes a restriction of competition under EC competition law and the recognition of the importance of quality and variety investment competition instead of just price competition.[182]

[180] Communication from the Commission providing Guidance on the Commission's Enforcement Priorities in Applying Article 82 of the EC Treaty to Abusive Exclusionary Conduct by Dominant Undertakings, COM(2009) 864 final, para 11 (hereinafter 'Commission Guidance on Article 82').

[181] Guidelines On The Assessment of Non-Horizontal Mergers Under the Council Regulation On The Control Of Concentrations Between Undertakings [2008] OJ C265/6, para 10; Guidelines On The Application of Art 81(3) [2004] OJ C101/97, para 25; DG Competition Discussion Paper on the Application of Art 82, n 178 above, para 24; Commission Guidance on Art 82, ibid, para 11.

[182] Competition based on quality (Q) or variety (V) increasing investment is equally as important as price competition. Richard Markovits defines QV investment

In contrast, US courts have not generally included as an equal consideration other parameters than price in the definition of market power and in their assessment of anticompetitive effects: non price competition has been a concern in some US cases but still remains a secondary concern or it is even not mentioned in others.[183]

There has been a considerable debate in the US case law also on the different sources of market power that are taken into account. For historical reasons, European competition law has given equal consideration to exclusionary and relational sources of market power than the ability to control price by restricting its own output. This is not the case in the US, where Stiglerian market power (insisting on the ability of a monopolist to restrict his output) has been a more important concern than Bainian power (where the source of market power is the ability of a firm to raise the costs and

competition as 'the process through which rival sellers compete away their potential supernormal profits by introducing additional QV investments until even the most profitable project in the relevant area of product space generates just a normal rate of return': R Markovits, *Truth or Economics. Is economic efficiency a sound basis upon which to make public policy or legal decisions?* (Yale University Press, 2008) 90. The importance of this type of competition has been recognized by the European Court of Justice in Case 26/76 *Metro SB-Großmärkte GmbH & Co KG v Commission* [1977] ECR 1875, para 21.

[183] See *Fortner Enterprises Inc v United States Steel Corp* 394 495, 503 (1986) ['market power is usually stated to be the ability of a single seller to raise price and restrict output']; *Jefferson Parish Hospital District No 2 v Hyde* 466 US 2, 27 n 46 (1984) ['as an economic matter, market power exists whenever prices can be raised above levels that would be charged in a competitive market']; *NCAA v Board of Regents of the University of Oklahoma*, 468 US 85, 109 n 38 (1984) ['market power is the ability to raise prices above those that would be charged in a competitive market']; *Ball Memorial Hospital Inc v Mutual Hospital Insurance Inc* 784 F 2d 1325 (7th Cir, 1986) 1335 ['market power comes from the ability to cut back the market's total output and so raise price']; *Wilk v American Medical Association* 895 F 2d 352, 359 (7th Cir, 1990) ['market power is the ability to raise prices above the competitive level by restricting output']; *PSI repair Services Inc v Honeywell Inc* 104 F 3d 811, 817 (6th Cir, 1997) ['the ability of a single seller to raise price and restrict output']; *Ryko Mfg Co v Eden Services* 823 F 2d 1215, 1232 (8th Cir, 1987) ['market power generally is defined as the power of a firm to restrict output and thereby increase the selling price of its goods in the market']; *Rebel Oil Co v Atlantic Richfield Co* 51 F 3d 1421, 1441 (9th Cir, 1995) ['the ability to control output and prices (is) the essence of market power']; *US v Microsoft Corp* 253 F 3d 34, 51 (DC Cir, 2001) ['a firm is a monopolist if it can profitably raise prices substantially above the competitive level']. See, however, US Department of Justice and Federal Trade Commission, 'Antitrust Guidelines for the Licensing of Intellectual Property' (1995) section 2.2 available at <http://www.usdoj.gov/atr/public/guidelines/0558.htm> ['Market power is the ability profitably to maintain prices above, or output below, competitive levels for a significant period of time. Market power can be exercised in other economic dimensions, such as quality, service, and the development of new or improved goods and processes. A buyer could also exercise market power (eg, by maintaining the price below the competitive level, thereby depressing output'.].

therefore reduce output of its competitors)[184] or relational market power.[185]

This example illustrates that economic transplants are influenced by the legal environment to which they are integrated and by the specific objectives pursued by the legal system. The same economic concept, market power, may have a different content when it is transplanted in EC competition law than it does in US antitrust law. As Robert Bork has once perceptively remarked, 'antitrust is necessarily a hybrid policy science, a cross between law and economics that produces a mode of reasoning somewhat different from that of either discipline alone'.[186] This is due to the effort made by the policy-makers and adjudicators to interpret economic transplants in conformity to the preferences of their legal system. The discourse is still presented as economic in nature, as the choice of the expression 'market power', instead of the legal concept of 'dominant position', or something else, shows. But the economic transplant is domesticated. The legal system 'reconstructs its own (legal) image of the external system within itself'.[187] It follows that even if two sub-systems use the same terms, they may understand them in different ways. For example, one could identify two different normative values that shape economic and legal discourse with regard to the definition of market power. If the purpose of the economic analysis of market power is to highlight a change in the current equilibrium of supply and demand, the ultimate purpose of legal discourse is to assign to this economic 'factual' nexus of market power the coding of either lawful or unlawful or, put differently, of interest for competition law intervention versus of no interest for competition law intervention. It follows, that if the economists do not hesitate to declare that every firm benefits from a degree of market power, in the sense that they have the ability to increase the price profitably to at least a category of consumers, this cannot be relevant for legal discourse, as only a certain kind or degree of market power will be qualified as 'unlawful' or 'of interest'. This may also explain the different content given to the economic

[184] On the distinction see TG Krattenmaker and SC Salop, 'Anticompetitive Exclusion: Raising Rivals' Costs to Achieve Power over Price' (1986) 96 *Yale Law Journal* 209–93; TG Krattenmaker, RH Lande and SC Salop, 'Monopoly Power and Market Power in Antitrust Law' (1987) 76 *Georgetown Law Review* 241, 249–50.

[185] W Grimes, 'Market Definition in Franchise Antitrust Claims: Relational Market Power and the Franchisor's Conflict of Interest' (1999) 67 *Antitrust Law Journal* 243–81.

[186] R Bork, *The Antitrust Paradox: A Policy at War with Itself* (Simon & Schuster, 1993) 8.

[187] Dwyer, n 67 above, 126

transplant of market power by each legal system, as internal considerations to the system—Is the regulator more risk-averse to false positives or false negatives? What is the acceptable level of substantive (error) costs?[188]—play an important role.

Consumer welfare

The integration of economic transplants in legal discourse may also aim to transform the legal order. This may or may not succeed, depending on the ability of the translator to attract the support of the most powerful actors in the formulation of legal rules and legal interpretation: the courts. The concept of 'consumer welfare' may provide some insights.

Consumer welfare denotes the idea that following the change from an equilibrium situation to another, the consumers of the specific product will benefit from a surplus and/or wealth transfer, in the sense that their ability to satisfy their preferences will increase. The choice of consumer welfare as an objective of competition law has distributive consequences. This concept is generally distinguished from the concept of total welfare that takes equally into account the benefits collected by other societal groups, such as the shareholders of the firm that adopts the specific commercial practice under investigation (consumer and producer surplus).

In competition law, the incorporation of consumer welfare as a valid objective of competition law implies that the outcome/consequences of a specific practice on consumers matters, before any decision on the lawfulness or unlawfulness of this practice has been reached. A reduction of competitive rivalry, following the exclusion of a competitor or an agreement between two competitors to cooperate with each other, will not be found unlawful, if they do not also lead to a likely consumer harm/detriment. A different approach would be a deontological emphasis on competitive rivalry, irrespective of any actual or potential consequences of a specific practice/conduct on consumers. Effects may indicate empirical observable findings on the worsening, in terms of price or quality, of the situation of specific groups of consumers, following the adoption of the anticompetitive practice (actual effects). It may also refer to situations where there are no observable findings of effects on these groups of consumers but there is 'a consistent theory of consumer harm' which is empirically validated. That is, 'the theory of harm should be consistent with factual observations' (ex ante validation) and 'that the market outcomes should be consistent with the

[188] A Stein, *Foundations of Evidence Law* (Oxford University Press, 2005) 1.

predictions of the theory' (ex post validation).[189] The theory of harm has the objective to establish a relation of causality between the specific practice and the consumer detriment. One could think in terms of a probability statement, that is, an evaluation of the 'inferential soundness' of this relationship,[190] or in terms of relative plausibility of the specific consumer harm story.[191]

This chapter will not discuss the relative merits of the possible integration of the concept of consumer welfare into EC competition law: this could be the subject of a specific study. The philosophical foundations of the concept,[192] as well as the methodology of revealed preferences that has permitted its measurement,[193] are put into question by scholars that criticize 'equilibrium economics'[194] and economic thinking emphasizing 'social preferences',[195] endogenous preference formation,[196] and more realist assessment of consumer behaviour,[197] thus leading to an integration of social, behavioural and institutional constraints in conceptualizing consumer choice.[198]

[189] P Papandropoulos, 'Implementing an Effects-based Approach Under Article 82', (2008) *Concurrences* 1–5, 3.

[190] J Cohen, *The Probable and the Provable* (Clarendon Press, 1977) 27

[191] RJ Allen, 'The Nature of Juridical Proof' (1991) 13 *Cardozo Law Review* 373; MS Pardo and RJ Allen, 'Juridical Proof and the Best Explanation' (2008) 27 *Law and Philosophy* 223.

[192] The two 'fundamental theorems' of welfare economics: see M Blaug, 'The Fundamental Theorems of Modern Welfare Economics, Historically Contemplated' (2007) 39(2) *History of Political Economy* 185– 207.

[193] P Samuelson, 'A Note on the Pure Theory of Consumer Behavior' (1938) 5 *Economica* 61–71; P Samuelson, 'Consumption Theory in Terms of Revealed Preference' (1948) 15 *Economica* 243; P Samuelson, 'The Problem of Integrability in Utility Theory' (1950) 17 *Economica* 355.

[194] eg, see N Kaldor, 'The Irrelevance of Equilibrium Economics' (1972) 82(3) *The Economic Journal* 1237–55; SAT Rizvi, 'The Microfoundations project in General Equilibrium Theory' (1994) 18(4) *Cambridge Journal of Economics* 357–77; F Ackerman, 'Still Dead After All These Years: Interpreting The Failure Of General Equilibrium Theory' (2002) 9 *Journal of Economic Methodology* 119–39.

[195] eg, see E Fehr and U Fischbacher, 'Why Do Social Preferences Matter—The Impact of Non-Selfish Motives on Competition, Cooperation and Incentives' (2002) 112 *Economic Journal* C1–33

[196] eg, see S Bowles, 'Endogenous Preferences: The Cultural Consequences of Markets and Other Economic Institutions' (1998) 36(1) *Journal of Economic Literature* 75–111.

[197] eg, see R Thaler, 'Towards a Positive Theory of Consumer Choice', (1980) 1 *Journal of Economic Behavior & Organization* 39–60; GA Akerlof and WT Dickens, 'The Economic Consequences of Cognitive Dissonance' (1982) 73(3) *American Economic Review* 307–19.

[198] For an analysis of the possible implications of these new constraints in competition law assessment, in particular under Article 82 EC, see I Lianos, 'Classification of

The concept has been introduced rather recently in competition law discourse, again through the means of guidelines and other soft law texts. The term first appeared in EC competition law discourse in 1997 in the Green Paper on vertical restraints, marking the debut of the 'modernization' of EC competition law.[199] Interestingly it also figures in the agreement between the European Commission and the US on the application of positive comity principles in the enforcement of competition law, adopted in 1998.[200] The US government was following with great interest and encouraged the progressive transformation of EC competition law towards an economic approach. Following the publication of the guidelines on vertical restraints the concept spread to other areas of EC competition law, such as the transfer of technology agreements,[201] some Article 81 cases,[202] some merger cases,[203] and then the horizontal merger guidelines in 2004,[204] the guidelines on the application of Article 81

Abuses: A Straight Story?' (forthcoming 2009) CLGE Working Paper Series 1/09, University College London.

[199] European Commission, Green Paper on Vertical Restraints in EC Competition Policy (1997) available at <http://europa.eu/documents/comm/green_papers/pdf/com96_721_en.pdf> para 25; See also, Communication From The Commission On The Application Of The Community Competition Rules To Vertical Restraints—Follow Up To The Green Paper On Vertical Restraints COM(1998) 544 final; Communication Pursuant to Art 5 of Council Regulation No 19/65/EEC on the application of Art 81(3) of the Treaty to categories of agreements and concerted practices [1999] OJ C270/7, para 3 ('EC competition policy in the field of vertical restraints has the following objectives—the protection of competition is the primary objective as this enhances consumer welfare and creates an efficient allocation of resources').

[200] Agreement Between the European Communities and the Government of the United States Of America on the Application of Positive Comity Principles in the Enforcement of their Competition Laws [1998] L173/28, point 3('(t)he purposes of this Agreement are to: (a) help ensure that trade and investment flows between the Parties and competition and consumer welfare within the territories of the parties are not impeded by anti-competitive activities for which the competition laws of one or both Parties can provide a remedy'). The concept of 'consumer welfare' becomes therefore a relevant concept for the interpretation of the scope of an international agreements between the European Communities and a third country.

[201] Commission Evaluation Report on the Transfer of Technology Block Exemption Regulation 240/96, COM(2001) 786 final, paras 29, 31; Commission Notice – Guidelines on the Application of Art 81 of the EC Treaty to Technology Transfer Agreements [2004] OJ C101/2, paras 5, 7.

[202] *Glaxo Wellcome*, Commission Decision, [2001] OJ L302/1, para 153.

[203] eg, see *Newscorp/Telepiù* (Case COMP/M.2876) Commission Decision [2004] OJ L 110/73, para 269; *Ryanair/Aer Lingus* (Case COMP/M.4439) Commission Decision [2008] OJ C 47/9, para 26.

[204] Guidelines on the Assessment Of Horizontal Mergers under the Council Regulation on the Control of Concentrations Between Undertakings [2004] OJ C31/5, para 61.

Table 5: Consumer welfare

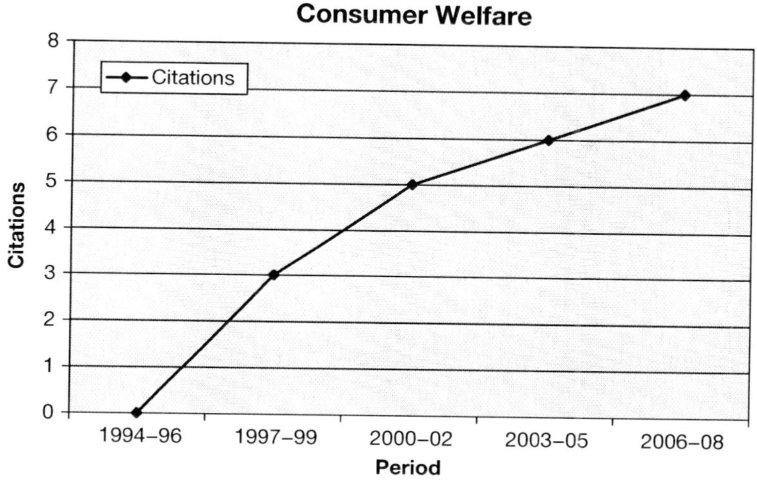

(3),[205] the white paper on damages actions in 2008[206] and, most recently, the Commission Guidance on Article 82.[207]

Its integration in EC competition law has been carefully designed and progressively found its way in the case law of the European Courts. The term was first used in the context of the case law of the European Courts by Advocate General Jacobs in his Opinion in SYFAIT in 2004 when he examined the economics of innovation in the pharmaceutical sector.[208] The ECJ did not address that issue in its decision as it declined to respond to the preliminary question sent by the Greek competition authority, the later not being formally a court under

[205] Communication from the Commission—Notice—Guidelines on the Application of Art 81(3) of the Treaty [2004] C101/97, paras 13, 21, 33, 104

[206] Commission Staff Working Paper *Accompanying the White Paper on Damages Actions for Breach of the EC Antitrust Rules*, COM(2008) 165 final, para 179.

[207] Commission Guidance on Art 82, n 180, above, paras 19, 29, 85, although the Commission also employs the terminology of 'consumer harm' without explaining if consumer welfare is a genus of consumer harm or if consumer harm and consumer welfare should be understood the same.

[208] Case C-53/03 Opinion of AG Jacobs, *Syfait and ors v GlaxoSmithKline plc and GlaxoSmithKline AEVE* [2005] ECR I-4609, paras 91, 92.

Article 234 of the EC Treaty. The concept then appeared in the *Microsoft* decision of the Court of First Instance in 2007, but only in a reference to the decision of the European Commission that was reviewed by the Court[209]. The concept took a more prominent role in the recent Opinion of AG Trstenjak in *Beef Industry Development* in September 2008.[210] The Advocate General adopted a theory according to which Article 81, paragraph 1 and Article 81, paragraph 3 of the EC Treaty take into account different aspects of 'consumer welfare':

> . . . the general conception of Article 81 EC is to ensure the optimal supply of consumers. However, different aspects of consumer welfare are taken into account under Article 81(1) EC and under Article 81(3) EC. Under Article 81 (1) EC, agreements which restrict competition between market participants and thus its function of supplying consumers optimally with a product at a lowest possible price or with innovative products are prohibited in principle. Such agreements directly affect consumer welfare and as such are prohibited in principle.[211]

The Court did not accept the position of AG Trstejnak and did not refer to the concept of 'consumer welfare'.[212]

The reaction of other members of the Court has not taken long to manifest. In her recent Opinion in *T-Mobile*, Advocate General Kokott defended a different perspective:

> Article 81 EC, like the other competition rules of the Treaty, is not designed only or primarily to protect the immediate interests of individual competitors or consumers, but to protect the *structure of the market* and thus *competition as such (as an institution)*. In this way, consumers are also indirectly protected. Because where competition as such is damaged, disadvantages for consumers are also to be feared.[213]

The Advocate General considers that the concept of anticompetitive object covers two forms of practices: first, practices that have a direct impact on consumers and the prices paid by them, referred to by the parties as practices affecting 'consumer welfare', and secondly, practices that have an indirect negative impact on consumers by restricting or distorting competition.[214] Advocate General Kokott takes care to not

[209] Case T-201/04 *Microsoft Corp v Commission* [2007] ECR II-3601, para 41.

[210] Opinion of AG Trstenjak in Case C-209/07 *Competition Authority v Beef Industry Development Society Ltd* [2008] (unreported).

[211] Ibid, para 56.

[212] *Beef Industry Development & Barry Brothers*, n 210 above.

[213] Opinion of AG Kokott in Case C-8/08 *T-Mobile Netherlands BV and ors* [2009] (unreported), para 58.

[214] Ibid, para 59.

employ the term, preferring instead a descriptive account of the form of the impact on consumers. At the doctrinal stage, she is careful to move away from economic terminology and economic transplants. First, she refers to the public interest of undistorted competition, indicating that maintenance of rivalry remains an important concern. Secondly, she suggests a limiting (outcome-based) principle to the scope of Article 81 (1) and the process-based definition of competition she advocates, which is, however, extremely ambiguous: 'the objective of European competition law must be *to protect competition and not competitors*, because indirectly that is of benefit also to consumers *and the public at large*'.[215] The reference to the 'public at large' seems to expand the beneficiaries of the principle of competition enshrined in Article 81(1) beyond the category of final, or even, intermediary consumers, thus implicitly questioning the utility of the concept of 'consumer welfare'. The Court of Justice accepted the formulation of Advocate General Kokott, although it carefully omitted any reference to 'the public at large', thus opening the possibility that this judgment could be interpreted as adopting a long term vision of 'consumer welfare' or being inspired by the principle of 'consumer sovereignty'.[216]

What these examples show is that the integration of the economic transplant of 'consumer welfare' along traditional objectives of EC competition law, such as market integration or the protection of the structure of competition, illustrate the effort made by policy-makers to render the interpretation of the competition law provisions of the Treaty more compatible with recent economic discourse. For some, the new economic discourse should set aside old principles. For others, the newly imported economic discourse should complement the existing values and principles. The instrument of economic transplant is flexible enough to accommodate both possibilities.

Economic Transplants as a Means to Preserve the Variety of Economic Discourse

The concept of 'barrier to entry' is of particular importance in EC competition law for the definition of a relevant market (barriers to existing competition) as well as for defining the existence of a restriction of competition in Article 81 of the EC Treaty, or of a dominant

[215] Ibid, para 71. Emphasis added.
[216] *T-Mobile Netherlands BV and ors*, n 213 above, para 38.

position in Article 82 of the EC Treaty (barriers to potential competition). There has been considerable literature on the economic concept of barriers to entry. In the neoclassical tradition of competition as an end-state, a barrier to entry is a market factor that prevents entry from occurring in the long-run. The economists are generally interested in determining whether there is an equilibrium in which entry will, or will not, occur: deterrence of entry, not simple delay of entry is of concern. By contrast, lawyers think of barriers to entry as factors that permit either substantial periods of monopolistic pricing (competition as an end-state) or factors that permit exclusion of competitors (competition as a process of rivalry), thus including factors slowing entry. Therefore, the competition lawyer's interest 'is not limited to those situations where the social loss caused by the monopolistic pricing is infinite, but where it is too large by some measure which is entirely a function of public policy' (for example, the regulator's preference on the degree of openness of markets). The incorporation of the concept of barrier to entry into different legal systems will not, therefore, produce similar effects. The concept may have a different meaning in US antitrust law from what it has in EC competition law and it may be different in competition law than in trade law.

Even within the paradigm of neoclassical economics, there are many traditions of the concept of barrier to entry. This chapter will focus on only two basic ones to make the point although one could list more: for example, according to new industrial economics behavioral approach, barriers to entry may be defined as absolute/natural or strategic and then divided between those that stem from endogenous sunk costs and those from exogenous sunk costs.[217]

The Bainian (from economist J Bain) approach to barriers to entry regards qualifying barriers to entry as market factors that deterred entry even if the firms already in the market were charging prices above the competitive level.[218] For example, a Bainian definition would define economies of scale as an entry barrier. Scale economies entail that a firm contemplating entry must always consider not merely the cost of producing, but also the cost of acquiring enough sales to make its own entry into the market profitable. If economies of scale are substantial, a dominant firm may be able to set a price above its costs and earn profits

[217] See, for instance, SC Salop, 'Strategic Entry Deterrence' (1979) 69 *American Economic Review* 335–8; On the various definitions of barriers to entry see RP McAfee, HM Mialon and M Williams, 'What is a Barrier to Entry?' (2004) 94 *American Economic Review* 461–5.

[218] J Bain, *Barriers to New Competition* (Harvard University Press, 1956) 3.

without causing new entry, for the residual market will not be large enough for a new firm to bring its costs down to the same level.

This position is not shared by the Stiglerian approach (from economist G Stigler) to the definition of barriers to entry. For Stigler, and the libertarian Chicago school, the notion that economies of scale can be entry barriers seems irrational because scale economies are themselves a form of efficiency.[219] The consideration of scale economies as barriers to entry will make efficiency an antitrust offence. Largely for these reasons, Stigler defines barriers to entry as 'a cost of producing (at some or every rate of output) which must be borne by a firm which seeks to enter an industry but is not borne by firms already in the industry'.[220] Concerning scale economies, it is clear that the costs for these are borne by firms already in the industry, therefore they should not be considered as barriers to entry. A Stiglerian perspective suggests more permissive antitrust standards than Bain's definition, as potential competition is socially desirable only if the new entrant has at least identical cost functions to the incumbent. Critical to Stigler's argument is the assumption of credit easiness. He questioned Bain's emphasis on imperfections in the capital market which would have dissuaded new as efficient as potential entrants to finance their investments up to the point where they would benefit from equivalent scale economies to these of a dominant firm. Stigler thought that large investment requirements could not impede the plans of a new firm to enter the market, given the wide-range funding options in financial and credit markets[221]. Is this assumption still valid in the era of the credit crunch?

It is thus clear that the choice of one or another definition of barrier to entry by a legal system is function of the values/preferences of this specific system regarding 'efficiency' or openness and market access as well as basic assumptions on the ability of firms to get the necessary credit to fund their entry into the market.

[219] G Stigler, *The Organization of Industry* (1968) 113–22; See also H Demsetz, 'Economics as a Guide to Antitrust Regulation' (1976) 19 Journal of Law & Economics 371–84, 382, 'alleged barriers to entry as advertising, vertical integration, and capital requirements all fall into the class of competitive tactics more likely to be associated with productive rivalry than unproductive monopolisation [. . .]'; H Demsetz, Barriers to Entry (1982) 72 *American Economic Review* 47–57.

[220] GJ Stigler, *The Organization of Industry* (RD Irwin: Homewood, Ill, 1968) 67.

[221] R Schmalensee, 'Sunk Costs and Antitrust Barriers to Entry' (2004) 94(2) *American Economic Review* 471–5, 472; A Gavil, WE Kovacic & JB Baker, *Antitrust Law in Perspective: Cases, Concepts and Problems in Competition Policy* (2nd ed, West, 2008) 983–7.

The case law of the courts in the US has been ambiguous regarding the definition of barriers to entry.[222] Some US circuit courts of appeal have followed a Stiglerian approach,[223] when others have followed a definition close to Bain[224] and finally some are inspired by both definitions.[225] In Europe, the courts have used the expression in various settings. There is not an authoritative definition of the concept in EC competition law although in *United Brands* the Court included economies of scale as an example of barriers to entry, thus following a Bainian definition.[226] The variety of the possible approaches to the definition of barriers to entry led the European Commission to adopt, in its vertical restraints guidelines, a position which seems closer to that defended by J Bain: 'Entry barriers are measured by the extent to which incumbent companies can increase their price above the competitive level, usually above minimum average total cost, and make supra-normal profits without attracting entry'.[227]

At the same time, however, the Commission accommodated new industrial economic literature by introducing an additional requirement for the qualification of entry barrier:

> The question whether certain of these factors should be described as entry barriers depends on whether they are related to sunk costs. Sunk costs are those costs that have to be incurred to enter or be active on a market but that are lost when the market is exited. Advertising costs to build consumer loyalty are normally sunk costs, unless an exiting firm could either sell its brand name or use it somewhere else without a loss.[228]

The most recent Commission's Guidance on its enforcement priorities in Article 82[229] explicitly cites economies of scale and scope as

[222] GJ Werden, 'Network Effects and Conditions of Entry: Lessons from the Microsoft Case' (2001) 69 Antitrust Law Journal 87–111, 103–9.

[223] eg, see *Advo Inc v Philadelphia Newspapers Inc* 51 F3d 1191, 1200-1202 (3d Cir, 1995).

[224] eg, see *Fortner Enterprises v United States Steel Corp* 394 US 495, 509 (1969); *Jefferson Parish Hospital District No 2 v Hyde* 466 US 2, 13 no 19, 14 (1984); *Eastman Kodak Co v Image Technical Services Inc* 504 US 451, 485 (1992); *Concord Boat Corp v Brunswick Corp* 207 F 3d 1039, 1059 (8th Cir, 2000).

[225] *Rebel Oil Co v Atlantic Richfield Co* 51 F3d 1421, 1439 (9th Cir, 1995) 'entry barriers are additional long-run costs that were not incurred by incumbent firms but must be incurred by new entrants, or factors in the market that deter entry while permitting incumbent firms to earn monopoly returns'; *Accord W Parcel Express v UPS* 190 F3d 974, 975 (9th Cir, 1999).

[226] Case 27/76 *United Brands v Commission* [1978] ECR 207, para 122.

[227] Guidelines on Vertical Rrestraints, above n. 126, para 126.

[228] Ibid, para 128.

[229] Commission Guidance on Article 82, n 180 above.

examples of barrier to entry. Interestingly, the Commission's Guidance does not employ the factor of sunk costs as an indicator of barriers to entry, thus retreating from the view it had adopted in the vertical restraints guidelines.[230] This may be justified by recent economic thinking that had cast doubt on the factor of sunk costs[231] and a more empirical turn in competition law discourse: indeed, the most recent OECD 'Best Practices' report on barriers to entry completely sidelines the issue of the definition of barriers to entry and concludes that 'what matters in actual cases is not whether an impediment satisfies this or that definition of an entry barrier, but rather the more practical questions of whether, when, and to what extent entry is likely to occur given the facts in each case'.[232]

In conclusion, the economic transplant of barrier to entry aims to maintain diversity in economic discourse.

This does not however mean that economic transplants should lead to a static view of the translated scientific discourse. The dual nature of economic transplants guarantees that this will not be the case. This chapter will conclude by developing some ideas on an interpretative theory that will preserve the specificities of economic transplants and will correspond to the paradigm of translation.

'Beyond Babel': Legal and Economic Discourses in the Age of 'Economic Transplants'

As Paul Ricoeur reminds us, the paradigm of translation is based on the principle of 'linguistic hospitality': '(w)e are called to make our language put on the stranger's clothes at the same time as we invite the stranger to step into the fabric of our own speech'.[233] Yet translation should remain a mediation between two distinct communities that stay loyal to their own discourse while being open to the 'betrayal' of translation. The risk for this delicate equilibrium is that of 'hegemonic' or 'deferent' translations. Establishing a diachronic dialectical interaction between the two discourses will prevent that from happening.

230 Commission Guidance on Article 82, ibid, para 17.

231 LMB Cabral and TW Ross, 'Are Sunk Costs a Barrier to Entry?' (2008) 17 *Journal of Economics and Management Strategy* 97–112.

232 OECD Competition Committee, 'Barriers to Entry' DAF/COMP(2005)42 available at <http://www.oecd.org/dataoecd/43/49/36344429.pdf> 17.

233 Ricoeur, n 17 above, 23.

The Risk of 'Hegemonic' and 'Deferential' Translations[234]

'Hegemonic translations' occur when the host legal system crystallizes existing economic discourse and adopts it regardless of the evolutionary potential of this discourse or the variety of this discourse in the foreign (economic) sub-system. In other words, the legal system builds its own image of economic discourse, appropriates it and cuts any link that may exist with the evolution of the source language/discourse.

One could consider that the concept of 'economic law' in the European continental tradition is an illustration of hegemonic translations.[235] Economic law is the law of the market organization: a branch of law more than a medium of communication between legal and economic discourse, as the law and economics conceives itself. If one looks to the concept more closely, however, it will be clear that the concept of economic law involves some form of communication between law and economics. The main difference with law and economics is that this communication takes place only at the moment of the translation of the economic concept into legal norm. The translation is domesticating the economic concept, which loses its distinctive character, or its original nature, and is crystallized into a term of the legal sub-system and subject to the auto-referential process of the latter. This constitutive moment ends the effort of communication: once the economic discourse becomes legal discourse/norm its origins are forgotten and it is interpreted as if it were any other form of legal discourse, without any particular attention to the concurrent evolution of the source concept in economic discourse. Most often, the translation effort involves the renaming of the concept, so as to make even clearer the dissociation between the concept and its origins (domesticated translation).

The concept of 'free competition' in ordoliberal thought is an illustration of this approach.[236] If one reads Walter Eucken's formulation of the principle in *Foundations of Economics* it is very clear

[234] Both terms are inspired by the discussion that followed the presentation of A Bayeux and F Ost at the *Séminaire interdisciplinaire d'études juridiques*: '*Traduction et Droits Européens-Enjeux d'une rencontre*' Facultés Universitaires de Saint Louis, Bruxelles, 19–20 February 2009. See also, A Bayeux, '*Traduction et droits européens—premiers jalons*' (on file with the author).

[235] Lianos, n 13 above, 69–81.

[236] W Möschel, 'The Proper Scope of Government Viewed from an Ordoliberal Perspective: The Example of Competition Policy' (2001) 157 *Journal of Institutional and Theoretical Economics* 3–13.

that the concept is intrinsically linked to an atomistic conception of competition, based on the perfect competition model.[237] Renaming the concept to 'free competition' ensures that the economic origins of the concept and its possible conceptual defects will not haunt the legal interpretative effort, sapping the epistemic legitimacy and, therefore, the authority of legal discourse. One could indeed perceive economic law as being essentially historically trapped to the economic imagery of its period of creation: a Pigouvian pre-1940 version of welfare economics before new challenges such as the 'new welfare economics' of Hicks and Kaldor, which gained prominence in the 1940s, or the Coasian new institutional economics in the 1960s challenged the Pigouvian church.[238] A parallel criticism of hegemonic translation can be made to the law and economics movement pioneered, among others, by Judge Richard Posner, essentially an importation in legal discourse of a different economic paradigm: that of new welfare economics based on a Coasean framework, without any regard to criticisms and oppositions to that model in economic discourse.

'Deferential translations' exist when the economic discourse is translated without any regard to the specific objectives of the legal system. For example a normative emphasis on economic efficiency only, without due regard to other objectives of the legal system, will render an unsatisfactory outcome, from a legitimacy point of view. The emphasis of economic analysis to economic efficiency may be understood from a methodological point of view. For example, the quest for respectability and conceptual coherence was particularly influential in the decision by welfare economists to ignore any ethical, social, distributive or psychological dimensions in the progressive construction of their ideal model of *homo economicus*. Economists were aware that their approach was, by definition, incomplete and essentially a purely methodological decision motivated by the logical positivism shift that attempted to conceive economics as a hard (natural) science.[239] 'Style is often an appeal to authority'.[240] In contrast, legal discourse is by

[237] W Eucken, *Foundations of Economics* (translated by TW Hutchison) (University of Chicago Press, 1951) 269–70.

[238] For an interesting discussion see M Blaug, 'The Fundamental Theorems of Modern Welfare Economics, Historically Contemplated' (2007) 39 *History of Political Economy* 185–207; H Hovenkamp, *Knowledge About Welfare: Legal Realism and The Separation of Law and Economics*, (2000) 84 Minnesota L. Rev 805–62.

[239] For an interesting analysis of this link see JR Hackney, *Under Cover of Science: American Legal-economic Theory and the Quest for Objectivity* (Duke University Press, 2007) ch 3.

[240] McCloskey, n 27 above, 11.

definition holist: it should incorporate all the dimensions of human existence if it is to be persuasive to the much broader group of constituents that it is addressed to. The translator should, therefore, be aware of the existence of areas of intranslability precisely because of the different methodologies and, more specifically, audiences to which the rhetoric of law and the rhetoric of economics aim to. The translator should also be attentive to the conditions that make scientific discourse blossom: that is, its openness, dialogue and continuous critical self-assessment. This will be the topic of the last section of this chapter.

The Need for a Diachronic Dialectic Interaction Between Legal and Economic Discourses

The dual nature of economic transplants and their potential impact on both legal and economic discourses should influence the choice of the method of interpretation that should be used to make them operational at the adjudicative stage, in different fact patterns and contexts. This method will be based on the default interpretation rule that the act of translation from economic to legal discourse maintains the economic nature of the concept and provides guidance to the interpreter to remain cognitively open to developments affecting the meaning and operation of this concept in economic discourse. In other words, the paradigm of translation, epitomized by the emergence of economic transplants, requires the establishment of a diachronic dialectic interaction between the legal and the economic discourses. A number of practical implications follow.

First, specialized tribunals or generalist tribunals with 'opinion specialization'[241] and a strong interdisciplinary capacity (clerks, research, and documentation units) should be preferred in areas with economic transplants, in order to ensure that economic analysis will still permeate the application of economic transplants following their translation to legal discourse. In other words, specialized adjudication will avoid the 'regression' to economic law and the epistemic asymmetry problem (between judges and 'experts') that could increase the risk of deferent translation from without (the judge appointed or party expert). This does not mean that we should appoint economists, or other social scientists without legal training and experience, as members of the

[241] See EK Cheng, 'The Myth of the Generalist Judge' (2008) 61 *Stanford Law Review* 519–72.

judiciary. This could increase the risk of deferent translation from within (the judge may have an intellectual bias towards his discipline), unless they form part of a judicial panel along with legally trained or experienced judges.

Secondly, particular attention should be brought to the conformity of interpretation with the preferences of the legal sub-system, in particular the consideration, in the effort of translation, of minority views in economic discourse, which may have been included by the policy-maker in the design of the economic transplant.

Thirdly, authoritative and close-system definitions of economic transplants in hard legal texts should be avoided in order to limit the risk of crystallization of economic discourse and the consequent risk of regression towards 'economic law'. This does not mean that hard texts, such as case law, cannot include references to economic transplants, but a particular effort should be made to establish a link with the guidelines that had first introduced these economic transplants, so as to emphasize the contingent and open to evolution character of their importation in legal discourse. This is of particular interest and importance, as economic orthodoxy can be questioned and economic discourse is currently undergoing an important shift.[242]

Conclusion

Umberto Eco's novel *The Name of the Rose* (1983) provides an interesting metaphor for the description of economic transplants. The main topic of the book is that the context of interpretation matters as much as empirical and deductive reasoning: William of Baskerville makes wide use of modern hermeneutics in attempting to solve the different murders occurring at the Benedictin monastery. But of particular interest for our purposes is the character of Salvatore. When Adso, who is the narrator in the book, first meets him he compares him to his image of a monster. He describes his face as a face put together with pieces from other people's faces. What Salvatore speaks is not Latin or any language at all: 'Salvatore spoke all languages, and no language'. He takes words sometimes from one language and sometimes from another. Salvatore was actually not inventing his own sentences but

[242] See GA Akerlof, 'The Missing Motivation in Macroeconomics' (2007) 97(1) *American Economic Review* 5–36.

using words he had heard in the past in different situations. The babelesque mutterings of Salvatore could appear as an adequate metaphor for the monstrous appearance of economic transplants to the devotees of the pure economic and legal discourses. Teubner was right to remark how this 'social science enlightenment' of law may lead to the production of 'an hybrid artifact with ambiguous epistemic status and unknown social consequences'[243]. Economic transplants are of this sort.

Yet the emergence of economic transplants, as challenging as it may appear for the 'familiar landmarks of our thought', offers the chance of a deeper interaction between economics and the law. Economic transplants are concepts developed in economics that are translated in law at the doctrinal stage. Their role can be better understood if one thinks of them as illustrations of the shift towards the paradigm of translation. In contrast to the closed-system hermeneutics of the pure legal or economic discourse, the paradigm of translation aims to put these two communities of law and economics in a diachronic and dialectic interaction with each other. In contrast to the concept of economic law and to the law and economics movement, economic transplants are a hybrid style of talk at the intersection of these two disciplines, evolving separately but also in congruence with each of them. Their interpretation should integrate the fact that they are the product of an act of translation: one could not expect that they are similar to the concept in their source language. Their subsequent interpretation and application should also not be cut off from the discourse of their community of origin. Lawyers and economists are, therefore, bound to work together in order to make sense of economic transplants. This is, after all, the main implication of the paradigm of translation.

[243] Teubner, n 66 above, 752.

Gauging the Cumbersomeness of EU Law

*Damian Chalmers**

Introduction

Europe matters. We know it matters because whenever reference is made to the presence of an EU provenance, lay perceptions of a legal provision change. Debate shifts to its general economic costs;[1] the economic benefits or costs for particular individuals;[2] how it threatens or reinforces perceptions of nationhood;[3] and the degree of national political unity or disunity it generates.[4] These extra associations constitute the cumbersomeness of EU law. They are the added significance or resonance attributed to a provision simply by virtues of its having an 'EU' tag. How to explain them? They cannot be said to emerge simply by reason of EU law's imposing too high regulatory costs, being culturally insensitive or politically divisive. These may be true of

* Professor of European Union Law, London School of Economics and Political Science.

[1] D Chalmers, 'The Positioning of EU Judicial Politics within the United Kingdom' (2000) 23 *West European Politics* 169, 188–90.

[2] M Gabel, 'Public Opinion and European Integration: An Empirical Test of Five Theories (1998) *60 Journal of Politics* 333. J Schild 'National v European Identities? French and Germans in the European Multi-Level System'(2001) 39 *Journal of Common Market Studies* 331; T Christin, 'Economic and Political Basis of Attitudes toward the EU in Central and Eastern European Countries in the 1990s' (2005) 6 *European Union Politics* 29.

[3] J Medrano, *Framing Europe: Attitudes to European Integration in Germany, Spain, and the United Kingdom* (Princeton University Press, 2003) chs 3, 9; A Menéndez-Alarcón, *The Cultural Realm of European Integration: Social Representations in France, Spain, and the United Kingdom* (Praeger: Westport, Conn, 2004); C Kentmen, 'Determinants of Support for EU Membership in Turkey: Islamic Attachments, Utilitarian Considerations and National Identity' (2008) 9 *European Union Politics* 487.

[4] L Hooghe and G Marks, 'Calculation, Community and Cues: Public Opinion on European Integration' (2005) 6 *European Union Politics* 419; M Gabel and K Scheve, 'Mixed Messages: Party Dissent and Mass Opinion on European Integration' (2007) 8 *European Union Politics* 37.

individual provisions but there is an inversion of cause and effect in such assertions as they beg the question as to the standards by which EU law is judged and why these standards are such powerful frames in its evaluation. Explanations referring to the 'foreignness' of EU law are equally unsatisfactory. This quality may impose higher duties of justification on EU law but its presence can say little about the content of EU law's associations.

Instead, it will be argued that this cumbersomeness can only be understood by reference to the claims that EU law makes about itself. For, whilst subjects' understandings of how EU law acts on them may be as heterogeneous as the human psyche and the legal contexts to which EU law contributes, in all circumstances EU law must perform certain common tasks. It must justify reasons for its presence, put forward qualities by which subjects can identify it and seek to bring about changes in its subjects' behaviour.

To undertake these tasks, EU law must make claims about itself. It must set out what counts as a justification; with what it identifies itself with and the behavioural ethos to which it appeals. Such claims are centred, it is argued, on a European *eudaimonia* which requires EU law to grant individuals the structures, entitlements, responsibilities and protection to make better and more successful lives for themselves.[5] There is a particularly intense relationship between it and EU law. This idea of self-betterment underpins the justification for any EU legal norm; the sense of what any EU legal norm is about and the instruction that EU law provides to its subjects on how to handle their lives.

The first half of this essay considers the distinctive features of the *eudaimonia* of EU law. All modern government is about the realization of *eudaimonia*, but a central feature of the European *eudaimonia* is that it sets out to realize goals for us and to better us in ways that other settlements are unable to. This is not simply a question of scale but also one of ideology as the EU, to do this, has to make claims that it knows what is good for our lives. Consequently, this *eudaimonia* imposes ambitious and irredeemable demands of EU law. Furthermore, as EU law imposes demands on multiple actors to realize these goals, this

[5] The term is first found in Aristotle's *Nichomachean Ethics*. It means happiness as a state that is secured by rational and virtuous activities premised on an adequate supply of entitlements and resources. Aristotle, *Nichomachean Ethics* (translated by W Ross) (Clarendon: Oxford, 1995) book I, paras 4–7.

European *eudaimonia* becomes a general benchmark for measuring institutional failure. Europe becomes the perennial, exigent voice reminding us of our collective insufficiency.

The considerable demands of European *eudaimonia* generate their own distributive concerns and politics. However, the strong focus on facilitating individual self-betterment has been at the expense of developing nuanced conceptions of these. A politics and conception of justice emerge but only in highly reactive ways. Justice concerns are addressed only through the formal interdependencies generated by EU law or the evident ones it cuts across rather than through resort to wider notions of community. The politics emerges only in a territorialized form whereby opposition to a particular standpoint becomes an entrenched stand-off between EU law and national defiance.

This *eudaimonia* provides not just teleologies and norms guiding EU law. It also provides a vision of how EU law is to govern its subjects and the entitlements and claims it can ask of them. The second half of this essay considers these. EU law's *eudaimonia* has led to its providing few entitlements whilst making many claims on its subjects. The need to offer something that cannot be offered by national law has led to EU law offering a very limited, unevenly distributed number of legal entitlements as most entitlements can easily be granted by national law. By contrast, the claim to regulate better than national law had led to EU law having to govern the most distant types of risks across a wide array of activities. It casts a cold hand across us, requiring us to consider dangers which are particularly difficult to gauge and which are thus hog-wired by anxiety.

A project demanding a lot, directly granting a little and always reminding us of our insufficiencies generates the style of reactions described at the beginning. Individuals may react by retreating into themselves, asking 'what's in it for me' or turning to false gods. None of this is to damn EU law. We are maybe condemned to seek better lives and EU law is simply a strong institutionalization of this which, notwithstanding these effects, brings many goods when viewed from a distance. But it does suggest that a central mission for EU law is not simply to better our lives but to mediate the cruelty of this by allowing individuals not just to lead better lives but to develop and realize accounts of their lives that they perceive as their own rather than set out for them.

A European Eudaimonia

To consider this *eudaimonia* less abstractly and in more detail, this essay examines three 2008 legislative proposals—those on carbon capture storage ('CCS'); patients' rights in cross-border health care ('PR'); and the provision of food information to consumers ('FI')—which were chosen because of their significance and difference.[6]

The CCS proposal is concerned with the aversion of catastrophe on a global scale.[7] It forms part of a strategy to reduce EU carbon dioxide emissions by 30 per cent by 2020 from 1990 levels. To that end, it is anticipated that 12 large-scale demonstration plants will be built by 2015 to 'capture' emissions and store them underground.[8] The proposal is concerned with regulation of these plants. It is about ecological risk and Man's relation to Nature. The risks are heterogeneous—those associated with emission of CO2 into the atmosphere, but also those associated with the contamination of the CO2 and those associated with leakage.

The PR proposal[9] consolidates the case law of the Court of Justice allowing EU nationals to seek publicly funded health care in another member state where such care could not be provided within their own within a reasonable period of time.[10] This pre-existing legal framework sets expectations so that a central debate in the proposal is whether an individual should still have to wait a reasonable period before seeking treatment abroad.[11] The subjects of the proposal are wide-ranging as entitlements are all given to all persons who might be seeking medical treatment and are entitled to these as social benefits in their state of

[6] The first two were mentioned in the 2008 programme as strategic initiatives, EC Commission, *Commission Legislative and Work Programme 2008*, COM (2007) 640, 14. The proposal on food information was in the 2007 Work Programme but only put forward in early 2008. It is one of the most significant 'simplifying' measures. EC Commission, *Commission Legislative and Work Programme 2007*, COM (2006) 629, 32

[7] EC Commission, *Proposal for a Directive on the geological storage of carbon dioxide and amending Council Directive (EEC) 85/337, Directive (EC) 96/61, Directive (EC) 2000/60, Directive (EC) 2001/80, Directive (EC) 2004/35, Directive (EC) 2006/12 and Regulation (EC) 1013/2006*, COM (2008) 18 ('CCS proposal').

[8] On this see EC Commission, *Limiting Global Climate Change to 2 Degrees Celsius, The Way Ahead for 2020 and Beyond*, COM (2007) 2, 5–6.

[9] EC Commission, *A Community framework on the application of patient's rights in cross-border health care*, COM (2008) 414 ('PR proposal').

[10] The most recent case in a long line is Case C-372/04 *Watts v Bedford Primary Care Trust* [2006] ECR I-4325, para 120.

[11] PR proposal, n 9 above, art 6.

affiliation. The substance of the proposal is about the conferral of a social right, the right to transnational health care, rather than the regulation of ecological risk. Redistributive questions are thus strongly to the fore as something (health care) traditionally considered a collective good, unitary and territorial, is unbundled and made a series of individual rights.[12]

The FI proposal is, in turn, distinctive.[13] The substance of the proposal is consumer rights with the central innovation being more detailed nutrition labelling requirements so that it will be mandatory to declare energy, fat, saturates and carbohydrates levels in food.[14] Like the PR proposal, it takes place within the framework of a settled EU legal background. This is, however, that of detailed legislation with the proposal bringing together eight pieces of legislation. Whilst wide-ranging it grants few, if any, directly effective entitlements to individuals. By contrast, extensive responsibilities are placed on the food industry.[15] The transnational economic dimension is more pressing than the other two proposals with intra-EU trade estimated to account for 75 per cent of all food trade within the EU.[16] Another feature of this proposal is that it occurs in a field—unlike the other two—already governed extensively by EC law where national food information laws are considered the exception, and, therefore, may only be adopted if they meet the conditions of the proposed Regulation.[17] How to look for commonality amongst such diversity? It is not unusual for common principles to be sought in heterogeneous laws which nevertheless enjoy the same formal pedigree. At the beginning of his Clarendon Law Lectures, Justice Breyer stated that 'the United States is a nation built upon the principles of liberty. That liberty means not only from freedom from government coercion but also the freedom to participate in the government itself'.[18]

Whether that is the case for the United States, these forms of liberty do not seem to be pivotal to informing and contouring the content of

[12] The Commission is quick to argue that the proposal will only have a limited effect on the organization and budgets of domestic health care, observing that over 90% of health care needs in the EU will be met by domestic systems. PR proposal, n 9 above, 8. It quotes the estimates of unmet medical need provided by the European Statistics on Income and Living Conditions.

[13] EC Commission, *Proposal for a Regulation on the provision of food information to consumers*, COM (2008) 40 ('FI proposal').

[14] FI proposal, n 13 above, arts 29–34.

[15] FI proposal, n 13 above, art 1(3).

[16] FI proposal, n 13 above, 9.

[17] FI proposal, n 13 above, Arts 37–43.

[18] S Breyer, *Active Liberty* (Oxford University Press, 2008) 9.

these legislative proposals. Instead, all proposals are concerned with securing the well-being of the EU citizenry. The CCS proposal's objective is 'permanent containment of CO_2 in such a way as to prevent or reduce as far as possible negative effect on the environment and any resulting risks to human health'.[19] The PR proposal seeks to establish 'a general framework for the provision of safe, high quality and efficient cross-border health care'.[20] The FI proposal is to provide the 'basis for the assurance of a high level of consumer protection in relation to food information, taking into account the difference in the perception of consumers and their information needs whilst ensuring the smooth functioning of the internal market'.[21]

It is a particular form of well-being that is being sought here. It is neither pleasure for EU citizens nor fulfilment of their desires nor securing of their contentment.[22] It is closer to the Aristotelian notion of *eudaimonia*—a form of self-fulfilment in which we flourish through exercising our human activities.[23] EU law becomes something enabling its subjects to fulfil their capacities to lead a successful and prosperous life. This life is not simply about flourishing but also about virtue as the idea of a prosperous life cannot readily be disentangled from that of a good life in the proposals.

The mission, therefore, at the heart of the FI proposal is to enable consumers to make more informed choices. Yet the information is not on the addictive qualities of food or how it can contribute to hallucinogenic experiences or be made into explosives or poisons. It is provided to enable consumers to lead healthy and ethical lives. The proposal, therefore, states that the information is a basis for consumers 'to make safe use of food, with particular regard to health, economic, environmental, social and ethical considerations'.[24] Food choices are not therefore just about the avoidance of allergens or salts but also about active contribution to a better society. Moreover, a process of identity-formation is to take place in the process. Provision of nutrition information is seen as central to educating the public in that form and heightening awareness of the issue.[25]

[19] CCS proposal, n 7 above, Art 1(2).

[20] PR proposal, n 9 above, Art 1.

[21] FI proposal, n 13 above, Art 1(1)

[22] An accessible and useful account of the literature on well-being can be found in D Haybron, *The Pursuit of Unhappiness: The Elusive Psychology of Well-Being* (Oxford University Press, 2008) 33–7.

[23] Aristotle, n 5 above.

[24] FI proposal, n 13 above, art 3(1).

[25] Ibid. Preamble, para 32.

The PR proposal follows a similar logic. The patient is to be an active guardian of her own health shopping around the single market for the best provider. She has both a freedom and a certain responsibility to secure the most healthy life for herself. For, if she does not, EU law provides no alternatives as to who will take care of it. The proposed Directive is therefore, *inter alia*, concerned to secure her accurate information about health care; clarity about the reimbursement rights; appropriate standards of care across the Union; and administrative rights in her state of affiliation which allow her a quick decision to go abroad for treatment.[26] It is about enlarging the possibilities for EU citizens to secure a healthy life for themselves by enabling them to make reliable choices about the quality of care provided for them and providing the administrative and financial support for those choices. However, this active citizenship does not extend to destabilizing the principles on which medical care is allocated where the perceived benefit is more contentious. They cannot seek treatment, therefore, that is not classified as a benefit in their state of affiliation, either because it is too costly or because its medical efficacy or ethics is challenged.[27]

The relationship between carbon capture and storage—an expensive, limited and tightly regulated process—and this idea of *eudaimonia* seems less apparent. Yet scratch below the surface and a similar story emerges. It is a technology central to the combating of climate change, a priority of the Sixth Environment Action Programme.[28] This programme seeks to decouple environmental pressure from economic growth and integrate ecological protection, balanced social development and economic prosperity of sustainable development in which each is valued and reconciled with the others.[29] The CCS proposal is not, therefore, about the imposition of some eco-centric straitjacket but focuses on allowing us to prosper according to received understandings, albeit adapted to new ecological sensitivities. Its benefits are seen not only to be combating climate change but also contributing to the security of energy supply and to innovation and competitiveness.[30] Certainly these goods are not individualized in the same way as the other two proposals but that is only because this proposal is underpinned by assumptions about the operations of the liberal market

[26] PR proposal, n 9 above, Arts 5–10.

[27] PR proposal, n 9 above, Art 6(1)

[28] Decision (EC) 1600/2002, laying down the Sixth Community Environment Action Programme [2002] OJ L242/1.

[29] Ibid, Preamble, paras 6–8.

[30] CCS proposal, n 7 above, 3.

economy. Debates, therefore, revolve about the effects of this technology on individual energy bills and the liability of operators in case of mishap.[31]

The Qualities of European *Eudaimonia*

But is not *eudaimonia* at the heart of all modern government? It may be but *eudaimonia* is not about a politics of affect or politics of happiness. It is about combining a politics of virtue with a politics of success in which demands of government, society and the citizen are made to be ever better. This perfectionism leads to an escalation of expectations of government and of the citizen that will not only ever be met but can also generate perceptions of breakdown or crisis.[32] In national systems, this vicious cycle is broken by the crucial distinction between state and government, which cuts across it in two important ways.

First, the distinction enables politics and competition for office to be the traditional palliative for the onset of a breakdown as it enables citizens to vote in or vote out governments without exiting from the political system of the state. If a government fails to meet expectations or the type of better life is too demanding or has too many costs, voters try a different medicine with a new government. They still remain part of the state, however. The personalization of the process enables citizens to believe that their national political system can deliver a better life over time as it offers the regular possibility for political renewal. Yet, as has been remarked for some time, this possibility to 'kick the rascals' out does not exist in the same way within the EU political system.[33] This absence not only weakens political accountability but, more importantly for the purposes of this essay, deprives the EU of the possibility of political catharsis with all the possibility for renewal of belief offered by that.

[31] *Analysis and Interpretation of responses from the carbon capture and storage internet consultation: Submission to the European Commission* (ICF International: London, 2007) 12–13 and 24–6.

[32] Haybron, n 22 above, provides a particularly strong critique at 159–170.

[33] The point was made early on in J Weiler, 'To Be a European Citizen—Eros and Civilisation' (2007) *Journal of European Public Policy* 495, 513–14. The strongest recent argument on how to hog-wire political competition more pervasively into the EU political system is in S Hix, *What's Wrong with the European Union and How to Fix It* (Polity: Oxford, 2008).

Secondly, the idea of the nation state carries with it the idea of a 'community of fate'. It is a community of strangers bound by a certain legacy. This legacy may generate a set of symbols or values for which citizens are willing to commit considerable sacrifices. Equally importantly, it generates a pragmatism by placing citizens in an institutional context which they simultaneously recognize as making them who they are but which also requires them to acknowledge limits on what is attainable. Put crudely, a British national would recognize the National Health Service as central to British political identity. Yet if it is a monument to the British political system, its historic under-funding compared to other Western health systems calibrates expectations accordingly. Nobody expects a British politician to realize German standards of public health care within a term of office. This absence of legacy catches EU law in a double bind. It has to offer more to compensate for the absence of affective ties yet also has no support of a historical context that can regulate people's expectations. The consequence is a heightened dependence on a *eudaimonia*, which is of a different scale and intensity, it will be argued, to the national one.

European Eudaimonia*: Realizing the Otherwise Unrealizable*

The Union competes with other tiers of government for the exercise of legislative power and must always show that, by virtue of the scale or imperative of the problem, it is best placed to address the problem.[34] This competition is legally formalized through the duty to demonstrate compliance with the subsidiarity requirement.[35] This contest is, moreover, a perennial one that takes place not only at the moment of adoption of a law but throughout its lifecycle as there is a continual need for justification and an ongoing possibility of review.[36] The goods

[34] On the strength of this see G Morgan, 'European Political Integration and the Need for Justification' (2007) 14 *Constellations* 332. See also the distinction made between performance legitimacy and polity legitimacy in N Walker, 'Constitutionalizing Enlargement, Enlarging Constitutionalism' (2003) 9 European Law Journal 365, 368–70.

[35] Protocol to the EC on the application of the Principles of Subsidiarity and Proportionality, para 4.

[36] The ongoing duty to justify is present in the review provisions attached at the end of most EC legislation committing the legislature to revisit the legislation after a number of years. It is now present in a more concerted manner in the 'Better Regulation' initiative. EC Commission, *A Strategy for the Simplification of the Regulatory Environment*, COM (2005) 535. This has led to 164 initiatives leading to removal of or Commission proposals to remove 2500 legislative acts by the end of 2007. EC

realized by EU law must, therefore, be goods that are, and continue to be, otherwise unattainable by these other tiers of government. This is not a simple question of scale in which EU law is able, for example, to counter trans-boundary effects in a way not possible through unilateral domestic action. EU law must also make a claim that it is ideologically best suited to realizing this level of *eudaimonia*. It must show not simply that it is big enough to realize certain goods but also that it is good enough to do so through its legal and political propensities. Academics refer to the Union as a 'special area of hope',[37] an institutional expression of cosmopolitanism[38] or a special place for civic solidarity.[39] Resonant statements are made in EU mobilizing documents about realizing an unprecedented range, scale and standard of goods.[40]

This percolates through to the micro-level in the style of justification and reflexivity shown in each of the proposals. The central justification for the CCS proposal is that national action cannot secure a sufficiently high level of 'environmental integrity'. In other words, there is more faith in EU law to set in play the appropriate ecological checks and balances than national law.[41] The justification for the FI proposal is not simply that it will realize a transnational good, the internal market,

Commission, *Second Strategic Review of Better Regulation in the European Union*, COM (2008) 32, 2–3.

[37] A Ferrara, 'Europe as a "Special Area for Human Hope" ' (2007) 14 *Constellations* 315.

[38] Z Baumann, *Europe: An Unfinished Adventure* (Polity: Cambridge, 2004) 34–8; A Giddens, *Europe in the Global Age* (Polity: Cambridge, 2007) 233; U Beck and E Grande, *Cosmopolitan Europe* (Polity: Cambridge, 2007) especially 6–11.

[39] J Habermas, *The Divided West* (Polity: Cambridge, 2007) 80–1.

[40] The Treaty of Lisbon amends the TEU so that the Treaty is now to draw inspiration 'from the cultural, religious and humanist inheritance of Europe, from which have developed the universal values of the inviolable and inalienable rights of the human person, freedom, democracy, equality and the rule of law': OJ 2007, C306/10. The European Union Charter of Fundamental Rights and Freedom seeks to assemble and synthesize fundamental rights and freedoms from an unprecedented array of documents—the constitutional traditions and international obligations common to the member states, the TEU, the ECHR, the Social Charters adopted by the Community and by the Council of Europe and the case-law of the Court of Justice and of the European Court of Human Rights (5th para of the Preamble) [2000] OJ C364/1. Perhaps most notoriously, the Lisbon Agenda set out in 2000 the goal to be, by 2010, 'the most competitive and dynamic knowledge-based economy in the world, capable of sustainable economic growth with more and better jobs and greater social cohesion'. *EU Bulletin* 3– 2000, 1–5.

[41] n 7 above, 6. Two other justifications are mentioned, namely the problem of transboundary storage sites and possible distortions of competition. The latter is explicitly couched as a secondary consideration, however, and the former would only justify legislation relating to transboundary sites.

but that it will also lead to lower regulatory costs for transnational companies and secure greater equity between EU citizens through the creation of a floor of consumer rights.[42] Finally, the PR proposal is to establish a new transnational good, cross-border health care, which not only operates in a legally transparent framework but is high quality, safe and efficient.[43]

The paradigm is not only set at an unusually high level, but EU law is also expected to demonstrate acute sensitivity to the heterogeneity of its *eudaimonia*. Appreciation is to be so elevated that EU law both has an awareness of when national laws are better placed to realize it and a capacity to incorporate these seamlessly within its normative schema. The FI proposal therefore allows national labelling laws to be taken for reasons relating to a limited number of public interests but these are subject to Community procedures of justification and authorization.[44] In like vein, the PR proposal notes that universality, access to good quality care, solidarity have been the organizing principles of national health systems across Europe. These 'overarching principles' are to be extended to patients from other member states but not in such a way as to prioritize the latter or act to the detriment of patients in the host state.[45] EU law's understanding of its *eudaimonia* must also be sensitive to its many hues and textures. All proposals are, therefore, subject to assessments measuring their economic, social and ecological impacts, which are, in turn, subject to procedures verifying their own quality.[46] They are to purse multiple goods and show sensitivity to surrounding goods. Mention has already been made of the CCS proposal, which posits itself as not just about limiting emissions, but also innovation and energy security.[47] The FI proposal not only insists that labelling laws are there to enable consumers to take account of a wide array of

[42] FI proposal, n 13 above, 9–10. [43] PR proposal, n 9 above, 7.

[44] Additional mandatory national labelling laws may be adopted for reasons relating to public health, consumer protection, prevention of fraud and protection of intellectual property rights. They must be notified and justified to the Commission. If they are not approved by the Commission, the Commission's draft decision is subject to the regulatory committee procedure. FI proposal, n 13 above, Arts 38, 42(2), 49.

[45] PR proposal, n 9 above, Preamble, para 12.

[46] In 2006 the Commission set up an Impact Assessment Board to monitor the quality of impact assessments. For the report of its activities see EC Commission, *Impact Assessment Board Report for the Year 2007*, SEC (2008) 120. The Commission has also subjected the procedures to external evaluation, *The Evaluation Partnership, Evaluation of the Commission's Impact Assessment Procedures, Final Report* (London, 2007) available at <http://ec.europa.eu/governance/impact/ia_carried_out/cia_2008_en.htm>.

[47] CCS proposal, n 7 above, 3.

policies[48] but is consistent with the Better Regulation Policy and the EU's Lisbon and Sustainable Development Strategies.[49] In like vein, the PR proposal sees itself as not interfering with a number of other policies (smooth coordination of social security schemes, data protection laws or laws on the recognition of professional qualifications) and as contributing to a number of others, notably racial equality, e-health and sharing assessments of new technologies.[50]

Certainly, it might be said that much of this is rhetorical. Little is binding and maybe the EU does not mean what it says. Yet even such a sceptical approach would beg the question why the EU justifies and identifies itself in this way. It can only be because there is a perception that this assuages some extra need. If the response is that the polity is weak and, therefore, must legitimate itself in a particularly shrill and urgent way, this still begs the question as to why 'this way' was chosen and further consideration as to the consequences of the choice of binding EU law so tightly to such a demanding and multi-dimensional understanding of *eudaimonia*.

The Irredeemability of European Eudaimonia

A feature of such a stringent benchmark is there is no mechanism for setting limits to its ambition. The EU can, thus, never be successful enough and consequently the demands it imposes on citizens to make their lives better can never be too exigent. But there is a further twist. If EU law claims that the goods it seeks to attain cannot be realized, it also acknowledges, almost without exception, that they cannot be realized by EU law alone. Indeed, as the objectives of EU law have expanded, a model has emerged in which EU law sets the ends or objectives for a policy regime whilst the means involve a wide array of international, EU, national, regional and local laws or other policy instruments. The mix can vary, and, because of this it has been subject to a wide number of appellations.[51] In some cases, the mix is of one of formal EU laws

[48] FI proposal, n 13 above, Art 3(1).

[49] Ibid. 4. Indeed, read like this, it seems almost as if the CCS and FI proposals are pursuing the same regulatory objectives!

[50] PR proposal, n 9 above, 4–6 and 18–20. See also EC Commission, 'A Community Framework on the Application of Patients' Rights in Cross-Border Healthcare', COM (2008) 415, 2–3.

[51] The formal objectives may be incorporated in directives, framework directives, resolutions, recommendations, benchmarks, targets, best practice. The titles for these arrangements in the literature include governance, multi-level governance, networked

and national laws and regulatory procedures. In other instances, EU law does little more than set general objectives within which member states have considerable latitude both as to means and as to strategy. These two ends of the spectrum cannot be categorized, furthermore, according to the formal pedigree of the instrument. There are situations, on the one hand, where framework directives, devolve almost complete autonomy about not just ways and means but targets and plans to member states.[52] By contrast, there are other circumstances, such as multilateral surveillance of economic policy, where soft law has been found to be highly constraining and to place tight controls on national autonomy.[53]

This division of labour in which the EU sets out the *telos* of a regime and in which it is granted guardianship over the ends and commitments of multiple policy fields reached a new level following the development of the Open Method of Coordination and the governance agendas at the turn of the millennium. These extended this division of labour to policy fields either not traditionally monitored by the Commission or ones that lay outside the formal Treaty limits.[54] A corollary escalation of expectations follows. European *eudaimonia* becomes unconfined in its demands and its dimensions. It sets ever more exacting demands across ever broader swathes of public life.

All this posits a particular relationship between EU law and national law. EU law becomes the superego of public life in Europe. It becomes the benchmark of the institutional measurement of all political and economic activity. As such, because of the irredeemability of European

governance, reflexive harmonization, condominium, consortio. All these titles carry differences but significant overlap. For categorizations see L Hooghe and G Marks, 'Unravelling the Central State, but How? Types of Multilevel Governance' (2003) 97 *American Political Science Review* 233.

[52] An example is the wide-ranging and important Framework Water Directive whose centrepiece is the identification of administrative procedures for river basis management, but leaves considerable leeway to member states as to how this is done and how to realize 'good water' status. Directive (EC) 2000/60 establishing a Community framework for the establishment of a Community Water Policy, [2000] OJ L327/1.

[53] See the excellent piece by Schelkle which emphasizes how the strengthening of the 'soft' procedures of multilateral surveillance whilst weakening the excessive deficit procedures actually led to a Communitarization of economic policy. W Schelkle, 'Hard Law in the Shadow of Soft Law in EU Economic Governance' (2007) 13 Columbia Journal of European Law 705.

[54] On the former see D Hodson and I Maher, 'The Open Method of Coordination as a New Mode of Governance: The Case of Soft Economic Policy Coordination' (2001) 39 *Journal of Common Market Studies* 716. On the latter see J Möllers, 'European Governance: Meaning and Value of a Concept' (2006) 43 Common Market Law Review 313.

eudaimonia, it is identified with the identification of failure and authoritative condemnation of public life across Europe.

In many cases, this is a failure of national laws or administration. This may be via enforcement actions, multilateral surveillance or peer review. So EU law is typically identified as having failed when it does not meet this minimum floor.[55] These processes of critique are also applied internally towards all EU law. The critique here is not that existing EU law does not seek *eudaimonia* but that it has done so inadequately. EU secondary legislation, therefore, invariably contains procedures for its own review. Yet this review habitually involves the paradox of subsequent legislation building upon existing law whilst critiquing its failure. The PR proposal follows the structure of the previous case law but does so on the basis that the latter is not sufficient to bring a general and effective application of the right to provide and receive health services, and is not sufficiently sensitive to the specificities of health services.[56] The FI proposal finds the extensive existing EU legislation on labelling to be piecemeal and of limited effectiveness as a communication tool so seeks to remedy this by making it more detailed and extensive.[57] The CCS proposal is particularly apt. Two international conventions have been amended to allow storage of CO_2 under the seabed.[58] There is, in no sense, any acknowledgment that these amendments build on the goals sought by these treaties. By contrast, the CCS proposal acknowledges the failures of the previous EU legal regime. As reduction of emissions to EU targets may not be possible, mitigation options have to be harnessed.[59] The proposal also states that existing EU legal mechanisms—be they emissions trading or waste legislation or integrated pollution prevention and control ('IPPC')—are insufficient to regulate the risks of carbon capture and storage.[60] If this is the justification for a special regime, however, it is accommodated within these regimes so any CCS plant has to meet waste, IPPC, environmental impact assessment and emissions legislation requirements as well as the further ones of the proposal.[61]

[55] B Laffan and C Shaw, 'Classifying and mapping OMCs in different policy areas', New Government Paper 02/D09 available at <http://www.eu-newgov.org/database/DELIV/D02D09_Classifying_and_Mapping_OMC.pdf>

[56] PR proposal, n 9 above, 2. [57] FI proposal, n 13 above, 5–7.

[58] The Convention on the Prevention of Marine Pollution by Dumping of Wastes and Other Matter ('1972 London Convention') and the Convention for the Protection of the Marine Environment of the North East Atlantic ('1992 OSPAR Convention')

[59] CCS proposal, n 7 above, Preamble, para 3. [60] Ibid, 5.

[61] CCS proposal, n 7 above, Arts 29–35.

The Politics of the European Eudaimonia

A feature of a combination of laws or institutions being harnessed to realize a common good is that law acquires a pre-eminent coordinating role. Its coercive effects are less salient. Instead, the expectations set by it about roles, relationships, commitments and responsibilities of actors are more to the fore. Coordination creates its own form of politics. The common good and the tasks asked by it may be contested. A vibrant example is the EU's anti-terror strategy which has a whole array of civil society established to police it and curb it.[62] A politics might also emerge from the coordination generating new vectors and institutional relations which undermine traditional checks and balances and legal constraints. The Open Method of Coordination has thus been seen as allowing national administrations avoiding being tied down by the usual processes.[63] Finally, contestation might take place even in the absence of such formal networks. For EU laws provide powerful norms enabling and requiring institutional actors to take measures that may background other goals or *modi vivendi*.[64]

If politics is a necessary condition therefore surrounding EU law, EU law's *eudaimonia* has led to its being a politics of unfalsifiable claims. By requiring multiple actors to combine to realize stringent long-term goals, EU law renders it impossible for the contribution of any actor to be gauged. This both diffuses accountability and escalates it exponentially, as the actions of the actors are perceived in everything or nothing terms. The contribution becomes something, therefore, which is exposed to an intractable claim and counterclaim. Greenpeace and the European Renewable Energy Council have, thus, opposed the development of carbon capture and storage partly out of concerns about the safety and viability of the technology. They also, however, believe the cost of the technology will displace investment in renewable energy, and, insofar as it might be subsidized, lead to new fossil fuel

[62] The current state of play is set out in EC Commission, *Revised Action Plan on Terrorism*, SEC (2006) 686. The most interesting account and critical observatory on this is the Statewatch Observatory available at <http://www.statewatch.org/observatory2.htm>.

[63] C Joerges, 'Integration through de-legalisation' (2008) 33 ELR 291, 310.

[64] Most persuasively on how EU legal frames cut across and disrupt national legal practices see C Schmid, 'Diagonal Competence Conflicts between European Competition Law and National Law: The example of book price fixing' (2000) 8 European Review of Private Law 155.

developments.[65] Such a claim may or may not be true but will never be tested because it would have to be assessed against all the other abatement measures taken within the Union and then against the counterfactual of what these might have been without this technology. Similarly, the FI information proposal is part of a regime designed to lead to more informed consumer choices and to healthier lifestyles. Even in a field governed so extensively by EU law, there is no information on how many people act on the information they read on labels, and the contribution of the latter takes place against a context of a blizzard of advertising and multifarious national health policies so that whilst, intuitively, labelling appears a good thing its contribution is highly uncertain. In terms of goods, all that can be measured in terms of each proposal is the amount of carbon dioxide stored and the amount of label information read by consumers.

If the politics of unfalsifiable claims permeate all governance regimes, even exclusively national ones, EU law adds an idiosyncratic feature. As EU law is associated with the *telos* of any regime, even if others contribute to its ways and means, it territorializes these tensions. Whilst it may be difficult to hold individual actors to account, it is possible to make general statements about the effectiveness or ideology of the overall regime[66] and the overall regime is tagged as European Union because it contributes to the European *eudaimonia*, and its overall performance is seen as something European for the same reason. Thus, whilst curbing climate change, health policy, etc, are not seen as something on which the Union has a monopoly, it enjoys a hegemony over the particularly regulatory route to realize these goods. Criticism of this route or this goal becomes constructed, therefore, as *anti-European*, and experience of, the disruption and the costs as *local*.[67] It is local constraints and controls that are lost; local people who suffer the risks of carbon capture and storage; local health services who might lose the capacity to operate under the principle of universality. To be sure, there is no *a priori* reason for this as these are experienced across the Union. It is the framing of the politics that makes it so.

[65] Greenpeace/European Renewable Energy Council, *Energy [r]evolution: A sustainable global energy outlook* (2008, Brussels) 133–4

[66] eg, see The Lisbon strategy could be said not to have realized its goals or the war on terror be criticized for its stance on civil liberties.

[67] G Teubner 'Legal Irritants: Good Faith in British Law and How Unifying Law Ends Up in New Divergences' (1998) 61 MLR 11.

To be sure, this territorialization in which ideological adversaries coalesce and consolidate around European Union and national poles can render political issues more salient and more acute.[68] However, the mechanisms or containers for mediating it or transforming it into innovative solutions are not apparent. Only two routes seem available. One is to reform the EU policy in question through participation in the EU public sphere. Yet, how realistic is this in a polity of half a billion people with many veto players for the majority of actors? It requires them, moreover, to frame their responses in pan Union terms—something that may not be readily accessible.[69] The alternative, because of the principle of the supremacy of Union law, is a decisionist logic in which opponents choose whether or not to comply with EU law and authorities decide whether or not to enforce it.

The Justice of the European Eudaimonia

The earlier quote from Breyer stated that the United States was not just founded upon the principle of liberty but was also a nation. As a political community of 'free and equals' the nation mediates the relationship between freedom and equality by insisting upon the public good securing a balance between the two. It is also important for reasons of identification as it sets out a series of claims as to why a particular interpretation of the good life with all its benefits and costs should be borne by a particular group of strangers at a certain place and time.[70] In this regard, the absence of a European Demos is significant. This is usually referred to as a form of sociological affect, an absence of sufficient belief in European-ness to see good reasons to bear significant sacrifices for the benefit of other

[68] D Chalmers, 'Reconciling European Risks and Traditional Ways of Life' (2003) 66 MLR 532, 558–62.

[69] An example of this is the decision of the Spanish Government not to comply with the requirement in Annex I of Directive 2007/23 on the placing of the market of pyrotechnic articles [2007] OJ L154/1, which requires the public to be at least 15 meters from certain types of fireworks. This is felt to compromise the nature of many Spanish festivals, most notably the Fallas of Valencia, notwithstanding that there are significant burns injuries in Spain every year because of this. It would be difficult for Spain to make a pan Union case here but the issue has generated considerable popular feeling in Eastern Spain: see <http://www.guardian.co.uk/world/2009/feb/21/spain-eu-fiestas-fires>.

[70] On this objection and its refutation see J Rubenfeld, *Freedom and Time: A Theory of Constitutional Self- Government* (Yale University Press: New Haven, 2001) 131–3.

Europeans.[71] Its absence is, however, also a failure of the imaginary. The absence of any idea of equivalent political community to that of the nation frames and limits the types of claim that EU law makes. It limits, in particular, the type of claim to justice it makes and the types of community for whose benefit it purports to act.

An immediate response might be that individual national laws do not justify themselves by references to vague notions of national political community and EU law is not insensitive to its distributive impacts and has distributive policies of its own. The argument is not that these are not present in EU law but that its notions of political community and social justice are markedly different from national ones. The starting point, drawn from Durkheim, is that two forms of social solidarity or justice are present in national systems.[72] These are mechanical solidarity, which is based on ideas of kinship and sameness (for example, religion or ethnicity) and organic solidarity which is based on the division of labour and notions of interdependence that flow from that and which lead interdependent parties to acknowledge mutual claims (for example employee rights, corporate law, consumer rights). National ideas of social justice and community rely on a dialectic between these two ideas of solidarity in which institutes the idea that there is something that binds a community beyond the division of labour and that the latter can never meet all the community's needs.[73] In this regard, ideas of nationhood have traditionally played an important role as the central receptacle for ideas of mechanical solidarity in modern societies with legal expressions of mechanical solidarity—family law, religious law, criminal law—all being predominantly governed by national law as these institutions have historically been seen as central to nation-building.

There is simply no equivalent at an EU level. The types of solidarity present in the European *eudaimonia* are centred around 'organic' ideas of solidarity generated by ideas of interdependence. In the three legislative proposals, those consulted and the impacts assessed were those

[71] The famous point by F Scharpf, *Governing in Europe: Effective and Democratic?* (Oxford University Press, 1998) 8–9.

[72] E Durkheim, *The Division of Labour in Society* (translated by L Coser) (Macmillan: London, 1984) chs II and III.

[73] R Unger, *Social Theory: Its Situation and Its Task* (Cambridge University Press: Cambridge, 1987) 1–4. For a critique see M Halberstam, *Totalitarianism and the Modern Conception of Politics* (Yale University Press: New Haven-London, 1999) 22–6.

considered to be most strongly affected by the proposals.[74] Within the proposals, notions of solidarity are, in turn, informed by the relations of interdependence between particular parties. The FI proposal recalibrates the relationship between food provider and final consumer;[75] the PR proposal that between the transnational patient, health care providers and public funders of health care; the CCS proposal that between operators and regulators but also, insofar as the processes will be governed by environmental impact assessment procedures, the public affected by the development.[76] The conception of justice as a form of quid pro quo is reflected in the policing of these regimes in which the central redress is restitutionary. Both the PR and CCS proposals rely on liability schemes. The *PR* proposal requires patients to have the possibility of making complaints and receiving compensation when they suffer harm from healthcare.[77] The CCS proposal provides for the extension of the environmental liability regime in Directive 2004/35/EC to apply to carbon capture and storage.[78] The FI proposal provides for no sanctions for non-compliance but does leave open the possibility that any contract would be void as a result of non-compliance and any harm suffered subject to redress under the Product Liability Directive.[79]

A feature of such solidarity is the formalism of its ties, with considerable attention to the effects of EU legislation on other interdependencies. The FI proposal, therefore, provides for special national regimes to continue to apply with regard to non pre-packed food, milk in glass bottles and most alcoholic beverages because it is acceptable that it is either extremely disruptive and in some cases impracticable to impose labelling rules on these or that other effectives means of imparting information have developed.[80] Likewise, food operators

[74] For the impact assessment of the three proposals see <http://ec.europa.eu/governance/impact/cia_2008_en.htm>

[75] The proposal therefore states that the Regulation shall provide 'the basis for the assurance of a high level of consumer protection in relation to food information' FI proposal, n 13 above, Art 1(1).

[76] The requirements of environmental impact assessment are incorporated in CCS proposal, n 7 above, Art 29. The duties of consultation are established in Directive 85/337/EEC on the assessment of the effects of certain public and private projects on the environment, [1985] OJ L175/40, Art 6(2).

[77] PR proposal, n 9 above, Art 5(1)(d).

[78] CCS proposal, n 7 above, Art 33

[79] See in particular the test of strict liability for damage caused from defective products in Directive 85/374/EC on the approximation of laws concerning liability for defective products [1985] OJ L210/29, Art 1.

[80] FI proposal, n 13 above, Arts 39–41.

below a certain size have been given additional two years to implement some of the proposal's requirement in acknowledgment of the latter's regulatory cost.[81]

This vision is narrow by virtue of its lack of affect. It has no regard to the feelings or symbols that might generate empathy or a sense of common enterprise. It cannot explain why EU citizens in one region should feel a commitment to marginalized groups in geographically distant regions within or beyond the Union. It is narrow in another sense. Solidarity is conceived in highly individualistic terms. The PR proposal refers to the 'patient' as a holder of entitlements[82] and the FI proposal premised on the notion of the 'average consumer'.[83] This individualization leads both to a disaggregration in which the private and the public are put on the same footing, and to an assimilation in which insensitivity is shown either to context or to differences in resources, endowments or capacities. Solidarity is levelled down in all this and shorn of its hue and seductive appeal. Equally importantly, it is denuded of its creative and reflexive dimensions. For a feature of many forms of solidarity is an ongoing concern with the insufficiency of current arrangements to respond fully to the needs and desires of everybody in which attention is focused recurringly not just on what is being distributed but on the singularity of different actors and their claims.[84]

The Claims of European *Eudaimonia*

The traits described in the previous section of the *eudaimonia* through which EU law is identified and justified tell us little about how EU law is to realize this *eudaimonia*. Yet EU law does not just set out a resonant picture of the good life. It is also a regulatory institution which seeks to secure it. This entails that legal instruments must be configured and coordinated in such a way that they do not just recognize this *eudaimonia*, but organize and direct behaviour towards it. This in turn

[81] FI proposal, n 13 above, Art 53.

[82] PR proposal, n 9 above, Art 4(f). Its definition excludes those who do not travel abroad for treatment.

[83] FI proposal, n 13 above, Preamble, para 38.

[84] The work of Axel Honneth therefore sees a commitment to symmetrical esteem in which the traits and values of each are symmetrically solidarity as a pre-requisite for solidarity. A Honneth, *Struggle for Recognition. The Moral Grammar of Social Conflicts* (Polity: Oxford, 1995) ch 5.

generates those microprocesses which govern how EU law is experienced—the types of claim made on individuals; the entitlements, responsibilities and powers granted; and the form of rule generated.

A Narrow Range of Entitlements

EU laws may benefit wide numbers of people but a feature of EU law is that it gives a very narrow range of positive entitlements which can be directly invoked and are actively invoked by its subjects. The following central entitlements are set out in the three proposals.

(1) The CCS procedure grants, subject to permits, operators the possibility to explore sites for carbon capture and storage and to store carbon dioxide at suitable sites.[85]

(2) The PR proposal grants persons covered by an EU public health scheme the entitlement to go to another member state for health care for something that is covered as a benefit by the legislation in their state of affiliation, and to have a number of procedural and substantive rights associated with that.[86]

(3) The FI proposal proposes mandatory food information for consumers on the identity and composition of the food, on protection of consumer's health and safe use and on the food's nutritional characteristics.[87]

The CCS proposal is self-avowedly for a small number—twelve—of capital intensive installations who have the capacity to install, supervise and maintain costly and complicated technology. If the other two proposals seem wide-ranging insofar as they affect patients and consumers of food, the pictures changes when one looks at the actual exercise of entitlements. With regard to food labelling, the number of consumers who look at labels is high and increasing. Most studies suggest that it is more than half of all consumers. More detailed studies, however, have suggested that self-reporting has exaggerated the extent to which consumers read labels with observational studies suggesting that the proportion of consumers who actually study labels rather than

[85] CCS proposal, n 7 above, Arts 5, 8.

[86] PR proposal, n 9 above, Art 6(1). These include, in the state of treatment, protection of personal data, equal treatment with that state's own nationals, information that will enable them to make an informed choice about the procedure; possibilities for complaints and remedies in the case of harm. Ibid, Art 5(1).

[87] FI proposal, n 13 above, Arts 4(1), 6.

glance at 'sell by dates' being less than 20 per cent. Whilst there is no research on the number of the consumers acting on the labels, one study suggests only 1 per cent read and understand nutritional information on labels—the central reform of the FI proposal.[88] The PR proposal is similar. The Commission is eager to minimize the resource implications, suggesting that very few individuals will exercise this transnational right. It notes that transnational care currently only accounts for about 1 per cent of national health care budgets and that 90 per cent of patient needs can be met through domestic systems.[89] To be sure, there is no comprehensive or reliable data on this.[90] Qualitative research suggests, however, that the patients who exercise their rights under the post *Kohll* case law to publicly funded health care abroad did so usually where they were both certified as fit to travel and for a narrow range of highly specialized health care services.[91]

This all begs the question whether there is selection bias here. After all, it is possible to think of EU law entitlements that are widely distributed and reasonably egalitarian. EU labour law is the most obvious example, but VAT law might be another. Yet, if the diffuse benefits of EU law might be more widely spread, it does seem that the direct grant of entitlements is narrow and highly contested. Highly dated research conducted by the author has suggested very little EU law is invoked in British courts. By the end of 1998, just 5 Directives accounted for 73 per cent of the instances in which Directives were invoked before British courts. Litigation was focused, furthermore, in a very narrow area of EC law. Five sectors accounted for 61 per cent of all the cases, and large policy areas, such as the single market, financial services, company law, consumer law, environmental law were marked by little or no litigation. Only 32.6 per cent of EC litigation involved disputes between private

[88] It was thus stated 'Consumers reported that they did understand the terms 'fat', 'calories/kilocalories', 'sugar', 'vitamins' and 'salt'. The concepts and terms reported as least well understood were the relationship between calories and energy; sodium and salt; sugar and carbohydrate; and the terms cholesterol and fatty acids. Consumers had difficulty in understanding the role that different nutrients mentioned on labels played in their diet. They also had difficulty converting information from g per 100 g to g per serving and serving size information also proved difficult to interpret. . .' G. Cowburn, & L. Stockley 'Consumer understanding and the use of nutrition labelling: a review' (2005) 8 *Public Health Nutrition* 21, 23.

[89] PR proposal, n 9 above, 8.

[90] European Commission, *High Level Group on Health Services and Medical Care* (DG Health and Consumer Protection, 2006) 6.

[91] M Rosenmöller, M McKee and R Baeten (eds) *Patient Mobility in the European Union: Learning from Experience* (European Observatory on Health Systems and Policies: Brussels, 2006)especially at 180.

parties, with two instruments, the Sex Discrimination and the TUPE Directives, accounting for 64.5 per cent of these instances.[92]

The reason for this derives from European Union law's *eudaimonia* having to secure goods not realizable by domestic action alone. Most entitlements can simply be granted through national law. The only reason for the grant of EU legal entitlements is when these would realize some new transnational good. This may take the form of some transnational right (for example, transnational health care) or the incidence of some collective good which, as a collective good, rarely depends on litigation to be realized.

In other instances, the justification for EU legal involvement involves either a deontological claim—it is good just because it is—or a claim that EU law knows better how to recognize and realize an existing good than national procedures. Yet both arguments are ones that are only politically sustainable in the most exceptional circumstances, and cannot be used to justify a wide-ranging intervention.

Turning first to the deontological argument, if we recognize something as so good for its own sake, it does not matter at what level it is regulated. In such cases, the argument is for universal regulation and EU law becomes simply an institutional expression of cosmopolitan values. Arguments surrounding Union or European regulation of abortion, holocaust denial or hate speech often seem to be underpinned by this.[93] One difficulty is what happens if a party disputes the presence of the good or the basis on which it is justified as a good.[94] An even more substantive difficulty is that the programming facilities of cosmopolitanism are very thin. It does not go to defining the limit or ways or means of realizing a good. It cannot set procedures for termination of a foetus or a complete definition of hate speech or denial.

[92] Chalmers, n 1 above, 178–83.

[93] See the notion of European Union demokratia promoted by T Garton Ash, 'We need a benign European hydra to advance the cause of democracy' *Guardian*, 17 April 2008, available at <http://www.guardian.co.uk/commentisfree/2008/apr/17/eu.usa>. On a pan-European right to abortion see Resolution 1607 of the Parliamentary Assembly of the Council of Europe, 'Access to safe and legal abortion' (2008) available at <http://assembly.coe.int/Mainf.asp?link=/Documents/AdoptedText/ta08/ERES1607.htm#1>.

[94] On the European Union criminalizing holocaust denial, the British *Daily Telegraph* stated, 'People who question the official history of recent conflicts in Africa and the Balkans could be jailed for up to three years for "genocide denial", under proposed EU legislation . . .' B Waterfield, ' EU plans far reaching "genocide denial" law' *Daily Telegraph*, 3 February 2007, available at <http://www.telegraph.co.uk/news/worldnews/1541411/EU-plans-far-reaching-genocide-denial-law.html>.

The other argument is premised on a good only acquiring normative status upon awareness of it as a good. A goal of law is therefore enquiry into what is good for us to do. In this, EU law may have advantages over other legal processes in this form of enquiry. Variations of this argument have been found in EU equal opportunities law where authors have argued that EU law has been able to develop a more progressive agenda than its national counterparts because the Court of Justice offers an arena for marginalized interests to escape the hegemony and capture of domestic institutions by regressive majorities or elites.[95] Unhappy with these institutions and unable to obtain sufficient voice there, these interests have been able to use the Court to express arguments that were otherwise pushed aside. There has thus been a freer market of ideas less dominated by entrenched interests before the Court of Justice in these fields.

There is something in this, but this argument creates the conditions for its own demise. Its starting point is that there is uncertainty surrounding what we know as good. We cannot know whether basing levels of pay on length of service is bad because it discriminates against women so EU law is to take a determinative judgment on this as other venues are suspect.[96] As the example shows, it assumes not only high contestation surrounding any judgment but also an element of normative absence. We are not sure of the reasons for action one way or another. Alongside this, the argument is a consequentialist one as it is based on the idea of something as good when we are confident of its consequences—it will lead to good things. Yet a body as remote as the Court of Justice from the heterogeneity surrounding the lives of half a billion people simply cannot know whether it is good for all of them or how it is good for them. Whatever the substantive merits of this argument, it begets a level of political contestation which suggests that EU law can only be deployed occasionally for this purpose.

The Unfair Distribution of Entitlements

The entitlements are not just narrowly confined—their distribution generates significant asymmetries. If the CCS proposal imposes

[95] From different traditions see M Poiares Maduro, *We, The Court: The European Court of Justice & the European Economic Constitution* (Hart: Oxford, 1998) 166–74; K Alter, 'The European Union's Legal System and Domestic Policy: Spillover or Backlash?' (2000) 154 *International Organization* 489.

[96] Case C-17/05 *Cadman v HSE* [2006] ECR 9583.

significant responsibilities and costs on the operators of 12 installations, it also empowers them. Carbon Capture storage is estimated at having the potential to reduce the cost of stabilizing CO_2 emissions by 30 per cent—an astronomical value in any emissions trading scheme.[97] The effects on the structure of the energy market are significant. The costs of the technology are high and they, therefore, push towards development of larger coal-fired power plants because of the economies of the scale of the latter. All this suggests a considerable concentration of industrial power.[98] With regard to the FI proposal, research suggests that labels are far more likely to be read by those of 'high educational achievement' who were women and lived in smaller households.[99] Whilst the PR proposal is adamant that that health care should be distributed on the basis of equity, universality and solidarity,[100] a new test is introduced—that of non-discrimination on nationality and respect for free movement.[101] It is a curious notion of non-discrimination, however. For it can only be invoked by patients who move for care from one state to another.[102] There are no entitlements in the proposal for patients in the state of affiliation to require the same level of treatment as those who are moving. Nor is there any for those in the member state of treatment to require the same level of care as mobile patients from other member states. It is a legal entitlement just given to mobile patients. There is not only a differentiation in legal entitlements between those who have the same ailment but, perhaps more importantly, a significant asymmetry emerges between patients with different types of condition. Those with a condition which requires specialized treatment but allows mobility are privileged vis-a-vis patients with other conditions. The former can demand resources to be spent on them, in particular access to specialized care in a way that is not available to other conditions and in a way that will be at the expense of the resources deployed on the latter.

How could this be so? It goes to the restricted imaginary of justice in the *eudaimonia* of EU law. Conceived around formalistic notions of

[97] On this see Integrated Pollution Prevention and Control Special Report, *Carbon Capture and Storage: A Special Report of Working Group III of the Intergovernmental Panel on Climate Change* (Cambridge University Press: Cambridge, 2005) 12.

[98] Ibid, 344ff.

[99] A summary of the research has been provided by the Foods Standards Agency, *Review and analysis of current literature on consumer understanding of nutrition and health claims made on food* (Food Standards Agency: London, 2007) available at <http://www.food.gov.uk/multimedia/pdfs/healthclaims.pdf>.

[100] PR proposal, n 9 above, Preamble, para 12

[101] Ibid, Preamble, para 12.

[102] Ibid, Art 5(1)(g).

interdependence, it lacks the scale of vision to countenance different styles of claim. There is thus no vision of public health which allows the different claims of different conditions and their treatments to be evaluated against one another. This restriction is not just one of range but also one of affect. Put simply EU law lacks an affective capacity which would enable it to gauge the value of treating one versus the value of treating another.

Subjection to Unimaginable Risks

A feature of all three proposals is that the risks in question are incalculable. If a feature of traditional risks is that they are seen as managed uncertainties whose incidence can be subjected to some form of calculation, many of the dangers regulated by EU law sit at the penumbra of this spectrum of calculation. It is not that they are necessarily more remote but they are particularly difficult to assess in any meaningful way.

With regard to the CCS proposal, there is almost no basis by which to gauge the economic and ecological risks of the technology. Current estimates on the financial cost of carbon capture and storage are linked to the costs of surveying the territory in question and those of pumping and transporting the CO_2. The costs of monitoring the site; post-closure obligations; and remediation of any leak are impossible to tell. There is then the imponderable of how much of this can be passed on to the customer. The ecological risks are even more uncertain. There are concerns that storage can increase the possibility of earthquakes and that leakage can lead to mass poisoning of the surrounding landscape. It is also uncertain how responsibility can be ascribed given the ubiquitous presence of CO_2 in the atmosphere. These ecological risks are considered remote but it is acknowledged that 'there is limited experience with geological storage, closely related industrial experience and scientific knowledge could serve as a basis for appropriate risk management'.[103] In other words, there is an element of speculation about the process because it is unprecedented and one has to proceed on the basis of apparently analogous processes. This was reflected in the Commission's consultation in which there was an extremely high proportion of 'don't knows' with parties unable to comment on the levels of ecological risk.[104] There is, consequently, increased emphasis on

[103] IPPC, n 97 above, 13.

[104] ICF International, *Analysis and Interpretation of responses from the CCS consultation* (Brussels, 2007) 10– 12.

procedure. The CO_2 stream must be kept as pure as possible and registers must be kept of the qualities and quantities of the CO_2 streams.[105] The operator is responsible for monitoring the injection facilities; storage complex; and surrounding environment for leakages or adverse ecological effects.[106] There must be regular reports to the authorities[107] and, in cases of significant irregularities or leakages, corrective measures must be taken.[108] These obligations all continue after closure of the site.[109]

The risks associated with the PR proposal derive from the patient being treated in another member state. There is an issue of continuity of care. How is after-care provided or follow-up treatment? The proposal has little to say on this but focuses on other dangers, namely lack of familiarity with the foreign health system and commensurability of health care standards across the different national systems. On the former, national contact points are to be established for cross-border health care. These are, *inter alia*, to provide patients with information on their rights and guarantees of quality and safety as well as helping to protect their rights and obtain out of court settlements where called for.[110] To secure commensurability of health care standards, European reference networks are to be put in place which promote not only cooperation between health care provider and maximize cost-effectiveness, but which also share knowledge and provide quality and safety benchmarks spreading best practice.[111] Combined, these networks created integrated reference points for the provision and allocation of health care in the European Union. Allocation is to take place through coordination and specialization. More broadly, they are also to change how health care is provided through enabling synergies between providers and the development of common approaches and methodologies, and these might be the most wide-ranging effects of the proposal.

A similar style of risk is found in the FI proposal. The central amendment is to provide labelling information on the nutritional qualities of food. All food must contain a nutrition declaration which provides information about the amounts of energy, fats, saturates and carbohydrates with specific reference to sugar and salt.[112] It may also include details on the amount of other nutrients which include

[105] CCS proposal, n 7 above, Art 12. [106] Ibid, Art 13. [107] Ibid. Art 14.
[108] Ibid. Art 16. [109] Ibid. Art 17(2). [110] Ibid. Art 12(2).
[111] Ibid, Art 15(2). [112] FI proposal, n 13 above, Arts 9(1)(l), 29(1).

protein, fibre, vitamins, transfats and mono- or poly-unsaturates.[113] A feature of nutrition is that it is the provision of cells, material and organisms to support life. A feature of almost all nutrients, and certainly all the ones on the mandatory list, is that none are bad or good per se. The problem arises if there is a deficiency or an excess. Nutritional science is notoriously inexact, therefore, as it must always look at the state of a body before and after the consumption of nutrients over a significant period during which a lot of other variables will come into play. Whilst there is course evidence of poor nutrition it is measured in outcomes, such as 30 per cent of the EU population being overweight in 2006.[114] The EU strategy on nutrition is therefore one based on precautionary politics. No food is banned because of its nutritional qualities on the grounds that the *ex ante* risk of excess is too great. Instead, individuals are encouraged to make healthy life style choices which integrate nutritional balance into this. Labelling has therefore become central to this strategy. If the FI proposal is about enabling individuals to make 'informed choices' by setting out the nutritional qualities of food, alongside it the Union has been eager to prevent manipulation of their choices by food providers, so we also find legislation not requiring the insertion of information but regulating the type of health or nutrition claims that may be made about food.[115]

The reasons for the management of this particular quality of risk lie in the European Union being concerned with the extension of *eudaimonia*. It does not reinvent the idea of a better life but aims to augment existing possibilities and understandings. This extension of opportunities is most obvious where it happens spatially. The PR proposal does not establish for the first time the idea of individual access to public health care but transnationalizes that right by making it an entitlement that stretches across a broader territory with a wider range of providers and types of provision. Yet *eudaimonia* stretches EU law in a more profound sense. As stated earlier, its ambition requires EU law to enable us not only to do things which would not otherwise be possible but to do them in a better way. This creates a particular relationship between EU law and risk. On the one hand, EU law is concerned to let

[113] Ibid, Art 29(2).

[114] EC Commission, *White Paper on A Strategy for Europe on Nutrition, Overweight and Obesity Related Health Issues*, COM (2007) 279, 2.

[115] Regulation 1924/2006 on nutrition and health claims made on foods [2007] OJ L12/3.

us to dare to do more things.[116] It enables us to experiment with biotechnology; complex financial markets; climate change; mass harvesting of fish stocks; diverse patterns of regulatory control, such as mutual recognition precisely because it is confident of its capacity to manage these things. On the other, it is concerned to manage these dangers more effectively than other regimes. The justification for EU regulation is that it can avert dangers that national authorities cannot. Once again, this is not simply a question of scale but of regulatory capacity and disposition. Commitments are thus made to high levels of safety and regulation.[117] Furthermore, the EU is to regulate those risks over which there are doubts about individual national capacity either because there is mistrust between regulators to realize this effectively or because the incidence, nature or scale of the risk is seen as particularly challenging to gauge. This is reflected in the institutional features of EU law. Mutual mistrust between regulators has led to a system where national regulators seek high guarantees from EU law which often go to inspection and certification.[118] A parallel process has emerged in situations, such as pharmaceuticals, food safety, and chemicals, where a European agency is set up to consider questions of market access. There is invariably provision for consultation of national regulators with the consequence that the agency acts as a meeting point for multiple regulators to reach a consensus and to verify each other's arguments.[119]

[116] Risk is said, therefore, to derive from *risicare*, from the Italian word 'to dare'. On the development of the term see P Bernstein, *Against the Gods: The Remarkable Story of Risk* (John Wiley: New York, 1996) especially chs 6–11.

[117] The strongest statement is in Art 95(3) of the EC Treaty which commits EU market regulation to a high level of health safety, environmental protection, and consumer protection.

[118] The point has been made by Majone with regard to the evolution of insurance and pharmaceuticals regulation. See G Majone, 'Mutual Trust, Credible Commitments and the Evolution of the Rules of the Single Market', EUI Working Paper RSC 95/1 (EUI: Fiesole). An equally strong case is the Whole Vehicle Type Approval process for the car market where since the early 1970s regulatory authorities have been required to comply with detailed testing and approval models. The process has been recast in Directive 2007/46 establishing a framework for the approval of motor vehicles and their trailers, and of systems, components and separate technical units intended for such vehicles [2007] OJ L263/1.

[119] This is formalized in duties upon Community agencies to resolve differences with and, in certain circumstances, liaise with national counterparts. Regulation (EC) 178/2002 establishing general principles for food safety and a European Food Safety Authority [2002] OJ L31/1, Arts 22(7), 30; Regulation (EC) 726/2004 laying down Community procedures for the authorisation and supervision of medicinal products for human and veterinary use and establishing a European Medicines Agency [2004] OJ L136/1, Arts 47, 50, 59(4); Regulation 1907/2006 concerning the Registration,

Substantively, this leads to EU law engaging with a particular style of activity in a particular way. EU law is granted guardianship over the most challenging form of risk because it claims a superior power of management. This power is justified in a claim to possess a better awareness of risk. This claim is founded partly on the authority of expertise—the use of multiple regulators—but it is also founded upon a claim to regulatory assurance in which the limits of scientific knowledge are perfectly understood. It is this which leads EU law to claim that it can regulate dangers whose parameters science or expertise does not fully understand or know. The most salient exposition of this is the prevalence of the precautionary principle in EU law, which allows for regulatory protection if the possibility of harm has been identified even if widespread scientific uncertainty persists.[120] A feature of this principle and analogous logics is that they are concerned not so much with gauging danger as managing the anxiety that arises from the failure to be able to do the former in a sufficiently compelling way. The principle allows recourse to heuristic and rule of thumb techniques on the grounds that expertise cannot provide the answer.[121] Yet what to do when having relied on expertise to secure jurisdiction, EU law rejects *a priori* the quest for scientific evidence as a model for decision-making?[122] Some have argued this space provides an opportunity for political participation[123] whilst others have decried the administrative freedom allowed by it.[124] Either political scenario is confronted with a context, however, which is the opposite to that promised. The promise of being allowed to do more things more safely is replaced by a reality of decision-makers and public having to confront unimaginable risks—dangers that cannot be fully gauged and for which only partial

Evaluation, Authorization and Restriction of Chemicals (REACH), establishing a European Chemicals Agency [2007] OJ L136/3, Arts 85(5) and 6(6).

[120] The literature is extensive but a particularly fine recent review is E Fischer, 'Opening Pandora's box: contextualizing the precautionary principle in the European Union' in M Everson and E Vos (eds) *Uncertain Risks Regulated* (Routledge-Cavendish: Abingdon, 2009).

[121] K Haggerty, 'From Risk to Precaution: The Rationalities of Crime Prevention' in R Ericson and A Doyle (eds) *Risk and Morality* (University of Toronto Press, Toronto, 2003) 193, 194–5.

[122] C Joerges, 'Sound Science in the European and Global Market: Karl Polanyi in Geneva', in M Everson and E Vos (eds) *Uncertain Risks Regulated* (Routledge-Cavendish: Abingdon, 2009) 415, 420.

[123] J Scott and S Sturm, 'Courts as Catalysts: Rethinking the Judicial Role in New Governance' (2007) 13 Columbia Journal of European Law 565.

[124] V Heyvaert, 'Facing the Consequences of the Precautionary Principle in European Community Law' (2006) 31 ELR 185.

reassurances and incomplete normative structures can be offered. This is no longer a reassuring world but one in which law institutes anxiety and a counter-impulse to do nothing.[125]

The Responsibilities of the European Subject

These risks fall on EU legal subjects. One style of risk is borne by those responsible for managing the quality of the operation—the providers of food or hospital services and the operators of carbon capture storage facilities. The other bearers of risks—the patient, the consumer, the public affected by carbon dioxide escape—are those required to adopt precautionary life strategies taking into account the risk to which they are being exposed. The levels of responsibility for the former are high in all three proposals. The CCS proposal imposes strong duties on site selection. The geological formation must be such that there is no significant risk of leakage or significant negative environmental or health impacts are likely to occur.[126] Similar duties apply to management of the stream. The operator must ensure concentrations of substances other than CO_2 do not affect the integrity of the site or pose a significant risk to the environment.[127] The operator is strictly liable for any environmental damage that occurs, irrespective of compliance with the Directive.[128] In like ilk, the PR proposal imposes new duties on providers of health services. There is intended to be a levelling up of quality so member states must create mechanisms to ensure compliance with recognized good medical practice. There must be monitoring and corrective action where this does not happen.[129] There must be systems of compensation and professional liability insurance schemes.[130] The standard of care in the FI proposal is also significant. Mandatory labelling has been introduced for more than nine nutrients (something estimated to be between seven to eleven times more costly than for three nutrients)[131] and minimum font sizes for all labels have been introduced to aid legibility—something also acknowledged as introducing significant

[125] On the politics of anxiety see D Chalmers, 'Risk, Anxiety and the European Mediation of the Politics of Life' (2005) 30 ELR 649, 663–74.

[126] CCS proposal, n 7 above, Art 4(2). [127] Ibid, Art 12.

[128] Ibid, Art 33. [129] PR proposal, n 9 above, Arts 5(1)(a), 5(1) (b).

[130] Ibid, Arts 5(1)(d), 5(1)(e).

[131] FI proposal, n 13 above, Art 29 and Annex VI. See EC Commission, *Impact Assessment Report on General Food Labelling Issues* (SEC, 2008) 92, 86.

extra cost for all industry.[132] There is a strict responsibility for this on all operators who place food on the market for the first time.[133] Yet there is also a responsibility on operators engaged in retail and distribution activities which do not affect food information to take due care to ensure that the requirements are met.[134] The regime is sufficiently onerous that there is a dispensation for five years from the nutrition elements for SMEs.[135]

If the levels of regulatory responsibility are high, the precautionary qualities of EU law add a twist by suggesting these can only ever be discharged in a partial way.[136] Dissatisfaction with orthodox calculative reasoning leads to recourse to multiple sources of validation in precautionary reasoning. The synthesis of these leads, in turn, to overall rule of thumb assessments beset by an element of contingency. In the CCS proposal, for example, as it is impossible for the operator to monitor the storage site itself for leakage, she is confined to monitoring the complex, the injection facilities and the surrounding environment in the hope that these will somehow provide indicative signs.[137] In the PR proposal, recourse to public funded treatment abroad will be had when sufficiently satisfactory specialized treatment is not available in the home state. This involves heuristic judgments by the specialist with the patient about the quality of treatment in the other hospital; the quality of the after-care; and the availability of substitute treatment in the home state. With regard to the question of nutrition labelling in the FI proposal, it is not simply a question of fat and salt being bad and fibre being good. In all cases, labels have to be read in the light of the life style of the consumer—a process that is inevitably situated and highly personalized to that consumer—and something that the retailer or food processor cannot advise on.

This leads EU law to adopt a Janus-faced approach to those exposed to risk by these operations. On the one hand, these are the subjects of EU law whose lives it seeks to better. In this regard, it delivers goods to them but, above all, opportunities for them to better their lives as it sees

[132] Ibid. Art 14(1). It will necessitate the redesign of 97% of all labels and the costs were estimated in the impact assessment at possibly 5.2 billion. Ibid, 43.

[133] FI proposal, n 13 above, Art 8(3).

[134] Ibid, Art 8(4).

[135] Ibid. Art 53.

[136] On the qualities of this logic see B Hebenton and T Seddon, 'From Dangerousness to Precaution: Managing Sexual and Violent Offenders in an Insecure and Violent Age' (2009) 49 *British Journal of Criminology* (forthcoming).

[137] CCS proposal, n 7 above, Art 13(1).

it and to realize the European *eudaimonia*. On the other hand, EU law is concerned with the effective management of risk. The understanding that the operators of risk activities cannot be insurers of risk leads it to ask its subjects to develop individual risk strategies. This development of opportunity and management of risk are brought together in all three proposals through the provision of information to subjects so that they can orient their lives. This is most obvious with the FI proposal and the details it requires of food labels, but the PR proposal provides for the provision of information to enable patients to make informed choices about their treatment and health care, including details on prices, outcomes, and liability coverage[138] by both the health care provider and through national contact points.[139] The CCS proposal provides, through incorporating the requirements of the integrated pollution prevention control and environmental impact assessment, that the public be consulted on the establishment of any installations or pipelines.[140] This right to be informed, on its face, is an entitlement enabling involvement and more aware life choices. Yet, in all cases, the exercise of this entitlement is not self-evident. It only makes sense to insist on consultation over carbon capture and storage if one is going to be actively involved in debate about the process. Similarly, acquiring information about treatment abroad involves a choice about two-centre treatment and questions of after-care that are not easy to resolve. Reading labels about nutrition is only meaningful if it contributes to leading an active and healthy life—something that is very challenging to do! Of course, individuals are free not to do this, but then they are simple disenfranchized. The legislation offers either no benefit to them or it is something to which they are simply exposed in some passive sense. In short, benefits are contingent on the exercise of significant responsibilities.

There is a strong paradox. EU law seeks to secure EU subjects a better life that is more effectively governed. The invocation of this better life leads it not only to expose its subjects to barely comprehensible dangers. It also creates asymmetries of power in which these dangers are created and governed for them by domineering processes—be it the energy operators in carbon capture and storage; health experts in the case of patients; or the food industry in the case of labelling—which

[138] PR proposal, n 9 above, Art 5(1)(c).
[139] PR proposal, n 9 above, Arts 5(1)(c), 12(1).
[140] CCS proposal, n 7 above, Arts 29, 30.

can provide only incomplete assurances about the dangers involved. Onerous duties are then placed on the subjects both to enable a better life for themselves and to deal with this absence of reassurance. Such a process, whatever its more diffuse benefits, lends itself to anomie and alienation.

Conclusion

An idea of self-betterment constitutes the cumbersomeness of EU law. Yet the idea of self-betterment is also central to the modern conception of the human condition and to government. And, indeed, if the EU were not there we would almost certainly reinvent equivalent processes to better ourselves. Yet, driven unrelentingly forward, self-betterment can become a pathology simultaneously making harsh demands and being blind to its costs. That is the danger for EU law. For it makes a number of harsh demands.

First, it drives its subjects on only to tell them they have never done sufficient. Secondly, if the benefits of EU law may at times be considerable (for example, a clean environment) they are also diffused and hidden as collective goods. By contrast, direct entitlements are granted only occasionally as EU law will only provide these where others cannot provide them. Meanwhile, the justice behind the arrangements is uneven and the politics poorly mediated. Thirdly, if the entitlements granted by EU law are few, the range, incidence and nature of responsibilities are considerable driven by the impulse to make us lead better lives and to regulate ever more activities ever more effectively. EU law creates therefore a law of fear in which through enabling us to do more, it also exposes us to more consequences, but provides limited assurances about the anxieties provoked and an insouciance about the sense of constraint it induces in the individual in the management of the entitlements and responsibilities established.

How to take this forward? This chapter is at an end but other writers who have written more generally about these conditions indicate two routes that will only be touched upon. In his work, Sen argues for the notion of freedom over that of well-being because it incorporates the idea of process as central to realization of a good life.[141] By this, he is

[141] A Sen, *Rationality and Freedom* (Harvard University Press: Cambridge, 2002) 585–7.

not referring to ideas about the public sphere but to the more intimate notion that individual ownership and praxis is vital to defining rather than just enjoying the good things in life. Others have talked about processes in which individuals are given more leeway to give an account of their own lives as whilst such accounts may only be partial and contingent they are the central medium through which we bind ourselves to others.[142] Surely this would call for more leeway from EU law in allowing us to define 'better' lives for ourselves and whether we want such lives. Alongside this, Fromm has famously talked about the fear of freedom in which individuals demanded to lead lives that they feel are their own seek a number of false gods—be these comforting symbols of authoritarianism; the approval of others in material or political conformism; or wanton destructiveness of the self or others.[143] Are these not many of the associations which arise in response to the claims of EU law? If so, this suggests that, irrespective of what is a better life, EU law must consider seriously what it demands subjects sacrifice of themselves in the collective pursuit of the distant horizon of betterment. And maybe what EU law needs to concern itself with is not its betterment or its reform but the conditions under which it allows individuals to escape from it to make their own lives.

[142] J Butler, *Giving an Account of Oneself* (Fordham University Press: New York, 2005) 30–40.

[143] E Fromm, *Fear of Freedom* (Ark: London, 1942) ch v.

European Tort Law: A Primer for the Common Lawyer

*Ken Oliphant**

Introduction

This chapter seeks to serve as a primer for the new legal category of European Tort Law. In the last two decades, this has been arguably the single most important intellectual enterprise relating to the law of tortious liability across our continent. Yet in the UK it is seen as somewhat of a niche endeavour, all too frequently ignored in the mainstream of tort scholarship. Such attention that it has received has all too often been negative. One of our greatest tort scholars, Tony Weir, anticipated that the increased European influence on our national tort law would be 'so painful to recount' that he opted to produce no further editions of his magnificently opinionated casebook[1] a loss that may be acknowledged even by the author of a rival work.[2]

The 'primer' of my title has a multiple meaning. It refers first to the provision of basic introductory information. It also bears the further meaning of preparing or equipping someone for a specific task, because my purpose here is not just the provision of information, but also to encourage and facilitate action. The final meaning I would invoke is 'to prepare an explosive for detonation.' If I succeed in this, I shall have achieved a further part of my purpose.

* Director of the Institute for European Tort Law in the Austrian Academy of Sciences, Vienna; Professor of Tort Law at the University of Bristol. A preliminary partial draft of this paper was delivered before the Torts Section of the Society of Legal Scholars at its annual conference at the LSE in September 2008. It draws upon previously published work in the yearbook published annually since 2001—H Koziol and BC Steininger (eds) *European Tort Law* (Vienna, 2002). I am grateful to Colm McGrath and Ali el Haj for their assistance in preparing the paper for publication.

[1] T Weir, *A Casebook on Tort* (10th edn, London, 2004) vii.

[2] M Lunney and K Oliphant, *Tort Law: Text and Materials* (3rd edn, Oxford, 2008).

The final words of my title—'for the common lawyer'—identify my intended audience. I have in mind, in particular (but not exclusively), tort lawyers in the English common law. For them, this primer is intended to provide basic introductory information about European Tort Law, packaged in such a way as to make it accessible to an English tort lawyer, and highlighting existing and future interactions between European and English tort law. I am also seeking to counter the typical English tort lawyer's scepticism towards European Tort Law, to demonstrate that it is already established as a legal category, albeit on a number of different planes of existence, and to encourage him or her towards active engagement with it, in particular by highlighting the ways such engagement can contribute to the improvement of domestic principles. Lastly, I hope to persuade that this encounter with European Tort Law has implications for the common law that are potentially explosive, but nevertheless positive, because explosive charges may assist in the demolition of outmoded and dilapidated structures to make way for renewal. Pursuing this line of thought, I shall argue that the English law of tort should be fundamentally deconstructed and redeveloped in the interests of justice and coherence, employing models derived from European Tort Law.

This argument unfolds in the course of an analysis of four planes on which a demonstrably European Tort Law may be identified. But I preface that with a short overview of research activity in European Tort Law, highlighting its principal centres and the major works produced to date, so as to provide a primer in the first sense described above.

Overview of European Tort Law Research Activity

A famous scene in Monty Python's film *The Life of Brian* makes fun of the factionalism of the revolutionary groups opposed to the Roman occupation of Judea: there's the Judean People's Front, the People's Front of Judea, the Popular Front of Judea and the Judean Popular People's Front. As the revolutionaries trade insults, one shouts: 'The People's Front of Judea. Splitters.' To be answered by his colleague, '*We're* the People's Front of Judea!' 'Oh,' says the first agitator, 'I thought we were the Popular Front.' European Tort Law can induce similar confusion. There's the European Group on Tort Law, the Institute (previously Research Unit) for European Tort Law, the European Centre of Tort and Insurance Law—and those are just the entities with which I have a personal affiliation. Add in the Study Group on a European Civil Code, the Common Core of European Private Law Group, the Joint Network on European Private Law, the Research Group on EC Private Law (also known as the Acquis Group), and several others I could name, and one might well be forgiven for feeling disorientated.

A bit of simple geography may help. The three main originating sources of ongoing research into European Tort Law are Osnabrück, Trento and Vienna. Let me give some indication of the vitality of scholarship in the area through a brief survey of the work emanating from each.

The University of Osnabrück, Northern Germany, is home to the Study Group on a European Civil Code, founded in 1997 and chaired by Professor Christian von Bar, whose own monumental study *The Common European Law of Torts* appeared in English in two volumes in 1998 and 2000.[3] The main focus of the Study Group's work, in collaboration with the Research Group on EC Private Law ('the Acquis Group'), has been the preparation of a *Draft Common Frame of Reference* (DCFR) containing principles, definitions and model rules of European Private Law. This work was conducted within the framework of a European Commission Action Plan,[4] with substantial EU funding. Though the initial focus was the law of contract, the scope of the project was extended to neighbouring areas of the law of obligations and property law so as to highlight the interaction of contract law with other categories.[5] It was, therefore, decided to incorporate in the DCFR the Study Group's independently-formulated principles of 'Non-Contractual Liability Arising out of Damage Caused to Another'.[6] An interim outline edition of the DCFR was published in 2008;[7] a full annotated version was expected shortly after this paper was submitted for publication. Further comparative material has also been

[3] C von Bar, *The Common European Law of Torts*, vol 1 (1998) and vol 2 (2000).

[4] Commission (EC), 'A More Coherent European Contract Law: An Action Plan' (Communication), COM (2003) 68 final, 12 February 2003.

[5] C von Bar and U Drobnig, *The Interaction of Contract Law and Tort and Property Law in Europe—A Comparative Study* (Munich, 2004).

[6] See further J Blackie, 'The Provisions for 'Non-Contractual Liability Arising out of Damage Caused to Another' in the Draft Common Frame of Reference' (2009) 20 King's Law Journal 215.

[7] C von Bar, E Clive and H Schulte-Nölke and ors (eds), *Principles, Definitions and Model Rules in European Private Law: Draft Common Frame of Reference (DCFR)* (interim outline edition) (Sellier: Munich, 2008). An interim edition followed in early 2009.

published in the series *Principles of European Law*, in which a forthcoming volume will deal with tort.[8]

The University of Trento, Northern Italy, is the institutional home for the project 'The Common Core of European Private Law', which held its first meeting in 1995. It is responsible for the book series of the same name, four of whose first 11 publications deal with issues in tort law: pure economic loss, strict liability, environmental liability, and pre-contractual liability.[9] Uniquely of the organizations considered here, the Trento project is committed to a neutral position neither for nor against further Europeanization of private law. Its aim is simply to identify what is common to the laws of the EU member states in the areas of contract, tort and property law, and what is different.[10]

In Vienna we find the European Centre of Tort and Insurance Law ('ECTIL') and the Institute for European Tort Law, both founded by the leading Austrian scholar Helmut Koziol, in 1999 and 2002 respectively. I succeeded him as Director of the Institute on 1 January 2009. These organizations are formally associated and work out of the same offices. Their scholarly output has included 25 titles in the series *Tort and Insurance Law*,[11] eight volumes of the yearbook *European Tort Law*, from 2001 on,[12] and the initial instalment (on factual causation) of a new 'digest' of European tort case law;[13] volume 2, which explores the concept of 'damage' from multiple tort law perspectives, is in preparation.

Naturally, important work on European Tort Law has also appeared outside the centres I have mentioned. The two Vienna-based organizations support the work of the European Group on Tort Law, founded

[8] C von Bar (ed), *Non-Contractual Liability Arising out of Damage Caused to Another* (Oxford, 2009, forthcoming).

[9] M Bussani and V Palmer (eds), *Pure Economic Loss in Europe* (Cambridge, 2003); F Werro and V Palmer (eds), *The Boundaries of Strict Liability in European Tort Law* (Durham, NC, 2004); M Hinteregger (ed), *Environmental Liability and Ecological Damage in European Law* (Cambridge, 2008); and J Cartwright and H Hesselink (eds) *Precontractual Liability in European Private Law* (Cambridge, 2008).

[10] See further M Bussani, M Infantino, and F Werro, 'The Common Core Sound: Short Notes on Themes, Harmonies and Disharmonies in European Tort Law' (2009) 20 King's Law Journal 239.

[11] Most recently H Koziol and V Wilcox (eds), *Punitive Damages: Common Law and Civil Law Perspectives* (Vienna, 2009).

[12] Beginning with H Koziol and BC Steininger (eds), *European Tort Law 2001* (Vienna, 2002).

[13] B Winiger and ors (eds), *Digest of European Tort Law, Volume 1: Essential Cases on Natural Causation* (Vienna, 2007).

in Tilburg in 1993 by Jaap Spier, then a professor at the University, later Advocate General of the Dutch Supreme Court. It is sometimes referred to as the Tilburg Group or the Tilburg-Vienna Group, but in fact it does not have a fixed home. The Group consists of leading tort experts from a range of European jurisdictions and elsewhere. Its main work to date has been the preparation of a set of *Principles of European Tort Law*, affectionately known by the acronym PETL, which were published in 2005.[14] The PETL were preceded by, and built upon, ten volumes in the series, *Unification of Tort Law*. The Group resumed work in January 2009 with a view to revising and updating PETL in the light of newly-undertaken comparative research.[15]

Other important work on European Tort Law has included Walter van Gerven's casebook on Tort in the *Ius Commune* series,[16] and Cees van Dam's very successful introductory text *European Tort Law*.[17] No published work has yet come out of the Cambridge-based 'European Legal Development project on liability for fault in the years 1850–2000, but this too is eagerly awaited.[18]

Notwithstanding the volume of the work being done in the major centres of European Tort Law and beyond, European Tort Law has been dismissed in some quarters as a misguided enterprise that is doomed to failure because of the incompatibility of different national systems, concepts and cultures.[19] My next aim in this paper is to demonstrate that European Tort Law is no mere pipedream—as is suggested by sceptics—but a present fact. Yes, European Tort Law already exists, though it is a multi-layered concept with several planes of existence.

[14] European Group on Tort Law, *Principles of European Tort Law: Text and Commentary* (Vienna, 2005). The text alone of the *Principles* is available at <http://www.egtl.org/Principles/index.htm>.

[15] See further BA Koch, 'Principles of European Tort Law' (2009) 20 King's Law Journal 203.

[16] W van Gerven, J Lever, and P Larouche, *Cases, Materials and Text on National, Supranational and International Tort Law* (Oxford, 2000).

[17] C van Dam, *European Tort Law* (Oxford, 2006).

[18] Details may be found on the project website at <http://www.eld.law.cam.ac.uk>.

[19] See (variously) P Legrand, 'European legal systems are not converging' (1996) 45 International and Comparative Law Quarterly 52; R Stevens, *Torts and Rights* (Oxford University Press: Oxford, 2007) 349–50; J Stapleton, 'Benefits of Comparative Tort Reasoning: Lost in Translation' (2007) Journal of Tort Law, vol 1, no 3, Art 6. For a cultural critique of some aspects of the European Tort Law project, see C van Dam, 'Who is Afraid of Diversity? Cultural Diversity, European Co-operation, and European Tort Law' (2009) 20 King's Law Journal 281.

European Tort Law: Planes of Existence

Principles of European Tort Law

An initial plane of existence for European Tort Law (the first of four I shall consider) is the idealized statement, or restatement,[20] of common rules and principles of tortious liability. These are the products of European Tort Law scholarship that have rightly attracted the most attention, though not all of it has been positive.[21] As previously mentioned, the two main products to date have been the European Group's *Principles of European Tort Law* ('PETL'),[22] and the provisions on non-contractual liability prepared by the Study Group on a European Civil Code and incorporated in the *Draft Common Frame of Reference* ('DCFR').[23]

The two documents exhibit considerable similarities in form and content.[24] Both texts commence with a basic norm or rule providing for liability for harm caused by fault or otherwise attributable to the defendant.[25] Both are structured around the essential triad of damage, causation and grounds of attribution or accountability. Both treat fault as only one possible ground of accountability, along with, for example, vicarious responsibility for harm caused by an employee, representative

[20] There is some analogy to be drawn here with the work of the American Law Institute on its successive Restatements of Torts. That explains why, eg, the American scholar, Michael D Green, one of the Co-Reporters for the Restatement (Third) of Torts: Liability for Physical Harm, was invited to become a member of the European Group of Tort Law. He joined the Group in succession to the late Gary T Schwartz, his former Co-Reporter.

[21] Even distinguished comparativists have expressed objections to such projects, eg, Sir Basil Markesinis describing them as 'at best, a utopian dream': Always on the Same Path: Essays on Foreign Law and Comparative Methodology (Oxford, 2001) 7. The express target of his criticism was 'codification' projects, but the context suggests his intent to refer to all efforts to promote (further) harmonization of national tort law regimes in Europe. See further P Legrand, 'Against a European Civil Code' (1997) 60 MLR 44; P Legrand, 'A Diabolical Idea' in A Hartkamp and ors (eds), *Towards a European Civil Code* (3rd edn, Kluwer: The Hague, 2004); P Giliker, 'Can 27(+) 'Wrongs' Make a Right? The European Tort Law Project: Some Sceptical Reflections' (2009) 20 King's Law Journal 257; and C van Dam, n 19 above.

[22] European Group on Tort Law, n 14 above.

[23] von Bar, n 7 above.

[24] See further K Oliphant, 'Introduction: European Tort Law' (2009) 20 King's Law Journal 189.

[25] PETL Art 1:101(1) (Basic Norm): 'A person to whom damage to another is legally attributable is liable to compensate that damage.' DCFR VI.—1:101(1) (Basic Rule): 'A person who suffers legally relevant damage has a right to reparation from a person who caused the damage intentionally or negligently or is otherwise accountable for the causation of the damage.'

or 'auxiliary'.[26] Both have features which might surprise a common lawyer, for example, a reduction of damages clause allowing the damages award to be reduced if requiring the defendant to pay full compensation would be 'oppressive' or 'disproportionate'.[27] So far as I know, such provisions are wholly alien to the common law but may be found in various forms in many continental systems.[28]

A feature of PETL that should be noted because of its relevance to what will emerge as a theme of this chapter is its explicit reliance on a 'flexible system' in establishing liability.[29] This is perhaps clearest in PETL's eschewal of fixed scope of liability rules in favour of a case-by-case assessment of the merits in the light of relevant factors: fore seeability, the nature and value of the protected interest, the basis of liability, the extent of the ordinary risks of life, and the protective purpose of the rule that has been violated.[30] The degree of protection provided to an interest may therefore reflect (amongst other things) whether the interference is intentional or merely negligent.[31] In apparent contrast with this flexible approach, the DCFR first posits a number of paradigm liabilities (for example, personal injury, infringement of dignity, liberty and privacy, and reliance upon incorrect advice or information) each subject to individualized requirements.[32] Then, in the residual class of cases falling outside these paradigm situations, it must be determined, first, whether the claimant has suffered the violation of a right or interest worthy of protection and, secondly, whether it would be fair and reasonable for there to be a right to compensation having regard to the ground of accountability, the nature and proximity of the damage, the reasonable expectations of the victim, and public policy.[33] So a flexible consideration of the individual case is also a feature of the DCFR—at least in cases outside the paradigm situations.

[26] PETL Art 1:101(2); DCFR VI—1:101(2) and 3:201.

[27] PETL Art 10:401; DCFR VI—6:202.

[28] PETL Art 10:401 commentary, para 1.

[29] Following W Wilburg, *Die Elemente des Schadensrechts* (Marburg ad Lahn, 1941). See PETL Commentary, General Introduction, para 22, and further W Wilburg (translated by H Hausmaninger) *The Development of a Flexible System in the Area of Private Law* (Vienna, 2000); BA Koch, 'Wilburg's Flexible System in a Nutshell' in H Koziol and BC Steininger (eds), *European Tort Law 2001* (Vienna, 2002) 545.

[30] PETL Art 3:201.

[31] PETL Art 2:102(5).

[32] DCFR VI—2:101(a) and 2:201ff.

[33] DCFR VI—2:101(1)(b) and (c), (2) and (3). Blackie, n 6 above, 221 aptly calls this the 'expansion joint' in the DCFR's tort provisions.

What is the utility of these 'principles projects'? Their aims are sometimes thought to be inextricably linked with advocacy of a European Civil Code but that is not in fact the case. Admittedly, the name of one protagonist, the Study Group on a European Civil Code, suggests such an ambition but the DCFR, in which the Group's work is now incorporated, has the more modest stated objective of providing principles, definitions and model rules to assist in the improvement of EU legislation (the *acquis communautaire*) and the drafting of future EU legislation.[34] In PETL, the express goal is 'the enhancement and harmonization of the law of torts in Europe'[35] but, again, there is no commitment to codification as such. So what alternative forms might harmonization take? An important distinction is between 'hard harmonization'—'the replacement of the national systems of contract and tort law by a binding European legal instrument'—and 'soft harmonization' whereby the fruits of comparative legal scholarship come to bear on legislative reform and judicial decision of hard cases.[36] I believe that only harmonization in the latter form provides a realistic objective, at least under current conditions. I also note that 'enhancement' is at least as important an objective as harmonization.

Already there is evidence that the work described above has contributed towards a soft harmonization as just described. In the huge regenerative efforts prompted by the fall of the Soviet Union and the fragmentation of East European nation states, many legal systems have begun the process of reforming their civil codes, under the acknowledged influence of European Tort Law in its various forms. Several reform projects of this nature draw explicitly on European Tort Law scholarship, even to the extent of taking PETL as an explicit model.[37] PETL, or its underlying ideas, have also had a decisive influence on a recent draft tort law revision in Austria.[38] The principles projects (plural) have yet to impinge on national court case-law to the same extent, but I should certainly mention here that the Spanish Supreme Court has on several occasions relied explicitly on PETL as an aid to the resolution of disputed questions of domestic law, putting PETL 'on an

[34] DCFR Introduction (interim edition), paras 60–76.

[35] PETL General Introduction, 30.

[36] G Wagner, 'The Project of Harmonizing European Tort Law' (2005) 42 CMLR 1269, 1270, and 1281ff.

[37] See A Dulak, 'Slovakia' in H. Koziol and BC Steininger (eds), *European Tort Law 2008* (Vienna, 2009) para 1ff.

[38] See BC Steininger, 'Austria' in H Koziol and BC Steininger (eds), *European Tort Law 2005* (Vienna, 2006).

equal footing' with the provisions of the Civil Code in determining the content of domestic liability rules and filling in the gaps between them.[39] This is a very striking confirmation of the impact of European Tort Law scholarship.

EC Tort Law[40]

A second plane of European Tort Law's existence is in the legislation of the EU, the decisions of the European Court of Justice (ECJ) and Court of First Instance, and the application of principles of EC law in national courts. English tort lawyers have traditionally seen EC law as marginal to their endeavours, intruding in them only in the form of the Product Liability Directive[41] and (to a lesser extent) state liability under the ECJ's *Francovich* jurisprudence.[42] But EC Tort Law is a larger and more significant category than is commonly appreciated, and itself takes a number of different forms. It embraces amongst other things: expressly created civil liability regimes (as under the Product Liability Directive); the judicially-developed principle of effective protection of Community rights, which may require the payment of compensation where a Community right is violated;[43] state liability; the non-contractual liability of community institutions under Article 288 II of the EC Treaty; the Regulations determining jurisdiction and applicable law in cross-border tort cases;[44] and the raft of other supporting laws—notably the Motor Insurance Directives[45]—that ensure the effective operation of tort liability rules.

Liability of Community Institutions

To demonstrate unequivocally that European Tort Law is a phenomenon already recognized in EC law, we need only turn to the non-contractual

[39] J Ribot and A Ruda, 'Spain' in H Koziol and BC Steininger (eds), *European Tort Law 2007* (Vienna, 2008) paras 27ff.

[40] See generally, H Koziol and R Schulze (eds), *Tort Law of the European Community* (Vienna, 2008). The following account draws intermittently on the present author's contribution to that volume, entitled 'The Nature and Assessment of Damages'.

[41] Directive (EEC) 85/374 on product liability.

[42] After Cases C-6 and 9/90, *Francovich v Italy* [1991] ECR I–5357.

[43] The principle may be traced back to Case 14/83, *von Colson and Kamann v Land Nordrhein-Westfahlen* [1984] ECR 1891.

[44] Regulation (EC) 44/2001 on jurisdiction and the recognition and enforcement of judgments in civil and commercial matters (Brussels I); Regulation (EC) 864/2007 on the law applicable to noncontractual obligations (Rome II).

[45] Directive (EEC) 84/5, Directive (EEC) 90/232, Directive (EC) 2000/26 and Directive (EC) 2005/14.

liability of Community institutions regulated by Article 288 II of the EC Treaty:

> In the case of non-contractual liability, the Community shall, in accordance with the general principles common to the laws of the Member States, make good any damage caused by its institutions or by its servants in the performance of their duties.

So where a contractor slips, falls and suffers injury on Community premises, the Community's liability as occupier is governed by 'general principles common to the laws of the Member States'.[46] The same common principles also apply where a Community official causes a road accident whilst driving on Community business, occasioning non-material damage to a secondary victim,[47] or where a would-be contractor detrimentally relies on an anticipated contract that never materializes.[48] Whether common general principles exist in a literal sense, other than at a high level of generality, has reasonably been doubted.[49] Nevertheless no one maintains that, to be 'common', a principle must be accepted in all of the member states: that would be 'virtually impossible' given the size of the Community's current membership.[50] It may be that, in future, PETL and the DCFR play a role in their identification. But in the meantime the Courts have in any case taken a sensibly robust approach to the identification and application of common general principles, even where divergent national practices exist.

An example is provided by the decision of the ECJ in the *Grifoni* case.[51] The applicant roofing contractor suffered a permanent disability of 35 per cent as a result of a fall from the roof of Institution premises in Italy and brought an action for damages under the equivalent of Article 288(2) of the EC Treaty. Following an initial ruling on liability, the case returned to the Court to determine the damages. A particular

[46] Case C-308/87, *Grifoni v European Atomic Energy Community (No 1)* [1990] ECR I-1203 and Case C-308/87, *Grifoni v European Atomic Energy Community (No 2)* [1994] ECR I-341. [47] Case 169/83, *Leussink v Commission* [1986] ECR 2801.

[48] Case T-203/96, *Embassy Limousines v European Parliament* [1998] ECR II-4239.

[49] F Jacobs, 'Some remarks on Community and Member State liability' in J Wouters and J Stuyk (eds), *Principles of Proper Conduct for Supranational, State and Private Actors in the European Union: Towards a Ius Commune* (Antwerp, 2001) 129–31, quoted by W van Gerven, 'Harmonization of private law: do we need it?' (2004) 41 CMLR 505, 515–6. See also 5/71, *Zuckerfabrik Schöppenstedt v Council* [1971] ECR 975, Opinion of AG Roemer, 989–90.

[50] Van Gervan, ibid, 516 (writing when membership of the Union as 15 was opposed to the current 27).

[51] Case C-308/87, *Grifoni* I [1990] ECR I-1203 and Case C-308/87, *Grifoni* II [1994] ECR I-341.

area of difficulty was the calculation of compensation for loss of future earnings. The extreme diversity of national laws on that issue made it almost impossible to identify 'common' principles.[52] In his Opinion, AG Tesauro identified three distinct approaches: 'the *in concreto* assessment practised in particular in Germany, the multiplier in force in the common law countries and the use of actuarial tables based mainly on the degree of invalidity and on a coefficient to take account of life expectancy',[53] for example, in Italy. Although a 'common' solution might be sought by calculating the damages according to the parameters used in each member state and then calculating a weighted average of the results obtained, that (said the Advocate General) would be 'an unrealistic manner of proceeding and in any event would be a long way from complying with the general principles common to the legal systems of the member states.'[54] In view of the difficulties inherent in any alternative approach, the Advocate General's preferred approach was that 'reference should be made to the common principles only in order to identify the nature of the loss to be compensated' and that there should be 'recourse to the method in use in the country in which the event occurs (place of the accident, nationality and residence of the injured party) in order to assess the loss in financial terms.'[55] The Court apparently followed this approach.

State Liability

The role of these common national principles of non-contractual liability in fact extends beyond Article 288 of the EC Treaty, because the ECJ has declared an equivalence between the rules of community liability and those governing the liability of member states. As it said in its *Brasserie du Pêcheur* judgment, 'the protection of the rights which individuals derive from Community law cannot vary depending on whether a national authority or a Community authority is responsible for the damage.'[56] So general principles common to the laws of the member states will play a decisive role in the further development of member state liability too, and therefore in national tort law, because it is for the national courts to provide an appropriate remedy. This is an

[52] Case C-308/87, *Grifoni* II [1994] ECR I-341, Opinion of AG Tesauro, para 8.
[53] Ibid. [54] Ibid. [55] Ibid.
[56] Joined Cases C-46/93 and C-48/93,*Brasserie du Pêcheur and Factortame* III [1996] ECR I-1029, para 42; Case C-352/98, *Bergaderm* [2000] ECR I-5291, para 41.

expanding jurisprudence, based on the satisfaction of three conditions, expressed as follows in *Brasserie du Pêcheur*:[57]

> the rule of law infringed must be intended to confer rights on individuals; the breach must be sufficiently serious; and there must be a direct causal link between the breach . . . and the damage . . .

Subsequent cases have confirmed that the *Francovich* liability applies not just to legislative failures (as in *Francovich* itself) but also to administrative actions and judicial rulings.[58]

In the United Kingdom, the Eurotort jurisprudence has already produced such well-known landmarks as the decisions in the *Factortame*[59] and *Three Rivers*[60] cases. The latter, arising out of the collapse of the Bank of Credit and Commerce International, foundered on the first of the requirements laid down by the ECJ—the intention to confer rights on individuals—a decision subsequently endorsed by the ECJ in the (unrelated) case of *Paul v Germany*.[61] There is an obvious analogy here with the domestic tort of breach of statutory duty, though it ought not to be pressed too far.[62]

With the increasing number of Directives, especially in such core areas of tort litigation as road traffic accidents, work injuries, and environmental damage, we can expect the Eurotort to be pleaded ever more frequently in domestic courts in the future. The Court of Appeal ruled in 2008, for example, that the United Kingdom had violated the claimant's rights under the Motor Insurance Directive in a sufficiently serious manner to give rise to liability in respect of a road traffic accident caused by an untraced driver.[63] The violation related to the Motor Insurers Bureau's application of a shorter limitation period than under general tort law to untraced driver claims, there being no provision for

[57] Joined Cases C-46/93 and C-48/93, *Brasserie du Pêcheur SA v Germany* [1996] ECR I-1029, paras 47–51.

[58] See respectively Case C–5/94, *R v Ministry of Agriculture, Fisheries and Food, ex parte Hedley Lomas (Ireland)* [1996] ECR I–2553 and Case C-224/01, *Köbler v Austria* [2003] ECR I-10239.

[59] *R v Secretary of State for Transport, ex parte Factortame Ltd (No 5)* [2000] 1 AC 524.

[60] *Three Rivers District Council v Governor and Company of the Bank of England (No 3)* [2003] 2 AC 1.

[61] Case C-222/02, *Paul v Germany* [2004] ECR I-9425.

[62] On the relationship between the Eurotort and normal principles of breach of statutory duty, see K Stanton, 'New Forms of the Tort of Breach of Statutory Duty' (2004) 120 LQR 324 at 328–30.

[63] *Byrne v Motor Insurers' Bureau* [2008] EWCA Civ 574, [2008] 3 WLR 1421. See also Case C-63/01, *Evans v Secretary of State for the Environment, Transport and the Regions* [2003] ECR I-14447, [2004] RTR 2.

the suspension of limitation till a child victim reached adulthood. The claimant had been three at the date of the accident. In another case, the court was faced with further *Francovich* claims arising out of accidents in the workplace and on the roads, though it rejected both on limitation grounds.[64] Nevertheless it is clear that the Eurotort cannot be ignored even in routine personal injuries practice.

Liability of Private Actors

A crucial development in the last decade has been the extension of the *Francovich* liability beyond the state and its application to defendants who are private actors. Since *Courage v Crehan*,[65] it has been established that an individual may be liable in an action for damages on the basis of the violation of a community right founded directly on the text of the Treaty itself. It has been suggested that this completes the circle uniting principles of community and state liability with the protection of community law rights under the *von Colson* case, and so provides the opportunity for a more integrated approach to tort liability under EC law.[66] If this is indeed so, it is clear that the common national principles mentioned in Article 288(2) of the EC Treaty (community liability) have the potential to play a considerable role in fleshing out the elements of the new integrated liability.

Effect on Existing Principles of National Tort Law

European Tort Law may, in addition, have an effect on existing liabilities in national law. This is already evident in other EU member states. For example, a decision of the Polish Supreme Court in 2007, considering state liability for unlawful court judgments, expressly relied on the ECJ's jurisprudence on the liability of member states for breach of EC law, with particular reference to the Court's judgment in *Köbler v Austria*,[67] which extended the *Francovich* liability to judicial decisions. It is said that the decision brings Polish law on state liability into

[64] *Spencer v Secretary of State for Work and Pensions*; *Moore v Secretary of State for Transport* [2008] EWCA Civ 750, [2009] 1 All ER 314 (claims for failure properly to implement, respectively, the Framework Health and Safety Directive and the Motor Insurance Directive (EEC) 84/5).

[65] Case C-453/99, *Courage v. Crehan* [2001] ECR I-6297.

[66] See, eg, W van Gerven, 'Harmonization of Private Law: Do We Need it?' (2004) 41 CMLR 505, especially 522–3; S Drake, 'Scope of Courage and the principle of 'individual liability' for damages: further development of the principle of effective judicial protection by the Court of Justice' [2006] ELR 841.

[67] Case C–224/01 *Köbler v Austria* [2003] ECR I-10239.

line with EC law.[68] The case is a very good illustration of how principles of EC tort law can exert a harmonizing influence even beyond areas strictly susceptible to the jurisdiction of the ECJ.

This development is especially noteworthy in the context of the present article because of the similarity it bears to a proposal to reform the English law of state liability advanced last year by the Law Commission in its Consultation Paper on *Administrative Redress.*[69] The paper recommends that the liability of public bodies for 'truly public' acts or omissions should be limited by a new requirement of 'serious fault', which it explicitly links with the ECJ's *Francovich* jurisprudence.[70] The Consultation Paper shows a commendable openness to the lessons to be learnt from experience elsewhere in Europe, both national and supranational, but I must strike a note of caution because it seems to me that the Law Commission has inadvertently transformed the ECJ test in adapting it to English law. What is in EC law a test of 'sufficiently serious breach' becomes in the Law Commission's proposal a test of 'serious fault'. But the ECJ test does not require fault as it is conceived in English law, even if the degree of fault exhibited is a relevant consideration in determining seriousness.[71] At first glance, the Law Commission's proposal therefore seems unduly restrictive as compared with state liability under EC law.

In considering the impact of EC Tort Law on national law, we should note that it is not just rules establishing individual causes of action that are in question. There may also be an impact on other rules of national tort law, for example, defences to liability. In this context, I must highlight a remarkable but (in the UK) little heralded decision of the ECJ that has potentially far-reaching consequences for English tort law. In *Candolin v Pohjola* in 2005,[72] there was a car accident in which the driver and all the passengers were drunk. One of the passengers was killed, and the others were seriously injured. Under Finnish law, compensation for personal injury in a road accident was expressly

[68] E Bagińska, 'Poland' in H Koziol and BC Steininger (eds), *European Tort Law 2007* (Vienna, 2008) para 78.

[69] Law Commission, *Administrative Redress: Public Bodies and the Citizen*, Consultation Paper No 187 (2008).

[70] Ibid, para 4.4. The proposed liability is further restricted to situations where the underlying legislative scheme was intended to confer rights or benefits on the individual claimant.

[71] *R v Secretary of State for Transport, ex parte Factortame Ltd (No 5)* [2000] 1 AC 524.

[72] Case C-537/03, [2005] ECR I-5745, [2006] RTR 1, [2005] 3 CMLR 17.

excluded where a passenger knew or should have known that the driver was above the limit unless there was 'a special reason' for paying compensation from the vehicle's insurance. The ECJ found that this limitation was contrary to EC law as it was a disproportionate interference with the passenger's right to be compensated by compulsory motor vehicle insurance, as provided under the Motor Insurance Directives.[73] There were restrictions, said the Court, on the appraisal under national civil liability laws of the extent to which a passenger contributed to the occurrence of his injuries.[74] Even leading proponents of European Tort Law have found this hard to digest, one remarking that it constituted 'another milestone in a series of cases blatantly disregarding the most fundamental principles of the law of delict'.[75] It is certainly surprising that a Directive on compulsory (liability) insurance should be interpreted as impacting on the principles of substantive liability law. Nevertheless, it is clearly binding on the English courts, and indeed is reflected in subsequent amendments to the Directive.[76]

How then does the *Candolin* decision affect English law? Let me limit myself to two short remarks. First, it is clear that the decision subjects the reduction of damages for contributory negligence in English courts to the supervisory scrutiny of the ECJ. Reductions in damages must not be 'disproportionate'.[77] In Norway, this was accepted by the Supreme Court in 2008.[78] The lower courts had applied a deduction of 60 per cent of the damages in a case where the passenger knew the driver was heavily intoxicated by alcohol. The Supreme Court —expressly relying on the EU Motor Insurance Directives and their interpretation in *Candolin*—found that this was disproportionate, especially in view of the claimant's age (18 at the time of the accident); it substituted a reduction of 40 per cent. Secondly, *Candolin* casts

[73] Directive (EC) 2005/14. Motor Insurance Directives, n 45 above.

[74] *Candolin*, n 72 above, paras 25–6.

[75] BA Koch, 'European Union' in H Koziol and BC Steininger (eds), *European Tort Law 2005* (Vienna, 2006) para 21.

[76] Directive (EEC) 90/232, Art 1.1A (as added by Directive (EC) 2005/14) precludes the exclusion of compensation cover by statutory provision or insurance contract clause on grounds of actual or imputed knowledge of the driver's intoxication. It does not apply to exclusions of cover resulting from principles of case-law, so has limited relevance to English law, where only contributory negligence (which reduces the compensation but does not exclude it) is a statutory defence.

[77] *Candolin*, n 72 above, para 29.

[78] Supreme Court 3 April 2008, noted by AM Anfinsen and B Askeland, 'Norway' in H Koziol and BC Steininger (eds), *European Tort Law 2008* (Vienna, 2009) paras 16 ff.

doubt on the legitimacy of judicial recourse in motor cases to any concept providing a complete defence to liability. Reliance on *volenti non fit iniuria*, it may be observed, is precluded by domestic legislation,[79] but in *Pitts v Hunt*[80] the Court of Appeal applied the defence of illegality (*ex turpi causa*) in a case where the claimant was a pillion passenger on the defendant's motorbike, knew he was drunk, and encouraged him to ride dangerously, speeding towards oncoming vehicles and swerving away at the last minute.[81] Arguably, that decision would fall foul of the ECJ principle. The mere element of illegality is certainly not enough to distinguish the case from the general run of cases in which the victim's contributory conduct is in issue, for much 'ordinary' contributory negligence involves some element of illegality, for example, failure to wear a seatbelt.[82]

Observations

Concluding this short overview of EC Tort Law, I would suggest that common lawyers have an obligation to participate in debates about 'general principles common to the laws of the member states', or those principles will be fashioned in a way that does not reflect common law systems. Common law private lawyers, in particular, must play a role. The development of European private law is too important to be left entirely to EC lawyers. I hope that the EC lawyers will forgive us our inexperience in their domain, and still find something of value in our input.

ECHR Tort Law

A third plane on which European Tort Law exists is to be found under the European Convention of Human Rights (ECHR) and the jurisprudence of the European Court of Human Rights (ECtHR). Though not conceived in terms of private law, it is increasingly recognized that the Convention performs a dual role: not simply as the upholder of fundamental rights but also as a source of compensation (just satisfaction) for human rights violations without effective remedy

79 Road Traffic Act 1988, s 149(3).

80 *Pitts v Hunt* [1991] 1 QB 24.

81 Ibid.

82 Second Directive (EEC) 84/5, Art 2(1) contemplates the exclusion of compensation in respect of passengers knowingly in a stolen vehicle, but in *Candolin*, n 72 above, the court stated that this should be interpreted strictly as it constituted a derogation from the general rule: see para 21.

in national courts.[83] This compensatory function is important and requires analysis, even if one accepts (as one should) that it must be subsidiary to the protection and vindication of human rights.[84]

Just Satisfaction Claims (Article 41 of the ECHR)

Human rights lawyers have understandably devoted little attention to how the Convention itself can be regarded as establishing a supranational system of tort liability. The principles by which the Strasbourg Court determines whether a violation of the Convention warrants an award of just satisfaction under Article 41 of the ECHR,[85] and sets the amount of compensation in individual cases, are widely (if unfairly) believed to be shrouded in uncertainty—or at least cloaked by the exercise of the court's 'equitable discretion'. As the court becomes more active in this area, there is an imperative need to clarify and evaluate the principles which (whether expressed or not) underlie the Court's approach to just satisfaction claims. This is the subject matter of current research undertaken by the Institute for European Tort Law in Vienna.[86] Amongst other objectives, this research is seeking to identify the categories of damage recognized in the court's jurisprudence, exploring the relationship between damage as such and 'mere' violations of the Convention, to examine the role of fault in establishing the liability of the Contracting parties under the Convention, and to test claims that the court takes a looser, more lenient approach to proof of causal connection than is normal in national systems.[87]

It is sometimes suggested that awards by the ECtHR are lower than those made by domestic courts, at least in the UK,[88] so it is important to remind ourselves that the court's own stated aim, at least as regards

[83] cf *Smith v Chief Constable of Sussex Police* [2008] UKHL 50, [2009] 1 AC 225, para 136 per Lord Brown.

[84] cf *Anufrijeva v London Borough of Southwark* [2003] EWCA Civ 1406, [2004] QB 1124, para 53 per Lord Woolf ('compensation. . . of secondary, if any, importance').

[85] According to the Court's Practice Direction on Just Satisfaction Claims of 28 March 2007, the award of monetary just satisfaction is subject to three preconditions: (1) the impossibility of complete reparation under domestic law; (2) the necessity for a monetary award in addition to the finding of violation itself; and (3) the justice of making such an award.

[86] Further details may be found on the Institute's website at <http://www.etl.oeaw.ac.at>.

[87] As suggested by Lord Brown in *Smith v Sussex Police*, para 138.

[88] *R (Greenfield) v Secretary of State for the Home Department* [2005] UKHL 14, [2005] 1 WLR 673, para 17 per Lord Bingham (awards for particular heads of non-pecuniary damage 'noteworthy for their modesty'); *Smith v Sussex Police*, para 58 per Lord Bingham.

pecuniary damage, is to place the applicant so far as possible in the position he or she would have been in if the violation had not taken place (ie *restitutio in integrum*).[89] It is not clear why this should produce a lower sum than under principles of damages in English law. There is perhaps greater justification for the suggestion with regard to non-pecuniary damage, as one cannot properly talk of *restitutio in integrum* here, but the perception that ECtHR awards are modest may well reflect the large number of cases where the non-pecuniary damage consists in purely mental injury falling short of a psychiatric condition (for example, stress, frustration or anxiety). Such injury is not normally compensated at all in English law. Where there is injury to health, ECtHR awards do not look so low. In *TP and KM v United Kingdom,*[90] concerning the actions of child care professionals in separating a mother from her daughter, who was erroneously perceived to be at risk from the mother's partner, the ECtHR awarded each applicant £10,000, an amount that the British judge, Arden LJ, noted was considerably in excess of what an English court would award for comparable psychiatric injury ('minor in nature'), the relevant guideline range being £500 to £2,250. She noted that the award of just satisfaction reflects factors apart from injury to health, for example, feelings of frustration and injustice.[91] Even taking such factors into account, however, she herself would have awarded each applicant the lesser sum of £6,000—providing further grounds for doubting the supposed parsimony of the Strasbourg court.

Another reason why some awards may appear to be rather low is that compensation for non-pecuniary damage, being incapable of precise calculation and so assessable only on an equitable basis,[92] may reflect prevailing economic conditions in the parties' home country, as the Court has occasionally acknowledged.[93] Awards in a prosperous Western European state cannot be directly compared with awards in the lower-waged economies emerging from the shadow of communism in Eastern Europe. On the present state of the case-law, however, it would

[89] Practice Direction on Just Satisfaction Claims, para 10.

[90] *TP and KM v United Kingdom* (App no 28945/95) ECHR 2001-V, 10 May 2001.

[91] Ibid, concurring opinion of Lady Justice Arden.

[92] Practice Direction, para 14. The Court expressly has regard to the standards which emerge from its own case-law, and has stated that 'domestic case-law is of limited relevance to the question of non-pecuniary damage in proceedings before it': *Gault v United Kingdom* (App no 1271/05) ECHR, 20 November 2007, para 30.

[93] *Svetoslav Dimitrov v Bulgaria* (App no 55861/00) ECHR, 7 February 2008, para 84; *Kostadinov v Bulgaria* (App no 55712/00) ECHR, 7 February 2008, para 100.

be rash to treat it as firmly established that such considerations may be taken into account.

Human Rights Act Claims

Turning to liability under domestic law, the Human Rights Act 1998 ('HRA') now provides a specific remedy for the violation of Convention rights, though it is available only against a public authority.[94] Section 8 (3) of the HRA limits the circumstances in which damages may be awarded for a breach of Convention rights to cases where 'the award is necessary to afford just satisfaction to the person in whose favour it is made.' The language is very close to that of Article 41 of the ECHR, but the requirements have 'been interpreted so strictly by the courts that the general view of legal commentators is that it is now very difficult to obtain damages under the HRA.'[95] In 2006, the Department of Constitutional Affairs, reviewing more than five years of the Act's operation, reported that there had been only three successful Section 8 claims. One of these, we now know, was subsequently reversed on appeal.

That was the first instance decision in *Van Colle v Chief Constable of the Hertfordshire Police*[96] upheld in 2007 by the Court of Appeal[97] but reversed a year later by the House of Lords.[98] A witness for the prosecution at the trial of a minor criminal received death threats. The police were aware, but failed to prevent his murder. His parents sued for damages, relying exclusively on the HRA; there was no concurrent claim for common law negligence. The House of Lords ruled that no liability arose under the Act because the threats were insufficient to establish a 'real and immediate risk' to the deceased's life. The Law Lords adapted the test applied by the ECtHR in its well-known *Osman* decision,[99] to be considered shortly, noting that it reflected the main policy arguments against holding the police liable for investigative

[94] HRA, ss 7–8.

[95] Department of Constitutional Affairs, Review of the Implementation of the Human Rights Act (2006), 18. See especially *Anufrijeva v Southwark London Borough Council* [2004] QB 1124.

[96] *Van Colle v Chief Constable of the Hertfordshire Police* [2006] EWHC 360 (QB), [2006] 3 All ER 963.

[97] *Van Colle v Chief Constable of the Hertfordshire Police* [2007] EWCA Civ 325, [2007] 1 WLR 1821.

[98] *Van Colle v Chief Constable of the Hertfordshire Police* [2008] UKHL 50, [2009] 1 AC 225.

[99] *Osman v United Kingdom* (App nos 87/1997/871/1083), [1999] 1 FLR 193, (2000) 29 EHRR 245, 28 October 1998.

failures, as the *Osman* Court had itself acknowledged.[100] The House of Lords has subsequently endorsed the application of the *Osman* test to cases not involving the police, for example, in a case of suicide by a person compulsorily detained in hospital under the mental health legislation,[101] and (with some equivocation) to a local authority landlord following a fatal attack by one tenant on another.[102]

This jurisprudence demonstrates that the HRA can potentially outflank limits on liability in general tort law, and serve as a conduit for the introduction into English law of approaches developed by the Court in Strasbourg, even if liability will arise under the Act only in very exceptional circumstances.

Human Rights and General Tort Law

Alongside the specific HRA claim for violation of a Convention right must be considered the way in which claims in general tort law may be affected by Convention principles. In other national systems, there has been occasional, but nonetheless significant, recourse to the Convention to support the judicial development of new principles. In Sweden, for example, it has been observed that '[t]he European Convention has become a natural part of national tort law.'[103] Here, and in several other countries, the jurisprudence of the European Court of Human Rights has had an expressly acknowledged impact on the award of compensation for non-pecuniary loss, in particular, inducing national courts to extend its availability in such areas as bereavement following the loss of a family member,[104] and non-pecuniary loss suffered by a corporation.[105]

[100] *Smith v Sussex Police*, para 91 per Lord Phillips; *Osman*, ibid, para 116.

[101] *Savage v South Essex Partnership NHS Foundation Trust* [2008] UKHL 74, [2009] 2 WLR 115 (claim remitted to trial).

[102] *Mitchell v Glasgow City Council* [2009] UKHL 11, [2009] 2 WLR 481 (no liability on the facts). Lord Rodger stated that the *Osman* test was irrelevant because it was not the council, but the police, who were potentially subject to the Art 2 obligation to counteract a threat to life (paras 69–71). Lord Brown (para 85) apparently agreed.

[103] H Andersson, 'Sweden' in H Koziol and BC Steininger (eds) *European Tort Law 2007* (Vienna, 2008) para 26. See further C Lebeck, 'Horizontal effect of the European Convention on Human Rights in Swedish law—A quiet constitutional change?' [2009] PL 25.

[104] eg, see H Gabartas and G Bžozeckaitė, 'Lithuania' in H Koziol and BC Steininger (eds), *European Tort Law 2007* (Vienna, 2008) paras 17ff; A Dulak, 'Slovakia', ibid, paras 20ff.

[105] E Navarretta and E Bargelli, 'Italy' in H Koziol and BC Steininger (eds), *European Tort Law 2007* (Vienna, 2008) paras 19ff.

What has been—and what will be in future—the influence of the Convention on English tort law? Under the HRA, the English courts *must* take account of decisions in Strasbourg (section 2), and *must* interpret legislation compatibly with the Convention rights (Section 3), but the former obligation is rather weak ('take account') and has been approached restrictively,[106] and the latter is of limited significance to our largely judge-made law of tort. Further, the courts still have to give an unequivocal answer to the question of the proper analysis of the court's own Section 6(1) duty not to act incompatibly with Convention rights, arising from the inclusion of courts amongst public authorities in section 6(3). Dicta could be cited in support of a range of possible positions, from full horizontality[107] to a purely procedural conception of the court's Section 6(1) duty,[108] with numerous shades of horizontality in between.[109] My own preferred analysis—supported by numerous dicta[110]—is that the Act requires the incremental development of existing causes of action in order to ensure compatibility with Convention rights, so long as this can be achieved 'without undermining the measure of certainty which is necessary to all law',[111] but not the creation of wholly new liabilities.

Rather than spilling yet more ink on this much discussed issue, let us instead consider the impact of Convention principles on English tort law to date. The three most important areas to consider are privacy, defamation and negligence.

Privacy

One cannot but remark upon the temporal coincidence of the implementation of the HRA and judicial recognition for the first time of a

[106] See M Arden, 'The Changing Judicial Role: Human Rights, Community Law and the Intention of Parliament' [2008] CLJ 487, 487.

[107] W Wade, 'Horizons of Horizontality' (2000) 116 LQR 217; SD Pattison and D Beyleveld, 'Horizontal Applicability and Horizontal Effect' (2002) 118 LQR 623.

[108] R Buxton, 'The Human Rights Act and Private Law' (2000) 116 LQR 48.

[109] For an overview, see M Hunt, 'The "Horizontal Effect" of the Human Rights Act: Moving Beyond the Public-Private Distinction', in J Jowell and J Cooper (eds), *Understanding Human Rights Principles* (Oxford, 2001) 163–7.

[110] *Venables v News Group Newspapers Ltd* [2001] Fam 430, 446 per Dame Elizabeth Butler-Sloss; *Douglas v Hello! Ltd* [2001] QB 967, 1002, per Sedley LJ, and 1011–12, per Keene LJ; *A v B plc* [2002] EWCA Civ 337, [2003] QB 195, para 4 per Lord Woolf; *Campbell v MGN Ltd* [2004] UKHL 22, [2004] 2 AC 457, para 132 per Baroness Hale; *Douglas v Hello! Ltd (No 6)* [2005] EWCA Civ 595, [2006] QB 125, para 53 per Lord Phillips.

[111] *Douglas v Hello! Ltd* [2001] QB 967, 1002 per Sedley LJ.

fully-fledged tort of invasion of privacy, cemented by the decision of the House of Lords in *Campbell v Mirror Group Newspapers Ltd.*[112] It is tempting to conclude that the development of a new liability for invasion of privacy should count amongst the achievements of the HRA. But the courts themselves have insisted that this is a development that is independent both of the HRA and the UK's Treaty obligations under the Convention: it reflects values inherent in the common law, and builds upon existing principle.[113] One advantage of this approach, for those who support the development, is that this liability will remain even if the HRA is repealed, as has been suggested by both the main political parties in recent times.

In our developing law of privacy, we see the English courts casting aside the established three-stage approach of the breach of confidence cases,[114] from which the new liability emerged, and adopting the structure of the Convention text itself. In fact, this was explicitly encouraged by the House of Lords in *Campbell*. The Convention rights, said Lord Nicholls, are 'now part of the cause of action'[115] which it would be 'misleading' to regard as an equitable liability concerned with unconscionability.[116] Similarly, for Lord Hoffmann there had been 'a shift in the centre of gravity' of the liability, which now focuses on the value of human autonomy and dignity rather than the defendant's good faith.[117] This approach had taken root in the Court of Appeal even before *Campbell*, and subsequent decisions have continued to refine it.[118]

For all their Lordships' emphasis that this development built on existing principles, and did not involve recognition of a wholly new cause of action, it seems that, in the result, we have two separate torts: one dealing with secrets under the traditional approach applicable to breach of confidence, the other dealing with privacy, with direct reference to the structure of the Convention right. The outcome of the two claims is not linked. A privacy claim may succeed where the

[112] *Campbell v Mirror Group Newspapers Ltd* [2004] UKHL 22, [2004] 2 AC 457.

[113] See especially *Campbell*, paras 13–18 per Lord Nicholls, and paras 49–51 per Lord Hoffmann.

[114] See especially *Coco v AN Clark (Engineers) Ltd* [1968] FSR 415, requiring (1) information of a confidential nature, (2) an obligation of confidence, and (3) unauthorized use.

[115] *Campbell*, n 112 above, para 17. cf Lord Woolf in *A v B plc* [2003] QB 195, para 4 ('absorbed').

[116] *Campbell*, n 112 above, para 13.

[117] *Campbell*, n112 above, para 51.

[118] See especially *Douglas v Hello! Ltd* [2001] 1 QB 967; *A v B plc* [2003] QB 195; *McKennitt v Ash* [2006] EWCA Civ 1714, [2008] QB 73; *HRH Prince of Wales v Associated Newspapers* [2006] EWCA Civ 1776, [2008] Ch 57.

'secrets' claims fails, and vice versa—as was the case with the now notorious Douglas-Zeta Jones wedding photos: *OK!* magazine could not rely on their private character, but their worth to the magazine as a 'scoop' was something that English law would protect.[119]

Defamation

The impact of the Convention on the law of defamation has been more subtle and uncertain. Reputation is not an explicit Convention right (though it is an aspect of the right under Article 8)[120] but it is expressly provided in the Convention that the necessity for protecting reputation is capable of justifying interference with the right to freedom of expression under Article 10(2) (restrictions, etc, 'necessary. . . for the protection of the reputation or rights of others'). In domestic law, the Convention has consequently been relied upon, not as a basis for tort liability, but to *resist* or *reduce* liability.

Three landmark cases prior to the implementation of the HRA may be mentioned: *Derbyshire County Council v Times Newspapers*,[121] barring defamation claims by democratically elected organs of government; *John v MGN Ltd*,[122] amending practice in respect of jury determinations of damages in order to preclude unduly high awards; and *Reynolds v Times Newspapers*,[123] on qualified privilege and the media. Each ruling was presented as the natural development of existing principles of English law, though the accord between common law and human rights jurisprudence was noted with satisfaction in the judgments in question.[124]

Following the implementation of the HRA, it has been argued on several occasions before the courts that the Convention right to freedom of expression requires, or at least allows, the introduction of new limitations on liability in the tort of defamation. For example, in *Loutchansky v Times Newspapers Ltd (No 2)*,[125] it was argued that Article 10 required the adoption of a 'single publication rule' whereby

119 *Douglas v Hello! Ltd sub nom OBG Ltd v Allan* [2007] UKHL 21, [2008] 1 AC 1.
120 *Radio France v France* (App no 53984/00) (2005) 40 EHRR 29, 30 March 2004.
121 *Derbyshire County Council v Times Newspapers* [1993] AC 534.
122 *John v MGN Ltd* [1997] QB 586. See previously *Rantzen v Mirror Group Newspapers (1986) Ltd* [1994] QB 670.
123 *Reynolds v Times Newspapers* [2001] 2 AC 127.
124 *Derbyshire v Times*, n 121 above, 551 per Lord Keith; *John v MGN*, n 122 above, 619 per Sir Thomas Bingham MR ('reinforcing and buttressing' the Court's conclusions); *Reynolds*, ibid, 207 per Lord Steyn.
125 [2001] EWCA Civ 1805, [2002] QB 783.

an article stored in an Internet archive would be published once and for all at the time of its initial posting, and therefore gave rise to only one cause of action no matter how many times it was accessed. The Court of Appeal disagreed, ruling that the existing 'multiple publication' rule did not have a 'chilling effect' going beyond what was necessary and proportionate in a democratic society for the protection of reputation. *Jameel v Wall Street Journal Europe SPRL*[126] provides another example. The defendants sought a restatement of the law comparable to that effected by the House of Lords in the *Derbyshire* case, arguing that the HRA required the introduction of a requirement of actual rather than presumed damage where a libel action was brought by a trading corporation. A bare majority of the House of Lords found that Article 10 required no such change, because the chilling effect of the existing rule was rather insignificant, and a company's reputation worth protecting.

To my knowledge, there have been so far only two successful attempts to change defamation law in the light of the recognition of Article 10 in English law by the HRA. First, in *O'Shea v MGN Ltd*,[127] Morland J created a special 'look alike' rule in a case where the claimant bore a close resemblance to, and was mistaken for, a glamour model photographed in an advert for an adult Internet service. It would be contrary to the Convention to apply the normal strict liability approach in determining whether the defamatory matter referred to the claimant. Secondly, in *Culnane v Morris*,[128] Eady J declined to follow the Court of Appeal's established interpretation[129] of Section 10 of the Defamation Act 1952,[130] which it construed as limiting the defence of privilege in respect of defamatory statements published by or on behalf of an election candidate. In the view of Eady J, it would be contrary to the Convention to deprive an election candidate or agent of the generally available defence of qualified privilege, and Section 3 of the HRA required that the Defamation Act provision should not be interpreted that way, notwithstanding the Court of Appeal authority.

A contrast may therefore be drawn between defamation and privacy in assessing the impact of the Convention, whether mediated by the

[126] *Jameel v Wall Street Journal Europe SPRL* [2006] UKHL 44, [2007] 1 AC 359.

[127] *O'Shea v MGN Ltd* [2001] EMLR 40.

[128] *Culnane v Morris* [2005] EWHC 2438 (QB), [2006] 1 WLR 2880

[129] *Plummer v Charman* [1962] 1 WLR 1469.

[130] This reads, so far as is material: 'A defamatory statement published by or on behalf of a candidate in any election. . . shall not be deemed to be published on a privileged occasion on the ground that it is material to a question in issue in the election. . .'

HRA or not. The changes to the protection of privacy have been monumental, but it is denied that the Convention has played more than a supporting role. The changes in defamation law have been more limited—as one would expect from a much more developed compartment of law—but they are nonetheless significant, and at least some of them were explicitly based on powers and obligations arising under the HRA.

Negligence

Turning to the tort of negligence, there remains here considerable uncertainty whether the HRA is to be a stimulus to the expansion of liability, filling in perceived gaps, or a factor militating against its expansion. The HRA can certainly be seen to have shifted the balance of policy considerations that determine whether a duty of care can be established. But in what direction? In *D v East Berkshire Community NHS Trust*,[131] concerning the liability of child care professionals for psychiatric harm done to a child they were trying to help, the Court of Appeal ruled that the policy arguments that had previously held sway in the House of Lords in the comparable case of *X v Bedfordshire, M v Newham*,[132] precluding recognition of a duty of care, were no longer decisive. They were premised on the undesirability of exposing child care professionals making delicate judgments in conflictual circumstances to the risk of civil liability, but they were significantly undermined if there was (as there would be in future) a claim under the HRA anyway. But in subsequent cases the balance has been tilted the other way, with the availability of an alternative claim under the HRA being seen as *obviating* the need for recognition of a claim at common law.[133] As Lord Brown stated in one recent case:[134]

> To the extent that articles 2 and 3 of the Convention and sections 7 and 8 of the Human Rights Act already provide for claims to be brought in these cases, it is quite simply unnecessary now to develop the common law to provide a parallel cause of action . . .

[131] *D v East Berkshire Community NHS Trust* [2003] EWCA Civ 1151, [2004] QB 558. The duty of care to the child was not in issue in the appeal to the House of Lords: [2005] UKHL 23, [2005] 2 AC 373.

[132] *X v Bedfordshire, M v Newham* [1995] 2 AC 633.

[133] eg, see *D v East Berkshire*, ibid, para 94 per Lord Nicholls; *Smith v Sussex Police*, n 83 above, para 136 per Lord Brown.

[134] *Smith v Sussex Police*, n 83 above, para 136.

A further issue, now frequently consigned to legal history, relates to the ECtHR's notorious decision in *Osman v United Kingdom*.[135] The case concerned the liability of the police for failing to prevent a fatal attack on the family of a schoolboy by one of his former teachers. I have already referred to the Article 2 reasoning in the case. My concern here is with the applicant's successful Article 6 claim. The gist of this claim was that the Court of Appeal, by striking out the applicants' negligence action against the police on the grounds that there was no arguable duty of care,[136] had deprived them of their right to a court, which is one aspect of the general Article 6 right to a fair trial: it was tantamount to the recognition that the police had an immunity from liability. In the ECtHR's view, this amounted to an unjustifiable restriction on the applicants' right to have a determination on the merits of their claim against the police. The Court attached particular significance to the English Court of Appeal's failure to have regard to considerations militating against the immunity on the facts of the individual case, for example, the very serious nature of the harm sustained and the (allegedly) grave negligence by the police.[137]

The *Osman* decision seemed to challenge some fundamental ideas of English tort law and procedure, but the storm quickly blew over as it emerged that that the Strasbourg Court had misunderstood the relevant principles of English law, as it admitted shortly afterwards in *Z v United Kingdom*.[138] There has been an 'unravelling' of the *Osman* Article 6 reasoning, which can now be safely forgotten.[139] That, in any event, is the standard interpretation of this chain of events.[140]

There is, however, an alternative interpretation, which I believe is more faithful to the ECtHR's revised Article 6 analysis in *Z v United Kingdom*. *Z* decides that Article 6 is not engaged by the non-availability of a cause of action which effectively prevents the applicant from suing in a given category of case,[141] and accepts that considerations of fairness, justice and reasonableness are properly taken into account in determining whether a duty of care should be recognized in a novel

[135] *Osman v United Kingdom* [1999] 1 FLR 193, (2000) 29 EHRR 245.

[136] *Osman v Ferguson* [1993] 4 All ER 344.

[137] *Osman*, n 135 above, para 151.

[138] *Z v United Kingdom* App no 29392/95), [2001] 2 FLR 612, (2002) 34 EHRR 97, 10 May 2001.

[139] cf C Gearty, '*Osman* Unravels' (2002) 65 MLR 87.

[140] eg, see *Matthews v Ministry of Defence* [2003] UKHL 4, [2003] 1 AC 1163 where it was conceded (correctly, in the view of the House of Lords) that only a procedural bar, and not a substantive limit on the claimant's right of action, was capable of interfering with the Art 6 right to a court.

[141] *Z v United Kingdom*, n 138 above, para 98.

category of case.[142] But it does not say that *Osman v United Kingdom* was wrongly decided, or detract from the core proposition advanced in that case, namely that there should be no denial of a duty of care on grounds of public policy without taking account of countervailing considerations arising on the facts, including the extent of the negligence and the gravity of the harm suffered.[143] Indeed, the ECtHR evidently tested the domestic decision in *X v Bedfordshire* against this very standard, concluding that the House of Lords had in fact carefully balanced 'the policy reasons for and against the imposition of liability. . . in the circumstances of the applicants' case.'[144]

We may conclude that it remains necessary for English courts to undertake a flexible balancing of the relevant factors in the circumstances of the individual case whenever it falls to be decided whether or not to recognize a duty of care in a novel category of case, and *a fortiori* where the issue is the weight to be attached to policy considerations in a recognized duty situation. Only in clear 'no duty' situations is there no such need. The *Osman* Article 6 reasoning may have been trimmed back, but the ECtHR has not abandoned it altogether.

I shall return to this point in my conclusion, but must first complete my survey of the different planes of existence of European Tort Law.

A Modern Ius Commune

A final layer of meaning in the concept of European Tort Law refers to the search for a common core of principles in the court practice of different national systems.[145] To what extent do tort law developments throughout the continent demonstrate trends that transcend national borderlines, the adoption of common solutions to common problems or—as the case may be—the divergence of national systems? To what extent can comparative research into other national tort laws clarify issues in English law and assist in further developments? I have to admit that the influence of European Tort Law in this sense has, in England, been rather limited to date, but there are some notable exceptions.

142 *Z v United Kingdom*, n 138 above, paras 96 and 100.

143 *Osman v United Kingdom*, n 135 above, para 151.

144 *Z v United Kingdom*, n 138 above, para 99. For a similar analysis, see T Hickman, 'Tort Law, Public Authorities, and the Human Rights Act 1998' in D Fairgrieve, M Andenas and J Bell (eds), *Tort Liability of Public Authorities in Comparative Perspective* (London, 2002).

145 This objective is particularly associated with the Common Core of European Private Law Project: see text accompanying nn 9–10 above.

A Case Study: *Fairchild v Glenhaven Funeral Services Ltd*[146]

The case of *Fairchild v Glenhaven Funeral Services Ltd*[147] provides an educational case study. This was the landmark decision of the House of Lords on causation under conditions of scientific uncertainty. The particular context was mesothelioma resulting from occupational exposure to asbestos. Mesothelioma is a particularly aggressive cancer with a long latency period—often 20–30 years. Science was unable to say whether it could result from exposure to a single 'rogue' fibre of asbestos, or only from cumulative exposure. So where the victim was exposed to asbestos in successive periods of employment, it could not be proven that *any* such period was a 'but for' cause of the cancer. The Law Lords were therefore invited to dispense with the fundamental requirement of factual causation.

The transcript of the hearing before the Lords reveals counsel's argument for the claimants to have been characterized, initially, by an almost total focus on British and Commonwealth case-law authorities, and a complete absence of comparative material from the civilian legal world. At the end of the first day of the hearing, the senior Law Lord (Lord Bingham) intimated that their Lordships would be interested in modern civilian European jurisprudence on the subject, and the claimants' legal team put itself to the task of tracking down relevant comparative material overnight. I have been told that their efforts extended to an after-hours telephone call to the offices of the European Centre of Tort and Insurance Law in Vienna, which obliged by arranging for material to be couriered to London over the weekend. Amongst the works to which the House of Lords was eventually able to refer were Walter van Gerven's *Casebook on Tort*[148] in the *Ius Commune* series, the European Group on Tort Law's collection *Unification of Tort Law: Causation*,[149] and Christian von Bar's *Common European Law of Torts*.[150] These researches revealed that, as Lord Bingham observed, although the problem with which the House of Lords was grappling was universal, judicial responses to it were not. In some jurisdictions,

[146] See further K Oliphant, '*Fairchild v Glenhaven Funeral Services Ltd* (2002)' in C Mitchell and P Mitchell, *Landmark Cases in the Law of Tort* (Hart, Oxford, forthcoming).

[147] *Fairchild v Glenhaven Funeral Services Ltd* [2002] UKHL 22, [2003] 1 AC 32.

[148] W van Gerven and ors, *Cases, Materials and Text on National, Supranational and International Tort Law* (Oxford, 1998).

[149] J Spier (ed) *Unification of Tort Law: Causation* (The Hague, 2000).

[150] C von Bar, *The Common European Law of Torts*, vol 1 (Oxford, 1998).

the claim would fail altogether. But, in a majority of jurisdictions, orthodox principles had been adapted to ensure the claimant received compensation.[151] This gave their Lordships confidence that the English law too might develop new principles, though only if this could be done, as Lord Bingham put it, 'coherently. . . so as to serve, even-handedly, the ends of justice.'[152] He cautioned that development of the law in England could not depend on 'a head count' of approaches adopted elsewhere, but recognized that national practice that offended basic justice should be anxiously reviewed if more acceptable outcomes resulted in the majority of other jurisdictions.[153] In the result, the House of Lords recognized an exception from the ordinary approach to factual causation in recognition of the obvious justice of the claimants' case. Considerations of European Tort Law evidently played some role in this decision, though it is impossible to quantify exactly their influence.

Four years later, the Law Lords were called upon to resolve an issue not settled by *Fairchild*, namely, whether a defendant liable under the exception should have a joint and several liability for the full loss, or only liability for a proportionate share reflecting his contribution to the total risk.[154] This time there was no reference to European Tort Law, though it may be noted that PETL could have been invoked in support of the proportionate liability solution adopted by the majority.[155] Obviously the House of Lords perceived there to be no need for such support on this occasion. The decision illustrates that recourse to civilian legal sources remains exceptional and somewhat inconsistent, even where important and novel questions of principle come to the House of Lords.

Other Examples of European Influence on English Tort Law

Still, *Fairchild* is naturally not the only example of explicit reference to continental European materials in support of a decision of the House of Lords. Lord Goff's opinions in *White v Jones*[156] and *Smith v Littlewoods Organisation Ltd*[157] spring immediately to mind. In more recent times, Lord Goff's mantle as the judiciary's leading comparativist has been

[151] *Fairchild*, n 147 above, para. 32. [152] ibid [153] ibid

[154] *Barker v Corus (UK) plc* [2006] UKHL 20, [2006] 2 AC 572. But see Compensation Act 2006, s. 3.

[155] See PETL Arts 3:103 and 3:106. As under *Barker*, this approach applies even where one source of the relevant risk was 'within the victim's sphere' (PETL art 3:106).

[156] *White v Jones* [1995] 2 AC 207.

[157] *Smith v Littlewoods Organisation Ltd* [1987] AC 241.

taken up by Lord Bingham, not just in *Fairchild*, but also (for example) in *Transco plc v Stockport Metropolitan Borough Council*,[158] where he stated his reluctance to abolish the strict liability rule of *Rylands v Fletcher* as to do so would tend to increase the disparity between English law and the laws of France and Germany, both of which recognize strict liability in disputes between neighbouring landowners.[159]

Insofar as *Fairchild* breaks new ground in terms of comparative law, it is in the *breadth* of its survey of foreign materials, which is no longer limited to the golden triangle of comparative law, England, France and Germany. In fact, the Law Lord's opinions' refer to the laws of no fewer than nine different European jurisdictions. This reflects the expanded horizons of European Tort Law scholarship, and the growing number of works available in English—which allows even the linguistically challenged (including myself) to take account of the legal positions in a wider range of national systems than ever before. Of course, the risk of misinterpretation or taking words out of context must always be borne in mind and guarded against,[160] but the correct precaution is more research, not closing one's eyes to the information that is available.

European Tort Law as Opportunity

This new era of European Tort Law should be regarded as an opportunity for English common lawyers, comparable to the decades following the abolition of the forms of action in the second half of the 19th century which for Pollock represented a 'classical period' in the history of English law. It was here (he thought) that '[t]he really scientific treatment of principles' began.[161] Current circumstances offer a similar chance to reconsider the conceptual foundations of our law of tort, and to eliminate inconsistencies, uncertainties and gaps.

[158] *Transco plc v Stockport Metropolitan Borough Council* [2003] UKHL 31, [2004] 2 AC 1.

[159] [2004] 2 AC 1, para 6.

[160] See J Stapleton, 'Benefits of Comparative Tort Reasoning: Lost in Translation' (2007) *Journal of Tort Law*, vol 1, no 3, Art 6. For a possible example of misunderstanding, see the criticism of the comparative analysis in the Law Lords' *Transco* decision by W van Boom, 'Some Remarks on the Decline of *Rylands v Fletcher* and the Disparity of European Strict Liability Regimes' [2005] *Zeitschrift für Europäisches Privatrecht* 618.

[161] F Pollock, *The Law of Torts: A Treatise on the Principles of Obligations Arising from Civil Wrongs in the Common Law* (1887), vii.

Of course, this is a long-term project: there is no quick fix. I would not look for results in five, or even 10, years. But I believe that the longer term trend will be towards further Europeanization in the interests of rationalization.

I cannot attempt a full reconceptualization of English tort law in the confines of this chapter, and therefore limit myself to a few remarks to indicate how a more European approach could enable a rationalization that would bring to an end the incoherence and injustice that sadly deface our present law of tort. A first step would be to rationalize the number of distinct liabilities we recognize in our law of tort. Bernard Rudden famously listed some 70 different torts that are recognized in one or other common law jurisdiction, but made no pretence of completeness and accepted that some of the liabilities listed could legitimately be broken down into further, more narrowly defined sub-torts.[162] Is this profusion of causes of action really necessary, or could Occam's razor be usefully applied to them? The continental systems, after all, make do with far fewer basic liability rules. It is no doubt necessary to note that our 'tort law' may be wider than that of other systems, and serve a variety of purposes ulterior to the compensation of the injured (and wronged) victim, for example, the determination of rights.[163] But there is too often a lack of any clear rationale for differences between overlapping causes of action,[164] while apparently common concepts are given different meanings even in torts that are closely connected, as recently highlighted with regard to the concept of 'unlawful means' in the economic torts.[165]

Of individual torts I shall address only one, albeit the broadest in scope and the most significant in practice. The law of negligence has disintegrated into a number of barely connected 'pockets of liability',[166] and all too frequently provokes expressions of regret from the

[162] B Rudden, 'Torticles' 67 *Tulane Civil Law Forum* 105 (1991–92).

[163] eg, see *Ashley v Chief Constable of Sussex Police* [2008] UKHL 25, [2008] 1 AC 962 and, generally, R Stevens, *Torts and Rights* (Oxford, 2007).

[164] eg, see Lord Rodger's Foreword to E Descheemaeker, *The Division of Wrongs: A Historical Comparative Study* (Oxford, 2009), vii–viii, referring to the conflict between principles of negligence and principles of defamation highlighted in *Spring v Guardian Assurance plc* [1995] 2 AC 296.

[165] Compare *OBG v Allan* [2008] 1 AC 1 (causing loss by unlawful means) and *Customs and Excise Commissioners v Total Network SL Customs and Excise Commissioners v Total Network SL* [2008] UKHL 19, [2008] 1 AC 1174 (unlawful means conspiracy).

[166] eg, see J Stapleton, 'Duty of care and economic loss: a wider agenda' (1991) 107 LQR 249; K Stanton, 'Professional negligence: duty of care methodology in the twenty-first century' (2006) 22 *Professional Negligence* 134.

judges who have to apply the law. Let me give just one example, out of many possible candidates.[167] In *Jain v Trent Strategic Health Authority*,[168] the claimants lost their nursing home business after the local health authority unreasonably made an *ex parte*, without notice application to a magistrate for cancellation of their statutorily required registration. By the time the claimants were able to present their side of the story, in the appeal hearing six months later, their business had suffered irreversible damage. They then lost their action for damages. The HRA was not effective at the relevant time, so the claimants had relied on common law negligence. The Law Lords rejected their claim on the basis that the authority owed them no duty of care, the loss being purely economic, though every one of their Lordships expressed regret at the outcome.[169]

Whose Responsibility: Parliament or the Courts?

Whose responsibility is it to deal with such injustice? In my opinion, the courts are too ready to say that the responsibility lies with parliament. The decision of the House of Lords in *White v Chief Constable of South Yorkshire Police*,[170] dealing with claims for post-traumatic stress disorder by police officers present at the Hillsborough football stadium disaster, represents a particular low point in the modern law of negligence. The Law Lords considered the law of nervous shock to be so far beyond judicial repair that the only sensible strategy for the courts was—in Lord Steyn's words—to say thus far and no further . . . [and] by and large to leave any expansion or development in this corner of the law to Parliament.'[171] As Lord Hoffmann observed, 'the search for principle' in this area of the law had been 'called off'.[172] All well and good, until one recalls who created the mess in which the House of Lords found itself. Even a child knows the maxim, 'You broke it—you fix it.'

The story does not end there. Lord Steyn's cautionary words were invoked recently by Lord Hope in the Lords' *Pleural Plaques* decision,

[167] See also *D v East Berkshire*, n 131 above, para 137 per Lord Brown ('legitimate grievances', 'paying the price of the law's denial of a duty of care'); *Rothwell v Chemical & Insulating Co Ltd* [2007] UKHL 39, [2008] 1 AC 281, para 59 per Lord Hope.

[168] *Jain v Trent Strategic Health Authority* [2009] UKHL 4, [2009] 2 WLR 248.

[169] Lord Scott (para 40), Lord Rodger (para 41 (implicitly)), Baroness Hale (paras 42 and 48), Lord Carswell (para.52) and Lord Neuberger (paras 53 and 57).

[170] *White v Chief Constable of South Yorkshire Police* [1999] 2 AC 455.

[171] Ibid, 500. [172] Ibid, 511.

which declined to extend the category of 'primary victim' to cover those suffering psychiatric illness as the result of their fear of developing cancer in the future in consequence of their past exposure to asbestos.[173] This delegation of responsibility to the legislature looks decidedly odd when one considers that, just five months before, the Department of Constitutional Affairs had published a Consultation Paper on *The Law of Damages*, in which it recommended that the courts continue to take responsibility for developing the law of liability for psychiatric injury.[174] The Government's expectation was that the courts would do so flexibly and incrementally; legislation, it was thought, would run the risk of imposing rigid requirements which would be unable to accommodate developments in medical knowledge and diagnoses. We seem therefore to be caught in a game of pass-the-parcel in which the music never stops, and no one gets closer to unwrapping the fundamental principles upon which rational legal development depends.

Flexibility or Rigidity?

I would argue that the judiciary should take responsibility for the development of a flexible approach to determining the scope of liability for negligence, in preference to the rigidity that now characterizes the common law. It is rigidity rather than certainty that I believe is the correct contrast, because English law's inflexible approach in fact tolerates a large number of uncertainties, as explained below.

The main obstacle to a more flexible approach to liability in negligence is 'the blunderbuss weapon' of the duty of care.[175] For some time now, a number of commentators have argued for a shift of emphasis from the question of duty to the question of breach.[176] Unfortunately, when the issue came before the House of Lords in *D v East Berkshire*,[177] a majority of the House declined to take the progressive course. The claimant had argued that the duty of care should be 'jettisoned' in

[173] *Grieves v FT Everard & Son, sub nom Rothwell v Chemical & Insulating Co Ltd* [2008] 1 AC 281.

[174] Department of Constitutional Affairs, *The Law* on *Damages* (Consultation Paper No 9/07, 2007), para 94.

[175] B Markesinis, 'Negligence, nuisance and affirmative duties of action' (1989) 105 LQR 104, 110.

[176] eg, see ibid; P Craig and D Fairgrieve, '*Barrett*, Negligence and Discretionary Powers' [1999] PL 626; D Fairgrieve, *State Liability in Tort* (Oxford, 2003) 84.

[177] *D v East Berkshire* [2005] 2 AC 373.

favour of a broader and more nuanced inquiry into fault (breach of duty), with the standard of care 'modulated' to reflect the applicable policy considerations. In his dissenting opinion, Lord Bingham stated that he would regard a shift of emphasis from consideration of duty to consideration of breach as 'welcome', adding that 'the concept of duty has proved itself a somewhat blunt instrument for dividing claims which ought reasonably to lead to recovery from claims which ought not.'[178] For the majority, Lord Nicholls admitted that the idea was 'not without attraction'. But he considered it would introduce too much uncertainty into the law, particularly in relation to currently clear 'no duty' situations, and was unnecessary because the HRA in any case provided a remedy in appropriate cases.[179] I hope that this debate is not yet finished, because there seems to be no doubt but that the rigidity in the current law leads to injustice, evidenced by repeated judicial expressions of regret at the outcomes of decided cases as noted above.

Uncertainties in the Current Law

Further, it must be recognized that the duty-based approach, though said to promote clarity and certainty, in fact results in a high degree of uncertainty, even obscurity, as is evident from the repeated visits to the House of Lords that have been necessary in many particular contexts, often without any final resolution of the disputed issues. A few examples should make this clear.

First, the last 15 years have seen four trips to the House of Lords to determine the liabilities of child care professionals (in *X v Bedfordshire*; *M v Newham*,[180] *Barrett v Enfield London Borough Council*,[181] *W v Essex County Council*,[182] and *D v East Berkshire*[183]). Yet significant uncertainties remain, for example, whether a duty of care is owed by a care worker to a child who it is feared is at risk of abuse. The House of Lords said 'no' in *X v Bedfordshire*; *M v Newham*, but the Court of Appeal concluded in *D v East Berkshire* that the policy considerations had shifted following the enactment of the HRA, and found that there was now a duty to a child taken into care. Yet this reasoning runs

[178] *D v East Berkshire*, n 131 above, para 49.
[179] *D v East Berkshire*, n 131 above, paras 92–4.
[180] *X v Bedfordshire*; *M v Newham* [1995] 2 AC 633.
[181] *Barrett v Enfield London Borough Council* [2001] 2 AC 550.
[182] *W v Essex County Council* [2001] 2 AC 592.
[183] *D v East Berkshire* [2005] 2 AC 373.

counter to the analysis of the House of Lords in subsequent cases, and the existence of a duty of care to the child in such circumstances has been regarded as at least open to question.[184]

Secondly, there is the liability of the police. In 20 years, three police negligence actions have reached the Lords: *Hill v Chief Constable of West Yorkshire*,[185] *Brooks v Commissioner of Police for the Metropolis*,[186] and *Smith v Sussex Police*.[187] Again, significant uncertainties remain. The last case of the three leaves open the question whether the police owe a duty of care in respect of their performance of operational tasks, for example, concerning public safety on the roads.[188] Established Court of Appeal authority says they do not,[189] but that may now be open to challenge.

Thirdly, we come to wrongful conception. In 10 years we have had three major decisions, two of them (*Macfarlane v Tayside Health Board*[190] and *Rees v Darlington Memorial Hospital NHS Trust*[191]) in the House of Lords. The third case, *Parkison v St James and Seacroft University Hospital NHS Trust*,[192] did not reach the Lords, so the issue it raised—whether damages for wrongful conception extend to additional costs attributable to the 'unwanted' child's disability—remains unresolved. The three Law Lords in the minority in *Rees* (Lord Steyn, Lord Hope and Lord Hutton) approved the decision that damages could be awarded. Of the majority, two (Lord Bingham and Lord Nicholls) were against it, and opposed to any exception on grounds of the child's disability, one (Lord Scott) thought that *Parkinson* was wrongly decided but that the award of damages might be appropriate where the very purpose of the sterilization was to protect against the birth of a child with an inherited disability. The final Law Lord (Lord Millett) expressly declined to voice an opinion.[193] So here too we have uncertainty.

184 *Jain v Trent Strategic Health Authority* [2009] 2 WLR 248, para 25 per Lord Scott.

185 *Hill v Chief Constable of West Yorkshire* [1989] AC 53.

186 *Brooks v Commissioner of Police for the Metropolis* [2005] UKHL 24, [2005] 1 WLR 1495.

187 *Smith v Sussex Police* [2009] 1 AC 225.

188 *Smith*, ibid, para 79 per Lord Hope and para 109 per Lord Carswell.

189 *Ancell v McDermott* [1993] 4 All ER 355.

190 *Macfarlane v Tayside Health Board* [2000] 2 AC 59.

191 *Rees v Darlington Memorial Hospital NHS Trust* [2003] UKHL 52, [2004] 1 AC 309.

192 *Parkison v St James and Seacroft University Hospital NHS Trust* [2001] EWCA Civ 530; [2002] QB 266.

193 *Rees*, n 191 above, paras 9 (Lord Bingham), 18 (Lord Nicholls), 35 (Lord Steyn), 57 (Lord Hope), 91 (Lord Hutton), 112 (Lord Millett) and 145 (Lord Scott).

Finally, we may return to the law of nervous shock. In 20 years, we have had six House of Lords decisions.[194] These have in no way improved the law as previously laid down in *McLoughlin v O'Brian*,[195] a decision in which the majority of the House of Lords did in fact adopt a flexible approach to establishing a duty of care,[196] only for a later panel of Law Lords[197] to reinterpret the decision to reflect Lord Wilberforce's more rigid, minority approach in that case.[198] Again, significant uncertainties remain, in particular about the correctness of the current approach to primary victims, based on the decision in *Page v Smith*, which has recently been doubted in more than one decision of the House.[199]

In truth, the search for certainty in an area of law where so much depends on judicial assessments of what is 'reasonable' is as likely to succeed as an attempt to catch a moonbeam. Uncertainty is the inevitable result of the instability of the concepts employed. Apparently firm boundary walls are prone to subsidence because of the insecurity of their foundations. On thorough scrutiny, many duty-restricting rules prove to be based on foreseeability or some variant upon it. For example, knowledge—which lies at the heart of the 'narrow' *ratio* of *Caparo v Dickman*[200]—is simply foreseeability of greater degree than that normally required, at least if one accepts imputed knowledge, and

[194] *Hicks v Chief Constable of the South Yorkshire Police* [1992] 2 All ER 65; *Alcock v Chief Constable of South Yorkshire* [1992] 1 AC 310; *Page v Smith* [1996] AC 155; *White v Chief Constable South Yorkshire Police* [1999] 2 AC 455; *W v Essex County Council* [2001] 2 AC 592; and *Rothwell v Chemical & Insulating Co Ltd* [2008] 1 AC 281.

[195] *McLoughlin v O'Brian* [1983] 1 AC 410.

[196] Every Law Lord bar Lord Wilberforce considered that the reasonable foreseeability of psychiatric injury raised a *prima facie* duty of care, all bar Lord Scarman accepting it might be rebutted in an appropriate case by countervailing policy considerations.

[197] In *Alcock v Chief Constable of South Yorkshire* [1992] 1 AC 310.

[198] For analysis, see A Mullis and K Oliphant, *Torts* (3rd edn, Basingstoke, 2003) 40–1.

[199] *White v Chief Constable of South Yorkshire* [1999] 2 AC 455, 473-80 per Lord Goff; *Rothwell v Chemical & Insulating* [2008] 1 AC 281, para 52 per Lord Hope; cf *Corr v IBC* [2008] UKHL 13, [2008] 1 AC 884, para 40 per Lord Walker ('a much simpler test').

[200] *Caparo v Dickman* [1990] 2 AC 605. See especially Lord Bridge at 621: 'the defendant knew that his statement would be communicated to the plaintiff, either as an individual or as a member of an identifiable class, specifically in connection with a particular transaction or transactions of a particular kind. . . and that the plaintiff would be very likely to rely on it for the purpose of deciding whether or not to enter upon that transaction or upon a transaction of that kind.' As I have remarked elsewhere, this language is so imprecise as to make us ask why the test was not satisfied on the facts of *Caparo* itself: Mullis and Oliphant, n 198 above, 74.

it remains a question of fact for the tribunal of fact in every case. A rule based on (actual or imputed) knowledge can never bring the hoped-for certainty.

The Way Ahead

So my argument would be for a more flexible approach to duty questions in English law, and a greater emphasis on the question of breach. A first step should be to recognize that the required standard of care can be modulated in the light of relevant policy considerations, which have to date been considered only in determining the existence of the duty, and consequently that the degree of fault by the defendant may be considered in deciding whether the standard is attained. At the same time, it should be accepted that the extent of the injury suffered by the victim in the individual case is a factor that can be weighed in the balance when considering the arguments, including the policy arguments, for and against the imposition of liability for negligence. I believe that such an approach is inherently attractive, but if support for it is needed, it may be derived from the decision of the ECtHR in *Osman v United Kingdom*. As was argued above, the core of the *Osman* Article 6 reasoning remains valid notwithstanding the Court's admission in *Z v United Kingdom* that it had revised its understanding of the role played in English law by considerations of fairness, justice and reasonableness. If the English courts fail to recognize *Osman*'s continued vitality, further Article 6 challenges to their practice cannot be ruled out.

Conclusion

In conclusion, I would briefly reiterate my view that English law has been, and will be further, shaped and reshaped by principles of European Tort Law in its various forms, whether through the tort law of the EC, the emerging principles of tort law under the European Convention of Human Rights (both directly and through the mechanisms introduced by the HRA), or from the influence of comparative research. Other national systems have felt these influences too. I have tried to show that this era of European Tort Law can act as a stimulus to beneficial change in English tort law and so represents an opportunity for common lawyers who are dissatisfied (as they should be) with the current lack of rationality and coherence at the heart of their law of tort.

The fruits of this engagement have already been seen in the development of new remedies before English courts, whether their origin is the ECJ or the House of Lords. Perhaps the most dramatic changes have been in the areas of privacy and defamation, where Convention arguments are routinely invoked and treated with due seriousness by the courts.

Negligence, however, remains largely resistant to such influences. It is an adolescent tort, gangly of limb and rude of manners. The well-groomed sophistication of its continental cousins provokes resentment and a surly reinforcement of its rude native ways. It has much to learn.

Team of Rivals? Toward A New Model of the Corporate Attorney/ Client Relationship

*David B Wilkins**

Introduction

From its founding, University College London ('UCL') has played a key role in defining—and critiquing—the traditional model of the attorney/client relationship. There is arguably no more quoted, or in the minds of many lawyers beloved, understanding of the duties owed by an advocate to his or her client than UCL's famous founder Lord Henry Brougham's speech in defence of Queen Caroline. Speaking on the floor of the House of Lords in 1820, Lord Brougham

* Lester Kissel Professor of Law and Faculty Director of the Program on the Legal Profession and the Center on Lawyers and the Professional Services Industry, Harvard Law School. This chapter was originally presented as the Current Legal Problems Lecture at University College London in March 2008. I wish to thank Colm O'Cinneide for arranging the lecture and for his outstanding comments on my initial draft. I also wish to thank the faculty and students who attended that event for their helpful comments. I would also like to thank faculty and students at Yale Law School, Georgetown Law Center, University of California at Hastings College of Law, Stetson University College of Law, University of Iceland Faculty of Law, University of Stockholm Faculty of Law, University of Vancouver Faculty of Law, and my home institution of Harvard Law School for helpful comments when I presented versions of the chapter at these institutions. In addition, John Coates, Ben Heineman, Robert Mnookin, Mari Sako, Bill Simon, Detlev Vagts, and Ben Zipursky, provided invaluable feedback on prior drafts. Chris Assise and Jason Silverstein also provided invaluable research support and feedback on prior drafts. Finally, I wish to thank my colleagues on the Harvard Law School Corporate Purchasing Project, Michele Beardslee, John Coates, Young-Kyu Kim, Ashish Nanda, and Sean Williams, for their outstanding work in helping to produce the data from that project discussed below. The phrase 'team of rivals' is used with apologies to Doris Kearns Goodwin and her book of the same title, which examines how the political rivals that made up Abraham Lincoln's wartime Cabinet succeeded in working closely together to bring the American Civil War to a successful conclusion, and to the current President, Vice-President, and Secretary of State of the United States, who some have referred to as comprising a modern-day 'team of rivals'.

eloquently stated what many still believe to be the essence of the lawyer's role:

> [A]n advocate, in the discharge of his duty, knows but one person in all the world, and that person is his client. To save that client by all means and expedients, and at all hazards and costs to other persons, and, amongst them, to himself, is his first and only duty; and in performing this duty he must not regard the alarm, the torments, the destruction which he may bring upon others. Separating the duty of a patriot from that of an advocate, he must go on reckless of the consequences, though it should be his unhappy fate to involve his country in confusion.[1]

For almost two centuries, these words have stood as the embodiment of the ideal of zealous advocacy that lawyers owe to their clients.[2] But of late, there have also been many who have questioned whether such an extreme standard of partisanship—ignoring the 'alarm,' 'torment,' and 'destruction' of others—is the proper standard for lawyers to take in all circumstances.[3] Specifically, I and others have argued that whatever the value of Brougham's conception in the context in which he made his famous claim—ie, the representation of an individual criminal defendant facing the unchecked power of the King in circumstances where the defendant's head was quite literally on the line—this understanding has much less to recommend it when we consider how corporate lawyers ought to conceive of their duties, particularly in the area of regulatory compliance.[4]

Today, these concerns are especially salient. As the spotlight of blame for the current economic meltdown shines its accusatory light on the cast of characters involved in the current economic meltdown, it is only a matter of time before the inside and outside lawyers who

[1] See MH Freedman, 'Henry Lord Brougham, Written by Himself' (2006) 19 Georgetown Journal of Legal Ethics 1215 (quoting Brougham).

[2] Ibid (discussing the many admiring references to Brougham's quote).

[3] William Simon was among the first to mount this critique, but there have now been many others. See WH Simon, 'The Ideology of Advocacy: Procedural Justice and Professional Ethics' (1978) Wisconsin Law Review 29–144; D Luban, *Lawyers and Justice: An Ethical Study* (Princeton University Press: Princeton, NJ, 1988); RW Gordon, 'The Independence of Lawyers' (1988) 68 Boston University Law Review 1–84; and D Rhode, *In the Interests of Justice* (Oxford University Press: Oxford and New York, NY, 2000).

[4] See DB Wilkins, 'Making Context Count: Regulating Lawyers after Kaye Scholer' (1993) 66 Southern California Law Review 1145–1220. For the classic argument that the criminal defence context may be ethically distinct from the other work lawyers do, see R Wasserstrom, 'Lawyers as Professionals: Some Moral Issues' (1975) 5 *Human Rights* 1–24.

represented the banks and other financial institutions we are currently bailing out will be called upon to take their turn in the dock.[5] When they do, it is unlikely enforcement officials or the public will have much sympathy for an ethic that appears to command lawyers for these powerful clients to proceed 'reckless of the consequences' even if it means casting 'the country in confusion'—let alone bankruptcy.

Given the current mood, there may be little the bar can do to avoid this 'unhappy fate' this time around. But as we prepare to enter into a brave new world in which all corporate actors—lawyers included—will almost certainly face increased scrutiny, I want to suggest that the profession and those we purport to serve would do well to consider whether there is something more fundamentally wrong with applying Brougham's conception of the lawyer's role to the corporate context than the conflation of the standards of advocacy appropriate to the criminal context with those that should govern in civil or regulatory matters.

At the heart of Brougham's understanding of the lawyer's role stands a simple but powerful assumption: that the attorney/client relationship is essentially one of agency. Of course a lawyer 'knows but one person in all the world' and is required to promote that person's interests 'by all means and expedients and at all hazards and costs to other persons, even to himself,' Brougham would likely say. These are simply the duties that an agent owes to his or her principal.[6] Lawyers are doing no more—and should be entitled to do no less—than

[5] The unfolding controversy over the role that lawyers for both Bank of America and Merrill Lynch played in the failure to disclose to the shareholders of either company the billions of dollars in bonuses that Merrill intended to pay out prior to the merger of the two institutions may very well be just the opening salvo in this line of attack. See TO Gorman, 'The SEC/Bank of America Settlement: The Lawyers Did it?' 25 April 2009 *SEC Actions* available at http://www.secactions.com/?p=1430 (reporting that '[a]ccording to the SEC, it was the advice of the lawyers that resulted in shareholders of both companies not being told about the billions of dollars in bonuses approved for Merrill employees when they voted on the acquisition of the broker by the bank'). If the blistering opinion by Judge Jed Rakoff rejecting the proposed settlement in the Bank of America/Merrill Lynch bonus case is any indication, the corporate bar could be in for a very bumpy ride indeed. See Z Kouwe, 'Judge Rejects Settlement Over Merrill Bonuses' *New York Times* 14 September 2009 available at <http://www.nytimes.com/2009/09/15/business/15bank.html> (reporting that '[g]iving voice to the anger and frustration of many ordinary Americans, Judge Jed S. Rakoff issued a scathing ruling' rejecting the settlement).

[6] See LR Patterson, 'Legal Ethics and the Lawyer's Duty of Loyalty' (1980) 29 Emory Law Journal 909 (characterizing the attorney/client relationship as primarily constituted by agency law).

others who are engaged by principals to protect their interests and pursue their goals.[7]

It is this traditional idea that I intend to question here. I do so in the spirit of another one of UCL's great founders Jeremy Bentham, whose auto-icon I had the pleasure of communing with when I delivered this paper in UCL in March 2008.[8]

Throughout his life, Bentham wrote many brilliant commentaries on law and legal ethics. In 1827, he delivered an especially devastating critic of the social utility of the attorney/client privilege. Bentham argued that the privilege was both unnecessary to protect the innocent (since any good lawyer should be able to persuade an innocent person that giving the lawyer all the facts would increase the client's chance of being acquitted) and socially pernicious with respect to the guilty (who would not be candid with their lawyers and therefore receive less effective legal representation, thereby making it more likely that they would be convicted—which is exactly what society should want!). It is in the spirit of this sceptical gaze that I want to examine the traditional claim that the corporate attorney/client relationship is best understood as being one of agency.

Specifically, I will argue that for all of its intuitive appeal, the agency model is no longer a helpful template for understanding the relationship between corporations and their outside firms. Instead, expanding on ideas that I first put forward in 1998,[9] I will argue that the relationship between these large and sophisticated clients and their increasingly large and sophisticated outside counsel is better conceptualized as a new kind of strategic alliance or partnership—or, to borrow a phrase that has been used to describe the long-term strategic partnerships between Japanese automakers and their suppliers, a new kind of 'legal *keiretsu*'—than as the typical agent-principal relationship envisioned by Brougham.

[7] See R Paul, 'The Lawyer as Tax Advisor' (1953) 25 Rocky Mountain Law Review 418 (arguing that 'the job entrusted to [the tax lawyer] by his client is to use all his learning and ability to protect his client's rights' and that the lawyer's 'notions of policy, and his personal view of what the law should be, are irrelevant'). Indeed, since lawyers are not only 'agents' but also 'fiduciaries,' their obligation to pursue the interests of their client-principals is arguably even stronger than agents who represent clients in more arms-length contexts. For an account of the heightened obligations of fiduciaries who purport to act for their principals in situations of trust and confidence, see T Frankel, 'Fiduciary Law' (1983) 71 California Law Review 795–836.

[8] Bentham remained thoughtfully silent with respect to my thesis so he bears no responsibility for what follows.

[9] See DB Wilkins, 'Do Clients Have Ethical Obligations to Lawyers? Some Lessons from the Diversity Wars' (1998) 11 Georgetown Journal of Legal Ethics 855–900.

My claim is both descriptive and normative. Descriptively, after spending most of the 1980s and 1990s acquiring in-house expertise that allowed them to break apart the bilateral monopolies that traditionally characterized the relationship between companies and their primary outside law firm and moving toward a spot-contracting model for procuring legal services, a growing number of corporate clients have reversed course and dramatically reduce the number of law firms that they use, particularly for high value work. At the same time, the law firms that serve these clients are consolidating as well—both through mergers and acquisitions of rival firms and by seeking new ways to consolidate and expand the work that they do for their best clients. As a result, clients and firms are increasingly entering into complex interdependent relationships that resemble the kind of strategic alliances that these same companies have entered into with many of their other suppliers.[10]

These changes, and the forces that have produced them, in turn raise important challenges for the legal profession's ability to fulfil its normative commitments to clients and to the public. Due in large measure to the growth of in-house legal departments, corporate clients today have a far greater ability to hold their lawyer-agents to full-throated standards of partisan advocacy than any client could have dreamed of during Brougham's day. Paradoxically, however, the spot-contracting model that exemplifies this new power often has failed to deliver the full range of benefits in terms of either quality or price that the in-house lawyers who led this charge believed that it would. This failure to deliver on the promise of market control has in turn led many of these clients to move from the 'logic of power,' that emphasizes the ability of stronger actors to gain by coercing their exchange partners into an asymmetric distribution of value, to a 'logic of embeddedness' which emphasizes the importance of reciprocity and mutual trust for the production of joint gains.[11] As a result, these companies and their primary firms are more likely to utilize strategies that emphasize 'voice' rather than 'exit' to

[10] For an excellent description and analysis of the characteristics of these increasingly important relationships, see RJ Gilson, CF Sabel and RE Scott, 'Contracting for Innovation: Vertical Disintegration and Interfirm Collaboration' (2009) 109 Columbia Law Review. I return to Gilson and ors analysis of the characterization of these relationships below.

[11] See R Gulati and M Sytch, 'Dependence Asymmetry and Joint Dependence in Interorganizational Relationships: Effects of Embeddedness on a Manufacturer's Performance in Procurement Relationships' (2007) 52 *Administrative Science Quarterly* 32–69 (discussing the difference between the 'logic of power' and the 'logic of embeddedness').

resolve problems that arise during the relationship—although, as we will see, exit always remains a credible threat.[12]

This new logic, however, arguably threatens the ability of outside counsel to function as public-regarding gatekeepers.[13] Although these concerns are legitimate, I will argue that the logic of embeddedness is no more corrosive of public regarding values than the logic of power that now typifies the relationship between companies and their outside firms. Indeed, this logic has the potential to be significantly less corrosive—particularly if we move away from an ethical and regulatory structures based on a principal-agent model that serves only to entrench the ability of powerful corporate-principals to impose their will on increasingly vulnerable lawyer-agents. Indeed as a wag like Bentham might say, current market conditions have largely turned the traditional justification for the agency model on its head. By withholding information and manipulating incentives sophisticated corporate clients now have the power to pressure their lawyers into taking risky or unethical actions that threaten to throw their law firms 'into confusion' in the form of legal peril or financial ruin. 'Innocent' lawyers who do not want to participate in such actions have no recourse other than to resign—or be fired. At the same time 'guilty' lawyers who have no interest in standing up to client pressure are given a pass on the ground that they are not responsible for the ends of the representation and are required to follow the client's direction so long as it is technically within the letter of the law. A model of the attorney/client relationship that recognizes that both clients and lawyers have reciprocal obligations of disclosure, forbearance, and fair dealing of the kind characteristic of

[12] See SR Helper and M Sako, 'Supplier Relations in Japan and the United States: Are they Converging?', in (Spring 1995) *Sloan Management Review* 77–84 (discussing the difference between 'voice' and 'exit' strategies in customer/supplier relationships in the automobile industry). For the classic formulation of the difference between voice and exit, see A Hirschman, *Exit, Voice and Loyalty* (Harvard University Press: Cambridge, Mass, 1970).

[13] Reiner Kraakman was the first to apply the term 'gatekeeper' to describe this aspect of the lawyer's role and, more importantly, to explore the factors that influence whether lawyers will be able to play this role effectively. See R Kraakman, 'Gatekeepers: The Anatomy of a Third Party Enforcement Strategy' (1986) 2 Journal of Law, Economics, & Organization 53–102. See also JC Coffee Jr, *Gatekeepers: The Professions and Corporate Governance* (Oxford University Press: Oxford and New York, NY, 2006). The idea that lawyers should be 'officers of the court' with responsibilities to the public purposes of the law, however, is as old as the profession itself. See ER Gaetke, 'Lawyers as Officers of the Court' (1989) 42 Vanderbilt Law Review 39–92.

strategic alliances, I will argue, provides a better foundation for dealing with these increasingly important problems.

The rest of this chapter proceeds in five parts. Part I briefly sets out the traditional agency model of the attorney/client relationship and explores how that model has always been in tension with the claim that corporate lawyers should also act as gatekeepers who protect and promote public norms. Part II tracks the evolution of the corporate attorney/client relationship with respect to these two competing dimensions through three stages of development: the traditional Golden Age marriage characterized by bilateral monopolies reinforced by information asymmetry between clients and lawyers and an oligopolistic cartel among firms; the divorce (circa 1989), typified by spot-contracting brought about by the growth of sophisticated in-house legal departments; and the development of a new legal *keiretsus* characterized by 'convergence' of law firm relationships by companies, 'consolidation' among firms, and integration and information exchange both within and across organizational boundaries, reinforced by a surprising amount of turnover among in-house lawyers. Part III then explores the implications of this third stage of development for clients, lawyers, and the public. Although there are risks for each of these constituencies in the hybrid model of cooperation and competition that characterize the new logic of embeddedness that informs these new strategic alliances, there are also important benefits —benefits that arguably minimize the traditional tension between the client-service and gatekeeping parts of the corporate lawyer's role. These potential benefits, however, will only be realized if the public regarding potential of legal *keiretsus* are reinforced by appropriate ethical and regulatory support. Part IV therefore begins the process of identifying ethical and regulatory changes that can promote the potential of these new strategic alliances while limiting their dangers. Part V concludes by briefly identifying questions for future research, particularly in light of the current economic crisis. Although I concede that the ultimate implications of the global slowdown for the relationship between large companies and their principal outside law firms have yet to be determined, initiatives such as the American Corporate Counsel Associationâs Value Challenge suggest that the new economic environment may very well accelerate the move toward the kind of partnering model I describe.

Can Agents be Gatekeepers?

Even at the time Lord Brougham uttered his famous pean to partisanship in 1820, it was well established that the client-centred duties he celebrated did not comprise the full measure of the lawyer's role. In addition to being faithful agents who pursued their client's interests, lawyers have traditionally also been expected to be 'officers of the court' who promote and uphold the public purposes of the legal framework.[14] For most of the profession's history, the bar has portrayed these twin obligations as being entirely consistent and harmonious. Lawyers promote the public good, according to this standard view, by zealously advocating for the interests of their private clients 'within the bounds of the law.'[15]

However, the public, and more specifically enforcement officials, have grown increasingly less sanguine about this alleged congruence. Beginning with a string of high profile enforcement actions in the 1970s, the Securities and Exchange Commission, for example, has pressed lawyers to take their public duties to investors more seriously when advising corporate clients on complying with federal securities laws.[16] In the 1980s and 1990s, the IRS and the Office of Thrift Supervision joined the chorus, bringing multimillion dollar enforcement actions and law suits against prominent law firms for advocating too zealously on behalf of their corporate clients in a manner that contravened applicable legal constraints.[17] Although prosecutions

[14] See Gaetke, 'Lawyers as Officers of the Court', n 13 above. As Robert Gordon emphasizes, this ideal was inherited from the traditions of the English bar and has been a part of the legal profession's self-understanding since the 18th century. See RW Gordon, 'The Ideal and the Actual in the Law: Fantasies and Practices of New York City Lawyers, 1870-1900' in GW Gawalt (ed), *The New High Priests: Lawyers in Post-Civil War America* (Greenwood Press: Westport, CN, 1984).

[15] The following statement in the old Model Code typifies this view: 'The duty of a lawyer, both to his client and to the legal system, is to represent his client zealously within the bounds of the law': see American Bar Association, *Model Code of Professional Conduct* (1981) [hereinafter Model Rules] Canon 7, EC 7-1. The Model Rules adopted in 1983 take a much more nuanced view of this connection. Although claiming that '[a] lawyer's responsibilities as a representative of clients, an officer of the legal system and a public citizen are usually harmonious,' the rules also concede that 'in the nature of law practice ... conflicting responsibilities are encountered among the lawyers various duties ... while [also] earning a satisfactory living.' See American Bar Association, *Model Rules of Professional Conduct* (1983) Preamble, paras 8 and 9.

[16] eg, see Coffee, n 13 above; LR Patterson, 'The Limits of the Lawyer's Discretion and the Law of Legal Ethics: National Student Marketing Revisited' (1979) Duke Law Journal 1251–74; LD Lowenfels, 'Expanding Public Responsibilities of Securities Lawyers: An Analysis of the New Trend in Stands of Care and Priorities of Duties' (1974) 74 Columbia Law Review 412–38.

[17] See Coffee, n 13 above, at 213–15.

against lawyers in the wake of Enron and other related corporate scandals in 2001 have been less numerous—and, it should be noted, less successful—there is nevertheless a growing consensus that it is no longer plausible to assume that the private interests of corporate clients will always, or even usually, be congruent with the public purposes of the legal framework, or that reputational incentives alone will always be sufficient to bridge this divide.[18]

Coming up with viable means for reinvigorating the lawyer's gate-keeping role, however, has proven to be substantially more allusive—and controversial. Reformers have tended to concentrate on two strategies: normative strategies designed to remind lawyers that they do in fact have duties to the legal framework that are as, if not more, important than their private duties to clients, and enforcement strategies that hold lawyers accountable for assisting—or in some cases for not preventing—client misconduct.[19] Both of these strategies have achieved important results—indeed, I have advocated both in the past and will do so again here. But with few exceptions, those who have advocated these strategies have done so without challenging the underlying characterization of the lawyer-client relationship as grounded in the principles of agency law that arguably have helped to create the tension between the lawyer's private and public duties in the first instance.[20]

It is hardly surprising that the agency model has remained strong, even as Brougham's overzealous characterization of it has lost favour. Clients, after all, hire lawyers to pursue their projects in their name and on their behalf. In addition, clients are generally held accountable for their lawyer's conduct.[21] Given these background characteristics, it is difficult to conceive of a plausible account of the attorney/client

[18] See Coffee, n 13 above (criticizing Easterbrook for assuming that reputational concerns will automatically make gatekeepers such as lawyers conform to public norms).

[19] For an example of a strategy that relies on changing the norms of legal practice, see WH Simon, 'Ethical Discretion in Lawyering' (1988) 101 Harvard Law Review 1083–145; Gordon, 'The Independence of Lawyers', n 3 above. My own prior work has tended to emphasize enforcement. See DB Wilkins, 'Who Should Regulate Lawyers?' (1992) 105 Harvard Law Review 799 (arguing for promoting public-regarding gate-keeping by increasing enforcement of existing public duties).

[20] David Luban has been one such exception. See Luban, n 3 above, 324–5 (arguing that the relationship between public interest lawyers and their clients is better understood as one between 'political comrades' than one of agency).

[21] eg, see *Link v Wabash RR Co* (1962) 370 US 626, 634 ('each party is deemed bound by the acts of his lawyer-agent and is considered to have "notice of all facts, notice of which can be charged upon the attorney"').

relationship that does not view the lawyer in some significant sense as the client's agent.

Nevertheless, the reality of the corporate attorney/client relationship has always been more complex than the simple agency model would suggest. To be sure, corporations have always tried to ensure that outside counsel follow their instructions and deliver high quality legal services that advance the company's objectives. And law firms have always worked hard at least to appear to be satisfying these expectations. But since Paul Cravath and his partners first put together the prototype of the modern large law firm in the waning decades of the 19th century, the actual balance of authority and decision-making responsibility between companies and their outside counsel has departed significantly from the standard agency account. Elite lawyers never conceived of themselves, to borrow Anthony Kronman's pejorative but nevertheless evocative phrase, as 'deferential servants' who merely carry out the client's bidding.[22] Instead, these early lawyers aspired to be wise counsellors, or 'lawyer-statesmen' to borrow another Kronman phrase, who played a key role in shaping their clients goals and in mediating between these private ends and the public purposes of the legal framework.[23] By the so-called 'Golden Age' of the large law firm in the middle decades of the 20th century, this 'Whiggish ideology' had become the accepted understanding of the corporate lawyer's role.[24]

In the next Part, I will explore how market conditions in the last decades of the 20th century made it increasingly difficult for lawyers to play this gatekeeping role—to the extent that they were actually serving this function before.[25] For present purposes, however, I want

[22] See A Kronman, *The Lost Lawyer: Failing Ideals of the Legal Profession* (Harvard University Press: Cambridge, Mass, 1993) 15.

[23] Ibid

[24] See E Smigel, *Wall Street Lawyer: Professional Organizational Man?* (Indiana University Press: Bloomington, Ind, 1963) 343–4. For the connection between this account of lawyer professionalism and the nobles oblige traditions of the early Whig party, see Gordon, 'The Ideal and the Actual' n 14 above. The scare quotes around 'Golden Age,' as Marc Gelernter wryly notes, are to remind us that the period in question was only golden for those with the right race, gender, and religion to be admitted to the club. See M Galanter, 'Lawyers in the Mist: The Golden Age of Legal Nostalgia' (1996) 100 Dickinson Law Review 549–62. I have made a similar critique of Kronman: see DB Wilkins, 'Practical Wisdom for Practicing Lawyers: Separating Ideals from Ideology in Legal Ethics' (1994) 108 Harvard Law Review 458–76.

[25] See Gordon, 'The Ideal and the Actual', n 14 above (acknowledging that lawyers have probably never lived up to their stated ideals about professional independence but citing examples in which the bar promoted projects that were not in the short-term interests of their corporate clientele).

to highlight how the agency model has contributed to this decline. By characterizing the relationship between corporate lawyers and their clients as fundamentally one of agency, the standard account systematically marginalizes, and indeed delegitimates, a lawyer's allegiance to this broader public role. Rather than being viewed as 'trusted advisors' who help to shape their clients' objectives in ways that ultimately serve both the clients' and the public's long-term goals, lawyers who seek to influence client ends are chastized as 'moral policemen' who constrain their clients' 'first class citizenship' by 'arrogating to themselves' decision-making authority that should belong exclusively to their client-principals.[26] The result has been an increasing tendency among even the most public-regarding segments of the corporate bar to embrace what Robert Gordon calls 'schizoid lawyering' in which practitioners confine their public commitments to their own (increasingly scarce) private time, while accepting uncritically the instructions of their private clients unmediated by any attention to public ends.[27]

Moreover as I argued in 1998, 'the agency model of the lawyer's role assumes that all ethical obligations flow from the lawyer-agent to the client-principal.'[28] Clients have only *rights*, not obligations.[29] To be sure, these rights may be limited by a lawyer's correlative obligations to the legal framework, and on occasion, even by 'the lawyer's own interest in remaining an upright person while earning a satisfactory living.'[30] As important and as controversial as these limitations may be, however, they do not disturb the basic framework in which clients have no obligations, save for their duty to pay for the services they receive.[31] As corporate clients have become increasingly sophisticated about their legal needs and interests—and increasingly capable of pressing their outside counsel to pursue these self-defined ends—the inattention to

[26] eg, see SL Pepper, 'The Lawyer's Amoral Ethical Role' (1986) *American Bar Foundation Research Journal* 613–36.

[27] Gordon, 'The Independence of Lawyers', n 3 above, 22–3.

[28] See Wilkins, 'Do Clients Have Ethical Obligations to Lawyers?', n 9 above, 856.

[29] See LR Patterson, 'The Function of a Code of Legal Ethics' (1980-81) 35 University of Miami Law Review, 699-700 (arguing that the Model Code implies 'that lawyers have only duties (not rights) in relation to clients, and that clients have only rights (not duties) in relation to lawyers'). Patterson goes on to argue against this understanding.

[30] Model Rules, n 15 above, Preamble.

[31] See Wilkins, 'Do Clients Have Ethical Obligations to Lawyers?', n 9 above, 855–6 (discussing the limited duties that client-principals owe to their lawyer-agents).

the obligations of clients sanctioned by the agency model has made it increasingly difficult to conceive of a plausible gatekeeping role for lawyers.

Before we proclaim the lawyer-statesman lost forever, however, it is important to remember that market conditions are by their very nature dynamic. In recent years, these conditions have been shifting back in the direction of a more collaborative relationship between companies and law firms. Understanding this shift, I will argue, highlights the need for a corresponding reinterpretation of the way in which we conceive of the normative obligations of both lawyers and clients.

From Spouses to Vendors to Partners

Over the last century the corporate attorney/client relationship has gone through three distinct, albeit overlapping, phases. The following sections present a stylized description of each of these periods.[32] Although important elements of the agency model are presented in all three, none conforms to the underlying assumptions upon which Lord Brougham's full-throated defence of the lawyer-as-agent model was based.

The Marriage: The Trusted—and Unaccountable—Advisor

As indicated above, corporate lawyers have always sought to be more than simply agents to their powerful clients. Instead, Wall Street lawyers and their counterparts in other cities fashioned a role for themselves as trusted advisors who would guide their clients through the complex web of problems at the intersection of law and business. As Robert Gordon explains, although '[n]ominally representing ... corporations, banking houses, or committees of security holders in

[32] It is important to note that each of these periods is more complex than these simple synopses suggest. Specifically, in each period particular companies and law firms deviated from the general tendencies I describe in some, or in some cases all, of their respective attorney/client relationships. This is particularly true, as I note below, of what I have characterized as the 'divorce' period in which even ardent advocates of breaking apart the bilateral monopolies that characterized the earlier period also recognized the value of 'partnering' with their most important outside firms on their most important matters. Notwithstanding this important gloss, however, most knowledgeable observers would concede that the overall ethos of this period was to move toward a spot contracting model of the attorney/client relationship characterized by the mantra that 'we hire lawyers not firms.'

bankruptcy proceedings,' this new breed of practitioners 'invented for themselves liaison roles in building or rebuilding the financial structures of American corporations that ensured the prosperity of the largest New York City law firms and came to seem indispensable to their clients.'[33]

As a result, companies and their principal law firms developed deep and enduring relationships that extended to every aspect of the company's business. Until well into the 1960s, it was not uncommon, for example, for a single law firm to handle all of the legal business for its major clients—from slip and fall cases to 'bet the company' litigation (to the extent such cases existed during this period) and important acquisitions or other structuring transactions.[34] Indeed, many law firms were located in the same buildings that housed the offices of their primary client, typically a bank, and it was not at all unusual for these longstanding business ties to be cemented through personal friendships and even marriages.

As Ronald Gilson argues, however, there were factors other than social ties that helped to perpetuate this state of affairs. In addition to the glue that undoubtedly comes from being members of the same small elite circle, the deep and enduring relationships between corporations and their outside counsel were also reinforced by pervasive information asymmetries between even the largest company and their outside counsel. Beginning with the New Deal and accelerating through the 'rights revolution' of the 1960s, the law governing corporate conduct became increasingly complex, subjecting corporations to a bewildering array of new regulations and potential liabilities. Few businesses, however, had any significant internal expertise to help them decipher and navigate these new legal risks. As a result, even sophisticated business executives were likely to defer to outside counsel to assess the company's legal risks and to define and implement an appropriate legal strategy.[35]

Given these information gaps, Gilson concludes, corporations traditionally found it efficient to invest in long-term relationships with a

[33] Gordon, 'The Ideal and the Actual', n 14 above, 59.

[34] See M Galanter and T Palay, *Tournament of Lawyers: The Transformation of the Big Law Firm* (Chicago University Press: Chicago, Ill, 1989) 34 (describing the enduring relationship between companies and firms during the 'golden age' and quoting clients as stating that 'outside counsel has been with us for many, many years' or that 'we have never given any thought to hiring another' firm).

[35] RJ Gilson, 'The Devolution of the Legal Profession: A Demand Side Perspective' (1990) 49 Maryland Law Review 869–916.

full-service outside firm that acted as both 'diagnostician' of the client's legal needs and as reliable 'referring agents' (often to another member of the same law firm) to ensure that the client's problems were handled correctly. These long-term relationships, in turn, created economic disincentives to lawyer switching that gave lawyers *de facto* power over even the largest corporate clients.[36]

To these structural aspects of the attorney/client relationship during the Golden Age, the legal historian Robert Gordon adds an important normative dimension.[37] In addition to their superior knowledge of the law and long-term client relationships that discouraged switching, lawyers during the Golden Age had the added advantage of the widespread belief among both lawyers and clients in the autonomy of law itself. Notwithstanding the 'legal realist' critique raised by left-leaning law professors in the 1930s, law schools, courts, law-makers, and popular culture spoke of law primarily as a set of formal rules separate and distinct from politics or even morality.

During the Golden Age, lawyers used this power in a variety of ways. Some of these ways undoubtedly benefited their corporate clients and were therefore consistent with the spirit of the agency model. The longstanding relationships between senior partners and corporate CEOs, for example, undoubtedly allowed the former to gain in-depth knowledge of the latter's business and to counsel the company in a manner consistent with its overall strategy and goals. At the same time, precisely because they were located in independent firms, these trusted advisors were also able to give their clients the benefit of their experience gained from representing other clients with similar problems.[38]

In addition, the stability of these lawyer/client relationships also helped to ensure that the valuable knowledge accumulated by senior lawyers would be passed on to the next generation. Clients were literally passed down from senior partners to their most promising protégés—protégés who had already worked on the client's matters for several years before assuming their new role.[39] Even junior associates were

[36] Galanter and Palay, n 34 above, 897–9.

[37] See Gordon, 'The Independence of Lawyers', n 3 above.

[38] See Smigel, n 24 above, 343 (arguing that as the law governing corporate conduct 'proliferated and increased in importance' corporate clients increasingly valued firms with the experience to interpret the new legal order).

[39] See Smigel, n 24 above, 117 (describing how 'chosen' associates 'are treated like heirs' and groomed to take over the firm's important client relationships).

likely to be well trained, both in the particulars of the client's work, having worked on a variety of problems under the close supervision of more senior lawyers, and more generally in the broad range of legal problems a client might confront, having rotated through the various areas of the firm's practice before settling into a particular specialty.[40]

These same structural and attitudinal features of the lawyer/client relationship between companies and firms during the Golden Age, however, also increased the ability of law firms to act as gatekeepers. As Gilson argues, high switching costs allow lawyers to 'shelter [the] gatekeeping function from the pressure of client demand.'[41] Even if a company knew that it disagreed with the advice given by outside counsel, it would still have to choose to incur both the cost of bringing another law firm up to speed and the loss of the relationship-specific capital of its prior counsel if it decided to move work from one law firm to another. Although some companies were willing to bear this expense, many others undoubtedly simply agreed to follow their original lawyer's advice, even if at some level corporate managers would have preferred to pursue other options. The fact that even Golden Age law firms had large enough client portfolios to ensure that 'no one client provide[s] enough income to materially or consciously influence the law office's legal opinion' also helped to ensure that firms were well positioned to see themselves as 'represent[ing] the law' with a duty to 'separate themselves from the client.'[42]

From the perspective of the lawyer's role as an officer of the court entrusted with safeguarding the administration of justice, the fact that law firms in the Golden Age were well positioned to constrain arguably harmful client conduct by exerting their market power is a good thing. From the perspective of the agency model, however this result is significantly more problematic. If, as Lord Brougham argued, an advocate should know 'only one person in the world' and pursue that client's interests single-mindedly, even if it risks 'throwing the country into confusion,' then anything short of counselling a client to engage in conduct that is clearly criminal or fraudulent should be a required part

[40] See Smigel, n 24 above, 52 (describing how law firms regarded the 'practice of law in the early years in the nature of an internship' and promised to provide young associates with both 'broad general experience' as well as specific grounding in the problems of particular clients).

[41] Gilson, n 35 above, 899.

[42] Smigel, n 24 above, 344.

of the agent's role.[43] To be sure, lawyers during the Golden Age continued to assert that there was in fact no conflict between these two positions. 'Independent legal opinion,' as Smigel glowingly reported, 'is perhaps *the* commodity [law firms'] offer, and the primary commodity for which they are paid.'[44] As these halcyon days for law firms drew to a close, however, it became increasingly clear that many corporate clients did not share the view that public gatekeeping duties were entirely congruent with their rights as principals to control the scope and direction of the representation.

Moreover, as legal costs continued to skyrocket, many corporate clients began to suspect that their 'trusted advisors' were engaged in violations of their agency duties that extended far beyond failing to push to (or beyond) the limits of the law. Whether these clients looked at staffing decisions (increasingly large teams of lawyers being thrown against every new problem), wasteful or duplicative effort (associates writing extensive memos to the file on problems that might never arise or having to review basic facts every time a new lawyer joined the team), or down right price gouging ($1 a page for Xeroxing or first class travel at the client's expense), companies began to feel that firms were using their market power to pad the partners' pockets at their expense. Given these discoveries, the traditional one line bill 'for services rendered ...' no longer seemed very appealing.

Indeed, many clients began to notice that their once staid law firms were taking on a distinctly entrepreneurial tone. Law firms grew rapidly in both size and scope during the 1970s and 1980s. At the same time, these institutions shed many of the gentlemanly norms that had traditionally governed relations among these institutions and began openly and aggressively competing for both talent and clients.[45]

Clients, in turn, both reacted to—and helped to spur—these developments by aggressively seeking ways to reduce their steadily escalating legal bills. As with many necessary but expensive services, a

[43] eg, see Pepper, n 26 above, (advocating this position). The constraint that a lawyer may not 'counsel or assist a client ... in conduct the lawyer knows to be criminal or fraudulent comes from Model Rules, n 15 above, Rule 1.2(d). Revealingly, Pepper argues that in order to maximize the autonomy of client-principals, lawyers should be required to construe even this standard constraint narrowly by giving clients access to the lawyer's 'legal realist' understanding of the law as little more than the price of the sanction discounted by the probability of enforcement. Ibid, 628.

[44] Smigel, n 24 above, 344.

[45] See Galanter and Palay, n 34 above, 58–62.

growing number decided that it would be cheaper to 'make' legal services internally rather than to 'buy' them on the open market.

The Divorce: 'We Hire Lawyers Not Firms'

By 1990 when Gilson chronicled the market inefficiencies that allowed lawyers during the Golden Age to act as gatekeepers with respect to their corporate clients, it was already apparent that the cosy relationships that facilitated this phenomenon were already going the way of the dinosaur. Throughout the 1980s corporate clients moved aggressively to close each of the three major information asymmetries that rendered them vulnerable to strategic manipulation—whether for benign purposes or otherwise—by their outside lawyers. The mechanism by which clients have accomplished this goal is simple. Instead of relying on outside firms to meet their diagnostic and referral needs, corporations began internalizing these functions by building sophisticated and extensive in-house legal staffs.[46] The result, as Gilson observed in 1990, has been 'a dramatic reduction in the switching costs facing clients and an elimination of lawyers' market power.'[47]

If Paul Cravath has become the public exemplar of the law firm as trusted advisor, then the General Electric Company's ('GE') long-time chief legal officer Ben Heineman is the symbol of the modern general counsel who helped to unravel the close connection between law firms and corporate clients that Cravath pioneered.[48] When Heineman took

[46] See RE Rosen, 'The Inside Counsel Movement, Professional Judgment, and Organizational Representation' (1989) 64 Indiana Law Journal 483–4.

[47] See Gilson, n 35 above, 903.

[48] The banner headline over the cover story in Corporate Counsel Magazine in which Heineman describes his role during this period captures this pride of place: 'In the Beginning.' See BW Jr Heineman, 'In the Beginning: GE's legendary general counsel explains how he revolutionized the role of in-house lawyer' (2006) 13/4 *Corporate Counsel* 84(5). In the interest of full disclosure, Heineman is a Senior Distinguished Fellow at the Harvard Law School Program on the Legal Profession. It is precisely because of this affiliation that I am particularly grateful for his graciousness in response to my decision to use him as the stylized exemplar of the tendency among general counsel during this period to move toward a more spot contracting model of the attorney/client relationship. As Heineman has made clear in our conversations about this project, GE always believed in partnering with its outside counsel on important matters and that most of the company's relationships with its primary outside firms were both collegial and productive. I have no doubt that this is true, as it undoubtedly was for many other companies and firms. However, as Heineman also concedes, the locus of these relationships was at the level of the 'matter' and not the 'firm'—and that the company's primary goal was to secure the best lawyer for the work regardless of where that lawyer was housed, whether inside GE's legal department or in a firm that the

over the legal department at GE in 1989, he moved systematically to break up the long-standing relationships that the company traditionally maintained with its principal law firms. Working with the express blessing of GE's legendary CEO Jack Welch,[49] Heineman recruited a cadre of talented lawyers from prestigious law firms to work in GE's legal department and then charged them with seeking out and eliminating unnecessary legal costs while improving the quality of the services the company received. By the conclusion of Heineman's tenure as General Counsel in 2006, GE had over 1,000 lawyers in its legal department—enough to rank it among the 20 largest law firms in size if it had been a free standing entity. These lawyers, in turn, substantially altered the relationship between inside and outside counsel and their respective roles in providing legal services to large companies.

Specifically, in-house counsel at GE and the many companies that began to emulate its policies, both took over much of the work that had previously been sent to outside lawyers, while also taking control over the process by which legal work that continued to go to firms was sourced, priced, and managed.[50] Law firms were made to compete for work in 'beauty contests' or 'bake offs' in which the winners were required to reduce their normal fees and to consent to exacting supervision over virtually every aspect of the services to be performed.[51] Not surprisingly, GE was the company that took this trend to its logical limit when in 2003 its subsidiary GE Commercial Finance required firms to compete in online auctions for the company's legal work.[52]

company may or may not have used before. It is this emphasis on finding the best 'horse for the course' that I believe characterizes the dominant ethos of this period.

[49] As Heineman emphasized in an email communication to me, business leaders play a crucial role in determining the nature and scope of a company's relationship to its lawyers—both inside counsel and outside firms. 'Inside counsel really are much, much more concerned about their relationship with the Business than they are with outside counsel,' he notes. The fact that Welch wanted lawyers who were intimately familiar with GE's culture and practices provided the key motivation for growing the company's inhouse capacity. See email communication from Ben Heineman to David Wilkins, 16 April 2009 (on file with the author). I return below to why business leaders might also want their outside counsel to have this kind of familiarity and how this is affecting the creation of a new relationship between companies and firms.

[50] See MC Daly, 'The Cultural, Ethical, and Legal Challenges in Lawyering for a Global Organization: The Role of the General Counsel' (2007) 46 Emory Law Journal 1057–112.

[51] eg, see Robert Nelson, *Partners with Power: The Social Transformation of the Large Law Firm* (University of California Press: Berkeley, Calif, 1988) 57–8; A Chayes and A Chayes, 'Corporate Counsel and the Elite Law Firm' (1985) 37 Stanford Law Review, 278.

[52] See A Lin, 'Like Any Vendor, Law Firms are Asked to Compete for Business on the Web', New York Law Journal 230, 6 November 2003, 1.

When competing for this work, a law firm's prior relationship with the company was expressly discounted. Instead, general counsel sought to break up existing relationships by requiring firms to compete for every new piece of significant business and choosing the winner based on some combination of price and perceived expertise of the particular lawyers who would be working on the matter. 'We hire lawyers, not firms' became the rallying cry of the day, with long-standing relationships with outside firms relegated to the graveyard of history.[53]

This shift in emphasis between the lawyer and the firm both reflected and helped to spur the transformation of many large law firms from the relatively sleepy professional enclaves of the Golden Age to the 21st century cut throat competitive businesses that these institutions have now become. These changes are familiar to anyone with even a passing interest in the legal profession and I will only briefly recount them here.[54] Suffice it to say that as competition for clients intensified, many firms began to compete aggressively for lawyers as well. Traditional taboos against lateral hiring of associates—and eventually partners—were discarded as firms moved to poach talented lawyers from their competitors, lawyers who were expected to bring their clients with them in tow. As more and more firms competed to hire the relatively static number of graduates from elite law schools, while trying to lure away 'star' associates, partners, and even whole practice groups from competitors, compensation levels soared, especially for 'rainmaking' partners believed to control important client relationships. Firms that either did not or could not compete, risked losing lawyers and clients, and as the century drew to a close, their very existence.

Collectively, these changes have substantially altered the value proposition that law firms made to their corporate clients. Rather than being 'wise counsellors' capable of guiding clients through the complex intersection of business strategy and legal rules, outside lawyers increasingly marketed (and I use the word advisedly) themselves as specialists capable of deploying large numbers of highly skilled experts at a

[53] DJ Dilucchio, '"We Hire the Lawyer, Not the Law Firm"—Really?' The Legal Intelligencer, 239/18 (2009), 5 (noting that '[t]his statement has been used for years, and will probably continue to be used' since '[t]his is what the general counsel want you to believe'). As Dilucchio's use of 'Really' at the end of his title implies, he is sceptical about whether this oft repeated claim is in fact true. I return to his scepticism below.

[54] For a catalogue of these familiar changes during the period between 1975 and 1995, see JB Heinz, R Nelson, R Sandeufur and EO Laumann, *Urban Lawyers: The New Social Structure of the Bar* (University of Chicago Press: Chicago, Ill, 2004).

moment's notice to handle the kind of emergencies that remain difficult for in-house lawyers to handle effectively.[55] The value proposition offered to associates and partners considering joining firms shifted as well. Rather than traditional incentives such as hands-on training, a reasonable (albeit never certain) chance for partnership, and collegiality, firms relied on money and prestige to entice law students and lawyers to join their organizations and to compete to win the tournament of lawyers.[56]

Finally, in addition to breaking up the bilateral monopolies between companies and firms, general counsel sought to bifurcate the two parts of the lawyer's role as well. On the one hand, corporate counsel sought to justify their importance to their clients on the ground that in their role as sophisticated diagnosticians and purchasing agents, in-house lawyers were able to ensure that the conduct of outside counsel *in fact* closely approximated the agency model's ideal of a perfect congruence between the principal's interests and the agent's actions. In a competitive market filled with sophisticated repeat players, the argument went, outside firms have little incentive to fail to seek their client's objectives. Although these firms undoubtedly would prefer to extract the highest possible price in return, these same market conditions suggest that in the vast majority of cases, firms that significantly overcharge their clients will not be able to escape detection for very long.[57]

On the other hand, general counsel argued that they were now better situated than outside counsel to play the wise counsellor and gatekeeping roles that law firms, because of the episodic and distant nature of their dealings with companies, were no longer in a position to play. Far from signalling their lack of independence (as law firm partners had traditionally claimed),[58] general counsel argued that their location inside the corporate hierarchy enabled them both to understand the client's business and to engage in risk assessment and preventative

[55] See Kronman, n 22 above, ch 5.

[56] For an extended discussion of the changing incentives for associates and partners during this period, see DB Wilkins and GM Gulati, 'Reconceiving the Tournament of Lawyers: Seeding, Tracking and Information Control in the Internal Labor Markets of Elite Law Firms' (1998) 84 Virginia Law Review 1581–682.

[57] See DB Wilkins, 'Who Should Regulate Lawyers?', n 19 above, 824–5.

[58] See Chayes and Chayes, n 51 above, 277 (noting that in-house counsel used to be referred to as 'kept lawyers' to underscore their lack of professional independence).

counselling more effectively than lawyers in outside firms. General counsel were therefore the lawyers who should be entrusted with the role of being both a 'partner' to the business in achieving its objectives and the 'guardian' of the company's long-term reputation and values.[59]

By the turn of the new century, this 'inside counsel movement,' as Robert Rosen has accurately labelled the push for authority and professional recognition by general counsel, appeared to have carried the day. General counsel in the model of Ben Heineman—indeed many were literally Heineman's protégés—occupied important positions in virtually every major company in the US, and a growing number outside of the United States as well.[60] Outside counsel typically report to the general counsel and are dependent upon these inside lawyers for crucial information about the client's goals. Indeed, it is fair to say that the general counsel has become the client of the outside law firm—leaving the top business people to be represented by in-house lawyers.[61] As a result, even critics who believe that outside firms can no longer act as 'lawyer-statesmen' hold out hope that in-house counsel will in fact fulfil the 'guardian' role that law firms have largely vacated.[62]

But a funny thing happened on the way to the coronation. Notwithstanding a significant investment in building up in-house capacities, many companies discovered that their outside spend on law firms continued to escalate throughout the 1990s and into the first decade of the 21st century.[63] Nor were all of the resources being devoted to monitoring and controlling law firms resulting in increased levels of client

[59] Not surprisingly, Ben Heineman has been the most vocal and articulate spokesperson for this view. See BW Jr Heineman, 'Caught in the Middle' *Corporate Counsel* 14/4 (2007) 9 (arguing that general counsel must be both 'partners' and 'guardians').

[60] See DA Deott, 'The Discrete Roles of General Counsel' (2005) 74 Fordham Law Review 960–61.

[61] See Nelson, n 51 above, 58.

[62] See Kronman, n 22 above, 284 (speculating that in house lawyers may be able to carry on the lawyer-statesman ideal that outside counsel are no longer capable of performing).

[63] See G Passerella 'Corporate Law Departments Hiring More and Spending More' The Legal Intelligencer, 27 September 2006 available at <http://www.law.com/jsp/ihc/PubArticleIHC.jsp?id=1159261524562> (reporting a survey by the consulting firm Altman & Weil finding an average growth in outside legal expenses of 5.5% among responding companies notwithstanding a 19% increase in hiring in-house lawyers).

satisfaction.[64] Finally, in the wake of the Enron related scandals in 2001, companies found themselves facing a new and more challenging regulatory environment in which enforcement officials were increasingly sceptical about the ability of corporate officers to detect and deter misconduct by their peers.

As a result, a growing number of companies have begun to rethink whether a spot-contracting model that simultaneously ruthlessly applies the agency model to outside firms while leaving all gatekeeping duties to in-house counsel is the most effective way to meet their legal needs. Although it is too early to say whether the movement to re-evaluate the Heineman bargain will result in as radical a restructuring of the relationship between companies and law firms as the one Heineman himself helped to introduce, there is enough evidence that an important change is underway to begin asking the question what such a new relationship might look like.

A New Partnership?

Five interlocking trends appear to be reshaping the relationship between corporate clients and their outside firms: 'convergence' in the number of law firms a company is likely to hire (at least for important work); 'consolidation' in the market for law firms capable of handling these kinds of assignments; 'integration' of personnel, systems and functions between clients and firms; 'corporate redesign' to replace top-down hierarchy with teams comprised of both inside and outside consultants; and a new kind of inside counsel 'movement' that is reshuffling the ranks of corporate general counsel. Collectively, these trends signal an important shift from spot contracting to a new partnership between clients and firms.

1. Convergence

Beginning in the mid-1990s, a growing number of companies have begun to dramatically reduce the number of outside firms to whom they give a significant percentage of their work. DuPont Chemical Corporation was among the first to move in this direction.

[64] JL Conley, 'GCs "Can't Get No Satisfaction" From Outside Counsel' *GC South*, 16 March 2006 available at <http://www.law.com/jsp/PubArticle.jsp?id=900005449198> (reporting a senior consultant from BTI as stating that 'satisfaction with outside law firms is "particularly low" right now').

Like most large companies DuPont spent most of the 1970s and 1980s diversifying its outside counsel while steadily beefing up its in-house legal department. But beginning in the 1990s, the company moved dramatically in the opposite direction. In just two years, DuPont reduced the number of US law firms to whom it gave significant business from 350 to 34.[65] Two of the company's in-house lawyers explained the reasons behind the company's change of heart in an article detailing a similar move in 2001 to reduce the number of firms that DuPont used for patent and trademark work internationally. Like most in-house lawyers raised on the spot-contracting model, the lawyers concede that they initially 'subscribed to the common wisdom . . . [that] competition between firms in the same country worked to our advantage in terms of fees and service.'[66] As a result, by the late 1990s the company had more than 300 outside firms handling its international patent and trademark work, in addition to 60 in-house lawyers and paralegals whose job it was to monitor their performance. But after engaging an outside consultant, the lawyers realized that this arrangement ended up raising, rather than reducing, the company's legal costs. As the lawyers explained:

> [S]preading patent and trademark work among a large number of firms limited rather than strengthened our bargaining power. Firms receiving a relatively small amount of work, ever from a perceived 'prestigious' client, were not inclined to offer discounts or give close management attention to the work. . . . Dealing with nearly 300 firms [also] made it difficult for the DuPont clerical staff to establish efficient internal procedures. Our bill paying practices were inconsistent and jeopardizing relationships.[67]

Worse yet, the lawyers came to believe that it also reduced the quality of the legal services the company received. 'We learned that the firms had little incentive to cooperate with one another on our behalf by sharing information and collaborating,' the lawyers complained. 'We needed to develop closer working relationships with all firms, not just the key ones, to ensure a good understanding of our business and IP strategies.'[68]

To move beyond these difficulties, the international group implemented a 'convergence' programme that was even more radical than the

[65] See J Gibeaut, 'The Outside Looking In' (2004) 90 *ABA Journal* 49.

[66] JE Dull and DJ Gould, 'DuPont's Legal Experiment' *IP Worldwide* 25 November 2002 available at <http://www.law.com/jsp/article.jsp?id=900005533284>.

[67] Ibid [68] Ibid

one the DuPont had gone through with respect to its US firms. In less than a year, the company reduced the number of firms handling its international work in this area from 300 to 48, with 28 of these handling more than 95 per cent of the company's international patent and trademark work.[69]

During the last decade, a growing number of companies have followed the DuPont model.[70] In a survey of corporate general counsel my colleagues and I conducted at Harvard Law School,[71] for example, as of 2003, 80 per cent of the companies in our sample reported that they gave 80 per cent of their important legal work to 25 or fewer law firms, with almost 40 per cent distributing this share of the company's important matters to 10 firms or fewer.[72] Although this trend remains unevenly distributed across firms, and there may even be some evidence that the overall trend toward convergence is slowing, [73] many of the

[69] Ibid

[70] See L Sander, 'In-House and Outside Counsel: Building a Solid Relationship' (2006) Chicago Lawyer 29 (citing several examples of convergence, including Allstate reducing its outside firms from 300–400 to 13 firms that would handle 80–90% of the company's work). Even those sceptical of the value of convergence concede that it is a growing trend among companies. See RW Morrison, 'Put Eggs in One Basket?' (2006) 29 Legal Times, 42 (acknowledging that '[f]or law departments in the last decade, convergence—that is, consolidating the number of outside firms used in order to save money—has been all the rage.') I will return to some of Morrison's criticisms below, but it is worth noting that even he advices companies to 'concentrate' their legal spending by 'lavishing 80% of its outside counsel budget on 10% of its law firms'). See Ibid. For present purposes, the difference between 'concentration' and 'convergence' is largely semantic with respect to the firms getting the 80%.

[71] In 2006, a group of scholars affiliated with the Harvard Law School Center on Lawyers and the Professional Services Industry conducted a study of how large publicly traded companies purchase legal services. Our data include (1) detailed interviews with 43 general counsel of S&P 500 corporations, and (2) a survey sent to CLOs of all S&P 500 companies as of 31 December 2006, which elicited a 28% response rate (n=139), for a total sample (interview and survey) of 166 companies, representing a third of the entire S&P. The survey respondents' companies accounted for between 30–40% of the S&P 500s revenues, assets and employees. After comparing both interview and survey respondents and non-respondents on a variety of metrics, we determined that in most respects the two sub-samples were similar, although respondents tended to be larger and have higher demand for legal services than did non-respondents. For a complete description of the study and a summary of its major findings, see M DeStefano Beardslee, JC Coates IV, A Nanda and DB Wilkins, 'Hiring Teams from Rivals: Theory and Evidence on the Evolving Relationship in the Corporate Legal Market', 22 June 2009 (unpublished manuscript on file with the author).

[72] Ibid, at 21–2.

[73] Although 40% of the firms in our sample decreased the number of law firms accounting for 80% of the companies' total legal spend between 2003 and 2006, just under 30% increased the number of firms in this category. The remaining 30% of respondents remained essentially unchanged. See Ibid. I return to the reasons why many companies may resist further converging their outside counsel relationships below.

largest companies (and therefore the most prized clients for firms) continue to move in this direction. Thus in 2005, the pharmaceutical giant Pfizer invited 120 law firms to compete for one of 20 coveted spots on the company's new preferred providers list.[74] Less than four years later, Pfizer further slashed the number of law firms on the list to 4.[75]

Moreover, the reasons companies give for moving toward this model also parallel the DuPont experience. Not surprisingly, cost is a significant factor. By concentrating their legal work in a smaller number of firms, companies hope to leverage their status as a 'trophy client' to exact deeper discounts and package rates. Moreover, as another general counsel in our sample emphasized, for many companies 'predictability is more important than the magnitude of the fee.'[76] General counsel ('GC'), like every other corporate manager, have to ensure that their department's spending stays within budgetary limits. By facilitating 'bundling' of cases and fixed fees, many GCs believe that convergence makes it easier to achieve this goal.[77]

The trend toward convergence, however, extends beyond the kind of commodity work where price is likely to be the sole—or even the predominate—criterion for selecting counsel.[78] Instead, companies that have slashed the number of firms who do the bulk of their outside work are giving these preferred providers access to 'premium' work as well. Indeed, GCs recognize that this is one of the major incentives for high quality firms to enter into these kinds of relationships. As a result, in return for discounted fees and some low-margin work, companies promise firms that they will also have preferential access to the company's more lucrative business.[79]

[74] E Gardner, 'Pfizer Litigators Endure Beast of a Beauty Contest' *Corporate Counsel* 31 October 2005 available at <http://www.law.com/jsp/article.jsp? id=1130499504777>.

[75] G Passarella, 'What's to Become of Wyeth Counsel in Pfizer Merger' *The Legal Intelligencer* 239/18 (2009) 1–2 (reporting Pfizer consolidation).

[76] Confidential interview on 1 April 2008. Of course, companies care about the overall size of the fee as well. As another GC dryly noted, he had no interest in 'buying every new partner at the firm a jaguar.' Interview with #7, General Counsel, Investment Bank, 2 November 2006, 5.

[77] Passerella, 'Wyeth's Counsel', n 75 above (describing how Pfizer has begun giving all of its work in a given area to a single firm in return for a fixed fee).

[78] Indeed, in our survey we specifically asked general counsel to discuss how they assigned 'important' legal work where price was not the overarching determination. Nevertheless, convergence remained an important theme.

[79] As we will see, in most cases 'preferential access' does not mean a guarantee, particularly for 'bet the company' cases or transactions as to which the company reserves the right to seek out the 'best' firm.

With respect to this higher-value work, cost is no longer the dominant factor. Instead, general counsels are looking for firms that will provide high quality service. But companies mean something different by 'quality service' than most commentators—and most outside lawyers—typically think. A recent survey by BTI consulting drives the point home.[80] When asked what they value most in an outside firm, the overwhelming plurality of general counsel responded 'client focus.' Not surprisingly, BTI found that this is what virtually every law firm believes that they are providing.[81] But when the consultants asked clients and law firms what they meant by 'client focus,' they received very different answers. Twenty-one per cent of GCs, again the overwhelming plurality, responded that 'client focus' means 'understanding our business.'[82] Only 10 per cent of law firm respondents suggested a similar understanding. Instead, 21 per cent of law firm respondents defined 'client focus' as 'doing what's best for the client.' Only 3 per cent of GCs offered this interpretation. Although it may not quite be fair to say that clients are from Mars and lawyers from Venus, our interviews confirm that general counsels put a high premium on finding lawyers who 'understand their business.'[83] An increasing number are attempting to ensure that their lawyers meet this goal through convergence.

Given all of these factors, it is not surprising that convergence has become the buzzword for GCs in the US, and increasingly abroad as well.[84] Indeed, as the DuPont example suggests, the trend toward convergence has been even more pronounced in Europe. In perhaps the most dramatic case, Tyco International recently reduced the number of

[80] Conley, n 64 above (discussing survey).

[81] See also RE Rosen, '"We're All Consultants Now": How Change in Client Organizational Strategies Influences Change in the Organization of Corporate Legal Services' (2002) 44 Arizona Law Review 671–2 (quoting a variety of law firm web sites with slogans that promise to put 'Clients First').

[82] Although this is obviously still only a minority of respondents, as BTI suggests many of the other answers commonly provided by GCs—eg responsiveness, following directions, even developing an early strategy for resolving disputes—can fairly be viewed as connected to the client's overall desire to have lawyers who understand how legal issues and disputes fit into the client's overall business strategy.

[83] As one typical respondent put it, 'They must understand our business and be able to work well with out business people. I generally select people that the business people trust. We might try different firms on different projects and the one that becomes the most trusted advisor is the one that I will use on an ongoing basis' Interview with #2, General Counsel, Investment Bank, 4 October 2006, 8.

[84] See Rosen, 'We're All Consultants Now', n 81 above, 665–6.

outside firms it uses in the UK, Europe, and the Middle East from 250 to 1—the UK based firm Eversheds.[85] I will return to Tyco's experience below. But although Tyco may be the most extreme example, other European companies are following suit. The Linde Group, for example, recently chose DLA Piper to handle all of its European work, with the rest going to four other firms. Similarly, Honeywell has selected the UK firm Lovells in much the same manner, while Brady Corp chose Eversheds.[86] Even GE is moving to reduce the 200 firms it currently uses in Europe to 25–30.[87]

A quick look at the law firms that have been selected to play the lead role in these new arrangements underscores a second trend that has helped to reshape the relationship between companies and outside firms during the last decade. Eversheds, DLA Piper, and Lovells are all international firms that have expanded rapidly since the 1990s and can credibly claim to have something approaching a global footprint (so long as one excludes the US from the map). Although the UK firms have been the leaders in international expansion, and indeed now rank among the largest firms in the world—both Eversheds and DLA each have over 2000 lawyers world-wide, with Magic Circle firms like Linklaters, Freshfields, and Clifford Chance topping the scales at close to 4000—their US cousins have not been far behind, and of course are far ahead with respect to their coverage in the US. Collectively this wave of consolidation among the world's top law firms has in turn facilitated a new rapprochement between companies and firms.

2. Consolidation

By any measure '[d]uring the last three decades, large law firms have mushroomed in size and geographic dispersion.'[88] In the 1960s, there were only 20 law firms in New York City with more than 50 lawyers, with the largest, Sherman & Sterling, consisting of 125 lawyers.[89] By the turn of the 20th century, there were more than 250 US firms larger than Sherman's old size, with more than 10 firms of over 1000 lawyers. The growth since 2000 has been even more torrid—until, of course, the fourth quarter of 2008. In 2006, the median size of the nation's

[85] See R Lloyd, 'Focus Europe: Firm Commitment' *American Lawyer* 30/7 (2008) S28-32. [86] Ibid.

[87] Ibid.

[88] M Galanter and W Henderson, 'Elastic Tournament: A Second Transformation of the Big Law Firm' (2008) 60 Stanford Law Review 1882.

[89] Smigel, n 24 above.

250 largest firms had ballooned to over 500, with more than 20 firms topping the scales at over 1000—and 4 breaking the 2000 lawyer barrier.[90] By some estimates, almost 10,000 lawyers—nearly one quarter of all school graduates—were expected to begin their careers in a large law firm in 2006.

Along with getting bigger, firms have also been expanding in geographic scope. Since 2000, for example, the 250 largest US-based law firms have more than double the number of lawyers in Europe and increased their headcount in Asia by more than 60 per cent.[91] UK based firms have been growing at an even faster pace.[92] Moreover, much of this growth has been accomplished through merger and acquisition. Until recently, law firm mergers were virtually unheard of. Between 2000 and 2008, merger activity among law firms increased in virtually every succeeding year, including mega combinations such as DC's Wilmer Cutler with Boston's Hale and Dorr to form Wilmer-Hale and New York's Dewey Ballentine and its long-time rival Loebuff Lamb & Green to form Dewey Loebuff.[93]

The result is that large global companies increasingly interact with law firms that are themselves large and globalized. Nor is this a coincidence. When asked to explain why their firms have grown so rapidly in recent years, firm leaders most often respond that they are simply responding to the demands of their clients.[94] Needless to say, the lack of agency implied by this characterization overlooks the firms' own interest in pursuing a growth strategy. There is plenty of evidence that firms are growing to increase their profits by acquiring new clients, and indeed whole new areas of practice. Nevertheless, even firms that are ruthlessly focused on increasing profits have come to see the importance of strengthening their relationships with their most important clients.[95] As a result, 'premium work for premium clients' has become as much of a buzz-phrase for law firms as finding lawyers who 'understand our business' has become for clients.

[90] 'The NLJ 250' The National Law Journal 29/11 (2006) S1.

[91] L Fortado, 'Steady Global Gains' (2006) 28/20 The National Law Journal 1.

[92] See 'The Global 100' *American Lawyer* 29/10 (2007) S1.

[93] See JD Bell and A Press, 'Law Firm Leaders Have Mergers on the Mind' *LawFirmInc*, 12 February 2007 available at <http://www.law.com/jsp/article.jsp?id=1170928976695>.

[94] See Galanter and Henderson, n 88 above, 1882 (citing increased demand as the reason why law firms have grown so dramatically over the last three decades).

[95] eg, see D Temporal, 'Beyond Client Care' *American Lawyer* 23/7 (2001) 65 (noting that '[a]t many firms, it is typical to see the top 50 clients generate between 45 and 60% of the firm's income')

The UK firm Linklaters is a case in point.[96] As my colleague Ashish Nanda documents, after a period of unprecedented growth between 2001 and 2004, in which the firm opened several new offices and completed five international mergers, Linklaters found that it was falling behind its US counterparts in profitability. The firm's chairman Tony Angel responded by instituting a dramatic plan to increase the firm's profitability and to place 'clear blue water' between it and its competitors. At the core of this plan was a mandate to concentrate the firm's resources on serving its largest and most important clients. In an internal study, the firm's management had determined these clients accounted for a disproportionately large share of the firm's profits and that when all costs were fully factored in, the firm actually lost money on many of its smaller client relationships.[97]

The firm therefore instituted a rigorous—and in the eyes of many—draconian policy to 'prune' its client list. Lawyers, and indeed whole offices, serving smaller more local clients were expressly told to drop these matters and to refocus their efforts on providing support for the firm's large global clients. Lawyers, and indeed whole offices, which were unable to do so were politely, but firmly, asked to leave the firm.[98] The result was a dramatic increase in the firm's profitability.

Although Linklaters policy is undoubtedly more drastic than most, in the last two years its strategy has been copied to a greater or lesser extent by virtually all of the top UK firms and by many US counterparts as well. Nor is this trend confined to firms like Linklaters that have global ambitions and seek only to compete for work at the top of the corporate food chain. As companies shrink the number of outside firms that they use and package even the legal work that they put out for competitive bid in ever larger bundles, there are fewer opportunities for firms to win new clients.[99] At the same time, the pressure by

[96] The following description is taken primarily from A Nanda and L Prusiner, 'Linklaters (A): Seeking Clear Blue Water' Harvard Law School Center on Lawyers and the Professional Services Industry, Case Study HLS 08-01 (2007). Some of the information discussed is from the (B) and (C) cases that are not yet publicly available.

[97] MD Goldhaber, 'Linklaters: Touched by an Angel' *American Lawyer* 29/10 (2007) 118 (reporting that the firm's 40 biggest clients and another 40 preferred global clients account for 52% of the firm's billing).

[98] Ibid, 118 (reporting that 'partners who do not serve the lucrative cross-border needs of priority clients are superfluous' and documenting that '125 partners left or retired in the last four years').

[99] This also helps to explain why firms have increasingly sought to acquire new clients by buying lawyers (and sometimes firms) with large books of business.

even longstanding clients to cut fees has led many firms to try to increase revenues by expanding the volume of work that they do for each client. Finally, the expanded size and geographic scope of most law firms has generated a relentless pressure in these institutions for partners to cross-sell the firm's services. The net result of all of these trends has been a growing awareness among firms that the best way to ensure their profitability is to leverage their relationships with their existing clients. This, in turn, has put pressure on firms to find ways to improve the level of service that they give to these increasingly important clients.

3. Integration

As companies and firms have moved closer together, the boundaries that have traditionally separated lawyer and client have grown increasingly permeable. Not surprisingly, companies like DuPont have been at the forefront of this trend. In return for getting on the company's list of 'preferred providers,' the law firms that work for DuPont are required to adopt common practices and systems that allow the company to both easily gain access to its files and billing information and to create virtual teams of lawyers across the network to work on the company's matters. To reinforce these common practices, the company meets regularly with various partners from the firms on its list to educate them about DuPont's issues and goals and to reinforce the need to work collaboratively to solve the company's problems.[100]

Many law firms have been taking similar actions to restructure their practices to ensure better service to their best clients. Thus, in addition to being organized by practice specialty and geography, many firms have adopted dedicated 'client teams' to service their most important client relationships.[101] In addition to providing interdisciplinary support, these teams often take various measures to integrate themselves into the client's business such as bringing in business people from the client to teach the lawyers about the company's practices and competitive position, and sending lawyers to train their in-house counterparts

[100] Dull and Gould, n 66 above.

[101] See Rosen, 'We're All Consultants Now', n 81 above, 672 (noting that consultants now advice law firms to organize themselves 'around industries rather than practice areas'); PD Zeughauser, 'Optimal Organization' *American Lawyer* 23/3 (2001) 63 (noting the growth in 'client relationship partners' in 'forward looking' law firms).

and business leaders about legal issues of particular relevance to the company.[102]

Indeed, many firms are going beyond seminars and periodic training to place associates (and sometimes even partners) to work full-time in the legal departments of their best clients for limited periods of time. These 'secondments' have been popular in the UK for some time.[103] Since 2000, however, the practice has gained considerable traction in the US as well.[104] Reverse transfers that allow in-house lawyers to spend six months or a year working in the office of the company's most important law firm have also begun to sprout up. And some clients and firms have taken to jointly interviewing law students that the firm intends to hire as a way of both getting the client's buy-in and as a means of signalling to new recruits the importance of getting to know the client's personnel and business.[105] Nor is such collaboration confined to the associate level. In one of our interviews, for example, the general counsel of a large brokerage company bragged that he had arranged for a partner who had done important work for the company, but whose firm did not, to move to another firm with which the company did substantial business.[106] Although our interviews suggest that this kind of aggressive matchmaking is relatively rare, it nevertheless underscores the degree to which the boundaries that have traditionally separated the companies and firms are becoming increasingly porous. As Robert Rosen explains:

> Outside counsel are quick to embrace outsourcing and porous borders because these organizational strategies can lead to more relational work, rather than one-shot transactions ... This allows for a 'rich two-way knowledge transfer

[102] See Rosen, 'We're All Consultants Now', n 81 above, 676 (noting that 'law firms also sell added value through improved corporate processes by selling training); see also R Dawson, *Developing Knowledge-Based Client Relationships: The Future of Professional Services* (Butterworth-Heinemann: Boston, Mass, 2000) 53 (arguing that 'it is increasingly common for corporate counsel to specifically request knowledge transfer from their legal firms')

[103] The practice began in the UK as a way for UK and European companies with relatively small general counsel offices to expand their internal legal capabilities without having to invest the resources in hiring lawyers full time. As the process became institutionalized, however, both companies and firms recognized that it was also a good way to build institutional knowledge and trust.

[104] See 'Loaning out Lawyers to get a Bigger Piece of the Corporation Pie' 27 October 2006, *Corporate Courses* available at <www.law.com/jsp/ihc/pwsArticleIHC.jsp?id=900005465738> (describing the use of secondment programs by US law firms to deepen their relationship with their best clients in an effort to increase business).

[105] S Qualters, 'Citigroup's New Hires to Take Long Route to Law Department' National Law Journal 12 October 2006 (describing a joint hiring program between Citigroup and three of its primary law firms).

[106] Confidential Interview.

and relationship development [as the proponents of outsourcing argue] . . . and [the client] becomes far more inclined to choose that law firm over others it knows less well.[107]

As Rosen goes on to explain, this trend has been facilitated by a set of connected trends in corporate America that encourage companies to invite outside 'consultants' inside the organization to be a part of corporate decision-making.

4. The Boundaryless Organization

Rosen argues that companies have implemented four interconnected practices that have fundamentally changed the way that these entities contract for, and utilize the services of, outside professionals such as lawyers: downsizing, outsourcing, self managing teams, and porous borders.[108] Throughout the 1990s, companies shed workers in an effort to 'reduce bloated bureaucracies' by eliminating middle managers and headquarters staff.[109] In place of these top-down controls, companies have created 'self-managing project teams' which are given wide discretion both to define their own goals and assemble expertise from both inside and outside the company to achieve their objectives.[110] The result, Rosen argues, is that companies have 'shift[ed] away from a 'transmission belt' delegation of powers from principal to agent towards one that emphasizes 'network coordination' among various constituencies, subject to an overall assessment of risks and rewards.[111]

At the same time, many companies have also turned to outsourcing what were once considered core organizational functions. In addition to reducing costs, Rosen argues that companies see outsourcing as a way to tap into expertise and experience held by outsiders who interact with multiple corporations. As a result, 'the strong boundaries that once separated firms have become less distinct, while . . . market transactions have become more intimate.'[112]

[107] Rosen, 'We're All Consultants Now', n 81 above, 670 (quoting Dawson, n 102 above, 162).

[108] Rosen, 'We're All Consultants Now', n 81 above, 641. Rosen also argues that these changes have transformed in-house counsel offices as well. I return to these observations below.

[109] Ibid.

[110] Ibid, 643–7.

[111] Ibid, 643.

[112] Ibid, 649 (quoting RJ Beninato, 'Employee and Executive Benefits' in WK Grollman (ed) *The Accountant as Business Advisor* (Wiley: New York, NY, 1986) 373, 400. See also J Badaracco, *The Knowledge Link: How Firms Compete Through Strategic Alliances* (Harvard Business School Press: Boston, Mass, 1991). I return to Badaracco's analysis below.

Rosen argues that these connected changes have fundamentally transformed the relationship between inside and outside counsel. In the heyday of the Inside Counsel Movement, powerful general counsel like Ben Heineman aggressively managed the interactions between outside firms and the company with the goal of reducing both the cost and scope of their work.[113] In companies that have been redesigned by downsizing, self-managing teams, outsourcing, and porous boundaries, outside firms are increasingly being invited to become part of the multidisciplinary project team that carries out the company's core functions. As Rosen concludes, 'in the modern corporation, relations between inside and outside counsel ... may be summarized in one word: partnering.'[114]

Recent trends in the career trajectories of in-house counsel are likely to accentuate these trends.

5. Inside Counsel Movement

When we prepared to send out our survey to general counsel in the S&P 500 we stumbled upon a surprising fact: a significant number of the chief legal officers listed in the most recent data bases we could find were no longer at their companies. In a separate paper, John Coates has probed further and discovered that contrary to the picture conveyed by well-known figures like Ben Heinemann who spent almost 20 years with General Electric, turnover rates among general counsel are surprisingly high. Indeed, in recent years turnover among general counsels has exceeded the rate at which CEOs have departed their companies by almost 50 per cent.[115] Thus in 2005, nearly, twice as many GCs turned over as CEOs (29 per cent to 15 per cent).[116] Although there are many reasons for these departures, a primary cause is the development of a burgeoning lateral market for GCs who want to move to similar positions in larger (and presumably better paying) companies.

High turnover rates among GCs are likely to increase the degree to which companies rely on their primary outside law firms. One of the principal arguments supporting the Inside Counsel Movement was that in-house lawyers would be a better source of institutional memory about the company's history and practices than outside firms. As lateral

113 Rosen, 'Inside Counsel Movement', n 46 above, 484–90.

114 Rosen, 'We're All Consultants Now', n 81 above, 670.

115 John C. Coates, IV 'CLO Turnover' (unpublished research on file with the author).

116 Ibid.

movement among associates and even partners escalated throughout the 1990s, this argument gained additional currency. As a result, companies no longer felt that they needed to have stable relationships with their outside counsel and instead could move work inside to preserve institutional memory. But as the careers of inside lawyers have become similarly volatile, the pendulum may be swinging back in the other direction. When a company hires a new general counsel—even one with previous experience in a similar position at another company—that person will inevitably have a steep learning curve to get up to speed on the company's legal history and preferred method for doing business. To fill in these gaps, the new GC is likely to look to the accumulated experience and knowledge of the company's primary outside lawyers. Similarly, general counsels who are contemplating making a move may fear tampering with their existing primary outside counsel relationships for fear that the speculative gains in cost and quality of bringing in a new firm either will not materialize, or will prove not to be worth the time and energy that the GC would have to expend to disrupt the status quo.

The fact that many general counsels' offices have downsized themselves in recent years reinforces this tendency. To be sure, in-house counsel has been the fastest growing segment of the legal profession for several years,[117] but this overall growth masks the significant number of cuts that have occurred in many companies. Rosen reports, for example, that all of the legal departments he interviewed in the mid-1980s had experienced at least one round of downsizing by the mid-1990s.[118] Similarly, there are many anecdotal reports of companies slashing their in-house staffs after a merger or other consolidation in an effort to reduce costs.[119] To be sure, there are companies like GE that continue to believe strongly in maintaining (and indeed expanding) their in-house legal staff. But for every GE, there are many others who have reduced the number of inside lawyers, or at a minimum, dramatically slowed the rate of growth. As a result, there is a wide variation in the size of general counsel offices among even the largest companies—with close to 50 per cent maintaining relatively modest departments with

[117] See Heinz, ors *Urban Lawyers*, n 54 above.

[118] See Rosen, 'We're All Consultants Now', n 81 above, 642.

[119] See Conley, n 64 above (reporting that 'some companies are spending more than ever on outside counsel following budget cuts that have forced GCs to slash their in-house staffs by 40% over the past 5 years').

fewer than 25 lawyers.[120] Teams of this size are likely to manage their relationships with outside counsel significantly differently than Ben Heinemann managed GE's external legal service providers from the company's 1000-plus lawyer in-house platform.[121]

6. A New Legal *Keiretsu*?

Collectively, these five interlocking trends—convergence of work in the hands of a limited number of 'preferred' firms; consolidation of the firms themselves through merger and acquisition; greater integration and knowledge transfer between companies and firms; changes in the organizational structure of companies that promote integration and blur the boundaries between the inside and the outside; and increasing instability and contraction in general counsel offices—are spurring the creation of a new working partnership between companies and their primary outside firms. Although general counsels continue to insist that they 'hire lawyers not firms,' in reality their relationship with their primary firms is a good deal stickier than this standard slogan would suggest.

To be sure, this is not the old fashioned marriage that firms and clients entered into during the Golden Age. Firms that manage to make it on a company's preferred provider list can lose their privileged status for reasons of incompetence or disloyalty. Even if they perform well, most companies still put the arrangement up for periodic review and renegotiation. And firms still compete with others on the list for particular assignments, or to grow their share of the relationship.

More fundamentally, outside firms and in-house lawyers still actively compete with each other for both work and influence. Companies compete by taking their work in-house or by switching (or threatening to switch) their business to other law firms. Firms compete by selling the knowledge they gain through their representation of a given company to other clients and by 'firing' existing clients in favour of new ones who can provide more lucrative work.

[120] See Corporate Counsel, 'In-House Tech Survey' (2007) available at <http://www.alacra.com/Incisive-Legal-Intelligence-Surveys-Lists-Rankings/In_House_Tech_Survey-inhouse_tech_survey>. Although accurate numbers are difficult to come by, this survey of Fortune 500 companies found that almost 50% had fewer than 25 in-house lawyers while less than 20% had departments over 100—and fewer than 2% with mega-departments of 500 or more. As this indicates, in this regard as in so many others, GE is an outlier.

[121] For a discussion of some of the potential differences, see Beardslee and ors, n 71 above.

Finally, firms and clients are engaged in a fierce war for talent. For years, companies have routinely cherry picked the best associates and partners working in their primary firms to join their in-house staff. In recent years, it has become increasingly common for law firms to return the favour by poaching senior in-house lawyers to return to private practice. Although these personnel exchanges are often mutually beneficial in that they strengthen the ties between the company and firm (another example of why these ties are increasingly strong) they also can pose competitive challenges for each party. A company that hires a partner who was previously handling its trademark work may no longer need to send this work outside. Similarly, a company that loses a senior in-house lawyer to one of its law firms risks seeing potentially valuable knowledge about the company's internal practices and procedures sold to competitors.[122] The consternation that many firms feel when general counsel berate them for their lack of diversity while at the same time hiring away their most promising minority lawyers underscores that even the most cooperative exchanges between parties and firms nevertheless contain an element of competition.

Indeed, it is precisely this paradoxical element of simultaneous cooperation and competition—'cooptition,' to use a phrase deployed by management scholars—that defines the modern relationship between companies and firms.[123] As a result, these relationships increasingly have come to resemble the kind of strategic alliances or partnerships that many companies have entered into with other long-term suppliers in order to achieve common objectives.[124] Like the partners in these arrangements, both corporations and law firms depend on each other to provide crucial information and expertise if the purposes of their cooperative venture—ie winning the case, successfully completing the deal, etc—are to be achieved. Corporations depend upon their lawyers to supply specialized legal knowledge; to

[122] Conflict of interest rules partially protect against this problem. See Model Rules, n 30 above, Rule 1.7. However, much of what a company may be afraid of losing may not be covered by such rules. See John Dzienkowski, 'Positional Conflicts of Interest' (1993) 71 *Texas Law Review* 457–540.

[123] C Loebbecke, 'The Future of Innovation … The Benefits of Being Realistic' in *The Future of Innovation* (Gower Press, forthcoming November 2009) (discussing cooptition).

[124] See Gilson and ors, n 10 above, 437 (observing that 'an interesting set of firms engages in a process of iterative co-design, in which suppliers contribute to the redefinition of interface specifications for new products by building on their experience in manufacturing existing models' and that 'these methods are today a familiar part of the new economy'); Badaracco, n 112 above.

gather information; to interface with competitors, consumers and government officials; and to monitor and mediate conflicts within the organization. For their part, firms depend upon their corporate clients to supply accurate information about corporate goals and practices; to follow the firm's instructions on matters of legal compliance; and, of course, to provide the firm with the capital that it needs for its survival, including reputational capital in the form of referral to other potential clients. In return for receiving these goods, each partner demands a certain level of control over the other partner's internal affairs. As Richard Painter argues, in their roles as 'monitors' and 'dealmakers,' outside counsel exercise substantial control over the corporation's internal affairs.[125] For the reasons set out above, corporate clients now exercise similar control over the internal affairs of outside firms.

The relationship between Chrysler corporation and its principal suppliers in the mid-1990s provides an instructive analogy—and as I will argue below, a cautionary one.[126] After years of losing market share to Japanese firms, Chrysler undertook a detailed benchmarking study of Honda, considered then—and now—to be one of the best-run companies in the world. As a result of this review, the American car company decided to try to institute some of its Japanese competitor's practices. At the core of this effort was a radical transformation of Chrysler's relationship with the parts manufacturers who constituted the firm's primary suppliers.

Chrysler, like all of its US competitors, was organized functionally by specialty and developed its products in a traditional sequential process in which Chrysler engineers designed components for its cars and then sent them out for competitive bids from all of its potential suppliers. Contracts were awarded to the lowest bidder with little attention to prior history or performance. As a result, 'the typical relationship between Chrysler and its suppliers was characterized by mutual distrust and suspicion' as each party tried to extract the maximum gain from what both sides viewed as a zero-sum game.[127]

[125] See R Painter, 'The Moral Interdependence of Corporate Lawyers and their Clients' (1994) 67 Southern California Law Review 520–53.

[126] The following account is taken from J Dyer, 'How Chrysler Created an American Keiretsu' (1996) 74/4 *Harvard Business Review* 42–56. For a description of the Japanese models which Chrysler attempted to copy, see M Sako, 'Supplier Development at Honda, Nissan, and Toyota: Comparative Case Studies of Organizational Capability Enhancement' (2004) 13(2) *Industrial and Corporate Change* 281–308.

[127] Dyer, n 126 above, 43.

Honda's organization and relationships with its primary suppliers were very different. At the Japanese company, workers were organized around multidisciplinary product development teams that were given 'cradle-to-grave' reasonability for all aspects of the development of a vehicle. Suppliers, who were chosen primarily on the basis of their past performance and relations with the company as opposed to price, were invited to participate in these product development teams at an early stage and, in return for continued high performance, were promised long-term contracts, typically lasting for the life of the vehicle. As a result, relations between Honda and its suppliers were characterized by a high degree of trust and collaboration.

Beginning in 1989, Chrysler began a campaign to adopt these practices. The company changed its internal organization from functional divisions to cross-functional teams. At the same time it cut the number of suppliers it would work with in half and began to involve them early in the design process by exchanging engineers and 'pre-sourcing' responsibility for particular components. Suppliers were given long-term contracts for the life of the vehicle and beyond. And while the company requested discounts in return, prices were set specifically to ensure that suppliers would be able to achieve reasonable and sustainable profits. As the company's chairman made clear 'All I want is your brainpower, not your margins.'[128]

Most radically of all, Chrysler rolled out a Supplier Cost Reduction Effort ('SCORE') under which suppliers were encouraged to provide suggestions about how Chrysler could improve its processes. In order to induce suppliers to participate, Chrysler agreed to share half of any resulting cost savings with the company that made the suggestion. In 1992, Chrysler made SCORE a formal part of its supplier rating system, along with more traditional measures such as price, quality and delivery. By the mid-1990s, SCORE accounted for 15 per cent of a supplier's performance and often made the crucial difference in whether a supplier would be able to expand its business with the company. Indeed, the programme became so successful that the company expanded it to provide incentives for suppliers to develop ideas that would reduce vehicle weight, warranty claims, and complexity. The programme has proven to be enormously successful, rising from 875 suggestions worth a total of $170.8 million in its first year of operation

[128] Ibid, 53.

to 5,300 suggestions generating $1.7 billion in savings when the programme was assessed in 1995.

More generally, by moving from a 'logic of power,' in which the company attempted to reap maximum advantage from its leverage over its suppliers, to a 'logic of embeddedness' in which the company worked to build a mutually cooperative relationship in which both parties would gain, Chrysler was able to dramatically reduce its overall costs while improving both the speed of its production process and the overall quality of its cars.[129] Throughout the 1990s, the company continued to find ways to give 'voice' to its suppliers, including establishing an advisory board of executives from its 14 biggest suppliers and holding an annual meeting with its top 150.[130] For their part, suppliers demonstrated their commitment to the relationship by creating a common technology platform with the automaker and establishing dedicated equipment, systems, processes, and staff exclusively to serve Chrysler's needs. Although the automakers current woes are well documented, as recently as 2007, Chrysler's collaborative relationships with its suppliers were continuing to produce impressive dividends.[131]

From the preceding sections, it should be clear that the evolving relationship between many companies and their principal outside law firms has come to take on many of the characteristics of the American *Keiretsu* that Chrysler forged with its suppliers in the 1990s. Although there are clearly differences between the two situations, the recent engagement between Tyco International and the UK law firm Eversheds underscores that the differences are not nearly as great as one might suspect.

[129] Ibid, 43 (noting that 'the cost of developing a new vehicle has plunged an estimate 20–40%' at the same time that 'the company has managed to produce one consumer hit after another' and 'profits per vehicle jumped from $250 to $2,110'). On the difference between the logics of power and embeddedness, and how the former can paradoxically diminish the putatively stronger party's ability to extract value from an exchange relationship see Gulati and Sytch, n 11 above, 59–60. As a Chrysler manager interviewed by the researchers summarized the difference between the company's orientation before and after the new initiative: 'The thinking used to be here that we'd like to see a supplier totally dependent on us and then we'd have the thumb over them. Now we recognize that neither extreme is good.' Ibid, 60.

[130] See also Helper and Sako, n 12 above, 79–80 (cataloguing measures taken by US auto companies to give voice to their suppliers).

[131] See Gulati and Sytch, n 11 above. As the authors demonstrate, Ford also pursued a similar strategy with its major suppliers with similar effects. See also Helper and Sako, n 12 above, 80–2 (demonstrating the correlation between voice relationships and improved performance).

7. The Smarter Model[132]

When Trevor Faure took over the legal department of Tyco International's operations for Europe, the Middle East, and Asia in 2004 the department was in a state of total disarray. Fresh from the major accounting scandal that nearly destroyed the parent company, Faure was given explicit instructions to improve the competence and integrity of the legal function. To achieve this objective, Faure instituted a systematic examination of how the company was spending its legal resources, both internally and with outside firms. What he quickly discovered was that notwithstanding significant increases in spending on both internal and external resources, the legal department was doing a poor job of managing its known legal expenses—and an even worse job of providing the kind of comprehensive legal coverage that could prevent legal problems from occurring in the first place.

Armed with this knowledge, Faure developed a plan to reallocate the company's legal spend in a manner that better protected its interests. At the core of Faure's strategy was a proposal to achieve the ultimate in convergence by slashing the number of outside firms the company used from 250 to a single provider. After interviewing several candidates, Faure settled on the 2000 lawyer UK firm Eversheds. The two year deal covered a wide-range of work, including labour and employment, IP, compliance, and litigation. All told, Eversheds was expected to gross $20 million per year in fees.

Implementing this plan, however, proved more difficult than either Tyco or Eversheds anticipated. Indeed, after the first year, Faure almost pulled the plug on the arrangement because Eversheds had not yet learned how to control the company's legal costs. For its part, the law firm claimed that the sheer volume of work—1,000 live matters followed by 100 new matters a month, spread over 30 jurisdictions—was simply too much for even such a large global firm to absorb. In the end, however, because of the significant investment that both parties had already made in the new relationship, the company and the law firm chose voice rather than exit and agreed to a new deal that brings the sides even closer together.

[132] The account below is taken primarily from a series of discussions with Tyco's Faure in connection with a forthcoming case study I am writing on the Tyco/Eversheds relationship as well as Faure's forthcoming book on the SMARTER Model. T Faure, *The Smarter Legal Model: More With Less* (Practical Law Company: New York, NY forthcoming 2010) (unpublished manuscript on file with the author).

Specifically, the new deal makes it even clearer than before that the company and firm will share both the risks and the rewards of Tyco's legal fate. To accomplish this objective, the company and the firm have agreed to a set of benchmarks for specific kinds of cases. For basic 'commodity work,' the company agrees to pay Eversheds for 10,000 hours of work at reduced rates. If the firm exceeds this pre-set number of hours, it will receive nothing for the first 1250 hours, and a dramatically reduced rate for any hour thereafter. If, on the other hand, the firm is able to complete the tasks in under the prescribed amount of time, the company will allow Eversheds to bill for 50 per cent of the hours that it *did not work* up to the 10,000 hours agreed upon to achieve this objective. For all litigation under $1 million, the firm will receive a 25 per cent success premium on top of its discounted fees for any case it wins—and will suffer a 10 per cent penalty from its discounted rates if the case is lost. With respect to higher value litigation and transactional work, the deal provides that Eversheds be paid its standard fees minus a smaller discount. Finally, premium work, such as 'bet-the-company' litigation and structuring transactions, is expressly not included in the deal, but Eversheds will be given an opportunity to compete for these matters along with other firms.

The most innovative aspects of the new arrangement between Tyco and Eversheds, however, fall outside of these typical parameters. These terms provide that in addition to making money on the fees the company pays it for its work, Eversheds can also profit if the firm hits a number of additional targets designed by the company to further what it considers to be important objectives. For example, the deal specifies that the firm will pocket a bonus in excess of $100,000 if the firm improves Tyco's 'client satisfaction' as measured by a survey given to the company's senior managers every October. The firm will also take home a six-figure bonus if it meets certain targets for diversifying its legal and support staff. Finally, the arrangement contains an incentive for Eversheds to help Tyco avoid getting into legal trouble in the first place. The firm will take home another six-figure bonus if it is able to reduce the number of law suits filed against Tyco by 15 per cent over the number filed in the previous year. To give Eversheds the chance to meet this target, Tyco promises to give the firm access (at the law firm's expense) to Tyco's business processes and people.

By providing specific rewards for helping the company to achieve its own objectives, Faure hopes to create a 'win-win' mentality between the company and Eversheds. As he told the *American Lawyer*, he hoped to avoid the 'winner-take-all' mentality that typically characterizes the relationship between outside counsel and firms and to create a relationship 'that encourages the right behaviour from both sides.'[133] As the editors of the magazine note, the result is a unique '[t]wo way partnership that ties the firm to the client but [also] ties the client to the firm.'[134]

As indicated above, the Tyco/Eversheds deal is indeed unique in both its scope and innovation. But it is also clear that other companies are looking closely at Tyco's experience. Since news of Faure's SMARTER model hit the press, a steady stream of general counsel have beaten a path to his door to see if they can adopt some or all of his methods. In 2009, Tyco's in-house team was named 'legal department of the year' by *The Lawyer*, which specifically praised the company's creation of 'win-win' incentives such as paying the firm a bonus for reducing litigation against the company. Given the overall trend toward convergence, it is only a matter of time before aspects of Faure's model will be copied by other companies.[135] Even companies that do not embrace all aspects of the SMARTER model are increasingly exploring mechanisms to encourage 'risk sharing' by their primary law firms through mechanisms like 'value billing' and the delivery of 'products' that standardize templates and tools in ways that are guaranteed to produce results.[136]

Indeed, in the last few years an entire industry has sprouted up to help companies and firms enter into collaborative relationships in which both the benefits and the costs of managing the company's legal risk are shared between client and lawyer. Consider, for example, eLawForum.[137] Begun as an on-line 'meeting' site designed simply to put companies with work to give out together with firms qualified to carry out these assignments, eLawForum has evolved into a full-fledged matchmaking service that works with both companies and firms to bundle and price legal work in a manner that allows an equitable sharing of both risks and rewards by both clients and firms.

[133] See Lloyd, n 85 above. [134] Ibid

[135] Indeed, Faure will soon be spreading the gospel himself. In February 2009, Faure left Tyco to become the worldwide general counsel for Ernst & Young. I return to the implications of this move below.

[136] Rosen, 'We're All Consultants Now', n 81 above, 677.

[137] Most of what follows comes from Clayton Christensen's excellent case study on the company. See CM Christensen and DA Scott, 'eLawForum: Transforming Legal Services' *Innosight*, 31 January 2003 available at <http://www.innosight.com/documents/elawforum.pdf>.

eLawForum works with clients to do the kind of 360-degree review of its legal problems and resources that Faure initiated at Tyco and then, crucially, to share this assessment with a group of law firms that the company has pre-cleared as being qualified to do the work.

Armed with this knowledge, the law firms then engage in a competitive bidding process for the fixed fee at which the law firm will undertake the representation. After an initial set of bids is received, eLawForum then works with both the company and the finalists to find the firm that the company feels will do the best job for the best price. Although the company is under no obligation to accept the lowest bid—and often does not—the agreed upon price is almost always significantly below what the company had historically paid for the services.[138] Once the basic terms have been agreed to, eLawForum then works with the two parties to produce a 'joint venture agreement' that clearly spells out how the work will be conducted—including the rights and obligations of each party to provide necessary information and cooperation,[139] the parameters for success, and how the risks and rewards of the work will be divided.[140] Similar services are already in the works.[141]

[138] The relationship between Unicol and the DC litigation firm Howrey is a case in point. After an 8 round bidding process conducted by eLawForum, Unicol hired Howrey to handle all of its environmental litigation for 5 years for a fixed fee paid quarterly and a variety of incentives. See H Smith, 'The Fix Is In: Cisco, Tyco, and Unocal Each Cut Flat-Fee Deals with Outside Litigators' *American Lawyer* 27/10 (2005) 54–63. Howrey was not the lowest bidder for the work. Instead, the firm, which had represented the oil company on insurance and commercial cases but not on environmental litigation, impressed the company's general counsel with its 'business-minded' approach that allowed the firm to tell the company 'how they and we would make money' on the deal. Ibid.

[139] Clients typically promise to provide the firm with accurate and complete information about cases and outcomes in a timely fashion. For their part, firms promise not to 'bait and switch' by ensuring that partners who say they will work on the client's matters actually do so. See Christensen and Scott, n 137 above, and Smith, 'The Fix Is In', n 138 above, 58.

[140] eg, in the Unocal/Howrey deal, the two parties will split any savings that Howrey generates by bringing in matters under the company's cost targets and will receive a performance bonus for every 20 cases that it resolves under the firm's historic cost of $500,000 per case. See Smith, 'The Fix Is In', n 138 above, 55. A similar deal negotiated through eLawForum between Tyco International and Shook Hardy & Bacon includes 6 different opportunities for the firm to be paid a bonus for achieving certain results.

[141] eg, Legal OnRamp is an invitation-only social networking site that connects in-house legal departments to outside lawyers. See A Oberthur, 'Virtual Connections: Lawyer-Only Site Help Boost Social Networking' *California Lawyer* available at <http://www.callawyer.com/story. cfm?pubdt=NaN&eid=892326&evid=1>.

Just like the *keiretsu* between Chrysler and its suppliers, the goal of all of these arrangements is the same: to 'encourage collaboration between client and law firm' in ways that both reduce costs and improve overall performance.[142] As one enthusiast put it:

> 'Rather than have the client wait until the proverbial brown stuff has hit the fan, we get involved much earlier, often before a lawsuit is filed – sometimes immediately when a complaint letter is sent, or even before, when an issue is identified. This is not only helpful for the [the client]. It is to our benefit as a firm to avoid mass litigation under this contract.'[143]

It is also to the firm's benefit to keep the relationship in place. And, like it or not, companies will often conclude that the same is true for them as well.

8. Turning the Titanic

In the end, the growing interdependence between companies and firms makes it increasingly difficult for either side to walk away from these new relationships. To be sure, all of these new partnerships contain formal escape clauses. Companies invariably reserve the right to scrap the deal if they are unhappy with the firm's performance.[144] And even if the firm performs admirably, the arrangements are always subject to periodic renegotiation and revision as was done by Tyco and Eversheds. Finally, in all but sole source agreements (and with respect to the most desirable work, even here as well), firms still have to compete with other preferred providers to gain a larger share of the client's work. Nevertheless, the collaboration, knowledge transfer, and personal connections that these deals are designed to foster has made these relationships a good deal stickier than the still too-often repeated mantra 'we hire lawyers not firms' would lead one to believe. The data from our corporate purchasing survey bears this out. Nearly 80 per cent of the general counsel in our sample claimed that at most they had terminated an important law firm relationship 'once or twice' between 2003–6, with almost a third (31 per cent) conceding that they had never done so during the period. Only 21 per cent claimed to have terminated such

[142] See Smith, 'The Fix Is In', n 138 above, 58.

[143] Smith, 'The Fix Is In', n 138 above, 60 (quoting the relationship partner for Morgan Lewis about its fixed fee contract with Cisco Systems to handle all the company's litigation for two years).

[144] See, Smith, 'The Fix Is In', n 138 above, 58 (noting that all of the contracts arranged by eLawForum she reviewed 'include provisions allowing the clients to end the arrangements if they're unhappy with the work.')

relationships more than twice, with only 1 per cent insisting that they had done so frequently.[145]

The fact that companies rarely terminate important law firm relationships should not be taken to mean that companies are generally satisfied with the service that they are receiving. To the contrary, there is widespread evidence that general counsel are often quite unhappy about the price, quality, and overall responsiveness of the work of their outside counsel. Rather, as Tyco's Faure discovered, the deeper and more multilayered these relationships become, the harder—and riskier—they are to change. As the former general counsel of a major financial firm once told me, changing these relationships is 'like turning the Titanic'—it takes an enormous amount of time and energy, and while you are trying to do it there is always the chance that you'll hit an iceberg.

Whether we call these new arrangements strategic alliances, partnerships, or a legal *keiretsu*, therefore, it is evident that the relationship between large companies and their primary outside law firms is increasingly being defined by the kind of cooperative/competitive relationships that have become ubiquitous in other parts of the new economy.[146] It is worth asking, therefore, how this new relationship is likely to affect the profession's core values of client service and professional independence.

Partners or Professionals?

Not surprisingly, the parties responsible for pressing these new arrangements do not see themselves as promoting a new model of the corporate attorney/client relationship—let alone creating a new paradigm for lawyer professionalism.[147] Nevertheless, the changes described in Part II are

[145] See Beardslee and ors, n 71 above, 29. See also RW Morrison, 'The Truth Behind those "Firings": How Many Law Departments Really Dump Their Firms so Abruptly' *Legal Times* 30/12 (2007) 44.

[146] As Gilson, Sabel, and Scott conclude about the ubiquity of such relationships generally: 'Under the name of Japanese production methods (a misnomer, because they have become common knowledge in manufacturing and design), these methods are today a familiar part of the new economy.' Gilson and ors, n 10 above, 436–37, 500.

[147] Indeed, when I called eLawForum's founder to discuss some of the issues in this paper, he professed great surprise that anyone would think his site had anything to do with professionalism or ethics. In this respect these entrepreneurs are quite different from the leaders of the Inside Counsel Movement, who Rosen describes as quite self-consciously engaged in a project to increase their professional standing by reorienting the normative understanding of the lawyer's role. See Rosen, 'Inside Counsel Movement, n 46 above, 479–554.

likely to have important consequences for how lawyers understand and carry out their various professional roles. These developments, in turn, may have important implications for clients, lawyers, and for the public.

Before proceeding, however, a word of caution is in order. As should be clear from the discussion above, the new model of the corporate attorney/client relationship I am describing is still very much in its nascent form. There is very little solid evidence of exactly what is going on, let alone about how these changes are affecting the conduct—and even more the professional self-understanding—of lawyers. Moreover, whether and how the new relationships that have been formed between companies and firms over the last decade will continue to develop is contingent on many factors, not the least of which are developments in the economy and the overall global market for legal services. My observations in this section will therefore be both preliminary and speculative. It is precisely because much remains to be determined, however, that it is so important to begin considering these consequences today while there is still time to shape an appropriate response.

Clients

At first blush, it might seem superfluous to discuss the impact of these new developments on clients. It is clients, after all, who have been pushing for the change. Moreover, as indicated above, the dominant theme over the last 30 years has been corporate clients' ability dramatically to reduce the information asymmetries that used to characterize their relationship with outside counsel. In such an environment, it would seem that there would be little danger that these sophisticated parties will not get what they want.[148] Indeed, as indicated below, in the minds of most commentators the real concern is whether corporate clients will use these new relationships to co-opt law firms in a manner that allows them to further entrench their power and influence.[149]

Nevertheless, there are critics who have raised a cautionary flag about whether, notwithstanding all of the hype, 'convergence'—particularly convergence in the kinds of large national or global firms that

[148] I made this point 15 years ago with respect to corporate clients' ability to prevent what I then described as 'agency delicts.' See DB Wilkins, 'Who Should Regulate Lawyers?', n 19 above. Given the growth in the number and sophistication of in-house counsel since then, this conclusion should be even more true today.

[149] For the classic formulation of this concern, see M Galanter, 'Why the "Have's" Come Out Ahead: Speculation on the Limits of Legal Change' (1974) 9 Law & Society Review 95–160.

are increasingly competing for this kind of work—is in the best interest of corporate clients. None other than Ben Heinemann has been in the forefront of this sceptical group. In a provocative article in the *American Lawyer*, Heinemann openly questioned whether global law firms promising 'one-stop-shopping' actually 'provide the claimed superior service, quality, or price.'[150] Heineman raises many trenchant criticisms about both the cost structure and the quality control of today's global law firms.[151] At the heart of his critique is what he labels as a profound 'disconnect' between how companies like GE think about productivity—achieving more for less—and the fact that too many law firms define the term as meaning boosting profits by increasing leverage and raising rates. He suggests that '[U]ntil the big, global firms candidly address the ultimate issue of productivity on a "total cost" (single price) per matter basis, they will have a hard time being on the same economic page as many corporate clients.'[152]

Ironically, it is precisely because many GCs agree with Heineman's assessment that they have moved to institute the kind of partnerships I have been discussing. As indicated in Part II, one of the main reasons why companies are concentrating their work in a smaller number of firms is to force these preferred providers to move toward fixed fees and other similar compensation systems in which both the costs and benefits of the representation are shared by both parties. Similarly, by building closer connections with their primary firms, companies hope to be able to monitor attorney performance more effectively, thereby reducing the danger of padding and waste.

More fundamentally, the way that Heineman frames the issue begs a central question that GCs who have decided to institute some version of the model I have been discussing see it as being at the core of what they are trying to achieve. For Heineman, each legal matter—'an antitrust issue under China's new competition laws,' 'environmental due diligence when purchasing Russian assets'—is potentially 'critical to the cross-border-transaction and requires separate counsel with specific expertise.'[153] But for many general counsel, such 'bespoke solutions', to borrow the quaint

[150] B Heineman, 'Bigger isn't Better: One Stop Shopping at Giant Global Law Firms has its Limits' *American Lawyer* 30/11 (2008) 71.

[151] Among Heineman's objections are that global firms have an inflated cost structure that requires them to 'bill until September' in order to be profitable and that these firms will inevitably have a large 'mediocre middle' and little or no common culture that should make companies sceptical of the firm's quality claims—particularly across specialties and geographies. See Ibid, 72.

[152] Ibid.

[153] Ibid.

British phrase Richard Susskind uses in his equally provocative new book *The End of Lawyers?*, are no longer what they are seeking.[154] As a legal consultant who has worked with many companies to consolidate their law firm relationships succinctly put it: 'A relatively small part of a corporation's legal function requires that kind of star lawyer.'[155]

To be sure some legal work is in fact the equivalent of brain surgery. Not surprisingly, arrangements like the one between Tyco and Eversheds exclude this work from the deal, although as indicated above Eversheds is entitled to compete for this 'premium work' along with other firms.[156] But it is also surely true that lawyers—even many in-house lawyers—systematically overestimate how much work truly qualifies for this designation. Moreover, as Susskind persuasively argues, there is a strong tendency for legal work to drift inexorably from 'premium' to 'commodity' over time.[157] As a result, clients adopting a 'risk assessment' perspective will often view lawyers as far more fungible than those who still think of legal services as fundamentally bespoke. For these clients, having lawyers who 'understand their business'—particularly how the business measures and evaluates risk, including legal risk—may be far more valuable than technical competence or skill. Once again, sophisticated corporate clients would appear to be in a good position to make these kinds of trade-offs.[158]

There is, however, an additional concern that, although still within the company's power to control, may nevertheless be more difficult for clients to address since by definition it will only arise once it is too late to correct. As indicated above, the interlocking connections between companies and firms engendered under the new preferred provider models mean that these relationships are a good deal stickier than the prior spot contracting arrangements. As a result, a company is vulnerable to being caught in the lurch if one of its primary firms fails. Such failures, although still rare, are nevertheless happening with increasing frequency, particularly in the

154 R Susskind, *The End of Lawyers? Rethinking the Nature of Legal Services* (Oxford University Press: Oxford and New York, NY, 2008).

155 See Sander, n 70 above (quoting Joel Henning).

156 Although this work is not guaranteed, Faure recently reported to me that Eversheds is now getting a significant percentage of this high-end work.

157 See Susskind, n 154 above.

158 The same analysis applies to the criticism that high turnover rates and poor internal control systems at many large law firms may limit the benefit that companies can expect to reap from convergence. To the extent that companies are worried about these problems—which, I should make clear, I believe that they should be—they have the resources at their disposal to require firms to take appropriate steps to limit the damage. I return to these controls below.

current economic environment. In the last year alone, three major firms —Heller Ehrman, Thelen Reed & Priest, and WolfBlock—have all closed their doors, and by almost every estimate others are sure to follow. Although many of the partners from these failed enterprises—and even some whole departments—have moved to other firms, the whole point of the kind of strategic alliance about which I have been speaking is that its value is extends beyond any particular lawyer or group.[159] Companies that partner with firms that fail will by definition lose this benefit.

As the 'junior' partner in the team, however, law firms are even more vulnerable to this kind of dislocation.

Firms

As with clients, it might seem self evident that the law firms that enter into these preferred provider relationships benefit from the arrangements. Clients are the 'mother's milk' of law firm life. Law firms that enter into long-term relationships with clients able to supply them with a steady supply of work would appear to have nothing to complain about.

In addition, firms can gain many other potential benefits that go beyond a steady supply of fees. One of the most important promises that firms make to those whom they recruit is that they will provide these young lawyers with excellent training in the skills and dispositions that they need to become accomplished and skilled practitioners.[160] In recent years, however, this promise has grown increasingly illusory. The reasons for this trend are undoubtedly multiple and mutually reinforcing. Clients, weary of an ever-changing cast of untrained—and undoubtedly relatively unproductive—junior lawyers shuffling in and out of their projects, are increasingly unwilling to pay for the work of first-and second-year associates.[161] At the same time, partners eager to boost their profits per partner are unwilling to absorb this cost either.

[159] To the extent that firms create dedicated 'client service teams' to handle a given company's matters across the entire range of the strategic partnership, the client will be able to minimize the lost value of the arrangement if its 'team' moves en masse to another firm in the event that the primary firm fails. Indeed, this may be one reason why, as I indicate below, our survey suggests that companies are increasingly looking toward the 'team' or 'group' as the important focus of their relationship with their primary outside firms. Nevertheless, even if an entire client team moves to a new firm—an occurrence, needless to say, that is surely not a given in the wake of a law firm failure —there are still likely to be costs associated with re-establishing the strategic partnership in the new firm.

[160] See Wilkins and Gulati, n 56 above, 1608–11.

[161] As one general counsel flatly told us: 'We finally told all our firms that we would not pay for first-year associates.'

The result, as Ben Heineman and I have elsewhere argued, is a 'lost generation' of associates who are coming of age in law firms without proper supervision or training.[162] This is a disaster for both firms and clients. Law firms (at least until the current downturn) were shedding associates at prodigious rates—in many cases up to 25 per cent per year. Although young lawyers change jobs for many reasons, recent research on the attitudes and careers of junior associates suggests that a perceived —and, I would argue real—lack of training and mentoring in large law firms is a significant cause.[163] For their part, clients are likely to have increasing difficulty finding trained third-and fourth-year associates—particularly ones with experience in handling (and understanding) their business—if most of the talented first and second year lawyers have already left.[164]

By giving both clients and firms a stake in a long-term relationship in which both sides have an interest in the other's success, the new partnerships offer at least some hope of breaking out of this gloomy state of affairs. Once they are freed from the tyranny of hourly billings, clients not only don't mind a young associate sitting in on a deposition or listening in on a phone call, they applaud the process.[165] For their part, firms welcome the prospect of having a junior lawyer interact with the

[162] See BW Heineman and DB Wilkins, 'The Lost Generation?' *American Lawyer* 30/3 (2008) 85. As I have also argued, this lack of training has a particularly devastating impact on black and other minority lawyers: DB Wilkins and GM Gulati, 'Why Are There So Few Black Lawyers in Corporate Law Firms' (1996) 84 *California Law Review* 493–626.

[163] R Dinovitzer and ors, *After the JD: First Results of a National Study of Legal Careers* (The NALP Foundation and the American Bar Foundation: Overland Park, Kans and Chicago, Ill, 2004) (reporting that junior associates in large law firms were dissatisfied with the training and mentoring that they received and that dissatisfaction in these areas is highly correlated with a lawyer's intention to leave his or her current employer within two years). We are in the process of analyzing the data from the study's second wave (examining respondents' careers after 7 or 8 years in practice) but preliminary results appear to confirm this finding. See R Dinovitzer and ors, *After the JD 2: A Preliminary Report* (forthcoming, 2009).

[164] Firms can try to ameliorate this danger by seeding their most promising associates, but as many partners will now concede—albeit candidly—it is becoming increasingly difficult to deliver on their promise of good training for even their most valued associates. See Wilkins and Gulati, n 56 above.

[165] Indeed, in a particular irony it is likely that many of the associates who leave firms will wind up working in the law departments of the very kind of companies that refused to train them in the first place. Although general counsel will certainly reply that they will be able to weed out those who have actually been trained at the point where they seek to hire these law firm refugees, the difficulty of gaining access to the private information about a given recruit's quality held by firms—information that neither the recruit nor the firm (or the headhunter) has any incentive to disclose—should make companies less than sanguine about their ability to make accurate judgments ex post.

client or trained to provide an important service, thereby freeing up the time of more experienced lawyers to seek out other opportunities.

But as was the case with clients, law firms also face risks from these new arrangements. As the smaller and more junior member of the partnership, firms face substantially more risks from the failure of their primary clients than the other way around. To see the magnitude of this danger, one needs only to return to the Chrysler analogy. As the bottom has fallen out of the auto market, the Obama administration has come to realize that it had to do more than bailout GM and Chrysler. It also had to pump billions of dollars into propping up their major suppliers.[166] *Keiretsus* links the fate of those in the strategic alliance in good times and in bad—and the more successful the alliance the more difficult it is for the parties to extract themselves from its grip. This is particularly true for the supplier in an economy in which other clients are already spoken for.

The recent tax product scandals involving the accounting firm of Ernst & Young and the Dallas law firm of Jenkens & Gilchrist provides a cautionary tale.[167] By all accounts, the accounting and law firms worked side-by-side developing and marketing a string of tax products that the IRS subsequently determined to be sham transactions whose sole purpose was to help clients avoid paying taxes. Indeed, if anything Ernst & Young was arguably more culpable since it designed the schemes and reaped most of the profits from the sale of the products. Jenkens's contribution was mainly to produce pre-packaged opinion letters blessing the deals for a fee. Yet when the house of cards came tumbling down and the IRS came calling, Ernst & Young was allowed to pay a fine albeit of several million dollars—that many knowledgeable observers considered to be little more than a slap on the wrist. Jenkens, on the other hand, was driven out of business.[168] Why? After the

[166] D Kiley, 'Billions for Auto Suppliers' Bailout' 19 March 2009 *Business Week* available at <http://www.businessweek.com/lifestyle/content/mar2009/bw20090319_960219.htm?chan=top+news_top+news+index+-+temp_news+%2B+analysis> (reporting that '[t]he Obama administration on March 19 created a $5 billion fund that guarantees payments to struggling auto suppliers, especially those tied to providing parts to General Motors (GM) and Chrysler that are facing the possibility of bankruptcy').

[167] See M Regan, 'Taxes and Death: The Rise and Demise of Jenkens & Gilchrist' (Unpublished manuscript on file with author, 2008). See also T Rostain, 'Sheltering Lawyers: The Organized Tax Bar and the Tax Shelter Industry' (2006) 23 *Yale Journal on Regulation* 77–120.

[168] See 'Tax Shelter Users Reach $75 Million Settlement with Firms that Gave Bad Advice' *LawCash.com*, 13 January 2005 available at <http://www.lawcash.com/attorney/3229/ernst-young-international- lawsuit.asp>.

demise of Arthur Andersen the government deemed Ernst & Young, like GM and Chrysler, too big too fail.[169] A 300-lawyer regional law firm, Jenkins had no similar protection.

Even less catastrophic changes in a client's fate can place the law firm supplier in a strategic alliance at risk. The Howrey/Unocal deal is again instructive. Notwithstanding delivering results that thrilled its corporate partner, Howrey ultimately lost its preferred provider deal when Unocal was acquired by Chevron, which already had its own law firm relationships. Indeed, even if ownership remains unchanged, the closer a firm gets to its corporate partner, the more the client is likely to view the firm as an extension of its own legal staff. Although obviously beneficial to a law firm in many respects, such closeness can also exact a price on the firm's other client relationships as 'preferred' clients seek to prevent 'their' lawyers from serving the preferred clients' business competitors, even in circumstances where no formal conflict exists or is likely to materialize.[170]

Indeed, law firms that enter into these kinds of relationships should be prepared for their client-partners to begin looking into many of their internal practices and procedures. Traditionally, general counsels have shown remarkably little interest in the internal management or practices of the law firms they employed. In our survey, for example, few general counsels rated such factors as the firm's compliance, compensation, or ownership structures as more than 'somewhat important' in awarding legal work.[171] But there are signs that this complacent attitude may be changing. In 2007, for example, Wal-Mart began asking

[169] KPMG avoided indictment in 2005 for similar reasons for conduct that was even more egregious. See R Schmidt and O Bilodeau, 'KPMG May Avoid Indictment as U.S. Pushes Settlement' *Bloomberg News*, 4 August 2005 available at <http://www.bloomberg.com/apps/news?pid=10000103&refer=us&sid=aAysChTpuW6E> (quoting several justice department officials as saying that they would not indict the firm for fear of 'eliminating thousands of jobs and reduce the number of big accounting firms to three').

[170] As one general counsel stated in a remark typical of what we heard from many others, 'We used [another firm] because [our main firm] had a conflict. We were pissed. We'd expect from our major providers that when taking on a matter if its crystal clear we're going to need help too that they don't take the matter ... hopefully someone from our law firms would call us and tell us and ask us if we want to engage them before they accept with a competition.'See Interview with #1, General Counsel, Investment Bank, 3 October 2006, 5. See also Heineman, n 150 above, 73 (noting the importance of firms not being on the other side of the client in sensitive policy level disputes). For a general discussion of the increasing importance of business or positional conflicts, see Dzienkowski, n 122 above.

[171] See Beardslee and ors, n 71 above, 25.

the firms on its preferred provider list whether the 'partners' working on the company's matters actually have an equity stake in the firm.[172] Similarly, the head of the Association of Corporate Counsel called for firms to push back against the 2007 salary increases for first-year associates and to begin inquiring about hours bonuses and other practices that arguably encourage lawyers to run the meter.[173]

As clients invest more in their relationships with their primary law firms, these questions are bound to increase. One can already see the trend with respect to companies that have recently had to terminate an important law firm relationship. Although, as indicated above, such terminations are relatively rare. When terminations do occur these actions appear to be positively correlated with a company's increased interest in internal law firm quality control systems. Thus, among firms in our survey that had not terminated an important law firm relationship in the past three years more than 50 per cent of GCs said that a firm's 'quality control systems' were not very important in determining whether a given firm would be hired.[174] Among those who had more frequent terminations, however, the opposite was true—almost two-thirds rated a law firm's quality control systems as being an important factor in the company's legal purchasing decisions. Whether experiencing a recent termination causes companies to be more concerned with quality control, or companies that have this orientation are more likely to be disappointed with the level of service they are receiving from their law firms,[175] this evidence suggests that at least some clients are beginning to draw the link between a firm's internal practices and the quality of its work product.

The fact that clients are beginning to look more carefully at a firm's internal structure and practices may end up being a boon for law firms. As many commentators have observed, law firms are probably the worst managed multibillion-dollar businesses in the world. Providing these organizations with an incentive to invest in internal compliance

[172] See 'Wal-Mart Puts Foot Down on Escalating Legal Fees,' *Law360*, 2 November 2007.

[173] A Press, 'The Change Agenda: A Long time Coming' *American Lawyer*, 15 December 2008 (reporting on the ACCA initiative). See also M Madison, 'Wal-Mart Memo Slams Associate Pay-Hikes' *Legal Week*, 9 November 2007 (reporting that Wal-Mart was refusing to pay increased rates based on higher associate salaries).

[174] See Beardslee and ors, n 71 above.

[175] Our survey does not allow us to tell in which direction the causation arrow points.

procedures, therefore, could potentially lead to important benefits that might help firms avoid situations like the one that sank Jenkens.[176]

Indeed, recent empirical work confirms that firms that adopt internal compliance mechanisms are less likely to commit certain kinds of ethical violations.[177] As I argue below, avoiding such situations benefits the public as well as firms.

It is important to concede, however, that the implications of the kind of increased scrutiny and control by clients that these new strategic partnerships tend to produce may not always be so benign, for the broader public purposes that lawyers as officers of the legal system are also supposed to serve.

The Public

In what has become one of the most iconic moments from the US savings and loan crisis of the late 1980s, Judge Stanley Sporkin famously asked '[w]here were [the attorneys]' and '[why] didn't any of them speak up or disassociate themselves from the[se] transactions?'[178] The question highlights the central tension in the traditional conception of the lawyer's role. In addition to being zealous advocates for the interests of their clients, lawyers are also supposed to play a broader gatekeeping role in which they both counsel their clients to conform their conduct to legal standards and refuse to cooperate, and in extreme cases, even blow the whistle when their clients seek to engage in conduct that undermines these standards. As we find ourselves in the grip of the latest round of corporate scandals that have made the S&L debacle look like petty larceny, it is fair to ask whether the new partnerships being forged by

[176] Elizabeth Chambliss and I first articulated this position in 2002. See E Chambliss and DB Wilkins, 'The Emerging Role of Ethics Advisors, General Counsel, and Other Compliance Specialists in Large Law Firms' (2002) 44 *Arizona Law Review* 559–92. Chambliss has gone on to become the most articulate defender of this position. eg, see E Chambliss, 'New Sources of Managerial Authority in Large Law Firms' (Unpublished manuscript on file with author, 2009); E Chambliss, 'The Professionalization of Law Firm In-House Counsel' (2006) 84 *North Carolina Law Review* 1551–76.

[177] See C Parker and S Mark, 'Regulating Law Firm Ethical Infrastructure: An Empirical Assessment of the Potential for Management Based Regulation of Legal Practice' (unpublished manuscript on file with the author, 2009) (testing Chambliss and Wilkins's claims about the value of internal compliance procedures in a sample of Australian law firms and finding a statistically significant correlation between procedures adopted and avoiding certain kinds of misconduct).

[178] *Lincoln Savings and Loan Assn v Wall* (1990) 743 F Supp 901, 920.

companies and their outside lawyers are likely to undermine the ability of lawyers to play this crucial gatekeeping role.

There is certainly reason to be concerned that it may. As Reineir Kraakman argued nearly a quarter of a century ago, whether lawyers or other professionals are able to act as gatekeepers depends crucially upon the characteristics of the market in which these intermediaries operate. As indicated above, this market has been moving steadily in the direction of transferring power from lawyers to clients. Moreover, to borrow William Simon's evocative phrase, there is now an active 'market for bad legal advice' in which clients actively shop for lawyers who are willing to give them legal opinions that can help to insulate them from liability or criticism.[179] As the market for legal services becomes increasingly competitive, there is a danger that lawyers will find it difficult to refuse such requests.

More to the point of the current discussion, convergence may very well increase this danger. As John Coffee notes, one of the factors that distinguishes external gatekeepers such as law firms from their internal counterparts such as in-house counsel is that the former have numerous clients and, therefore, are less likely to be beholden to any one. But the more a company concentrates its legal work in a single law firm, the larger the potential loss of this client's business will loom in the law firm's decision-making—particularly in a world in which other clients are doing the same thing with their preferred providers. Indeed, it is precisely this hope of becoming a 'star' client that has been one of the most important drivers of the current convergence boom. It is certainly plausible to expect that clients who enter into such arrangements will expect those who serve them to treat them with the unquestioning deference that 'star' status often affords.

Indeed, more may be at stake than simply an increased danger of client pressure. The switch to a 'partnering' ethos among outside counsel may threaten the very professional self-conception that made lawyers want to act as gatekeepers in the first place. As Robert Gordon succinctly notes, no gatekeeping regime can survive unless lawyers have a strong desire to be independent from their clients.[180] Although one

[179] See W H Simon, 'The Market for Bad Legal Advice: Academic Professional Responsibility Counseling as an Example' (2008) 60 Stanford Law Review 1556–7. Although there has been heated criticism of Simon's contentions about the conduct of academic ethics advisers, no one has seriously challenged his basic claim that clients often demand that their lawyers bless transactions with little or no legal merit.

[180] See Gordon, 'The Independence of Lawyers', n 3 above.

can certainly argue how much lawyers have ever displayed this desire in fact—let alone been willing to act on the basis of their status as independent professionals in circumstances where their clients were pressuring them to do otherwise[181]—lawyers who have wanted to embrace this mantle have been aided by a professional ethos that sharply differentiates law from business. But as Robert Rosen argues, the more lawyers become enmeshed in the client's business, the more they are likely to take on a view of 'independence' that stresses the importance of protecting the client from competition from competitors and regulatory oversight, as opposed to encouraging the client to comply with legal and policy norms.[182] Recent empirical research suggests that this may have already happened to many inside lawyers.[183] By instructing outside lawyers to become 'partners' with their major clients who are encouraged to see their primary value as helping client teams deploy legal knowledge to maximize competitive advantage, the new strategic alliances between companies and firms risk turning 'independent' lawyers into just another consultant serving business ends.[184]

There is clearly merit in these concerns. Indeed, as I will argue below, this is precisely why it is unhelpful and unwise for scholars and professionals interested in maintaining the lawyer's gatekeeping role to either ignore these developments or to leave them entirely to the realm of private ordering. Nevertheless, before we bemoan a world in which 'we are all consultants now,' it is important to see that strategic alliances don't so much eliminate the space for gatekeeping as reorient its dynamics.

One can begin to see this point by remembering the prevailing account of why outside lawyers were increasingly unable to play their traditional 'wise counsellor' role during the heyday of the In-house Counsel Movement. In that not-so-distant past, many commentators laid the blame for the decline of the 'lawyer statesman' on the fact that partners in law firms no longer had sustained relationships with their

[181] Ibid, 34. See also RL Nelson, 'Ideology, Practice, and Professional Autonomy: Social Values and Client Relationships in the Large Law Firm' (1985) 37 Stanford Law Review 503–51 (discussing how corporate lawyers have beliefs similar to their clients). But see WH Simon, '*Babbit v Brandeis: The Decline of the Professional Ideal*' (1985) 37 Stanford Law Review 565–'87 and Gordon, 'The Ideal and the Actual', n 14 above.

[182] See Rosen, 'We're All Consultants Now', n 81 above. I discuss the difference between these two meanings of 'independence' in Wilkins, 'Who Should Regulate Lawyers?', n 19 above, 1179–80.

[183] See RL Nelson and LB Neilsen, 'Cops, Counsel, and Entrepreneurs: Constructing the Role of Inside Counsel in Large Corporations' (2000) 34 Law & Society Review 457–94.

[184] Rosen, 'We're All Consultants Now', n 81 above, 671–9.

corporate clients but were instead only brought in to handle discrete transactions, often at the last minute.[185] As a result, these critics asserted, lawyers no longer had the opportunity to get to know their clients' business in manner that would allow them to function like the trusted advisors of old.[186] Moreover, by shifting work around among many firms, corporate clients were able to play these competing advisors against each other while ensuring that no single firm knew enough to be able to detect or deter the misconduct.[187] As John Coffee evocatively puts it: 'monogamy has thus given way to polygamy, as the company flirts with many outside counsel' thereby 'providing less shelter . . . within the firm for the independent professional who resists the client.'[188]

The new partnering models provide a hedge against these dangers. As indicated above, the whole point of these new arrangements is to ensure sustained contact between the company and its primary outside firms. Although rarely monogamous (but see Tyco and Eversheds) convergence dictates that these arrangements will not have the characteristics of speed dating inherent in the old spot-contracting model either. Lawyers who work in these new arrangements therefore have the potential to see the big picture in a way that their colleagues in firms with more transactional relationships with their clients will have a harder time doing.

Moreover as the Tyco/Eversheds deal underscores, partnering relationships often provide incentives for firms to assist companies in reducing their overall legal costs by recommending measures that help the company prevent legal problems in the first place. Thus, Tyco has agreed to pay Eversheds a bonus of $100,000 if it successfully reduces lawsuits against the company below historic levels. Such a payment is pureprofit for the firm and also a significant benefit to the company, which not only saves the cost of legal fees, potential damage awards, and (frequently overlooked) managerial distraction, but also stands to

[185] eg, see Kronman, n 22 above.

[186] Kronman, n 22 above, 271–315. Many contemporary commentators continue to echo this sentiment. See Coffee, n 13 above 194–5 (noting that the relationship between law firms and their corporate clients is now 'less intimate, ongoing, or fully informed than is the relationship between the same corporation and its outside auditor').

[187] See Coffee, n 13 above, 226. See also Dennis Thompson, *Political Ethics and Public Office* (Harvard University Press, 1987) 40–66 (describing the difficulties created by situations in which there are 'many hands'). As I explain below, this is precisely what Charles Keating did in the famous *Lincoln Savings & Loan* case that gave rise to Judge Sporkin's lament about 'where were the lawyers?' that began this section.

[188] Coffee, n 13 above, 230.

gain significantly from increased customer satisfaction and overall goodwill.[189] As the recent multi-million dollar fines paid out by Siemens Corporation for violations of the Foreign Corrupt Practices Act underscore, the cost of failing to prevent, or at a minimum detect, illegal conduct by company employees can have consequences for the bottom line that far exceed the cost of legal fees.[190] It should go without saying that preventing illegal actions by company employees also benefits the public and the rule of law generally.[191]

Moreover, the long-term nature of these new strategic partnerships gives each side an incentive to invest in the long-term health of the other. As indicated above, clients and firms who enter into these arrangements remain distinct entities—and, more importantly, in significant respects competitors. As the Chrysler example underscores, a cooperative relationship between such quasi-competitors will only succeed if each side can credibly signal that they will use the power that it will inevitably gain over the other party during the course of the relationship responsibly.[192] As Gomes-Casseres argues, such relationships depend upon partners exercising 'mutual forbearance' by which 'they forgo short-run opportunistic actions in the interest of maintaining the relationship, which they expect will yield long-run benefits.'[193]

To achieve these long-term benefits, both parties must remain 'healthy' in every sense of the word. As indicated above, at a minimum this means that both the client and the firm must remain economically viable. But as leading thinkers in both business and the professions underscore, the long-term health and viability of either a company or a professional service firm depends upon more than dollars. To survive and prosper, both kinds of organizations must also have legitimacy

[189] Significantly, prevention also benefits the self-interest of general counsels who are constantly trying to get management to see that their value lies primarily in reducing the company's exposure to risk. See Coffee, n 13 above (on GCs being good at prevention even though they are not really independent).

[190] D Crawford and M Esterl, 'Siemens Pays Record Fine in Probe: $800 Million Settlement Will End U.S. Bribery Case for German Conglomerate' *Wall Street Journal*, 16 December 2008.

[191] It is possible that firms may try to reduce lawsuits by helping employees to hide misconduct rather than by eliminating it. This is, however, a risky strategy for both the firm and the company since if the misconduct is eventually detected the potential exposure could increase dramatically because of the perceived cover-up.

[192] See B Gomes-Casseres, *The Alliance Revolution: The New Shape of Business Rivalry* (Harvard University Press: Cambridge, Mass, 1996) 95 (arguing that alliance partners must 'walk a fine line between rivalry and collaboration').

[193] Ibid, 35.

among all of their respective core constituencies both inside and outside the organization.

For companies, this means maintaining a strong culture of integrity that will allow the organization both to attract and retain top talent and to engender trust among consumers and regulators.[194] Indeed, according to one of the most respected voices in business, the more challenging the times the more important it is for a company to have a strong set of core values that it adheres to even in the face of economic uncertainty.[195]

The same is true for law firms. Although the firms surely need to be profitable to survive in today's competitive culture, they also must credibly signal that they exemplify strong ethical values if they want to attract and retain the best lawyers. This was the central value proposition trumpeted by firms during the Golden Age.[196] Although much has changed since those times, evidence from a study of recent law school graduates suggests that maintaining a core commitment to values such as craft and professionalism are still central to recruiting and retaining top talent.[197] In the absence of this commitment to some distinctive

[194] Ben Heineman has been one of the most ardent and articulate defenders of this view. See BW Jr Heineman, *High Performance with High Integrity* (Harvard University: Cambridge, Mass, 2008) 1, '[C]ontemporary corporations should strive to fuse high performance with high integrity—the twin goals of capitalism'.

[195] See J Rheingold, 'Jim Collins: How great companies turn crisis into opportunity' *Fortune* 159/2 (2009) 48–52 (quoting Collins as arguing that what distinguishes companies that succeed is that they have core values that explain 'why it is important that [the company continue to] exist[]' and that ' the more challenged you are, the more you have to have your values') Collins goes on to give the example of Proctor & Gamble during the depression, 'One of the things that was very distinctive about P&G ... was that they said a customer will always be able to depend on the fact that a product is what we say it is—we will always build our reputation on quality. When they were under pressure to start cutting corners or use cheaper ingredients, they just didn't do that.' It is important to note that Collins is, as the article describes, a highly respected 'business guru' whose books *Built to Last* and *Good to Great* have sold more copies than any others in the genre. As a result, whether or not his diagnosis of what makes companies succeed in difficult times is in fact true, it is likely to be very influential among business leaders.

[196] As a particularly effusive advocate of this view put it, '[Large law firms provide] an exceptional opportunity to acquire a liberal education in modern government and society. Such partnerships are likely in the future, as they have in the past, to prepare and offer for public service men exceptionally qualified to serve. The very nature of such a partnership permits a man to do more, not less civic work, and permits him, as a true officer of the court and a responsible citizen, more readily to enter public service for various periods and to serve society to his full professional capacity.' A Dean, *William Nelson Cromwell 1854- 1948: An American Pioneer in Corporation, Comparative and International Law* (Ad Press: New York, NY, 1957) 86.

[197] See Dinovitzer and ors, 'ADJ1', n 163 above (reporting that the primary reason reported by respondents for why they went to law school was to have a 'satisfying career' as opposed to high salaries or prestige).

notion of lawyer-professionalism, it is difficult to see why ambitious young women and men should go to law school, or if they do, pursue a legal career, as opposed to a potentially more lucrative career in fields such as investment banking or private equity.[198]

Lawyers can, and should, play a central role in maintaining a company's core values.[199] Indeed, many general counsels assert that this is at the core of what they do.[200] But as many commentators have noted, although their position inside the company gives general counsel unique access to, and understanding of, the company's core values, it also can make it difficult for these captive lawyers to distance themselves from the business imperatives that can lead these values to be corrupted for short-term gain.[201] Outside counsel, therefore, can and should play a role in helping their internal counterparts to counteract this pressure. By ensuring that a company's primary outside counsel have both access to and a stake in the company's long-term future, the new strategic partnerships described above make it more likely that firms will have both the incentive and ability to play this supportive role.

The Tyco/Eversheds deal is once again instructive. When Trevor Faure took over the legal department in 2004, Tyco had just emerged from a series of ethics scandals that nearly destroyed the company. Faure therefore viewed restoring the company's core values and

[198] I have elsewhere called this the paradox of professional distinctiveness. In order to compete both with each other and with other professionals, law firms are under tremendous pressure to become more 'business-like.' But if they become too much like any other business than those seeking only money will rationally move to alternative careers with shorter qualification standards and potentially much higher returns. See DB Wilkins, 'Partner Shmartner! *EEOC v Sidley Austin Brown & Wood*' (2007) 120 Harvard Law Review 1264–78. Of course, whether alternative careers such as investment banking will remain more lucrative than practicing law after the current economic collapse remains to be seen. See N Raymond, 'Former UBS Banker, Tired of Bonus Politics, Heading to Linklaters' *Am Law Daily*, 9 April 2009 (describing the decision by a former Cravath partner who left that firm in 2005 to join UBS to leave the investment bank in 2009 and join the UK law firm Linklaters).

[199] See Painter, 'The Moral Interdependency of Corporate Lawyers and Their Clients', n 125 above 520–53 (noting the substantial power that outside firms have in structuring the internal dynamics of their corporate clients).

[200] See Heineman, 'Caught in the Middle', n 59 above.

[201] See Rosen, 'We're All Consultants Now', n 81 above, 657 (noting that because inside lawyers work on business teams, that legal work is done in a 'managerial frame' creating a danger that these lawyers will view themselves as just another consultant who 'adds value' and not as 'a carrier of independent professional judgment').

instilling a culture of compliance to be among his highest priorities. At the same time, Faure had to ensure that the company was able to return to profitability so that it could survive in an increasingly competitive marketplace in which its reputation had been shattered. To accomplish these twin objectives, Faure and his legal team developed a series of training courses about the difference between 'sinning' and 'winning'—and the importance of obtaining customized legal advice in differentiating between the two in close cases. To be effective, however, the lessons learned in this training had to be reinforced in the business managers' dealings with both inside and outside lawyers. Faure therefore required Eversheds to engage in a range of activities designed to facilitate the development of a common set of values and approach between the company and the firm. Specifically, Faure waited to ensure that when business managers were confronted with difficult ethical challenges that they had an incentive to seek advice from the outside lawyers, and that the advice they received would be consistent with the company's policies and values. To achieve this objective, Eversheds was required as part of the deal to give managers 30 minutes of free legal advice on any matter when requested, to develop and update a set of policies, templates and checklists on key legal and ethical issues facing each of the company's businesses, to participate in Tyco's legal department training and to include the company's inside lawyers in its training, and eventually to take over the function of training business clients on matters of law and company policy. Although the firm was not directly paid for any of these services, the fact that it would receive a significant bonus for both improving customer satisfaction and reducing the number of law suits against the company gave the firm an incentive to take these responsibilities seriously—and, equally important, to press the legal department to ensure that it was doing the same.

One can see a similar set of incentives with respect to the stake that companies have in the long-term reputational health of their outside firms. Corporations need more from their lawyers than simple economic viability. They also seek to appropriate the legitimacy that lawyers receive in virtue of their status as officers of the legal system. Society has given lawyers broad, and in many instances exclusive, access to one of society's most precious and important resources—the law. In return, lawyers are expected to use their power in ways that benefit, or at a minimum do not subvert, the public interest. Notwithstanding the public's ambivalent attitude toward lawyers, this social bargain gives the profession a privileged status in the eyes of state officials and, in many cases, the public as a whole. This legitimacy is one of the benefits corporations receive when they hire outside firms.[202] In order to maintain this privileged status, however, corporate law firms must not be seen as consistently undermining the public purposes of the law. Corporations, therefore, have a stake in ensuring that law firms do not squander this valuable resource by placing the firm's short-term economic gain above its long-term interest in its own legitimacy.

Return again to the Tyco/Eversheds agreement. In addition to providing Eversheds a bonus for reducing the number of cases against the company, the deal also specifies that the firm will receive a $100,000 bonus if it achieves certain diversity targets. The fact that elite firms are almost as racially segregated today as they were at the time of *Brown v Board of Education* stands as an important critique of the profession's adherence to the core-legitimating norm of 'Equal Opportunity Under Law.'[203] Even if law firms are willing to forgo this legitimacy for the sake of short-term profits, corporations have a stake in helping firms resist this destructive impulse. For it is only if law firms can continue plausibly to hold themselves out as legitimate protectors of public norms that the long-term cooperative venture between these firms and their corporate clients will succeed. This connection between demography and legitimacy helps to explain why diversity initiatives have managed to obtain so much traction in the organized bar. Indeed, in the decade since I first drew this connection it is fair to say that companies have been more willing to intervene in the internal practices of law firms in the diversity area than in almost any other aspect of a firm's business with the exception of its billing practices.[204]

Experience in the diversity area, however, also underscores the potential danger of relying too heavily on private market incentives to achieve public goals. As I have argued extensively elsewhere, the

[202] Indeed, in the eyes of many, corporate firms have been the principal beneficiaries of this legitimacy. See Kronman, n 22 above, 273 (arguing that 'for a hundred years, the large corporate law firm has been the principal standard-bearer of the lawyer-statesman ideal in the sphere of private practice').

[203] See Luban, n 3 above, 252–6 (arguing that 'Equal Justice Under Law' is the legal profession's core legitimating ideal).

[204] eg, see K Schmidt, 'Corporate Diversity Demands put Pressure on Outside Counsel' *The Recorder*, 28 December 2006. Needless to say, one can certainly question how effective—or even sincere—many of these efforts have been. I return to the issue of effectiveness below. But as damning as this evidence is, it remains clear that companies —and increasingly firms—believe it is important to be seen as being committed to this issue. Firms that are not seen as committed, risk losing legitimacy with core constituencies.

movement to shift the justification for efforts to diversify the legal profession from the civil rights paradigm of 'separate is inherently unequal' to a market-based paradigm based on the claim that 'diversity is good for business' is fraught with peril.[205] By their very definition, market-based diversity arguments tie the achievement of diversity goals to the logic of the marketplace. That logic, however, is likely to be a good deal less hospitable to diversity as a profitmaximizing goal—and a good deal more troubling in its normative implications—than those who promote this shift typically acknowledge. Thus, while many companies claim to value diversity, when the chips are really on the table far fewer are prepared to make it an important criteria when selecting outside counsel in important cases.[206] Moreover, in those cases where companies do see a clear business justification for hiring minority lawyers it is often in situations—for example, when looking for a lawyer to defend the company against an employment discrimination suit—that raise troubling implications for both the lawyers involved and for the overall goal of promoting equality. The bottom line is that too much focus on the bottom line runs the risk of promoting the appearance of a commitment to diversity at the expense of producing real results.

The danger is that the new partnering model between clients and firms will have similar consequences with respect to professional independence generally. As Robert Rosen worries, companies that seek to integrate lawyers into their business functions may only value the 'appearance of "independence"' as opposed to any real commitment to public purposes or detachment from client aims.[207] Clients, after all, want to minimize risk, not wholly eliminate it. As a result, lawyers who come to identify too closely with business teams may begin to 'approach managing legal risks with non-compliance as a viable option.'[208] More fundamentally, even if one concedes that both clients and firms have a mutual interest in preventing misconduct and reducing risk, there is a danger that the 'risk management' perspective that

[205] See DB Wilkins, 'From "Separate is Inherently Unequal" to "Diversity is Good for Business": The Rise of Market-Based Diversity Arguments and the Fate of the Black Corporate Bar' (2004) 117 Harvard Law Review 1548–616. See also Beardslee and ors, n 71 above, 29.

[206] See Wilkins, Ibid 1575. Our research on corporate counsel bears this out. Although many general counsels told us that diversity was important to them in our qualitative interviews, in the survey itself this factor was ranked by most GCs as 'unimportant' when making important legal purchasing decisions.

[207] Rosen, 'We're All Consultants Now', n 81 above, 649.

[208] Ibid, 660.

this shared interest engenders will paradoxically diminish 'a lawyer's *individual* responsibility for making moral judgments about his role in law and society,' inducing 'a kind of moral apathy' that will ultimately 'hobble professional independence.'[209]

As I indicated at the outset, there is merit to these concerns. Nevertheless, as even the harshest critiques of this approach concede, 'risk management forces attention to the practical consequences of professional responsibility decisions, at least insofar as consequences are measured in liability.'[210] Indeed, as the defenders of this approach emphasize, policies and practices that *institutionalize* the process of uncovering, evaluating, and minimizing risk are essential to combat the organizational dynamics that both contribute to individual misconduct and restrict the ability of lawyers to act as independent gatekeepers.[211] To understand why, it is necessary to look more closely at the relationship between risk, ethics, and rewards in the kind of strategic partnerships being forged by companies and firms.

The Ethics and Enforcement of Professional Alliances

Like Tyco and Eversheds, when companies enter into long-term relationships with key suppliers, their respective rights and obligations are typically defined by contract.[212] Because alliance partners are entering into an ongoing relationship that will inevitably change over time, however, these agreements tend to be 'open-ended,' containing 'gaps' that must be filled in at a later date by some form of joint

[209] A Alfieri, 'The Fall of Legal Ethics and the Rise of Risk Management' (2006) 94 Georgetown Law Journal 1939. See also M Regan, 'Risky Business' (2006) 94 Georgetown Law Journal 1966 (arguing that 'conceptualizing ethics as a matter of avoiding liability can influence [personal] dispositions, attitudes, and motives, and therefore how someone exercises her discretion'); WH Simon, 'The Ethics Teacher's Bittersweet Revenge: Virtue and Risk Management' (2006) 94 Georgetown Law Journal 1985–92.

[210] Simon, ibid, 1897.

[211] See A Davis, 'Legal Ethics and Risk Management: Complimentary Visions of Lawyer Regulation' (2008) 21 Georgetown Journal of Legal Ethics 96 (arguing that 'far from 'undermin[ing] the aspirational tradition of legal professionalism,' as suggested by Professor Alfieri, risk management is actually about institutionalizing precisely those values, and giving them concrete form'). See also Chambliss and Wilkins, 'Ethics Advisers', n 176 above.

[212] For an excellent description of the contractual problems caused by these new forms of alliances and the complex ways that customers and suppliers attempt to work around these problems, see Gilson and ors, n 10 above.'

decision-making.[213] Although alliance partners often develop institutional arrangements to resolve these unexpected events or to renegotiate difficulties in performance,[214] ultimately the success of the collaborative venture depends upon their ability to nurture and maintain an ethical value, namely trust.[215] Ethics, in addition to economics, is therefore at the core of these arrangements. Defining the ethical norms that should govern these ventures—and the connection between these norms and the standard conception of legal ethics—is therefore critical in evaluating whether the move to this new kind of partnership between companies and firms will promote or undermine professional independence.[216]

Although defining appropriate ethical values is therefore necessary, as we have learned from long experience in the field of legal ethics, it is rarely sufficient to ensure compliance with appropriate ethical norms. Ethical duties must be reinforced through institutional mechanisms that promote and monitor compliance—and include a realistic threat of sanctions if those norms are routinely violated or ignored. Enforcement as well as aspiration, therefore, must be a part of any plausible regime of professional ethics.[217] Once again, understanding the range of actual—and potential—enforcement mechanisms, both public and

[213] See Gomes-Casseres, n 192 above, 34. See also Gulati and Sytch, n 11 above, 41 (arguing that 'relationships characterized by high joint dependence foster a culture of 'mutual reliance' in which exchange partners exhibit a decreased proclivity for opportunistic behaviour'), citing Oliver Williamson, *The Economics of Institutions of Capitalism: Firms, Markets, Relational Contracting* (The Free Press: New York, NY, 1985) 190.

[214] The Tyco/Eversheds deal, for example, was scheduled to run for 2 years but because significant problems arose in the first year, in part because neither party had fully anticipated the difficulty of shifting all of the company's work in such a short space of time, the parties renegotiated important aspects of the deal after the first year. See Lloyd, n 85 above.

[215] See R Gulati, 'Does Familiarity Breed Trust? The Implications of Repeated Ties for Contractual Choice in Alliances' (1995) 38 *The Academy of Management Journal* 85–112.

[216] As Gilson and ors underscore, to maintain these relationships requires a complex combination of normative and structural elements that are 'more formal than 'relationships,' but designed to facilitate learning among collaborating peers by means much less formal than hierarchical ordering.' Gilson and ors, n 10 above, 446.

[217] The classic text on the relationship between norms and their enforcement is Duncan Kennedy, 'Form and Substance in Private Law Adjudication' (1981) 89 Harvard Law Review 1685–778. For my application of Kennedy's insight about the relationship between the content of a norm and its enforcement to legal ethics, see Wilkins, 'Who Should Regulate Lawyers?', n 19 above, 809–11 (discussing the connection between 'content' and 'compliance' arguments in legal ethics). See also DB Wilkins, 'Legal Realism for Lawyers' (1991) Harvard Law Review 468–524.

private, is critical to reaching an overall judgment about the implications for the ideal of professional independence of the move toward strategic alliances between companies and firms.

Each of these dimensions—ethics and enforcement—are large and complex, and what follows neither catalogues the full range of possibilities nor purports to develop a definitive account on either topic. Instead, I want to suggest why neither ethics nor enforcement concerns provide an *a priori* reason to oppose strategic alliances between companies and firms and to suggest some avenues for using both of these domains to help ensure that the movement that appears to be taking place in this direction will not unduly undermine the legitimate purposes of professional independence, and may even promote these goals.[218]

The Ethics of Alliance

The idea that companies and firms must learn to trust each other if they are to forge an effective partnership might at first blush seem not to require any adjustment in ethical norms. After all, the traditional model of legal ethics is expressly premised on encouraging a trusting relationship between lawyers and clients.[219] For anyone who has been paying attention to the actual relationship between clients and law firms of late, however, it is painfully evident that there is a significant

[218] I use the qualifier 'legitimate' advisedly. There is a long history of lawyers speaking as if 'professional independence' is a good unto itself. eg, see Kronman, n 22 above (arguing that the ideal that lawyers should be 'statesman' who are sympathetic but ultimately detached from the aims of their clients is ultimately grounded in the professional moral development of lawyers themselves). But while the legal profession cannot survive unless those who enter into it find their careers satisfying—a non-frivolous question in today's profession—the content of professional norms cannot rest solely (or even largely) on what is good for lawyers. See Wilkins, 'Practical Wisdom for Practicing Lawyers', n 24 above, 472 (making this point with respect to Kronman's book). Given that the bar has often used the ideal of professional independence as a sword to defeat the kinds of external regulation that might actually give corporate lawyers the incentive to resist the improper demands of their powerful clients, we should be particularly careful about uncritically accepting arguments of this kind as a reason not to explore the types of ethical and regulatory alternatives described below. On the bar's use of independence arguments to restrict public participation in the development of ethical norms, see D Rhode, 'Why the ABA Bothers: A Functional Perspective on Professional Codes' (1991) 59 Texas Law Review 690–2. For a more detailed analysis of how external enforcement can promote independence from clients, see Wilkins, 'Who Should Regulate Lawyers?', n 19 above, 863–73.

[219] eg, see M Freedman, *Understanding Lawyers' Ethics*, (3rd edn, LexisNexis: Newark, NJ, 2004) (arguing that legal ethics is premised on the client's need to be able to trust their fate to their lawyer).

gap between the ideal and the actual when it comes to mutual trust. Ironically, this is particularly true in the corporate sector, where theory would suggest that the interests of client and firm would be most aligned.[220] Although inside and outside lawyers are not quite Hatfields and McCoys, these two parts of what is purportedly a common profession have become increasingly distant and antagonistic, often communicating through duelling pronouncements from their respective bar organizations.[221] Communication at the micro level is often not much better, with each side accusing the other of using it as a cash or a debit machine respectively.[222] The result is relationships every bit as mistrustful and adversarial as those that characterized the relationship between Chrysler and its suppliers before it moved to the *keiretsu* model.[223]

To move beyond this impasse and create effective collaborative relationships, companies and firms will have to develop what Gomes-Casseres calls 'relationship capital' by honouring their stated commitments and adhering to norms of 'fairness' and 'reciprocity.'[224] Although the parties can achieve a good deal of what is required by contractual means, for example by moving to fixed fees, supporting the broader normative aspects of the relationship discussed in the proceeding section will require ethical as well as contractual support. This, in turn, will require revisiting the standard principal/agent conception of the attorney/client relationship.

[220] See JB Heinz and E Laumann, *Chicago Lawyers: The Social Structure of the Bar* (Russell Sage Foundation: New York, NY, 1982) 380 (characterizing the corporate sector of the bar as a 'patronage type occupation ... where corporate clients to a large degree dictate the nature of the work done').

[221] Note, eg, the competing positions taken by the American Bar Association and the American Corporate Counsel Association on the issue of multidisciplinary practice in the late 1990s. See AL Kaufman and DB Wilkins, *Problems in Professional Responsibility for a Changing Profession* (4th edn, Carolina Academic Press: Durham, NC, 2002) 651–62 (discussing this debate).

[222] Compare Smith, 'The Fix Is In', n 138 above, 58 and 60 (quoting Cisco's general counsel as lamenting that the firms the company used before moving to its current preferred provider relationship 'shed crocodile tears when they heard we got sued') with N Koppel and A Jones, '"Billable Hour" Under Attack: In Recession, Companies Law Firms for Flat-fee Contracts' *The Wall Street Journal* 24 August 2009 available at <http://online.wsj.com/article/SB125106954159552335.html> (noting that the shift by some companies to flat fees 'could squeeze earnings at law firms' and quoting a partner complaining that 'a client can't expect to have the absolute best team of [trial] lawyers from a firm and have the lawyers give up all the other work they could be doing on a regular fee basis, to work 18 hours a day for months at a time on a flat fee engagement').

[223] One final anecdote. My colleagues at Harvard Law School and I were considering designing a joint executive education programme for lawyers from both law firms and general counsel offices but abandoned the idea when too many general counsels indicated that they would not come to such an event.

[224] See Gomes-Casseres, n 192 above, 34.

As indicated above, in theory the agency model gives clients near plenary control over the terms and conditions of the lawyer/client relationship. Although this helps to ensure loyalty by lawyers, it raises significant problems for developing and preserving a relationship of mutual trust—particularly one that incorporates public-regarding commitments on both sides.[225]

Consider the client's unqualified right to dismiss a lawyer for any reason.[226] This right is a natural outgrowth of the agency model.[227] It also hands corporate clients a potent sword to pressure lawyers into engaging in risky or unethical conduct. In the infamous Lincoln Savings and Loan debacle, for example, Charles Keating deftly used this authority to put pressure on lawyers from the law firm of Kaye Scholer Fireman Handler & Hays not to question his actions regarding the management of the thrift. Thus, when the law firm initially handling the regulatory audit insisted that Lincoln disclose certain questionable transactions to regulators, Keating fired it and brought in Kaye Scholer.[228] The lesson was not lost on lawyers at the newly hired firm, who vowed to avoid the 'situation of mutual distrust and animosity' that was caused by the prior firm's tough stance regarding Keating's questionable practices.[229] To make matters worse, under the governing ethical rules applicable at the time the prior firm not only had no power to contest the dismissal on grounds of public policy, but was equally

[225] Jack Coffee cites exactly this problem as the reason for dismissing legal ethics as a plausible foundation for establishing an effective gatekeeping role for corporate counsel:'Because legal ethics at its core views the attorney as a client-serving professional who is not permitted to dominate the relationship (and because market conditions make it unlikely that lawyers could do so today), legal ethics does not hold out a practical remedy for gatekeeper failure. One must therefore look beyond legal ethics and the moral exhortations it provides to find a realistic means to empower the attorney as gatekeeper'. Coffee, n 13 above, 229. The fact that the move toward strategic alliances between lawyers and firms alters the market conditions that inhibit gatekeeping implies that a move away from the client-serving agency model might actually produce real results.

[226] See Model Rules, n 15 above, Rule 1.16 comt. 4 (noting that a client has an unqualified right to fire his or her lawyer 'at any time and for any reason').

[227] See Henry, *Walden & Davis v Goodman* (1987) 741 SW2d 233, 236 ('The relationship between the attorney and his client must be based upon the utmost trust and confidence ... [T]he exercise of the right to discharge an attorney with or without cause does not constitute a breach of contract because it is a basic term of the contract implied by law into it by reason of the nature of the attorney/client relationship').

[228] See WH Simon, 'The Kaye, Scholer Affair: The Lawyer's Duty of Candor and the Bar's Temptations of Evasion and Apology' (1998) 23 Law and Social Inquiry 243–96. For my own take on the case, see Wilkins, 'Making Context Count', n 4 above.

[229] See Wilkins, Ibid n 4 above, 1208 fn 56 (quoting an internal Kaye, Scholer memorandum).

powerless to disclose what it almost certainly suspected to be criminal or fraudulent conduct by Lincoln—even to Kaye Scholer.[230]

Nor was this the only way in which Keating sought to exploit his power as principal in Lincoln's relationship with its lawyer-agents. In addition to holding the sword of Damocles over Kaye Scholer's head, Keating also assiduously controlled the information that was given to any of the many firms representing the thrift. As a result, no single law firm working for the thrift—let alone any single lawyer—had a complete understanding of Lincoln's practices, thereby making it easier for Keating to hide his illegal conduct. Reports about the conduct of company officials at Enron and WorldCom suggest that Keating was far from alone in using this power to ensure that legal work is sufficiently fragmented that no one can take the long view, and 'the broader interests of the corporation . . . go unrepresented.'[231] Although critics of these practices have urged lawyers to reject this kind of narrow framing,[232] as John Coffee accurately notes such calls 'exist[s] in considerable tension with traditional legal ethics,' which, consistent with the agency model, gives clients sole authority to 'define the objectives of representation.'[233] Consequently, as Coffee concludes, in many recent scandals the problem is not so much that lawyers were at the scene of the crime but chose to look the other way, but rather that 'lawyers were nowhere near the scene of the crime, thereby enabling others to orchestrate the fraud'.[234]

[230] See Model Rules, n 15 above, Rule 1.6 (1983) (providing that a lawyer may only breach confidentiality to prevent a 'future crime' involving death or seriously bodily harm, or in a dispute with the client or in a proceeding involving the lawyer's representation of the client). See also PB Heymann and L Liebman, *The Social Responsibility of Lawyers: Case Studies* (Foundation Press: Westbury, NY, 1988) 195 (describing the infamous OPM Leasing case in which a lawyer who resigned because he discovered evidence that his client was engaged in a massive fraud felt compelled by the confidentiality rules not to reveal what he knew to successor counsel). Ironically, the successor lawyer involved in OPM was none other than Peter Fishbine, who subsequently was the lead lawyer for Kaye Scholer in the Lincoln Savings and Loan case. I discuss the changes to Rule 1.6 and other related rules that would have altered what would have been permissible for lawyers in the Lincoln and OPM cases below.

[231] See Coffee, n 13 above, 226.

[232] eg, see R Gordon, 'A New Role for Lawyers? The Corporate Counselor after Enron' (2003) 35 *Connecticut Law Review* 1185–216.

[233] See Coffee, n 13 above, 226 (quoting Model Rules, n 15 above, Rule 1.2). As Coffee goes on to say, 'If the organization as client wants to use outside counsel in a narrow fashion, asking them only technical questions and structuring the relationship so that outside counsel is neither invited nor equipped to provide 'holistic' advice, the organization would seem entitled to do so.' Ibid.

[234] Coffee, n13 above, 231.

To move beyond this state of affairs, it is necessary to construct an account of legal ethics that helps to place lawyers in a position to detect client misconduct—and to give them the power to try to deter what they see. Structurally, as indicated above, the new strategic alliances between companies and firms are likely to place lawyers in a better position to be at the 'scene of the crime'—or better yet, the place where the crime may be averted—than the spot-contracting model manipulated by Charles Keating. But if the lawyers are to utilize their newfound knowledge, the ethical restrictions that discourage them from doing so ought to be removed. The logic of embeddedness that characterizes these cooperative relationships suggests that parties should not engage in deception, coercion, or other forms of pressure tactics designed to force the other partner into violating a legal or ethical duty.[235] To the extent that a company has breached this ethical duty to its outside firm, there would seem to be little reason to reward it for transgressing such a fundamental part of the joint relationship. Although a contrary rule surely raises difficult questions about how such an obviously strained attorney/client relationship will be managed, courts do not hesitate to compel lawyers to continue representing clients in circumstances where the *lawyer* does not want to continue because of a disagreement with the client.[236] At a minimum, the logic of these new relationships suggest that clients should pay some penalty for dismissing an attorney for failing to breach one of the lawyer's own ethical duties.

Indeed, one can see the recent changes in the confidentiality rules enacted by the American Bar Association as nodding in the direction of acknowledging the fundamental unfairness of the traditional agency model in a world in which lawyers are almost as vulnerable to client manipulation as the other way around. After steadfastly resisting the imposition of all but the most minimal gatekeeping—let alone whistle

[235] See Gulati and Sytch, n 11 above, 61 (emphasizing that the logic of embeddedness is mediated by the amount of 'joint action' between the parties and that this factor significantly 'contributes to the enhanced performance of the relationship as a whole and its increased value-generating potential').

[236] See Tennessee Board of Professional Responsibility Formal Op 96-F-140 (1996) (refusing to allow a lawyer appointed to represent a minor seeking an abortion to resign because the lawyer was morally opposed to the procedure under any circumstances). Given that corporate clients are sophisticated repeat players who must operate everyday in relationship that are less than ideal, the argument that the rule allowing clients to fire their lawyers for any reason is necessary to preserve the client's right to effective legal representation rings hollow in the face of cases that require individual lawyers with strong moral objections to do otherwise.

blowing—duties, the ABA amended the Model Rules in 2002 and 2003 to give lawyers significantly greater latitude to disclose client fraud. Thus, Model Rule 1.6 governing confidentiality has been changed to allow lawyers to disclose information when reasonably necessary to prevent a client from 'committing a crime or fraud that is reasonably certain to result in substantial injury to the financial interests or property of another' or to 'prevent mitigate or rectify' financial injury 'that is reasonably certain to result or has resulted from the client's commission of a crime or fraud.'[237] In both of these instances, however, the lawyer can only blow the whistle if the client has used the lawyer's services in furtherance of the criminal or fraudulent conduct.[238] In other words, clients like Charles Keating who involve their lawyers unknowingly in their fraudulent schemes, or who dismiss their lawyers for failing to cooperate in further misconduct, risk empowering their former advisors to disclose the fraud in order to protect themselves from the deleterious consequences of their client's overreaching.[239]

The amendments to Model Rule 1.13, which governs the duties of lawyers who represent 'organizational' clients such as corporations, arguably go even further. Beginning in 2003, lawyers who believe that a corporate manager has, or is about to, act—or refuse to act—in a manner that constitutes 'a violation of a legal obligation to the organization' or that may result in a 'violation of law that reasonably might be imputed to the organization' are given three interlocking protections against being ensnared in the client's wrongdoing. First, the lawyer is required to report what he knows to 'the highest authority in the organization, including, if warranted ... to the highest authority that can act on behalf of the organization as determined by applicable law.'[240] Secondly, if that authority 'insists upon or fails to address in a timely and appropriate manner' conduct that the lawyer believes is 'clearly a violation of law' *and* is 'reasonably certain to result in substantial injury to the organization,' the lawyer 'may reveal' whatever information the lawyer 'reasonably believes necessary to prevent

[237] See Model Rules, n 15 above, Rules 1.6(b)(2) and 1.6(b)(3). [238] Ibid.

[239] Of course, if the lawyer did know about the fraud (or turned a blind eye under circumstances in which such knowledge can reasonably be inferred) and continued to actively assist the client, he or she would not only be guilty of violating the ethics rules but (most likely) the substantive law as well. See Model Rules, n 15 above, Rule 1.2(d) ('a lawyer shall not counsel a client to engage, or assist a client, that the lawyer knows is criminal or fraudulent') I return to the question of how the substantive law regulates lawyer conduct below.

[240] Model Rules, n 15 above, Rule 1.13(a).

substantial injury' to her organizational client.[241] Finally, a lawyer who 'reasonably believes that he or she has been discharged' or 'forced to withdraw' for reporting conduct under either of the above two provisions, 'shall proceed as the lawyer reasonably believes necessary to assure that the organization's highest authority is informed of the lawyer's discharge or withdrawal.'[242] Collectively, these three provisions both require that lawyers ensure that their real client—the 'organization' (at least as represented by the board)—is aware of any potential misconduct by corporate managers or employees that might harm the organization's real long-term interests, while giving them at least some leverage against retaliation by those who might be tempted to ignore the lawyer's advice or punish him or her for trying to give it.

To be sure, these reforms continue to leave the heart of the agency model in place. None of these changes, for example, alter a corporate client's fundamental right to exclude lawyers from the venues where important decisions are made or to strategically manipulate the information the lawyer receives. A complete account of the ethics of lawyer/client strategic alliances would have to define client obligations as well as lawyer rights. To begin to articulate such an account of 'client ethics,' however, necessarily requires moving beyond the domain of legal ethics. Whatever their other virtues, the Model Rules of Professional Conduct cannot bind non-lawyers. Although one can try to infer client duties from either the general moral commitments that all members of society share, or the special responsibilities that corporations owe to society, any system that purports credibly to bind companies to adhere to norms of trust and reciprocity with law firms that acknowledge that lawyers have public duties to the legal framework as well as private obligations to clients will inevitably require an engagement with substantive law.[243]

Regulating Reciprocity

Even the modest progress that the profession has achieved since 2002 in moving away from a completely client-centric agency model of legal

241 Model Rules, n 15 above, Rule 1.13(c).

242 Model Rules, n 15 above, Rule 1.13(e).

243 See Coffee, n 13 above, 372 (arguing that regulation will be required to allow gatekeepers to function in a world where they can 'demand fuller disclosure to report misconduct up the ladder, and to search for information the corporation wanted not to disclose'). For my prior analysis of the limited ability of 'general moral' and 'corporate social responsibility' arguments to generate robust ethical duties by clients to promote diversity in law firms, see Wilkins, 'Client Ethics', n 9 above, 868-875

ethics toward one that gives lawyers at least some tools to protect themselves against client-opportunism can be traced to the threat of state regulation. The rules permitting lawyers to disclose contemplated or completed financial frauds were proposed as part of the original text for the Model Rules of Professional Conduct in 1981, only to be repeatedly and vociferously voted down for almost 20 years. Only the public outcry over Enron and related scandals and the threat of the imposition of even more fulsome reporting requirements by Congress galvanized the bar to adopt these provisions. Indeed, the ABA's House of Delegates refused to impose mandatory 'up-the-ladder' reporting requirements in Model Rule 1.13 until the beating of the wings of the Sarbanes-Oxley Act ('SOX') made it painfully clear that in the absence of some amendment, the profession's entirely discretionary version of that rule would soon be rendered entirely superfluous. Even then, the bar adopted a version of Rule 1.13 that is significantly weaker than the statutory duty imposed by SOX.[244]

It is not surprising that Congress passed rules of conduct creating more stringent gatekeeping duties on lawyers than the profession was inclined to impose on itself. The bar is well aware that what I have elsewhere called 'institutional controls' such as SEC enforcement is far more likely to detect a lawyer's violation of public gatekeeping duties than the profession's own disciplinary system, and, even more importantly, to impose significant sanctions when violations are brought to the surface.[245] Indeed, this realization helps to explain the curious phenomenon of bar leaders actively lobbying against the Securities and Exchange Commission's ('SEC') proposed rule requiring a lawyer who discovers that his corporate client has used his work product to engage in criminal or fraudulent conduct to make a 'noisy withdrawal' in which the lawyer expressly disavows his prior work product, even though such conduct is arguably already permissible in approximately

[244] Although the trigger for up-the-ladder reporting under SOX is notoriously murky, the Act nevertheless sets an objective standard for defining the lawyer's duties in this area. See Section 307 (mandating up-the- ladder reporting if there is 'credible evidence based upon which it would be unreasonable ... for a prudent and competent attorney not to conclude that it is reasonably likely that a material violation has occurred'). Model Rules, n 15 above, Rule 1.13, on the other hand, still requires that the lawyer has actual knowledge of a material violation before he or she is required to report conduct to a higher authority in the organization. See Model Rules, n 15 above, Rule 1.0(f) (defining 'knows' as 'denot[ing] actual knowledge of the fact in question').

[245] See Wilkins, 'Who Should Regulate Lawyers?', n 19 above, 835–8.

40 states.[246] The question remains, however, whether these and other recent statutory attempts to regulate lawyer conduct can play a positive role in encouraging lawyers to take their public gatekeeping roles seriously notwithstanding the fact that the developments described in this paper are likely to place outside counsel in long-term relationships with clients that blur the traditional boundary between law and business.

Although the evidence is both preliminary and mixed, there is at least some indication that these regulatory changes are having a positive effect on lawyer independence. Tanina Rostain, for example, reports that interviews with 10 general counsels from large companies revealed a much higher commitment by respondents to 'assert jurisdiction over questions of legal risk,' and to embrace 'broad gatekeeping duties' than reported in earlier studies.[247] Although Rostain is careful not to read too much into these findings given both the small sample size and the many factors that potentially distinguished her respondents from those involved in prior studies, she nevertheless finds support for the view that SOX has empowered general counsel to play a more active role in gatekeeping. As one respondent summarized:

> [directors and senior managers] are afraid of going to jail. It is very effective in that way, in my view. It is almost to the point where you have to bend over backwards not to be shrill. And when you play the compliance card, make sure you mean it because you are going to stop these guys in their tracks. ... Once you say compliance, you are very, very empowered. The thing about Sarbanes-Oxley that I don't like ... I think it is overkill in a variety of areas, but the power ... to mandate a culture of compliance is very strong.[248]

Surveys of the attitudes of general counsel after the passage of the Act appear to support this conclusion, as does the fact that many companies increased their spending on outside counsel during this period.[249]

[246] See Coffee, n 13 above, 221–2 (describing the bar's successful efforts to beat back this rule).

[247] See T Rostain, 'General Counsel in the Age of Compliance, Preliminary Findings and New Research Questions' (2008) 21 Georgetown Journal of Legal Ethics 465-90. Rostain compares her results to the relative unwillingness by general counsels to act as 'cops' found in studies conducted by Nelson and Neilsen and Robert Rosen in the 1990s and 1980s respectively. See Nelson and Nielsen, 'Cops, Counsel, and Entrepreneurs', n 182 above; Robert Rosen, 'Inside Counsel Movement', n 46 above.

[248] Rostain, ibid, 489 (quoting the general counsel of a medical devise company).

[249] See MC Daks, 'Compliance, Not Legal Fees Named as GCs Chief Concern' New Jersey Law Journal, 1 November 2006 available at <http://www.law.com/jsp/ihc/PubArticleIHC.jsp?id=1162289115195> (reporting that in a survey of general counsel

This dynamic highlights a key feature of the current approach to regulating corporate conduct. In addition to setting out mandates and penalties, contemporary regulatory schemes governing corporate conduct employ incentives to encourage companies to create internal compliance regimes that diffuse regulatory norms throughout the organization. As Rostain explains, in these new regulatory schemes '[c]orporations are expected to install controls—including ethics codes, self-audit mechanisms, compliance training, whistleblower protections, and the designation of compliance personnel—at every organizational level to minimize the risk of unlawful and unethical behavior.'[250]

These regulatory regimes make it clear that responsibility for compliance will be jointly shared among lawyers, managers, and other professionals who possess relevant technical competence or expertise. The growth of the kind of strategic alliances between companies and law firms discussed above further highlights that the 'lawyers' involved in helping to establish and operate these new compliance mechanisms will come from both inside and outside the company. All of this underscores the need to develop an account of how these diverse professionals can collaborate in ways that further, rather than frustrate, the public goals underlying these new compliance systems.

John Coffee, for example, proposes that companies be required to have their annual and quarterly disclosure documents reviewed by an 'independent' attorney from outside the company, who, 'after reasonable inquiry,' would then be required to certify that the disclosures were not materially misleading.[251] Lawyers who failed to discharge this new duty competently under Coffee's proposal could be sued under the securities laws for aiding and abetting their client's fraud.[252]

By highlighting how regulation can be used to impose duties on clients that in turn support the public gatekeeping responsibilities of outside counsel, Coffee's proposal is a step in the right direction. But in trying to 'restor[e] the principal-agent relationship between lawyers and investors' by creating a special role for 'disclosure counsel,' while keeping the

in 169 companies, 86% listed 'keeping track of company activities that might have legal implications' as their number one concern). See also Conley, n 64 above (reporting that 'GCs—buffeted by regulatory changes from the Sarbanes-Oxley Act, an increasingly risk-averse corporate environment and CEOs who want cost containment and more value from in-house departments—are turning to outside lawyers with greater frequency').

[250] Rostain, n 247 above, 480. Examples of this new regulatory approach can be found in fields as diverse as environmental protection policy to anti-terrorism and employment discrimination regulation. See ibid, 466–7.

[251] See Coffee, n 13 above, 349.

[252] Coffee, n 13 above, 351.

traditional 'hired gun' model of the lawyer-agent endorsed by Lord Brougham in place for the rest of the company's counsel, Coffee risks minimizing the effectiveness of the former while exacerbating the problems of the latter. Although companies would presumably have to share information with their 'disclosure counsel,' these same clients would have no incentive to do so with all of the other lawyers involved in the company's complex compliance machinery. Nor would the hired-gun agents have any power or incentive to protest this fate. Indeed, it is entirely possible that Coffee's proposal could drive the vast majority of lawyers not acting as 'disclosure counsel' to give up their gatekeeping roles altogether while at the same time encouraging the company to treat their 'disclosure counsel' as little more than an agent of the government who the company should regard in the same way that it views the SEC.[253]

Moreover, as important as the goal of ensuring proper disclosure under the securities laws is to the overall functioning of our market economy, this is hardly the only place where we want lawyers to act as public gatekeepers. As indicated above, the new regulatory focus on compliance has resulted in the creation of numerous gatekeeping regimes. It is difficult to see, however, how Coffee's proposal could be replicated across all of these diverse regulatory domains. Should Congress seek to create a dedicated 'compliance counsel' in every instance in which the statutory scheme contemplates public gatekeeping? If so, how would these new compliance specialists interact with each other, and with lawyers not in this role who, according to Coffee, would continue to operate under Brougham's hired gun agency model? As others have noted, there is already a burgeoning industry of 'law consultants' claiming to assist companies in defining and operationalizing these new compliance mandates.[254] Although creating a separate

[253] Although any proposal to create a class of specialists with enhanced responsibilities for gatekeeping runs the risk of diminishing the importance that lawyers not in this role place on these public duties, Coffee's proposal seems particularly likely to produce this result. A law firm general counsel, for example, is specifically charged with interacting with the firm's partners and associates in order to remind them of their individual professional obligations. See Davis, n 210 above. Coffee's proposal, on the other hand, seems to contemplate that disclosure counsel, who by definition will come from a different law firm than the other lawyers working for the corporation, should perform their role independently without seeking to influence what the company's other lawyers are doing. Indeed, given that 'disclosure counsel' would be assuming all of the risks on non-disclosure, it may even be difficult to get lawyers to assume this new role since malpractice insurance and other related costs would likely be quite high.

[254] See T Rostain, 'The Emergence of "Law Consultants"' (2006) 75 Fordham Law Review 1397–428; C Parker, *The Open Corporation: Effective Self-Regulation and Democracy* (Cambridge University Press: Cambridge and New York, NY, 2002).

'compliance counsel' might prevent the legal profession from losing market share to these new competitors (many of whom, as Rostain notes, are themselves lawyers) it might also entrench the kind of turf wars that will only work to obscure the fundamental purpose underlying these regulatory schemes—that achieving effective compliance is the joint responsibility of legal and business professionals. To achieve this goal it is necessary to move beyond a regulatory focus that assumes that gatekeeping duties are the sole responsibility of a single actor.

Conclusion: Where Do We Go From Here Community or Chaos?[255]

As I write this article, the market for corporate legal services is being radically transformed—or at least so it seems. Law firms are shedding associates—and even partners—faster than GM is laying off autoworkers. And perhaps in a harbinger of GM's fate, many brand name law firms have already shuttered their doors and more are almost certain to follow.

If anything, fate (or to be more accurate greed) has been even less kind to many of the clients who have traditionally supported these legal giants. There are no more investment banks anymore (unless you count Raymond James), and there is precious little left of the deal market that these former trophy clients helped to support.

Needless to say, I do not pretend to know where all of this is heading even in the next six to 12 months, let alone in the next five to 10 years. My guess is that nobody does. Specifically, although it appears that we have reached a significant fork in the road that could bring about a fundamental restructuring of the Cravath model of the large law firm, it is wise to remember that reports of the model's demise have been greatly exaggerated in the past.[256]

Nevertheless, it DOES feel like the ground is shifting in important ways. I close by saying a few words about what these changes might portend for the legal *keiretsus* discussed here.

[255] With apologies to the Reverend Dr Martin Luther King.

[256] The consulting firm McKinsey & Company famously wrote a report in the late 1990s predicting that Cravath would no longer exist as an independent firm by the turn of the century. We all know how that one worked out.

First, it seems likely that the contraction in both client and law firm markets will accelerate many of the trends cited above. Even those companies who survive the downturn in tact are going to look aggressively for places to cut costs. The legal department, with its high fixed costs and indirect contribution to the bottom line, is likely to be a prime candidate. Although all of the headlines have been about law firm layoffs, many companies have already begun downsizing their general counsel offices as well.[257] As in-house legal offices shrink, companies are likely to become even more dependent upon their relationships with outside firms.

Consider, for example, the 'Value Challenge' initiative recently launched by the American Corporate Counsel Association ('ACC'). Based on a series of off the record discussions between companies and firms, the 'Value Challenge' seeks to 're-establish trust and improve [the attorney/client] relationship, on both sides' by assuring 'an adequate flow of work so that outside lawyers understand the client better and can be more efficient in what they do,' while at the same time 'get[ting] junior lawyers better trained' and creating incentives to 'better budget and manage costs and staffing.'[258] To further these goals, clients and lawyers are asked to sign a 'Covenant' under which both sides agree to undertake affirmative duties to create a new mutually productive partnership between companies and firms. Companies are asked to take a number of measures, including 'defin[ing] our objectives in the engagement' and 'provid[ing] training opportunities for your associates,' designed to signal the corporation's 'understand[ing] that our relationship is built on mutual trust' and to 'help nurture an enduring relationship with the firm, not just individual lawyers.'[259] Outside counsel, in turn, is asked to promise that it will 'learn your business and strategic objectives,' 'use the most appropriate staffing' to '[s]eek to reduce our costs creatively and constantly', and to '[w]ork hard to retain and reward personnel that embrace these concepts, and to ensure that every member working on your project walks this talk.'[260] As the blog entry from Sun Microsystems general counsel Mike Dillon featured prominently on the ACC's home page for the

[257] See L Marek, 'Layoff Pain Migrates In-House' National Law Journal 31/29 (2009) 1 (reporting attorney layoffs at Hyatt, Cigna, eLoyalty, Motorola, Yahoo—and even GE).

[258] See ACC Value Challenge Briefing Package July 2009 available at <http://www.acc.com/valuechallenge/resources/upload/ACC-Value-Challenge-Briefing-Package.pdf>.

[259] Ibid. [260] Ibid.

'Value Challenge' makes clear, the fact that 'we are in the early stages of a seismic shift in the traditional cost and delivery model for legal services' will only accelerate the need for the kind of commitments by both clients and firms set out in the 'Covenant'.

Secondly, although many law firms will undoubtedly try to resist the move to flat fees and other similar initiatives proposed by client initiatives like the 'Value Challenge', in the end many will come to realize that they have little choice but to do whatever it takes to solidify and deepen their relationships with their primary clients. As the number of such 'trophy' representations shrink—along with the legal budgets of those clients who remain—a spot on a company's preferred provider list will become as precious as it is rare. Law firms are likely to compete aggressively for the honour.

Although such intense competition could easily further suppress the willingness of firms to carry out their public gatekeeping responsibilities, the increased regulatory scrutiny that is certain to follow on the heels of the current crisis will push against this natural tendency. Companies in the financial services industry are about to face the kind of regulatory onslaught not seen since the New Deal. And just like that historic period, this new environment will ultimately be a boon for lawyers—particularly lawyers who can help companies credibly signal to regulators and the public that they are operating in a manner that will not threaten to drive the proverbial bus, as President Obama likes to refer to the economy, into a ditch again anytime soon.[261] In such an environment, it is at least plausible that independence could become the new cool. Indeed, since some of the new regulatory attention is bound to be directed toward sharpening the bar's gatekeeping duties, lawyers are likely to have a personal stake in insuring their—and their client's—rectitude.

Needless to say, there are likely to be other less happy consequences as well. Law firms that are squeezed for cash are less likely to devote some of these scarce resources to causes that they still think of as charity, such as pro bono and diversity—particularly if shell shocked law students and associates stop inquiring about these issues. Given that

[261] See Peter Sher, 'Lessons for US Corporate Law Firms from the Great Depression' 2009 (unpublished manuscript on file with the author) (documenting how many of todayâs leading law firms rose to prominence during the great depression by displaying a flexibility to changed circumstances that allowed them to take advantage of the regulatory and market reforms of the New Deal and speculating that there will be similar winners emerging out of the current crisis).

the attention devoted to these issues even in good times is relatively low, this could be a substantial blow.

Even here, however, there is the potential for a silver lining. In a tacit recognition of the important role that pro bono and diversity have come to play in defining the legitimacy of the attorney/client relationship, the ACC's 'Value Challenge Covenant' specifically calls on clients and firms to both maintain and support their own, and each otherâs, pro bono and diversity efforts.[262] Moreover, to ease the pain of deferred start dates and mandatory furloughs, many firms are giving their erstwhile associates stipends to work in public interest or government jobs while partners wait to see if the Obama stimulus package can jump start the corporate legal market.[263] Some of those who take advantage of this option will undoubtedly like their public jobs and stay. Most, however, will probably decide to return to the firms that have furloughed them—but hopefully with a renewed commitment to public ideals to go along with their new understanding of the reality that even the safest choices may be less safe than one has been led to believe.

This movement between public and private is, of course, simply the latest (if unexpected) manifestation of the increasing volatility of legal careers. In the After the JD Study we found that even after 2 to 3 years, many young lawyers had not only changed jobs but also moved across sectors.[264] Our preliminary analysis of Wave II suggests that this trend has only accelerated as the class of 2000 moves toward early middle age.[265]

The fact that lawyers are likely to move across sectors with greater frequency in the coming years, however, raises an important challenge for the kind of analysis I have presented here. The model of the attorney/client relationship I have been exploring is based on the particular dynamics of the relationship between large companies and equally large law firms. In the prevailing sociological account, these actors constitute a distinct 'hemisphere' of legal practice that is separate from what these theorists charmingly called the 'personal plight' sector of the bar.[266] But as lawyers increasingly move across this divide—often repeatedly—we will have to rethink whether the jurisdictional boundaries between different areas of practice, and different kinds of

[262] ACC Value Challenge Briefing Package, n 268.

[263] S Chen, 'For Jobless Lawyers, Plan B includes Good Works' *CNN Money and Main Street*, 13 April 2009.

[264] Dinovitzer and ors, n 163 above, 'AJD1'.

[265] Dinovitzer and ors, n 163 above, 'AJD2'.

[266] See Heinz and Laumann, n 220 above.

client relationships, will continue to hold—and if not, what to make of it.

The same point can be made about law firm boundaries. In our study of how corporations purchase legal services, we found a surprising willingness for companies to treat the 'team' or 'work group' as being even more important than either the firm or the individual in deciding how to administer punishment when it is disappointed in the services it receives on a particular matter.[267] If this trend continues, the important unit of analysis might shift significantly—undermining the ability of 'companies' and 'firms' to forge the kind of cooperative relationships examined here.

As I indicated at the outset, developing a model of the attorney/client relationship that adequately accounts for these rapidly moving changes is a large and difficult task and I certainly make no claim to have delivered the last word here.[268] Instead, I will simply plead that no plausible account of legal ethics can avoid these vexing questions. The nature of the lawyer's role inevitably places those who occupy this position at the intersection of competing normative and institutional worlds—law, business, policy, family, and nation. It is up to those of us who have the luxury to think about these issues at some remove from the front lines to help those in the trenches—and those who depend on lawyers to carry out both their public and their private duties—to navigate among these competing domains without either being crushed, or, to return for one final time to Brougham, 'involv[ing] the country in [too much] confusion.'

[267] See Beardslee and ors, n 71 above.

[268] For my prior punting of this issue, see Wilkins, 'Legal Realism for Lawyers', n 217 above.

Index